1OOO LIGHTS

eds. Charlotte & Peter Fiell

1000 LIGHTS

1878 to present

1000 Leuchten
1878 bis heute

1000 Luminaires
1878 à aujourd'hui

TASCHEN

HONGKONG KÖLN LONDON LOS ANGELES MADRID PARIS TOKYO

Contents/Inhalt/Sommaire

The evolution of artificial light

Die Evolution des künstlichen Lichts
L'évolution de l'éclairage artificiel

◁◁ Isamu Noguchi with Akari lights, c. 1960 /
Isamu Noguchi mit Akari Leuchten, c. 1960 /
Isamu Noguchi parmi ses luminaires Akari, vers
1960

▷ Cartoon published in Punch, 25 June 1881 /
Cartoon im Punch vom 25. Juni 1881 / Dessin
humoristique publié dans Punch, 25 juin 1881

"WHAT WILL HE GROW TO?"

In the beginning

Of all the great achievements of science and invention, the production and application of artificial light ranks amongst the highest. Few human endeavors have had such a far-reaching influence upon the development of civilization. Today we take electric lighting for granted, yet just over a hundred years ago transforming night into day at the flick of a switch was hailed as nothing short of miraculous. Since humankind's earliest origins, the patterns of daily life had been determined largely by the sun – the greatest light source of them all. In many ancient societies, the sun was perceived as no less than the giver of life and was used to define the world in symbolic terms. The development of artificial light, on the other hand, provided a vital means of independence from the rhythms of nature and increasingly enabled humans to redefine the world around them. The progress of civilization has been inextricably linked with the evolution of artificial light, which can be seen both as an economic factor and as an artistic medium that has long influenced our health, safety, efficiency and happiness. The advances in man-made light – from the humble oil lamp to the first practical incandescent electric light bulb and on to fluorescent tube lighting

Am Anfang

Unter allen großen Erfindungen und Errungenschaften der Wissenschaft gehören die Herstellung und der Einsatz von künstlichem Licht zu den bedeutendsten. Nur wenige menschliche Leistungen hatten einen so weitreichenden Einfluss auf die Entwicklung der Zivilisation. Heute betrachten wir elektrische Beleuchtung als eine Selbstverständlichkeit, doch ist es nur knapp hundert Jahre her, dass die Verwandlung der Nacht in den Tag durch bloßes Betätigen eines Schalters geradezu als Wunder bejubelt wurde. Seit den Ursprüngen der menschlichen Existenz wurde der Rhythmus des täglichen Lebens hauptsächlich von der Sonne bestimmt, in vielen Gesellschaften des Altertums galt sie als Lebensspender und Symbol des Universums. Die Entwicklung des künstlichen Lichts ermöglichte den Menschen, sich vom Rhythmus der Natur zu emanzipieren und ihre Umwelt neu zu definieren. Das elektrische Licht kann als ein wirtschaftlicher Faktor wie auch als künstlerisches Medium betrachtet werden, das seit seinen Anfängen unsere Gesundheit, Sicherheit, Leistungsfähigkeit und unser Glück beeinflusst. Die Fortschritte in der Herstellung des Kunstlichts – von der primitiven Öllampe über die erste elektrische Glühbirne

Au commencement

De toutes les inventions scientifiques, la production et l'utilisation de la lumière artificielle comptent parmi les plus éblouissantes. Peu de découvertes ont eu un impact aussi profond sur le développement de la civilisation. De nos jours, nous appuyons sur l'interrupteur sans même y penser, mais, il y a à peine plus d'un siècle, le fait même de transformer ainsi les ténèbres en lumière aurait relevé du pur miracle. Dès les origines de l'humanité, la vie quotidienne est rythmée principalement par le soleil – première source de lumière et de vie, et symbole de l'univers pour bien des sociétés primitives. La lumière artificielle, en revanche, a peu à peu affranchi l'homme des rythmes de la nature et lui a permis de redéfinir le monde qui l'entourait. Le progrès de la civilisation est etroitement lié à l'évolution de la lumière artificielle, laquelle, aussi bien par son rôle économique que par sa dimension artistique, a influé sur notre santé, notre sécurité, notre efficacité et notre bonheur. Les progrès de la lumière artificielle – depuis la modeste lampe à huile jusqu'au tube fluorescent, en passant par la première ampoule électrique à incandescence – ont progressivement allongé notre temps de veille, de sorte que nous pouvons sans exagération

AQUARIUM LUMINEUX

◁ *Page from a trade catalog published by Leroy, Paris, c.1867 – featuring the Aquarium Lumineux designed by Willaeys and manufactured by A. Biloret & C. Mora / Seite aus einem von Leroy veröffentlichten Verkaufskatalog, Paris, ca. 1867 – mit dem von Willaeys entworfenen und von A. Biloret & C. Mora produzierten Aquarium Lumineux / Page d'un catalogue commercial publié par Leroy, Paris, env. 1867, où l'on peut voir l' Aquarium Lumineux conçu par par Willaeys et fabriqué par A. Biloret & C. Mora*

"I am much in the dark about light."

„Was das Licht anbelangt, tappe ich im Dunkeln."

«Pour ce qui est de la lumière, je tâtonne dans le noir.»

– Benjamin Franklin

– have progressively lengthened our waking hours so that now we can truly state that we live in a non-stop 24-hour society. Even today the electric light is still seen as a potent symbol of progress.

This book focuses on domestic lighting design from the late 1870s to present day and aims to show how the development of electric lighting at the end of the 19th century coincided with the emergence of the new profession of industrial design. Artists, architects, engineers and designers took up the challenges provided by this new and exciting technology and applied it to the design of many different types of light fixture – hanging, floor, table and so on – often in very unique and individual ways. While many designers concentrated on producing functional lighting solutions, others preferred to explore the expressive potential of electric light through the use of a variety of natural and synthetic materials and a wide range of production techniques and technologies. During the early years of domestic electrification, lighting products were often designed as integral elements of complete interior schemes and were therefore almost always labor-intensive and expensive to produce. During the inter-war period, however, as the reality of the Machine Age and large-scale industrial manufactur-

bis zu Leuchtstoffröhren – haben unsere Tage so verlängert, dass wir heute in einer 24-Stunden-Gesellschaft leben. Auch heute noch gilt elektrisches Licht als ein starkes Symbol des Fortschritts.

Das vorliegende Buch konzentriert sich auf das Leuchtendesign vom Ende der 1870er Jahre bis in die heutige Zeit und zeigt, wie die Verbreitung elektrischen Lichts gegen Ende des 19. Jahrhunderts zeitlich mit dem Aufkommen des Industriedesigns zusammenfiel. Künstler, Architekten, Ingenieure und Designer nahmen die Herausforderungen dieser neuen Technologie an und wandten sie auf die Gestaltung von Beleuchtungskörpern wie Hänge-, Steh-, Tischleuchten an. Während sich viele Gestalter auf funktionale Lösungen konzentrierten, zogen es andere vor, mit einer Vielzahl von Materialien und Produktionstechniken das expressive Potenzial von elektrischem Licht auszuloten. Während der Anfangszeit der Elektrifizierung von Privathaushalten wurden Leuchten häufig als Bestandteile ganzer Inneneinrichtungen gestaltet und waren folglich sehr teuer. Im Lauf der Zwischenkriegszeit, in der das Maschinenzeitalter und die Massenerzeugung von Industriegütern immer mehr zur Realität wurden, begannen Produktgestalter jedoch nach ökonomischeren Lösungen zu suchen. In der

affirmer que notre société «ne dort jamais». Aujourd'hui encore, l'éclairage électrique est perçu comme un puissant symbole de progrès.

Ce livre a pour objet l'éclairage domestique de la fin des années 1870 à aujourd'hui. Nous y montrons que le développement de l'éclairage artificiel à la fin du XIXᵉ siècle coïncide avec l'apparition de la profession de dessinateur industriel. Artistes, architectes, ingénieurs et dessinateurs ont mis leur talent au service de cette nouvelle et fascinante technologie, créant une grande variété de luminaires – lampadaires, suspensions, lampes de table, etc. – d'un style souvent unique et très personnel. Alors qu'un grand nombre de créateurs s'attachaient avant tout à l'aspect pratique, d'autres choisirent d'explorer une plus grande variété de matières (organiques et artificielles) et de techniques de production afin de mettre en valeur la lumière électrique dans tout ce qu'elle avait de plus expressif. Au début de l'ère électrique, les luminaires faisaient généralement partie intégrante de la décoration intérieure, d'où leur coût élevé en argent et en heures de travail. Ce n'est qu'à l'entre-deux-guerres, avec l'essor de l'industrialisation, qu'on a commencé à rechercher des systèmes plus universels, économiques et compatibles avec

introduction

the evolution of artificial light

◁ Aurora Globe *scientific electrical demonstration instrument made by Benjamin Pike, 294 Broadway, New York, c.*1867–78 / Aurora Globe, *ein von Benjamin Pike, 294 Broadway, New York, hergestelltes elektrisches Instrument für wissenschaftliche Demonstrationen, ca.* 1867–78 / Aurora Globe, *instrument électrique de démonstration scientifique, réalisé par Benjamin Pike, 294 Broadway, New York, env.* 1867–78

▷ *Portable and hanging metal oil lamps, 17th and 18th century* / *Tragbare und hängbare Öllampen aus Metall, 17. und 18. Jahrhundert* / *Suspensions et lampes à huile portatives en métal, XVIIe et XVIIIe siècles*

ing grew, designers began to look for more universal and affordable solutions that speculated on serial production. The post-war era subsequently ushered in a period of remarkable formal experimentation that considerably extended the esthetic parameters of lighting design. In comparison to other areas of consumer product design, such as automotive, seating and domestic appliances, lighting products do not have to adhere so closely to ergonomic requirements and this allows for a much greater freedom of compositional expression. The many lighting designs featured in the following pages have been carefully selected as among the finest and most important examples of their kind. Not only do they best reflect the styles and movements that have defined design during the 20th century and early 21st century, they are also among the most innovative in articulating the uniquely expressive quality of emitted light. Quite simply, artificial lighting has enlightened the world by illuminating our path towards civilization.

Oil Lamps to Gaslight

The first lamps are believed to have appeared around 70,000 BC and would have been made of shells or hollowed rocks plugged with dried plant matter,

Nachkriegszeit begann eine Phase bemerkenswerter formaler Experimente, welche die ästhetischen Dimensionen des Leuchtendesigns erweiterten. Im Vergleich zu anderen Bereichen des Produkt- oder Industriedesigns, wie etwa Fahrzeuge, Sitzmöbel und Haushaltsgeräte, müssen sich Beleuchtungskörper nicht so streng an ergonomischen Anforderungen ausrichten, was eine wesentlich größere Freiheit im gestalterischen Ausdruck erlaubt. Die in diesem Band präsentierten Entwürfe wurden sorgfältig ausgewählt. Sie reflektieren nicht nur die Stile und Tendenzen, die das Design im 20. und zu Beginn des 21. Jahrhunderts prägen, sondern bringen auch die einzigartige Ausdruckskraft von Licht zum Vorschein, denn künstliches Licht hat die Welt auch geistig erleuchtet, indem es unseren Weg in die Zivilisation erhellend begleitete.

Von der Öllampe zum Gaslicht

Man nimmt an, dass die ersten Lampen aus der Zeit um 70.000 v. Chr. datieren und aus Muscheln oder ausgehöhlten Steinen gefertigt waren, gefüllt mit getrockneten Pflanzen, die man mit Tierfett getränkt hatte. Um 3.000 v. Chr. tauchten die ersten steinernen Öllampen auf, und bereits ab dem 7. Jahrhun-

une production en série. Par la suite, la période d'intense expérimentation qui suivit la Seconde Guerre mondiale permit d'élargir considérablement le champ des critères esthétiques de l'éclairage électrique. Contrairement à d'autres produits de consommation comme l'automobile, les sièges et les appareils ménagers, les luminaires ne sont pas soumis aux considérations ergonomiques, ce qui laisse d'autant plus de liberté au créateur. Les nombreux exemples de luminaires présentés au fil des pages suivantes ont été soigneusement choisis parmi les plus représentatives de leur genre. Non seulement ils illustrent les principaux styles et mouvements décoratifs du XXe et du début du XXIe siècle, mais leur manière de diffuser et de mettre en valeur la lumière est aussi totalement nouvelle. En bref, l'éclairage artificiel a illuminé le monde en éclairant notre voie vers la civilisation.

De la lampe à l'huile à l'éclairage au gaz

On estime que les premières lampes sont apparues environ soixante-dix mille ans avant notre ère. Elles étaient vraisemblablement faites de coquillages ou de pierres creuses remplies de matières végétales séchées, de la

such as moss, that had been soaked in animal fat. Around 3,000 BC stone oil lamps began appearing and by the 7th century BC the Greeks were making terracotta oil lamps to replace hand-held torches. Indeed, the word "lamp" derives from the Greek *lampas*, meaning torch. During the Roman period, molded-clay oil lamps, often embellished with hunting, allegorical or erotic scenes, were serially produced in some of the world's first "factories". For the next 2000 years candles, rush-lights and oil lamps made of pottery, stone or metal were used to generate artificial light, and it was not until 1792, when the Scottish engineer William Murdock (1754–1839) invented coal-gas lighting to illuminate his own house in Redruth, Cornwall, that oil was superseded as the lighting fuel of choice. By 1799 Murdock's employer, the great engineering firm of Boulton & Watt, was manufacturing gas lighting equipment, and just four years later gas street lamps were installed to illuminate Pall Mall in London. Westminster Bridge was subsequently lit by gaslight in 1813 and within a few years gas lighting was being used in other countries as well. Baltimore became the first American city to use gas lighting in 1816 and Paris was gas-lit from 1820. It was not until the advent of incandescent burners and mantles in 1900,

dert v. Chr. stellten die Griechen Öllampen aus Terrakotta her, die Fackeln ersetzten. Das Wort „Lampe" leitet sich von „lampas", dem griechischen Wort für Fackel ab. Während der Römerzeit wurden in den ersten „Fabriken" der Welt aus Ton geformte Öllampen, häufig verziert mit Jagdszenen, allegorischen oder erotischen Motiven, produziert. Im Lauf der folgenden zweitausend Jahre wurden Kerzen, Binsenlichter und Öllampen aus Keramik, Stein oder Metall verwendet, um künstliches Licht zu erzeugen. Erst als im Jahr 1792 der schottische Ingenieur William Murdock (1754–1839) für sein Haus in Redruth, Cornwall, eine Beleuchtung mit Kohlengas erfand, wurde Öl als Brennmaterial abgelöst. Bereits 1799 begann Murdocks Arbeitgeber, die bedeutende Firma Boulton & Watt, Gasbeleuchtungen zu produzieren, nur vier Jahre später wurden Gasstraßenlaternen aufgestellt, um die Londoner Pall Mall zu illuminieren. Wenige Jahre nachdem 1813 die Westminster Bridge mit Gasbeleuchtung ausgestattet worden war, wurde diese Technik auch in anderen Ländern eingeführt. 1816 war Baltimore die erste Stadt der Vereinigten Staaten mit Gasbeleuchtung, 1820 folgte Paris. Erst 1900 jedoch, mit dem Aufkommen von Glühbrennern und Glühstrümpfen, konnten Gaslampen ein hell leuchtendes, weißes Licht produzieren.

mousse par exemple, trempées dans de la graisse animale. La lampe à huile est sans doute apparue autour de 3000 avant J.-C. ; au VIIᵉ siècle avant J.-C., les Grecs utilisaient déjà des lampes à huile en terre cuite qui, peu à peu, détrônèrent les traditionnelles torches. Le mot « lampe » provient d'ailleurs du mot grec *lampas*, qui signifie « torche ». Les Romains produisaient déjà des lampes à huile en série dans leurs « usines ». Moulées en argile, elles étaient souvent décorées de scènes mythologiques, érotiques ou cynégé-

"Who will change old lamps for new ones? … new lamps for old ones?"

„Wer tauscht alte Lampen gegen neue? … neue Lampen gegen alte?"

« Qui veut échanger des vieilles lampes pour des neuves ? … des lampes neuves pour des vieilles? »

– Aladdin from *The Arabian Nights*

tiques. Au cours des deux mille ans qui suivirent, on s'éclaira au moyen de bougies, de chandelles et de lampes à huile en argile, en pierre ou en métal. L'huile

▷ Benham & Sons *catalog illustrating* Rickets's
Ventilating Gas Globe-Lights, *19ᵗʰ century /
Katalog von* Benham & Sons *mit der Abbildung
von* Rickets' *Ventilationsgaslampenglocken,
19. Jahrhundert / Catalogue de* Benham &
Sons *où l'on peut voir les lampes sphériques à
gaz de ventilation de* Rickets, *XIXᵉ siècle*

▷▷ *The* Sheffield United Gas Light Company
*advertisement showing various gas fixtures,
19ᵗʰ century / Werbeanzeige der* Sheffield
United Gas Light Company *Gasleuchten, 19. Jahrhundert / Réclame de la*
Sheffield United Gas Light Company *où l'on
peut voir divers appareils d'éclairage au gaz,
XIXᵉ siècle*

---

however, that gaslight was able to
produce a dazzling and brilliant white
light.

Early electric lighting
experiments

Prior to the introduction of gaslight in
the late 18th and early 19th century,
there had been a number of experimental attempts to source another and different type of light from electric energy.
The German physicist Otto von Guericke (1602–1686) is usually credited
with producing the first man-made electric light in 1663, by means of a revolving sulphur-filled glass globe which,
when rubbed against a cloth, produced
sparks of static electricity. By 1709
Francis Hauksbee (1666–1713) had
made significant improvements to von
Guericke's rotating frictional generator
by adding a small amount of mercury
to the glass globe and evacuating most
of the air from it. Once a sufficiently
strong charge of static electricity had
been built up, Hauksbee's globe glowed
when he placed his hands on it. Unbe-
knownst to him, he had created the
world's first proto-neon light.

After Hauksbee's electrostatic generating experiments, it took nearly a century of research by numerous other scien-

Frühe Experimente mit
elektrischem Licht

Bereits vor der Einführung des Gas-
lichts im späten 18. und frühen 19. Jahrhundert waren Experimente unternom-
men worden, um eine zusätzliche und
alternative Art von Lichtquelle aus elektrischer Energie zu gewinnen. Im Allgemeinen wird dem deutschen Physiker
Otto von Guericke (1602–1686) zugeschrieben, das erste elektrische Licht
erzeugt zu haben, als er 1663 Versuche
mit einer schwefelgefüllten Glaskugel
durchführte, die bei Reibung an einem
Stoff Funken aus statischer Elektrizität
erzeugte. 1709 nahm Francis Hauksbee (1666–1713) entscheidende Verbesserungen am rotierenden Reibungs-
elektrizitätsgenerator vor, den von
Guericke entwickelt hatte, indem er
etwas Quecksilber in die Glaskugel
füllte und den größten Teil der Luft
absaugte. Hatte sich dann die Kugel
in ausreichendem Maß mit statischer
Elektrizität aufgeladen, leuchtete sie,
wenn Hauksbee seine Hand darauf
legte. Ohne es zu wissen, hatte er damit
das erste Neonlicht der Welt produziert.

Nach Hauksbees elektrostatischen
Experimenten bedurfte es fast eines
ganzen Jahrhunderts der Forschung,
bevor Antoine François de Fourcroy
(1755–1809), Louis Nicolas Vauquelin

resta le principal combustible utilisé jusqu'à ce que l'ingénieur écossais William
Murdock (1754–1839) invente l'éclairage au gaz de houille en 1792, pour sa
maison de Redruth en Cornouailles. En
1799, la grosse firme Boulton & Watt,
où Murdock travaillait, avait commencé
à fabriquer des appareils d'éclairage au
gaz et, à peine quatre ans plus tard, sur
le Pall Mall, à Londres, était équipé de
réverbères à gaz. En 1813, le pont de
Westminster était éclairé au gaz.
L'exemple ne tarda pas à être suivi dans
d'autres pays : Baltimore, en 1816, fut
la première ville américaine éclairée au
gaz et Paris lui emboîta le pas en 1820.
Ce n'est toutefois qu'avec l'invention
des brûleurs et des manchons à incandescence, en 1900, que l'on put obtenir
une lumière blanche éclatante et vive à
partir du gaz.

Les balbutiements
de l'éclairage électrique

Avant même l'invention de l'éclairage
au gaz à la fin du XVIIIᵉ et au début du
XIXᵉ siècle, quelques tentatives pour
produire de la lumière grâce à l'énergie
électrique avaient déjà eu lieu. C'est au
physicien allemand Otto von Guericke
(1602–1686) qu'on attribue généralement l'invention de la première lumière
électrique : en 1663, il produisit des

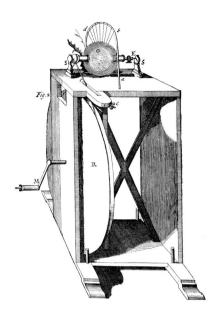

◁ Electrical machine, 1730, a type of apparatus first devised by Otto von Guericke / Elektro-maschine, 1730 – das ist die Art von Apparat, wie sie zuerst von Otto von Guericke entwickelt wurde / Machine électrique, 1730 – Otto von Guericke fut le premier à concevoir ce genre d'appareils

tists before Antoine François de Four-croy (1755–1809), Louis Nicolas Vauquelin (1763–1829) and Louis Jacques Thenard (1777–1857) con-ducted the first important demonstra-tion of the igniting power of large gal-vanic battery plates. With knowledge of these French scientists' pioneering work and the larger-scale experiments undertaken by a now long-forgotten "Mr. Children"¹, the eminent British sci-entist Sir Humphry Davy (1778–1829) conducted his first electrical discharge lighting experiments in the laboratory of the Royal Institution, London, in 1802. As the Royal Institution's journal noted, "When two small pieces of well burned charcoal, or a piece of charcoal and a metallic wire, were made to complete the circle [i.e. circuit], in water, vivid sparks were perceived, gas was given out very plentifully, and the points of the charcoal appeared red-hot in the fluid … [Another] experiment was made by means of a small glass tube contain-ing a slip of platina [sic] hermetically sealed into it, and having a piece of charcoal attached to its lower extremity: the communication was effected by means of iron wires; and the charcoal was made white-hot, by successive con-tacts continued for nearly two hours."²

Davy's early experiments fuelled inter-est in the idea of electric lighting using

(1763–1829) und Louis Jacques Thenard (1777–1857) in einer ersten Demonstration die Zündkraft galvani-scher Akkumulatorenplatten vorführten. In Kenntnis dieser Pionierarbeit und der umfassenden Versuche eines heute längst vergessenen „Mr. Children"¹, unternahm Sir Humphry Davy (1778–1829), einer der bedeutendsten briti-schen Chemiker, 1802 seine ersten Experimente zur Erzeugung von Licht mittels elektrischer Entladung im Labo-ratorium der Londoner Royal Institution. Im Journal der Royal Institution hieß es dazu: „Als mit zwei kleinen Stückchen stark verbrannter Holzkohle oder einem Stück Holzkohle und einem Metalldraht der [Strom]Kreis geschlossen wurde, wurden im Wasser leuchtende Funken wahrgenommen, Gas strömte in sehr großen Mengen aus und die Spitzen der Kohlestücke erschienen rotglühend in der Flüssigkeit. [Ein weiteres] Experi-ment wurde mittels einer kleinen Glas-röhre durchgeführt, die einen Streifen Platina [sic] enthielt, welcher herme-tisch in dieser verschlossen worden war und an deren unterem Ende ein Stück Holzkohle angebracht war. Die Übertra-gung trat in Kraft mittels Eisendrähten; und die Kohle wurde weißglühend gemacht, durch aufeinander folgende Kontakte, die beinahe zwei Stunden lang fortgesetzt wurden."²

étincelles d'électricité statique grâce à un globe de verre rempli de soufre qu'il faisait tourner en le frottant avec un chiffon. En 1709, Francis Hauksbee (1666–1713) avait bien amélioré ce « générateur » en y ajoutant un peu de mercure et le vidant de presque tout son air. Une fois suffisamment chargé en électricité statique, le globe de Hauksbee se mettait à luire quand on le touchait avec les mains. Sans le savoir, il avait inventé l'ancêtre du néon.

Presque un siècle de recherches plus tard, Antoine François de Fourcroy (1755–1809), Louis Nicolas Vauquelin (1763–1829) et Louis Jacques Thenard (1777–1857) furent les premiers à démontrer que de grandes plaques gal-vaniques chargées d'électricité avaient un pouvoir d'ignition. Fort des expé-riences de ces savants français et de celles menées par un certain « Mr Children »¹, aujourd'hui oublié, l'éminent savant britannique Sir Humphry Davy (1778–1829) tenta de produire de la lumière au moyen d'une décharge élec-trique dans son laboratoire de la Royal Institution, à Londres, en 1802. L'expé-rience est relatée dans le journal de la Royal Institution : « Lorsque deux mor-ceaux de charbon bien brûlés ou un morceau de charbon et un fil de métal fermaient le cercle circuit, dans l'eau, on observait de vives étincelles, une gran-

▷ Drawing by Francis Hauksbee, the Curator of Experiments at the Royal Society, London, showing his own electrical machine, c.1709 / Zeichnung von Francis Hauksbee, dem Kurator der Experimente an der Londoner Royal Society, von seiner eigenen Elektromaschine, ca. 1709 / Dessin de Francis Hauksbee, Conservateur Scientifique à la Royal Society, Londres, représentant sa propre machine électrique, env. 1709

the incandescent principle, which is based on the observation that solids and gases when heated to a temperature above 525° centigrade will emit light. His researches, however, also highlighted a seemingly insurmountable obstacle – the fact that filaments burned rapidly when exposed to air. Rather than trying to overcome this problem, Davy focused his attention instead on arc lighting.

Arc lighting

By 1809 Humphry Davy had perfected the first electric carbon arc and the following year demonstrated his new invention at the Royal Institution in London. This type of electric discharge apparatus did not have a filament; it relied instead upon two carbon rods placed very close to one another, but not touching. The electric current sparked across the small gap to form an arc of glowing vapor, while the carbon points, becoming white hot, produced a dazzling light. Amongst Davy's notes – collected into two volumes by his assistant Michael Faraday (1791–1867) and now held in the library of the Royal Society – is a description of one of his lecture-experiments: "… the charcoal became ignited to whiteness, and by withdrawing the points from each

Die frühen Experimente Davys weckten das Interesse an der Erzeugung elektrischen Lichts nach dem Prinzip der Glühhitze. Es basiert auf der Beobachtung, dass Festkörper wie auch Gase, wenn man sie auf über 525° Celsius erhitzt, Licht ausstrahlen. Davys Forschungsarbeiten brachten jedoch auch ein scheinbar unüberwindliches Hindernis zutage: die Tatsache nämlich, dass Glühfäden an der Luft sehr schnell verbrannten. Statt dieses Problem zu lösen, widmete Davy sich fortan der Entwicklung von Bogenlampen.

Das Bogenlicht

Bis zum Jahr 1809 hatte Humphry Davy den ersten elektrischen Kohlelichtbogen perfektioniert und führte ihn im Jahr darauf an der Royal Institution in London vor. Bei dieser Art von Gasentladungslampe wurden statt eines Glühfadens zwei Kohlestäbe verwendet, die sich fast berührten. Der elektrische Zündfunke sprang über den schmalen Spalt und bildete einen Bogen aus Leuchtgas, während die Spitzen der Kohlestäbe weißglühend wurden und ein blendend helles Licht ausstrahlten. In Davys Notizen, die von seinem Assistenten Michael Faraday (1791–1867) gesammelt wurden und sich heute im Besitz der Royal Society befinden, wird

de quantité de gaz se dégageait et les incandescents morceaux de charbon jetaient des lueurs rouges dans le liquide … Nous fîmes une [autre] expérience avec un infime morceau de platina [sic] hermétiquement enfermé dans un petit tube de verre, à l'extrémité inférieure duquel on avait attaché un morceau de charbon. Des fils de fer assuraient la conduction. Après presque deux heures de contacts ininterrompus, nous parvînmes à chauffer le charbon à blanc. »

Par la suite, de plus en plus de chercheurs s'inspirèrent des expériences de Davy pour essayer de produire de la lumière par incandescence, principe selon lequel tout gaz ou solide chauffé à plus de 525° C émet de la lumière. Mais il restait un problème apparemment insurmontable : le fait qu'un filament exposé à l'air se consumait rapidement. Plutôt que d'essayer de le résoudre, Davy concentra son attention sur l'arc électrique.

Les lampes à arc

En 1809, Humphry Davy avait mis au point le premier arc électrique au carbone. L'année suivante, il en fit une démonstration à la Royal Institution de Londres. L'appareil était capable de

Engraved portrait of Sir Humphry Davy – after a painting by T. Phillips / Gestochenes Porträt von Sir Humphry Davy – nach einem Gemälde von T. Phillips / Portrait gravé de Sir Humphry Davy, d'après une peinture par T. Phillips

Humphry Davy's "great battery" set up in the basement of the Royal Institution – this device was used to power his electrical experiments including his demonstration of the electric arc principle / Sir Humphrey Davys „große Batterie", die im Keller der Royal Institution aufgebaut war; sie wurde zur Stromversorgung

für seine Experimente verwendet, einschließlich seiner Demonstration des Lichtbogenprinzips / «Grande pile» montée par Sir Humphry Davy dans le sous-sol de la Royal Institution – celle-ci le fournissait en électricité pour ses expériences, notamment pour sa démonstration du principe de l'arc électrique

other, a constant discharge took place through the heated air, in a space at least equal to four inches, producing a most brilliant ascending arch of light, broad and conical in form in the middle".[3] It was not until 30 years after Davy's spectacular arc-light demonstration, however, that commercial arc-lighting systems began to be developed for locations that needed very strong bright light, such as streets and large public buildings.

In 1834 the British scientist William Edwards Staite (1809–1854) embarked on a series of experiments with arc lighting, which resulted in him filing a number of patents for lamp mechanisms and the production of carbon rods. Prior to Staite's pioneering work the carbon rods used in arc lamps had to be regulated by hand, but in 1836 he devised a system that allowed the rods to be controlled by clockwork. The eminent French physicist Jean-Bernard-Léon Foucault (1819–1868) also patented a similar clockwork-controlled regulating system in the early 1840s. In 1846 Staite discovered that the carbon rods were consumed less rapidly if they were enclosed in a glass vessel that did not freely admit air. Two years later he demonstrated his improved arc lamp – developed in conjunction with William Petrie (1821–1908) – by illuminating

eines seiner Experimente geschildert: „… die Kohle entzündete sich bis zum Weißglühen, und indem sich ihre Spitzen voneinander entfernten, fand eine stetige Entladung durch die erhitzte Luft statt, in einem Raum, der mindestens zehn Zentimeter maß, was einen überaus hellen, aufsteigenden Bogen aus Licht erzeugte, dessen Form in der Mitte breit und konisch war".[3] Nach Davys Vorführung sollten jedoch noch dreißig Jahre vergehen, bis kommerzielle Bogenlampen für Standorte entwickelt wurden, die eine besonders starke und helle Beleuchtung benötigten, wie Straßen und öffentliche Gebäude.

Im Jahr 1834 unternahm der britische Wissenschaftler William Edwards Staite (1809–1854) eine Reihe von Experimenten mit Bogenlicht und meldete mehrere Patente für Lampenmechanismen und die Herstellung von Kohlestäben an. Vor Staites bahnbrechenden Arbeiten mussten die in Bogenlampen verwendeten Kohleelektroden per Hand reguliert werden. Er aber ersann 1836 eine Methode, die es ermöglichte, die Stäbe mittels eines Uhrwerks einzustellen. Auch der bedeutende französische Physiker Jean-Bernard-Léon Foucault (1819–1868) ließ sich zu Beginn der 1840er Jahre ein ähnliches System patentieren. 1846 entdeckte Staite, dass sich die Kohlestäbe in einem ver-

produire une décharge électrique sans filament, au moyen de deux bâtonnets de carbone placés très près l'un de l'autre sans se toucher. Lorsque le courant électrique traversait ce mince espace, un arc de vapeur lumineuse se formait et les extrémités des tiges de carbone chauffées à blanc émettaient une vive lumière. Les notes de Davy – rassemblées par son assistant Michael Faraday (1791–1867) en deux volumes, aujourd'hui conservés à la bibliothèque de la Royal Society – décrivent ces expériences : « … le charbon était chauffé à blanc, et lorsqu'on écartait les électrodes l'une de l'autre, une décharge continue se produisait à travers l'air chauffé sur une distance d'au moins 10 cm. On observait un arc ascendant fort lumineux, dont la forme en son milieu évoquait un large cône. »[3] Il s'écoula encore trente ans, cependant, avant la commercialisation des premières lampes à arc lumineux destinées à l'éclairage des rues, bâtiments publics et autres lieux nécessitant une lumière vive et très puissante.

En 1834, l'ingénieur britannique William Edwards Staite (1809–1854) entama une série d'expériences sur l'arc lumineux, lesquelles se concrétisèrent par un grand nombre de brevets sur la mécanique des lampes et la production des tiges de carbone. Avant Staite,

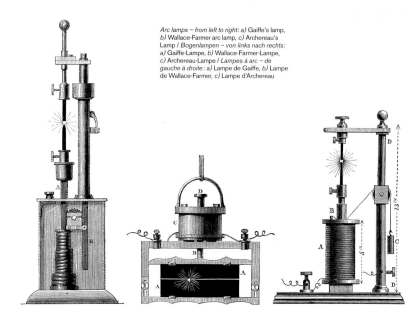

Arc lamps – from left to right: a) Gaiffe's lamp,
b) Wallace-Farmer arc lamp, c) Archereau's
Lamp / Bogenlampen – von links nach rechts:
a) Gaiffe-Lampe, b) Wallace-Farmer-Lampe,
c) Archereau-Lampe / Lampes à arc – de
gauche à droite : a) Lampe de Gaiffe, b) Lampe
de Wallace-Farmer, c) Lampe d'Archereau

the National Gallery in London, and
went on to present it at other venues
across Britain. It was not until 1857,
however, that the French inventor Victor
Serrin introduced the first really satis-
factory arc lamp, which incorporated an
electro-magnetic mechanism to regulate the gap between the carbon rods.
Unfortunately at this stage arc lamps
required batteries, which meant they
were far too expensive for large-scale
application. Some 20 more years would
pass, before the advent of practical
generators – first developed by the
French engineer and inventor Zénobe-
Théophile Gramme (1826–1901) in
1870 – and the availability of cheaper
batteries meant that attention was once
again turned to light sources powered
by electricity.

In 1876, while working in France, the
Russian engineer Paul Jablochkoff
(1847–1894) developed his electric
"candle" using Gramme's generators to
provide the necessary supply of electricity. The carbon rods in Jablochkoff's
design were positioned not end to end
but in parallel, like a candle with a double wick, while the two electrodes were
kept apart not by any kind of mechanism, but by kaolin. The resulting electric light was both cheaper and easier
to use than earlier arc lamps and at the
same time brighter and safer than exist-

schlossenen Glasgefäß weniger schnell
verzehrten. Zwei Jahre später beleuchtete er im Rahmen der ersten Präsenta-
tion seiner verbesserten Bogenlampe,
die er mit William Petrie (1821–1908)
entwickelt hatte, die National Gallery in
London. Anschließend führte er sie an
weiteren Schauplätzen in ganz Großbritannien vor. Doch erst 1857 stellte der
französische Erfinder Victor Serrin die
erste wirklich überzeugende Bogenlampe vor, die einen elektromagnetischen
Mechanismus verwendete, um den Ab-
stand zwischen den Kohlestäben zu
regulieren. Allerdings benötigten die
Bogenlampen damals Batterien, was
bedeutete, dass sie für einen großflächi-
gen Einsatz viel zu teuer waren. Deshalb
vergingen fast zwanzig weitere Jahre,
bis sich mit den Generatoren, die 1870
von dem französischen Ingenieur und
Erfinder Zénobe-Théophile Gramme
(1826–1901) entwickelt worden waren,
und der Verfügbarkeit billigerer Batterien die Aufmerksamkeit erneut auf
Lichtquellen richtete, die elektrische
Energie nutzten.

Während seiner Tätigkeit in Frankreich
im Jahr 1876 entwickelte der russische
Ingenieur Paul Jablochkoff (1847–
1894) seine elektrische „Kerze" unter
Verwendung von Grammes Generatoren, die für die nötige Energiezufuhr
sorgten. Die in Jablochkoffs Entwurf

celles-ci étaient ajustées à la main. En
1836, l'ingénieur inventa un mécanisme
permettant de les régler de manière
automatique. L'éminent physicien
français Jean-Bernard-Léon Foucault
(1819–1868) avait breveté un système
semblable de réglage mécanique dès le
début des années 1840. En 1846,
Staite découvrit que les bâtonnets de
carbone se consumaient moins vite
lorsqu'on les plaçait dans un récipient
en verre plus ou moins étanche à l'air.
Cette lampe à arc améliorée – mise au
point avec la collaboration de William
Petrie (1821–1908) – éclaira la National Gallery de Londres, avant d'être utilisée, quelques années plus tard, dans
d'autres lieux publics en Angleterre.
Il fallut toutefois attendre 1857 pour
que la première lampe à arc digne de
ce nom fasse son apparition : mise au
point par l'inventeur français Victor
Serrin, elle possédait un mécanisme
électromagnétique permettant de régler
l'espace entre les bâtonnets de carbone. À cette époque, hélas, les lampes
à arc fonctionnaient encore avec des
piles, et étaient donc bien trop chères
pour une utilisation courante. Près de
vingt ans furent encore nécessaires
pour que l'avènement des générateurs
pratiques – mis au point en 1870 par
l'ingénieur et inventeur français Zénobe-
Théophile Gramme (1826–1901) –
et l'apparition de piles moins chères,

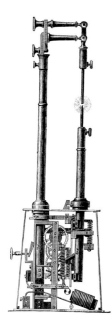

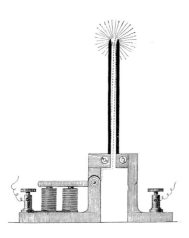

Arc lamps, 1870s – from left to right: a) Wilde's Candle, b) Serrin's Lamp, c) Rapieff's Lamp / Bogenlampen – von links nach rechts: a) Serrin-Lampe b) Wilde-Lampe c) Rapieff-Lampe / Lampes à arc – de gauche à droite : a) Lampe de Serrin, b) Lampe de Wilde, c) Lampe de Rapieff

introduction
the evolution of artificial light

ing gas lamps. During the 1880s Jablochkoff's candle became the first arc lamp to be used in significant numbers. The design was still problematic, however, because although the carbon rods burnt down at roughly the same rate, they had to be replaced after only a few hours of use.

The inherent problem of regulating the gap between carbon electrodes meant that arc lighting often had a variable intensity and could be unreliable in operation. In fact arc lighting was not truly improved until around 1878, when Charles Brush (1849–1929) developed a new system that regulated the size of the gap between the electrodes by the means of an electromagnet and a simple "ring clutch". Brush's arc light system was subsequently adopted throughout the United States and also widely abroad. In 1893 William Jandus introduced an even better arc lamp, which was successfully enclosed and could be operated at 80 volts (earlier arc lamps relied on much lower voltages). Despite the numerous hard-won improvements that took place during the 19th century, however, there was still an insurmountable problem with arc lighting – its almost blinding luminosity, which meant that it was completely unsuitable for use in domestic environments.

verwendeten Kohlestäbe waren nicht Ende an Ende, sondern parallel zueinander positioniert. Bei dieser Konstruktion, die einer Kerze mit doppeltem Docht ähnelte, wurde Kaolin eingesetzt, um die Elektroden für eine Lichtbogenbildung weit genug auseinander zu halten. Das daraus resultierende elektrische Licht war sowohl billiger und einfacher in der Anwendung als frühere Bogenlampen als auch heller und sicherer als Gaslampen. Im Lauf der 1880er Jahre wurde Jablochkoffs Kerze als erste Bogenlampe in großer Stückzahl installiert. Doch ein Problem blieb: Obwohl die Kohlestäbe darin nicht schneller niederbrannten als bei anderen Lampen, mussten sie nach nur wenigen Stunden ausgewechselt werden.

Das Problem der Regulierung des Abstands zwischen den Kohlestäben führte dazu, dass Bogenlampen häufig mit unterschiedlicher Intensität brannten und nicht zuverlässig funktionierten. Eine wirkliche Verbesserung des Bogenlichts wurde erst um 1878 erzielt, als Charles Francis Brush (1849–1929) den Zwischenraum mithilfe eines Elektromagneten und einer einfachen „Ring-Kupplung" regulierte. Das von Brush erfundene Bogenlicht fand in der Folge weite Verbreitung in den Vereinigten Staaten und auch in anderen Ländern. 1893 stellte William Jandus eine

apportent à la recherche sur la lumière électrique un réel regain d'intérêt.

En 1876, lors d'un séjour en France, l'ingénieur russe Paul Jablochkoff (1847–1894) mit au point sa « bougie » électrique, alimentée en électricité par les générateurs de Gramme. Ses bâtonnets de carbone étaient non pas placés bout à bout mais disposés parallèlement l'un à l'autre, ce qui lui donnait l'air d'une bougie à deux mèches. Elle n'était dotée d'aucun mécanisme permettant de maintenir les électrodes de carbone séparées l'une de l'autre, mais utilisait pour cela le kaolin. La lampe ainsi créée était moins onéreuse et plus simple à utiliser que les anciens modèles de lampes à arc, tout en étant plus sûre et plus lumineuse que les lampes à gaz encore en vigueur à l'époque. Au cours des années 1880, la « bougie » de Jablochkoff fut la première lampe à être utilisée à assez grande échelle. Mais un problème subsistait : les bâtonnets avaient beau brûler plus ou moins à la même vitesse, il fallait tout de même les remplacer après quelques heures seulement.

En raison de la difficulté du réglage de l'écart entre les électrodes, les lampes à arc variaient d'intensité et étaient peu fiables à l'usage. Ce n'est qu'en 1878 que ce problème fut en grande partie

"Light is the first of painters.
There is no object so foul
that intense light will not
make it beautiful."

„Licht ist der hervor-
ragendste Maler. Es gibt
keinen Gegenstand, der so
abscheulich wäre, dass ihn
intensives Licht nicht schön
machen kann."

« La lumière est le premier
des peintres. Il n'est point
d'objet si immonde qu'une
lumière vive ne puisse
embellir. »

– Ralph Waldo Emerson

◁ Jandus *arc lamp, 1895 – an enclosed arc lamp
whose glass cover restricted the flow of air /
Jandus-Bogenlampe, 1895 – eine in Glas ein-
gefasste Bogenlampe zur Verminderung des
Luftstroms / Lampe à arc* Jandus, *1895 – lampe
à arc munie d'un couvercle en verre qui la
protégeait des courants d'air*

The glare of arc lighting (which is still used today for floodlights) was in fact so strong that it led the eminent British author Robert Louis Stevenson (1850–1894) to humorously advocate a return to softer-toned gas lighting. "The word ELECTRICITY now sounds the note of danger … a new sort of urban star now shines out nightly, horrible, unearthly, obnoxious to the human eye; a lamp for a nightmare! Such a light as this should shine only on murders and public crime, or along the corridors of lunatic asylums, a horror to heighten horror. To look at it only once is to fall in love with gas, which gives a warm domestic radiance." Luckily for those who concurred with these sentiments and disliked the blinding effect of arc lighting, other scientists seeking a reliable light source powered by electricity were exploring a different avenue: the principle of incandescence.

Incandescent electric lighting

Probably the earliest mention of an incandescent lamp is found in a paper written by William Robert Grove (1811–1896) and published in the *Philosophical Magazine* in 1840 – the same year he was elected a fellow of the Royal Society. In his article, Grove describes how he inserted a coil of platinum wire

bessere Bogenlampe vor, die von einem Gefäß umschlossen war und mit 80 Volt betrieben werden konnte (frühere Bogenlampen arbeiteten mit sehr viel niedrigeren Voltzahlen). Trotz all dieser Verbesserungen im 19. Jahrhundert gab es jedoch immer noch ein unüberwindliches Problem bei der Anwendung von Bogenlicht: seine blendende Helligkeit, die es für den Einsatz im häuslichen Bereich völlig ungeeignet machte.

Das Licht der Bogenbeleuchtung (das heute noch für Scheinwerfer verwendet wird) war so grell, dass es den britischen Schriftsteller Robert Louis Stevenson (1850–1894) veranlasste, auf humoristische Weise die Rückkehr zum gedämpfteren Gaslicht zu propagieren. Er schrieb: „Das Wort ELEKTRIZITÄT schlägt nun einen gefährlichen Ton an – ein neuer Stern erstrahlt allnächtlich am städtischen Firmament, schrecklich, schauerlich, abscheulich für das menschliche Auge; eine Lampe für einen Albtraum! Ein Licht wie dieses sollte nur auf Mörder und Staatsverbrechen scheinen oder auf den Gängen von Irrenhäusern, um den Schrecken, um den Schrecken zu steigern. Es nur ein einziges Mal zu erblicken heißt, sich sofort in Gas zu verlieben, das einen warmen, wohnlichen Glanz ausstrahlt." Zum Glück gab es zu dieser Zeit jedoch auch Forscher, die auf der Suche nach

résolu, grâce à Charles Francis Brush (1849–1929), qui mit au point un système d'électro-aimant assorti d'une « bague de serrage ». Par la suite, les lampes à arc de Brush furent adoptées à travers tous les États-Unis et même au-delà des frontières. En 1893, William Jandus conçut un modèle encore plus perfectionné, présentant le double avantage d'être fermé et de fonctionner avec du courant de 80 volts (les modèles précédents nécessitaient un voltage beaucoup plus faible). Pourtant, malgré tous ces laborieux progrès qui jalonnèrent le XIXᵉ siècle, les lampes à arc souffraient d'un handicap insurmontable : leur luminosité éblouissante, qui les rendaient impropres à une utilisation domestique.

L'intensité lumineuse des arcs électriques (aujourd'hui utilisés dans les projecteurs) était telle que l'éminent écrivain britannique Robert Louis Stevenson (1850–1894) en vint, sur le ton de la plaisanterie, à prendre la défense des bonnes vieilles lampes à gaz. « Le mot ÉLECTRICITÉ est à présent empreint de danger – une étoile urbaine d'un nouveau genre, horrible, terrifiante ou inconnue, odieuse pour l'œil humain, brille dans nos nuits – une lampe de cauchemar ! Une telle lumière ne devrait servir qu'à démasquer les criminels, dénoncer les meurtriers ou éclairer les couloirs des asiles de fous,

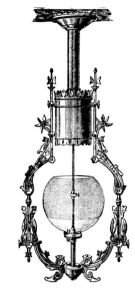
▷ Jablochkoff Candle *in a converted gas streetlight* / Elektrische Kerze von Jablochkoff *in einer umgerüsteten Gasstraßenlaterne* / Réverbère à gaz converti *équipé d'une bougie de Jablochkoff*

▷▷ Brush *arc lamp* / Brush-Bogenlampe / Lampe à arc de Brush

attached to two charged copper wires inside an inverted glass tumbler placed in a bowl of distilled water.[5] Grove maintained that this incandescent lamp had emitted sufficient light to "read for hours". A year later, in 1841, Frederick de Moleyn designed and built a similar lamp featuring a spiral of platinum wire which, like Grove's, was made "incandescent" (radiant) when an electric current was passed through it. In 1845 de Moleyn improved his incandescent lamp by expelling as much air as possible from his glass bulb, which helped to retard the rapid destruction of the metallic filament. During this period it was only possible to obtain a rather imperfect vacuum and this led to the widespread belief that no lamp based on the incandescent principle would be able to be produced at anything like a reasonable cost.

In 1845 William Staite, who had earlier invented a clockwork mechanism for regulating the distance between carbon electrodes in arc lamps, demonstrated a lamp with a metallic filament at a conference held at the Sunderland Athenaeum. Among the audience at this event was a 17-year old student by the name of Joseph Swan (1828–1914). Indeed, it was this youthful encounter that led Swan to become interested in the development of practi-

einer zuverlässigen, elektrisch betriebenen Lichtquelle einen anderen Weg ersannen: das Prinzip des Glühlichts.

Das elektrische Glühlicht

Die wahrscheinlich früheste Erwähnung der Glühlampe, eines Vorläufers der heutigen Glühbirne, findet sich in einer von William Robert Grove (1811–1896) verfassten Abhandlung, die 1840 im *Philosophical Magazine* veröffentlicht wurde – im selben Jahr, in dem Grove zum Fellow der Royal Society gewählt wurde. In diesem Artikel beschreibt er, wie er einen spulenförmig gedrehten Platindraht, befestigt an zwei aufgeladenen Kupferdrähten, in einen umgedrehten Glaskrug einsetzte, der in einer Schüssel mit destilliertem Wasser stand. Grove behauptete, diese Glühlampe habe genügend Licht gegeben, um bei ihrem Schein stundenlang zu lesen.[5] Im Jahr darauf, 1841, entwarf und konstruierte Frederick de Moleyn eine ähnliche Lampe, die aus einem Platinspiraldraht bestand, der, wie bei Grove, zum „Weißglühen" (Leuchten) gebracht wurde, wenn man elektrischen Strom durch ihn fließen ließ. Im Jahr 1845 verbesserte Moleyn seine Glühlampe, indem er so viel Luft wie möglich aus dem Glaskolben absaugte, wodurch das Verglühen des Leuchtfadens verzögert werden

horreur révélant l'horreur. La voir une fois seulement, c'est tomber amoureux du gaz et de sa chaleureuse, familière clarté. »[4] Heureusement pour ceux qui partageaient ses sentiments sur la lumière éblouissante des lampes à arc, d'autres scientifiques, bien décidés à trouver une source fiable de lumière électrique, cherchaient dans une direction sensiblement différente : celle du principe d'incandescence.

L'éclairage électrique à incandescence

William Robert Grove (1811–1896) a sans doute été le premier à faire allusion à une lampe à incandescence, dans un article publié dans le *Philosophical Magazine* en 1840 – l'année où il fut élu membre de la Royal Society. Selon cet article, Grove avait relié une spirale de fil de platine relié à deux fils de cuivre chargés, le tout étant enfermé dans un gobelet de verre retourné et placé dans un bac d'eau distillée. Grove soutenait que la lampe incandescente ainsi formée avait émis assez de lumière pour permettre de « lire pendant des heures ».[5] L'année suivante, Frederick de Moleyn conçut et construisit une lampe semblable, faite d'une spirale de fil de platine, laquelle, comme celle de Grove, devenait « incandescente » (radiante)

Brush arc lamps *in New York City, 1881* /
Brush-Bogenlampen *in New York City, 1881* /
Lampes à arc de Brush à *New York, 1881*

Page from Siemens arc lamp catalog, 1908 /
Seite aus dem Bogenlampenkatalog von
Siemens, 1908 / Page du catalogue de lampes
à arc de Siemens, 1908

▷ William Grove's incandescent lamp, 1840 /
William Groves Glühlampe, 1840 / Lampe à
incandescence de William Grove, 1840

cal electric lighting. That same year a
patent specification for a new electric
lighting device was published on behalf
of a young American inventor, John
Wellington Starr (d. 1846). The patent
described an apparatus consisting of a
short carbon rod positioned above a
column of mercury, which was placed in
a Torricellian vacuum. Unfortunately for
Starr, the glass used in this experimental light bulb blackened too rapidly to
make it a viable proposition.

Captivated by Staite's demonstration
and intrigued by Starr's *in vacuo* concept, Joseph Swan began conducting
experiments with a view to developing
the first economical incandescent electric lamp. "It appeared to me evident", he
declared, "that an advantage would be
gained by making the incandescent
carbon filament as thin as possible, and
my first experiments were directed to
the attainment of this object by means
of carbonized paper and carbonized
cardboard".⁵ In 1848, via a process
which involved saturating paper strips
and coils with tar and treacle, placing
them into a mass of powdered charcoal
and then kiln-burning them in a fireclay
crucible, Swan managed to obtain
extremely thin and flexible spirals and
strands of carbon. By 1855 at the very
latest he had perfected his method of
"carbonization" and was able to make

konnte. Das Vakuum, das sich zu dieser
Zeit herstellen ließ, war jedoch unvoll-
kommen, was zu der Annahme führte,
man könne eine solche Lampe unmöglich zu vernünftigen Kosten produzieren.

Ebenfalls im Jahr 1845 präsentierte
William Staite, der zuvor den Uhrwerk-
mechanismus zur Abstandsjustierung
zwischen den Kohleelektroden in Bogenlampen erfunden hatte, während
einer Konferenz im Sunderland Athe-
näum eine Metallglühfadenlampe. Im
Publikum befand sich auch der sieb-
zehnjährige Student Joseph Swan
(1828–1914), den das Erlebnis dieser
Vorführung dazu brachte, sich für die
Entwicklung des elektrischen Lichts zu
interessieren. Im selben Jahr erschien
unter dem Namen des jungen amerikanischen Erfinders John Wellington Starr
(gest. 1846) eine Patentschrift, in der
ein Apparat zur Erzeugung von elektrischem Licht beschrieben wurde. Er bestand aus einem kurzen Kohlestab über
einer Quecksilbersäule, in der eine „torri-
cellisches Vakuum" genannte Luftleere
herrschte. Zum Leidwesen von Starr
wurde das für diese Glühlampe verwendete Glas zu schnell geschwärzt, als
dass diese zu einer entwicklungsfähigen
Konstruktion hätte werden können.

Fasziniert von William Staites Vorführung und J. W. Starrs Vakuum-Methode,

lorsqu'un courant électrique la parcou-
rait. En 1845, Moleyn améliora sa
lampe incandescente en ôtant autant
d'air que possible de l'ampoule de verre,
ce qui eut pour effet de retarder la destruction du filament métallique. À cette
époque, on ne savait obtenir qu'un vide
imparfait, d'où l'opinion largement
répandue qu'aucune lampe utilisant le
principe d'incandescence ne pourrait
être fabriquée à un prix abordable.

En 1845, William Staite qui, auparavant,
avait inventé un mécanisme automatique pour ajuster la distance entre les
électrodes de carbone dans les lampes
à arc, présenta une lampe à filament
métallique lors d'une conférence au
Sunderland Atheneum. L'un des audi-
teurs était un étudiant de dix-sept ans,
Joseph Swan (1828–1914), pour qui
cette rencontre eut l'effet d'un déclic.
La même année, un brevet
fut publié au nom d'un jeune inventeur
américain, John Wellington Starr (mort
en 1846), décrivant un appareil électrique lumineux composé d'un court
bâtonnet de carbone placé au-dessus
d'une colonne de mercure, tout placé
dans un vide torricellien. Malheureuse-
ment pour Starr, le verre de cette
ampoule expérimentale noircissait trop
vite et sa découverte ne suscita pas
l'attention qu'elle méritait.

very strong yet highly elastic carbon filaments. In 1860 he undertook a partially successful experiment using a glass bottle, an air pump, a rubber stopper, a battery and one of his carbonized strips, which proved on the one hand that his thin filaments were suitable for producing incandescent light and on the other that it was crucial to achieve a better type of vacuum, as any trace of air led to the carbon becoming distorted.

Another drawback in 1860 was the continuing absence of a cheap supply of power that would make electric lighting economically viable. Over the next few years, however, considerable progress was made in this field, with the development of practical dynamos by pioneers such as Samuel Alfred Varley (1832–1921), Charles Wheatstone (1802–1875), Zénobe-Théophile Gramme, Werner von Siemens (1816–1892), Charles Brush, Henry Wilde (b. 1833) and Frederick Hale Holmes (c. 1840–1875).[7] These new dynamo-based generators could illuminate up to ten arc lamps at once, making them practical for use in large factories, mills or workshops. Being so powerful, however, they were not suitable for smaller light points, or "the subdivision of the electric light", as it was described. Brilliantly, Swan saw that the problem of subdividing electricity could be circum-

begann Joseph Swan die erste im Verbrauch sparsame elektrische Glühlampe zu entwickeln. Er erklärte dazu: „Es erschien mir einleuchtend, dass es von Vorteil wäre, den Kohlestoffglühfaden so dünn wie möglich zu machen, und meine ersten Experimente waren darauf ausgerichtet, dieses Ziel mittels karbonisierten Papiers und Kartons zu erreichen".[6] 1848 gelang es Swan, äußerst dünne und flexible Kohleelektroden herzustellen, indem er zuvor in Teer oder Melasse getränkte Papierstreifen und -spiralen mit Holzkohlenstaub umhüllte und anschließend in einem feuerfesten Tiegel brannte. Spätestens bis zum Jahr 1855 hatte Swan diese Methode der „Verkohlung" perfektioniert, mit der es ihm gelang, sehr haltbare und dennoch biegsame Kohlenstoffglühfäden herzustellen. Im Jahr 1860 unternahm er ein Experiment unter Verwendung einer Glasflasche, einer Luftpumpe, eines Gummistöpsels, einer Batterie und eines seiner Kohlestreifen. Er bewies, dass die von ihm entwickelten dünnen Leuchtfäden, so genannte „Wendel", für die Herstellung von Glühlampen geeignet waren, und zum anderen, dass es von entscheidender Bedeutung war, ein besseres Vakuum zu erzielen, da die kleinste Menge Luft zum Verglühen und somit zur Zerstörung der Kohleelektrode führte.

Fasciné par la démonstration de William Staite et intrigué par le concept de vide mis en avant par J. W. Starr, Joseph Swan s'attacha à développer la première lampe électrique à incandescence qui fût aussi économique. « Il m'est apparu clairement », expliqua-t-il, « qu'on aurait tout avantage à utiliser un filament de carbone aussi fin que possible. Mes premières expériences étaient donc menées dans ce but, à l'aide de papier et carton carbonisés.»[6] En 1848, Swan parvint à obtenir des spirales et des brins de carbone très fins et très souples à partir de languettes et de rouleaux de papier trempés dans le goudron et la mélasse puis enfouis dans de la poudre de charbon et chauffés dans un creuset d'argile. En 1855, voire un peu plus tôt, il avait perfectionné ce processus de « carbonisation » et était en mesure de fabriquer des filaments de carbone à la fois très résistants et très élastiques. En 1860, il obtint un succès mitigé avec une expérience utilisant une bouteille de verre, une pompe à air, un bouchon en caoutchouc, une pile et l'une de ses languettes de papier carbonisé. L'essai prouva, d'une part, que ses minces filaments étaient à même de produire une lumière incandescente, mais de l'autre, qu'il était crucial d'obtenir un vide aussi parfait que possible, puisque le carbone se déformait en présence de la moindre trace d'air.

William Staite holding an early incandescent bulb, c.1842 / William Staite mit einem frühen Modell einer Glühbirne, ca. 1842 / William Staite tenant l'une des toutes premières ampoules à incandescence, env. 1842

navigated not by using complicated apparatus for dividing the current, but by using thin filaments that had a high specific resistance *in vacuo.* Acknowledging that the key to domestic electric lighting lay in the development of a practical incandescent lamp, Swan began working on ways of producing more resistant filaments and better vacuums.

"I am now able to produce a perfectly durable electric lamp by means of incandescent carbon."

„Mir ist es gelungen, mithilfe von leuchtendem Kohlestoff eine haltbare elektrische Lampe zu produzieren."

« Je suis à présent en mesure de produire une lampe électrique parfaitement durable fonctionnant au carbone incandescent. »

– Sir Joseph Swan

During this period of intense experimentation, Swan – assisted by Charles Stearn – discovered a method that at

Ein weiteres Hindernis bestand darin, dass es um 1860 noch keine billige Energieversorgung gab, die den Einsatz von elektrischem Licht ökonomisch sinnvoll gemacht hätte. Im Lauf der folgenden Jahre wurden in dieser Hinsicht jedoch beachtliche Fortschritte erzielt, im Zusammenhang mit der Entwicklung brauchbarer Dynamos durch Pioniere wie Samuel Alfred Varley (1832–1921), Charles Wheatstone (1802–1875), Zénobe-Théophile Gramme, Werner von Siemens (1816–1892), Charles Brush, Henry Wilde (geb. 1833) und Frederick Hale Holmes (ca. 1840–1875).[7] Diese neuen Systeme auf Dynamobasis konnten bis zu zehn Bogenlampen gleichzeitig beleuchten, was diese für große Fabrikhallen, Mühlen oder Werkstätten geeignet machte. Aber gerade weil ihr Licht so stark war, waren sie nicht für kleinere Lichtquellen geeignet – oder für die „Unterteilung von elektrischem Licht", wie man es nannte. Klugerweise erkannte Swan, dass man dieses Problem nicht durch komplizierte Apparate lösen konnte, sondern nur durch den Einsatz dünner Leuchtfäden, die im Vakuum einen hohen Leistungswiderstand aufwiesen. Da der Schlüssel zur elektrischen Beleuchtung von Privathaushalten in der Entwicklung einer brauchbaren Glühlampe lag, begann Swan an Methoden zur Erzeugung von widerstandsfähigeren Leuchtfäden und

L'absence d'un approvisionnement électrique bon marché dans les années 1860 était un obstacle supplémentaire au développement d'une lumière électrique économiquement viable. Pendant les années qui suivirent, de grands progrès furent cependant accomplis dans ce domaine, grâce aux dynamos mises au point par les pionniers qu'étaint Samuel Alfred Varley (1832–1921), Charles Wheatstone (1802–1875), Zénobe-Théophile Gramme, Werner von Siemens (1816–1892), Charles Francis Brush, Henry Wilde (né en 1833) et Frederick Hale Holmes (vers 1840–1875).[7] Ces nouveaux générateurs pouvaient alimenter jusqu'à dix lampes à arc en même temps et s'avéraient par conséquent utiles dans de grandes usines, fabriques et autres ateliers. Mais ils étaient trop puissants pour ce qu'on appelait la « sous-division de l'éclairage électrique », à savoir son utilisation en plusieurs points de lumière plus faibles. Swan eut alors une idée de génie : plutôt que d'essayer de trouver un système compliqué pour diviser le courant, il décida d'utiliser de minces filaments ayant une extrême résistance dans le vide. Convaincu que la lampe à incandescence était l'avenir de l'éclairage domestique, Swan se mit à essayer de produire des filaments plus résistants et un vide plus parfait.

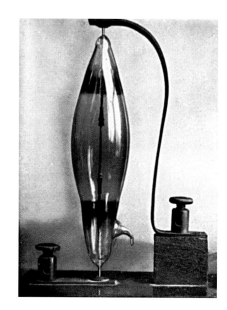

Joseph Swan's first incandescent lamp, presented in Newcastle in December 1878 / Joseph Swans erste Glühlampe, der Öffentlichkeit im Dezember 1878 in Newcastle präsentiert / Première lampe à incandescence mise au point par Joseph Swan et présentée au public en décembre 1878

last allowed him to rid a light bulb of troublesome residual air. He used the mercury vacuum pump invented by Hermann Sprengel (1834–1900) in 1865 to create as near perfect a vacuum as possible while the carbon was cold, and then passed a strong current through the filament to exhaust the remaining small quantity of air before the bulb was finally sealed. This landmark discovery appears to have been made towards the end of 1878: Swan gave the first demonstration of his practical incandescent lamp at the Newcastle-upon-Tyne Chemical Society on December 18 that year. Strangely, Swan did not immediately patent his ground-breaking invention, in the erroneous belief that the principle of incandescent electric lighting had already been in the public domain too long. Although Stearn urged Swan to file a patent for his incandescent lamp, he resisted and was eventually beaten to it by the American inventor Thomas Edison (1847–1931), who obtained a very broad British patent on 10 November 1879. In fact it was not until the following year that Swan finally patented his lamp. This confusion over patent applications explains why there is often a misunderstanding as to who actually invented the first practical electric light bulb. Although Swan's name is frequently linked to that of Thomas Edison, the

eines besseren Vakuumsystems zu arbeiten.

Während dieser Phase intensiven Experimentierens entdeckte Swan, assistiert von Charles Stearn, eine Methode, die es ihm endlich ermöglichte, einen Lampenkolben von dem problematischen Luftrückstand zu befreien. Mit dieser Technik ließ sich unter Einsatz einer 1865 von Hermann Sprengel (1834–1900) erfundenen Quecksilbervakuumpumpe eine annähernd perfekte Luftleere herstellen, während die Kohleelektrode kalt war. War dieser Punkt erreicht, wurde ein starker Stromstoß durch den Leuchtfaden geleitet, um die kleine Menge an Restluft abzupumpen, bevor der Kolben schließlich versiegelt wurde. Diese bahnbrechende Entdeckung scheint Ende 1878 gemacht worden zu sein, und am 18. Dezember dieses Jahres präsentierte Swan seine Glühlampe zum ersten Mal in den Räumen der Chemical Society in Newcastle upon Tyne. Merkwürdigerweise ließ Swan seine bedeutende Erfindung nicht sofort patentieren, weil er fälschlicherweise annahm, das Prinzip der elektrischen Beleuchtung sei bereits seit langem in staatlichem Besitz und deshalb nicht patentierbar. Obgleich Stearn ihn drängte, ein Patent für seine Kohlefadenlampe zu beantragen, kam ihm der amerikanische Elektrotechniker und

C'est pendant cette période d'intense expérimentation que Swan, aidé de Charles Stearn, découvrit une méthode pour vider l'ampoule de son air résiduel. À l'aide d'une pompe à vide à mercure inventée en 1865 par Hermann Sprengel (1834–1900), on obtenait un vide aussi parfait que possible pendant que le carbone était froid, puis, une fois ce point atteint, on faisait passer un fort courant dans le filament pour épuiser les derniers résidus d'air, avant de sceller l'ampoule. Cette découverte de taille date vraisemblablement de la fin de l'année 1878 ; le 18 décembre de cette même année, Swan fit une première démonstration de sa lampe à incandescence à la Chemical Society de Newcastle upon Tyne. Assez bizarrement, il tarda à faire breveter cette fracassante découverte : il pensait, à tort, que le principe de l'éclairage électrique à incandescence était tombé depuis déjà longtemps dans le domaine public. Stearn l'encouragea vivement à déposer un brevet, mais il résista et fut finalement devancé par l'inventeur américain Thomas Edison (1847–1931), qui obtint un brevet britannique très étendu le 10 novembre 1879. Swan, en fait, attendit l'année suivante pour faire breveter sa lampe. Ceci explique que beaucoup de gens de nos jours aient encore du mal à se mettre d'accord sur la paternité de la première ampoule élec-

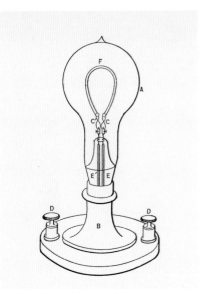

two worked entirely independently and it was actually Swan who was the first to develop a successful electric incandescent light bulb – if only by a matter of months.

While Joseph Swan was clearly leading the way in Europe, important contributions to the development of practical electric lighting were also being made in America from the 1850s onwards by such inventors as Moses Farmer (1820–1893), Hiram Maxim (1840–1916) and William Edward Sawyer (d. 1883). Indeed, Sawyer initially appeared to be the front-runner in the race to develop the first practical incandescent lamp. In August 1877 he patented a system using parallel circuits that regulated the distribution of electricity and thus produced the subdivision of electricity necessary to allow "constant illumination [to be] maintained in every part of the system".* In January 1878 Sawyer established the Electric-Dynamic Light Company of New York in collaboration with the Manhattan patent attorney Albon Man, but this partnership was up against a formidable opposition.

Erfinder Thomas Edison (1847–1931) zuvor, der am 10. November 1879 ein sehr umfassendes britisches Patent erwarb. Dies ist wohl die Erklärung dafür, warum es bei der Frage, wer die erste praktisch anwendbare Glühlampe erfand, zu einem Missverständnis kam. Häufig wird Swan im Zusammenhang mit Thomas Edison genannt. Doch die beiden Erfinder arbeiteten vollkommen unabhängig voneinander, und eigentlich entwickelte Swan als Erster mit Erfolg eine elektrische Glühlampe.

Während Joseph Swan in Europa eindeutig eine führende Rolle zukam, gab es in den Vereinigten Staaten einige Erfinder, wie etwa Moses Farmer (1820–1893) und William Edward Sawyer (gest. 1883), die ab den 1850er Jahren wesentlich zur Entwicklung des elektrischen Glühlichts beitrugen. Ursprünglich schien William Sawyer das Rennen um die erste elektrische Glühlampe gemacht zu haben. Im August 1877 nahm er ein Patent auf eine Konstruktion, die Parallelkreise zur Regulierung der Stromverteilung verwendete. Damit konnte die notwendige Unterteilung von Elektrizität stattfinden, welche „die Aufrechterhaltung einer konstanten Illumination in jedem Teil des Systems"* möglich machte. Gemeinsam mit dem New Yorker Patentanwalt Albon Man grün-

trique. Bien que le nom de Swan soit souvent associé à celui de Thomas Edison, chacun travaillait de son côté, et c'est en fait Swan qui mit au point la première ampoule électrique à incandescence digne de ce nom – même s'il n'avait que quelques mois d'avance sur son concurrent.

Alors qu'en Europe, Joseph Swan faisait figure de pionnier, d'autres inventeurs, depuis le milieu du XIXᵉ siècle, faisaient avancer la recherche sur l'éclairage électrique domestique aux États-Unis : parmi eux, Moses Farmer (1820–1893), Hiram Maxim (1840–1916) et William Edward Sawyer (décédé en 1883). Au départ, William Sawyer était en tête de file : en 1877, il breveta un système de circuits parallèles permettant de contrôler la distribution d'électricité de manière à obtenir ces fameuses sous-divisions offrant « une illumination constante d'un bout à l'autre du système ».* En collaboration avec Albon Man, l'avocat new-yorkais spécialiste des brevets, Sawyer fonda la Electric-Dynamic Light Company of New York en janvier 1878, qui rencontra une très grande opposition.

The wizard of Menlo Park

As a young but already very successful inventor, Thomas Edison had turned his attention to the "subdivision of light" at the beginning of 1878. In an article that appeared in the *New York Tribune* on 28 September 1878, he declared: "I have let the other inventors get the start of me in this matter somewhat, because I have not given much attention to electric lights; but I believe I can catch up to them now … There is [now] no difficulty about dividing up the electric currents and using small quantities at different points. The trouble is in finding a candle that will give a pleasant light, not too intense, which can be turned on or off as easily as gas"." The announcement of Edison's intention to develop a safe and inexpensive electric light bulb caused the price of illuminated gas stocks to tumble on both the New York and London stock exchanges, while shares in the Edison Electric Lighting Company (founded in 1878) soared from practically nothing to an astonishing $1,200 each.

Like Swan, Edison realized that the use of high-resistance filaments was the key to producing smaller units of light. At his well-equipped Menlo Park laboratory in New Jersey, Edison and some 100 assistants proceeded to conduct

dete Swan im Januar 1878 die Electric-Dynamic Light Company of New York, die es jedoch mit einer mächtigen Gegnerschaft zu tun bekommen sollte.

Der Zauberer von Menlo Park

Als junger, aber bereits sehr erfolgreicher Erfinder hatte Thomas Edison Anfang 1878 seine Aufmerksamkeit auf die Unterteilung von Licht konzentriert. In einem Artikel im *New York Herald Tribune* vom 28. September 1878 erklärte er: „Ich habe es zugelassen, dass mir die anderen Erfinder in dieser Sache zuvorgekommen sind, denn ich habe elektrischen Beleuchtungen keine besondere Beachtung geschenkt. Ich glaube jedoch, sie nun einholen zu können … Es ist [jetzt] keine schwierige Sache [mehr], den elektrischen Strom zu unterteilen und kleine Mengen an unterschiedlichen Stellen zu verwenden. Die Schwierigkeit liegt darin, ein Beleuchtungsmittel zu finden, das ein angenehmes Licht ausstrahlt, nicht zu intensiv, und das sich ebenso leicht ein- und ausschalten lässt wie Gas."[8] Edisons Absicht, eine sichere und günstige elektrische Lampe zu konstruieren, ließ den Preis von Brenngas sowohl an der New Yorker als auch an der Londoner Börse ins Bodenlose stürzen, während der Preis von Anteilen

Le magicien de Menlo Park

Le jeune et très précoce inventeur Thomas Edison avait commencé à s'intéresser la « sous-division de la lumière » dès les premiers mois de 1878. Le 28 septembre 1878, il déclara, dans un article du *New York Herald Tribune*, avoir « laissé les autres inventeurs prendre une certaine avance dans ce domaine, n'ayant pas beaucoup réfléchi au problème de la lumière électrique et à leur utilisation en faibles quantités à différents endroits sont [à présent] résolues. Il reste à trouver une bougie capable de donner une lumière agréable, point trop intense, pouvant s'allumer et s'éteindre aussi facilement que le gaz. »[8] À l'annonce du projet d'Edison de mettre au point une ampoule électrique bon marché et sans danger, les valeurs de l'éclairage au gaz chutèrent à la bourse de New York comme à celle de Londres, tandis que les actions de l'Edison Electric Lighting Company (fondée en 1878) qui, jusque-là ne valaient pratiquement rien, grimpèrent jusqu'à $1 200 chacune.

Tout comme Swan, Edison comprit que l'utilisation de filaments hautement résistants était la indispensable condi-

◁ Sarah Jordan's boarding house in Menlo Park, New Jersey, 1879 – Thomas Edison is standing in his shirtsleeves. Many of his assistants roomed here and it was the first residence to be lit by Edison lighting / Sarah Jordans Pension in Menlo Park, New Jersey, 1879 (Thomas Edison in Hemdsärmeln); viele seiner Assistenten wohnten hier und es war das erste von Edison elektrisch beleuchtete Wohnhaus / Pension tenue par Sarah Jordan à Menlo Park dans le New Jersey, 1879 – Thomas Edison, est debout, en bras de chemise. Plusieurs de ses assistants y logeaient, et ce fut la première habitation à être éclairée à l'électricité par ses soins

around 1,600 different experiments in the search for a suitable filament. The materials they tested included carbonized cotton thread, carbonized strips of bamboo and filaments made of platinum and platinum/iridium alloys. Eventually, on 22 October 1879, Edison and his team produced their first successful incandescent lamp, which employed a horseshoe-shaped carbonized paper burner. (Joseph Swan was later to claim he had first experimented with similar-shaped burners some fifteen years earlier.[10]) Edison noted that his first bulb "burnt like a star at night for 45 hours, and it went out with unexpected quickness."[11] During the next couple of months, Edison filed patent applications for high-resistant carbon filaments and for his revolutionary incandescent lamp with its carbonized paper burner. On New Year's Eve of 1879, the first public demonstration of Edison's new light bulbs took place at Menlo Park and was witnessed by over 3,000 visitors. In early 1880 Edison's company installed its first commercial light system on the SS *Columbia* – a new steamship built by the Oregon Railway and Navigation Company. The SS *Columbia*'s maiden voyage from New York to Portland caused quite a sensation, and with its 115 twinkling lights the steamship greatly publicized Edison's achievements, most notably through an exten-

an der 1878 gegründeten Edison Electric Lighting Company von praktisch Null auf 1.200 Dollar hochschnellte.

Ebenso wie Swan erkannte Edison, dass der Einsatz hochohmiger Leuchtdrähte, also solcher mit hohem elektrischem Widerstand, der Schlüssel zur Erzeugung kleinerer Lichteinheiten war. In seinem Labor in Menlo Park, New Jersey, führte Edison mit etwa hundert Assistenten circa 1.600 verschiedene Experimente durch, um ein geeignetes Material für Glühfäden zu finden. Zu den getesteten Materialien gehörten karbonisierter Baumwollfaden, karbonisierte Bambusstreifen sowie Wendel aus Platin und aus einer Platin-Iridium-Legierung. Endlich, am 22. Oktober 1879, gelang Edison und seinem Team die Fertigung ihrer ersten erfolgreichen Glühlampe, die einen hufeisenförmigen Papierbrenner aufwies. Joseph Swan sollte später behaupten, er habe gut fünfzehn Jahre zuvor als Erster mit ähnlich geformten Lampenbrennern experimentiert.[10] Edison notierte, seine erste Glühlampe habe „45 Stunden lang gebrannt wie ein Stern bei Nacht, und dann erlosch sie mit unerwarteter Schnelligkeit."[11] Im Lauf der folgenden Monate stellte Edison mehrere Patentanträge für hochohmige Kohlefäden und für seine revolutionäre Glühlampe mit karbonisiertem Papierbrenner. Am

tion pour la production de plus petites unités de lumière. Dans son laboratoire bien équipé de Menlo Park, dans l'État du New Jersey, Edison et une centaine d'assistants menèrent quelque mille six cents expériences pour tenter de trouver le matériau le plus propice à la fabrication de filaments. Ils testèrent, entre autres, des fils de coton et des baguettes de bambou carbonisés, ainsi que des filaments faits de platine et d'un alliage de platine et d'iridium. Finalement, le 22 octobre 1879, Edison et son équipe fabriquèrent leur première lampe à incandescence munie d'un brûleur à papier carbonisé en forme de fer à cheval (Joseph Swan devait plus tard prétendre qu'il s'était servi de brûleurs du même type quelque quinze ans auparavant[10]). Selon Edison, la première ampoule « brûla comme une étoile pendant 45 heures, puis s'éteignit soudainement ».[11] Pendant les deux mois qui suivirent, Edison déposa des demandes de brevets pour ses filaments de carbone hautement résistants et pour une lampe révolutionnaire à brûleur à papier carbonisé. Le 31 décembre 1879, plus de trois mille personnes assistèrent à la première démonstration publique des nouvelles ampoules d'Edison à Menlo Park. Au début de l'année 1880, un nouveau paquebot de la Oregon Railway and Navigation Company (Compagnie des chemins de fer et de naviga-

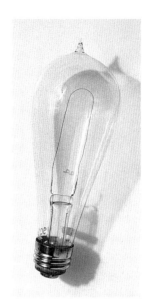

▷ Edison lamp *with screw fitting, c.1880 –
the first incandescent lamp to be successfully
mass-produced* / Edison-Glühbirne *mit
Schraubfassung, ca. 1880 – die erste
erfolgreich in Massenproduktion gefertigte
Glühbirne* / Lampe Edison *à culot à vis, env.
1880 – première lampe à incandescence
fabriquée à grande échelle avec succès*

sive article published in the prestigious journal *Scientific American*.

By November 1879 the commercial production of incandescent light bulbs had begun at Menlo Park. Already at this early stage the two main methods of connecting bulbs to an electrical source had been established – Edison having chosen the screw fitting and Swan the bayonet. Unsurprisingly, the two inventors decided to go into partnership in Britain and in 1880 founded the Edison & Swan United Lamp Company, which later became known as Ediswan.

Despite having achieved his momentous goal of producing the world's first commercial incandescent light, Edison was fully aware that, without a power network to supply it, electric lighting could never be economically viable. Recognizing that "the issue is factories or death!"[12] but finding the other directors of the Edison Electric Light Company reluctant to invest further, he was left with no alternative but to borrow money and sell his own stock-holdings. With the cash thus raised, he built new plants to manufacture the equipment needed to bring electric light into people's homes – from dynamos, junction boxes and underground tubing right down to sockets and switches. Even

Neujahrsabend 1879 fand die erste öffentliche Vorführung von Edisons neuer Glühbirne vor mehr als 3.000 Besuchern in Menlo Park statt. Zu Beginn des Jahres 1880 installierte Edisons Firma ihr erstes kommerzielles Beleuchtungssystem an Bord der S.S. Columbia, eines neuen, von der Oregon Railway and Navigation Company gebauten Dampfschiffs. Die Jungfernfahrt der S.S. Columbia von New York nach Portland, Oregon, sorgte für großes Aufsehen und mit den 115 blinkenden Lichtern des Schiffes wurden auch Edisons Leistungen in den Medien gewürdigt, insbesondere in einem ausführlichen Artikel im *Scientific American*.

Im November 1879 wurde in Menlo Park die gewerbliche Produktion von Glühlampen aufgenommen. Bereits in diesem frühen Stadium hatten sich die beiden maßgeblichen Anschlussmethoden mit Edisons Schraubfassung, auch Edison-Sockel genannt, und Swans Bajonettfassung oder Swan-Sockel durchgesetzt. Die beiden Erfinder beschlossen schließlich – wenig überraschend – sich in Großbritannien miteinander zu assoziieren und gründeten 1880 die Edison & Swan United Lamp Company, die später unter dem Namen Ediswan bekannt wurde.

Obgleich er sein Ziel erreicht hatte, die

tion de l'Oregon), le *Columbia*, fut équipé du tout premier système d'éclairage commercialisé par la compagnie d'Edison. Le voyage inaugural du paquebot de New York à Portland, Oregon, fit sensation : ses cent quinze lumières scintillantes révélaient au monde le travail de l'inventeur et un long article fut publié dans la prestigieuse revue *Scientific American*.

En novembre 1879, les ateliers de Menlo Park avaient commencé à fabriquer des ampoules à incandescence en série. Déjà à cette époque, il existait deux manières de relier l'ampoule à la source électrique : la vis, choisie par Edison, et la baïonnette, préférée par Swan. Les deux inventeurs finirent naturellement par s'associer et fondèrent, en 1880, en Grande-Bretagne, la Edison & Swan United Lamp Company, qui serait connue plus tard sous le nom d'Ediswan.

Edison avait atteint son ambitieux objectif : commercialiser la première lampe à incandescence, mais il ne s'arrêta pas là. Il avait compris que sans une infrastructure permettant de distribuer le courant électrique, l'éclairage électrique ne serait jamais viable économiquement. « Créer des usines ou mourir »[12] était le choix qui s'imposait à lui. Les autres directeurs de la Electric Light Company Edison étant réticents

◁ Early Sawyer-Man lamp *with fibrous carbon filament* / *Frühes Modell einer* Sawyer-Man-Lampe *mit Glühfaden aus Kohlestofffaser* / *Une des premières lampes* Sawyer-Man *á filament en carbone fibreux*

▽▽ *Diagram of a Sawyer-Man incandescent lamp* / *Diagramm einer Glühlampe der Firma Sawyer-Man* / *Schema d'une lampe à incandescence Sawyer-Man*

▽ *Sawyer-Man Electric Co. advertisement,* Electrical Review, *18 February 1888* / *Werbeanzeige der Sawyer-Man Electric Company im* Electrical Review *vom 18. Februar 1888* / *Réclame de la Sawyer-Man Electric Co.,* Electrical Review, *18 février 1888*

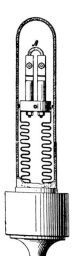

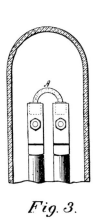

Fig. 1.

Fig. 2.

Fig. 3.

Fig. 4.

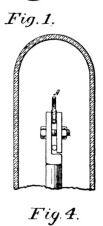

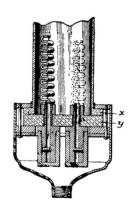

Fig. 5.

▷ Early Sawyer-Man lamp *with metal filament /*
Frühes Modell einer Sawyer-Man-Lampe *mit*
Metallglühfaden / Une des premières lampes
Sawyer-Man *à filament métallique*

with the founding of these factories and his establishment of the world's first electrical supply system for domestic use, introduced to New York City in 1882, Edison was up against stiff competition. The 1880s namely produced a veritable "Gold Rush" in the electric lighting sector, with competitors filing a plethora of patents, suing each other for infringements and merging their companies into larger entities. And whereas the "Wizard of Menlo Park" had favored the direct current system, by the early 1890s alternating current systems had become the preferred choice. In 1892 over seven million light bulbs were manufactured. The Electric Age had finally become a reality.

Lighting design in the age of electricity

Edison's incandescent light bulb extended the possibilities of lighting design immeasurably, and for designers, architects, engineers and artists the advent of electric light brought a whole new typology to their oeuvre. By dealing with the technical side of electric lighting, Edison had given designers the freedom to explore the functional and esthetic potential of a cheaper, safer and more reliable source of artificial light. Not surprisingly, some of the very

erste industriell gefertigte Glühlampe der Welt zu produzieren, erkannte Edison, dass der kommerzielle Erfolg des elektrischen Lichts von der Entwicklung einer Infrastruktur für die Stromverteilung abhing. Edison sah ganz deutlich, dass „die Frage lautet: Fabriken oder Tod!"[12] Da sich die anderen Direktoren der Edison Electric Light Company jedoch weigerten, weitere Investitionen zu tätigen, hatte er keine andere Wahl, als Geld zu borgen und seinen eigenen Aktienbesitz zu veräußern. Mit dem Geld baute er neue Fabriken, um all die Vorrichtungen herzustellen, die gebraucht wurden, um elektrisches Licht in Privathaushalte zu bringen: von Dynamos, Abzweigdosen und Erdkabeln bis zu Steckdosen und Schaltern. Aber auch mit dem Bau dieser Fabriken und der Gründung des weltweit ersten Energieversorgungssystems für Privathaushalte, das 1882 in New York City eingeführt wurde, sah sich Edison einer starken Konkurrenz gegenüber. Die „Goldrausch"-Phase der 1880er Jahre erlebte eine Unmenge an Patentanmeldungen seiner Konkurrenten, die einander wegen Patentrechtsverletzungen mit Klagen überzogen oder ihre Firmen zu immer noch größeren Unternehmen fusionierten. Zu Beginn der 90er Jahre des 19. Jahrhunderts waren Wechselstromsysteme zur bevorzugten Energieversorgung gegenüber Edisons Gleich-

à investir davantage, il lui fallut donc emprunter et vendre ses propres parts de la compagnie. Les fonds ainsi rassemblés servirent à construire des usines pour fabriquer des dynamos, des boîtes de raccordement, des tuyaux souterrains, des prises, des interrupteurs et autres appareils permettant d'acheminer l'électricité jusque dans les foyers. Même avec ces usines et bien qu'il eût fourni à la ville de New York, en 1882, le premier système au monde d'approvisionnement domestique en électricité, Edison dut faire face à une concurrence sans merci. L'industrie de l'éclairage électrique, pendant les années 1880, était en plein essor – on assistait alors à une véritable « ruée vers l'or », faite de courses aux brevets, de procès pour contrefaçons et de fusions d'entreprises. De plus, alors que le « magicien de Menlo Park » s'était montré favorable au courant continu, le courant alternatif fut largement adopté dès le début des années 1890. En 1892, plus de sept millions d'ampoules électriques furent fabriquées. L'Âge de l'Électricité était enfin devenu réalité.

La création de luminaires lampes à l'Âge de l'Électricité

L'avènement des ampoules à incandescence d'Edison fut, pour nombre

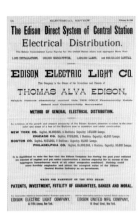

▽ An early illustration of bulb manufacture /
Zeichnung von den Anfängen der Glühbirnen-
herstellung / Dessin montrant la fabrication des
toutes premières ampoules

Edison Electric Light Co. advertisement,
Electrical Review, 18 February 1888 /
Werbeanzeige der Edison Electric Light Co.
im Electrical Review vom 18. Februar 1888 /
Réclame de l'Edison Electric Light Co.,
Electrical Review, 18 février 1888

first electric lights were adapted from
existing gaslight models, while others
were cobbled together using Edison-
patent switches and sockets. These
somewhat utilitarian designs found
themselves quickly surpassed, however,
by more decorative models by Art Nouveau designers, which better explored
the expressive potential of electric
light.

Already highly skilled in working with
glass and metal, the first generation of
professional designers – who included
William Arthur Smith Benson (1854–
1924), Louis Comfort Tiffany (1848–
1933), Émile Gallé (1846–1904) and
Josef Hoffmann (1870–1956) – combined new electric lighting technology
with avant-garde esthetic trends to
create some of the most beautiful lights
ever made. The Art Nouveau esthetic of
the fin-de-siècle period gave way in the
early 20th century to a more austere
approach to lighting, as embodied by
the utilitarian arc lights designed for
AEG in 1908 by Peter Behrens (1868–
1940). The Functionalist cause pioneered by Behrens and his associates
at the Deutscher Werkbund was taken
up during the 1920s and 1930s by
associates of the De Stijl movement
and designers at the Bauhaus, who
combined a Modernist idiom with lighting solutions that speculated on large-

stromsystemen geworden, und 1892
wurden bereits über sieben Millionen
Glühlampen produziert. Das elektrische
Zeitalter war endlich Realität geworden.

Lampendesign im Zeitalter der Elektrizität

Edisons Glühlampe sorgte für zahllose
Gestaltungsmöglichkeiten von Beleuchtungskörpern und erweiterte damit das
Tätigkeitsfeld von Designern, Architekten, Ingenieuren und Künstlern. Edison
hatte sich nur mit der technischen Seite
der elektrischen Beleuchtung auseinander gesetzt und dadurch den Ge-
staltern die Freiheit gelassen, das funktionale und ästhetische Potential dieser
billigen, sicheren und zuverlässigen
Lichtquelle auszuloten. Dabei über-
raschte es kaum, dass einige der ersten
elektrischen Lampen Gaslichtmodellen
nachgebildet waren, während andere
aus Edison-Fassungen und -Schaltern
mit beliebten Versatzstücken zusam-
mengeschustert wurden. Bald wurden
diese mehr auf Funktionalität bedach-
ten Modelle jedoch von dekorativeren
Jugendstil-Modellen abgelöst, in denen
die expressiven Möglichkeiten des
Kunstlichts besser zur Geltung kamen.

Die in der Arbeit mit Glas und Metall
bereits sehr bewanderte erste Genera-

d'artistes, de fabricants, d'architectes
et d'ingénieurs, une véritable révolution.
Edison s'était occupé de l'aspect technique de l'éclairage électrique, laissant
à d'autres le loisir d'explorer les possibilités fonctionnelles et esthétiques de
cette nouvelle source de lumière artificielle économique et sûre. Les toutes
premières lampes électriques – cela
n'a d'ailleurs rien d'étonnant – étaient
d'anciens modèles au gaz convertis.
D'autres furent bricolées à partir de
prises et d'interrupteurs des usines
Edison. Ces appareils utilitaires furent
toutefois rapidement surpassés par
des modèles plus décoratifs, de style
Art Nouveau, qui mettaient bien mieux
en valeur le potentiel expressif de la
lumière.

La première génération de créateurs
professionnels, dont William Arthur
Smith Benson (1854–1924), Louis
Comfort Tiffany (1848–1933), Émile
Gallé (1846–1904) et Josef Hoffmann
(1870–1956) était déjà
fort habile au travail du verre et du
métal. Mariant les technologies modernes et les tendances d'avant-garde
en matière d'esthétique, leurs lampes
étaient en fait de purs bijoux. Le mouvement Art Nouveau fit place au début
du XXᵉ siècle à une esthétique plus
austère, illustrée par les lampes à arc
utilitaires que Peter Behrens (1868–

Cover of Popular Electric Lighting by Captain E. Ironside Bax, published 1891 / Buchumschlag des 1891 veröffentlichten Titels Popular Electric Lighting von Captain E. Ironside Bax / Couverture du livre du Capitaine E. Ironside Bax, Popular Electric Lighting, publié en 1891

Cover of The Age of Electricity from Amber-Soul to Telephone by Park Benjamin, published 1887 / Buchumschlag von Park Benjamins 1887 veröffentlichtem Titel The Age of Electricity from Amber-Soul to Telephone / Couverture du livre de Park Benjamin, The Age of Electricity from Amber-Soul to Telephone, publié en 1887

scale production for the masses. Paradoxically, the ascendancy of the sumptuous Art Deco style during the same 1930s era saw designers such as Jean Perzel (1892–1986) and René Lalique (1860–1945) creating ever more decorative light fixtures, incorporating luxury materials such as bronze and alabaster, for an elite clientele. This remarkable period of design endeavour

"To invent, you need a good imagination and a pile of junk."

„Zum Erfinden braucht man eine gute Vorstellungskraft und einen Haufen Trödel."

« Pour inventer, il vous faut une bonne dose d'imagination et un tas de bric à brac. »

– Thomas Edison

saw the creation of a number of iconic lights: Wilhelm Wagenfeld (1900–1990) designed his *Model No. ME1* table light at the Bauhaus in 1924, Poul Henningsen (1894–1967) began developing his landmark *PH* range of lighting in 1927, George Carwardine (1887–1948) invented the *Anglepoise*

tion professioneller Designer, zu der William Arthur Smith Benson (1854–1924), Louis Comfort Tiffany (1848–1933), Émile Gallé (1846–1904) und Josef Hoffmann (1870–1956) gehörten, wusste die neue Technologie mit avantgardistischen Trends zu verbinden. Die Jugendstil-Ästhetik des ausgehenden 19. Jahrhunderts wurde zu Beginn des 20. Jahrhunderts von einem sachlicheren Zugang zum Leuchtendesign abgelöst, wie ihn die zweckmäßigen Bogenlampen verkörperten, die 1908 von dem Architekten Peter Behrens (1868–1940) für AEG entworfen wurden. Während der 1920er und 1930er Jahre wurde diese funktionalistische Richtung von den Bauhaus-Gestaltern und deren Mitstreitern aus der De Stijl-Bewegung fortgesetzt, indem sie Leuchten in einer modernistischen und für eine industrielle Massenproduktion konzipierten Formsprache entwarfen. Paradoxerweise brachte der ebenfalls während der 1930er Jahre vorherrschende üppige Stil des Art Déco Designer wie Jean Perzel (1892–1986) und René Lalique (1860–1945) hervor, die für eine elitäre Klientel immer dekorativere Beleuchtungskörper aus kostbaren Materialien schufen. Während dieser bemerkenswert produktiven Phase wurde eine Reihe von Leuchten entworfen, die in die Designgeschichte eingingen: Wil-

1940) créa en 1908 pour la firme AEG. Au cours des années 1920 et 1930, les membres du Bauhaus et du mouvement De Stijl poursuivirent le travail fonctionnaliste amorcé par Behrens et ses amis du Deutscher Werkbund, imaginant des appareils d'éclairage d'inspiration moderniste compatibles avec une production démocratique à grande échelle. Paradoxalement, c'était aussi l'époque de l'Art Déco dans toute sa somptuosité : plusieurs fabricants, notamment Jean Perzel (1892–1986) et René Lalique (1860–1945), produisaient des lampes de plus en plus sophistiquées, dont les plus luxueuses, usant de matériaux tels que le bronze et l'albâtre, étaient destinées à une clientèle d'élite. Plusieurs luminaires légendaires virent le jour pendant cette période d'extraordinaire raffinement esthétique : Wilhelm Wagenfeld (1900–1990) créa sa lampe de table *Modèle n° ME1* au Bauhaus en 1924 ; Poul Henningsen (1894–1967) lança sa célèbre série *PH* en 1927 ; George Carwardine (1887–1948) inventa la lampe *Anglepoise* en 1933 et Jacob Jacobsen (1901–1996) conçut sa classique lampe de travail *Luxo L-1* en 1937. Après la guerre, quelques compagnies américaines proposèrent de nouveaux types d'éclairage, tels que les systèmes *Lytepole* et *Lytespan* de Lightolier. C'était aussi le début du

Lighting design in the age of electricity   29

introduction

the evolution of artificial light

▷ Wolfram Lamp poster designed by F. Schön, Germany c.1908–10 / Von F. Schön gestaltetes Plakat mit Wolfram-Lampe, Deutschland, ca. 1908–10 / Lampe Wolfram, affiche de F. Schön, Allemagne, env. 1908–10

▽ Le Gaz Electrique, poster designed by P. Carrère, France, c.1910 / Von P. Carrère für Le Gaz Electrique gestaltetes Plakat, Frankreich, ca. 1910 / Affiche de P. Carrère pour le Gaz Électrique, France, env. 1910

light in 1933 and Jacob Jacobsen (1901–1996) designed the classic Luxo L-1 task light in 1937. The subsequent post-war period saw American companies introducing important new lighting typologies, such as Lightolier's Lytespan pole light systems. The 1940s also witnessed the emergence of the New Look, with designers creating lighting products that were strongly influenced by trends in contemporary fine art as well as by new materials developed during wartime. This new direction in lighting design rested on the concept of industrial sculpture and was chiefly pioneered by Italian designers, notably Gino Sarfatti (1912–1984), who combined style and imagination with low-tech manufacturing techniques in the development of products that explored the emotional potential of artificial light. This exhilarating time for lighting designers was bolstered by the widespread economic prosperity of the 1950s and the general public's pervasive desire to banish the war-torn past in order to embrace a bright new future. During this period of social reconstruction, the lighting industry came to be dominated by Italian companies, which operated as concept factories producing innovative lighting products that pushed both esthetic and technical boundaries to their limits.

helm Wagenfeld (1900–1990) entwarf 1924 am Bauhaus seine Tischleuchte Modell Nr. ME1, 1927 begann Poul Henningsen (1894–1967) mit der Entwicklung seiner berühmten PH-Serie, 1933 erfand George Carwardine (1887–1948) die Anglepoise und 1937 gestaltete Jacob Jacobsen (1901–1996) den Schreibtischleuchtenklassiker Luxo L-1. In den Nachkriegsjahren führten amerikanische Firmen bedeutende Neuerungen ein, wie etwa Lightolier mit seinen „Pole-Light" genannten Lytespan-Lichtsystemen. In diese Zeit fällt auch das Aufkommen des „New Look" mit Leuchten, deren Gestaltung von Trends in der zeitgenössischen Kunst und neuen Materialien beeinflusst war. Diese vom Konzept der industriellen Skulptur ausgehende Richtung im Leuchtendesign wurde hauptsächlich von italienischen Designern, insbesondere von Gino Sarfatti (1912–1984), angeführt. Begünstigt wurde diese aufregende Phase vom wachsenden materiellen Wohlstand der 1950er Jahre und von der Sehnsucht der breiten Öffentlichkeit, die vom Krieg überschattete Vergangenheit hinter sich zu lassen. Während dieser Phase wurde die Beleuchtungsindustrie zunehmend von italienischen Firmen beherrscht, die konzeptionell wegweisende Leuchten produzierten, welche sowohl ästhetisch als auch technisch das Äußerste wagten.

« New Look », période durant laquelle les créateurs se tournaient volontiers vers les beaux-arts et les nouvelles matières inventées pendant la guerre. Cette nouvelle tendance, qui s'inspirait du concept de sculpture industrielle, était particulièrement vivace en Italie, notamment avec Gino Sarfatti (1912–1984), dont les luminaires combinaient élégance, imagination et simplicité technique, tout en explorant le potentiel émotionnel de la lumière électrique. Toute cette effervescence avait comme toile de fond la croissance économique des années 1950 et la volonté du public d'oublier la guerre et de croire en un avenir radieux. Les entreprises italiennes, pendant cette période de reconstruction, étaient à l'avant-garde de l'industrie de l'éclairage, proposant sans cesse de nouveaux concepts et repoussant toujours plus loin les limites des défis techniques et esthétiques.

Éclairer les années 1960 et 1970

Depuis les débuts de l'électrification à la fin du XIXᵉ siècle, la conception des appareils d'éclairage a été influencée par les développements de la technologie de production de lumière (de la première ampoule à incandescence jusqu'aux toutes récentes diodes lumineuses), plus que par n'importe quel

Lightolier advertisement for the Lytegem high-intensity light, c. 1967 – this commercially successful light designed by Michael Lax in 1965 was one of the first high-intensity lights to be introduced into the domestic environment / Werbung von Lightolier für die hochintensive Leuchte Lytegem, ca. 1967 – die von Michael Lax 1965 entworfene Leuchte verkaufte sich sehr gut und war eine der ersten hochintensiven Leuchten für den Wohnbereich / Publicité Lightolier pour le spot basse tension Lytegem, vers 1967. Ce spot de Michael Lax (1965) connut un grand succès commercial et fut l'un des premiers éclairages haute intensité proposé pour un environnement domestique.

Lighting up the 1960s and 1970s

Since the beginning of electrification, in the late 19th century, the design of light fixtures has more than anything else been influenced by developments in lamp technology – from the first incandescent light bulb to the latest LEDs. For the first half of the 20th century most designers were happy to use regular filament bulbs – indeed, this is still the most popular light source for domestic environments – and it was not until the 1960s and early 1970s that designers really began to experiment with other sources of illumination, such as halogen bulbs and fluorescent and neon tubes. Ettore Sottsass dramatically incorporated arched neon tubes in his totem-like *Asteroide* light (1968), for example, while Joe Colombo's *Alogena* series (1970) was one of the first domestic lighting ranges to exploit the potential of low-voltage halogen bulbs. Importantly for future generations of lighting designers, this period also saw the development in 1962 of the very first visible-spectrum light-emitting diode (LED) by Nick Holonyak, Jr. (b. 1928), who was then working as a consultant to General Electric Company's laboratory. It is only recently, however, that LEDs have become powerful enough in terms of luminosity to be used effectively in lighting design.

Leuchtendesign in den 1960er und 1970er Jahren

Seit dem Beginn der Elektrifizierung Ende des 19. Jahrhunderts wurde die Gestaltung der Beleuchtungskörper in erster Linie durch Neuerungen in der Lampentechnik beeinflusst – von der ersten Glühbirne bis hin zu modernsten Leuchtdioden (LEDs). In der ersten Hälfte des 20. Jahrhunderts beschränkten sich die meisten Designer darauf, die üblichen Glühbirnen zu verwenden – tatsächlich sind sie nach wie vor die beliebteste Lichtquelle in der Wohnraumbeleuchtung –, und erst in den 1960ern und Anfang der 1970er Jahre begannen sie, mit anderen Leuchtmitteln zu experimentieren, wie etwa Halogenlampen oder Leuchtstoff- und Neonröhren. Ettore Sottsass zum Beispiel bezog gebogene Neonröhren auf sehr wirkungsvolle Weise in die Gestaltung seiner skulpturalen Stehleuchte *Asteroide* (1968) ein, und Joe Colombos *Alogena*-Reihe (1970) war eine der ersten Wohnraum-Leuchtenserien, die das Potenzial von Niedervolt-Halogenlampen nutzten. In dieselbe Zeit, genauer in das Jahr 1962, fällt auch die für spätere Beleuchtungsdesigner wichtige Entwicklung der allerersten Leuchtdiode (LED) im sichtbaren Spektrum durch den 1928 geborenen Nick Holonyak Jr., der damals als Berater

autre facteur. Au cours de la première moitié du XXᵉ siècle, la plupart des designers se contentèrent d'utiliser les classiques ampoules à filament – qui restent la source lumineuse la plus répandue dans l'environnement domestique – et ce n'est pas avant les années 1960 et le début des années 1970 qu'ils commencèrent réellement à expérimenter d'autres pistes, comme celle des ampoules halogènes, des tubes fluorescents et au néon. Avec son fameux sens du spectaculaire, Ettore Sottsass utilisa des tubes au néon cintrés dans son luminaire-totem *Asteroide* de 1968, par exemple, tandis que la série *Alogena* de Joe Colombo (1970) fut l'une des premières gammes de luminaires pour la maison à exploiter le potentiel des ampoules halogènes basse tension. Cette période cruciale pour les futures générations de designers spécialisés dans ce domaine, vit également la mise au point, en 1962, de la première diode lumineuse à spectre visible (LED) par Nick Holonyak Jr. (né en 1928), alors consultant auprès du laboratoire de la General Electric Company. Ce n'est que récemment, cependant, que les diodes sont devenues suffisamment puissantes en termes de lumens pour être sérieusement utilisées dans la conception de luminaires.

Les années 1960 et le début des

◁ Ennio Lucini, Cespuglio table light, 1968 – an iconic Pop design, with its glowing acrylic diffusers this light provocatively contested the esthetic parameters of lighting design / Ennio Lucini, Tischleuchte Cespuglio, 1968 – diese Ikone des Pop-Designs stellte mit ihren leuchtenden Acryldiffusoren die ästhetischen Parameter des Beleuchtungsdesigns auf provokante Weise in Frage / Ennio Lucini, lampe de table Cespuglio, 1968, icône du design pop. Ses diffuseurs en acrylique luminescent contestaient de façon provocante les dogmes esthétiques de la conception classique des luminaires.

▷ Poltronova publicity photograph of a contemporary interior showing the Sanremo floor light designed by Archizoom Associati, c. 1968 – an early Radical lighting design / Werbefoto von Poltronova, Aufnahme eines zeitgenössischen Interieurs mit Stehleuchte Sanremo von Archizoom Associati, ca. 1968 – ein frühes Beispiel des Radical Designs / Photographie publicitaire Poltronova d'un intérieur de l'époque montrant le lampadaire Sanremo conçu par Archizoom Associati, vers 1968. C'est un des premiers projets de lampe du mouvement radical.

The 1960s and early 1970s also saw newly available plastics broadening the designer's choice of materials – from spray-on "Cocoon" (a self-skinning PVC) to translucent Perspex (methacrylate). But if the growing use of synthetic polymers had a major influence on lighting design, even more dramatic was the impact of the huge cultural shifts that occurred during these years. The social freedoms that epitomized the era were directly translated into experimental anything-goes designs that challenged the boundaries of lighting and art. These "light sculptures," such as those by Yonel Lébovici, were not intended to be particularly functional in the traditional sense, but were instead provocative three-dimensional projections inspired by futuristic utopian visions.

The Middle East Oil Crisis that impacted on world economies in the early 1970s shattered these beautiful dreams and helped to concentrate the minds of both designers and manufacturers. Expensive oil meant that cheap plastics were a thing of the past, while the ensuing global recession necessitated a return to the Functionalist principles of the Modern Movement. For the most part, lighting from the mid-to-late 1970s was characterized by a strictly rational approach that sought to achieve maximum effect with minimum means.

des Labors von General Electric tätig war. Erst in jüngerer Zeit gelang es jedoch, LEDs mit einer für das Beleuchtungsdesign ausreichenden Effizienz zu entwickeln.

In den 1960ern und Anfang der 1970er Jahre standen erstmals auch neu entwickelte Kunststoffe zur Verfügung, die den Designern mehr Gestaltungsmöglichkeiten boten – von der aufspritzbaren „Cocoon"-Glasfaserhaut (ein PVC-Integralschaum) bis zu lichtdurchlässigem Perspex (Methacrylat). Hatte die zunehmende Verwendung von synthetischen Polymeren schon einen großen Einfluss auf das Beleuchtungsdesign, so wirkten sich die gewaltigen kulturellen Umwälzungen dieser Jahre noch viel dramatischer aus. Das für diese Zeit charakteristische Sprengen der Konventionen wurde nach dem Motto „Alles ist möglich" in experimentelles Design übersetzt, die Grenze zwischen Beleuchtung und Kunst aufgebrochen. Die „Lichtskulpturen" eines Yonel Lébovici zielten nicht auf Funktionalität im traditionellen Sinn ab, sondern waren provokante dreidimensionale Entwürfe, die sich aus futuristisch-utopischen Visionen speisten.

All diese schönen Träume zerbrachen und die Designer wie die Hersteller begannen umzudenken, als Anfang der

années 1970 bénéficièrent également d'un élargissement du choix de matériaux grâce à l'apparition de nouveaux plastiques, du plastique projeté « Cocoon » au Perspex translucide (méthacrylate). Mais si l'usage grandissant des polymères synthétiques a exercé une influence majeure sur le design, l'impact de la puissante évolution culturelle durant cette décennie est tout aussi important. La libération des contraintes sociales qui marqua fortement cette période se retrouva spectaculairement traduite en audacieux projets expérimentaux bousculant les frontières entre l'art et l'éclairage. Ces « sculptures lumineuses », comme celles de Yonel Lébovici, ne se voulaient pas particulièrement fonctionnelles, au sens traditionnel, mais jouaient la provocation par leur projection en trois dimensions inspirée de visions futuristes utopiques.

La crise du pétrole qui frappa les économies mondiales au début des années 1970 ruina ces rêves et incita les designers et les fabricants à davantage de concentration. Un pétrole cher signifiait que les plastiques bon marché appartenaient dorénavant au passé, et la récession globale qui s'ensuivit favorisa un retour au fonctionnalisme du Mouvement moderne. Pour sa plus grande part, l'éclairage du milieu à la

Richard Sapper's *Tizio* task light (1972) and Ernest Gismondi's *Sintesi* (1975) both epitomized the short-lived High-Tech style, which was born out of the "Less is More" dictum first voiced by Ludwig Mies van der Rohe. The Oil Crisis also served to draw attention to the finite nature of the world's energy sources, a realization that prompted the development of General Electric's first energy-saving compact fluorescent lamp (CFL) in 1973. Other manufacturers also conducted laboratory trials of CFLs but deemed them too costly to mass-produce. In fact it was not until 1994, when Philips introduced its *New Generation TL* lamps, that CFLs really caught on. These new lamps not only had an increased life expectancy but also a much lower mercury content.

New technologies and the emotional aspect of light

By the late 1970s many product designers, particularly in Italy, had grown bored of the objective and highly constrained traditional approach to industrial design. In an effort to combat what they saw as the overwhelming banality of mainstream products, they pursued a radical Anti-Design agenda, the seeds of which had been sown in the late 1960s. The extraordinary experimental lights

1970er Jahre die Weltwirtschaft im Zeichen der Ölkrise im Nahen Osten stand. Die Verteuerung des Erdöls führte dazu, dass der ehemals billige Kunststoff zu einem teuren Werkstoff wurde, und die nun folgende weltweite Rezession machte die Rückbesinnung auf die funktionalistischen Grundsätze der Moderne erforderlich. In der zweiten Hälfte der 1970er Jahre war das Beleuchtungsdesign größtenteils von einer streng rationalen Haltung und dem Bemühen um maximale Wirkung bei minimalem Materialeinsatz bestimmt. Die Arbeitsleuchten *Tizio* (1972) von Richard Sapper und *Sintesi* (1975) von Ernesto Gismondi verkörpern beide den kurzlebigen Hightech-Stil, der auf dem ursprünglich von Ludwig Mies van der Rohe propagierten Grundsatz des „Weniger ist mehr" beruhte. Die Ölkrise führte auch vor Augen, dass fossile Brennstoffe nur begrenzt vorhanden sind, was General Electric dazu veranlasste, 1973 die erste energiesparende Kompakt-Leuchtstofflampe auf den Markt zu bringen. Andere Hersteller experimentierten ebenfalls mit diesem neuen Lampentyp, hielten ihre Serienfertigung aber für zu kostenintensiv. Erst als Philips 1994 seine Leuchten *TL New Generation* auf den Markt brachte, setzten sich die Kompakt-Leuchtstofflampen durch. Die neuen Leuchtmittel hatten nicht nur eine längere

fin des années 1970 se caractérisa par une approche strictement rationnelle qui cherchait à obtenir le maximum d'effets avec le minimum de moyens. La lampe de travail *Tizio* de Richard Sapper (1972) et la *Sintesi* de Ernesto Gismondi (1975) exprimaient toutes deux un style high-tech qui ne dura guère, inspiré d'une application du célèbre « Moins c'est plus » de Ludwig Mies van der Rohe. La crise du pétrole servit également à attirer l'attention sur la nature non renouvelable des réserves mondiales, ce qui accéléra le développement par la General Electric des premières ampoules compactes fluorescentes à économies d'énergie (CFL) apparues en 1973. D'autres fabricants menèrent également des essais en laboratoire, mais les jugèrent trop coûteuses à produire. En fait, il fallut attendre le lancement par Philips, en 1994, de ses ampoules *Nouvelle génération TL*, pour que les ampoules CFL se répandent vraiment. Non seulement elles duraient beaucoup plus longtemps mais elles contenaient aussi nettement moins de mercure.

Les nouvelles technologies et l'émotion de la lumière

À la fin des années 1970, de nombreux designers produit, en particulier en Italie,

New technologies and the emotional aspect of light   33

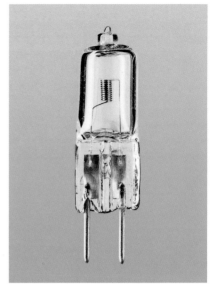

designed by Alessandro Mendini and Michele De Lucchi for Studio Alchimia in the late 1970s and early 1980s, for example, used ironic wit, bold color and unusual forms to erode the austerity of Modern Movement dogma. This early foray into Post-Modern lighting design was followed by the Memphis design studio, which used patterned laminates and unusual totemic forms to create lighting products that were symbolically rich, if somewhat functionally deprived. The credit-fueled economic boom of the 1980s supported this more expressive approach to lighting design, especially now that "functional" lighting (i. e. recessed halogen downlighters, spotlights etc.) had become so unobtrusive as to be almost invisible. With the technical aspects of lighting by now highly refined, the designers of the 1980s were free to explore the more symbolic implications of "enlightenment" and the idea of lighting as metaphor.

The 1990s brought huge advances in lamp technology, including the introduction of cool-running CDM (ceramic discharge mercury) bulbs. Not only was the light emitted by CDMs more powerful and focused than existing halogen bulbs, but it was also whiter and hence provided better color rendering – an important consideration in the retail sector in particular. In place of halogen

Lebensdauer, sondern enthielten auch deutlich weniger Quecksilber.

Neue Technologien und der emotionale Aspekt des Lichts

Ende der 1970er Jahre hatten viele Produktdesigner, vor allem die italienischen, genug von der vernunftbestimmten und sehr eingeengten traditionellen Haltung im Industriedesign. Um gegen die ihrer Meinung nach erdrückende Banalität der Mainstream-Produkte anzukämpfen, nahmen sie eine radikale Anti-Design-Haltung ein, deren Ursprung in den ausgehenden 1960er Jahren lag. Die außergewöhnlich experimentellen Leuchten, die zum Beispiel Alessandro Mendini und Michele De Lucchi Ende der 1970er und Anfang der 1980er Jahre für Studio Alchimia entwarfen, setzten Ironie, kräftige Farben und ungewohnte Formen ein, um die dogmatische Strenge der Moderne aufzubrechen. Diesem frühen Vorstoß in das postmoderne Beleuchtungsdesign schloss sich das Studio Memphis an, das äußerst symbolträchtige, wenn auch funktional etwas reduzierte Leuchten aus bunt gemusterten Laminaten und mit ungewöhnlichen Formen gestaltete. Der durch Kredite gespeiste Wirtschaftsboom der 1980er Jahre trug zu dieser expressiveren Haltung zum

s'étaient lassés de l'approche traditionnelle, par objectifs cadrés, du design industriel. Pour combattre ce à quoi ils attribuaient la banalité étouffante des produits de grande consommation, ils se lancèrent dans une démarche radicale d'anti-design, dont les premières graines avaient été semées dès la fin des années 1960. Les extraordinaires luminaires expérimentaux d'Alessandro Mendini et Michele De Lucchi pour Studio Alchimia à la fin des années 1970 et au début des années 1980, par exemple, mettaient en œuvre des formes inhabituelles, des couleurs audacieuses, une ironie et un esprit qui bousculaient l'austérité des dogmes modernistes. Cette première avancée vers le postmodernisme fut suivie par l'apparition du Studio Memphis, qui utilisait des plastiques strafiés à motifs et de curieuses formes totémiques pour créer ses luminaires riches en symbolique mais parfois bien peu fonctionnels. Le boom économique, gavé par le crédit, de la fin des années 1980, alimenta cette approche plus expressive, et ce d'autant que l'éclairage «fonctionnel» (ampoules halogènes discrètes, spots, etc.) était maintenant devenu si discret qu'il frisait l'invisibilité. Les aspects techniques étant résolus par des moyens raffinés, les designers des années 1980 étaient libres d'explorer les implications plus symboliques de

◁◁ *Richard Sapper, Tizio task light for Artemide, 1972 – low-voltage current is carried through arms to halogen bulb in the head / Richard Sapper, Arbeitsleuchte Tizio für Artemide, 1972 – der Niederspannungsstrom wird durch die Arme zur Halogenlampe im Leuchtenkopf geleitet / Richard Sapper, lampe de bureau Tizio pour Artemide, 1972. Le courant basse tension alimente directement l'ampoule halogène.*

◁ *Low-voltage halogen bulb made by Philips, 2001 / Niedervolt-Halogenlampe von Philips, 2001 / Ampoule halogène basse tension Philips, 2001*

▷ *Ernesto Gismondi, Track lighting system for Artemide, c.1980 – could be used in conjunction with heads from the Aton and Sintesi ranges / Ernesto Gismondi, Leuchtschienensystem für Artemide, ca. 1980 – kombinierbar mit Leuchtenköpfen aus den Serien Aton und Sintesi / Ernesto Gismondi : système d'éclairage sur rail pour Artemide, vers 1980. Ce système acceptait à la fois les spots des gammes Aton et Sintesi.*

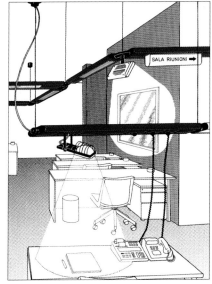

bulbs, too, compact fluorescents were now developed for use in spotlights in order to reduce energy consumption. Today's low-energy mini fluorescent lamps are up to 80% more efficient than conventional tungsten filament bulbs and last eight times longer.

"Over and above its symbolic value, light allows us to read, interpret and change reality."

„Über seinen symbolischen Wert hinaus ermöglicht uns das Licht, die Umgebung zu erkennen, zu interpretieren und zu verändern."

« Au-delà de sa valeur symbolique, la lumière nous permet de lire, de décrypter et de changer le réel. »

– Claudio Salocchi

These developments went hand in hand with the increasing realization that light can affect moods and work levels. Natural daylight is constantly changing, from pink-tinged morning light to bright midday light to the warm orange of sunset, yet the majority of artificial lighting systems still offer a constant, unchang-

Design bei, vor allem da die „funktionalen" Beleuchtungskörper (d. h. Halogen-Deckeneinbauleuchten, Strahler usw.) formal so dezent geworden waren, dass man sie kaum mehr wahrnahm. Auch die Lichttechnik war inzwischen so ausgereift, dass sich die Designer auf die symbolischen Implikationen der „Erleuchtung" und das Licht als Metapher konzentrieren konnten.

Die 1990er Jahre brachten wieder bedeutende Fortschritte in der Lichttechnik, unter anderem auch die Einführung der wenig Hitze abstrahlenden Quecksilberdampf-Entladungslampen mit Keramikkolben. Sie erzeugen nicht nur ein stärkeres und konzentrierteres Licht als Halogenlampen, es ist auch weißer und sorgt für eine bessere Farbwiedergabe, was vor allem für Warenpräsentationen eine wichtige Rolle spielt. Für Strahler wurden nun statt Halogenlampen die im Stromverbrauch viel sparsameren Kompakt-Leuchtstofflampen entwickelt. Die heutigen energiesparenden Mini-Leuchtstofflampen sind um bis zu 80% effizienter als konventionelle Wolframbirnen und haben eine achtmal so lange Lebensdauer.

Parallel zu diesen technischen Entwicklungen stellte sich auch immer mehr heraus, dass das Licht einen Einfluss auf unsere Stimmung und Arbeitsleis-

« l'illumination » et de l'idée même d'éclairage comme métaphore.

Les années 1990 furent marquées par d'importants progrès, dont l'apparition d'ampoules « froides » CDM (céramique à décharge de mercure). Non seulement l'éclairage émis était plus puissant et plus concentré qu'avec les halogènes, mais la lumière était plus blanche et permettait donc un meilleur rendu des couleurs, facteur important pour le secteur de la distribution, entre autres. Détrônant les halogènes, des ampoules fluorescentes compactes équipaient les spots afin de réduire la consommation d'énergie. Aujourd'hui les lampes fluorescentes basse consommation sont jusqu'à 80% plus efficaces en rendement que les ampoules conventionnelles à filament de tungstène et durent huit fois plus longtemps.

Ces développements sont allés de pair avec la prise de conscience croissante que la lumière peut affecter l'humeur et la productivité. La lumière naturelle change constamment, passant du rose de l'aurore à l'éclat de midi et à l'orangé du coucher de soleil. Pourtant, la majorité des systèmes d'éclairage offre un éclairage constant. Ceci peut affecter nos biorythmes et nos niveaux de sérotonine, et il est établi que la privation de la lumière du jour peut provo-

ing light. This can play havoc with our biorhythms by affecting our seratonin levels. It is a well-established fact that sunlight deprivation can cause depression, or SAD (Seasonal Affective Disorder), as it is known in medical circles. But it was only in the late 1990s that lighting manufacturers – notably Erco and iGuzzini – began devising systems that mimicked the natural fluctuations of sunlight that occur as clouds sail across the sun's path while it makes its passage from east to west. From the mid-1990s onwards, companies such as Artemide began exploring a new kind of feel-good lighting that offered variable degrees of brightness and hues of light to suit one's mood. This human-centered approach to lighting was intended to promote a sense of well-being and provided an exceptional degree of user interaction. The emotional aspect of lighting is now seen as highly relevant by manufacturers and it looks set to become an even bigger issue in the future.

Lighting today and tomorrow

The last few years have witnessed unprecedented levels of innovation in the lighting industry, particularly in Europe. Indeed, to judge from a stroll round the biannual "Euroluce" trade fair in Milan

tung hat. Das natürliche Tageslicht verändert sich ständig – vom schwachen Rosaton am Morgen über das grelle Licht am Mittag bis zum warmen Orange bei Sonnenuntergang –, während die meisten künstlichen Beleuchtungssysteme nach wie vor für konstant gleich bleibendes Licht sorgen. Das kann sich auf unseren Seratoninhaushalt auswirken und unseren Biorhythmus kräftig durcheinander bringen. Es ist erwiesen, dass ein Mangel an Sonnenlicht depressiv machen kann – die Mediziner sprechen von SAD (saisonabhängige Depression). Aber erst Ende der 1990er Jahre versuchten Beleuchtungsfirmen – insbesondere ERCO und iGuzzini – mit ihren Produkten die natürlichen Veränderungen des Sonnenlichts nachzuahmen. Ab Mitte der 1990er Jahre begannen Firmen wie Artemide eine neue Art von „Wohlfühl-Beleuchtung" zu erproben, bei der man die Helligkeitsgrade und Farbtönungen je nach Stimmung variieren kann. Diese Art der Beleuchtung stellt den Menschen und sein Wohlbefinden in den Mittelpunkt und lässt dem Benutzer außergewöhnlich viel Interaktionsspielraum. Heute messen die Hersteller dem emotionalen Aspekt der Beleuchtung große Bedeutung bei, und es sieht ganz danach aus, dass er in Zukunft noch wichtiger werden wird.

quer une dépression saisonnière. Mais ce n'est qu'à la fin des années 1990 que les fabricants d'appareils d'éclairage – en particulier ERCO et iGuzzini – ont commencé à mettre au point des systèmes reproduisant les fluctuations naturelles de la lumière du jour, ce qui arrive, par exemple, lorsqu'un nuage masque le soleil. À partir du milieu des années 1990, des entreprises comme Artemide commencèrent à travailler sur un nouveau type d'éclairage de confort offrant des degrés de puissance et des nuances lumineuses adaptables à l'atmosphère recherchée. Cette approche centrée sur l'homme entendait promouvoir un sentiment de bien-être tout en apportant à l'usager un exceptionnel potentiel d'interactivité. L'aspect émotionnel de la lumière est aujourd'hui pris en compte par les fabricants et promet d'être à l'avenir un enjeu encore plus important.

Éclairer aujourd'hui et demain

Ces dernières années, l'industrie de l'éclairage a connu des niveaux d'innovation sans précédent, en particulier en Europe. Si l'on en juge par une visite du salon biennal «Euroluce» de Milan, de la boutique du Design Museum à Londres, ou par la lecture de n'importe quel magazine traitant de design, il

◁◁ *Ceramic discharge lamp (CDL) manufactured by Philips, 2001 / Entladungslampe mit Keramikbrenner, hergestellt von Philips, 2001 / Ampoule céramique à décharge (CDL) fabriquée par Philips, 2001*

◁ *Compact fluorescent bulbs manufactured by Philips, 2000 / Kompakt-Leuchtstofflampen, hergestellt von Philips, 2000 / Ampoules compactes fluorescentes fabriquées par Philips, 2000*

▷ *SAD-A-LITE light manufactured by Northern Lights of Canada, c. 1980–85 – this was the first prescribable light used to treat Seasonal Affective Disorder; it emitted a whopping 10,000 lumens / Leuchte SAD-A-LITE, hergestellt von Northern Lights of Canada, ca. 1980–85 – die erste Leuchte, die zur Behandlung der saisonabhängigen Depression verschrieben werden konnte, mit einer Leuchtintensität von gigantischen 10.000 Lumen / SAD-A-LITE, fabriquée par Northern Lights of Canada, vers 1980–85. Ses 10 000 lumens ont fait d'elle la première lampe prescrite dans le traitement de la «dépression saisonnière».*

or the Design Museum shop in London, or even a casual perusal of any design-related magazine, it would seem that many of the most interesting break throughs in product design are now happening in lighting. Newly developed synthetic materials and technologies continue to transform the possibilities for lighting design, while at the same time a shift in cultural emphasis from the functional to the emotional has granted designers a broader esthetic freedom. The preoccupation of contemporary designers with the sensual and poetic potential of lighting has in turn fueled the increasing interest in lighting demonstrated by today's mainstream consumers. Many recent designs, such as Jurgen Bey's *Light Shade Shade* hanging light (1999) and Tord Boontje's *Blossom* chandelier (2002), more often resemble quasi-artworks than functional tools for illumination.

Electric lighting has today reached another major turning-point in its evolution. The technology it has relied upon almost exclusively for over a century – the incandescent filament light bulb – is likely to be succeeded by a new generation of discreetly small low-voltage LEDs that are much more energy-efficient. These remarkable semi-conductor devices can already last 40 to 50 years before they burn out. In terms of

Beleuchtung heute und morgen

Die Beleuchtungsindustrie, ganz besonders die europäische, hat in den letzten Jahren einen nie dagewesenen Innovationsschub erlebt. Und wenn man sich auf der alle zwei Jahre in Mailand stattfindenden Messe „Euroluce" oder im Shop des Londoner Design Museums umsieht, ja sogar wenn man nur eine Designzeitschrift durchblättert, bekommt man den Eindruck, dass viele der interessantesten Entwicklungen im Produktdesign derzeit im Bereich des Beleuchtungsdesigns stattfinden. Nach wie vor verändern neu entwickelte synthetische Werkstoffe und neue Technologien die Gestaltungsmöglichkeiten, während zugleich die Verschiebung des kulturellen Schwerpunkts vom Funktionalen zum Emotionalen den Designern mehr ästhetische Freiheit ermöglicht. Viele in den letzten Jahren entstandene Entwürfe, wie etwa die Hängeleuchte *Light Shade Shade* (1999) von Jürgen Bey und der Kronleuchter *Blossom* (2002) von Tord Boontje, ähneln eher einem Kunstwerk als einem funktionalen Beleuchtungskörper.

Derzeit steht das elektrische Licht wieder an einem wichtigen Wendepunkt in seiner Entwicklung. Die Technik, auf der es seit mehr als einem Jahrhundert fast ausschließlich beruht – die Glüh-

semble que nombre des avancées les plus intéressantes dans le domaine du design produit concernent aujourd'hui l'éclairage. De nouveaux matériaux de synthèse, de nouvelles technologies transforment sans cesse les possibilités de création, tandis que dans le même temps le passage du fonctionnel à l'émotionnel a apporté aux designers une plus grande liberté esthétique. L'intérêt des designers contemporains pour le potentiel sensuel et poétique de l'éclairage alimente chez les consommateurs un attrait grandissant pour les lampes. De nombreux modèles récents, comme la suspension de Jurgen Bey *Light Shade Shade* (1999) et le lustre *Blossom* (2002) de Tord Boontje, sont plus proches de l'œuvre d'art que de l'outil d'éclairage fonctionnel.

L'éclairage aborde aujourd'hui un tournant crucial. À la technologie sur laquelle il s'appuyait depuis plus d'un siècle – l'ampoule à filament incandescent – va probablement succéder une nouvelle génération de minuscules diodes électroluminescentes (LED) à basse tension, beaucoup moins gourmandes en énergie. Ces remarquables semi-conducteurs peuvent déjà durer quarante à cinquante ans avant d'être remplacés. En termes de luminosité, dix LED équivalent à une ampoule classique et il n'est donc pas inconcevable qu'au cours

"Light is one of the most difficult properties to pin down!"

„Licht ist eine der am schwierigsten einzufangenden Eigenschaften."

« La lumière est l'une des choses les plus difficiles à saisir. »

– Ezio Manzini

luminosity, about ten LEDs equal one regular bulb, so it is not inconceivable that within the next decade they will begin to replace traditional filaments. In fact this has already started to happen, with LEDs being used by the automobile industry in its latest-generation car tail lights.

In 2002 Joseph C. Oberle, General Manager of Technology at GE Lighting, predicted that the 20 lumens per watt that a single LED could produce would double within five years. Remarkably, just two years on from that pronouncement, the Silicon Valley-based company Lumileds developed a LED capable of producing 120 lumens per single source, spectacularly surpassing Oberle's prediction. Important for the

lampe –, wird aller Wahrscheinlichkeit nach durch eine neue Generation von unauffälligen kleinen Niedervolt-Leuchtdioden (LEDs) abgelöst werden, die mit wesentlich weniger Energie auskommen. Diese bemerkenswerten, auf der Halbleitertechnologie beruhenden Lichtemitter haben schon heute eine Lebensdauer von vierzig bis fünfzig Jahren. Was die Lichtausbeute betrifft, entsprechen etwa zehn LEDs einer normalen Glühbirne. Es ist also nicht undenkbar, dass die LEDs in den nächsten zehn Jahren die traditionellen Lampen allmählich ersetzen werden. Dieser Prozess hat in Wirklichkeit bereits begonnen, denn die Automobilindustrie verwendet die LED-Technik bereits seit längerem für ihre Rückleuchten.

2002 sagte der General Manager for Technology von General Electric Joseph C. Oberle voraus, dass die 20 Lumen pro Watt, die eine LED damals erzeugte, innerhalb von fünf Jahren verdoppelt werden könnten. Erstaunlicherweise entwickelte die im Silicon Valley ansässige Firma Lumileds nur zwei Jahre später eine LED, die 120 Lumen pro Lichtquelle erzeugt, und übertraf damit Oberles Prognose deutlich. Wichtig für eine breite Akzeptanz der LED in der Zukunft ist auch die Tatsache, dass es inzwischen nicht nur bunte, sondern auch weiße LEDs gibt. Vorläufig gibt es

de la prochaine décennie, elles commencent à remplacer les filaments traditionnels. En fait, l'industrie automobile en utilise déjà pour équiper les feux arrières des voitures.

En 2002, Joseph C. Oberle, directeur général de la technologie à GE Lighting, prédisait que les 20 lumens par watt qu'une diode peut produire doubleraient dans les cinq ans. Deux ans plus tard, la société Lumileds, basée dans la Silicon Valley, a annoncé une diode capable de produire 120 lumens par source, dépassant, et de loin, la prédiction d'Oberle. La diffusion de ces diodes sera d'autant plus importante qu'elles sont maintenant disponibles en lumière blanche et non seulement de couleur. Un inconvénient persiste cependant : les diodes à lumière blanche semblent avoir une durée de vie plus courte, car leur protection en époxy s'assombrit lorsqu'elle est exposée aux UV de la lumière émise. Mais il est inévitable que dans un futur sans doute proche, ce problème soit résolu par de nouveau progrès dans la technologie des matériaux.

Une nouvelle technologie s'ouvre actuellement aux explorations de l'industrie : les O-LED (diodes lumineuses organiques) souples et transparentes, qui devraient encore renforcer la mobilité des appareils d'éclairage. Parfois

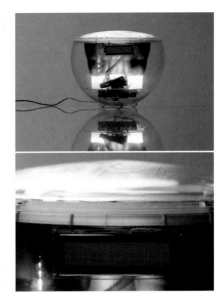

future widespread acceptance of LEDs, they are now available not just in color but also in white. There is, however, a temporary drawback: white LEDs appear to have a shorter lifespan, because the epoxy casing housing them darkens when it is exposed to the emitted UV light. But it is inevitable that in the not-too-distant future this shortcoming will be resolved through advances in materials technology.

There is yet another field of next-generation technology undergoing development in the lighting industry – O-LEDs (organic light-emitting devices) that are flexible and transparent and look set to bring even greater portability to lighting. Also known as Electro-Luminescence (EL) film, O-LEDs will radically change the esthetic vocabulary of lighting design in the future. Progressive young designers, such as Sam Buxton, are already integrating them into their product solutions. These films essentially consist of layers of incredibly thin yet flexible sheets of plastic that contain phosphorescent material sandwiched between electrodes. Today, light-emitting films are used to backlight the liquid crystal displays of wristwatches, mobile phones, pagers and consoles of hand-held computer games, but in the future it is very likely they will transform many other products, includ-

jedoch noch eine Schwierigkeit: Weiße LEDs haben eine kürzere Lebensdauer, da die Kunstharzummantelungen durch das emittierte UV-Licht getrübt werden. Dieser Nachteil wird aber zweifellos in nicht allzu ferner Zukunft durch Fortschritte in der Materialtechnik beseitigt werden können.

Auch bei einer anderen Zukunftstechnologie ist es die Beleuchtungsindustrie, die ihre Weiterentwicklung vorantreibt: die organischen Lichtdioden (O-LEDs), die flexibel und transparent sind und die Beleuchtung voraussichtlich noch viel mobiler machen werden. Die manchmal auch als Elektroluminiszenz- oder EL-Folie bezeichneten O-LEDs werden das ästhetische Formenvokabular des Beleuchtungsdesigns radikal verändern. Progressive junge Designer wie Sam Buxton integrieren sie bereits in ihre Produktlösungen. Die Folien bestehen im Wesentlichen aus Schichten von extrem dünnen, flexiblen Kunststoffschichten, die ein zwischen Elektroden gepacktes phosphoreszierendes Material enthalten. Heute werden lichtemittierende Folien für die Hintergrundbeleuchtung der LCD-Anzeigen von Armbanduhren, Mobiltelefonen, Pagern und Computerspielkonsolen eingesetzt, aber in der Zukunft werden sie sehr wahrscheinlich viele weitere Produkte verändern. Die deut-

appelés film électroluminescent (EL), les O-LED changeront radicalement le vocabulaire esthétique du design de luminaires. De jeunes designers progressistes comme Sam Buxton les intègrent déjà dans leurs projets. Ces films sont en fait des couches de feuilles de plastique incroyablement fines et souples, qui contiennent des matériaux phosphorescents pris en sandwich entre des électrodes. Aujourd'hui, ils servent déjà à rétro-éclairer des cristaux liquides sur les écrans de montres, de téléphones mobiles, de consoles de jeux d'ordinateurs, mais dans le futur, il est très probable qu'ils transformeront de multiples autres produits, dont les téléviseurs. La société allemande Bree, qui collabore avec le Bayer Material Sciences Lab, a même utilisé des films EL pour un nouveau sac à main : grâce à des couches de plastique électroluminescent connectées à une pile de 9 volts, le contenu du sac s'éclaire lorsqu'il s'ouvre. Ainsi plus de gouffre noir lorsque vous cherchez désespérément vos clés de voiture… Des constructeurs d'automobiles ont commencé à utiliser le film EL à l'intérieur de certains modèles, la Mercedes-Benz Maybach étant la première voiture à bénéficier de ce progrès technologique. Deux des principaux avantages du film EL sont qu'il génère beaucoup moins de chaleur que les ampoules à filament

ing televisions. The German company Bree, working in conjunction with Bayer Material Sciences Lab, has even employed EL film for a new handbag: by incorporating layers of plastic electroluminescent sheet connected to a 9-volt battery, when the bag is opened its contents are illuminated. So no more bottomless black holes while searching for those elusive keys … Automotive manufacturers have also begun using EL film for car interiors, with the Mercedes-Benz *Maybach* being the first car to incorporate this advanced technology. Two of the major benefits of EL are that it has a low degree of heat-generation in comparison to regular filament bulbs and it gives uniform luminescence that does not produce glare.

The quest for energy-efficient lighting technologies has been given fresh impetus by the recent uncertainties regarding oil supply, and it is only a question of time before solar power will become a viable alternative for certain types of lighting application. Perhaps, one day in the future, buildings will be constructed from a membrane-like material that incorporates, on the outside, photovoltaic cells to store the energy from the sun and, on the inside, an O-LED film coating to turn this stored power into light. In the meantime, the lighting industry will continue to

sche Firma Bree hat in Kooperation mit Bayer Material Science sogar eine Handtasche mit einer EL-Folie ausgestattet. Öffnet man die Tasche, so wird ihr Inhalt durch die eingearbeitete EL-Folie, die an eine 9-Volt-Batterie angeschlossen ist, beleuchtet. Die Automobilindustrie verwendet neuerdings ebenfalls EL-Folien, und zwar für die Innenbeleuchtung von Autos. Der erste mit dieser modernen Technologie ausgestattete PKW ist der *Maybach* von Mercedes-Benz. Zwei der wichtigsten Vorteile der EL-Folien sind ihre im Vergleich zu konventionellen Glühlampen geringe Wärmeentwicklung und die Tatsache, dass sie ein absolut gleichmäßiges, blendfreies Licht abgeben.

Die Suche nach energiesparenden Beleuchtungstechnologien hat durch die jetzt wieder ins Bewusstsein dringende Ungewissheit der Erdölversorgung einen neuen Impetus erhalten, und es ist nur noch eine Frage der Zeit, bis die Sonnenenergie eine realistische Alternative für bestimmte Beleuchtungsformen bieten wird. Es könnte gut sein, dass eines Tages Gebäude aus einem membranähnlichen Material entstehen, das auf der Außenseite Fotovoltaik-Zellen enthält und damit die Sonnenenergie speichert, und auf der Innenseite mit einer EL-Folie beschichtet ist, die die gespeicherte Energie in

et qu'il fournit une luminescence uniforme, sans éblouissement.

La quête de technologies d'éclairage faibles consommatrices d'énergie a retrouvé une nouvelle actualité à l'occasion des incertitudes récentes sur l'approvisionnement en pétrole et son coût. L'arrivée de l'énergie solaire alternative viable dans certains types d'application d'éclairage n'est plus qu'une question de temps. Un jour, peut-être, les façades des immeubles seront une membrane équipée de cellules photovoltaïques pour emmagasiner l'énergie solaire et, à l'intérieur, de films O-LED pour la restituer sous forme de lumière. Dans le même temps, l'industrie continuera à rechercher au point des sources lumineuses qui fourniront une meilleure couleur (c'est-à-dire aussi proche que possible du blanc), plus petites et écologiquement plus efficaces. Comme il l'a fait par le passé, le designer se devra alors de trouver la meilleure façon d'exploiter ces technologies pour produire des objets qui transcenderont le simple utilitarisme et sauront capter l'authentique beauté de la lumière.

◁◁ *Alberto Meda and Paolo Rizzatto, StarLed table light for Luceplan, 2001 – this 21ˢᵗ-century candlestick incorporates white LEDs / Alberto Meda and Paolo Rizzatto, Tischleuchte StarLed, 2001 – dieser Kerzenständer des 21. Jahrhunderts verwendet weiße LEDs und ist dank aufladbarer Batterien tragbar / Alberto Meda et Paolo Rizzatto, lampe de table Star Led, 2001 – ce bougeoir du XXIᵉ siècle à LED blanches est alimenté par une batterie rechargeable qui le rend facilement déplaçable.*

◁ *Carlotta de Bevilacqua, Sui table light for Artemide, 2001 – incorporates 18 white LEDs as its light source / Carlotta de Bevilacqua, Tischleuchte Sui, 2001 – mit 18 weißen LEDs als Lichtquelle bestückt und „dazu gedacht, direkt auf dem Körper aufzuliegen" / Carlotta de Bevilacqua, lampe de table Sui, 2001 – dotée de 18 LED blanches, cette lampe est conçue pour « encourager le contact avec le corps ».*

▷ *Ingo Maurer, Stardust for Ingo Maurer, 2000 – this remarkable luminaire incorporates blue-colored O-LEDs that are reminiscent of star clusters / Ingo Maurer, Leuchte Stardust für Ingo Maurer, 2000 – für diese bemerkenswerte Leuchte wurden blaue O-LEDs verwendet, die an einen Sternenhimmel erinnern / Ingo Maurer, Stardust, pour Ingo Maurer, 2000. Ce remarquable luminaire est équipé de O-LED bleues qui évoquent un ciel étoilé.*

research and develop light sources that achieve a better color (i.e. as close as possible to white) and that are smaller and ecologically more efficient. And in the future as in the past, the role of the designer will be to find the best way to exploit these technologies so as to produce objects that transcend utility and capture the true poetic beauty of light.

Editors Note

For this project we have drawn on the expertise of a team of contributors, who have provided insightful texts to accompany the illustrations. To them we offer our warmest thanks. For ease of reference the lights are grouped according to decade, and the index at the back of this publication should prove useful in finding specific designs and designers. The contact details for manufacturers of lights that are still in production can also be found at the end of this book. In distilling the superlative achievements in lighting design since 1878 into the present *1000 Lights*, we have tried to be as objective as possible. There are just so many great lighting products out there, and if there are omissions in the following pages, it is only because of space constraints. We have nevertheless attempted to include all the acknowledged design "classics" as well as a few obscure though highly innovative

Licht umwandelt. Bis dahin wird die Beleuchtungsindustrie weiterhin an der Erforschung und Entwicklung von Lichtquellen arbeiten, die eine bessere Farbwirkung (d. h. so nahe wie möglich an Weiß) erzielen, kleiner und ökologisch effizienter sind. Und wie bisher wird es auch in Zukunft die Aufgabe der Designer sein, diese Technologien optimal einzusetzen, um Objekte zu schaffen, die über den praktischen Nutzen hinausgehen und die wahre poetische Schönheit des Lichts einfangen.

Anmerkungen der Herausgeber

Wir haben uns bei diesem Buchprojekt auf die Sachkenntnis eines Autorenteams gestützt, die die Abbildungen mit informativen Texten versehen haben. Ihnen gilt unser herzlicher Dank. Um den Überblick zu erleichtern, wurden die vorgestellten Leuchten nach Jahrzehnten geordnet. Der Index am Ende des Buches ist als Hilfestellung bei der Suche nach bestimmten Modellen oder Designern gedacht. Auch die Kontaktadressen der noch produzierenden Leuchtenhersteller sind am Ende des Buches zu finden. Bei der Auswahl der bedeutendsten Beispiele des Beleuchtungsdesigns seit 1878 waren wir um größtmögliche Objektivität bemüht. Aber es gibt so viele wichtige Leuchten, dass es unmöglich war, alle zu berück-

Notes des Editeurs

Cette publication a bénéficié de la collaboration d'une équipe de spécialistes, qui signent les textes d'accompagnement des illustrations. Nous les remercions chaleureusement. A fin de faciliter les recherches, les lampes sont regroupées par décennies et un index des designers et des fabricants figure en fin du livre. Les références des fabricants de luminaires toujours en production se trouvent également à la fin de ce livre. En décrivant les remarquables réussites de la conception de luminaires de 1878 à nos jours, nous avons essayé d'être aussi objectifs que possible. Seul le manque d'espace nous a dicté certaines omissions. Nous nous sommes efforcés de présenter tous les « classiques » reconnus ainsi que quelques modèles pratiquement inconnus mais qui restent néanmoins des exemples d'innovation, dans l'espoir que cet ouvrage servira non seulement de référence utile et fiable, mais aussi de source d'inspiration pour les futurs créateurs de luminaires.

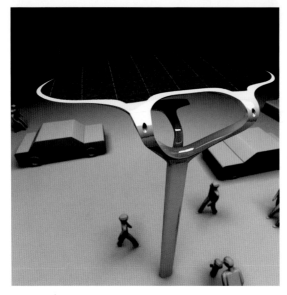

examples, in the hope that this book will
serve not only as a reliable and useful
sourcebook but also as a font of inspiration for future lighting designers.

sichtigen. Es war uns ein Anliegen, alle
anerkannten „Klassiker" sowie einige
weniger bekannte, aber dafür besonders innovative Beispiele aufzunehmen
in der Hoffnung, dass dieses Buch nicht
nur als zuverlässiges und nützliches
Nachschlagewerk, sondern auch als
Inspirationsquelle für künftige Beleuchtungsdesigner dienen wird.

1. Davy, Sir Humphry, Elements of Chemical
Philosophy, J. Johnson & Co., London 1812,
p. 151
2. Journals of the Royal Institution of Great Britain,
London 1802, pp. 210 and 212–13
3. Davy, Op. cit., p. 153
4. Stevenson, Robert Louis, "A Plea for Gas Lamps"
in: Virginibus Puerisque and Other Papers,
Kegan Paul, London 1881
5. Philosophical Magazine, Third Series, vol. XXVII,
p. 422, quoted in: Pope, Franklin Leonard,
Evolution of the Electric Incandescent Lamp,
Henry Cook, New Jersey 1889, p. 19
6. Swan, Kenneth R., Sir Joseph Swan and the
Invention of the Incandescent Electric Lamp,
Longmans, Green & Co., London 1946, p. 16
7. Holmes is best remembered for inventing the
generator that powered the first arc lamp to be
used in a lighthouse, at South Foreland on the
southeast coast of England, in 1858.
8. Pope, Evolution, p. 10
9. Ibid., p. 15
10. Nature, 1 January 1880; quoted in: Swan, Sir
Joseph, p. 26
11. Sudjic, Deyan, The Lighting Book, Mitchell
Beazley, London 1985, p. 24
12. Cox, J. A., A Century of Light, The Benjamin
Company Inc., New York 1979, p. 33

1 Davy, Sir Humphry, Elements of Chemical Philosophy, J. Johnson & Co., London 1812, S. 151
2 Journals of the Royal Institution of Great Britain,
London 1802, S. 210, S. 212–213
3 Davy, Elements, S. 153
4 Stevenson, Robert Louis, „A Plea for Gas Lamps"
in Virginibus Puerisque and Other Papers,
Kegan Paul, London 1881
5 Philosophical Magazine, 3rd series, vol. XXVII,
London 1840, S. 422; zitiert in Pope, Franklin
Leonard, Evolution of the Electric Incandescent
Lamp, Henry Cook, New Jersey 1889, S. 19
6 Swan, Kenneth R., Sir Joseph Swan and the
Invention of the Incandescent Electric Lamp,
Longmans, Green & Co., London 1946, S. 16
7 Holmes wurde für die Erfindung des Generators
bekannt, der die erste Bogenlampe betrieb,
welche 1858 in einem Leuchtturm an der
Südostküste von England installiert wurde.
8 Pope, Evolution, S. 10
9 Pope, ibd., S. 15
10 In Nature, 1. Januar 1880; zitiert in Swan, Sir
Joseph, S. 26
11 Sudjic, Deyan, The Lighting Book, Mitchell
Beazley, London 1985, S. 24
12 Cox, J. A., A Century of Light, The Benjamin
Company Inc., New York 1979, S. 33

1. Davy, Sir Humphry, Elements of Chemical
Philosophy, J. Johnson & Co., Londres, 1812,
p. 151
2. Journals of the Royal Institution of Great Britain,
Londres, 1802, pp. 210 et 212–213
3. Davy, Op. cit., p. 153
4. Robert Louis Stevenson, « A Plea for Gas
Lamps »/ Virginibus Puerisque, Kegan Paul,
Londres, 1881
5. Philosophical Magazine, 3e série, vol. XXVII,
p. 422/Pope, Franklin Leonard, Evolution of the
Electric Incandescent Lamp, Henry Cook, New
Jersey, 1889, p. 19
6. Swan, Kenneth R., Sir Joseph Swan and the
Invention of the Incandescent Electric Lamp,
Logmans, Green & Co., Londres, 1946, p. 16
7. Holmes est surtout connu pour avoir inventé le
générateur qui alimentait la première lampe à arc
utilisée dans un phare, à South Foreland en 1858.
8. Pope, Op. cit., p. 10
9. Pope, Op. cit., p. 15
10. Nature, 1er janvier 1880/ Swan, Kenneth R., op.
cit., p. 26
11. Sudjic, Deyan, The Lighting Book, Mitchell
Beazley, Londres, 1985, p. 24
12. Cox, J. A., A Century of light, The Benjamin
Company Inc., New York, 1979, p. 33

Lights from 1878 to present
Leuchten von 1878 bis heute
Les luminaires, de 1878 à aujourd'hui

Joseph Swan in his laboratory at Holland Park, London, c.1900 / Joseph Swan in seinem Laboratorium in Holland Park, London, ca. 1900 / Joseph Swan dans son laboratoire de Holland Park, Londres, vers 1900

Joseph Swan became captivated with the idea of producing the first practical incandescent light bulb after having read an account in the *Repertory of Patent Inventions* of an incandescent carbon *in vacuo* lamp devised by the American inventor John Wellington Starr, and having attended a number of lectures in Sunderland given by William Edwards Staite which demonstrated not only arc lamps but also a lamp that incorporated a platinum alloy filament. (CF/PF)

Der englische Erfinder Joseph Swan war von der Idee eingenommen, die erste brauchbare Glühlampe zu produzieren, nachdem er im *Repertory of Patent Inventions* die Beschreibung einer vom amerikanischen Erfinder John Wellington Starr konstruierten Vakuumglühfadenlampe gelesen und eine Reihe von Vorlesungen in Sunderland besucht hatte, bei denen William Edwards Staite nicht nur Bogenlampen, sondern auch eine Lampe vorführte, die einen Glühfaden mit Platinlegierung enthielt. (CF/PF)

Joseph Swan se consacra à la fabrication de la première ampoule à incandescence après avoir lu, dans le *Repertory of Patent Inventions* (Répertoire des inventions brevetées), la description d'une lampe à carbone sous vide conçue par l'inventeur américain J. W. Starr. Il avait aussi assisté à plusieurs conférences données par William Staite à Sunderland, lequel avait présenté non seulement plusieurs lampes à arc, mais aussi une lampe possédant un filament en alliage de platine. (CF/PF)

"It appeared to me evident that an advantage would be gained by making the incandescent carbon filament as thin as possible … by means of carbonized paper."

„Es erschien mir einleuchtend und von Vorteil, den Kohlefaden so dünn wie möglich zu machen … mithilfe von karbonisiertem Papier."

« Il m'est apparu clairement qu'on aurait tout avantage à utiliser un filament de carbone aussi fin que possible… fait de papier carbonisé. »

– Joseph Swan

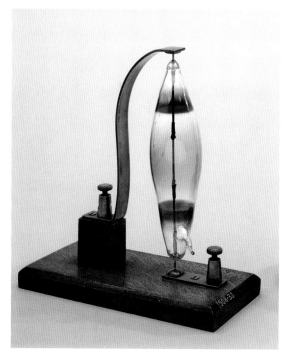

Joseph Swan's first incandescent light bulb, 1878 / Joseph Swans erste Glühlampe, 1878 / Première ampoule à incandescence mise au point par Joseph Swan, 1878

In 1848, after three years of experimentation, Joseph Swan perfected the "carbonization" of thin strips or spirals of paper and card that had been soaked in syrup, treacle or tar and then heated in a mass of powdered charcoal. The resulting carbonized filaments were thin yet flexible, but any residual trace of air left in the glass "bulb" caused them to break down quickly. It was only after Hermann Sprengel's invention of the mercury vacuum pump in 1865 and William Crookes's perfecting of vacuums while developing his radiometer in 1875, that Swan and his colleague, Charles Stearn, were able to achieve the sufficient vacuum required to make the first practical light bulb based on the incandescent principle in December 1878. (CF/PF)

Im Jahr 1848 perfektionierte Swan die „Verkohlung" mittels dünner Streifen oder Spiralen aus Papier oder Karton, die in Sirup, Melasse oder Teer getränkt und anschließend in einer Masse aus Kohlenstaub erhitzt worden waren. Die daraus gewonnenen Kohlenstoffglühfäden waren dünn und dennoch biegsam. Aber die kleinste im Glaskolben verbliebene Menge an Restluft ließ diese rasch verdampfen. Erst nachdem Hermann Sprengel 1865 die Quecksilbervakuumpumpe erfunden und William Crookes im Verlauf der Entwicklung seines Radiometers den Vakuumprozess optimiert hatte, gelang es Swan und seinem Mitarbeiter Charles Stearne, ein ausreichendes Vakuum zu erzielen und im Dezember 1878 die erste brauchbare Glühlampe herzustellen. (CF/PF)

En 1848, après trois années d'expérimentation, Swan mit au point la « carbonisation » de fils et spirales de papier trempés dans du sirop, de la mélasse ou du goudron, puis chauffés dans de la poudre de charbon. Les filaments carbonisés ainsi obtenus étaient minces et flexibles, mais se désagrégeaient rapidement en présence de la moindre trace d'air. Ce n'est qu'avec la pompe à vide à mercure, inventée en 1865 par Hermann Sprengel, et les techniques mises au point par William Crooke en 1875 alors qu'il travaillait à son radiomètre, que Swan et son collègue Charles Stearn parvinrent à obtenir un vide suffisant et, en décembre 1878, à créer la première ampoule fonctionnant selon le principe d'incandescence. (CF/PF)

The first commercial incandescent light bulb manufactured by Swan's factory in South Benwell, Newcastle upon Tyne, 1881 / Die erste kommerzielle Glühlampe, hergestellt von Joseph Swans Fabrik in South Benwell, Newcastle upon Tyne, 1881 / Première ampoule à incandescence fabriquée à des fins commerciales par l'usine de Swan à South Benwell, Newcastle upon Tyne, 1881

On 3 February 1879, Joseph Swan publicly demonstrated his incandescent electric light bulb at a lecture at the Chemical Society of Newcastle upon Tyne. He did not, however, apply for a patent to protect his invention until 1880. The same year Swan installed electric lighting in Sir William Armstrong's house, Cragside, the first house in Britain other than Swan's own to be lit by electricity. Around this time the Swan Electric Lamp Company Limited was also established in South Benwell, Newcastle, and by the early months of 1881 the commercial manufacture of a modified light bulb had begun. (CF/PF)

Am 3. Februar 1879 führte Joseph Swan seine elektrische Glühlampe im Rahmen einer Vorlesung in der Chemical Society in Newcastle upon Tyne erstmals öffentlich vor. Er beantragte jedoch erst 1880 ein Patent, um seine Erfindung urheberrechtlich zu schützen. Im selben Jahr installierte Swan eine elektrische Beleuchtung im Haus von Sir William Armstrong in Cragside, dem ersten Haus in Großbritannien, abgesehen von Swans eigenem, das elektrisches Licht erhielt. Um diese Zeit wurde auch die Swan Electric Lamp Company Limited in South Benwell, Newcastle, gegründet, und bereits zu Beginn des Jahres 1881 lief dort die kommerzielle Herstellung einer modifizierten Glühlampe an. (CF/PF)

Le 3 février 1879, Joseph Swan fit une démonstration publique de son ampoule électrique à incandescence à la Chemical Society de Newcastle upon Tyne. Il attendit 1880, cependant, avant de déposer un brevet pour protéger son invention. La même année, Swan installa un éclairage électrique au domicile de Sir William Armstrong à Cragside, première maison en Grande-Bretagne, après celle de Swan, à être éclairée à l'électricité. À peu près à la même époque, la Swan Electric Lamp Company fut créée à South Benwell, Newcastle. Dès les premiers mois de 1881, la production d'ampoules modifiées destinées au commerce avait commencé. (CF/PF)

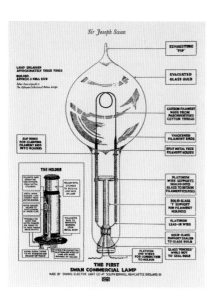

◁ Drawing showing Joseph Swan's first commercial incandescent light bulb, 1881 / Zeichnung der ersten von Joseph Swan entwickelten kommerziellen Glühlampe, 1881 / Dessin de la première ampoule à incandescence mise en vente par Joseph Swan, 1881

▽ Contemporary print showing "Mr Swan's Electrical Workshop in Newcastle", 1881 / Zeitgenössischer Druck mit der Darstellung von „Mr Swan's Electrical Workshop in Newcastle", 1881 / Gravure d'époque de « L'Atelier électrique de M. Swan à Newcastle », 1881

Although Thomas Edison was not the inventor of the first incandescent light bulb, he devised the first practical example to be successfully commercialized. After a frenzied year of research and experimentation at his Menlo Park laboratory, Edison and his team produced their first incandescent light bulb in October 1879. It incorporated a carbon filament, which was shaped like a horseshoe and glowed when an electric current was passed through it. The glass bulb had only a small residual amount of oxygen remaining in it, which meant that even though the filament became very hot it did not actually catch fire. (CF/PF)

Obwohl Thomas Edison nicht der Erfinder der ersten Glühlampe war, entwickelte er das erste kommerziell erfolgreiche Modell. Nach einem aufregenden Jahr des Forschens und Experimentierens in seinem Labor in Menlo Park produzierten Edison und seine Mitarbeiter im Oktober 1879 die erste Glühbirne. Sie enthielt einen hufeisenförmigen Kohlenstoffglühfaden, der zu leuchten begann, sobald elektrischer Strom ihn durchfloss. In dem Glaskolben war nur noch eine kleine Restmenge an Sauerstoff verblieben, was bedeutete, dass der Kohlefaden, obwohl er sehr heiß wurde, nicht Feuer fing und verglühte. (CF/PF)

Bien que Thomas Edison n'ait pas inventé l'ampoule à incandescence, c'est à lui que l'on doit le premier modèle commercialisé avec succès. Après une année d'intenses recherches à son laboratoire de Menlo Park, Edison et son équipe créèrent leur première ampoule à incandescence en octobre 1879. Elle possédait un filament de carbone en forme de fer à cheval qui luisait lorsqu'il était parcouru d'un courant électrique. L'ampoule en verre ne contenait qu'un infime résidu d'oxygène, de sorte que le filament pouvait atteindre des températures très élevées sans prendre feu. (CF/PF)

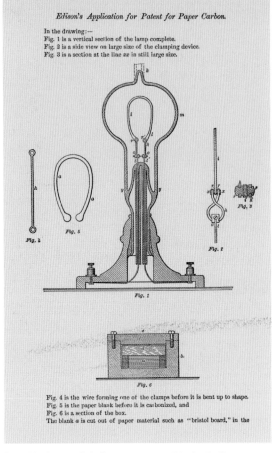

Edison's Application for Patent for Paper Carbon.

In the drawing:—
Fig. 1 is a vertical section of the lamp complete.
Fig. 2 is a side view on large size of the clamping device.
Fig. 3 is a section at the line xx in still large size.

Fig. 4 is the wire forming one of the clamps before it is bent up to shape.
Fig. 5 is the paper blank before it is carbonized, and
Fig. 6 is a section of the box.
The blank a is cut out of paper material such as "bristol board," in the

Thomas Edison's patent application for paper carbon filament light bulb, filed 8 December 1878 / Thomas Edisons Patentantrag für eine Glühbirne mit Kohlenstoffglühfaden, eingereicht am 8. Dezember 1878 / Demande de brevet pour une ampoule à filament de papier carbonisé, déposée par Thomas Edison le 8 décembre 1878

▷ Thomas Edison's carbon filament incandescent light bulb, c.1880 / Thomas Edisons Glühbirne mit Kohlenstoffglühfaden, ca. 1880 / Ampoule à incandescence à filament de carbone conçue par Thomas Edison, vers 1880

"If there is a way to do it better … find it."

„Wenn es einen Weg gibt, es besser zu machen … finde ihn."

« S'il existe une meilleure façon de faire… trouvez-la. »

– Thomas Edison

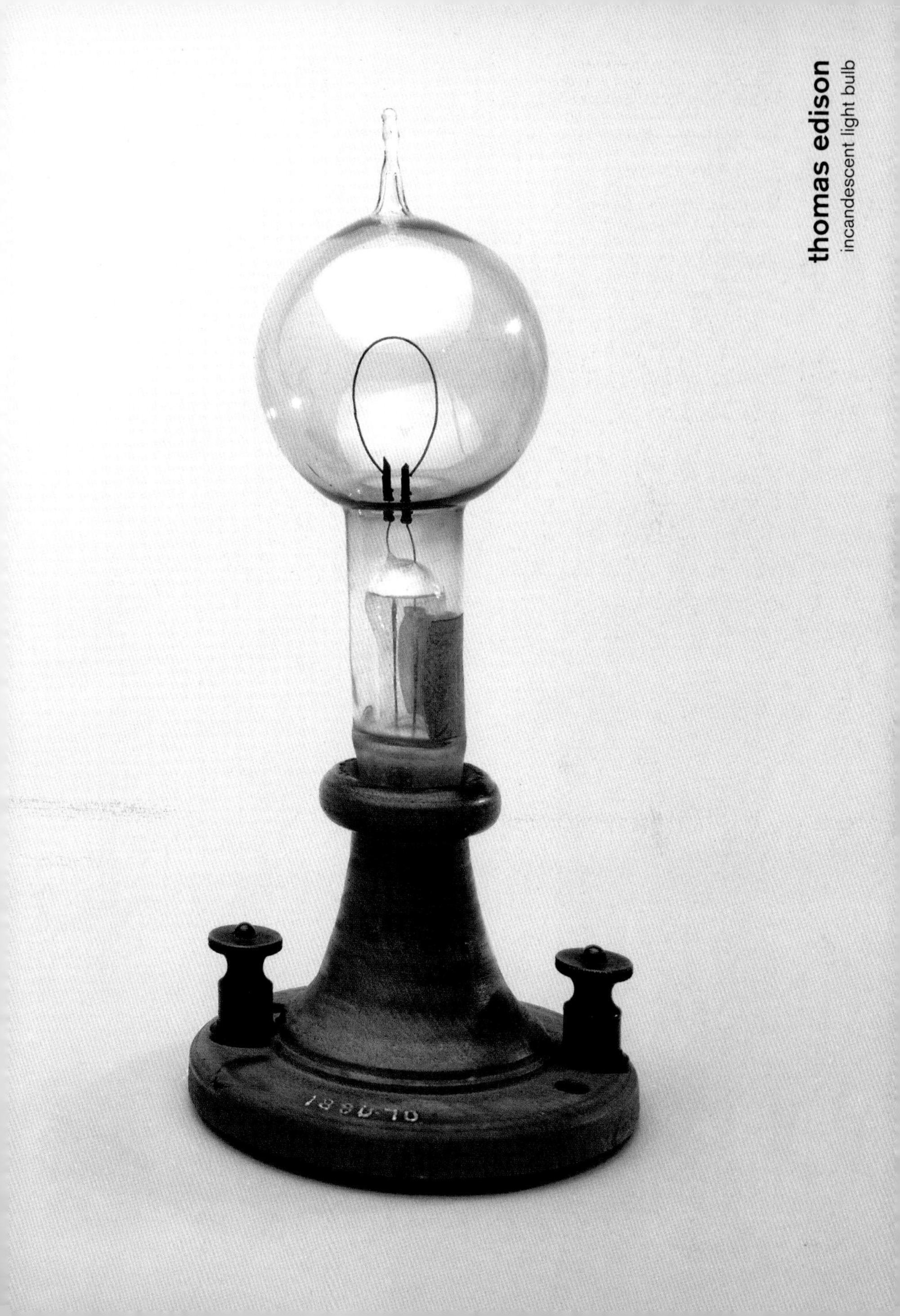

thomas edison
incandescent light bulb

Only a month or so after Thomas Edison had produced his first successful light bulb, it was patented and put into industrial mass-production. Despite achieving this remarkable goal, Edison realized that domestic electric lighting would not become a widespread reality unless there was an effective infrastructure established to distribute electricity. Over the next few years he worked tirelessly to provide the necessary system equipment and in September 1882 opened the world's first permanent central power station on Pearl Street, New York – initially the enterprise had only 59 customers. (CF/PF)

Nur etwa einen Monat nachdem Thomas Edison seine erste erfolgreiche Glühbirne hergestellt hatte, wurde sie patentiert und ihre industrielle Massenproduktion wurde aufgenommen. Trotz dieser bemerkenswerten Leistung war Edison klar, dass sich eine elektrische Beleuchtung der Privathaushalte ohne entsprechende Infrastruktur zur Stromverteilung nicht umfassend verwirklichen ließe. Während der folgenden Jahre arbeitete er unermüdlich an den erforderlichen Anlagen und Geräten, bevor er im September 1882 das weltweit erste Kraftwerk für den Dauerbetrieb in der New Yorker Pearl Street eröffnete. Das Unternehmen hatte zu Beginn lediglich 59 Kunden. (CF/PF)

Un mois à peine après qu'Edison eût créé sa première ampoule, elle fut brevetée et fit l'objet d'une production industrielle de masse. Mais Edison ne s'arrêta pas là: il comprit que l'éclairage domestique à l'électricité n'aurait aucun avenir tant qu'il n'existerait pas d'infrastructure efficace pour distribuer l'électricité. Pendant les quelques années qui suivirent, il travailla sans relâche pour produire le matériel nécessaire et, en septembre 1882, inaugura la première centrale électrique permanente sur Pearl Street à New York. Au départ, l'entreprise ne comptait que cinquante-neuf clients. (CF/PF)

Thomas Edison experimenting in his Menlo Park laboratory, 1880s / Thomas Edison bei einem Experiment in seinem Labor in Menlo Park, 1880er Jahre / Thomas Edison se livrant à une expérience dans son laboratoire de Menlo Park, années 1880

During the 1880s and 1890s, Thomas Edison continued to perfect his light bulb – he quickly abandoned his carbon "horse-shoe" filament in favor of thinner and more flexible filaments made of carbonized cotton threads. During this period he also designed safety fuses, insulating materials, light sockets and on/off switches in order to enhance the commercial viability of his light bulb. Through his development of a safe, reliable and inexpensive light source, Edison heralded the dawn of the Electric Age and opened up a whole new world of possibilities for lighting designers. (CF/PF)

Im Lauf der 1880er und 1890er Jahre perfektionierte Thomas Edison seine Glühlampe weiter. So gab er bald den hufeisenförmigen Papierkohlefaden zugunsten dünnerer und flexiblerer Wendel aus karbonisiertem Baumwollfaden auf. In dieser Zeit entwarf er auch Sicherungen, Isolierstoffe, Lampenfassungen und Ein-Aus-Schalter, um den kommerziellen Erfolg seiner Glühbirne zu steigern. Mit seiner Entwicklung einer sicheren, verlässlichen und wirtschaftlich günstigen Lichtquelle leitete Edison das Zeitalter der Elektrifizierung ein und eröffnete eine ganz neue Welt der Möglichkeiten für Beleuchtungsdesigner. (CF/PF)

Pendant les années 1880 et 1890, Edison continua à perfectionner son ampoule – il abandonna rapidement le filament de carbone en «fer à cheval» au profit de filaments plus minces et plus flexibles faits de fils de coton carbonisé. Pendant la même période, il conçut également des fusibles de sûreté, des isolants, des prises de courant et des interrupteurs afin d'assurer davantage de viabilité commerciale à son ampoule. À travers ses efforts pour mettre au point une source de lumière économique, fiable et sans danger, Edison préparait l'arrivée de l'Ère Électrique et ouvrait tout un monde de possibilités aux créateurs de luminaires. (CF/PF)

thomas edison
incandescent light bulb

The main office of the Edison United Manufacturing Company, New York (NY), 1880s / Der Sitz der Edison United Manufacturing Company, New York City, 1880er Jahre / Siège de la Edison United Manufacturing Company à New York, années 1880

Early Edison incandescent light bulb, with clamps for carbon filaments, 1879 / Ein sehr frühes Modell von Edisons Glühbirne mit Klammern für Kohlenstoffglühfäden, 1879 / L'une des toutes premières ampoules à incandescence, munie d'attaches pour les filaments de carbone, conçue par Edison en 1879

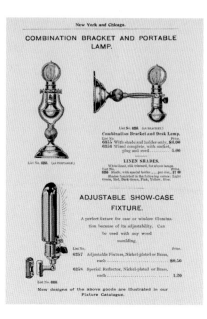

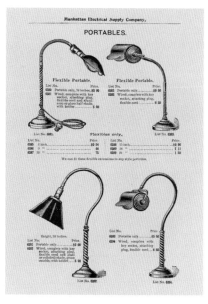

Manhattan Electrical Supply Company,

PORTABLES.

Plain Portable.

Standard Portable.

Adjustable Lamp.

Bracket or Portable.

Some new designs of these goods in our Fixture and Portable Catalogue.

New York and Chicago.

COMBINATION BRACKET AND PORTABLE LAMP.

LINEN SHADES.

ADJUSTABLE SHOW-CASE FIXTURE.

A perfect fixture for case or window illumination because of its adjustability. Can be used with any wood moulding.

New designs of the above goods are illustrated in our Fixture Catalogue.

New York and Chicago.

PORTABLES.

SLATE BASE.

Our Fixture and Portable Catalogue illustrates a complete line of these goods.

Manhattan Electrical Supply Company,

PORTABLES.

Flexible Portable.

Flexible Portable.

Flexibles only.

We can fit these flexible extensions to any style portable.

Some of the earliest electric lights manufactured in the United States incorporated sockets and switches that were made by the Edison Company. This example (late 1890s) is very similar to a model illustrated in the lighting catalog of the Manhattan Electrical Supply Company and could be used either as a wall-mounted bracket light or as a portable desk light. Dating from the 1890s, this "Combination" brass light was produced by the Dale Company and had an innovative counterweight element that incorporated an Edison-patented socket. Originally costing $5, the light was intended for use in conjunction with a linen shade. (CF/PF)

Einige der frühesten in den Vereinigten Staaten hergestellten elektrischen Leuchten waren mit Fassungen und Schaltern der Edison Company ausgestattet. Das hier gezeigte Beispiel hat große Ähnlichkeit mit einem im Beleuchtungskatalog der Manhattan Electrical Supply Company abgebildeten Modell und ließ sich sowohl als Wandleuchter als auch als tragbare Tischleuchte verwenden. Die aus den 1890er Jahren stammende „Kombinationslampe" aus Messing wurde von der Dale Company hergestellt und war mit einem innovativen Schwenkmechanismus und einer Edison-Fassung ausgestattet. Die Leuchte kostete ursprünglich fünf Dollar und war für den Gebrauch mit einem Lampenschirm aus Leinen gedacht. (CF/PF)

Les toutes premières lampes électriques faites aux États-Unis étaient parfois munies de prises et d'interrupteurs fabriqués par la compagnie Edison. Un modèle très semblable à celui-ci est présenté dans le catalogue de luminaires de la Manhattan Electrical Supply Company et pouvait être utilisé soit comme applique murale, soit comme lampe de bureau mobile. Ce modèle « combiné » en laiton fabriqué par la compagnie Dale date des années 1890 et possédait un système novateur de contrepoids muni d'une prise Edison. Coûtant $5 à l'origine, cette lampe était censée être utilisée avec un abat-jour en tissu. (CF/PF)

◁ *Pages from the Manhattan Electrical Supply Company's catalog, 1890s / Seiten aus dem Katalog der Manhattan Electrical Supply Company, 1890er Jahre / Pages du catalogue de la Manhattan Electrical Supply Company, années 1890*

Combination bracket and portable table/wall light, late 1890s

Brass base with articulated holder, Edison-manufactured socket and switch, 30.5 cm high / Messingfuß mit Gelenkhalterung, Edison-Fassung und -schalter, 30,5 cm hoch / Socle en laiton, bras articulé, prise et interrupteur Edison, 30,5 cm de hauteur
Dale Company, USA

Manufactured in the United States, this early brass electric light could be height-adjusted from 23 inches to 27 inches, while its milky-glass shade could be positioned at various angles along its swan-necked brass stem. Dating from the late 1890s, this type of simple yet practical design was known as a "Portable" (i.e. not fixed to a wall). Although highly utilitarian, early electric lighting products such as this often incorporated classically inspired decoration – in this case the simple fluted motif on its base. (CF/PF)

Diese frühe, in den Vereinigten Staaten gefertigte Messingleuchte war von 58 cm bis 69 cm höhenverstellbar, während ihr Lampenschirm aus Milchglas entlang des gebogenen Halses in verschiedene Winkel positioniert werden konnte. Dieses einfache, aber praktische Design stammt aus den späten 1890er Jahren und wurde unter der Bezeichnung „tragbar" (d.h. nicht an der Wand befestigt) bekannt. Obgleich in hohem Maß auf den praktischen Nutzen bedacht, waren frühe elektrische Leuchtenmodelle wie dieses häufig mit klassisch inspiriertem Dekor versehen – in diesem Fall ein schlichtes Riffelmotiv auf dem Leuchtenfuß. (CF/PF)

La hauteur de cette lampe électrique en laiton fabriquée aux États-Unis pouvait se régler de 58 à 69 cm. Son abat-jour en verre blanc pouvait être ajusté à des angles différents le long de sa tige en col de cygne. Ce type de modèle simple et pratique des années 1890 était appelé « mobile » (par opposition à ceux que l'on accrochait au mur). Bien que très utilitaires, les tout premiers appareils d'éclairage électrique étaient souvent ornés de motifs d'inspiration antique – comme les cannelures sur le socle de celui-ci. (CF/PF)

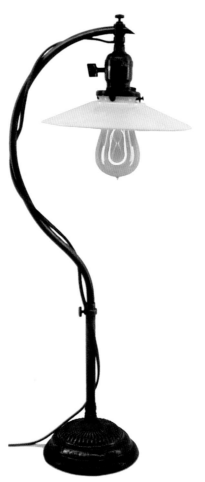

△ **Portable desk light, late 1890s**

Brass base with Edison-made socket and General Electric switch and opalescent glass shade, 58.5–69 cm high / Messingfuß mit Edison-Fassung und GE-Schalter sowie Lampenschirm aus Opalglas, 58,5–69 cm hoch / Socle en laiton, prise Edison, interrupteur General Electric, abatjour en verre opalescent, hauteur ajustable de 58,5 à 69 cm
USA

▷ **Extension/Portable table light, late 1890s**

Height-adjustable brass base with opalescent glass shade, 51–71 cm high / Höhenverstellbarer Messingfuß mit Lampenschirm aus Opalglas, 51–71 cm hoch / Socle en laiton à hauteur réglable de 51 à 71 cm, abatjour en verre opalescent
Dale Company, USA (attrib.)

Dating from the 1890s, this American-made light is very similar to other models manufactured by the Dale Company. It incorporated an Edison-made socket and switch and featured a height-adjustable arm that allowed it to be extended by about eight inches (20 cm). Although a relatively utilitarian design, the light features an elegant brass stem with barley-twist detailing and classically inspired finials. When completely wired, this early "Extension/Portable" table light would have retailed for around $8. (CF/PF)

Diese in den Vereinigten Staaten produzierte Leuchte datiert aus den 1890er Jahren und weist große Ähnlichkeit mit anderen Modellen aus der Produktion der Dale Company auf. Sie ist mit einer Fassung und einem Schalter aus der Edison-Fabrikation und einem höhenverstellbaren Arm ausgestattet, der sich um circa 20 cm verlängern ließ. Die Leuchte war zwar in der Gestaltung recht funktional, hatte aber einen eleganten Messingfuß, der mit Spiralmuster und klassisch inspiriertem Blätterknauf verziert war. Komplett verdrahtet kostete diese frühe auszieh- und tragbare Tischleuchte im Einzelhandel ungefähr acht Dollar. (CF/PF)

Cette lampe américaine, qui date des années 1890, est très semblable aux autres modèles fabriqués par la Dale Company. Elle est munie d'une prise et d'un interrupteur Edison ainsi que d'un bras réglable pouvant être allongé d'environ 20 cm. Bien que relativement utilitaire de conception, elle possède une élégante tige torsadée en laiton et des fleurons d'inspiration antique. Équipée de tous ses raccords, cette lampe mobile à rallonge se serait vendue environ $8. (CF/PF)

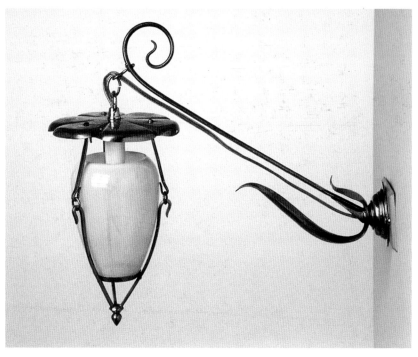

◁ **Table light, c.1880s–1890s**

Brass and copper base with Vaseline glass
shade, 50 cm high / Fuß aus Messing und
Kupfer mit Lampenschirm aus Vaselineglas,
50 cm hoch / Socle en laiton et cuivre,
abatjour en verre opalescent dit verre Vaseline,
50 cm de hauteur
W. A. S. Benson & Co., London, Great Britain
(base) / James Powell, London, Great Britain
(shade)

Wall light, c.1880s–1890s

Brass and copper mounts with Vaseline glass
shade, 17.8 cm high, 40 cm long / Halterung
aus Messing und Kupfer mit Lampenschirm aus
Vaselineglas, 17,8 cm x 40 cm / Montures en
laiton et cuivre, abat-jour en verre Vaseline,
17,8 x 40 cm
W. A. S. Benson & Co., London, Great Britain
(mounts) / James Powell, London, Great Britain
(shade)

After training as an architect, William
Arthur Smith Benson turned his
attention to the design of metalwork
at the suggestion of Edward Burne-
Jones and William Morris and subsequently became the greatest lighting
designer of the British Arts & Crafts
Movement. Unlike other designers affili-
ated with this reforming "New Art" cru-
sade, however, Benson embraced
rather than rejected the use of machinery to produce his beautiful brass and
copper designs. He designed literally
thousands of chandeliers, wall lights
and table lights, which were manufactured in his metalworking workshop
(est. 1880) and later in his own well-
equipped factory in Hammersmith.
(CF/PF)

Nach seiner Ausbildung als Architekt
wandte sich William Arthur Smith Benson auf Anregung von Edward Burne-
Jones und William Morris der Gestaltung von Metallarbeiten zu und wurde
in der Folge zum wichtigsten Leuchtendesigner der britischen Arts & Crafts-
Bewegung. Im Gegensatz zu anderen,
die sich dieser künstlerischen Reform-
bestrebung verschrieben hatten und
den Einsatz von Maschinen ablehnten,
nahm Benson diese jedoch bereitwil-
lig an, um seine schönen Messing-
und Kupfergebilde zu produzieren. Er
entwarf buchstäblich Tausende unterschiedlicher Leuchten, die zunächst in
seiner 1880 gegründeten Metallwerkstatt und später in seiner eigenen Fabrik im Londoner Stadtteil Hammersmith hergestellt wurden. (CF/PF)

Après ses études d'architecture,
William Arthur Smith Benson s'orienta
vers la ferronnerie sur les conseils
d'Edward Burne-Jones et de William
Morris, et devint le plus grand créateur
de luminaires du mouvement Arts and
Crafts en Grande-Bretagne. À l'in-
verse des autres sympathisants de
ce courant visant au renouveau des
arts décoratifs, Benson était favorable
à l'utilisation de machines dans la production de ses somptueux objets de
cuivre et de laiton. Plusieurs milliers de
lustres et de lampes murales et de
table sortirent de son atelier, ouvert en
1880, et, plus tard, de son usine per-
formante de Hammersmith. (CF/PF)

◁ **Chandelier, 1880s**

Brass frame and mounts with Vaseline glass shades, 125 cm drop / Montierung aus Messing mit Lampenschirmen aus Vaselineglas, 125 cm lang / Cadre et montures en laiton, abat-jour en verre Vaseline, 125 cm de hauteur
W. A. S. Benson & Co., London, Great Britain (mounts) / James Powell & Sons, London, Great Britain (shades)

Wall light, 1880s

Brass and copper mounts with Vaseline glass shade, 27 cm long / Montierung aus Messing und Kupfer mit Lampenschirm aus Vaselineglas, 27 cm tief / Structure en laiton et cuivre, abat-jour en verre Vaseline, 27 cm de profondeur
W. A. S. Benson & Co., London, Great Britain (mounts) / James Powell & Sons, London, Great Britain (shade)

Often using a combination of brass and copper, "Mr. Brass Benson" – as he was nicknamed by his friend and colleague William Morris – produced lights that accentuated the glowing warmth of these metals through the use of unornamented surfaces and sinuous forms that were reminiscent of unfurling fronds. The opalescent and Vaseline glass shades incorporated into his designs were similarly inspired by forms found in the natural world. Benson's well-designed Arts & Crafts-style lighting reflected the organicism of continental Art Nouveau and was exhibited in Siegfried Bing's famous Paris gallery – the Maison de l'Art Nouveau. Benson also retailed his designs through his own Bond Street showroom in London. (CF/PF)

Der häufig mit einer Kombination aus Messing und Kupfer arbeitende „Mr. Brass Benson" (brass = Messing), wie er von seinem Freund und Kollegen William Morris genannt wurde, entwarf Leuchten, die den warmen und glänzenden Charakter dieser Metalle durch die Verwendung glatter Oberflächen und gewellter, an Blattwerk erinnernder Formen akzentuierten. Auch die Lampenschirme aus Opaleszent- oder Vaselineglas waren von natürlichen Formen inspiriert. Bensons gelungene Leuchtengestaltung im Arts & Crafts-Stil korrespondierte mit den organischen Formen des Art Nouveau. So wurden seine Leuchten etwa in Siegfried Bings berühmter Galerie in Paris, dem Maison de l'Art Nouveau, ausgestellt. (CF/PF)

Benson – que son ami et collègue William Morris surnommait « Mr Brass Benson » ('M. Benson Laiton') – était un adepte de la combinaison cuivre/laiton, dont il savait mettre en valeur les chauds reflets au moyen de surfaces non décorées et de formes sinueuses évoquant des feuillages entrelacés. Les formes de ses abat-jour en verre Vaseline s'inspiraient également de la nature. Apparentés au style Arts and Crafts, les luminaires de Benson évoquent le courant continental de l'Art Nouveau par leurs formes organiques. Ils furent d'ailleurs exposés dans la célèbre Maison de l'Art Nouveau de Siegfried Bings à Paris. Benson vendait aussi ses modèles dans son salon d'exposition de Bond Street à Londres. (CF/PF)

Unlike fellow members of the Arts & Crafts Movement, W. A. S. Benson embraced mechanization and the majority of his metalwork designs were intended for machine production. He approached manufacturing from the perspective of an engineer rather than that of a handcraftsman and ensured that his products were logically designed so that they were suited to compartmentalized industrial production. By reconciling art manufacturing with mechanized production, Benson was an important and early proponent of modern design. His pioneering efforts drew high praise from the German design critic Hermann Muthesius, who thought that Benson's manufacture of artistic wares should serve as a future model for German industrial production. (CF/PF)

Im Gegensatz zu anderen Mitgliedern der Arts & Crafts-Bewegung begrüßte W. A. S. Benson die Mechanisierung und konzipierte die Mehrzahl seiner Metalldesigns für die maschinelle Herstellung. Er sah die industrielle Fertigung mehr aus der Perspektive des Ingenieurs als aus der des Handwerkers und achtete auf den logischen Aufbau seiner Entwürfe, so dass sie sich für die segmentierte industrielle Produktionsweise eigneten. Indem er Kunst mit Mechanisierung versöhnte, wurde Benson zu einem wichtigen und frühen Verfechter des modernen Designs. Seine wegweisenden Bemühungen brachten ihm hohes Lob durch den deutschen Designkritiker Hermann Muthesius ein, der sein Verfahren als Modell für die deutsche Industrie pries. (CF/PF)

Contrairement à d'autres membres du mouvement Arts and Crafts, Benson était favorable à la mécanisation, et la plupart de ses modèles de métal étaient conçus pour pouvoir être fabriqués à la machine. Il raisonnait comme un ingénieur plutôt que comme un artisan, s'efforçant de penser ses modèles logiquement et de les rendre compatibles avec la division industrielle du travail. Par sa volonté de réconcilier production artistique et mécanisation, Benson est un important précurseur du design moderne. Il reçut les éloges du critique allemand Hermann Muthesius, qui l'érigea comme exemple pour l'industrie allemande. (CF/PF)

◁ **Chandelier, c.1900**
Brass and copper frame and mounts with Vaseline glass shades, 114 cm drop / Montierung aus Messing und Kupfer mit Lampenschirmen aus Vaselineglas, 114 cm lang / Structure en laiton et cuivre, abat-jour en verre Vaseline, 114 cm de hauteur
W. A. S. Benson & Co., London, Great Britain (mounts) / James Powell & Sons, London, Great Britain (shades)

Page from W. A. S. Benson & Company's "Price List of Fittings for Electric Light", c.1901 / W.A.S. Benson & Co. Preisliste für elektrische Beleuchtungskörper, ca. 1901 / Catalogue-tarifs de luminaires électriques, W. A. S. Benson & Co., vers 1901

Hanging light, c.1900

Metal shade with leaded glass inserts, 16.5 cm
drop / Lampenschirm aus Metall mit Einsätzen
aus Bleiverglasung, 16,5 cm hoch / Abat-jour
métallique incrusté de pièces de verre serties
de plomb, 16,5 cm de hauteur
Glasgow, Scotland

▷ *Drawing room of the Mackintoshes' house at
18 Southpark Avenue, featuring light fixture
designed for their previous Mains Street flat /
Der Salon im Haus der Familie Mackintosh in
der Southpark Avenue 18 mit der bereits für
ihre Wohnung in der Mains Street entworfenen
Hängeleuchte / Le salon de la maison des
Mackintosh, 18 Southpark Avenue, où l'on
peut voir la suspension créée pour leur ancien
appartement de Mains Street*

Originally designed for Charles Rennie
Mackintosh's own flat at 120 Mains
Street in Glasgow, this hanging light
(c.1900) was initially used to cover
a gas-fitting. When Mackintosh and
his wife moved in 1906 to their new
house at 18 Southpark Avenue, they
took it with them and adapted the
metal shade for use with electric light.
With its simple geometry – a cube sur-
mounted by a half-sphere – and
abstracted petal motif, this light was
remarkably forward-looking in comparison to other more elaborate *fin-de-
siècle* lighting designs. Mackintosh
designed a number of variations of
this light, including those used for the
White Room at the Ingram Street Tea
Rooms (1900) and a musician's light
with two shades. (CF/PF)

Diese für Charles Rennie Mackintoshs
eigene Wohnung im Haus Mains Street
120 in Glasgow entworfene Hängeleuchte (ca. 1900) war ursprünglich für
den Gasbetrieb konzipiert. Als Mackintosh und seine Frau 1906 in ihr neues
Haus in der Southpark Avenue zogen,
adaptierten sie den Metallschirm für
eine elektrische Beleuchtung. Mit ihrer
schlichten geometrischen Form und
ihrem abstrakten, blätterförmigen Motiv
war diese Leuchte bemerkenswert fortschrittlich im Vergleich zu anderen,
kunstvolleren Leuchten der Jahrhundert-
wende. Mackintosh entwarf eine Reihe
von Variationen dieses Modells, so
1900 für den White Room in den
Ingram Street Tea Rooms oder eine
Leuchte für Orchestermusiker mit zwei
Schirmen. (CF/PF)

Créée à l'origine pour l'appartement de
Mackintosh situé au 120 Mains Street
à Glasgow, cette suspension était prévue pour recouvrir une lampe à gaz.
Lorsque, en 1906, Mackintosh et son
épouse s'installèrent au 18 Southpark
Avenue, ils l'emportèrent et modifièrent
l'abat-jour métallique pour pouvoir l'utiliser avec un appareil électrique.
Sa simplicité géométrique – un cube
surmonté d'une demi-sphère – et ses
motifs de pétales stylisés font qu'elle
est très en avance sur son époque, où
la mode était aux modèles fin de siècle
plus élaborés. Mackintosh en créa plusieurs variantes dont celle utilisée dans
le Salon blanc des Salons de thé d'Ingram Street (1990) et une lampe de
musicien munie de deux abat-jour.
(CF/PF)

***Bulles de savon* appliques, *c.*1900**

Patinated bronze mounts with glass shades,
28 cm high / Montierungen aus patinierter
Bronze mit Lampenschirmen aus Glas, 28 cm
hoch / Montures en bronze patiné, abat-jour
en verre, 28 cm de hauteur
France

The increased use of electricity as a
source of domestic lighting around the
close of the 19th century stimulated the
imaginations of numerous designers.
The Paris "Exposition Universelle et
Internationale" of 1900 provided a spectacular showcase for lighting design.
The French led the fashion for sculpted
figural subjects as the basis for light
designs and their creators, often distinguished artists rather than industrial
designers, would use considerable
ingenuity to incorporate the light bulb or
shade as an integral element in the concept. In this instance the shades represent giant soap bubbles. (PG)

Die gegen Ende des 19. Jahrhunderts
wachsende Verbreitung elektrischer
Beleuchtung in den Privathaushalten
regte die Phantasie zahlreicher Designer an, und die Weltausstellung in
Paris von 1900 bot ihnen eine spektakuläre Präsentationsfläche. Frankreich
war Trendsetter bei der Verwendung
von plastisch gearbeiteten, figurativen
Themen, und französische Gestalter,
bei denen es sich häufig eher um bekannte Künstler als um Industriedesigner handelte, verwandten beträcht-
lichen Einfallsreichtum darauf, dass
Leuchte oder Lampenschirm integrale
Gestaltungselemente des Gesamtent-
wurfs bildeten. In diesem Beispiel stellen die Schirme riesige Seifenblasen
dar. (PG)

L'utilisation croissante de l'électricité
comme source d'éclairage domestique
vers la fin du XIXᵉ siècle inspira
de nombreux créateurs. L'Exposition
Universelle qui se tint à Paris en 1900
offrit un aperçu spectaculaire de la
création de luminaires. La France était
à la pointe de la mode pour les figurines sculptées qu'on intégrait parfois
aux lampes. Ses créateurs, qui, étaient
souvent des artistes distingués plutôt
que de simples dessinateurs industriels, déployaient des trésors d'inventivité pour faire de l'ampoule et de
l'abat-jour une partie intégrante du tout.
Dans ce modèle-ci, les abat-jour évoquent d'énormes bulles de savon. (PG)

The "femme-fleur" was among the most distinctive motifs of French Art Nouveau. The dreamy-eyed maiden, lightly clothed in diaphanous fabric and entwined with giant flowers, appeared in posters and decorative prints and in small-scale domestic objects. Typically, she would be in ceramic or cast in bronze and gilded as a desk ornament. In this functional sculpture by Georges Flamand (c.1900), the bulbs represent flowers. They have no shades – this was often the case, for the bulbs would have been of a low wattage and were a novelty to be admired rather than concealed. (PG)

Die „femme-fleur" gehörte zu den charakteristischen Motiven des französischen Jugendstils. Es handelte sich dabei um die Figur eines Mädchens mit verträumten Augen, leicht bekleidet in transparentem Stoff und umschlungen von riesigen Blumen. Sie erschien auf Plakaten und dekorativen Drucken oder diente als Wohnaccessoire. Meist wurde diese Figur aus Keramik oder vergoldeter Gussbronze hergestellt und als Schreibtischschmuck verwendet. In dieser funktionalen Skulptur (ca. 1900) von Georges Famand stellen die Leuchtkörper Blumen dar. Dieses Modell hat keine Lampenschirme. Das war häufig der Fall, da die Glühbirnen mit einer niedrigen Wattzahl brannten und eine Novität darstellten, die eher bestaunt als verdeckt werden sollte. (PG)

La « femme-fleur » était l'un des motifs caractéristiques de l'Art Nouveau français. Jeune fille aux yeux rêveurs drapée d'étoffes diaphanes et enveloppée de fleurs géantes, elle apparaissait sur des affiches, des gravures décoratives et de petits objets de la vie courante. En règle générale, les figurines étaient en céramique ou coulées en bronze, puis dorées, et servaient d'ornement de bureau. Les ampoules, dans cette sculpture fonctionnelle de Flamand (vers 1900), évoquent des fleurs. Elles n'ont pas d'abat-jour – c'était souvent le cas lorsque, comme ici, on utilisait un courant de faible intensité. De plus, les ampoules étaient une nouveauté digne d'admiration et ne se cachaient plus. (PG)

Figural table light, *c.*1900

Gilt-bronze construction / Figur aus vergoldeter Bronze / Sculpture en bronze doré
Georges Flamand, near Paris, France

Narcissus wall appliques, c.1900

Patinated bronze mounts with frosted glass shades and details, 92 cm high / Montierungen aus patinierter Bronze mit Lampenschirmen und Details aus Mattglas, 92 cm hoch / Montures en bronze patiné, abat-jour et ornements en verre corrodé, 92 cm de hauteur
France

▷ **Dragonfly chandelier, c.1900**

Bronze mounts with glass shade, 30 cm drop / Montierung aus Bronze mit Lampenschirm aus Glas, 30 cm lang / Montures en bronze, abat-jour en verre, 30 cm de hauteur
France

Jean-Auguste Dampt was a sculptor who specialized in finely executed works in mixed media. He is less well known than his pupil Jean Dunand, yet his exquisite productions deserve greater recognition than their rarity allows them. Here he has taken the motif of the narcissus and developed it into a pair of Art Nouveau wall appliques (c.1900) that involve a characteristic contrast of materials. The unsigned French chandelier similarly combines bronze and glass, and elegantly exploits the fashionable dragonfly motif in a cohesive design in which form and decoration are one. (PG)

Jean-Auguste Dampt war ein Bildhauer, der sich auf fein gearbeitete Objekte aus verschiedenen Materialien spezialisiert hatte. Obgleich weniger bekannt als sein Schüler Jean Dunand, verdienen seine exquisiten Arbeiten von Seltenheitswert doch große Anerkennung. Hier hat er das Motiv des Narziss in einem Paar Wandapplikationen (ca. 1900) aufgegriffen, die den für den Jugendstil charakteristischen Kontrast von Materialien aufweisen. Bei den unsignierten französischen Kronleuchtern wurden Bronze und Glas auf ähnliche Weise kombiniert; das modische Libellenmotiv ziert einen Entwurf, in dem Form und Dekor eine Einheit bilden. (PG)

Sculpteur de profession, Dampt se spécialisait dans la production d'objets finement travaillés de matières diverses. Quoique moins connu que son élève Jean Dunand, il mérite reconnaissance pour ses œuvres rares mais néanmoins ravissantes. Ces deux appliques murales Art Nouveau en forme de narcisses (vers 1900) illustrent bien son style par leur textures contrastées. De la même manière, ce lustre français non signé marie le bronze et le verre et intègre avec élégance le motif de la libellule très en vogue, dans un tout harmonieux, où forme et ornement ne font qu'un. (PG)

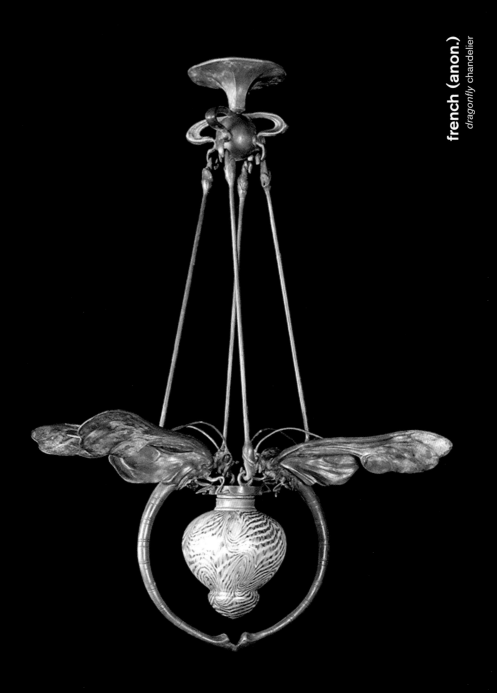

Around 1900, the provincial town of Nancy became a rival to Paris in the quality of work produced by local designers and manufacturers. Inspired by Émile Gallé, they formed an association, the École de Nancy, to develop and promote a decorative style that drew its inspiration from nature. Their stylistic ambitions coincided with the lush lines and motifs of fashionable continental Art Nouveau and the leading creators achieved considerable national and international acclaim. Both the table light (c.1900) and chandelier (1900s) are the product of a collaboration between the Daum Frères glass works and the Louis Majorelle furniture and metalwork manufactory. (PG)

Um 1900 rivalisierte die Provinzstadt Nancy mit Paris im Hinblick auf die Qualität der von lokalen Entwerfern und Manufakturen produzierten Arbeiten. Angeregt von Émile Gallé gründeten sie eine Vereinigung, die École de Nancy, um einen ornamentalen Stil zu entwickeln, der seine Inspiration aus der Natur bezog. Ihre künstlerischen Ambitionen korrespondierten mit den reich verzierten Formen und Motiven des Jugendstil, der in ganz Kontinentaleuropa Mode war, und so erzielten die führenden Vertreter der École de Nancy große Erfolge im In- und Ausland. Tisch- und Deckenleuchte (ca. 1900) sind beide aus der Zusammenarbeit der Glasmanufaktur Daum mit der Möbel- und Metallwarenfabrik Louis Majorelle hervorgegangen. (PG)

Vers 1900, Nancy, ville de province se mit à concurrencer Paris par la qualité des produits réalisés par ses créateurs et ses industriels. Suivant la voie tracée par Émile Gallé, ceux-ci fondèrent l'École de Nancy afin de développer et de promouvoir un style décoratif inspiré par la nature. Leurs motifs et leurs lignes opulentes s'inscrivaient dans le courant Art Nouveau alors en vogue, et les plus grands d'entre eux connurent un succès phénoménal, en France comme à l'étranger. Cette lampe et ce lustre (vers 1900) sont tous deux nés d'une collaboration entre la Verrerie Daum et la manufacture de Louis Majorelle, qui fabriquait du mobilier et des articles de ferronnerie. (PG)

Table light, *c.*1900
Wrought-iron base with etched glass shades, 59.5 cm high / Fuß aus Schmiedeeisen mit Lampenschirmen aus geätztem Glas, 59,5 cm hoch / Socle en fer forgé, abat-jour en verre gravé, 59,5 cm de hauteur
Majorelle, Nancy, France (base) / **Daum Frères**, Nancy, France (shades)

▷ **Chandelier, 1900s**
Bronze mounts with glass shades, 177.8 cm drop / Montierung aus Bronze mit Lampenschirmen aus Glas, 177,8 cm lang / Montures en bronze, abat-jour en verre, 177,8 cm de hauteur
Majorelle, Nancy, France (mounts) / **Daum Frères**, Nancy, France (shades)

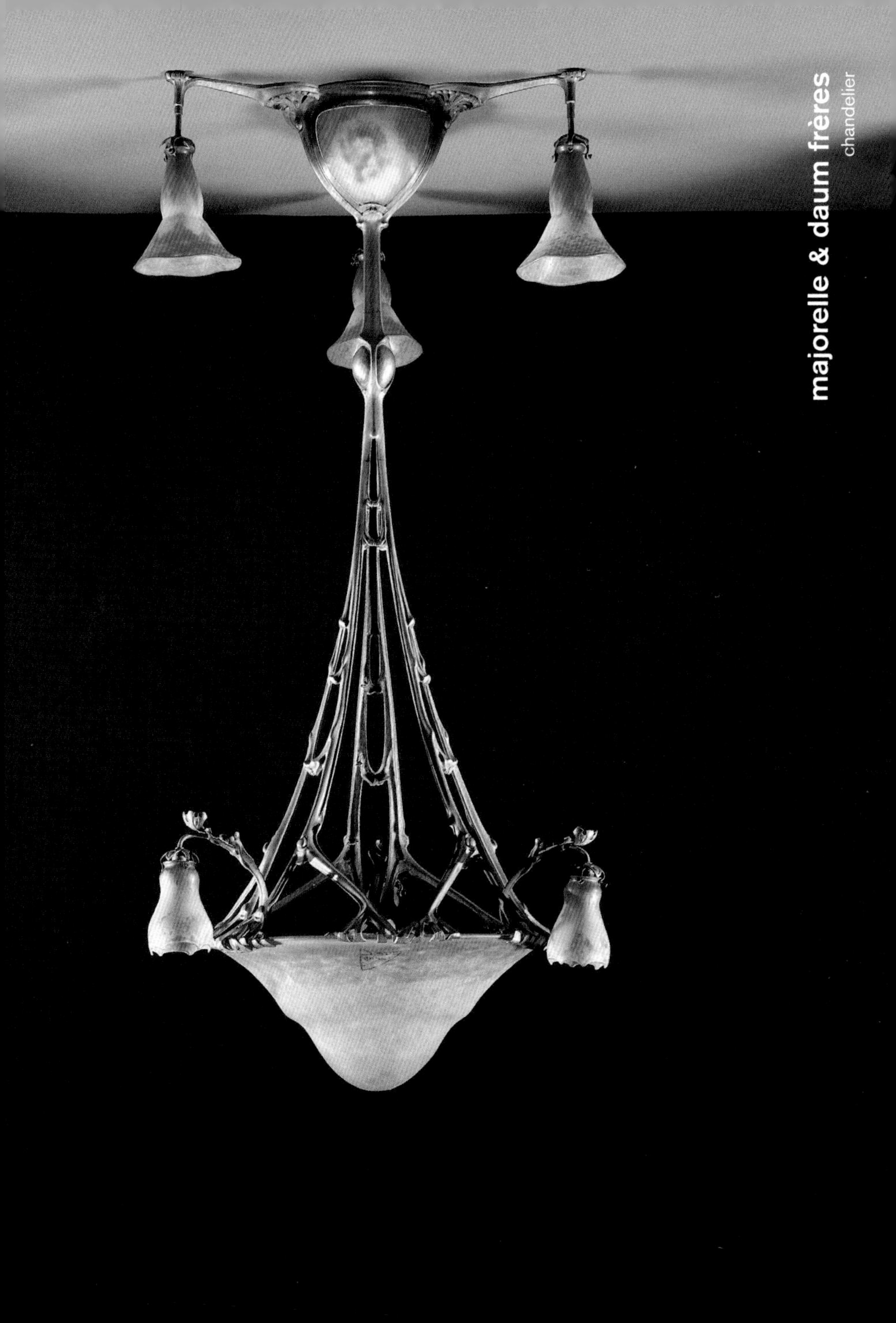

majorelle & daum frères
chandelier

Magnolia table lights, *c.*1903

Gilt-bronze bases with carved glass shades, 79.7 cm high / Fuß aus vergoldeter Bronze mit Lampenschirmen aus geformtem Glas, 79,7 cm hoch / Socles en bronze doré, abat-jour en verre sculpté, 79,7 cm de hauteur
Majorelle, Nancy, France (base) / **Daum Frères**, Nancy, France (shades)

▷ *Page from Majorelle catalog, c.1903 / Seite aus einem Katalog der Firma Majorelle, ca. 1903 / Page du catalogue Majorelle, vers 1903*

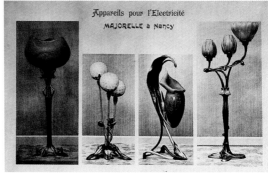

Appareils pour l'Électricité
MAJORELLE à Nancy

The mirror pair of lights (c.1903) conceived in the form of flowering magnolia stems are among the most sumptuous creations generated by the Daum-Majorelle collaboration. The use of gilt bronze makes these appropriate complements to the rich gilt-bronze mounted furniture created by Majorelle. The glass shades are sculpted in full relief. The single-stem table light (c.1903) is also representative of the highest level of quality from these makers – here the cameo decoration has the subtlety achieved by hand carving rather than acid etching. (PG)

Das spiegelgleiche Paar Tischleuchten (ca. 1903) in Form von blühenden Magnolien gehört zu den herrlichsten Kreationen, die aus der Zusammenarbeit zwischen den Firmen Daum und Majorelle entstanden sind. Die Verwendung von vergoldeter Bronze macht sie zur passenden Ergänzung für die ebenfalls reich mit vergoldeter Bronze verzierten Möbel von Majorelle. Die Glasschirme sind in Form von erhabenen Reliefs plastisch gestaltet. Auch die einzelne Tischleuchte (ca. 1903) repräsentiert die höchste Qualitätsstufe in der Arbeit dieser Gestalter. Hier ist der Überfangdekor von einer zarten Feinheit, die eher durch den Handschnitt als durch Säureätzung erzielt wird. (PG)

Évoquant des branches de magnolia en fleurs, cette paire de lampes en miroir (vers 1903) compte parmi les créations les plus somptueuses de la collaboration Daum-Majorelle. Leurs éléments en bronze doré en faisaient un complément idéal de l'opulent mobilier Majorelle, dont les cadres étaient souvent faits du même métal. Les abat-jour en verre sont sculptés en haut-relief. La lampe de table à un pied (vers 1903) est, elle aussi, représentative du style des deux fabricants dans tout ce qu'il avait de plus luxueux : la décoration en camée est ici réalisée à la main plutôt que gravée à l'acide, d'où sa finesse. (PG)

majorelle & daum frères
table light

Table light, c.1903
Bronze base with wheel-carved glass shade, 71.8 cm high / Bronzefuß mit Lampenschirm aus Glas mit Hochschnittdekor, 71,8 cm hoch / Socle en bronze, abat-jour en verre gravé à la roue, 71,8 cm de hauteur
Majorelle, Nancy, France (base) / Daum Frères, Nancy, France (shades)

Les Coprins (designed in 1902) is rightly regarded as one of Émile Gallé's masterpieces. In this object we see the scope of his vision as a Symbolist artist, and we are confronted with the evidence of his readiness to push his chosen materials to their limits in his search for inventive and expressive form. This light, conceived in the shape of three vastly over-scaled mushrooms, is an extraordinary artifact by any standards – it is a *tour de force* of virtuoso glasswork and exudes a sinister, quasi-erotic sensuality. (PG)

Die Tischleuchte *Les Coprins* (Entwurf von 1902) gilt zu Recht als eines der Meisterwerke von Émile Gallé. In diesem Objekt wird sowohl seine visionäre Kraft als symbolistischer Künstler als auch seine Bereitschaft sichtbar, auf der Suche nach neuen, ausdrucksstarken Formen das Potential seiner Materialien bis an ihre Grenzen auszuschöpfen. Diese in der Form von drei überdimensionalen Pilzen gestaltete Leuchte ist in jeglicher Hinsicht ein außerordentliches Objekt: Es stellt eine *Tour de Force* virtuoser Glaskunst dar und strahlt eine unheimliche, quasi-erotische Sinnlichkeit aus. (PG)

La lampe *Les Coprins*, créée en 1902, est considérée à juste titre comme l'un des chefs-d'œuvre d'Émile Gallé. Cet objet, qui révèle la sensibilité symboliste de l'artiste visionnaire, montre combien sa recherche de formes novatrices et expressives le menait à repousser toujours plus loin les limites de la matière. *Les Coprins*, qui emprunte sa forme à trois champignons surdimensionnés, est extraordinaire à tous points de vue. Il émane, de cette prouesse technique du maître verrier, une sensualité morbide et quasi érotique. (PG)

Les Coprins table light, 1902
Cameo glass stems and shades with bronze fittings, 83 cm high / Fuß und Lampenschirme aus überfangenem Glas mit Bronzemontierung, 83 cm hoch / Ornements de bronze, tiges et abat-jour en verre gravé en camée, 83 cm de hauteur
Cristallerie de Gallé, Nancy, France

◁ Sketch of maker's mark by Émile Gallé, c.1900 / Zeichnung des Markenzeichens von Émile Gallé, ca. 1900 / Croquis de la signature de la Cristallerie, par Émile Gallé, vers 1900

"All objects have a defining contour, yet from where come those shapes with the power to move men?"

„Alle Gegenstände haben eine individuelle Form, doch woher kommen die Formen, welche die Menschen berühren?"

« Tous les objets ont des contours, mais d'où vient la forme qui émeut ? »

– Émile Gallé

Morning Glory table light, c.1900
Wrought-iron mounts with intaglio glass shade, 50.5 cm high / Montierung aus Schmiedeeisen mit Lampenschirm aus Glas mit Schnittdekor, 50,5 cm hoch / Montures en fer forgé, abat-jour en verre gravé en intaille, 50,5 cm de hauteur
Cristallerie de Gallé, Nancy, France

When Émile Gallé first turned his attention to the creation of lights incorporating his now distinctive cameo glass, he and his studio evolved a range of works that are a perfect expression of Art Nouveau as it was developed in Nancy. The starting point was a plant form, represented accurately, though of course over-scaled, but subtly stylized and with a fluid elegance of line. As well as reflecting Gallé's passionate interest in nature, this light is true to the Art Nouveau principle of a perfect synthesis of form and decoration. (PG)

Als Émile Gallé damit begann, Leuchten unter Verwendung seines berühmten geschliffenen oder geätzten Überfangglases zu kreieren, schufen er und seine Mitarbeiter eine Reihe von Arbeiten, die auf vollkommene Weise den Stil des Art Nouveau ausdrücken, wie er in Nancy entwickelt wurde. Den Ausgangspunkt seiner Gestaltung bilden Pflanzenformen in exakter, wenn auch vergrößerter Darstellung, zart stilisiert und mit elegant fließenden Linien. Diese Leuchte spiegelt nicht nur Gallés leidenschaftliches Interesse an der Natur, sondern verbindet auch getreu nach dem Prinzip des Art Nouveau in einer perfekten Synthese Form und Dekor. (PG)

Émile Gallé était déjà connu pour son verre camée lorsqu'il décida, en collaboration avec son atelier, d'appliquer cette technique à la production de lampes, lesquelles sont de parfaits exemples de l'Art Nouveau tel qu'il était en train de se développer à Nancy. Chacune s'inspirait d'une plante, qui était représentée fidèlement, quoique agrandie et finement stylisée, en lignes fluides et élégantes. Ce luminaire, qui témoigne de la passion que Gallé vouait à la nature, est aussi typique de l'Art Nouveau par la synthèse qu'il opère entre la forme et l'ornementation. (PG)

tiffany studios
lily table light

"Handicraft which pos-
sesses beauty and origi-
nality is independent
of passing fashion."

„Handwerk, das Schönheit
und Originalität besitzt,
ist unabhängig von vorüber-
gehenden Moden."

« Un objet à la fois beau
et original n'a que faire
des caprices de la mode. »

– Louis Comfort Tiffany

◁ **Twelve-light *Lily* table light,
c.1900–02**
Bronze base with Favrile glass shades, 51.5 cm
high / Bronzefuß mit Lampenschirmen aus
Favrile-Glas, 51,5 cm hoch / Socle en bronze,
abat-jour en verre Favrile, 51,5 cm de hauteur
Tiffany Studios, New York (NY), USA

▷ **Eighteen-light *Lily* table light,
c.1900–02**
Bronze base with Favrile glass shades, 53.5 cm
high / Bronzefuß mit Lampenschirmen aus
Favrile-Glas, 53,5 cm hoch / Socle en bronze,
abat-jour en verre Favrile, 53,5 cm de hauteur
Tiffany Studios, New York (NY), USA

Believing that "nature is always beautiful," Louis Comfort Tiffany used stylized representations of flora and fauna to bring beauty into the home, which according to him would enhance the quality of life. These lights (c.1900–02) fashioned after waterlilies were among his firm's most prized designs. Sometimes referred to as the "Pond Lily" lights, they featured trumpet-like shades made of iridescent amber Favrile glass supported on cast-bronze bases decorated in high relief with overlapping lily pads and buds. Sumptuous and elegant in design, the 18-light model epitomizes the virtuoso craftsmanship of the Tiffany workshop. (CF/PF)

In der Überzeugung, dass die Natur immer schön sei, arbeitete Louis Comfort Tiffany mit stilisierten Darstellungen von Flora und Fauna, um Schönheit in das Heim zu bringen, was seiner Meinung nach die Lebensqualität erhöhte. Die Wasserlilien nachempfundenen Leuchten (ca. 1900–02) gehörten zu den begehrtesten Objekten seiner Firma. Die auch als „Pond Lily" bezeichneten Leuchten waren mit trompetenförmigen Lampenschirmen aus Favrile-Glas bestückt mit Stielen aus Gussbronze, die mit plastisch geformten Lilienblättern und Knospen verziert waren. Prächtig und elegant im Design vermittelt das mit achtzehn Lampen ausgestattete Modell einen lebhaften Eindruck von der virtuosen Handwerkskunst der Tiffany Werkstatt. (CF/PF)

Partant de sa conviction que « la nature est toujours belle », Louis Comfort Tiffany faisait entrer la beauté à l'intérieur des maisons et pensait pouvoir améliorer la qualité de vie de leurs habitants grâce à ses représentations stylisées de flore et de faune. Cette lampe (vers 1900–02), qui s'inspire d'un nénuphar et était parfois appelée « Pond Lily » (« lis des étangs »), comptait parmi ses modèles les plus recherchés. Ses abat-jour en forme de trompettes étaient fabriqués en verre Favrile et reposaient sur des socles en bronze coulé en formes de feuilles et de boutons de nénuphars. La somptueuse élégance du modèle à dix-huit ampoules donne une bonne idée de l'extrême virtuosité dont les Ateliers Tiffany étaient capables. (CF/PF)

The *Wistaria* table light (*c*.1904) was devised by one of Tiffany's most important designers, Mrs. Curtis Freschel, and was one of the few lights manufactured by the firm where the shade and base were designed as a unified composition. According to the Tiffany Studios Price List of 1906, the light originally retailed for $400. This model was known as *Wistaria* rather than *Wisteria*, as the plant which inspired it was named in tribute to Caspar Wistar – an anatomy professor at the University of Pennsylvania. A similarly successful design in terms of color and composition, the *Apple Blossom* table light (*c*.1902–06) incorporates the same realistic tree-trunk-like bronze base. (CF/PF)

Die *Wistaria* Tischleuchte (ca. 1904) wurde von Mrs. Curtis Freschel, einer der bedeutensten Designerinnen der Tiffany Studios, entworfen und gehört zu den wenigen von dieser Firma hergestellten Leuchten, bei denen Lampenschirm- und Fuß eine kompositorische Einheit bilden. Laut der Preisliste der Tiffany Studios aus dem Jahr 1906 wurde die Leuchte damals für 400 Dollar verkauft. In Gedenken an den Anatomieprofessor Caspar Wistar an der Universität von Pennsylvania wurde das Modell *Wistaria* benannt und trägt nicht den lateinischen Namen der Pflanze *Wisteria*, die dem Entwurf als Vorbild zugrunde lag. Ein im Hinblick auf Farbe und Komposition ähnlich erfolgreiches Design, die *Apple Blossom* Tischleuchte (ca. 1902–06), ist mit dem modellgleichen Bronzefuß in Form eines Baumstammes ausgestattet. (CF/PF)

La lampe de table *Wistaria* (vers 1904) est l'œuvre de Mme Curtis Freschel, l'un des créateurs les plus importants de chez Tiffany. C'est aussi un exemple rare de lampe dont le pied et l'abat-jour étaient conçus comme un tout. Selon les tarifs des Ateliers Tiffany Studios pour 1906, elle était vendue $400. Son nom était une version rare du mot « wisteria » (« glycine ») et faisait référence à Caspar Wistar, le professeur d'anatomie à l'Université de Pennsylvanie qui donna son nom à la plante. Tout aussi réussie dans sa couleur et sa composition, la lampe *Apple Blossom (Fleurs de pommier,* vers 1902–06*)* est elle aussi dotée d'un socle en bronze évoquant un tronc d'arbre. (CF/PF)

△ / ▽ **Apple Blossom** table light, *c.*1902–06

Bronze base with leaded glass shade, 74.6 cm high / Bronzefuß mit bleiverglastem Lampenschirm, 74,6 cm hoch / Socle en bronze, abat-jour en verre vitrail, 74,6 cm de hauteur **Tiffany Studios,** New York (NY), USA

▷ **Wistaria** table light, *c.*1904

Bronze base with leaded glass shade, 66 cm high / Bronzefuß mit bleiverglastem Lampenschirm, 66 cm hoch / Socle en bronze, abat-jour en verre vitrail, 66 cm de hauteur **Tiffany Studios,** New York (NY), USA

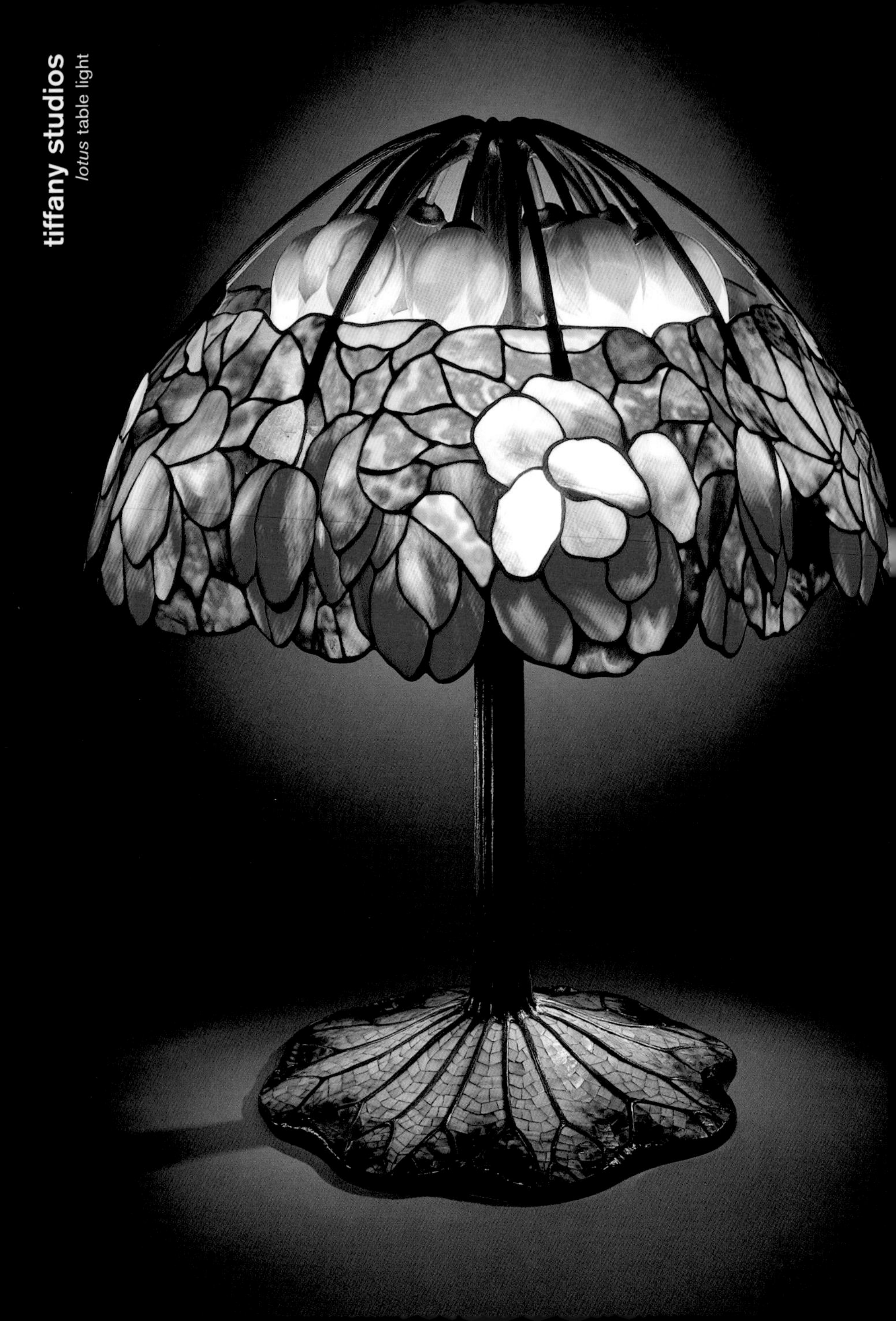

tiffany studios
lotus table light

◁ **Lotus table light, c.1900–06**
Bronze and glass mosaic base with leaded
glass and favrile glass shades, 88.3 cm high /
Bronzefuß mit Glasmosaikeinlage, Lampenschirme aus Bleiverglasung und Favrile-Glas,
88,3 cm hoch /
Tiffany Studios, New York (NY), USA

Tiffany Studios workshop, c.1900 / Tiffany
Werkstätte in Corona, ca. 1905 – die Arbeiter
sind mit der Herstellung von bleiverglasten
Lampenschirmen beschäftigt /

Perhaps the most beautiful of all the
lighting designs manufactured by
Tiffany Studios, the *Lotus* table light
(c.1900–06) was the second most
expensive model produced by the firm,
retailing in 1906 at the princely sum
of $750. What makes this model so
special is the three-dimensionality of its
composition – a ring of bud-like shades
are circled by a leaded glass screen
with a stylized pattern of open lotus
flowers. The choice of the lotus flower
not only reflects the influence of both
Oriental and Islamic art on the Art
Nouveau style but also the contemporary fascination with forms taken from
nature. (CF/PF)

Das vielleicht schönste aller von den
Tiffany Studios hergestellten Lampen-
designs, die Tischlampe *Lotus*, war
auch gleichzeitig das zweitteuerste
Modell im Sortiment dieser Firma, das
im Jahr 1906 für die stolze Summe von
750 Dollar verkauft wurde. Was dieses
Modell so besonders macht, ist die
Dreidimensionalität seiner Komposition:
ein Ring aus knospenartigen Schirmen
wird von einem Bleiglasschirm umgeben, der mit einem stilisierten Muster
aus offenen Lotusblüten verziert ist. Die
Wahl der Lotusblume spiegelt nicht nur
den Einfluss wider, den orientalische
und islamische Kunst auf den Stil des
Art nouveau hatten, sondern auch die
damalige Faszination für Formen aus
der Natur. (CF/PF)

Peut-être le plus beau luminaire jamais
sorti des Tiffany Studios, la lampe de
table Lotus était la deuxième en terme
de prix et se vendait pour la somme
astronomique de $750. Son appa-
rence si particulière vient de sa conception tridimensionnelle – plusieurs abat-
jour en forme de boutons de fleurs
sont disposés en cercle et entourés
d'un écran en verre de plomb orné de
fleurs de lotus stylisées. Le choix du
lotus reflète non seulement l'influence
orientale et islamique qui régnait sur
l'Art Nouveau, mais aussi la fascination
de l'époque pour les formes emprun-
tées à la nature. (CF/PF)

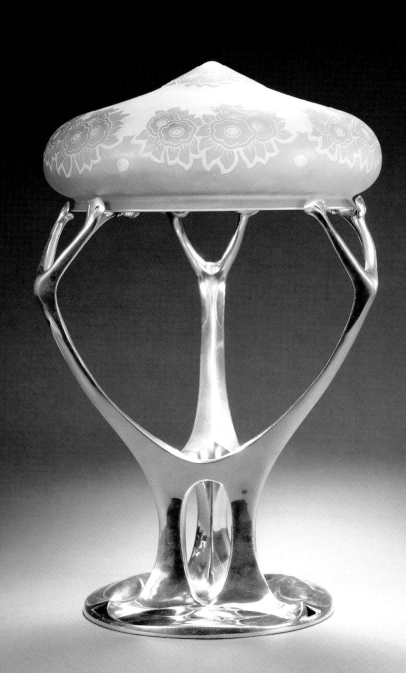

In 1899 Friedrich August Scherf and his son, Walter, founded the small Osiris factory in Nuremberg and began producing elegant lighting designs. In 1902 the company developed a new metal alloy known as "Isis", which although more expensive than existing types of pewter was eminently suitable for the firm's beautiful organic Art Nouveau products. Some of the leading German designers and architects of the day produced designs for the Osiris factory, including Peter Behrens, Joseph Maria Olbrich, Friedrich Adler, Bruno Paul and Richard Riemerschmid. Walter Scherf was also responsible for some of the 1,300 products manufactured by the factory between 1899 and 1909 (when the company closed). (CF/PF)

Im Jahr 1899 gründeten Friedrich August Scherf und sein Sohn Walter die kleine Fabrik Osiris in Nürnberg und begannen, elegante Leuchten herzustellen. 1902 entwickelte die Firma eine neue Metalllegierung mit dem Namen „Isis", die zwar teurer war als bestehende Zinnlegierungen, sich aber ausgesprochen gut für ihre schönen, organisch geformten Jugendstilobjekte eignete. Einige der führenden deutschen Designer und Architekten jener Zeit fertigten Entwürfe für Osiris, so Peter Behrens, Joseph Maria Olbrich, Friedrich Adler, Bruno Paul und Richard Riemerschmid. Auch Walter Scherf selbst gestaltete einige der 1.300 Zinnartikel, welche die Fabrik in den Jahren zwischen 1899 und 1909, dem Jahr ihrer Schließung, produzierte. (CF/PF)

En 1899, Friedrich August Scherf et son fils Walter fondèrent la petite usine Osiris de Nuremberg et commencèrent à fabriquer d'élégants luminaires. En 1902, la société mit au point un nouvel alliage métallique appelé « Isis » qui, même s'il était plus cher que les types d'étain déjà connus, s'avéra parfaitement adapté aux beaux luminaires Art Nouveau d'inspiration organique que fabriquait la compagnie. Plusieurs grands dessinateurs et architectes allemands de l'époque, dont Peter Behrens, Joseph Maria Olbrich, Friedrich Adler, Bruno Paul, et Richard Riemerschmid, mirent leur talent au service de l'usine Osiris. Quant à Walter Scherf, il signa plusieurs des mille trois cents modèles qui en sortirent entre 1899 et 1909 (l'année de sa fermeture). (CF/PF)

◁ *Model No. 787 Osiris* table light, *c.*1901–02

Pewter base with etched glass shade, 53 cm high / Fuß aus Zinn mit Lampenschirm aus geätztem Glas, 53 cm hoch / Socle en étain, abat-jour en verre gravé, 53 cm de hauteur
Walter Scherf & Co., Nuremberg, Germany

Model No. 751 Osiris table light, *c.*1901–02

Pewter base with opalescent glass shade, 41.9 cm high / Fuß aus Zinn mit Lampenschirm aus Opalglas, 41,9 cm hoch / Socle en étain, abat-jour en verre opalescent, 41,9 cm de hauteur
Walter Scherf & Co., Nuremberg, Germany

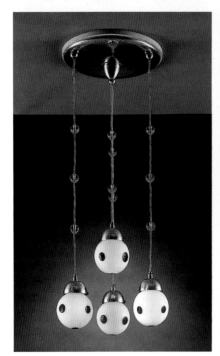

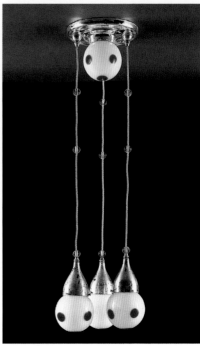

△ **Hanging light, c.1902**

Brass mounts with glass beads and shades, 35.6 cm diameter / Montierung aus Messing mit Glasperlen, Lampenschirme aus weißem Opalglas mit blauen Tupfen, 35,6 cm Durchmesser / Montures en laiton, pendeloques de verre, abat-jour en verre blanc opalescent à pois bleus, 35,6 cm de diamètre
E. Bakalowits & Söhne, Vienna, Austria (attrib.)

△▷ **Hanging light, c.1902**

Silver-plated brass mounts with glass beads and shades, 111.8 cm drop / Montierung aus versilbertem Messing mit Glasperlen, Lampenschirme aus weißem Opalglas mit roten Tupfen, 111,8 cm lang / Montures en laiton argenté, pendeloques de verre, abat-jour en verre blanc opalescent à pois rouges, 111,8 cm de hauteur
E. Bakalowits & Söhne, Vienna, Austria (attrib.)

▷ **Chandelier, c.1900**

Gilt-metal mounts with glass beads and shades, 96.5 cm drop / Montierung aus vergoldetem Metall mit grünen Glasperlen, Lampenschirme aus weißem, irisierendem Glas, 96,5 cm lang / Montures en métal doré, pendeloques en verre vert, abat-jour en verre blanc irisé, 96,5 cm de hauteur
E. Bakalowits & Söhne, Vienna, Austria (attrib.)

In 1903, in collaboration with the architect Josef Hoffmann and the banker Fritz Wärndorfer, Koloman Moser set up the famous Wiener Werkstätte, or Vienna Workshops, sharing the post of artistic director with Hoffmann until 1907. As well as producing numerous designs for the Wiener Werkstätte, Moser also worked for the Viennese glassware manufacturers E. Bakalowits & Söhne from about 1900 onward, designing a wide range of modern glassware and lighting fixtures. As an artist and craftsman, Moser helped shape the Secessionist style, and his works were quickly copied by other designers and manufacturers. (TB)

1903 gründete Koloman Moser zusammen mit dem Architekten Josef Hoffmann und dem Bankier Fritz Wärndorfer die berühmte Wiener Werkstätte, als deren künstlerischer Direktor er gemeinsam mit Hoffmann bis 1907 fungierte. Neben seinen zahlreichen Entwürfen für die Wiener Werkstätte war Moser vor allem als Entwerfer für die Wiener Glaswarenhandlung E. Bakalowits & Söhne tätig, für die er ab ca. 1900 zahlreiche moderne Glaswaren und Beleuchtungskörper entwarf. Mosers kunstgewerbliche Entwürfe prägten den Stil der Wiener Secession und wurden schon bald von anderen Entwerfern und Herstellern kopiert. (TB)

En 1903, en collaboration avec l'architecte Josef Hoffmann et le banquier Fritz Wärndorfer, Koloman Moser fonda les célèbres Wiener Werkstätte, ou Ateliers de Vienne, dont il partagea le poste de directeur artistique avec Hoffmann jusqu'en 1907. Non seulement il y créa de nombreux objets, mais, à partir de 1900 environ, il travailla aussi pour la manufacture viennoise E. Bakalowits & Söhne, où il signa toutes sortes d'articles en verre et de luminaires modernes. En tant qu'artiste et artisan, Moser contribua à la formation du style sécessionniste. D'autres créateurs et industriels ne tardèrent pas à le copier. (TB)

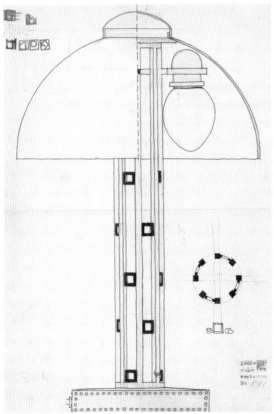

The *Model No. M109* table light designed by Josef Hoffmann in 1903 was one of the first lights produced by the Wiener Werkstätte. A contemporary photograph taken *c.*1904 shows a pair of these lights above a radiator in the Wiener Werkstätte's Neustiftgasse showroom. Among buyers of this type of light were Hirschwald, the Berlin applied arts specialists, and the Purkersdorf Sanatorium, which Hoffmann also designed. The table light, a reproduction of which is currently made by Woka Lamps of Vienna based on the original design, is striking for the classical architectural form that lends it a timeless elegance. (TB)

Bei der Tischleuchte *Modell Nr. M109* nach einem Entwurf von Josef Hoffmann aus dem Jahr 1903 handelt es sich um eine der ersten von der Wiener Werkstätte produzierten Leuchten. Eine zeitgenössische Fotografie von ca. 1904 dokumentiert ein Paar dieser Leuchten auf einer Heizkörperverkleidung im ersten Ausstellungsraum der Wiener Werkstätte in der Wiener Neustiftgasse. Als Abnehmer dieses Leuchtentyps fungierten das auf modernes Kunstgewerbe spezialisierte Berliner Kunstgewerbehaus Hirschwald und das ebenfalls von Hoffmann entworfene Sanatorium Purkersdorf. Die Tischleuchte, die heute von der Wiener Firma Woka Lamps in Anlehnung an den alten Entwurf reproduziert wird, überzeugt durch ihre klassisch architektonische Formgebung, die der Leuchte eine zeitlose Eleganz verleiht. (TB)

Conçue par Josef Hoffmann en 1903, la lampe de table *Modèle n° M109* est l'un des premiers luminaires à être sorti des Wiener Werkstätte. Une photographie d'époque, prise vers 1904, en montre deux exemplaires posés sur un cache-radiateur dans le salon d'exposition des Wiener Werkstätte à la Neustiftgasse. Le spécialiste berlinois en arts appliqués Hirschwald en acheta une, de même que le Sanatorium de Purkersdorf, dont les bâtiments étaient aussi signés Hoffmann. La lampe, dont la compagnie viennoise Woka Lamps produit aujourd'hui une réplique d'après les dessins d'origine, étonne par sa forme classique, qui lui confère une élégance intemporelle. (TB)

◁ *Model No. M109* **table light, 1903**
Nickel-plated brass base with opalescent glass shade, 55 cm high / Fuß aus vernickeltem Messing mit Lampenschirm aus Opalglas, 55 cm hoch / Socle en laiton nickelé, abat-jour en verre opalescent, 55 cm de hauteur
Wiener Werkstätte, Vienna, Austria (reissued by Woka Lamps, Vienna, Austria)

△ *Design drawing for the* Model No. M109 *table light by Josef Hoffmann, 1903 / Entwurfszeichnung für die Tischleuchte* Modell Nr. M109 *von Josef Hoffmann, 1903 / Dessin de la lampe de table* Modèle n° M109 *par Josef Hoffmann, 1903*

▷ *Wiener Werkstätte showroom at Neustiftgasse 32, Vienna, c.1904 / Ausstellungsraum der Wiener Werkstätte in der Wiener Neustiftgasse 32, ca. 1904 / Salon d'exposition des Wiener Werkstätte au 32 Neustiftgasse, Vienne, vers 1904*

The work of Belgian architect and designer Henry van de Velde is distinguished by its strong individuality and what was for the period astounding modernity. For his many building projects and interior design schemes, always planned as a *gesamtkunstwerk* (total work of art), van de Velde created a whole series of lights, to which he devoted as much care and attention as he would to a complex ground plan or an elaborate façade. The design for this 1903 hanging light continues to show strong Jugendstil influences. Lights similar to this were also fitted at van de Velde's famous Villa Esche in Chemnitz. (TB)

Die Entwürfe des belgischen Architekten und Designers Henry van de Velde zeichnen sich durch eine starke Individualität und eine für die damalige Zeit erstaunliche Modernität aus. Für seine zahlreichen Bauprojekte und Inneneinrichtungen, die immer als Gesamtkunstwerk angelegt waren, entwarf van de Velde auch neue Beleuchtungskörper, deren Gestaltung er genauso viel Aufmerksamkeit widmete wie etwa dem Entwurf eines komplizierten Grundrisses oder einer aufwendigen Fassade. Der Entwurf der Hängeleuchte aus dem Jahr 1903 ist noch stark dem Jugendstil verpflichtet. Verwendung fand die Leuchte u. a. in van de Veldes berühmter Villa Esche in Chemnitz. (TB)

L'œuvre de l'architecte et dessinateur belge Henry van de Velde est à la fois très originale et extraordinairement moderne pour son époque. Chaque fois qu'il construisait une maison ou qu'il en assurait la décoration intérieure (projets qu'il envisageait toujours comme une « œuvre d'art totale »), il réalisait aussi les luminaires, y mettant autant de soin et d'attention qu'à l'élaboration d'un plan ou d'une façade. Cette suspension de 1903 est encore fortement marquée par l'influence du Jugendstil. La célèbre Villa Esche de van de Velde à Chemnitz était équipée de plusieurs modèles semblables. (TB)

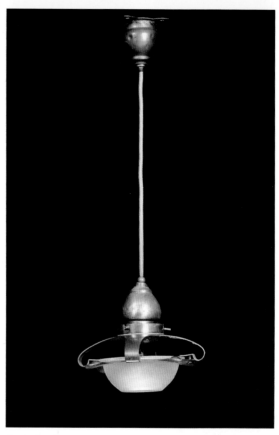

Hanging light, 1903
Copper mounts with frosted glass shade, 23 cm diameter / Montierung aus Kupfer mit Lampenschirm aus Mattglas, 23 cm Durchmesser / Montures en cuivre, abat-jour en verre dépoli, 23 cm de diamètre
Otto Seyffart, Altenburg, Germany

"The joy of having shaken off the nightmare of the imitation of styles."

„Die Freude darüber, den Albtraum der Imitation von Stilen abgeschüttelt zu haben."

« Quelle joie de s'être débarrassé du cauchemar de l'imitation. »

– Henry van de Velde

In 1906 Henry van de Velde was commissioned to design and build a tennis club in Chemnitz. The design showed fewer Jugendstil influences and moved toward a more down-to-earth, functional style. Nevertheless, the unmistakable elegance and fondness for detail made it typical of van de Velde. The ceiling lights (1906–08) for the clubhouse lounge were based on the geometric shapes of the triangle, circle and cylinder, in contrast to the sinuous curves that characterized van de Velde's creations dating from around 1900. (TB)

1906 erhielt Henry van de Velde den Auftrag zur Planung und Einrichtung eines Tennisclubs in Chemnitz. Der Stil der Einrichtung war nicht mehr so stark dem Jugendstil verpflichtet, sondern weist bereits in Richtung einer mehr sachlichen, von der Funktion abgeleiteten Gestaltung. Typisch für van de Velde ist jedoch die unverkennbare Eleganz und die Liebe für das Detail. Die für den Aufenthaltsraum im Clubhaus der Tennisanlage entworfene Deckenleuchte (1906–08) basiert in ihrer Formgebung auf den geometrischen Grundformen Dreieck, Kreis und Zylinder. Sie steht damit in Kontrast zu van de Veldes Entwürfen um 1900, die als gestalterisches Element die geschwungene Linie bevorzugten. (TB)

En 1906, Henry van de Velde fut chargé de la conception et de la construction d'un club de tennis à Chemnitz. Il opta pour un style fonctionnel et sans façons, qui s'éloignait de l'influence du Jugendstil. On y reconnaît bien, en revanche, l'élégance propre à l'architecte et sa prédilection pour les détails. Le salon du club était équipé de suspensions (1906–08) dont les formes géométriques (triangle, cercle, cylindre) contrastaient avec ses œuvres tout en courbes sinueuses des alentours de 1900. (TB)

△△ **Hanging light for the Chemnitz Tennis Club, 1906–08**

Brass and painted wood mounts with opalescent glass shades, 33 cm drop / Montierung aus Messing und lackiertem Holz mit Lampenschirmen aus Opalglas, 33 cm lang / Montures en laiton et bois émaillé, abat-jour en verre opalescent, 33 cm de hauteur
Otto Bergener, Weimar, Germany

△ *The Chemnitz Tennis Club, designed by Henry van de Velde, 1906–08 / Interieur des 1906–08 von Henry van de Velde gestalteten Chemnitzer Tennisclubhauses / Vue intérieure du tennis club de Chemnitz, réalisé en 1906–08 par Henry van de Velde*

△ **Table light for the Susan Lawrence Dana House, Springfield, (IL), c.1903**

Bronze base with leaded glass panels, 62.2 cm high / Fuß und Montierung aus Bronze mit Bleiverglasung, 62,2 cm hoch / Socle en bronze, panneaux de verre serti de plomb, 62,2 cm de hauteur /
Linden Glass Co., Chicago (IL), USA

◁ *Interior of the Susan Lawrence Dana House, Springfield, Illinois / Interieur des Susan Lawrence Dana House in Springfield, Illinois / Intérieur de la Maison de Susan Lawrence Dana à Springfield, Illinois*

▷ **Table light for the Susan Lawrence Dana House, Springfield, (IL), c.1903**

Bronze base with leaded glass panels, 56.5 cm high / Fuß und Montierung aus Bronze mit Bleiverglasung, 56,5 cm hoch / Socle en bronze, panneaux en verre serti de plomb, 56,5 cm de hauteur
Linden Glass Co., Chicago (IL), USA

In 1902 Frank Lloyd Wright designed a large house in Springfield, Illinois, for the widowed socialite Susan Lawrence Dana. It was Wright's first "blank check" commission, which meant he was able to design numerous site-specific furnishings and fittings in order to create a veritable *gesamtkunstwerk*. For this extensive project, which comprised 12,000 square feet of living space, Wright designed over 200 light fixtures and skylights, including these two remarkable leaded glass and bronze table lights (*c.*1903). In 2002 Christie's sold the larger double pedestal model for $1,989,500, setting a world auction record for a work by Wright. (CF/PF)

Im Jahr 1902 entwarf Frank Lloyd Wright ein Wohnhaus in Springfield, Illinois, für Susan Lawrence Dana, eine verwitwete Dame der Gesellschaft. Es war Wrights erster „Blankoscheck"-Auftrag, bei dem er zahlreiche maßgeschneiderte Möbel und Einrichtungsgegenstände entwerfen und damit ein tatsächliches Gesamtkunstwerk kreieren konnte. Für dieses umfangreiche Projekt mit über 1000 m² Wohnfläche entwarf Wright über 200 Beleuchtungskörper und Laternen, so die beiden Tischleuchten (ca. 1903) aus Bronze und Bleiverglasung. Im Jahr 2002 erzielte Christie's für das größere Modell mit 1.989.500 Dollar den höchsten Preis, der je bei einer Auktion für eine Arbeit von Wright gezahlt wurde. (CF/PF)

En 1902, Frank Lloyd Wright réalisa une grande maison à Springfield, dans l'État d'Illinois, pour une veuve de la haute société, Susan Lawrence Dana. Pour la première fois, Wright avait carte blanche et était libre d'imaginer toutes sortes de mobilier et d'aménagements sur mesure, ce qui lui permit de créer une véritable *œuvre d'art totale*. Pour ce projet de grande envergure (plus de mille mètres carrés d'espace habitable), Wright créa plus de deux cents luminaires et lucarnes, dont ces deux extraordinaires lampes de table en bronze et verre senti de plomb. En 2002, le grand modèle à deux pieds se vendit chez Christie's pour $1 989 500 – le prix le plus élevé jamais atteint aux enchères par une œuvre de Wright. (CF/PF)

These bronze and leaded-glass wall lights (c.1902 and c.1909) were designed site-specifically for two of Frank Lloyd Wright's so-called Prairie Houses. The lights echoed the strong geometry of these buildings with their jutting horizontal gables and soaring vertical elements, while the choice of glass color reflected the hues of the surrounding landscape with its lush green trees and golden grasses. Inspired by Japanese screens, this type of leaded-glass fixture produced a warm indirect light, which gave Wright's interiors a charming and cozy ambience. (CF/PF)

Die Wandleuchten (ca. 1902 und ca. 1909) aus Bronze und Buntglas wurden speziell für zwei von Frank Lloyd Wrights so genannten „Prärie-Häusern" entworfen. Die Leuchten spiegelten die kraftvolle Geometrie dieser Häuser mit ihren vorspringenden horizontalen Giebeln und hoch aufragenden vertikalen Elementen wider, während die Färbung des Glases die Farbtöne der umgebenden Landschaft mit ihren üppig grünen Bäumen und gelbgoldenen Weiden aufgriff. Die von japanischen Wandschirmen inspirierten Wandleuchten mit Buntglas erzeugten ein warmes, indirektes Licht, das Wrights Innenräumen eine bezaubernde, behagliche Atmosphäre verlieh. (CF/PF)

Ces appliques murales en bronze et verre vitrail (vers 1902 et 1909) furent réalisées sur mesure pour deux des maisons dites « de la prairie » de Frank Lloyd Wright. Leurs corniches saillantes et leurs longues lignes verticales reflétaient l'architecture très géométrique des bâtiments, tandis que les tons verts et dorés du verre évoquaient la végétation environnante. Ce type de luminaire s'inspirait des paravents japonais et émettait une douce lumière indirecte qui donnait aux intérieurs de Wright leur charmante et chaleureuse ambiance. (CF/PF)

◁◁ **Wall light for the Francis W. Little House, Peoria, Illinois, c.1902**

Bronze mount with glass panels, 33.5 cm high / Bronzemontierung mit Glasfüllungen, 33,5 cm hoch / Monture en bronze, panneaux de verre, 33,5 cm de hauteur
Linden Glass Co., Chicago (IL), USA

△ **Wall lights for the E. P. Irving House, Decatur, Illinois, c.1909**

Bronze mounts with glass panels, 15.2 cm high / Bronzemontierung mit Glasfüllungen, 15,2 cm hoch / Montures en bronze, panneaux en verre, 15,2 cm de hauteur
Linden Glass Co., Chicago (IL), USA

◁ *Living room from the Francis W. Little house at The Metropolitan Museum of Art, New York / Installation des Wohnzimmers aus dem Francis W. Little Haus im Metropolitan Museum of Art, New York / Décor de la salle de séjour de la maison de Francis W. Little exposé au Metropolitan Museum of Art, New York*

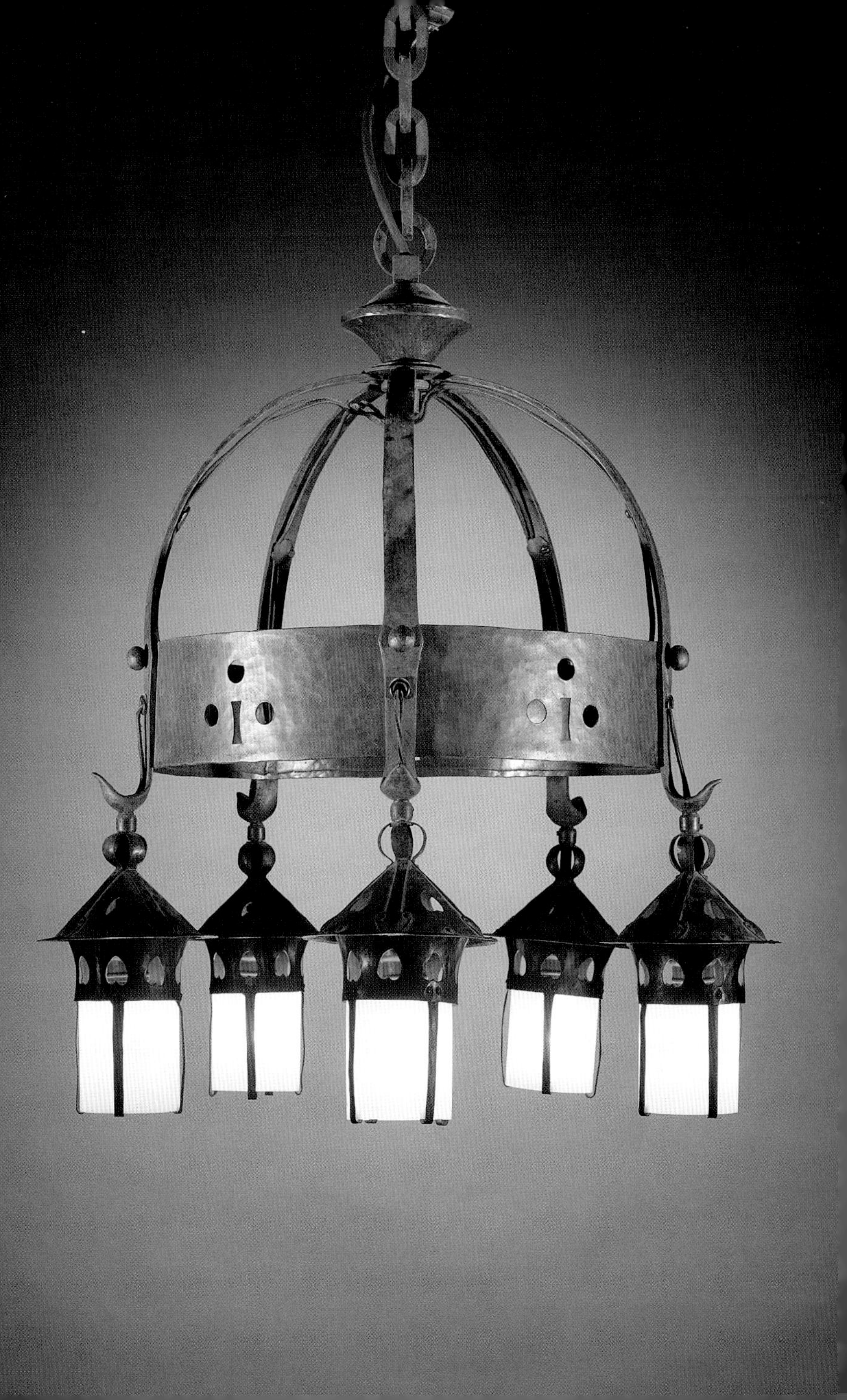

gustav stickley
model no. 223 chandelier

◁ *Model No. 223* chandelier, *c.*1905
Wrought-iron and hammered copper mounts
with copper and glass lanterns, 40.5 cm high /
Montierung aus Schmiedeeisen und gehämmertem Kupfer mit Laternen aus Kupfer und
Glas, 40,5 cm hoch / Montures en fer forgé
et cuivre martelé, lanternes en cuivre et verre,
40,5 cm de hauteur
Craftsman Workshop, Eastwood (NY), USA

▷ Table Light, *c.*1905
Hammered copper base with hammered copper
and amber glass shade, 76.2 cm high / Fuß aus
gehämmertem Kupfer mit Lampenschirm aus
gehämmertem Kupfer und Bernsteinglas,
76,2 cm hoch / Socle en cuivre martelé, abat-
jour en cuivre martelé et verre ambré, 76,2 cm
de hauteur
Craftsman Workshop, Eastwood (NY), USA

Gustav Stickley was one of the leading protagonists of the Arts & Crafts
Movement – sometimes referred to
as the Craftsman movement – in the
United States. As he noted, "In the
beginning there was no thought of
creating a new style, only a recognition
of the fact that we should have in our
homes something better suited to our
needs and more expressive of our
character as a people than imitations
of the traditional styles." His lighting
designs lovingly crafted from hammered copper reflect not only these
sentiments, but also his belief in the
primacy of plain surfaces and simplified
structure. (CF/PF)

Gustav Stickley war einer der führen-
den Protagonisten der als Arts &
Crafts-Bewegung, manchmal auch als
Craftsman Movement bezeichneten
Stilrichtung in den Vereinigten Staaten.
„Am Anfang", notierte er, „gab es
keinen Gedanken daran, einen neuen
Stil zu erschaffen, sondern nur die
Anerkennung der Tatsache, dass wir in
unseren Wohnungen Dinge haben sollten, die unseren Bedürfnissen besser
entsprechen und unseren Charakter als
Volk besser zum Ausdruck bringen als
Imitationen traditioneller Stile." Seine
liebevoll aus gehämmertem Kupfer
gefertigten Leuchten sind nicht nur ein
Spiegel dieser Empfindungen, sondern
auch seiner Überzeugung von der Vor-
rangigkeit glatter Oberflächen und ver-
einfachter Strukturen. (CF/PF)

Gustav Stickley était l'un des protago-
nistes principaux du mouvement Arts &
Crafts aux États-Unis – parfois connu
sous le nom de « Craftsman ». « Au
départ », écrivit-il, « nous n'avions aucune intention de créer un style nouveau.
Nous voulions simplement créer pour
nos maisons des objets répondant
davantage à nos besoins, et exprimant
notre identité en tant que peuple, mieux
que ne le faisaient les modèles inspirés
des styles traditionnels.» Ses luminaires, qu'il fabriquait amoureusement à
la main en utilisant du cuivre martelé,
reflètent non seulement cette conviction, mais aussi son intérêt pour les surfaces lisses et les structures simplifiées.
(CF/PF)

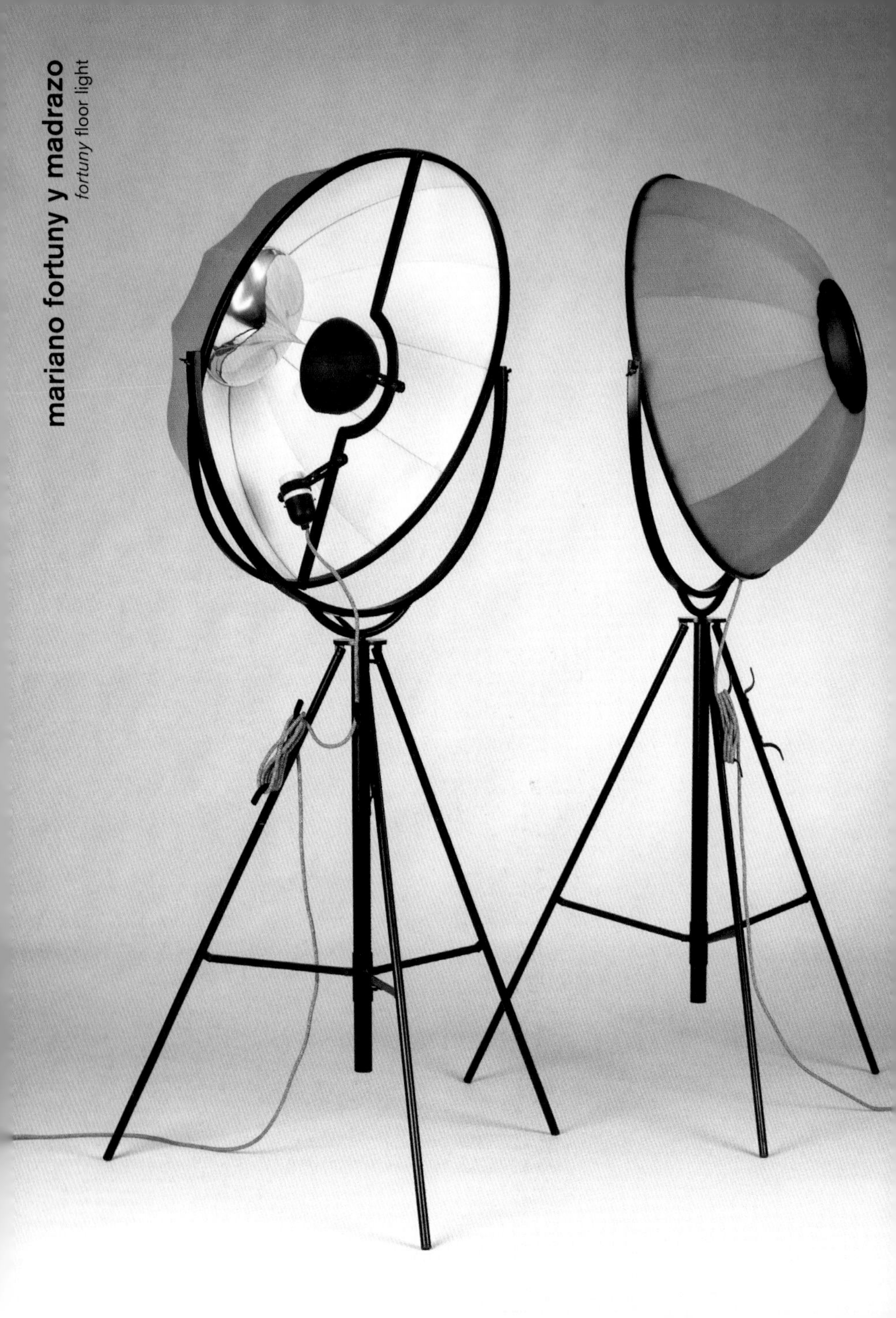

mariano fortuny y madrazo
fortuny floor light

Although best remembered for his exquisite silk pleated dresses, Mariano Fortuny was also a highly innovative lighting designer. Realizing that electricity had the potential to transform theatrical lighting, he developed in his Venetian palazzo-atelier-laboratory a system that used concave reflectors to reduce glare. He outlined this innovative, patented system in his treatise *Éclairage Scénique* (1904) and utilized this technique in his desk light (1903) and floor light (1907). The latter helped to transform both theatrical and photographic lighting. Never intended for domestic use, the design, with its folding tripod base and umbrella-like reflector, is also known as the *Projector* light. (CF/PF)

Obwohl in erster Linie für seine exquisiten Seidenplisseekleider bekannt, war Mariano Fortuny auch ein höchst innovativer Leuchtendesigner. Da er das Potential von elektrischem Licht für die Veränderung der gesamten Bühnenbeleuchtungstechnik erkannt hatte, entwickelte er ein System mit konkaven Reflektoren zur Reduzierung von Blendlicht. Diese innovative und patentierte Technik setzte er auch bei seiner Schreibtischleuchte von 1903 und der Stehleuchte von 1907 ein. Letztere trug dazu bei, die Beleuchtungen sowohl für die Bühne als auch für Fotografen zu verbessern. Der nie für den Einsatz im häuslichen Bereich gedachte Beleuchtungskörper mit zusammenlegbarem Stativ und reflektorartigem Schirm ist auch unter dem Namen *Projektor*-Leuchte bekannt. (CF/PF)

On connaît surtout de Mariano Fortuny pour ses ravissantes robes plissées en soie, mais il est aussi l'auteur de luminaires très novateurs. Ayant compris que l'électricité pourrait révolutionner l'éclairage scénique, il mit au point, dans le palais vénitien qui abritait son atelier laboratoire, un système pour réduire l'intensité lumineuse avec des réflecteurs concaves. Il présenta ce système breveté dans son traité *L'Éclairage Scénique* (1904) et l'utilisa pour sa lampe de bureau (1903) et son lampadaire (1907) qui contribua à révolutionner l'éclairage dans les milieux du spectacle et de la photographie. Doté d'un trépied pliant et d'un réflecteur en parapluie, l'appareil, qui ne fut jamais destiné à un usage domestique, est aussi connu sous le nom de lampe *Projector*. (CF/PF)

◁ **Fortuny** floor lights, 1907

Adjustable enameled metal base with cotton umbrella shade, 240 cm high (max) / Verstellbarer Stativfuß aus Metall mit Lampenschirm aus Baumwolle, 240 cm hoch (max.) / Socle ajustable en métal émaillé, abat-jour en coton en forme de parapluie, hauteur maximale 240 cm
Reissued by **Pallucco Italia**, Castagnole Di Paese, Italy

△△ **Desk light, 1903**

Enameled aluminum base with metal arm and brass shade with chrome-plated exterior and enameled interior, 61 cm high / Lackierter Aluminiumfuß mit Metallarm und Lampenschirm aus Messing, außen verchromt und innen lackiert, 61 cm hoch / Socle en aluminium émaillé, bras en métal, abat-jour en laiton chromé à l'extérieur et émaillé à l'intérieur, 61 cm de hauteur
Reissued by **Ecart**, Paris, France

△ *Original version of desk light, c.1910 / Tischlampe in ihrer Originalversion, ca. 1910 / La lampe de bureau dans sa version d'origine datant des années 1910*

The collaboration between the German architect and designer Peter Behrens and the Berlin-based Allgemeine Elektrizitäts-Gesellschaft (better known as AEG) began in 1907, when Behrens was appointed the firm's artistic adviser. As such, he was responsible for AEG's overall public image and over the next few years created an early example of a successful corporate identity. He planned new factory and office buildings, developed a modern typeface for the firm's graphics and publicity material, and redesigned a large proportion of the product range. In the field of lighting, the plain, functional lines of his *Bogenlampe* (1907) marked a move beyond *Jugendstil*, paving the way for the trend toward greater simplicity that characterized German design in the late 1920s. (TB)

Die Zusammenarbeit zwischen dem deutschen Architekten und Designer Peter Behrens und der Allgemeinen Elektrizitäts-Gesellschaft (AEG) begann 1907 mit seiner Ernennung zum künstlerischen Beirat der Firma. In dieser Funktion war Behrens für das gesamte äußere Erscheinungsbild der AEG verantwortlich und schuf in den Folgejahren ein frühes Beispiel einer erfolgreichen *Corporate Identity*. Er plante neue Fabrik- und Verwaltungsgebäude, entwickelte eine einheitlich moderne Firmentypographie für Geschäftsdrucksachen sowie Reklame und war für die Neugestaltung großer Teile der Produktpalette des Elektrokonzerns zuständig. Im Bereich des Leuchtendesigns waren es seine so genannten Bogenlampen, die durch ihre nüchterne, funktionale Formensprache den Jugendstil überwanden und die sachlichen Tendenzen des deutschen Designs der späten 1920er Jahre vorwegnahmen. (TB)

La collaboration entre l'architecte et créateur allemand Peter Behrens (1868–1940) et l'Allgemeine Elektrizitäts-Gesellschaft (plus connue sous le nom d'AEG) débuta en 1907, date à laquelle Behrens fut nommé directeur artistique de la société. En tant que tel, il était chargé de son image extérieure et, pendant les années qui suivirent, il réussit à lui donner une forte identité visuelle. Il dessina les plans de nouveaux bureaux et ateliers, inventa des caractères modernes pour son département de graphisme et de publicité et repensa plusieurs de ses produits. Dans le domaine de l'éclairage, les lignes simples et fonctionnelles de sa *Bogenlampe* s'éloignaient du Jugendstil et annonçaient l'esthétique plus dépouillée qui allait dominer les arts décoratifs allemands à la fin des années 1920. (TB)

▽◁ **AEG Sparbogen** hanging light, 1907

Enameled and part-gilded metal mounts with white opalescent glass shade, 82 cm drop / Montierung aus lackiertem und teilweise vergoldetem Metall mit Lampenschirm aus weißem Opalglas, 82 cm hoch / Montures en métal émaillé et partiellement doré, abat-jour en opaline blanche, 82 cm de hauteur
AEG, Berlin, Germany

▽▷ **Model No. 67216 AEG Bogenlampe** hanging light, 1907

Enameled and part-gilded metal mounts and shade / Montierung und Lampenschirm aus lackiertem und teilweise vergoldetem Metall / Montures et abat-jour en métal émaillé et partiellement doré
AEG, Berlin, Germany

▷ *AEG Metallfadenlampe poster by Peter Behrens, 1907 / Plakat AEG Metallfadenlampe von Peter Behrens, 1907 / Affiche de Peter Behrens vantant la Metallfadenlampe d'AEG, 1907*

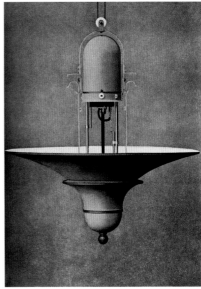

ALLGEMEINE ELEKTRICITÆTS GESELLSCHAFT

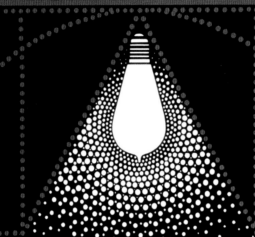

A·E·G·METALLFADENLAMPE

ZIRKA EIN WATT PRO KERZE

Working in the Arts & Crafts idiom, Charles Sumner Greene and Henry Mather Greene designed numerous lights for their integrated architectural schemes. Strongly influenced by Japanese art and architecture, the brothers' work was distinguished by a quasi-Oriental style that frequently incorporated abstracted branch-like motifs and rounded edges, which emphasized handcraft skills and conveyed a level of refinement not generally associated with the American Arts & Crafts movement. Greene & Greene's approach to design centered on identifying what is functionally necessary and then giving it a beautiful and honestly expressed form. (CF/PF)

Der Formensprache der Arts & Crafts-Bewegung verhaftet, entwarfen Charles Sumner Greene und Henry Mather Greene zahlreiche Leuchten für ihre Inneneinrichtungsprojekte. Die stark von japanischer Kunst und Architektur beeinflusste Arbeit der beiden Brüder zeichnete sich durch einen annähernd orientalischen Stil aus mit häufig abstrahierten, zweigartigen Motiven und abgerundeten Kanten, die eine handwerkliche Geschicklichkeit und Raffinesse aufwiesen, die man im Allgemeinen nicht mit dem amerikanischen Arts & Crafts-Stil assoziiert. Der gestalterische Zugang von Greene & Greene konzentrierte sich darauf, das in funktionaler Hinsicht Notwendige mit einer schönen und im Ausdruck ehrlichen Form zu verbinden. (CF/PF)

Charles Sumner Greene et Henry Mather Greene, qui travaillaient dans la tradition de l'Arts & Crafts, créèrent de nombreuses lampes pour leurs projets d'architecture intégrée. Fortement influencé par l'art et l'architecture du Japon, le travail des deux frères se reconnaissait à son style quasi-oriental qui faisait souvent appel à des motifs de branches stylisées et à des angles arrondis, mettait en avant le savoir-faire artisanal et créait une impression de raffinement que l'on n'associe pas d'ordinaire, au mouvement Arts & Crafts américain. Greene & Greene commençaient par identifier ce qui était nécessaire d'un point de vue fonctionnel, puis s'attachaient à lui donner une forme aussi belle et honnête que possible. (CF/PF)

△△ **Lantern for the Robert R. Blacker House (Pasadena),** *c.*1907–09

Copper frame with iridescent glass panels, 85 cm drop / Montierung aus Kupfer mit Einsätzen aus irisierendem Glas, 85 cm lang / Structure en cuivre, panneaux en verre irisé, 85 cm de hauteur
The Workshops of Peter Hall & Emil Lange, Pasadena (CA), USA

◁ *Dining room of Gamble House showing light fixture designed site-specifically by Greene & Greene in 1908 / Esszimmer im Gamble House mit der 1908 von Greene & Greene speziell für diesen Raum entworfenen Leuchte / Salle à manger de la maison Gamble, où l'on peut voir des luminaires réalisés sur mesure par Greene & Greene en 1908*

△ **Wall lights for the Robert R. Blacker House (Pasadena),** *c.*1907–09

Inlaid mahogany brackets with leaded iridescent glass panels, 48.5 cm high / Montierungen aus intarsiertem Mahagoni mit irisierenden Bleiglasscheiben, 48,5 cm hoch / Supports en marqueterie d'acajou, panneaux de verre irisé serti de plomb, 48,5 cm de hauteur
The Workshops of Peter Hall & Emil Lange, Pasadena (CA), USA

The glassworks of Émile Gallé and Daum Frères have become synonymous with the best of Art Nouveau glass and with the École de Nancy. Both companies often worked closely with contemporary metalworkers providing shades for lights, but they also produced all-glass models. Early examples of these featured enameled decoration, often floral and with gilt highlights. In 1889 Gallé exhibited his first cameo glass at the Exposition universelle et internationale in Paris, and cameo glass production subsequently flourished in both companies, resulting in both commercial and artistic vases and lights, including this rare Gallé model with its landscape decoration. (VT)

Die Glasmanufakturen von Émile Gallé und Daum Frères sind zu Synonymen für die besten Glasarbeiten des Art Nouveau und für die École de Nancy geworden. Beide Firmen arbeiteten häufig mit zeitgenössischen Metallhandwerkern zusammen, die die Lampenschirme lieferten. Sie fertigten aber auch ganz aus Glas bestehende Modelle an. Frühe Beispiele weisen lackierte, oft florale und mit Gold unterlegte Verzierungen auf. Nachdem Gallé auf der Pariser Weltausstellung von 1889 seine ersten Arbeiten aus geätztem oder geschnittenem Überfangglas präsentiert hatte, florierte die Produktion beider Manufakturen, was sich in eher kommerziell aber auch künstlerisch anspruchsvoll gestalteten Vasen und Leuchten äußerte, zu denen auch das seltene Modell von Gallé (ca. 1910) mit Landschaftsdekor zählt. (VT)

Le nom d'Émile Gallé et celui des Frères Daum évoquent aujourd'hui de superbes objets en verre de style Art Nouveau et sont devenus synonymes de l'École de Nancy. Les deux entreprises collaboraient fréquemment avec des ateliers de ferronnerie qui leur fournissaient des abat-jour, mais ils produisaient aussi des luminaires entièrement en verre. Leurs premiers modèles étaient ornés d'émaux, souvent d'inspiration florale et soulignés de dorures. En 1889, Gallé montra son premier verre gravé en camée à l'Exposition Universelle de Paris. Très vite, le verre gravé en camée remporta un vif succès et les deux sociétés se mirent à produire des vases et des lampes à des fins tout artistiques que commerciales, dont ce rare modèle de Gallé représentant un paysage. (VT)

Table light, c.1905

Etched, enameled and gilded glass base and shade with metal fittings, 35.6 cm high / Fuß und Lampenschirm aus geätztem, lackiertem und vergoldetem Überfangglas mit Metallmontierung, 35,6 cm hoch / Pied et abat-jour en verre gravé, émaillé et doré, garnitures métalliques, 35,6 cm de hauteur
Daum Frères, Nancy, France

▷ **Waterfall** table light, c.1910

Double overlaid cameo glass base and shade with metal fittings, 67 cm high / Fuß und Lampenschirm aus geätztem Überfangglas mit Metallmontierung, 67 cm hoch / Pied et abat-jour en verre double couche gravé en camée, 67 cm de hauteur
Cristallerie de Gallé, Nancy, France

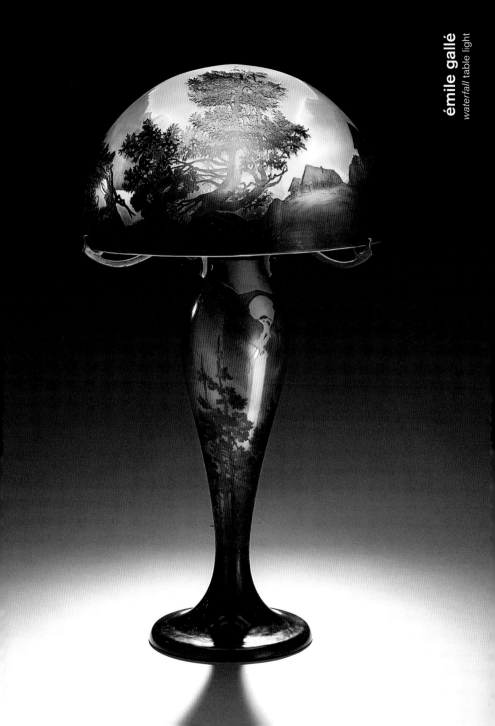

In an attempt to counteract the excesses of the Art Nouveau style, Maurice Dufrêne co-founded the Société des Artistes Français in 1904. While his table light (c.1902–04) incorporates a quintessentially Art Nouveau motif – peacock feathers – the design has a boldness of form that belongs to the Art Deco style. The extraordinary chandelier (c.1913) he designed almost a decade later for Paul Watel epitomizes his belief that "it is essential to study conscientiously the balance of volume, the silhouette and the proportion in accordance with the chosen material and the technique imposed by this material." Versatile and prolific, Dufrêne promoted an unusual design language that married Modern elements to traditional forms. (CF/PF)

In dem Versuch, den Exzessen des Art Nouveau entgegenzutreten, gründete Maurice Dufrêne im Jahr 1904 zusammen mit Gleichgesinnten die Société des Artistes Français. Zwar ist seine Tischleuchte (ca. 1902–04) mit einem typischen Motiv des Art Nouveau versehen – Pfauenfedern –, doch zeichnet sich der Entwurf durch eine Kühnheit in der Form aus, die den Stil des Art Déco vorwegnimmt. In dem ungewöhnlichen Kronleuchter, den er ca. 1913 für Paul Watel entwarf, drückt sich seine Überzeugung aus: „Es ist unbedingt erforderlich, die Balance der Form, die Silhouette und die Proportion in Übereinstimmung mit dem gewählten Material und der durch dieses Material diktierten Technik gewissenhaft zu studieren." Vielseitig und produktiv in seiner Arbeit, propagierte Dufrêne eine außergewöhnliche Formensprache, die moderne Elemente mit traditionellen Formen verband. (CF/PF)

Maurice Dufrêne fut l'un des fondateurs de la Société des Artistes en 1904, dont le but était de contrecarrer les excès de l'Art Nouveau. Sa lampe de table (vers 1902–04) conjugue l'Art Nouveau – avec son emblématique motif de plumes de paon – et les formes audacieuses de l'Art Déco. L'extraordinaire lustre que Dufrêne conçut pour Paul Watel vers 1913 reflète sa conviction que « l'équilibre du volume, la silhouette et la proportion méritent une étude soigneuse qui prenne en compte le matériau choisi et les techniques qu'il nécessite ». Dufrêne, dont l'œuvre était abondante et éclectique, prônait un style singulier mariant éléments modernes et styles traditionnels. (CF/PF)

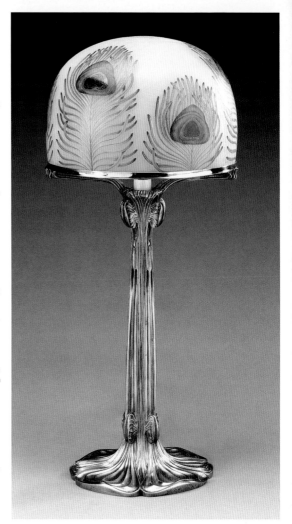

Table light, c.1902–04

Gilt bronze base with etched, gilt and enameled cameo glass shade, 47.6 cm high / Fuß aus vergoldeter Bronze mit Lampenschirm aus geätztem, vergoldetem und emailliertem Überfangglas, 47,6 cm hoch / Socle en bronze doré, abat-jour en verre gravé en camée, doré et émaillé, 47,6 cm de hauteur
Daum Frères, Nancy, France

▷ **Chandelier for Paul Watel, c.1913**

Carved wood frame with opalescent shades, 230 cm drop / Montierung aus geschnitztem Holz mit Lampenschirmen aus Opalglas, 230 cm lang / Structure en bois ajouré, verrines en opaline, 230 cm de haut
France

Between 1906 and 1913 Tiffany Studios manufactured around 300 different lighting designs. The types of lights illustrated here, which incorporate Favrile glass shades, are less well known than the colorful leaded glass models that have become synonymous with the Tiffany name. These designs, however, while more utilitarian in nature, were just as exquisitely executed and stylistically inventive. The floor light (c.1910), for example, features a "Pompeian" base that is wittily topped with an Aladdin-style oil lamp, while the *Model No. 417* desk light (c.1910) has a serpentine arm that is beautifully counterbalanced. (CF/PF)

In den Jahren zwischen 1906 und 1913 wurden bei den Tiffany Studios ca. dreihundert verschiedene Leuchten hergestellt. Die hier abgebildeten Leuchten mit Schirmen aus Favrile-Glas sind weniger bekannt als die Modelle mit den bunten, bleiverglasten Lampenschirmen, die zu einem Synonym für den Namen Tiffany wurden. Diese Leuchten waren zwar zweckmäßiger, in ihrer Ausführung jedoch genauso edel und stilistisch innovativ. So ist zum Beispiel die Stehleuchte (ca. 1910) mit einem „pompejisch" anmutenden Fuß und einem geistreich auf Aladdins Wunderlampe verweisenden Gefäß an der Spitze ausgestattet, während der geschwungene Arm der Schreibtischleuchte *Modell Nr. 147* (ca. 1910) ein ästhetisch gelungenes Gegengewicht erhielt. (CF/PF)

De 1906 à 1913, Tiffany fabriqua environ trois cents modèles différents de luminaires. Les lampes représentées ici, chacune dotée d'un abat-jour en verre Favrile, sont moins connues que les objets en verre vitrail aujourd'hui associés avec la marque Tiffany. Leur inventivité et leur finesse d'exécution n'en sont pas moins remarquables, même si elles se veulent par nature plus utilitaires. Notez, par exemple, le socle « pompéien » du lampadaire (vers 1910) et son amusant motif en forme de lampe d'Aladin, ainsi que la belle courbe du bras qui soutient le contrepoids de la lampe de bureau *Modèle n° 417* (vers 1910). (CF/PF)

◁ **Floor light,** *c.*1910

Patinated bronze base with Favrile glass shade,
137.2 cm high / Fuß aus patinierter Bronze
mit Lampenschirm aus Favrile-Glas, 137.2 cm
hoch / Socle en bronze patiné, abat-jour en
verre Favrile, 137.2 cm
Tiffany Studios, New York (NY), USA

▷ **Model No. 417 desk light,** *c.*1910

Gilt bronze base with Favrile glass shade,
38.1 cm high / Fuß aus vergoldeter Bronze mit
Lampenschirm aus Favrile-Glas, 38.1 cm hoch /
Socle en bronze doré, abat-jour en verre Favrile,
38.1 cm
Tiffany Studios, New York (NY), USA

▽ **Double student light,** *c.*1910

Patinated bronze base with Favrile glass
shades, 60.3 cm high / Fuß aus patinierter
Bronze mit Lampenschirmen aus Favrile-Glas,
60.3 cm hoch / Socle en bronze patiné, abat-
jour en verre Favrile, 60.3 cm
Tiffany Studios, New York (NY), USA

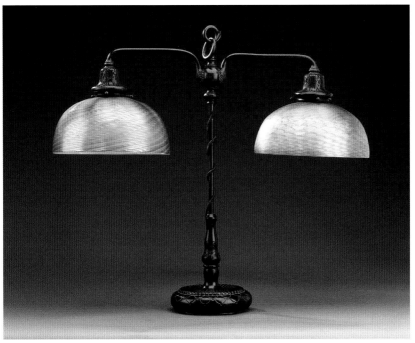

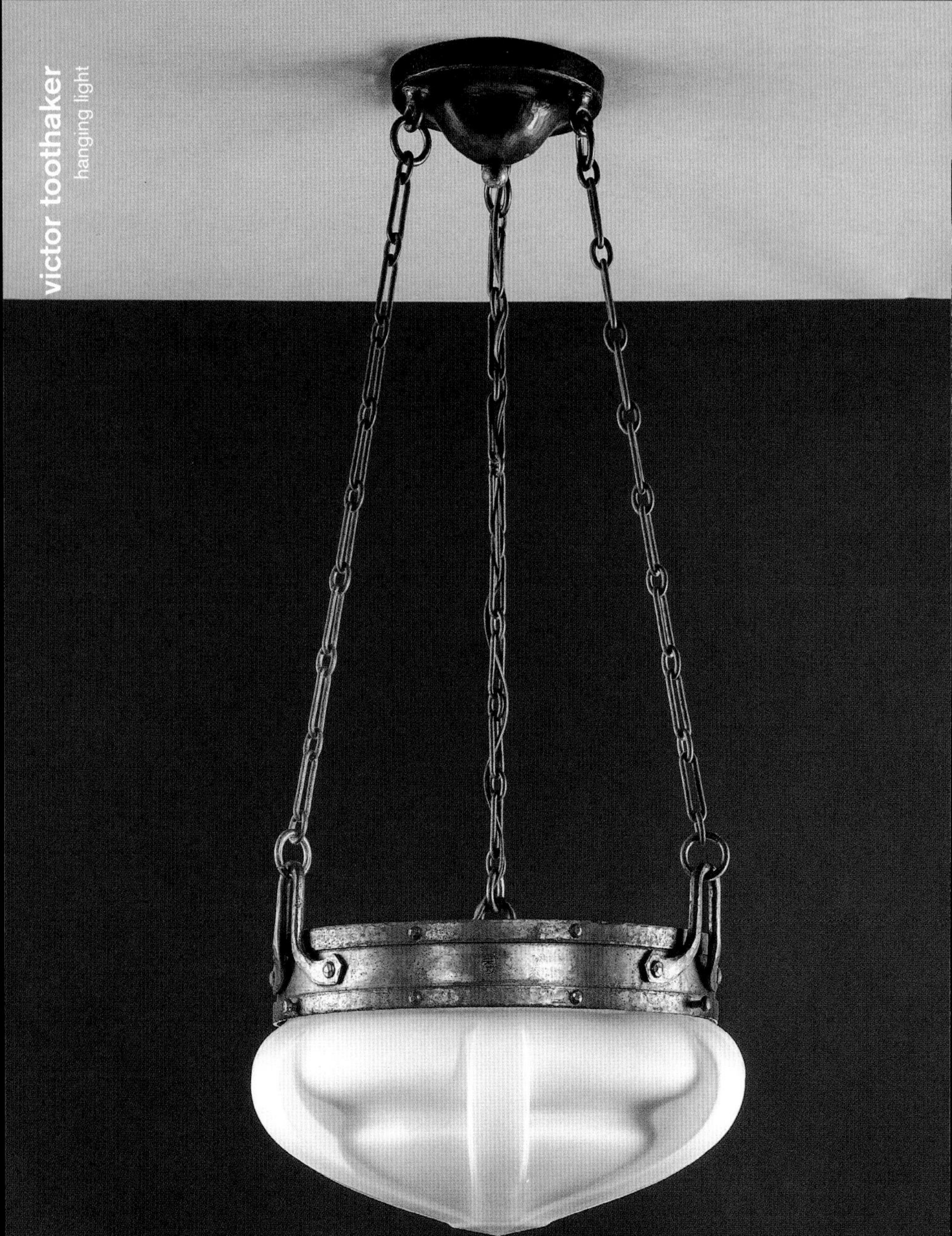

victor toothaker
hanging light

◁ **Hanging light, *c.*1912**
Hammered copper mounts with molded glass shade, 91.5 cm drop / Montierung aus gehämmertem Kupfer mit Lampenschirm aus Pressglas, 91,5 cm lang / Montures en cuivre martelé, abat-jour en verre moulé, 91,5 cm de hauteur
Roycroft Metalwork Shop, East Aurora (NY), USA

Hanging light, *c.*1910
Hammered copper mounts with mica glass panels, 45.7 cm drop / Montierung aus gehämmertem Kupfer mit Einsätzen aus Mica-Glas, 45,7 cm lang / Montures en cuivre martelé, plaquettes de mica, 45,7 cm de hauteur
Roycroft Metalwork Shop, East Aurora (NY), USA

Inspired by the utopian ideals of the British Arts & Crafts movement, Elbert Green Hubbard founded the Roycrofters community in 1895. Based in East Aurora, New York, Roycrofters had its own press, a furniture workshop, and an inn for tourists. In 1902 its Copper Shop was built and by 1906 the first Roycroft copper wares were being sold. These two chandeliers (*c.*1912 and *c.*1910) epitomize the community's output – plain yet well-crafted durable objects that reflected a desire for a return to a simpler life. Victor Toothaker not only designed for Roycrofters but also for Gustav Stickley's workshop. (CF/PF)

Inspiriert von den utopischen Idealen der britischen Arts & Crafts-Bewegung gründete Elbert Green Hubbard im Jahr 1895 die Gemeinschaft der Roycrofters. Die in East Aurora, New York, ansässigen Roycrofters betrieben ihre eigene Druckerpresse, eine Möbeltischlerwerkstatt und ein Gasthaus für Touristen. 1902 wurde eine Kupferschmiede eingerichtet, 1906 kamen die ersten Kupferarbeiten der Roycroft-Werkstätte auf den Markt. Die beiden Deckenleuchten (ca. 1912 und ca. 1910) sind exemplarisch für die Produktion der Künstlergruppe: einfache, doch handwerklich gut gemachte und solide Einrichtungsgegenstände. Victor Toothaker entwarf nicht nur für die Roycrofters, sondern auch für die Werkstatt von Gustav Stickley. (CF/PF)

S'inspirant des idéaux utopiques du mouvement britannique Arts & Crafts, Elbert G. Hubbard fonda les Roycrofters à East Aurora, dans l'État de New York, en 1895. La communauté possédait sa propre imprimerie, un atelier de mobilier et une auberge pour les touristes. Une fabrique d'objets en cuivre y fut construite en 1902 et, quatre ans plus tard, ses premiers produits étaient commercialisés. Ces deux lustres (vers 1912 et 1910) sont de bons exemples du style Roycroft : simples, durables et de bonne facture, ils exprimaient un désir de revenir à une vie plus simple. Le créateur Victor Toothaker collabora avec les Roycrofters, ainsi qu'avec l'atelier de Gustav Stickley. (CF/PF)

dirk van erp
table light

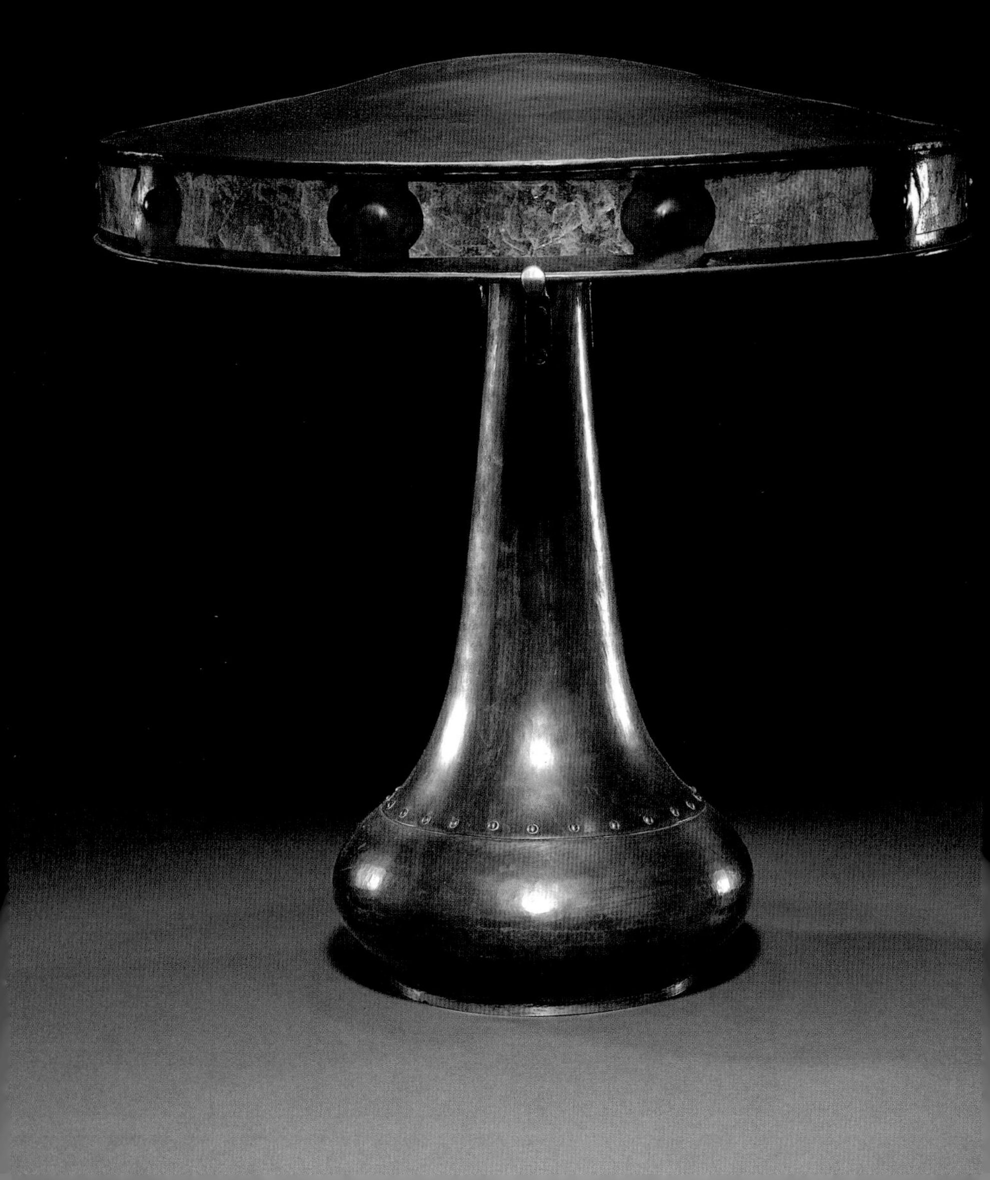

◁ **Table light, c.1911**
Hammered copper base and shade with mica panels, 47 cm high / Fuß und Lampenschirm aus gehämmertem Kupfer mit Mica-Glasfüllungen, 47 cm hoch / Socle et abat-jour en cuivre martelé, plaques de mica, 47 cm de hauteur
Dirk Van Erp Studio/Copper Shop, San Francisco (CA), USA

Table light, c.1911
Hammered copper base and shade with mica panels, 56.5 cm high / Fuß und Lampenschirm aus gehämmertem Kupfer mit Mica-Glasfüllungen, 56,5 cm hoch / Socle et abat-jour en cuivre martelé, plaques de mica, 56,5 cm de hauteur
Dirk Van Erp Studio/Copper Shop, San Francisco (CA), USA

The renowned American metalwork designer Dirk van Erp learnt craft skills working in his family's hardware business in The Netherlands prior to emigrating to the United States in 1886. While employed at the US Navy shipyard near San Francisco, he began making vases out of spent brass shell casings. In 1908 van Erp established the Copper Shop in Oakland and started production of "art" metalwork, which included his famous lights that were marketed from around 1911. The hammered copper bases and translucent mica shades gave these lights a soft amber glow that enhanced the cozy feeling of fashionable Mission-style interiors. (CF/PF)

Der bekannte amerikanische Metalldesigner Dirk van Erp erlernte handwerkliche Fertigkeiten in der Metallwerkstatt seiner Familie in den Niederlanden, bevor er 1886 in die Vereinigten Staaten auswanderte. Im Jahr 1908 gründete van Erp den Copper Shop in Oakland und nahm die Produktion von künstlerischen Metallarbeiten auf, zu denen seine berühmt gewordenen Leuchten gehören, die ab 1911 verkauft wurden. Die Füße aus gehämmertem Kupfer und die durchscheinenden Lampenschirme aus Glimmerglas, auch Mika-Glas genannt, ließen diese Leuchten in einem sanften Licht leuchten, von dem die anheimelnde Atmosphäre der Inneneinrichtungen im damals modischen „Mission Style" noch gesteigert wurde. (CF/PF)

Le célèbre créateur de luminaires américain Dirk Van Erp s'initia au travail manuel dans la quincaillerie familiale aux Pays-Bas, avant d'émigrer aux États-Unis en 1886. Alors qu'il travaillait sur un chantier naval de la marine américaine près de San Francisco, il se mit à bricoler des vases à partir d'enveloppes vides d'obus en laiton. En 1908, Van Erp mit sur pied la Maison du cuivre à Oakland et commença à fabriquer des objets d'«art» en métal, dont ses célèbres lampes, qui furent sur le marché à partir de 1911. Leur pied en cuivre martelé et leur abat-jour en mica translucide diffusaient une douce lumière ambrée, soulignant l'ambiance douillette des intérieurs de style «Mission». (CF/PF)

Table light, *c*.1911

Hammered copper base and shade with mica panels, 52 cm high / Fuß und Lampenschirm aus gehämmertem Kupfer mit Einlagen aus Mica-Glas, 52 cm hoch / Socle et abat-jour en cuivre martelé, panneaux de mica, 52 cm de hauteur
Dirk Van Erp Studio/Copper Shop, San Francisco (CA), USA

▷ **Table light, *c*.1915**

Hammered copper base and shade with mica panels, 43.2 cm high / Fuß und Lampenschirm aus gehämmertem Kupfer mit Einlagen aus Mica-Glas, 43,2 cm hoch / Socle et abat-jour en cuivre martelé, panneaux de mica, 43,2 cm de hauteur
Dirk Van Erp Studio/Copper Shop, San Francisco (CA), USA

Although Dirk van Erp eschewed the use of machinery, he adopted the division of labor for the manufacture of more complex products at his Copper Shop. The hammered surfaces of his lights and their exposed rivets were manifestations of the Arts & Crafts movement's credo of "truth to materials" and "revealed construction". Although van Erp's manufacturing operation was small-scale and his handcrafted lights were relatively expensive (most originally retailing at between $20 and $50), he managed to popularize the use of mica for light shades and helped to forge a distinctively American Arts & Crafts style. (CF/PF)

Dirk van Erp vermied zwar den Einsatz von Maschinen, machte sich aber für die Produktion komplexerer Objekte in seinem Copper Shop einen arbeitsteiligen Herstellungsprozess zu Eigen. In den gehämmerten Oberflächen seiner Leuchten und ihren unverdeckten Nietverbindungen manifestierte sich das Credo der Arts & Crafts-Bewegung von der „Treue zum Material" und der „sichtbaren Konstruktion". Obgleich van Erps handgearbeitete Leuchten in Einzelanfertigung produziert wurden und mit Verkaufspreisen zwischen 20 und 50 Dollar relativ teuer waren, gelang es ihm, die Verwendung von Mika-Glas für Lampenschirme populär zu machen und zu der Ausbildung eines spezifisch amerikanischen Arts & Crafts-Stils beizutragen. (CF/PF)

Van Erp se passait de machines, mais il avait volontiers recours à la division du travail pour la fabrication des objets les plus complexes de son Copper Shop. Les surfaces martelées de ses lampes et leurs rivets apparents étaient fidèles à l'esprit du mouvement Arts & Crafts qui prônait un retour à la « vérité des matériaux » et à la « construction révélée ». Van Erp fabriquait ses objets à petite échelle et ses lampes artisanales étaient relativement onéreuses (la plupart coûtaient entre $20 et $50), ce qui ne l'empêcha pas de lancer la mode des abat-jour en mica et de contribuer à la formation d'un style Arts & Crafts proprement américain. (CF/PF)

fulper pottery company
vasekraft table light

After a period of intense experimentation, the Fulper Pottery Company began production of art pottery in 1909 and the following year introduced its first lighting products. These ceramic wares were retailed under the *Vasekraft* name and were widely recognized for their innovative forms and unusual glazes. In 1912 Fulper developed a unique technical innovation, whereby domed ceramic lampshades were inset with small panels of colored opalescent glass – a risky manufacturing process because each material has a different heating and cooling temperature – and the table lights it produced using this combination of materials are considered among the factory's greatest achievements. (CF/PF)

Nach einer Phase des intensiven Experimentierens begann die Fulper Pottery Company im Jahr 1909 mit der Produktion von künstlerischen Töpferwaren und produzierte im Jahr darauf die ersten Leuchten aus Keramik. Diese Objekte, die unter dem Markennamen *Vasekraft* verkauft wurden, waren weithin anerkannt für ihre innovativen Formen und außergewöhnlichen Glasuren. 1912 entwickelte Fulper eine einmalige technische Neuerung, mit der es gelang, gewölbte Lampenschirme aus Keramik mit Einlegearbeiten aus kleinen, farbigen Opalglasscheiben zu verzieren. Dieser Herstellungsprozess war riskant, da die beiden Materialien unterschiedliche Erhitzungs- und Abkühlungstemperaturen haben. Die so gefertigten Tischleuchten zählen zu den größten Leistungen der Manufaktur. (CF/PF)

Après une période d'intense expérimentation, la Compagnie de Poteries Fulper commença à fabriquer de la poterie d'art en 1909 et, l'année suivante, lança ses premiers luminaires. Ces objets en céramique étaient vendus sous le nom de *Vasekraft* et se reconnaissaient à leurs formes nouvelles et à leur glaçure originale. En 1912, Fulper inventa une nouvelle technique consistant à incruster les abat-jour arrondis en céramique de petits morceaux de verre coloré opalescent. L'opération était délicate, car les matières chauffaient et se refroidissaient à des températures différentes. Les lampes de tables fabriquées selon cette technique sont considérées comme les plus grandes réussites de l'usine. (CF/PF)

◁ **Vasekraft** table light, *c.*1915
Glazed earthenware base and shade with opalescent glass inserts / Fuß und Lampenschirm aus glasierter Keramik mit Opalglaseinlagen / Socle et abat-jour en faïence, incrustations de verre opalescent
Fulper Pottery Co., Flemington (NJ), USA

▷ **Vasekraft** table light, *c.*1915
Glazed earthenware base and shade with opalescent glass inserts, 40.6 cm high / Fuß und Lampenschirm aus glasierter Keramik mit Opalglaseinlagen, 40,6 cm hoch / Socle et abat-jour en faïence, incrustations de verre opalescent, 40,6 cm de hauteur
Fulper Pottery Co., Flemington (NJ), USA

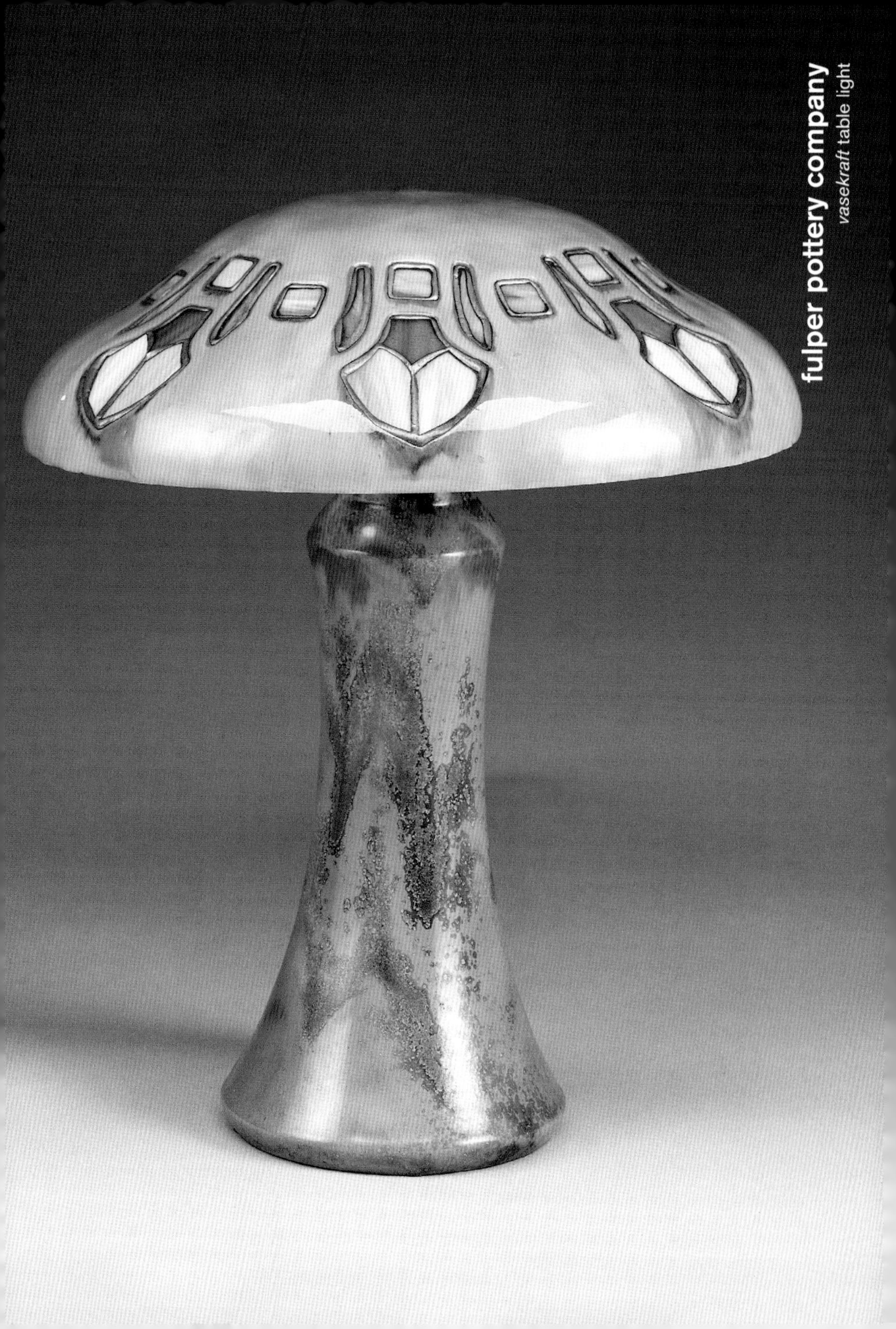

fulper pottery company
vasekraft table light

This is the largest and most spectacular light (c.1920) produced in series by the Gallé workshops. It is possible, even likely, that this model dates from after Gallé's death in 1904. The serial manufacture of cameo glass lights was a key element of the workshop production and these lights enjoyed an ongoing commercial success. As with most of the production lights, the form – rather like that of a mushroom – lacks the fluid grace of Gallé's earlier, more sculptural, Art Nouveau pieces. The lush decoration and colors compensate for this rigidity of silhouette. (PG)

Bei dieser Leuchte (ca. 1920) handelt es sich um das größte und spektakulärste in Serie gefertigte Leuchtobjekt der Manufaktur Gallé. Es ist möglich, sogar wahrscheinlich, dass dieses Modell aus der Zeit nach Gallés Tod im Jahr 1904 datiert. Die Serienfabrikation von Leuchten aus veredeltem Überfangglas war ein Hauptbestandteil der Firmenproduktion, und sie war ein anhaltender kommerzieller Erfolg. Wie den meisten Serienausführungen fehlt der pilzartigen Form dieses Modells die fließende Anmut von Gallés früheren und mehr skulptural gestalteten Entwürfen im Stil des Art Nouveau. Allerdings entschädigen das reiche Dekor und die satten Farben für diesen Mangel an formaler Eleganz. (PG)

La lampe ci-contre (vers 1920) est la plus grande et sans doute la plus spectaculaire de toutes celles qui furent fabriquées en série dans les ateliers Gallé. Il est possible et, même vraisemblable, qu'il ait été réalisé après la mort de Gallé en 1904. Les activités de l'atelier reposaient largement sur la fabrication en série de ce type de luminaires en cameo glass, qui jouissaient d'un succès durable. Comme dans la plupart des lampes industrielles, la forme de celle-ci – qui évoque un champignon – n'a pas la grâce fluide et sculpturale des œuvres antérieures, de style Art Nouveau, de Gallé. La luxuriance des couleurs et des ornements vient ici compenser la rigidité de la silhouette. (PG)

△△ *Photograph of Émile Gallé working in his studio, c.1900 / Aufnahme von Émile Gallé in seinem Atelier, ca. 1900 / Photographie d'Émile Gallé au travail dans son atelier, vers 1900*

△ *The display room at the Nancy factory, c.1900 / Ausstellungsraum der Fabrik in Nancy, ca. 1900 / Salle d'exposition de la Cristallerie à Nancy, vers 1900*

▷ **Wisteria table light, c.1920**
Cameo glass base and shade, 76.2 cm high / Fuß und Lampenschirm aus geätztem und geschliffenem Überfangglas, 76,2 cm hoch / Socle et abat-jour en verre multicouche gravé en camée, 76,2 cm de hauteur
Cristallerie de Gallé, Nancy, France

Although the design of this table light (*c*.1920) bears the Gallé name, it is a posthumous production. It demonstrates, nonetheless, that Émile Gallé had established a studio capable of inventiveness both in concept and in technique. This is one of the most spectacular lights produced by the Gallé workshops. It involves multiple stages of etching to achieve the range of colors, and it exploits to great effect a technique known as "blow-out" (*soufflé*). The layers of colored glass are blown into a mold that anticipates not just the basic silhouette, but also the sculptural and well-detailed high relief of the floral decoration. (PG)

Obgleich diese Tischleuchte (ca. 1920) den Namen Gallé trägt, ist sie ein posthumes Erzeugnis. Damit demonstriert sie überzeugend, dass Émile Gallé ein Atelier etabliert hatte, das einfallsreiche Arbeiten zu produzieren vermochte, sowohl im Hinblick auf Entwurf als auch auf Technik. Dieses Leuchtenmodell ist eines der großartigsten, das die Gallé Werkstätten produziert haben. Seine Fertigung erforderte mehrere Ätzungsvorgänge, um die vielen Farbnuancen zu erzielen, und es wurde auf sehr wirkungsvolle Weise eine Technik eingesetzt, die als „ausgeblasen" oder „soufflé" bezeichnet wird. Hierbei wird das in mehreren Schichten farbig überfangene Glas in eine Form geblasen, die nicht nur die grundlegenden Umrisslinien vorgibt, sondern auch bereits das plastische und detaillierte Relief des Blumendekors. (PG)

Cette lampe (vers 1920) est signée Gallé, mais c'est en fait une œuvre posthume. Elle démontre néanmoins que l'atelier fondé par Émile Gallé était capable d'inventivité conceptuelle autant que technique, et compte parmi les modèles les plus spectaculaires à en être sortis. Ses couleurs ont été obtenues par phases successives de gravure et c'est un exemple très réussi de la technique dite « soufflé » : plusieurs couches de verre coloré étaient soufflées dans un moule qui leur donnait non seulement leur forme générale, mais faisait aussi apparaître chaque détail de la décoration florale en haut relief. (PG)

◁ / ▷ *Rhododendron* table lights,
*c.*1920

Mold-blown double overlaid and etched cameo glass base and shade, 48.3 cm and 47 cm high / Fuß und Lampenschirm aus formgeblasenem, doppelt überfangenem und geätztem Glas, 48,3 und 47 cm hoch / Socle et abat-jour en verre pressé soufflé double couche, décor gravé, 48,3 cm et 47 cm de hauteur
Cristallerie de Gallé, Nancy, France

armand-albert rateau

model no. 1318 floor lights for jeanne lanvin

The interior of fashion designer Jeanne Lanvin's home was among Armand-Albert Rateau's most important commissions. These floor lights (1920–22), designed for her bedroom, continued the daisy theme requested by Mme Lanvin in honor of her daughter, Marguerite. Rateau's superior craftsmanship is evident in the detailed casting of the birds and flowers and the finishing touch of the original ivory switch. So pleased was Rateau with the result that he later used the model in other interiors, including his own. A pair of these floor lights was exhibited at the Metropolitan Museum of Art, New York, in 1926. (VT)

Die Inneneinrichtung von Jeanne Lanvins Haus gehörte zu Armand-Albert Rateaus wichtigsten Aufträgen. Diese Stehleuchten (1920–22), die für das Schlafzimmer entworfen wurden, führten das von Mme Lanvin zu Ehren ihrer Tochter Marguerite gewünschte Margeritenthema fort. Rateaus überragende Handwerkskunst offenbart sich in der detailgenauen Ausführung der Vögel und Blumen sowie des meisterlich gestalteten Lichtschalters aus Elfenbein. Rateau war so angetan von dem Ergebnis, dass er dieses Modell später auch in anderen Innenraumausstattungen, einschließlich seiner eigenen Wohnung, verwendete. 1926 wurde eines dieser Leuchtenpaare im Metropolitan Museum of Art in New York ausgestellt. (VT)

La décoration intérieure de la maison de Jeanne Lanvin compte parmi les commandes les plus importantes jamais faites à Rateau. Ces deux lampadaires (1920–22), conçus pour la chambre à coucher de Mme Lanvin, reprennent le thème de la marguerite en l'honneur de sa fille, qui portait ce nom. L'habileté consommée de Rateau est visible dans les délicats ornements en formes d'oiseaux et de fleurs, de même que dans le détail de l'interrupteur d'origine en ivoire. Rateau était tellement satisfait du résultat qu'il réemploya plus tard ce modèle dans d'autres intérieurs, y compris le sien. Une paire de lampadaires identiques fut exposée au Metropolitan Museum of Art de New York en 1926. (VT)

◁ **Model No. 1318 floor lights for Jeanne Lanvin**, *c.*1920–22

Patinated bronze bases and glass shades, 167.7 cm high / Füße aus patinierter Bronze mit Lampenschirmen aus Glas, 167,7 cm hoch / Socles en bronze patiné, abat-jour en verre, 167,7 cm de hauteur
Armand-Albert Rateau, Levallois, France

▽ *Jeanne Lanvin's bedroom with* Model No. 1318 *floor lights, c.1922 / Jeanne Lanvins Schlafzimmer mit den Stehleuchten* Modell Nr. 1318, *ca. 1922 / Chambre de Jeanne Lanvin, où l'on peut voir deux lampadaires* Modèle n° 1318, *vers 1922*

Renowned for its porcelain, Sèvres also manufactured many lights, from figural models to shades. These might involve up to three artisans – one responsible for the shape, another for the decoration, and one for the actual execution – although the roles often overlapped. Typically, the bases were outsourced. Similar in design and using the stylized flower motifs characteristic of the time, is the light (c.1922) by Raymond Subes, one of the foremost French ironworkers of the 1920s and 1930s. His oeuvre ranged from architectural commissions to decorative objects. This table light was shown at the 1922 Salon des Artistes Décorateurs. (VT)

Die für ihr Porzellan berühmte Staatsmanufaktur Sèvres produzierte zahlreiche Beleuchtungskörper, von figuralen Modellen bis zu Lampenschirmen, an denen teilweise bis zu drei Kunsthandwerker arbeiteten: Einer war für die Formgebung, einer für das Dekor und ein dritter für die Ausführung verantwortlich, wobei sich diese Rollen häufig überschnitten. Die Leuchtenfüße wurden meistens von anderen Firmen bezogen. Ähnlich in der Gestaltung und verziert mit den für die damalige Zeit charakteristischen stilisierten Blumenmotiven, stellt sich die Tischleuchte (ca. 1922) von Raymond Subes dar, einem der bedeutendsten französischen Kunstschmiede der 1920er und 1930er Jahre. Sein Œuvre reichte von Gebäudeausstattungen bis zu kleinen Ziergegenständen. Die Tischleuchte wurde im Salon des Artistes Décorateurs von 1922 gezeigt. (VT)

Renommée pour sa porcelaine, la manufacture de Sèvres fabriquait toutes sortes de luminaires, des modèles figuratifs jusqu'aux abat-jour. Jusqu'à trois artisans pouvaient travailler à un même modèle : l'un en dessinait la forme, un autre la décoration et le troisième exécutait le tout, même si les rôles pouvaient se recouper. Le socle était le plus souvent fabriqué par une entreprise extérieure. La lampe de Raymond Subes (vers 1922), l'un des plus grands ferronniers des années 1920 et 1930, est semblable par son style et par ses motifs de fleurs stylisées caractéristiques de l'époque. Sa production allait de commandes architecturales à des objets décoratifs. Cette lampe de table fut exposée en 1922 au Salon des artistes décorateurs. (VT)

◁ **Table light, 1922**
Gilt bronze base and glazed porcelain shade, 50.5 cm high / Fuß aus vergoldeter Bronze mit Lampenschirm aus glasiertem Porzellan, 50,5 cm hoch / Socle en bronze doré, abat-jour en porcelaine vernissée, 50,5 cm de hauteur
Manufacture Nationale de Sèvres, Sèvres, France (shade)

Table light, c.1922
Wrought-iron base with glass shade, 60 cm high / Fuß aus Schmiedeeisen mit Lampenschirm aus Glas, 60 cm hoch / Socle en fer forgé, abat-jour en verre, 60 cm de hauteur
Raymond Subes, Paris, France (base) / Schneider Frères, Epinay-Sur-Seine, France (attrib. shade)

▷ **Table light, 1923**
Shagreen and palm wood base with card shade, 57.7 cm high / Fuß aus Rochenhaut und Palmholz mit Lampenschirm aus Karton, 57.7 cm hoch / Socle en galuchat et bois de palmier, abat-jour en carton, 57.7 cm de hauteur
Clément Rousseau, Neuilly, France

Seagull table light, c.1920
Wrought-iron base with cameo glass shade, 49.5 cm high / Schmiedeeiserner Fuß mit Lampenschirm aus geätztem und poliertem Überfangglas, 49.5 cm hoch / Socle en fer forgé, abat-jour en verre gravé en camée, 49.5 cm de hauteur
Cristallerie de Gallé, Nancy, France (shade)

The *Seagull* table light (*c.*1920) bears the Gallé name but has little to do with the artist. A posthumous creation from his workshops, it testifies to the enduring value of his brand name. The iron stem is possibly an improvised solution to a broken glass base. The design by Clément Rousseau (1923) is of around the same date, but represents another level of quality and true innovation. In its understated, yet faultless proportions and in the use of exotic but discreet materials – palm wood and tinted shagreen – it exemplifies the best of French Art Deco. (PG)

Die Tischleuchte mit dem Mövenmotiv (ca. 1920) trägt zwar den Namen Gallé, hat aber wenig mit dem Künstler zu tun, da sie erst nach seinem Tod in der Manufaktur kreiert wurde. Dennoch zeugt sie vom bleibenden Wert seines Markennamens. Bei dem schmiedeeisernen Fuß handelt es sich möglicherweise um eine spätere Ergänzung. Das Design von Clément Rousseau (1923) ist zwar etwa zeitgleich entstanden, zeichnet sich jedoch durch ein höheres Qualitätsniveau und echte Innovation aus. In ihren zurückhaltenden, aber makellosen Proportionen und der Verwendung exotischer, aber dezenter Materialien – Palmholz und getönte Rochenhaut – ist diese Gestaltung exemplarisch für den Höhepunkt des französischen Art Déco. (PG)

Bien qu'elle soit signée Gallé, cette lampe *Mouette* (vers 1920) doit peu à l'artiste du même nom. Créée par son atelier de manière posthume, elle témoigne tout au plus de la longévité de la marque. Le pied en fer a sans doute été improvisé pour suppléer à un socle en verre cassé. Le modèle de Clément Rousseau date à peu près de la même époque (1923), mais il est bien d'une qualité et d'une nouveauté bien supérieurs. D'un style très simple, il est néanmoins parfait dans ses proportions et dans l'utilisation discrète qu'il fait de matériaux exotiques – comme le bois de palmier et le galuchat teinté. Il incarne le summum de l'Art Déco français. (PG)

René Lalique's *Oiseau de feu (Firebird)* table light (*c.*1920) uses a motif that recalls the imagery of the Art Nouveau jewels that made his reputation around 1900. The exotic creature, part-woman, part-bird, derives from the iconography of the Symbolist movement, adapted into an Art Deco idiom. Lalique was exceptional in maintaining his individuality throughout significant shifts in fashion and taste. His first important commission as a glassmaker was to design perfume bottles for Coty, and the *Apple Blossom* table light (*c.*1920) echoes the bottle-and-stopper forms of those earlier years. (PG)

René Lalique setzte bei seiner Tischleuchte *Oiseau de Feu* (ca. 1920) ein Motiv ein, das an die Bildersprache seiner Glanzstücke des Art Nouveau erinnert, mit denen er um 1900 berühmt wurde. Hier wurde die der Ikonographie des Symbolismus entstammende exotische Kreatur, halb Frau, halb Vogel, in einen Art-Déco-Entwurf übertragen. Lalique verstand es auf einzigartige Weise, seine Individualität trotz gravierender Veränderungen in Mode und Geschmack zu bewahren. Sein erster bedeutender Auftrag als Glaskünstler war die Gestaltung von Parfumflakons für die Firma Coty, und in seiner Tischleuchte *Apple Blossom* (ca. 1920) klingen die flakonartigen Formen dieser frühen Jahre wieder an. (PG)

La lampe de table *Oiseau de feu* (vers 1920) de René Lalique déploie un motif appartenant au registre des bijoux Art Nouveau qui firent la gloire du créateur au tournant du siècle. Mi-femme, mi-oiseau, l'étrange créature qui l'orne relève de l'iconographie symboliste, tout en répondant aux canons de l'Art Déco. Lalique était passé maître dans l'art suivre les tendances du moment sans pour autant renier sa personnalité. Le parfumeur Coty fut l'un des premiers à lui commander des objets en verre et la forme de cette lampe *Fleurs de pommier* (vers 1920) n'est pas sans affinités avec les flacons de parfum de ses débuts. (PG)

△△ **Apple Blossom table light,** *c.*1920
Molded and etched glass diffuser and base, 40.6 cm high / Diffusor und Sockel aus formgegossenem und geätztem Glas, 40,6 cm hoch / Diffuseur et socle en verre moulé et gravé, 40,6 cm de hauteur
René Lalique, Wingen-Sur-Moder, France

△ **Oiseau de feu table light,** *c.*1920
Molded and etched glass diffuser and base, 43 cm high / Diffusor und Sockel aus formgegossenem und geätztem Glas, 43 cm hoch / Diffuseur et socle en verre moulé et gravé, 43 cm de hauteur
René Lalique, Wingen-Sur-Moder, France

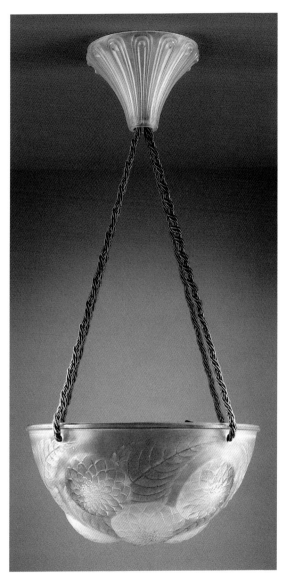

René Lalique's lighting designs, such as the well-known *Dahlias* chandelier (1921), which was probably his most commercially successful design, are notable for their exquisite frosted surfaces. Guillaume Janneau wrote of Lalique's opalescent glass in his book *Modern Glass* (published c.1932) that it "has the ethereal brilliance of Arctic ice. Its texture is hardly visible, and one can scarcely believe that it was once a thick opaque substance, shaped by running into a mold; it would seem rather to consist of immaterial ether, the frozen breath of a Polar night." (CF/PF)

René Laliques Leuchten, so die bekannte *Dahlien*-Hängeleuchte (1921), wahrscheinlich sein kommerziell erfolgreichster Entwurf, zeichnen sich durch ihre äußerst fein mattierten Oberflächen aus. Guillaume Janneau schrieb in seinem ca. 1932 veröffentlichten Buch *Modern Glass* über Laliques Opalglas: „Es hat das ätherische Leuchten von arktischem Eis. Seine Oberfläche ist kaum sichtbar, und es ist schier unglaublich, dass es einmal eine dicke, opake Masse war, die ihre Gestalt durch eine Gussform erhielt. Es scheint vielmehr aus körperlosem Äther zu bestehen, dem gefrorenen Atem einer Polarnacht." (CF/PF)

Les luminaires signés René Lalique, dont le célèbre lustre *Dahlias* (1921), sans doute l'un de ses succès les plus populaires, et l'amusant lustre *Madagascar*, se reconnaissent à leurs magnifiques surfaces dépolies. Dans son livre *Le Verre moderne* (publié en 1932), Guillaume Janneau décrivit le verre opalescent de Lalique en ces termes : « Il a la brillance éthérée de la glace arctique. Sa texture est à peine visible, et on a du mal à croire qu'elle est née d'une épaisse substance opaque, à laquelle on a donné forme en la faisant couler dans un moule ; on le dirait fait plutôt d'éther impalpable, du souffle glacé d'une nuit polaire. » (CF/PF)

Dahlias chandelier, 1921
Sandblasted and molded glass shade and mounts with cord, 30.5 cm diameter / Lampenschirm aus geformtem und sandgestrahltem Glas, gehalten von Schnüren, 30.5 cm Durchmesser / Abat-jour en verre sablé et moulé soutenu par des cordelettes, 30.5 cm de diamètre
René Lalique, Wingen-Sur-Moder, France

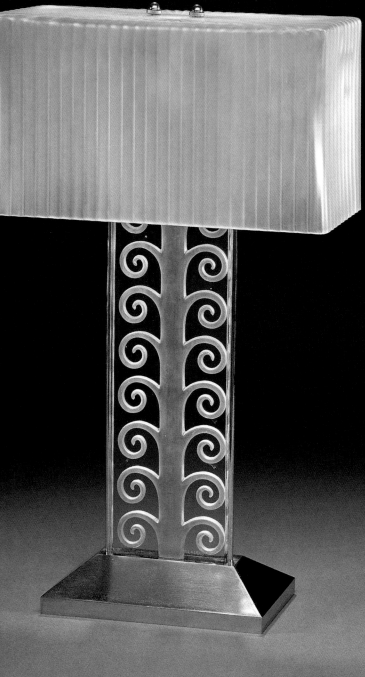

rené laliqu

cardamine table l

By the late 1920s René Lalique had abandoned naturalistic motifs in favor of more stylized and geometric decoration. His *Cardamine* and *Camélia* table lights (*c.*1928) eloquently reflect this change of stylistic emphasis. The lights are basically the same model with the only difference being their size and the etched decoration on their central supporting glass panels. Unashamedly Art Deco in style, these lights exemplify Lalique's masterful handling of glass and his work's remarkable sense of lightness. (CF/PF)

Gegen Ende der 1920er Jahre hatte René Lalique naturalistische Motive zugunsten eines mehr stilisierten und geometrischen Dekorationsstils aufgegeben. Seine Tischleuchten *Cardamine* und *Camélia* (ca. 1928) belegen diesen stilistischen Wandel sehr deutlich. Bei den Leuchten handelt es sich im Wesentlichen um das gleiche Modell, wobei der einzige Unterschied in ihrer Größe und den geätzten Verzierungen auf den Glasfüßen besteht. Eindeutig Art Déco im Stil, sind die Leuchten beispielhaft für Laliques meisterliches Geschick in der Verarbeitung von Glas und für das bemerkenswerte Gefühl von Leichtigkeit, das seine Arbeiten auszeichnet. (CF/PF)

À la fin des années 1920, René Lalique avait abandonné le naturalisme au profit de motifs plus stylisés et géométriques. Ses lampes de table *Cardamine* et *Camélia* (vers 1928) illustrent parfaitement cette évolution stylistique. Les deux lampes sont *grosso modo* construites sur le même modèle, à l'exception de leur taille et des ornements gravés sur les piliers de verre qui soutiennent l'ensemble. D'un style résolument Art Déco, les deux modèles prouvent à quel point Lalique maîtrisait le travail du verre, dans un style d'une remarquable légèreté. (CF/PF)

rené lalique
camélia table light

◁ *Cardamine* **table light**, *c.*1928
Molded and sandblasted glass shade on molded intaglio glass and metal base, 40.8 cm high / Fuß aus Intaglio-Pressglas auf Metallsockel, Lampenschirm aus sandgestrahltem Pressglas, 40,8 cm hoch / Abat-jour en verre moulé et sablé, socle en métal et verre moulé et intaillé, 40,8 cm de hauteur
René Lalique, Wingen-Sur-Moder, France

▷ *Camélia* **table light**, *c.*1928
Molded and sandblasted glass shade on molded intaglio glass and metal base, 45.1 cm high / Fuß aus Intaglio-Pressglas auf Metallsockel, Lampenschirm aus sandgestrahltem Pressglas, 45,1 cm hoch / Abat-jour en verre moulé et sablé, socle en métal et verre moulé et intaillé, 45,1 cm de hauteur
René Lalique, Wingen-Sur-Moder, France

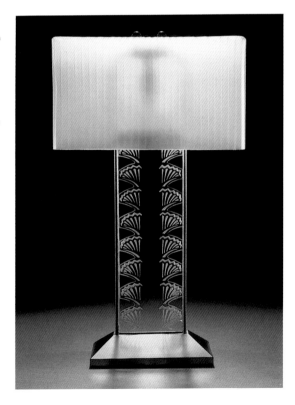

A recurring theme in Edgar Brandt's work, the snake appears in his andirons, urn handles, vases, jardinières and other forms, but nowhere does he use it more powerfully than in his serpent lights: *Le Serpent Naja*, *La Tentation*, and *Cobra*, all fashioned in bronze. *La Tentation* (c.1920), produced from 1920 to the 1930s, featured prominently in Brandt's advertisements and was made to order in either floor or table models. Approximately 100 examples of each were made. The precise detailing of the serpent's scales, eyes and tongue and the basket-patterned base make this floor light among Brandt's most elegant designs. (VT)

Die Schlange ist ein immer wiederkehrendes Motiv im Werk von Edgar Brandt, man findet es in seinen Kaminböcken, Urnengriffen, Vasen, Blumenständern und anderen Objekten. Aber nirgendwo setzte er es kraftvoller um als in seinen Leuchtenmodellen *Le Serpent Naja*, *La Tentation* und *Cobra*, die alle aus Bronze gearbeitet waren. Die augenfällig in Brandts Werbeanzeigen präsentierte Leuchte *La Tentation* (ca. 1920) wurde von 1920 bis in die 1930er Jahre produziert und war auf Bestellung als Steh- oder Tischleuchte lieferbar. Von jedem Modell wurden ungefähr hundert Stück hergestellt. Die präzise Ausführung von Schuppen, Augen und Zunge der Schlange und des korbartig gestalteten Sockels machen diese Stehleuchte zu einem von Brandts elegantesten Entwürfen. (VT)

Le serpent était un thème récurrent de l'œuvre de Brandt : il apparaissait, entre autres, dans ses chenets, les poignées de ses urnes, ses vases, ses jardinières et autres objets, mais c'était dans ses lampes serpents qu'il était le plus impressionnant. Celles-ci étaient élaborées en bronze et baptisées *Cobra*, *Le Serpent Naja* et *La Tentation*. Le modèle *La Tentation* (vers 1920), qui figurait souvent dans la réclame des produits Brandt, fut fabriqué sur commande entre 1920 et 1926, tant en lampadaire qu'en lampe de table, chaque type étant produit à une centaine d'exemplaires. La finesse des écailles, des yeux et de la langue du serpent, de même que le socle en forme de panier faisaient de ce lampadaire l'un des modèles les plus élégants de Brandt. (VT)

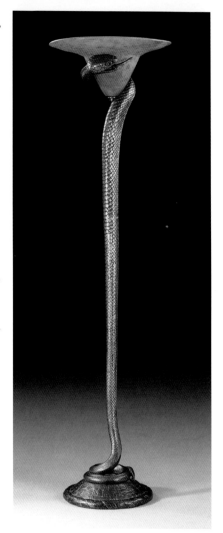

La Tentation floor light, c.1920

Patinated bronze base with alabaster shade, 166.4 cm high / Fuß und Schaft aus patinierter Bronze mit Lampenschirm aus Alabaster, 166,4 cm hoch / Socle en bronze patiné, abatjour en albâtre, 166,4 cm de hauteur
Edgar Brandt, Paris, France (base) / **Daum Frères**, Nancy, France (shade)

▷ *Edgar Brandt advertisement showing* La Tentation *floor light, 1931 / Werbeanzeige von Edgar Brandt mit der Stehleuchte Edgar Brandt, 1931 / Réclame pour la maison Edgar Brandt, 1931, où l'on distingue le lampadaire* La Tentation

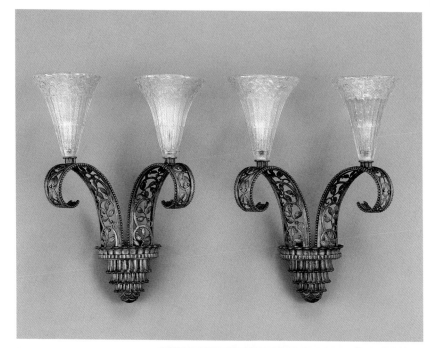

Wall appliques, c.1925

Silver-plated wrought-iron mounts and acid-etched glass shades, 52 cm high / Montierungen aus versilbertem Schmiedeeisen mit Lampenschirmen aus geätztem Glas, 52 cm hoch / Montures en fer forgé argenté, abat-jour en verre gravé à l'acide, 52 cm de hauteur
Edgar Brandt, Paris, France (mounts) / **Daum Frères**, Nancy, France (shades)

▷ Table light, c.1925

Patinated wrought-iron base and stem with glass shades, 53.6 cm high / Fuß und Montierung aus patiniertem Schmiedeeisen mit Lampenschirmen aus Glas, 53,6 cm hoch / Socle et tige en fer forgé patiné, abat-jour en verre, 53,6 cm de hauteur
Edgar Brandt, Paris, France (base) / **Daum Frères**, Nancy, France (shades)

▷▷ Floor light, c.1925

Wrought-iron base and stem with acid-etched glass shade, 143 cm high / Fuß, Schaft und Montierung aus Schmiedeeisen mit Lampenschirmen aus geätztem Glas, 143 cm hoch / Socle et tige en fer forgé, abat-jour en verre gravé à l'acide, 143 cm de hauteur
Louis Katona, Paris, France (base) / **Daum Frères**, Nancy, France (shade)

Scrollwork was a common motif in Art Deco ironwork. Edgar Brandt's decorative wall appliques (c.1925), which use the scroll as their form, are a variant of a magnificent chandelier he exhibited at the 1925 Paris Exposition internationale des arts décoratifs et industriels modernes and, more precisely, of three-branch wall appliques featured in his gallery. His decorative exuberance is slightly more restrained in the table light. Louis Katona makes more spartan use of decoration in his floor light (c.1925). All the lights incorporate shades from the Daum glass factory in Nancy, which often collaborated with metalworkers, providing custom shades as well as these more commercial models. (VT)

Spiral- und Blattverzierungen waren ein beliebtes Motiv in den Kunstschmiedeeisenarbeiten des Art Déco. Edgar Brandts dekorative Wandleuchten (ca. 1925), bei denen die Spiralform als Grundform verwendet wurde, sind eine Variante des großartigen Kronleuchters, den Brandt 1925 auf der Pariser Exposition Internationale des Arts Décoratifs et Industriels Modernes ausstellte sowie der dreiarmigen Wandleuchten, die in seiner Galerie hingen. Der ornamentale Reichtum seiner Entwürfe fällt bei der Tischleuchte etwas gemäßigter aus. Louis Katona macht bei seiner Standleuchte (ca. 1925) nur sparsamen Gebrauch von Verzierungen. Alle diese Leuchten sind mit Lampenschirmen der Glasmanufaktur Daum in Nancy ausgestattet, die häufig mit Metallkunsthandwerkern zusammenarbeiteten. (VT)

La volute était un motif fréquent du fer forgé de style Art Déco. Elle donne sa forme ici à ces deux appliques murales décoratives d'Edgar Brandt (vers 1925), qui sont en fait une variante d'un superbe lustre montré à Paris en 1925 lors de l'Exposition internationale des arts décoratifs de 1925 et, plus précisément, d'une applique à trois branches qu'on pouvait voir dans sa galerie. L'exubérance de la décoration s'assagit quelque peu dans la lampe de table, tandis que le lampadaire de Louis Katona (vers 1925) en est une version épurée. Chacun de ces modèles était doté d'abat-jour de Daum. La Verrerie de Nancy travaillait fréquemment avec des ferronniers, fabriquant aussi bien des abat-jour sur mesure que des modèles plus commerciaux, comme ici. (VT)

louis katona & daum frères
floor light

eileen gray
floor light

This highly important light is one of three lights by Irish designer Eileen Gray from around 1923. One of the floor lights was part of an ambitious interior project for the XIV Salon des artistes décorateurs in Paris entitled "a bedroom-boudoir for Monte Carlo". Influenced by Oceanic Art and the Cubist, Surrealist and Dutch De Stijl movements, the light was a radical and much talked-about design at the salon. The vellum shade was decorated with abstract motifs and stitched together with raffia, and the base was constructed of lacquered and stained exotic woods. (AP)

Diese beeindruckende Leuchte ist eines von drei Leuchtenobjekten der irischen Gestalterin Eileen Gray aus der Zeit um 1923. Eine der Stehleuchten gehörte zu einem ambitionierten Raumgestaltungsprojekt für den XIV. Salon des artistes décorateurs Français in Paris mit dem Titel „ein Schlafraum-Boudoir für Monte Carlo". Die von Kunst aus Ozeanien, den Kubisten, Surrealisten und der Gruppe De Stijl beeinflusste Leuchte war ein radikaler und im Salon viel diskutierter Entwurf. Der Pergamentschirm ist mit abstrakten Motiven verziert und mit Raphiabast zusammengenäht, während der Fuß aus lackierten und gebeizten exotischen Hölzern besteht. (AP)

Cette lampe très importante appartient à un groupe de trois luminaires conçus par la créatrice irlandaise Eileen Gray autour de 1923. Un des lampadaires faisait partie d'un ambitieux projet d'intérieur nommé « chambre-boudoir pour Monte Carlo » et exposé au XIVᵉ Salon des artistes décorateurs à Paris. Affirmant un style assez révolutionnaire influencé par l'art océanien, le cubisme, le surréalisme, et le mouvement néerlandais De Stijl, elle y fit beaucoup parler d'elle. L'abat-jour en vélin était décoré de motifs abstraits et piqué en raphia, tandis que le pied était en bois exotiques laqués et teints. (AP)

◁◁ **Floor light, c.1923**

Lacquered and stained exotic wood base with parchment and raffia shade, 186.8 cm high / Fuß aus lackiertem und gebeiztem Holz mit Lampenschirm aus Pergament und Bast, 186,8 cm hoch / Socle en bois exotique laqué et teinté, abat-jour en vélin et raphia, 186,8 cm de hauteur
Eileen Gray, Paris, France (attrib.)

△◁ *Vellum hanging light designed by Eileen Gray, 1920s / Hängeleuchte von Eileen Gray aus Pergament, 1920er Jahre / Suspension en vélin piqué réalisée par Eileen Gray, années 1920*

△△▷ Japonaise *lantern designed by Eileen Gray, c.1923 /* Japonaise *Laterne von Eileen Gray ca. 1923 / Lanterne «japonaise» créée par Eileen Gray, vers 1923*

△ *Display at Jean Désert, Paris, showing Eileen Gray's* Pirogue *sofa and assymetrical floor light, c.1923 / Schauraum von Jean Désert, Paris mit Eileen Grays* Pirogue *Sofa und asymmetrischer Stehleuchte, ca. 1923 / Décor exposé dans la galerie de Jean Désert à Paris on y voit le sofa* Pirogue *d'Eileen Gray, ainsi qu'un lampadaire asymétrique, vers 1923*

◁ *Another version of Eileen Gray's floor light missing its shade, c.1923 / Eine weitere Version von Eileen Grays Stehleuchte mit fehlendem Pergamentschirm, ca. 1923 / Autre exemplaire du lampadaire d'Eileen Gray, sans son abat-jour en vélin et raphia, vers 1923*

△ Dining room designed by René Herbst,
c.1928 / Esszimmer nach Entwurf von René
Herbst, ca. 1928 / Salle à manger conçue par
René Herbst, vers 1928

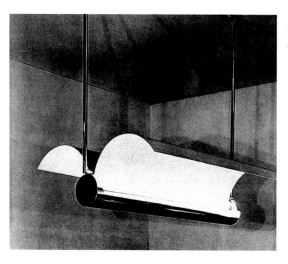

◁ Suspended ceiling light designed by René
Herbst, c.1928 / Pendelleuchte nach Entwurf
von René Herbst, ca. 1928 / Suspension à
deux ailettes créée par René Herbst, vers
1928

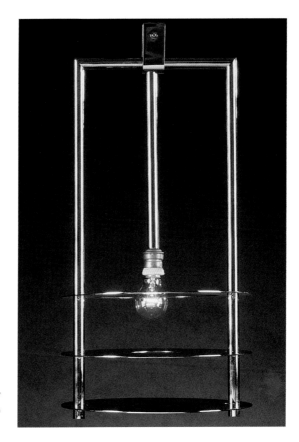

Suspended ceiling light, 1929
Nickel-plated mounts and disks, 70 cm drop /
Konstruktion aus vernickeltem Metall, 70 cm
lang / Tubes et disques d'acier nickelé, 70 cm
de hauteur
Établissements René Herbst, Paris, France

Between 1929 and 1932 René Herbst
contributed four articles on lighting to
the specialist journal *Lux* in which he
suggested that readers should seek
the expertise of lighting engineers.
Practicing what he preached, Herbst
consulted Perféleca's lighting engineer,
André Salomon, when designing his
own lights, including the double-winged
ceiling fixture that was displayed at the
1928 Salon d'Automne in Paris.
The suspended ceiling light (1929) not
only reflects the stylistic purity of French
Modernism, but also Herbst's rigorous
rejection of ornament in favor of an
industrial esthetic. (CF/PF)

In den Jahren zwischen 1929 und
1932 verfasste René Herbst für die
Fachzeitschrift *Lux* vier Artikel, in denen
er den Lesern nahe legte, sich von
Beleuchtungsingenieuren beraten zu
lassen. Er selbst folgte diesem Rat und
konsultierte den Beleuchtungsingenieur
der Firma Perféleca, André Salomon,
wenn er seine eigenen Leuchten entwarf, so die zweiflügelige Deckenleuchte, die 1928 im Salon d'Automne
in Paris ausgestellt wurde. Die Pendelleuchte (1929) spiegelt nicht nur den
stilistischen Purismus des französischen Modernismus wider, sondern
auch Herbsts konsequenten Verzicht
auf Ornamentierung zugunsten einer
industriellen Ästhetik. (CF/PF)

Entre 1929 et 1932, René Herbst
écrivit quatre articles sur l'éclairage
pour la revue spécialisée *Lux*, dans
lequel il suggérait à ses lecteurs de
demander conseil à des ingénieurs
éclairagistes. C'est d'ailleurs ce qu'il
fit lui-même : chacun de ses luminaires,
y compris la suspension à deux ailes
qu'il exposa au Salon d'Automne de
1928 à Paris, fut réalisé avec l'aide
d'André Salomon, qui était ingénieur
éclairagiste chez Perféleca. Le lustre
(1929) reflète la pureté stylistique du
Modernisme français, mais aussi
le choix de Herbst de rejeter tout
ornement au profit d'une esthétique
industrielle. (CF/PF)

Suspended ceiling light, c.1925

Wrought-iron mounts with sandblasted
glass panels, 35.6 cm drop / Montierung
aus Schmiedeeisen mit Lampenschirm aus
sandgestrahlten Glasscheiben, 35,6 cm lang /
Montures en fer forgé, plaques de verre sablé,
35,6 cm de hauteur
Atelier Primavera, Paris, France

▷ **Table light, c.1925**

Nickel-plated metal base with alabaster band,
bulb-holder and shade, 47 cm high / Fuß aus
vernickeltem Metall mit Zierband, Lampenfassung und -schirm aus Alabaster, 47 cm hoch /
Socle en métal nickelé à bandeau d'albâtre,
cache-ampoule et abat-jour en albâtre, 47 cm
de hauteur
Albert Cheuret, Paris, France

With its faceted sunburst form, Louis
Sognot's suspended ceiling light
(c.1925) displays the influence of
Cubism on French decorative art during
the mid-1920s. He incorporated this
design in the bedroom installation of the
Primavera Pavilion at the 1925 Paris
Exposition internationale des arts
décoratifs et industriels modernes.
Albert Cheuret's alabaster and metal
table light (c.1925) similarly reflects the
sculptural opulence and material sump-
tuousness of the French Art Deco style.
Like Sognot, Cheuret regularly showed
his work at the salon of the Société des
artistes décorateurs. (CF/PF)

Mit ihrer facettierten, rosettenförmigen
Gestaltung lässt die von Louis Sognot
entworfene Deckenleuchte (ca. 1925)
den Einfluss des Kubismus auf die
französische dekorative Kunst der
1920er Jahre erkennen. Sognot nahm
dieses Leuchtenobjekt in seine Schlaf-
zimmereinrichtung auf, die 1925 im Primavera Pavillon auf der Pariser Exposition internationale des arts décoratifs
et industriels modernes ausgestellt
wurde. Albert Cheurets Tischleuchte
(ca. 1925) aus Alabaster und Metall
spiegelt in Form und Material die Opu-
lenz des französischen Art Déco wider.
Ebenso wie Sognot präsentierte auch
Cheuret seine Arbeiten regelmäßig im
Salon de la Société des artistes
décorateurs. (CF/PF)

Cette suspension à facettes «plissé-
soleil» réalisée par Louis Sognot (vers
1925) trahit l'influence du Cubisme sur
les art décoratifs français au milieu des
années 1920. Le modèle faisait partie
du décor de chambre à coucher du
Pavillon Primavera à l'Exposition internationale des arts décoratifs et industriels modernes de Paris en 1925.
La lampe de table en albâtre et métal
signée Albert Cheuret (vers 1925)
reflète, elle aussi, le goût de l'Art Déco
français pour les formes opulentes et
les matières somptueuses. Comme
Sognot, Cheuret exposait régulièrement
ses œuvres au Salon de la Société des
artistes décorateurs. (CF/PF)

Jacques-Émile Ruhlmann's interiors were the essence of luxury and refinement in the 1920s, in part because he designed almost every element of each room, including the furniture, rugs, wallpaper, mirrors and lighting. Both of these lights (*c.*1925) attest to Ruhlmann's insistence on using sumptuous materials throughout, and they illustrate his affinity with clean lines. Yet they also display characteristics of much of his furniture design, such as the fluting on the table light mount and the swirls on the applique, reminiscent of the burled veneers he often used. (VT)

Jacques-Émile Ruhlmanns Interieurs galten in den 1920er Jahren als die Quintessenz von Luxus und edlem Raffinement, was im Wesentlichen daran lag, dass er jede Raumausstattung bis ins letzte Detail selbst entwarf, einschließlich der Möbel, Teppiche, Tapeten, Spiegel und Beleuchtungskörper. Beide hier präsentierten Leuchten (ca. 1925) belegen seine Vorliebe für kostbare Werkstoffe und seine Affinität zu klaren Formen. Gleichzeitig enthalten sie dekorative Elemente, die man auch in vielen seiner Möbelentwürfe entdecken kann, wie die Riffelung auf der Montierung der Tischleuchte und die wirbelige Ornamentik der Wandapplikation, die an die häufig von ihm verwendeten Wurzelholzfurniere erinnert. (VT)

Pendant les années 1920, les intérieurs de Ruhlmann représentaient le summum du luxe et du raffinement, en partie parce qu'il concevait pratiquement tous les éléments, depuis le mobilier jusqu'aux tapis en passant par les papiers peints, les miroirs et les luminaires. Les deux modèles (vers 1925) représentés ici témoignent du goût de Ruhlmann pour les matières somptueuses, qu'il tenait à utiliser en toutes circonstances, de même qu'elles illustrent son amour des lignes pures. Elles rappellent aussi son mobilier par certains détails, comme les cannelures sur la monture de la lampe de table et les lignes sinueuses des appliques, qui évoquent les placages qu'il utilisait souvent. (VT)

Table light, *c.*1925
Alabaster shade with gilt bronze stem on black marble base, 35 cm high / Lampenschirm aus Alabaster mit Montierung aus vergoldeter Bronze auf Sockel aus schwarzem Marmor, 35 cm hoch / Vasque en albâtre, fût en bronze doré sur un socle en marbre noir, 35 cm de hauteur
Établissements Ruhlmann et Laurent, Paris, France

▷ **Wall applique, *c.*1925**
Alabaster diffuser on gilt bronze mount, 35.5 cm diameter / Montierung aus vergoldeter Bronze mit Lampenschirm aus Alabaster, 35,5 cm Durchmesser / Cache-ampoule en albâtre, monture en bronze doré, 35,5 cm de diamètre
Établissements Ruhlmann et Laurent, Paris, France

In 1917 the Hungarian-born painter Vilmos Huszár became a founding member of the De Stijl group and the following year began designing primary-colored interiors, furniture, textiles, glass and lights. His table light (c.1920) with its simple geometric form and primary colors encapsulates the group's desire to create a universal language of abstracted cubism. Gerrit Rietveld joined the De Stijl group in 1919 and also designed a number of lights that reflected the group's interest in the spatial relationships between elements. The reductivist formal geometry of his table light (1925) is startlingly Modern for its date. (CF/PF)

Im Jahr 1917 wurde der in Ungarn geborene Maler Vilmos Huszár zum Mitbegründer der Künstlergruppe De Stijl und begann im Jahr darauf mit der Gestaltung von Innenausstattungen, Möbeln, Stoffen, Glasobjekten und Leuchten in Primärfarben. Seine Tischleuchte (ca. 1920) mit ihren einfachen geometrischen Formen und Grundfarben verkörpert das Bestreben der Gruppe, eine universelle Sprache des abstrakten Kubismus zu kreieren. Gerrit Rietveld wurde 1919 Mitglied von De Stijl. Auch er entwarf eine Reihe von Leuchten, die das Interesse der Gruppe an den räumlichen Verhältnissen zwischen einzelnen Gestaltungselementen widerspiegeln. Die reduzierte formale Geometrie seiner Tischleuchte (1925) ist überraschend modern für ihre Zeit. (CF/PF)

En 1917, Vilmos Huszár, peintre d'origine hongroise, fut l'un des membres fondateurs du groupe De Stijl. L'année suivante, il commença à réaliser des intérieurs, des meubles, des textiles, des objets en verre et des luminaires aux couleurs primaires. Les formes simples et géométriques de sa lampe de table (vers 1920), de même que ses couleurs primaires, résument bien la volonté du groupe d'inventer un langage universel à partir du cubisme abstrait. En 1919, Gerrit Rietveld se joignit au groupe et réalisa plusieurs luminaires reflétant leur intérêt commun pour les relations spatiales entre les éléments. Les formes géométriques et minimales de sa lampe de table (1925) sont étonnamment modernes pour l'époque. (CF/PF)

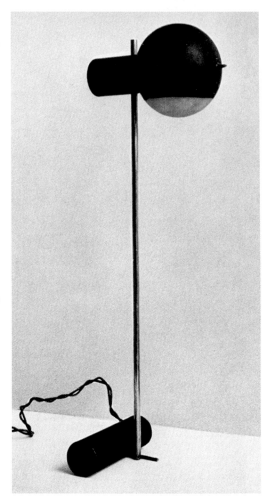

Table light, 1925
Nickel-plated and painted iron base with enameled iron and glass shade, 38 cm high / Fuß aus vernickeltem und lackiertem Metall mit Lampenschirm aus lackiertem Metall und Glas, 38 cm hoch / Socle en fer nickelé et peint, abat-jour en fer émaillé et verre, 38 cm de hauteur
Gerard A. van de Groenekan, Utrecht, The Netherlands

▷ **Table light, c.1920**
Tubular steel column mounted on rectangular painted wood sections, 22 cm high / Fuß aus verchromtem Stahlrohr auf rechteckigen Elementen aus lackiertem Holz, 22 cm hoch / Colonne tubulaire en acier montée sur des rectangles de bois peint, 22 cm de hauteur
Vilmos Huszár, Voorburg, The Netherlands

gerrit rietveld

It was while designing a consulting room for Dr. Hartog of Maarssen in The Netherlands in 1922 that the Dutch architect and designer Gerrit Rietveld developed the first prototype of a ceiling light consisting of elements arranged at right angles to each other and hanging freely in space. The light, along with his famous *Red/Blue* chair (1917–23), would become synonymous with De Stijl. Inspired by the work of Rietveld, Walter Gropius designed very similar ceiling lighting for the director's office (1923–24) at the Bauhaus's Weimar headquarters, but it was constructed as a component of an interior design scheme organized on strict Constructivist principles. (TB)

Im Zusammenhang mit dem Entwurf einer Sprechzimmereinrichtung für den Arzt Dr. Hartog in Maarssen (1922) entwickelte der niederländische Architekt und Designer Gerrit Rieveld den ersten Prototypen einer Deckenleuchte aus rechtwinklig zueinander angeordneten, scheinbar frei im Raum hängenden Soffitten, die neben seinem berühmten *Rot/Blau Stuhl* zu einem Synonym des De Stijl-Designs werden sollten. Angeregt durch den Entwurf Rietvelds, der zu Beginn der 1920er Jahre in regem Austausch mit dem Bauhaus stand, entwarf Walter Gropius für sein Direktionszimmer (1923–24) am Bauhaus Weimar eine formal sehr ähnliche Deckenbeleuchtung, die Bestandteil einer streng konstruktivistisch gegliederten Raumgestaltung war. (TB)

C'est en concevant un cabinet de consultation pour le Dr. Hartog à Maarsen aux Pays-Bas en 1922, que l'architecte et créateur néerlandais Gerrit Rietveld mit au point le prototype d'une lampe dont les éléments, disposés à angles droits les uns par rapport aux autres, flottaient librement. Ce luminaire, comme sa célèbre chaise *Red/Blue*, allait devenir le symbole du mouvement De Stijl. S'inspirant de Rietveld, qui, pendant les années 1920, était impliqué dans d'intenses débats d'idées avec le Bauhaus, Walter Gropius créa un éclairage de plafond très semblable pour le bureau du directeur du Bauhaus à Weimar (1923–24) mais celui-ci faisait partie d'un projet de décoration intérieure organisé selon des principes constructivistes très stricts. (TB)

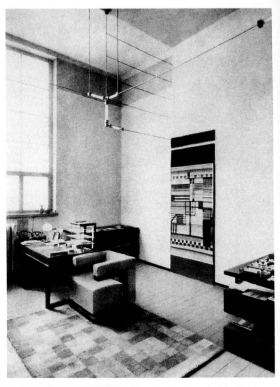

△ *Director's office at the Weimar Bauhaus, designed by Walter Gropius, 1923–24 / Direktionszimmer am Bauhaus Weimar, entworfen von Walter Gropius, 1923–24 / Bureau du directeur au Bauhaus de Weimar, réalisé par Walter Gropius, 1923–24*

◁ *Surgery at Dr. A. M. Hartog's practice in Maarssen designed by Gerrit Rietveld, 1922 / Sprechzimmer in der Praxis von Dr. A. M. Hartogh in Maarssen, entworfen von Gerrit Rietveld, 1922 / Cabinet du Dr. A. M. Hartog à Maaarsen, réalisé par Gerrit Rietveld, 1922*

▷ **Hanging light, 1922**

Wood and glass construction with glass tube lights, 155 cm drop (max.) / Konstruktion aus Holz und Glas mit Glasröhrenlampen, 155 cm lang (max.) / Structure en bois et verre, tubes lumineux en verre, 155 cm de hauteur maximale
Gerrit Rietveld, Utrecht, The Netherlands; later manufactured by Gerard A. van de Groenekan, Utrecht, the Netherlands (reissued by Tecta, Lauenförde, Germany)

Wilhelm Wagenfeld's iconic *ME1* table light (*c.*1923–24), designed in conjunction with Carl Jakob Jucker at the Weimar Bauhaus, set out the school's new functionalist agenda, which speculated on the development of standardized goods for industrial mass-production. With its elemental construction of an opalescent domed shade, glass and metal cylindrical stem, and circular glass base, this remarkable light clearly showed that through the application of Modern design principles – purity, simplicity, self-effacement – a certain stylishness could be achieved in everyday objects. As a prototype for industrial production, the *ME1* light also reflected the symbiosis of art and technology, which was at the core of Bauhaus philosophy. (CF/PF)

Wilhelm Wagenfelds Designikone, die zusammen mit Carl Jakob Jucker am Bauhaus Dessau entworfene Leuchte *ME1* (ca. 1923–24) war ein Signal für das neue Programm der Schule, das auf die Entwicklung standardisierter Gebrauchsgüter für die industrielle Massenproduktion setzte. Mit der elementaren Konstruktion, bestehend aus einem kuppelförmigen Opalglasschirm, einem zylindrischen Ständer aus Metall und Glas und einem kreisförmigen Glasfuß, bewies dieses Design, dass durch die Anwendung moderner Gestaltungsprinzipien – Reinheit, Schlichtheit, Zurückhaltung – eine stilvolle Eleganz gelingen konnte. Als Prototyp für die maschinelle Fertigung verkörpert die Leuchte zudem die Symbiose von Kunst und Technologie, die den Kern der Bauhaus-Philosophie ausmachte. (CF/PF)

Le légendaire modèle *ME1* de Wilhelm Wagenfeld, créé au Bauhaus de Dessau avec Carl Jacob Jucker (vers 1923–24), clamait le nouveau credo fonctionnaliste de l'école, qui visait à créer des biens standardisés compatibles avec une production de masse. Avec son abat-jour arrondi en verre opalescent, son pied cylindrique en verre et en métal, et son socle circulaire en verre, cette superbe lampe était d'une simplicité extrême et prouvait que les objets de la vie courante pouvaient prétendre à une certaine élégance répondant à des critères modernistes de pureté, de simplicité et de discrétion. Le *ME1*, prototype du luminaire industriel, opérait la symbiose entre art et technologie qui était au cœur de la philosophie du Bauhaus. (CF/PF)

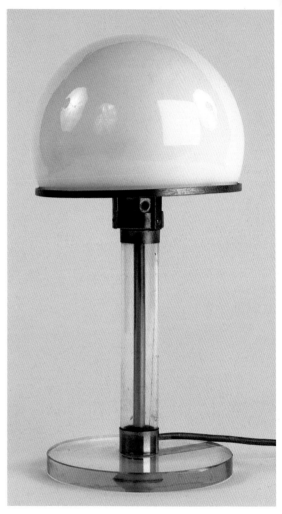

Model No. ME1 table light, c. 1923–24

Brass, nickel-plated steel and glass base with opalescent glass shade, 35.5 cm high / Fuß aus Messing, vernickeltem Stahl und Glas mit Lampenschirm aus Opalglas, 35,5 cm hoch / Socle en laiton, acier nickelé et verre, abat-jour en verre blanc opalin, 35,5 cm de hauteur **Bauhaus**, Weimar/Dessau, Germany (reissued by **Tecnolumen**, Bremen, Germany)

▷ △ *Dismantled* Model No. ME1 *table light, c.1924 /* Modell Nr. ME1 *Tischleuchte, ca. 1924 /* La lampe Modèle n° ME1 *démontée, vers 1924*

▷ ▽ *Original Bauhaus Dessau catalog designed by Herbert Bayer showing Model Nos. ME1 and ME2 table lights, 1925 /* Von Herbert Bayer gestalteter Katalog des Bauhaus Dessau mit den Tischleuchten Modell Nr. ME1 und ME2, 1925 / Extrait d'un catalogue du Bauhaus présentant les lampes de table Modèle n° ME1 et ME2, conception graphique Herbert Bayer, 1925*

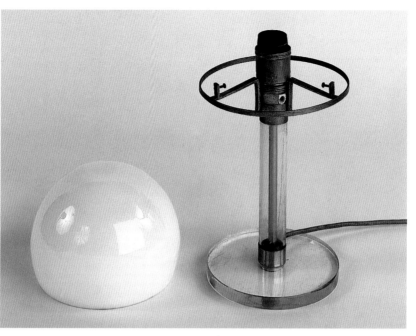

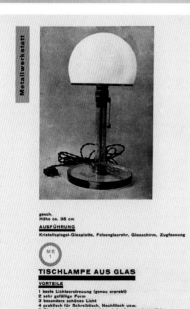

Metallwerkstatt

gesch.
Höhe ca. 35 cm
AUSFÜHRUNG
Kristallspiegel-Glasplatte, Felsenglasrohr, Glasschirm, Zugfassung

ME
1

TISCHLAMPE AUS GLAS

VORTEILE
1 beste Lichtzerstreuung (genau erprobt)
2 sehr gefällige Form
3 besonders schönes Licht
4 praktisch für Schreibtisch, Nachttisch usw.
5 Glocke festgeschraubt bleibt in jeder Lage unbeweglich

Metallwerkstatt

gesch.
Höhe ca. 35 cm
AUSFÜHRUNG
Messing vernickelt, Glasschirm, Zugfassung

ME
2

TISCHLAMPE AUS METALL

VORTEILE
1 beste Lichtzerstreuung (genau erprobt) mit Jenaer Schottglas
2 sehr stabil
3 einfachste, gefällige Form
4 praktisch für Schreibtisch, Nachttisch usw.
5 Glocke festgeschraubt, bleibt in jeder Lage unbeweglich

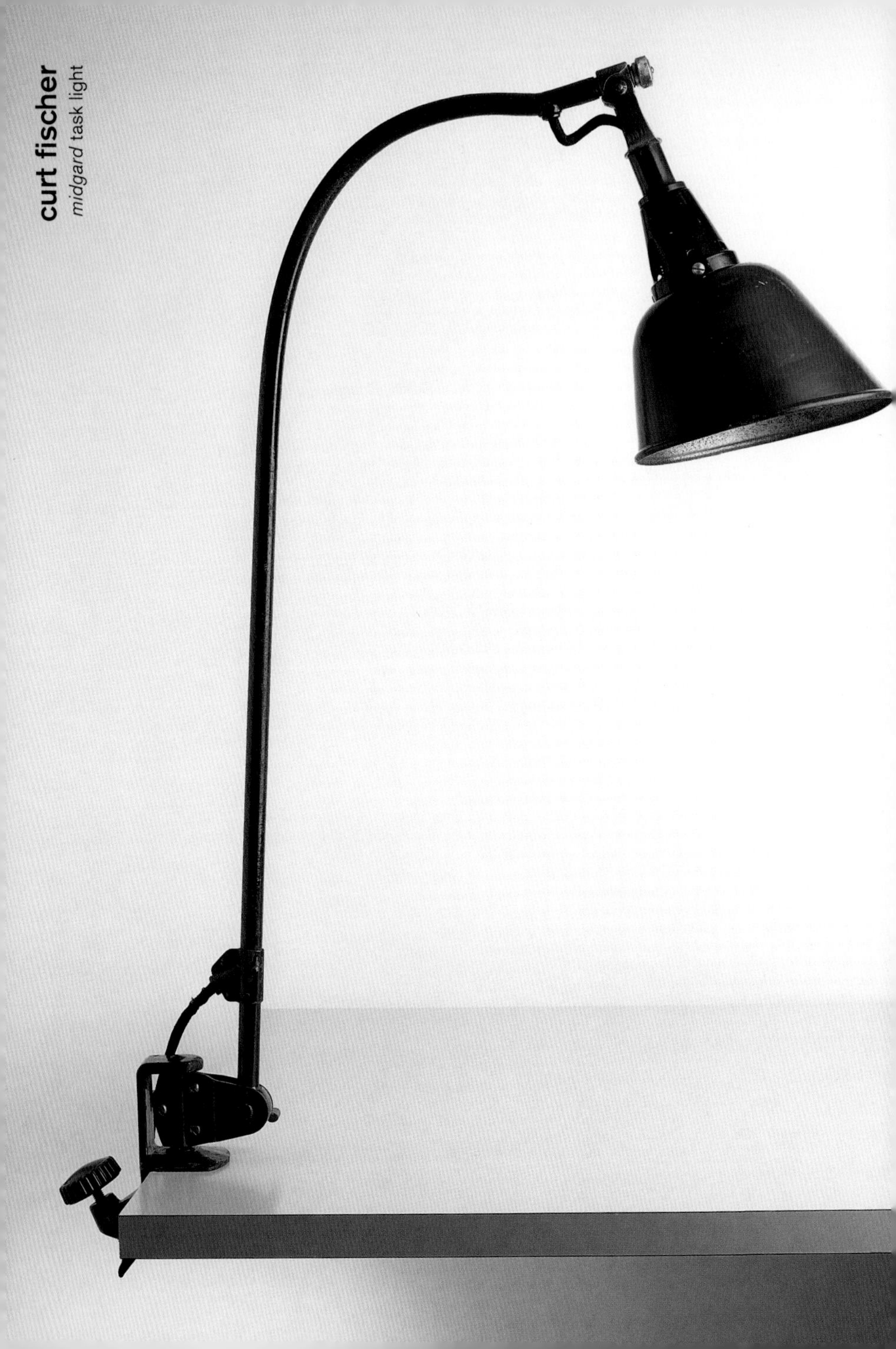

curt fischer
midgard task light

◁ **Midgard** task light, *c.*1923–25

Enameled metal clamp, stem and shade with nickel-plated metal mounts, 72 cm high / Klemmvorrichtung, Fuß und Lampenschirm aus lackiertem Metall, 72 cm hoch / Pince étau, tige et abat-jour en métal émaillé, montures en métal nickelé, 72 cm de hauteur
Industriewerk Auma, Ronneberger & Fischer, Auma/Thuringia, Germany / W. Goy & Co., Frankfurt/Main, Germany

Ise and Walter Gropius in their Master's house at the Dessau Bauhaus, c.1926–27. A Midgard-task light is attached to the shelving unit / Ise und Walter Gropius im Wohnzimmer des Gropius-Meisterhauses, Bauhaus Dessau, ca. 1926–27. An einem der Bücherregale ist eine Midgard-Leuchte angebracht / Ise et Walter Gropius dans la salle de séjour de la maison du directeur qu'ils occupaient au Bauhaus de Dessau, vers 1926–27. Une lampe Midgard est pincée sur les étagères.

The *Midgard* task light, designed by Curt Fischer *c.*1923–25, must have provided an important model for the skilled artisans in the Bauhaus's metal workshop in Dessau when, in 1925, they set about developing modern lighting fixtures. The multifunctional task light was part of the furniture and fittings at the Weimar Bauhaus and is known to have been used in the living room of the Master's house occupied by Ise and Walter Gropius at the Dessau Bauhaus. Fischer's uncompromising design is especially striking for the non-dazzle reflector and the mechanism of the arm, which enabled the light to be adjusted to almost any angle. (TB)

Die *Midgard* Arbeitsleuchte, um 1923–25 von Curt Fischer entworfen, zählte sicherlich zu den großen Vorbildern für die Mitarbeiter der Metallwerkstatt am Bauhaus in Dessau, die sich ab 1925 intensiv mit der Entwicklung von modernen Beleuchtungskörpern auseinandersetzten. Die multifunktionale Arbeitsleuchte fand schon in der Einrichtung der Metallwerkstatt am Bauhaus Weimar Verwendung und ist später auch in der Wohnzimmereinrichtung von Ise und Walter Gropius in deren Meisterhaus am Dessauer Bauhaus belegbar. Der kompromisslose Entwurf von Fischer überzeugt durch den blendfreien Reflektor und die Mechanik des Lampenarms, der nahezu jede Einstellung der Leuchte ermöglicht. (TB)

Réalisée par Curt Fischer vers 1923–25, la lampe de travail *Midgard* servit vraisemblablement de modèle aux artisans qualifiés de l'atelier de ferronnerie du Bauhaus à Dessau lorsque, en 1925, ceux-ci commencèrent à fabriquer des luminaires modernes. La lampe de travail polyvalente faisait partie du mobilier du Bauhaus de Weimar, et l'on sait qu'il en existait un exemplaire dans la maison du directeur à Dessau, où logeaient Ise et Walter Gropius. D'un style pour le moins austère, le modèle surprend par son réflecteur anti-éblouissant et par le mécanisme de son bras, grâce auquel on peut orienter la lampe à presque n'importe quel angle. (TB)

The hanging light with pulley fitting, known as *Model No. ME78b*, was designed in 1926 by Marianne Brandt and Hans Przyrembel as part of the furniture and fittings of the Dessau Bauhaus. Lights of this type, which were initially produced only on a small scale in the Bauhaus's metal workshops in Dessau, were installed in various parts of the building, including the weaving and metal workshops and the architecture department's drawing office. The same model was also used to light the dining room of Walter Gropius's Master's house. (TB)

Die Deckenleuchte *Modell Nr. ME78b* mit Zugvorrichtung ist 1926 von Marianne Brandt und Hans Przyrembel als Teil der Einrichtung des Dessauer Bauhauses entworfen worden. Verwendung fand die Leuchte, die zunächst nur in kleiner Serie in der Metallwerkstatt des Dessauer Bauhauses hergestellt wurde, in verschiedenen Räumen des Bauhausgebäudes (Weberei, Metallwerkstatt, Zeichensaal der Architekturabteilung). Sie diente aber auch als Esszimmerleuchte im Meisterhaus von Walter Gropius. (TB)

Cette suspension à poulie, connue sous le nom de *Modèle n° ME78b*, fut créée en 1926 par Marianne Brandt et Hans Przyrembel et faisait partie des aménagements du Bauhaus Dessau. Fabriqué au départ à petite échelle dans les ateliers de ferronnerie du Bauhaus à Dessau, ce type de lampe fut installé un peu partout dans le bâtiment, y compris dans les ateliers de ferronnerie et de tissage. Le même modèle éclairait la salle à manger de la maison du directeur occupée par Walter Gropius. (TB)

Model No. ME 78b hanging light, 1926

Nickel-plated aluminum counterweights, mounts and shade, 250 cm drop (max.), 50 cm diameter / Ausgleichgewichte, Montierung und Lampenschirm aus vernickeltem Aluminium, 250 cm lang (max.), Lampenschirm 50 cm Durchmesser / Contrepoids, montures et abat-jour en aluminium nickelé, 250 cm de hauteur maximale, 50 cm de diamètre (abat-jour)
Bauhaus Dessau (1926–27) / **Metallwerke** vorm. Paul Stotz, Stuttgart, Germany (1927–29) / **Schwintzer & Gräff**, Berlin, Germany (1929–c.1939) (reissued by **Tecnolumen**, Bremen, Germany)

▷ *The weaving workshop in the Dessau Bauhaus studio building, c.1927 / Die Webwerkstatt im Studiogebäude des Bauhauses Dessau, ca. 1927 / Atelier de tissage du Bauhaus Dessau, vers 1927*

marianne brandt & hans przyrembel

model no. me 78b hanging light

At the time when fixtures and fittings were being installed in the new Bauhaus buildings in Dessau, the Bauhaus's metal workshop paid increased attention to developing modern, up-to-date lighting fixtures which would later be industrially manufactured under license on a larger scale. Among the spaces lit by the *Model no. ME 27* ceiling light and the *Model no. ME104* hanging light, made in 1926 to a design by Marianne Brandt, was the Master's house of László Moholy-Nagy, who was artistic director of the metal workshop from 1923 until 1928. (TB)

Im Zusammenhang mit der Einrichtung des Dessauer Bauhauses beschäftigte sich die Metallwerkstatt des Bauhauses vermehrt mit der Entwicklung von modernen, zeitgemäßen Beleuchtungskörpern, die später gegen Lizenzgebühren auch in größeren Stückzahlen industriell gefertigt werden sollten. Die Deckenleuchte *Modell Nr. ME27* und die Hängeleuchte *Modell Nr. ME104* aus dem Jahr 1926 nach Entwürfen von Marianne Brandt fanden u. a. im Meisterhaus von László Moholy-Nagy Verwendung, der von 1923 bis 1928 als künstlerischer Leiter der Metallwerkstatt fungierte. (TB)

Alors que les nouveaux bâtiments du Bauhaus à Dessau étaient en train d'être aménagés, les ateliers de ferronnerie de l'école multipliaient leurs efforts pour mettre au point des luminaires modernes susceptibles d'être un jour fabriqués sous licence à grande échelle. Les suspensions *Modèle n° ME27* et *ME104*, fabriquées en 1926 d'après une idée de Marianne Brandt, y éclairaient, entre autres, l'atelier, situé dans la résidence du directeur, de László Moholy-Nagy. Ce dernier remplissait les fonctions de directeur artistique à l'atelier de ferronnerie entre 1923 et 1928. (TB)

◁ **Model No. ME27 suspended ceiling light, 1926**
Nickel-plated brass mount with white opalescent glass shade, 40 cm diameter (shade) / Montierung aus vernickeltem Messing mit Lampenschirm aus weißem Opalglas, Lampenschirm 40 cm Durchmesser / Monture en lation nickelé, abat-jour en verre blanc opalescent, 40 cm de diamètre (abat-jour)
Bauhaus Dessau, Dessau, Germany (reissued by **Tecnolumen**, Bremen, Germany)

Model No. ME104 hanging light, 1926
Nickel-plated brass mount with white opalescent glass shade / Montierung aus vernickeltem Messing mit Lampenschirm aus Opalglas / Monture en lation nickelé, abat-jour en verre blanc opalescent
Bauhaus Dessau, Dessau, Germany / **Schwintzer & Gräff**, Berlin, Germany

◁ *PH* table light, 1927

Enameled copper shades on patinated bronze base, 53 cm high / Lampenschirme aus lackiertem Kupfer auf Fuß aus patinierter Bronze, 53 cm hoch / Abat-jour en cuivre émaillé, socle en bronze patiné, 53 cm de hauteur
Louis Poulsen & Co., Copenhagen, Denmark

▷ *PH* table light, c.1927

Opaque glass shades on polished brass base, 44,5 cm high / Lampenschirme aus Opakglas auf Fuß aus poliertem Messing, 44,5 cm hoch / Abat-jour en verre opaque, socle en laiton poli, 44,5 cm de hauteur
Louis Poulsen & Co., Copenhagen, Denmark

In 1924 Poul Henningsen developed a series of multi-shaded hanging and table lights that were designed to reduce the dazzling glare of the modern electric light bulb. The same year he began designing lights for Louis Poulsen and in 1925 his first *PH* light was awarded a gold medal at the Exposition internationale des arts décoratifs et industriels modernes in Paris. The configuration of the elegantly curved, light-diffusing *PH* shades – made of either opaque glass or enameled copper – was reputedly inspired by a stacked cup, bowl, and saucer. (CF/PF)

Im Jahr 1924 entwickelte Poul Henningsen eine Serie von Hänge- und Tischleuchten mit mehreren Schirmen, die so konzipiert waren, dass sie das grelle Licht der modernen elektrischen Glühbirne dämpften. Im selben Jahr begann er, Leuchten für Louis Poulsen zu entwerfen, und ein Jahr später, 1925, wurde die erste Leuchte seiner *PH* Serie auf der Exposition Internationale des Arts Décoratifs et Industriels Modernes in Paris mit einer Goldmedaille ausgezeichnet. Die Anordnung der elegant geschwungenen, ein weiches Licht streuenden *PH* Lampenschirme, entweder aus Opakglas oder lackiertem Kupfer gefertigt, war angeblich von einem aus Tasse, Schüssel und Untertasse bestehenden Geschirrstapel inspiriert. (CF/PF)

En 1924, Poul Henningsen réalisa une série de suspensions et lampes de table à plusieurs abat-jour permettant d'adoucir la luminosité des ampoules électriques modernes. La même année, il se mit à créer des luminaires pour Louis Poulsen et, en 1925, sa première lampe *PH* reçut une médaille d'or à l'Exposition internationale des arts décoratifs et industriels modernes de Paris. On raconte que Henningsen s'inspira de la forme d'une tasse, d'un bol et d'une soucoupe empilés lorsqu'il imagina les courbes élégantes des abat-jour en cuivre émaillé, qui produisaient une lumière diffuse. (CF/PF)

Following the success of the first *PH* lights, Poul Henningsen developed a new hanging light known as the *PH Septima* (1927–28), which was first shown as a prototype at the Danske Kunstindustrimuseum, Copenhagen in 1928. The configuration of the bowl-like glass shades was based on Henningsen's earlier *PH5/5* hanging light (1927), whereby four additional diffusers were inserted into the overall design, giving a total of seven – hence the name *Septima*. The shades were made of clear glass, which were part-sandblasted in order to reduce glare. In 1929 an amber-colored version of the light was introduced. (CF/PF)

Nach dem Erfolg der ersten *PH* Leuchten entwickelte Poul Henningsen eine neue Hängeleuchte mit dem Namen *PH Septima* (1927–28), die 1928 zuerst als Prototyp im Kopenhagener Kunstgewerbemuseum präsentiert wurde. Die Anordnung der schalenartigen Glasschirme dieser Leuchte basierte auf Henningsens früherer Hängeleuchte *PH5/5* (1927), nur dass dieses Modell mit vier zusätzlichen Diffusoren ausgestattet war, was eine Gesamtzahl von sieben ergab – daher der Name *Septima*. Die Schirme waren aus Klarglas gefertigt, die teilweise sandgestrahlt wurden, um das Blendlicht zu reduzieren. 1929 wurde eine bernsteinfarbene Version dieser Leuchte auf den Markt gebracht. (CF/PF)

Encouragé par le succès de ses premières lampes *PH*, Poul Henningsen mit au point une nouvelle suspension bapti´se *PH Septima* (1927–28), qui fut exposée pour la première fois en tant que prototype au Danske Kunstindustrimuseum de Copenhague en 1928. La configuration de ses abat-jour en forme de bols rappelait son modèle antérieur, *PH5/5* (1927), mais comprenait quatre diffuseurs supplémentaires, ce qui faisait sept au total – d'où son nom. Les abat-jour étaient en verre transparent, qui était en partie dépoli de manière à réduire l'intensité lumineuse. En 1929, une version de couleur ambrée en fut réalisée. (CF/PF)

Plan for the Louis Poulsen stand at the 1929 Exposición Internacional de Barcelona showing the full PH lighting range including the Septima / Aufbauplan für den Stand von Louis Poulsen auf der Weltausstellung in Barcelona von 1929 mit der kompletten von Poul Henningsen entworfenen PH Leuchtenserie, einschließlich der Hängeleuchte Septima / Plan du stand de Louis Poulsen à l'Exposición Internacional de Barcelona, où l'on pouvait voir toute la gamme des luminaires PH créée par Poul Henningsen, y compris la suspension Septima

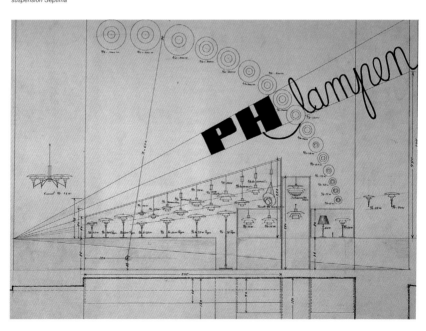

△ *PH Septima* hanging light, 1927–28
Brass mounts with sandblasted glass diffusers,
40 cm (small) or 50 cm (large) diameter /
Montierung aus Messing mit Diffusoren aus
sandgestrahltem Glas, 40 cm (klein) oder
50 cm (groß) Durchmesser / Montures en
laiton, diffuseurs en verre dépoli de 40 cm à
50 cm de diamètre
Louis Poulsen & Co., Copenhagen, Denmark

◁ *Design drawing of the* PH Septima *hanging
light, c.1929–31 / Entwurfszeichnung für die
Hängeleuchte* PH Septima, *ca. 1929–31 /
Dessin de la* PH Septima, *vers 1929–31*

◁ Desk light, 1927

Aluminum shade with Bakelite lever, tubular brass arm with counterbalance weight and upright on stained beech base, 60 cm high / Sockel aus gebeizter Buche, Fuß, Arm und Gegengewicht aus Messing, Lampenschirm aus Aluminium mit Bakelitschalter, 60 cm hoch / Abat-jour en aluminium, levier en bakélite, bras tubulaire à contrepoids et montant en laiton, socle en hêtre teinté, 60 cm de hauteur **Buquet**, Paris, France (reissued by **Tecnolumen**, Bremen, Germany)

▷ Floor light, 1927

Aluminum shade with Bakelite lever, metal arms with counterbalance weights on telescopic metal base, 210 cm high / Aluminiumschirm mit Bakelitschalter, Metallarme mit Ausgleichgewicht auf ausziehbarem Metallfuß, 210 cm hoch / Abat-jour en aluminium à levier en bakélite, bras métalliques à contrepoids, fût métallique téléscopique, 210 cm de hauteur **Buquet**, Paris, France

In 1925 Edouard-Wilfrid Buquet designed an innovative adjustable light, which predated George Carwardine's *Anglepoise* light by some seven years. In 1927 he patented a modified version of this counterbalanced design, which set a new standard for task lighting and became one of the most popular lights of the period. Although the light was exhibited at the 1929 Salon d'Automne in Paris and was widely illustrated in French magazines during the 1930s, it was not until the 1970s that Buquet was finally credited for its design. His floor light is a rare batch-produced variation of his task light. (CF/PF)

Im Jahr 1925 entwarf Edouard-Wilfrid Buquet eine innovative, verstellbare Arbeitsleuchte – gut sieben Jahre bevor George Carwardine seine *Anglepoise* Leuchte entwickelte. 1927 ließ sich Buquet eine modifizierte Version der verwendeten Ausgleichgewichtskonstruktion patentrechtlich schützen. Dieses Modell setzte neue Maßstäbe für die Gestaltung von Arbeitsleuchten und wurde zu einem der beliebtesten Entwürfe der Zeit. Doch obwohl sie 1929 in Paris ausgestellt und in den 1930er Jahren häufig abgebildet wurde, erhielt Buquet erst in den 1970er Jahren die ihm gebührende Anerkennung für seine Gestaltung. Bei der Stehleuchte handelt es sich um eine seltene, in Serie produzierte Variante seiner Arbeitsleuchte. (CF/PF)

En 1925, Edouard-Wilfrid Buquet inventa une lampe réglable d'un type nouveau, devançant George Carwardine et son *Anglepoise* d'environ sept ans. En 1927, il breveta une version modifiée de ce modèle à contrepoids, qui allait révolutionner l'éclairage de travail et devenir l'une des lampes les plus populaires de l'époque. Bien qu'elle fût exposée au Salon d'Automne de Paris en 1929 et abondamment publiée dans les magazines français pendant les années 1930, ce n'est qu'en 1970 que Buquet reçut la reconnaissance qui lui était due en tant que son auteur. Le lampadaire ci-contre en est une variante rare fabriquée en petite série. (CF/PF)

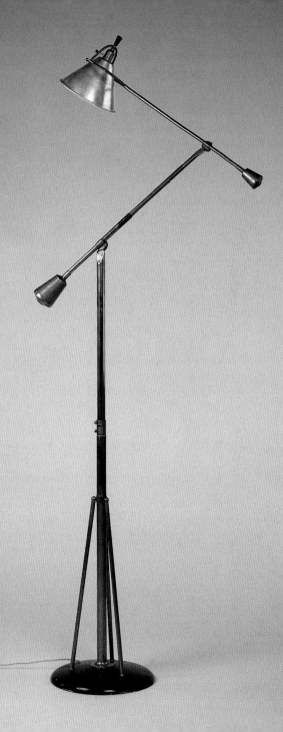

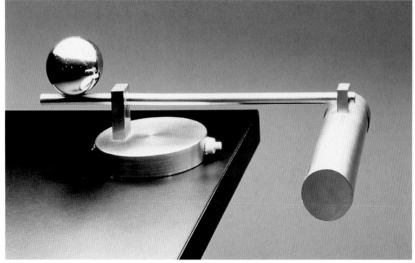

△ Model No. 404 Giso *piano light, 1927 –
this version has a push-button switch and
was produced from 1939 /* Modell Nr. 404
Giso *Klavierleuchte, 1927 – diese Version
hat einen Druckknopfschalter und wurde von
1939 an produziert /* Lampe de piano Modèle
n° 404 Giso *, 1927 cette version est dotée
d'un interrupteur à bouton-poussoir et fut
fabriquée à partir de 1939*

▷ *Photograph from* W. H. Gispen *catalog
showing* Model No. 404 Giso *piano light,
1927 – this version has a black-bronzed
shade /* Abbildung aus dem Katalog von W. H.
Gispen *mit der Klavierleuchte* Modell Nr. 404
Giso, *1927–28 – diese Version hat einen
schwarz-bronzierten Lampenschirm /* Photographie extraite du catalogue de W. H.
Gipsen, *montrant la lampe de piano* Modèle
n° 404 Giso *dans une version à abat-jour en
bronze noirci*

In 1927, in collaboration with Willem Hendrik Gispen, the Dutch architect Jacobus Johannes Pieter Oud designed a prototype piano light whose elemental form revealed the functionalist approach to design promoted by the Bauhaus. A version of this light was given as a wedding present in 1927 to their mutual friend, the painter Harm Kamerlingh Onnes. Without consulting Oud, the following year Gispen began serially producing a modified version of this light. Comprising only six elements, the *404 Giso*, as this later version became known, cantilevered over the edge of the piano in order to optimize the illumination of the sheet music and keyboard below. (CF/PF)

Im Jahr 1927 entwarf der holländische Architekt Jacobus Johannes Pieter Oud in Zusammenarbeit mit Willem Hendrik Gispen den Prototyp einer Klavierleuchte, in deren strenger Formgebung der Einfluss des funktionalen Bauhausdesigns deutlich zu erkennen ist. Eine Version dieser Leuchte wurde 1927 einem gemeinsamen Freund der beiden Designer, dem Maler Harm Kamerlingh Onnes, zur Hochzeit geschenkt. Ohne vorherige Absprache mit Oud begann Gispen im Jahr darauf mit der Serienproduktion eines leicht modifizierten Modells dieser Leuchte. Die aus nur sechs Elementen bestehende *404 Giso*, wie diese spätere Version bezeichnet wurde, ragte über den Rand des Klaviers hinaus, um eine optimale Beleuchtung der Notenblätter und der Tastatur zu erzielen. (CF/PF)

Aux alentours de 1927, l'architecte néerlandais Jacobus Johannes Pieter Oud mit au point, en collaboration avec Willem Hendrik Gispen, un prototype de lampe de piano, dont la forme fonctionnaliste chère au Bauhaus. En 1927, un exemplaire en fut offert en cadeau de mariage à leur ami commun, le peintre Harm Kamerlingh Onnes. L'année suivante, Gispen commença, sans consulter Oud, à la produire en série dans une version modifiée. Baptisée *404 Giso*, cette version plus tardive ne comprenait que six pièces et était placée en porte-à-faux sur le piano de manière à éclairer au mieux la partition et le clavier. (CF/PF)

▽ *Model No. 404 Giso*
piano light, 1927

Nickel-plated and chromed brass base, shade and counterweight, 29.8 cm deep / Fuß, Lampenschirm und Ausgleichgewicht aus vernickeltem und verchromtem Messing, 29,8 cm tief / Socle, abat-jour et contrepoids en laiton nickelé et chromé, 29,8 cm de profondeur
W. H Gispen & Co., Rotterdam, The Netherlands

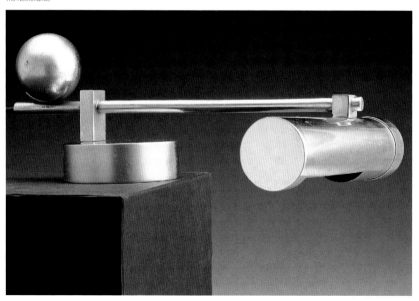

willem hendrik gispen
model no. 312 giso wall light

In 1911 Willem Hendrik Gispen traveled to England, where he was exposed to the idea of "art manufactures". On his return to The Netherlands, he became a member of the Netherland Union of Handicraft & Industrial Art and later in 1916 founded a metalworking company in Rotterdam to produce mainly architectural fittings made of tubular metal. In 1924 the factory embraced mechanization and three years later launched its *Giso* range of lighting. Combining functionalism with geometric purity, these lights were exceptionally avant-garde for their day and went on to become key elements in most Dutch Modernist interiors during the late 1920s and 1930s. (CF/PF)

Im Jahr 1911 unternahm Willem Hendrik Gispen eine Reise nach England, wo er mit der Idee der „fabrikmäßigen Erzeugung von Kunst" in Berührung kam. Nach seiner Rückkehr in die Niederlande wurde er Mitglied der niederländischen Vereinigung für Kunstgewerbe und Handwerk und gründete 1916 eine Metallwarenfabrik in Rotterdam, wo hauptsächlich Möbel und Wohnaccessoires aus Stahlrohr produziert wurden. 1924 wurde die Fabrik umfassend mechanisiert und drei Jahre später die *Giso* Leuchtenserie auf den Markt gebracht. In ihrer Verbindung aus Funktionalismus und geometrischer Klarheit waren diese Leuchten außergewöhnlich fortschrittlich für ihre Zeit und wurden während der späten 1920er und 1930er Jahre zu einem wichtigen Ausstattungselement in den meisten modernen Wohnraumgestaltungen in Holland. (CF/PF)

En 1911, Willem Hendrik Gispen se rendit en Angleterre, où il eut son premier contact avec les « art manufactures » (usines d'art). À son retour aux Pays-Bas, il devint membre de l'Union néerlandaise d'artisanat et d'art industriel, puis, en 1916, il fonda une entreprise de ferronnerie fabriquant surtout les équipements architecturaux en tube de métal. En 1924, l'entreprise fut mécanisée et, trois ans plus tard, elle lança sa gamme de luminaires *Giso*. À la fois fonctionnelles et d'une grande pureté géométrique, ces lampes étaient exceptionnellement avant-gardistes pour l'époque. À la fin des années 1920 et pendant les années 1930 aux Pays-Bas, tout intérieur moderniste digne de ce nom en possédait une. (CF/PF)

△ *Gispen poster advertising* Giso *lights, 1928 / Werbeplakat von Gispen für* Giso *Leuchten, 1928 / Affiche publicitaire pour les lampes* Giso *de Gispen, 1928*

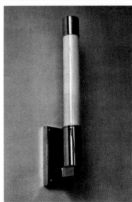

◁ *Model No. 312 Giso wall light, 1929*
Chrome-plated metal mounts with cylindrical bulb, 37.5 cm high / Montierung aus verchromtem Metall mit zylindrischem Leuchtkörper, 37,5 cm hoch / Montures en métal chromé, ampoule cylindrique, 37,5 cm de hauteur
W. H Gispen & Co., Rotterdam, The Netherlands

Model No. 32 Giso suspended ceiling light, 1927

Metal mounts with opalescent glass shade and etched glass disks, 34 cm drop / Montierung aus Metall mit Lampenschirm aus Opalglas und geätzten Glasscheiben, 34 cm lang / Montures métalliques, abat-jour en verre opalescent, disques de verre gravé, 34cm de hauteur
W. H Gispen & Co., Rotterdam, The Netherlands

The remarkable success of the *Giso* lighting range was due to not only Willem Hendrik Gispen's ability to combine industrial production with artistic expression, but equally to his use of bold, eye-catching posters, which helped to advertise his Modernist products. In 1927 Gispen displayed his furniture and lights at the Deutscher Werkbund's *Die Wohnung* exhibition in Stuttgart and received so many orders there that two years later he was able to open a larger factory in Culemborg to mass-produce his designs. (CF/PF)

Der außerordentliche Erfolg der *Giso* Leuchtenkollektion lag nicht nur an der Fähigkeit von Willem Hendrik Gispen, fabrikmäßige Produktionsmethoden mit künstlerischer Ausdruckskraft zu kombinieren, sondern auch an der Verwendung auffallender Werbeplakate, die halfen, seine modernistischen Produkte zu verbreiten. 1927 präsentierte Gispen seine Möbel und Beleuchtungskörper auf der Ausstellung *Die Wohnung* des Deutschen Werkbunds in Stuttgart und erhielt daraufhin so viele Bestellungen, dass er zwei Jahre später eine größere Fabrik in Culemborg für die Massenfertigung seiner Objekte eröffnen konnte. (CF/PF)

Le succès phénoménal de la gamme de luminaires *Giso* s'explique par le talent déployé par Willem Hendrik Gispen pour réconcilier production industrielle et expression artistique, mais il doit aussi beaucoup à ses audacieuses affiches publicitaires, qui vantaient les mérites de ses créations modernistes. En 1927, Gispen participa à l'exposition *Die Wohnung* du Deutscher Werkbund. Il y reçut tellement de commandes que, deux ans plus tard, il ouvrit une usine plus grande à Culemborg où ses modèles étaient fabriqués en grande série. (CF/PF)

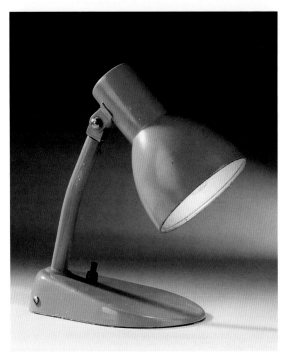

Model No. 702 Kandem table light, 1928

Enameled steel base, adjustable arm and shade, 25 cm high / Fuß, verstellbarer Arm und Lampenschirm aus lackiertem Stahl, 25 cm hoch / Socle, bras et abat-jour réglables en acier émaillé, 25 cm de hauteur
Körting & Mathiesen (Kandem), Leipzig, Germany

▷ **Model No. 756 Kandem desk light, 1927**

Enameled steel base, adjustable arm and shade, 43 cm high (max.) / Fuß, verstellbarer Arm und Lampenschirm aus lackiertem Stahl, 43 cm hoch (max.) / Socle, bras et abat-jour réglables en acier émaillé, 43 cm de hauteur maximale
Körting & Mathiesen (Kandem), Leipzig, Germany

Marianne Brandt, the only woman in the Bauhaus metal workshop, became the school's most successful lighting designer. Her diminutive bedside light (1928), designed in collaboration with Hin Bredendieck, could be easily turned on in the dark with its push-button switch, while its adjustable arm and narrow focus ensured that the light could be efficiently directed so as not to disturb a sleeping partner. Her desk light (1927), again a collaboration with Bredendieck, was also designed to give an even and easily directed light, while its sculptural wedge-like base neatly directed the electric cable to the rear. (CF/PF)

Marianne Brandt, die einzige in der Metallwerkstatt des Bauhauses tätige Frau, wurde zur erfolgreichsten Leuchtendesignerin der Schule. Ihre zusammen mit Hin Bredendieck entworfene kleine Nachttischleuchte (1928) ließ sich mittels Druckknopfschalter bequem im Dunkeln einschalten, während man sie durch ihren verstellbaren Arm und schmalen Lichtstrahl präzise einstellen konnte, so dass ein schlafender Partner nicht durch ihr Licht gestört wurde. Auch ihre ebenfalls mit Bredendieck gestaltete Schreibtischleuchte (1927) war so konstruiert, dass sie ein gleichmäßiges und einfach zu richtendes Licht gab. Durch ihren keilförmig geformten Fuß wurde das Stromkabel nach hinten geführt. (CF/PF)

Seule femme à travailler dans l'atelier de ferronnerie du Bauhaus, Marianne Brandt devint la personnalité la plus en vue de l'école dans le domaine des luminaires. Cette minuscule lampe de chevet (1928), créée en collaboration avec Hin Bredendieck, s'allumait facilement dans l'obscurité grâce à son interrupteur à poussoir. En même temps, son bras réglable et l'étroitesse de son champ lumineux permettaient d'orienter le faisceau de façon à ne pas déranger son compagnon de lit. Autre collaboration avec Bredendick, la lampe de bureau (1927) était elle aussi étudiée de manière à émettre une lumière uniforme et facile à orienter. Le câble électrique était dirigé vers l'arrière grâce au socle triangulaire. (CF/PF)

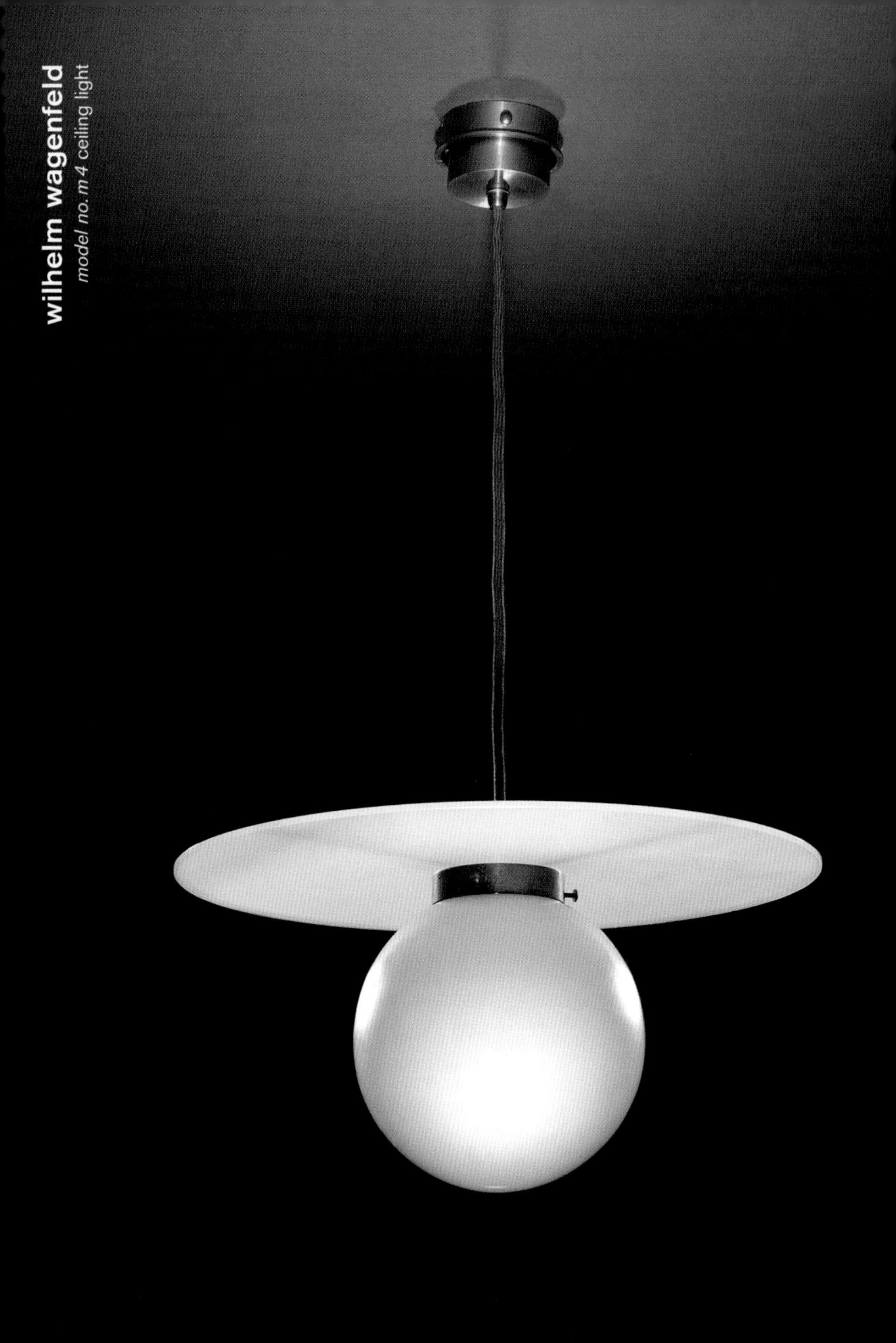

wilhelm wagenfeld

model no. m 4 ceiling light

◁ Model No. M4 ceiling light, c.1926–27

Nickel-plated metal mounts with glass disk and globe shade, 40 cm, 50 cm diameter / Montierung aus vernickeltem Metall mit Glasscheibe und kugelförmigem Lampenschirm aus Glas, 40 cm, 50 cm Durchmesser / Montures en métal nickelé, disque et abat-jour sphérique en verre, 40 cm, 50 cm de diamètre
Staatliche Bauhochschule, Weimar, Germany

Ceiling light for the Werkbund Weissenhofsiedlung exhibition, 1927

Nickel-plated brass mounts with glass shades, 111 cm drop / Montierung aus vernickeltem Messing mit Lampenschirmen aus Glas, 111 cm lang / Montures en laiton nickelé, abat-jour en verre, 111 cm de hauteur
Kunstgewerbeschule Burg Giebichenstein, Halle/Saale, Germany

In 1923 Karl Müller was appointed director of the metal workshop at the Kunstgewerbeschule Burg Giebichenstein. During his tenure, the school became one of the leading German centers for avant-garde metalware production. His ceiling light for the Werkbund's *Weißenhof* exhibition (1927) reflects the Halle school's tempered approach to functionalism, and its embrace of a gentler form of Modernism than the Bauhaus. Wilhelm Wagenfeld's *Model No. M4* ceiling light, in contrast, demonstrates the strictly rational approach to design espoused by the Bauhaus and can be seen to typify the output of the Staatliche Bauhochschule Weimar, which was founded in Weimar after the Bauhaus moved to Dessau. (CF/PF)

Im Jahr 1923 wurde Karl Müller zum neuen Leiter der Metallwerkstatt an der Kunstgewerbeschule Burg Giebichenstein ernannt, die während seiner Amtszeit zu einem der führenden Zentren des deutschen Metallkunsthandwerks wurde. Seine für die vom Deutschen Werkbund organisierte *Weißenhof*-Ausstellung entworfene Deckenleuchte (1927) ist von dem gemäßigten Funktionalismus der Haller Kunstgewerbeschule geprägt, die eine mildere Form des Modernismus propagierte als das Bauhaus. Im Gegensatz dazu demonstriert Wilhelm Wagenfelds Deckenleuchte *M4* (ca. 1926–27) den streng rationalen Designansatz, wie ihn das Bauhaus verfolgte. Damit ist sie ein typisches Produkt der Staatlichen Bauhochschule Weimar. (CF/PF)

En 1923, Karl Müller fut nommé directeur de l'atelier de ferronnerie de la Kunstgewerbeschule Burg Giebichenstein, et dès lors, celle-ci devint l'un des principaux centres de fabrication d'articles métalliques avant-gardistes d'Allemagne. La lampe de plafond (1927) qu'il réalisa pour l'exposition *Weißenhof* du Werkbund reflète le fonctionalisme modéré des arts appliqués de l'École de Halle, plus souple que le Bauhaus dans sa vision du Modernisme. En revanche, le plafonnier *M4* (vers 1926–27) de Wilhelm Wagenfeld, témoigne de l'approche strictement rationnelle associée au Bauhaus et est un bon exemple du type de lampes produit à la Staatliche Bauhochschule Weimar, fondée après le Bauhaus déménagea à Dessau. (CF/PF)

The *Rondella Polo* desk light, designed by Christian Dell in 1928–29, came with an important technical innovation in the form of a ball-and-socket joint. This not only enabled the arm of the lamp to swivel through 360 degrees, but also allowed variations to the vertical angle of inclination. The ball-and-socket joint was used again later in Dell's 1929 *Polo Populär* task light, which, like the *Rondella* (1927–28), had a parabolic reflector as a shade. A similar shade featured in another model manufactured at the same period by Bünte & Remmler of Frankfurt. Dell's influence is unmistakable. (TB)

Die *Rondella Polo* Schreibtischleuchte nach einem Entwurf von Christian Dell aus dem Jahr 1928–29 verfügt als wichtige technische Neuerung über ein Kugelgelenk, das nicht nur ermöglicht, den Leuchtenarm um 360 Grad zu schwenken, sondern auch den vertikalen Neigungswinkel der Leuchte zu verändern. Das Kugelgelenk fand auch bei Dells späterer *Polo Populär* Arbeitsleuchte aus dem Jahr 1929 Verwendung. Wie schon bei der *Rondella* (1927–28) und der *Polo Populär* dient ein paraboloider Reflektor als Lampenschirm. Ein ähnlicher Lampenschirm fand auch bei einem anderen Leuchtenmodell der Frankfurter Firma Bünte & Remmler aus der gleichen Zeit Verwendung. Der Einfluss von Dell ist unverkennbar. (TB)

La lampe de bureau *Rondella Polo*, créée par Christian Dell en 1928–29, était équipée de rotules, ce qui constituait une innovation technique importante. Non seulement elles pouvaient faire pivoter le bras de la lampe à 360°, mais permettaient aussi de varier l'angle d'inclinaison vertical. La rotule fut réutilisée par la suite dans la lampe de travail *Polo Populär*, que Dell créa en 1929 et qui, à l'instar de la *Rondella* de 1927–28, était munie d'un réflecteur en guise de coiffe. Un autre modèle fabriqué à la même époque par Bünte & Remmler de Francfort était doté d'un abat-jour semblable, où l'on reconnaît clairement l'influence de Dell. (TB)

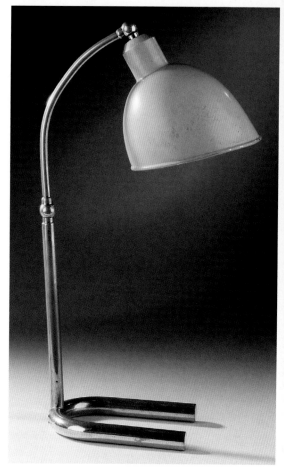

Desk light, c.1929
Chrome-plated tubular metal base and arm with enameled metal shade, 45 cm high / Fuß und Arm aus verchromtem Metallrohr mit Lampenschirm aus lackiertem Metall, 45 cm hoch / Base et bras tubulaires en métal chromé, abat-jour en métal laqué, 45 cm de hauteur
Bünte & Remmler, Frankfurt/Main, Germany

▷ *Rondella Polo* **desk light, 1928–29**
Nickel-plated cast-iron base with nickel-plated brass adjustable arm and nickel-plated copper shade, 33.5 cm high / Fuß aus vernickeltem Gusseisen mit verstellbarem Arm aus vernickeltem Messing und Lampenschirm aus vernickeltem Kupfer, 33,5 cm hoch / Socle en fonte nickelée, bras réglable en laiton nickelé, abat-jour en cuivre nickelé, 33,5 cm de hauteur
Beleuchtungskörperfabrik Rondella GmbH, Oberusel, Germany; later manufactured by Bünte & Remmler, Frankfurt/Main, Germany

christian dell
polo populär desk light

In 1926 Christian Dell, former master of the metal workshop at the Weimar Bauhaus, was appointed director of the newly established metalwork course at the Frankfurt School of Art, a post he held until his dismissal by the Nazis in 1933. In Frankfurt, as well as teaching and practising as a silversmith, he launched his career as a lighting designer. Among his earliest and most successful models were the *Polo Populär* (1929) and *Rondella* (1927–28) desk lights. Both were manufactured first by the Rondella factory at Oberursel and later by Bünte & Remmler in Frankfurt/Main. (TB)

1926 übernahm Christian Dell, der ehemalige Werkmeister der Metallwerkstatt am Bauhaus Weimar, die Leitung der neu gegründeten Metallklasse an der Frankfurter Kunstschule, die er bis zu seiner Entlassung durch die Nationalsozialisten 1933 leitete. Neben seiner pädagogischen Arbeit und der Ausführung von Silbergeräten begann er hier seine Karriere als Entwerfer für Beleuchtungskörper. Zu seinen frühesten und erfolgreichsten Modellen für Beleuchtungskörper zählen die Tischleuchten *Polo Populär* (1929) und *Rondella* (1927–28), die beide zunächst von der Beleuchtungskörperfabrik Rondella in Oberursel und später von der Firma Bünte & Remmler in Frankfurt/Main hergestellt wurden. (TB)

En 1926, Christian Dell, ancien maître artisan à l'atelier de métal du Bauhaus de Weimar, fut nommé directeur de la toute nouvelle section de ferronnerie de l'École d'art de Francfort, poste qu'il garda jusqu'à ce qu'il en fût renvoyé par les Nazis en 1933. En même temps qu'il enseignait et pratiquait le métier d'orfèvre à Francfort, il démarra une carrière de créateur de luminaires. Deux de ses premiers modèles et aussi les plus populaires, sont les lampes de table *Polo Populär* (1929) et *Rondella* (1927–28). Les deux furent fabriquées tout d'abord par l'usine Rondella à Oberursel, puis par Bünte & Remmler à Francfort-sur-le-Main. (TB)

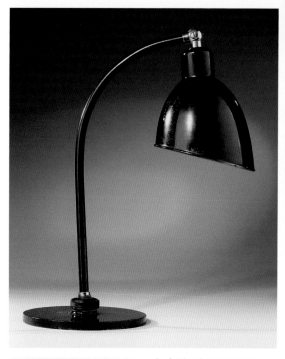

DAS FRANKFURTER REGISTER **1**
„RONDELLA" TISCH- UND STÄNDER- (ATELIER) LAMPE

◁ *Das Frankfurter Register, No. 1, 1928, showing* Rondella *lights designed by* Christian Dell / *Das Frankfurter Register, Nr. 1, 1928, mit Abbildungen der von Christian Dell entworfenen* Rondella *Schreibtisch- und Stehleuchte /* N° 1 de Das Frankfurter Register, *1928, sur lequel sont représentés la lampe de bureau* Rondella *et le lampadaire* Rondella *créés par* Christian Dell

◁ *Polo Populär* **desk light, 1929**

Enameled and nickel-plated metal base, stem
and shade, 40 cm high / Fuß, Arm und Lampenschirm aus lackiertem und vernickeltem Metall,
40 cm hoch / Socle, tige et abat-jour en métal
émaillé et nickelé, 40 cm de hauteur
Beleuchtungskörperfabrik Rondella, Oberusel,
Germany; later manufactured by Bünte &
Remmler, Frankfurt/Main, Germany

Rondella **desk light, 1927–28**

Nickel-plated metal stem and arm with copper
base and enameled metal shade, 54 cm high
(max.) / Fuß aus Kupfer, Schaft und Arm aus
vernickeltem Metall mit Lampenschirm aus
lackiertem Metall, 54 cm hoch (max.) / Tige et
bras en métal nickelé, socle en cuivre, abat-jour
en métal émaillé, 54 cm de hauteur maximale
Beleuchtungskörperfabrik Rondella, Oberusel,
Germany; later manufactured by Bünte &
Remmler, Frankfurt/Main, Germany

The lights designed by Christian Dell in
the 1920s were extremely functional
and highly standardized. Building on his
early experience of modern lighting
design in the Weimar Bauhaus metal
workshop, where between 1922 and
1925 he worked with the workshop's
artistic director László Moholy-Nagy and
students such as Wilhelm Wagenfeld,
Carl Jakob Jucker and Gyula Pap, he
successfully developed a prototype task
light, the *Rondella*. He continued to
make changes and improvements and
to adapt its features for use in a range
of products. The parabolic reflectors
ensuring dazzle-free task lighting were
a hallmark of Dell's early designs. (TB)

Christian Dells Leuchtenentwürfe aus
den 1920er Jahren zeichnen sich durch
extreme Funktionalität und starke Typi-
sierung aus. Aufbauend auf seinen
Erfahrungen in der Metallwerkstatt am
Bauhaus Weimar, wo er zwischen
1922 und 1925 in Zusammenarbeit mit
dem Bauhausmeister László Moholy-
Nagy und einigen Schülern erste Erfahrungen mit dem Entwurf von modernen
Beleuchtungskörpern sammelte, entwickelte Dell den erfolgreichen Grundtyp
der Arbeitsleuchte, die *Rondella*
Arbeitsleuchte, die er später immer
wieder variierte und auf unterschiedliche Anforderungsprofile übertrug. Typisches Merkmal der frühen Leuchtenentwürfe von Dell sind die paraboloiden
Reflektoren, die ein blendfreies Arbeiten ermöglichen. (TB)

Les luminaires créés par Christian Dell
dans les années 1920 étaient extrêmement fonctionnels et très standardisés.
Fort de son expérience acquise au
Bauhaus Weimar où, de 1922 à 1925,
il avait travaillé avec László Moholy-
Nagy, directeur artistique de l'atelier de
ferronnerie, et ses étudiants dont
Wilhelm Wagenfeld, Carl Jakob Jucker
et Gyula Pap, il parvint à mettre au
point un prototype de lampe de travail,
la *Rondella*. Il ne cessa de l'améliorer
et d'en adapter les pièces afin de les
réutiliser dans d'autres modèles.
Comme toutes les lampes que Dell
conçut au début de sa carrière, celle-
ci est équipée de réflecteurs paraboliques permettant d'en adoucir la
luminosité. (TB)

Model No. NT922 table light, 1927

Polished chrome-plated brass base, stem and arm with linen shade, 48 cm high / Fuß, Schaft und Arm aus verchromtem Messing mit Lampenschirm aus Leinen, 48 cm hoch / Socle, tige et bras en laiton chromé et poli, abat-jour en toile, 48 cm de hauteur
Nessen Studio, New York (NY), USA (currently produced by **Nessen Lamps, Mamaroneck** (NY), USA)

In 1927 the German émigré Walter von Nessen established Nessen Studio in New York in order to specialize in the design and manufacture of modern architectural lighting. The same year he developed a completely new lighting feature – the swing arm – leading a contemporary critic to note: "The ingenuity of a German immigrant, Walter von Nessen, has had far-reaching effects on contemporary lamp design." Using innovative soldering techniques and incorporating special screw machined fittings, the arms of von Nessen's elegant lights could be swung round 340 degrees. (CF/PF)

Im Jahr 1927 gründete der deutsche Einwanderer Walter von Nessen das Nessen Studio in New York, um sich auf die Gestaltung und Produktion moderner Beleuchtungskörper zu spezialisieren. Noch im selben Jahr entwickelte er mit dem Schwingarm ein vollkommen neues Leuchtenelement, das einen zeitgenössischen Kritiker zu der Bemerkung veranlasste: „Die Genialität eines deutschen Immigranten, Walter von Nessen, hatte weitreichende Auswirkungen auf das zeitgenössische Lampendesign." Durch innovative Löttechniken und formgedrehte Spezialmontierungen waren die Arme von Nessens eleganten Leuchten um 340 Grad schwenkbar. (CF/PF)

En 1927, l'émigré allemand Walter von Nessen fonda les Ateliers Nessen à New York qui se spécialisaient dans la conception et la réalisation d'éclairage architectural moderne. La même année, il mit au point un tout nouvel accessoire – le bras pivotant, qu'un critique contemporain décrivit en ces termes : « L'ingéniosité de l'immigré allemand Walter von Nessen a laissé sa marque indélébile sur l'éclairage contemporain ». Les pièces des élégantes lampes de von Nessen étaient soudées grâce à de toutes nouvelles techniques, et articulées au moyen d'un système de vis travaillées à la machine. Le bras pouvait pivoter à 340°. (CF/PF)

Model No. NF987 **floor light, 1927**

Chrome-plated brass base, stem and arm with linen shade, 125 – 152.5 cm high / Fuß, Schaft und Arm aus verchromtem Messing mit Lampenschirm aus Leinen, 125 – 152,5 cm hoch / Socle, tige et bras en laiton chromé, abat-jour en toile, 125 à 152,5 cm de hauteur
Nessen Studio, New York (NY), USA (currently produced by **Nessen Lamps, Mamaroneck** (NY), USA)

One of the great trailblazers of American industrial design during the late 1920s and 1930s, Walter von Nessen applied the highly refined manufacturing techniques he had learnt while training in his native Germany to the serial manufacture of stylish lighting products that typified the American Moderne style. These swing-arm designs were among his most commercially successful products, thanks to the fact that they look as good with antiques as with modern furnishings. It is a testament to the timeless appeal of these lights that, 70 years after they were first designed, they remain in production today. (CF/PF)

Einer der großen Pioniere des amerikanischen Industriedesigns, der in Deutschland geborene Walter von Nessen, wandte in den späten 1920er und 1930er Jahren die hoch entwickelten Fertigungstechniken, die er während seiner Ausbildung in Deutschland kennen gelernt hatte, auf die Serienproduktion eleganter Leuchten an, die den amerikanischen Moderne style verkörperten. Diese mit schwenkbarem Arm ausgestatteten Modelle gehörten zu seinen kommerziell erfolgreichsten Entwürfen, was sicher auch daran liegt, dass sie ebenso gut zu modernen Möbeln wie zu Antiquitäten passen. Es zeugt von der zeitlosen Eleganz dieser Leuchten, dass sie 70 Jahre nach ihrem Entwurf immer noch produziert werden. (CF/PF)

Walter von Nessen, l'un des chefs de file de la création industrielle américaine des années 1930, mettait en pratique des techniques de fabrication sophistiquées. Il les avait acquises en se formant, dans son Allemagne natale, à la production en série de luminaires chic caractéristique du Moderne style américain. Ses modèles à bras pivotant remportèrent un vif succès commercial, dû au fait qu'ils s'harmonisaient au mobilier moderne comme aux meubles anciens. Hommage à leur intemporelle séduction soixante-dix ans plus tard, on les fabrique toujours.

walter von nessen
model no. nf 987 floor light

In 1927 Donald Deskey and Philip Vollmer established Deskey-Vollmer Inc. – a studio that concentrated on the design and manufacture of exclusive Art Deco metal furniture and lighting, which was specially commissioned by wealthy clients such as Adam Gimbel (president of Saks Fifth Avenue), Helena Rubinstein and John D. Rockefeller. Both these lights (c.1927–29) reflect Deskey's extraordinary ability to create striking forms that epitomize the Moderne style. His lighting designs from this period are characterized by the bold use of geometry and gleaming metal surfaces. (CF/PF)

Im Jahr 1927 gründeten Donald Deskey und Philip Vollmer die Firma Deskey-Vollmer Inc. – ein Studio, das auf die Gestaltung und Produktion exklusiver Einrichtungsgegenstände und Beleuchtungskörper aus Metall spezialisiert war. Ihre Entwürfe im Stil des Art Déco waren maßgeschneiderte Kunden wie den Präsidenten der Kaufhauskette Saks Fifth Avenue, Adam Gimbel, Helena Rubinstein und John D. Rockefeller. Beide hier vorgestellten Leuchten (ca. 1927–29) offenbaren Deskeys außergewöhnliches Geschick in der Gestaltung eindrucksvoller Formen, die exemplarisch sind für den Moderne style. Seine Leuchtenentwürfe aus dieser Zeit zeichnen sich durch kühne geometrische Linien und glänzende Metalloberflächen aus. (CF/PF)

En 1927, Donald Deskey et Philip Vollmer fondèrent la Deskey-Vollmer Inc. – atelier qui se spécialisait dans la conception et la fabrication de mobilier et de luminaires métalliques de style Art Déco et recevait des commandes de riches clients tels qu'Adam Gimbel (président de Saks Fifth Avenue), Helena Rubinstein et John D. Rockefeller. Chacune de ces deux lampes (vers 1927–29) reflète l'extraordinaire aptitude de Deskey à créer des formes révolutionnaires résumant le Moderne style. Les luminaires qu'il réalisa à cette époque se reconnaissent à leur audace géométrique et à leurs surfaces métalliques miroitantes. (CF/PF)

◁ **Desk light, c.1927–29**
Chrome-plated steel shade and stem on painted wood base, 31.7 cm high / Verchromter Hals und Lampenschirm auf lackiertem Holzsockel, 31,7 cm hoch / Abat-jour et tige en acier chromé, socle en bois peint, 31,7 cm de hauteur
Deskey-Vollmer Inc., New York (NY), USA

▷ **Desk light, c.1927–29**
Nickel-plated metal shade and base, 12.25 cm high / Fuß und Lampenschirm aus vernickeltem Metall, 12,25 cm hoch / Abat-jour et socle en métal nickelé, 12,25 cm de hauteur
Deskey-Vollmer Inc., New York (NY), USA

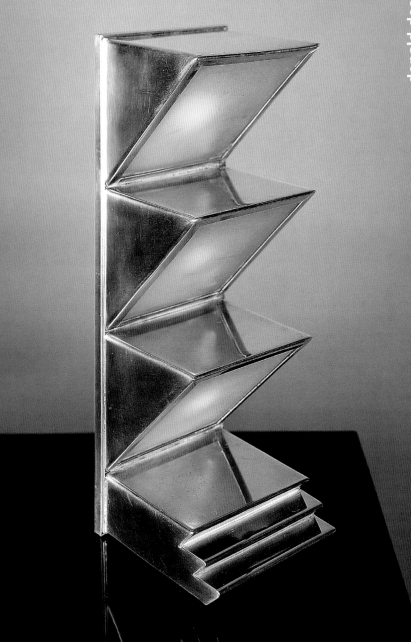

△ Luminator *floor light for the DAF shop, Milan, 1935 /* Luminator *Stehleuchte für das Stoffgeschäft DAF, Mailand, 1935 / Lampadaire* Luminator *pour la boutique DAF à Milan, 1935*

△▷ *Sketch of the Italian Pavilion at the Exposición Internacional de Barcelona showing the* Luminator *floor light, 1929 / Zeichnung vom italienischen Pavillon auf der Weltausstellung in Barcelona mit der* Luminator *Stehleuchte, 1929 / Croquis pour le Pavillon italien de l'Exposición Internacional de Barcelona sur lequel on peut voir le lampadaire* Luminator, *1929*

▷ **Luminator** floor light, 1929
Chrome-plated metal pillar with enameled tubular metal rotating arm and glass shade, 184 cm high / Säule aus verchromtem Metall mit drehbarem Arm aus lackiertem Metallrohr und Lampenschirm aus Glas, 184 cm hoch / Fût en métal chromé, bras tubulaire pivotant en métal laqué, abat-jour en verre, 184 cm de hauteur
Luciano Baldessari, Trento, Italy (reissued by Luceplan, Milan, Italy)

Inspired by experimental German design, the Futurist artist-cum-architect Luciano Baldessari conceived his *Luminator* floor light (1929) as an abstraction of an "illuminated mannequin" with the curved tubular metal section representing the arms. Initially designed for the Italian Pavilion at the 1929 Exposición Internacional de Barcelona, the *Luminator* was one of the few Rationalist lighting designs put into production in Italy during the late 1920s and 1930s. A variation of the light with integral wood plinths was designed in 1935 for the DAF textile shop in Milan. (CF/PF)

Inspiriert vom experimentellen deutschen Design gestaltete der zu den Futuristen zählende Künstler und Architekt Luciano Baldessari seine Stehleuchte *Luminator* (1929) als abstrahierte Darstellung einer „beleuchteten Schaufensterpuppe" mit geschwungenen Metallrohrelementen als Arme. Die für den italienischen Pavillon auf der Weltausstellung in Barcelona von 1929 entworfene *Luminator* Leuchte war einer der wenigen Leuchtendesigns des „Rationalismus", der in Italien in der Zeit der späten 1920er und 1930er Jahre umgesetzt wurde. Eine Variante der Leuchte, die mit einer Sockelplatte aus Holz ausgestattet war, wurde 1935 für das Mailänder Stoffgeschäft DAF entworfen. (CF/PF)

S'inspirant du design expérimental allemand, l'artiste/architecte futuriste Luciano Baldessari voyait son lampadaire *Luminator* (1929) comme un « mannequin lumineux » stylisé, dont les tubes courbés en métal représentaient les bras. Conçu au départ pour le Pavillon italien de l'Exposición Internacional de Barcelona de 1929, le *Luminator* est l'un des rares modèles rationalistes à avoir été fabriqué en Italie à la fin des années 1920 et pendant les années 1930. Une variante dotée d'un socle en bois d'une seule pièce en fut réalisée en 1935 pour la boutique de textile DAF à Milan. (CF/PF)

◁ **Desk light, c.1930**

Bakelite and wood base with aluminum shade,
28 cm high / Fuß aus Bakelit und Holz mit
Lampenschirm aus Aluminium, 28 cm hoch /
Socle en bakélite et bois, abat-jour en alu-
minium, 28 cm de hauteur
France

Wall lights, c.1930

Aluminum constructions, 18.4 cm high /
Aluminiumkonstruktionen, 18,4 cm hoch /
Strcutures en aluminium, 18,4 cm de hauteur
France

Jacques Le Chevalier proved himself
adept at creating light fittings in a very
particular vein. He was a functionalist
working in the new Modernist ethic,
seemingly aware of the ideas emanating
from the Bauhaus and conscious of the
work of other French avant-garde innovators. He used materials associated
with industrial rather than domestic
design – Bakelite and aluminum. Yet,
typically French, he was evidently concerned as much with issues of style as
of function, and he created a range of
lights that are a chic interpretation of a
mechanistic esthetic. (PG)

Das Talent von Jaques Le Chevalier lag
darin, einen ganz speziellen Typus von
Beleuchtungskörpern zu kreieren: Auf
der einen Seite war er ein Funktionalist,
der seine Entwürfe mit der neuen
modernistischen Ethik und im Bewusstsein sowohl der Ideen des Bauhauses
als auch der Arbeiten anderer französi-
scher Avantgarde-Gestalter schuf.
Dabei verwendete er Materialien, die
eher dem industriellen als dem häuslichen Design zugeordnet werden –
Bakelit und Aluminium. Auf der anderen Seite jedoch setzte er sich – was
vielleicht typisch französisch ist – offensichtlich ebenso intensiv mit Fragen
des Stils wie mit Fragen der Funktion
auseinander und entwarf eine Reihe von
Leuchten, die man als stilvolle Interpretation einer mechanistischen Ästhetik
ansehen kann. (PG)

Les luminaires créés par Le Chevalier
avaient un style particulier. Fonctionnaliste dans l'âme, il travaillait dans
l'esprit tout nouveau du Modernisme,
et semblait réceptif aux idées émanant
du Bauhaus ainsi qu'à celles d'autres
créateurs avant-gardistes français. Les
matériaux qu'il utilisait – la bakélite et
l'aluminium – étaient alors davantage
associés à l'industrie qu'à la décoration
intérieure. Pourtant, en bon Français,
il s'intéressait au style autant qu'à la
fonction, et créa toute une série de
lampes qui s'inspiraient d'une esthétique industrielle tout en restant élégantes. (PG)

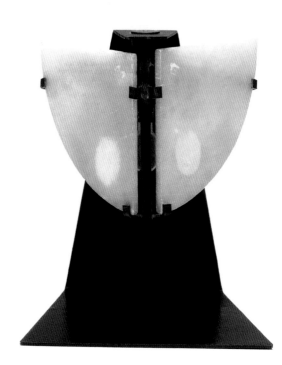

"Only new images excite our emotions!"

„Nur neue Erscheinungs-formen reizen unsere Emotionen!"

«Seules les nouvelles images suscitent chez nous des émotions!»

– Pierre Chareau

Model No. LP180 table light, c.1930
Wrought iron base with alabaster diffusers, 29.2 cm high / Fuß aus Schmiedeeisen mit Alabaster-Diffusoren, 29,2 cm hoch / Socle en fer forgé, plaques d'albâtre, 29,2 cm de hauteur
France

▷ **Model No. LA550 wall appliques, 1930s**
Metal mounts with alabaster diffusers, 35.5 cm high / Montierungen aus Schmiedeeisen mit Alabaster-Diffusoren, 35,5 cm hoch / Armatures en métal, abat-jour en albâtre, 35,5 cm de hauteur
France

Having started his career as a draughtsman, Pierre Chareau went on to become one of the most important architects and designers of the first half of the twentieth century. He exhibited at the salon of the Société des artistes décorateurs and was a major patron of modern avant-garde art of the period. In the late 1920s Chareau shifted his style from a decorative mode, similar to his contemporaries of the period such as Ruhlmann, Gray and Mallet-Stevens, to a more "machine-age" and modernist language, as these Cubist-inspired alabaster lights demonstrate. (AP)

Pierre Chareau wurde im Lauf seiner als technischer Zeichner begonnenen Laufbahn zu einem der bedeutendsten Architekten und Designer der ersten Hälfte des 20. Jahrhunderts. Er beteiligte sich an den Ausstellungen der Société des artistes décorateurs und war ein wichtiger Förderer der künstlerischen Avantgarde seiner Zeit. Gegen Ende der 1920er Jahre wandelte sich sein dekorativer Stil, der dem seiner Zeitgenossen wie Ruhlmann, Gray und Mallet-Stevens glich, zu einer eher dem „Maschinenzeitalter" entsprechenden, modernistischen Formensprache, wie es diese vom Kubismus inspirierten Alabaster-Leuchten (ca. 1930) demonstrieren. (AP)

Après des débuts de dessinateur, Pierre Chareau devint l'un des architectes et créateurs les plus importants de la première moitié du vingtième siècle. Il exposait ses œuvres au Salon de la Société des artistes décorateurs et était l'un des principaux défenseurs de l'art avant-gardiste de l'époque. À la fin des années 1920, il abandonna son style orné, semblable à celui de ses contemporains Ruhlmann, Gray et Mallet-Stevens, au profit d'un langage plus moderniste et plus «industriel», comme le montrent ces lampes en albâtre d'inspiration cubiste. (AP)

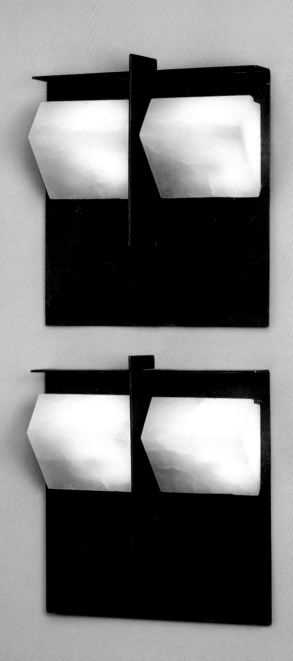

A masterpiece of modern 1930s design, this table light bears a strong resemblance to the architectural works that were beginning to take the world by storm. From 1928 Louis Sognot worked closely with Charlotte Alix and together the pair did some of their most famous work for the Maharaja of Indore. The Maharaja's palace, designed by the German-born architect Eckart Muthesius, housed furnishings by some of the most important designers of the day and included a spectacular dressing table and swivel chair in the Maharani's bedroom and the Maharaja's own bed, all created by the French duo. (AP)

Diese Tischleuchte, ein Meisterwerk des modernen 30er-Jahre-Designs, hat große Ähnlichkeit mit Architekturformen, die die Welt im Sturm zu erobern begannen. Ab 1928 arbeitete Louis Sognot eng mit Charlotte Alix zusammen. Gemeinsam schufen sie einige ihrer berühmtesten Entwürfe für den Maharadscha von Indore. Der von dem in Deutschland geborenen Architekten Eckart Muthesius gestaltete Palast enthielt Möbel von einigen der wichtigsten Designer jener Zeit, darunter auch einen Toilettentisch und einen Drehstuhl im Schlafzimmer der Maharani sowie das Bett des Maharadscha, die von dem französischen Künstlerpaar Sognot und Alix entworfen wurden. (AP)

Véritable chef-d'œuvre moderniste des années 1930, cette lampe de table évoque le style architectural qui commençait à faire fureur à l'époque. À partir de 1928, Louis Sognot travailla en étroit partenariat avec Charlotte Alix. Certaines de leurs œuvres les plus célèbres furent créées pour le Maharadjah d'Indore. Le palais de ce dernier avait été construit par Eckart Muthesius, architecte d'origine allemande, et les meubles étaient signés des plus grands créateurs du moment. La spectaculaire coiffeuse et le fauteuil pivotant qui se trouvaient dans la chambre de la Maharani, ainsi que le lit du Maharadjah, étaient dûs aux deux Français. (AP)

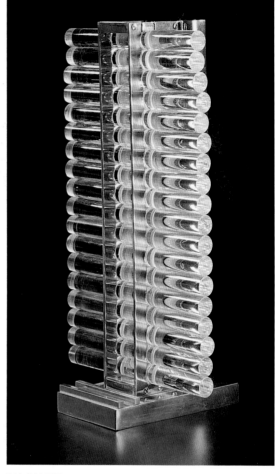

Table light, 1930s

Nickel-plated metal base with glass rod reflectors, 39.5 cm high / Fuß aus vernickeltem Metall mit Reflektoren aus Glasstäben, 39,5 cm hoch / Socle en métal nickelé, réflecteurs en tiges de verre, 39,5 cm de hauteur
France

Established in 1927, La Maison Desny collaborated with numerous avantgarde designers and decorators such as Alberto and Diego Giacometti, Djo-Bourgeois, Jean-Michel Frank and the architect Robert Mallet-Stevens, with whom the firm was closely associated on several interiors and designs. This chromed metal and stacked square glass table light (c.1935) concealed the naked bulbs to produce a gentle glow, while at the same time sending a strong avant-garde message. Most Desny items bear the impressed signature "Desny Paris Made in France déposé." Some, however, show variations of this or are unsigned. (AP)

Die im Jahr 1927 gegründete Firma La Maison Desny arbeitete mit zahlreichen fortschrittlichen Designern und Innenarchitekten zusammen, wie etwa Alberto und Diego Giacometti, Djo-Bourgeois, Jean-Michel Frank und dem Architekten Robert Mallet-Stevens, mit dem gemeinsam das Unternehmen etliche Interieurs und Wohnaccessoires schuf. Diese Tischleuchte aus verchromtem Metall und übereinander angeordneten, quadratischen Glasscheiben (ca. 1935) verbarg die nackten Glühbirnen, um ein weiches und warmes Licht auszustrahlen, und war gleichzeitig ein überzeugendes Plädoyer für Avantgarde-Design. Die meisten Objekte von Desny tragen den Prägestempel „Desny Paris Made in France déposé". Allerdings gibt es auch einige Objekte mit differierendem Stempel oder ohne Bezeichnung. (AP)

Fondée en 1927, La Maison Desny travaillait avec de nombreux créateurs et décorateurs avant-gardistes, dont Alberto et Diego Giacometti, Djo-Bourgeois, Jean-Michel Frank et l'architecte Robert Mallet-Stevens. L'entreprise réalisa avec ce dernier plusieurs objets et intérieurs. Les ampoules de cette lampe de table carrée en verre et métal chromé (vers 1935) étaient cachées de manière à émettre une lumière douce, tout en arborant un style résolument avant-gardiste. La plupart des objets Desny portent l'inscription « Desny Paris Made in France déposé » en guise de signature. On en trouve toutefois des variantes et certains objets ne sont pas signés. (AP)

la maison desny
table lights

△△ Circular version of chromed metal and glass table light by La Maison Desny, c.1935 / Runde Version der Leuchte aus Metall und Glas von La Maison Desny, ca. 1935 / Version circulaire de la lampe en métal chromé et verre fabriquée par La Maison Desny, vers 1935

△ **Table light,** *c.***1935**
Chrome-plated metal base with glass diffusers, 16.7 cm high / Fuß aus verchromtem Metall mit Glasdiffusoren, 16,7 cm hoch / Socle en métal chromé, diffuseurs en verre, 16,7 cm de hauteur
La Maison Desny, Paris, France

Model No. 66 Giso hanging light, 1931

Gilt metal mounts with opalescent glass globe
and etched glass rings, 30 cm diameter /
Montierung aus vergoldetem Metall mit Opal-
glaskugel und geätzten Glasringen, 30 cm
Durchmesser / Montures en métal doré, globe
en verre opalescent, anneaux en verre gravé,
30 cm de diamètre
W. H. Gispen & Co., Rotterdam,
The Netherlands

As one of the foremost proponents of
the Dutch avant-garde, Willem Hendrik
Gispen was involved in the great
functionalism-versus-formalism debate.
In his own work, however, he skillfully
managed to reconcile both approaches
and in so doing exerted much influence
both at home and abroad. With its bold
outline, Gispen's Model No. 66 hanging light (1931) also reflects the strong
graphic quality so characteristic of
Dutch design. Very often Gispen would
modify his designs over a period of
time – Model No. 66, for example, can
be seen as an evolution of his earlier
Model No. 32 hanging light, which was
designed in 1927. (CF/PF)

Als einer der führenden Vertreter der
holländischen Avantgarde war Willem
Hendrik Gispen auch an der großen
Debatte zum Thema „Funktionalismus
kontra Formalismus" beteiligt. In seiner
eigenen Arbeit gelang es ihm jedoch,
beide Konzepte auf geschickte Weise
miteinander zu verbinden, womit er sowohl in seinem Land als auch international einen stilbildenden Einfluss aus-
übte. Mit ihren markanten Umrisslinien
ist Gispens Hängeleuchte Modell Nr.
66 (1931) auch ein gutes Beispiel für
die grafische Qualität, die so charakteristisch für das holländische Design ist.
Da Gispen häufig seine Entwürfe im
Laufe der Zeit veränderte, lässt sich
Modell Nr. 66 als eine Fortentwicklung
seiner früheren Hängeleuchte Modell
Nr. 32 aus dem Jahr 1927 sehen.
(CF/PF)

Figure de proue de l'avant-garde
néerlandaise, Willem Hendrik Gispen
prenait part au débat virulent qui
opposait les partisans du fonctionnalisme à ceux du formalisme. Son
œuvre, en revanche, réconciliait avec
bonheur les deux approches, et était
de ce fait fort imitée, aux Pays-Bas
comme à l'étranger. La forme auda-
cieuse de sa suspension Modèle n° 66
(1931) est typique du style très graphique qui était alors en vogue aux
Pays-Bas. Gispen modifiait très souvent ses modèles après un laps de
temps – le Modèle n° 66, par exemple,
semble découler de sa suspension
Modèle n° 32, créée en 1927. (CF/PF)

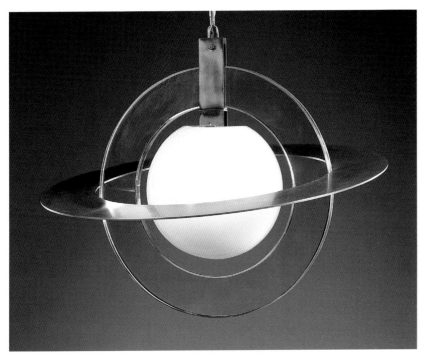

Saturn hanging light, c.1930

Metal mounts with white glass shade held within glass and nickel-plated rings, 56.75 cm diameter / Montierung aus Metall mit Lampenschirm aus Opalglas, umgeben von zwei Ringen aus Glas bzw. vernickeltem Metall, 56,75 cm Durchmesser / Montures métalliques, abat-jour en verre blanc enchâssé dans des anneaux en verre et métal nickelé, 56,75 cm de diamètre DIM (Décoration Intérieure Moderne), Paris, France

René Joubert and Georges Mouveau founded the Parisian interior design company DIM (Décoration Intérieure Moderne) in 1914. In 1923 Pierre Petite joined the firm, which had its own workshop specializing in the production of fine quality furniture, textiles and light fixtures. Apart from lights designed by Joubert and Petite, the company also manufactured lighting by other notable designers including Jacques Le Chevalier, Gabriel Guévrékian, Jean Prouvé, Jean Lesage and Daniel Stéphan. The *Saturn* hanging light (c.1930) displays the strong stylistic influence of the Modern Movement on DIM. (CF/PF)

René Joubert und Georges Mouveau gründeten 1914 die Pariser Firma für Inneneinrichtung DIM (Décoration Intérieure Moderne). 1923 trat Pierre Petite in das Unternehmen ein, das eigene auf die Produktion hochwertiger Möbel, Textilien und Beleuchtungskörper spezialisierte Werkstätten hatte. Neben den von Joubert und Petite entworfenen Leuchten stellte die Firma auch Beleuchtungskörper von anderen bekannten Designern her, wie etwa Jacques Le Chevalier, Gabriel Guévrékian, Jean Prouvé, Jean Lesage und Daniel Stéphane. Die Hängeleuchte *Saturn* (ca. 1930) offenbart den starken Einfluss, den der Stil der Moderne auf die Gestalter von DIM hatte. (CF/PF)

En 1914, René Joubert et Georges Moureau fondèrent l'entreprise parisienne DIM (Décoration Intérieure Moderne). En 1923, ils furent rejoints par Pierre Petite. L'entreprise avait alors son propre atelier spécialisé dans la fabrication de meubles, de textiles et de luminaires de haute qualité. En plus des lampes créées par Joubert et Petite, elle fabriquait aussi des luminaires dessinés par d'autres créateurs connus, tels que Jacques Le Chevalier, Gabriel Guévrékian, Jean Prouvé, Jean Lesage et Daniel Stéphan. La suspension *Saturne* montre combien l'entreprise DIM était influencée par le Mouvement Moderne. (CF/PF)

Table light, 1930s

Nickel-plated metal ring stand with spherical nickel-plated metal shade, 25 cm high / Ringförmiger Fuß mit kugelförmigem Lampenschirm aus vernickeltem Metall, 25 cm hoch / Abatjour sphérique en métal nickelé sur un socle en anneau de métal nickelé, 25 cm de hauteur
Damon, Paris, France

Wall light, 1930s

Nickel-plated metal mounts and arm with nickel-plated metal shade, 31.5 cm high / Montierung, Arm und Lampenschirm aus vernickeltem Metall, 31,5 cm hoch / Platine de fixation, bras et coiffe en métal nickelé, 31,5 cm de hauteur
La Maison Desny, Paris, France

▷ **Floor light, c.1930**

Nickel-plated metal base, stem and adjustable shade, 204 cm high / Fuß, Schaft und verstellbarer Lampenschirm aus vernickeltem Metall, 204 cm hoch / Socle, fût et abat-jour réglable en métal nickelé, 204 cm de hauteur
La Maison Desny, Paris, France

As is the case with La Maison Desny, little is known of the history of Damon. Echoing the shape of the popular vases and planters used by many decorators at the time, this spherical table light (c.1930s) with its Cyclops-like "eye" could be revolved on its hoop stand to illuminate a specific area as required. Damon and Desny were pioneers in completely eliminating fashionable materials such as parchment and wood from their designs and creating instead ultra-modern, sleek pieces in either chromed or nickel-plated metal. (AP)

Wie im Fall von La Maison Desny weiß man nur wenig über die Geschichte der Firma Damon. Die kugelförmige Tischleuchte (1930er Jahre) mit ihrem zyklopenartigen „Auge", die an Vasenformen erinnert, die zu jener Zeit bei vielen Innenraumgestaltern beliebt waren, ließ sich auf ihrem Reifenfuß beliebig drehen, um einen gewünschten Bereich gezielt zu beleuchten. Damon und Desny waren die ersten Leuchtendesigner, die völlig auf edle Werkstoffe wie Pergament und Holz verzichteten und stattdessen hypermoderne, raffinierte Leuchten aus verchromtem oder vernickeltem Metall herstellten. (AP)

On ignore pratiquement tout de l'histoire de Damon, comme de celle de La Maison Desny. Cette lampe de table (années 1930), dont la forme sphérique rappelle les vases et jardinières en vogue à l'époque, évoquait l'œil d'un cyclope et pouvait pivoter sur son socle circulaire de manière à éclairer telle ou telle partie de la pièce. Damon et Desny furent parmi les premiers à ne pas utiliser le parchemin, le bois, ou autres matières à la mode dans leurs modèles. Fabriqués en métal chromé ou nickelé, ceux-ci étaient lisses et ultra-modernes. (AP)

The Modernist architectural form evident in this floor light (*c.*1930) is typical of the work of La Maison Desny. It has an adjustable shade so that light can either be directed upward, thus creating an uplighter, or downward, to cast a pool of light into the room. This model was illustrated in numerous avant-garde journals, including *Art et Décoration* (March 1931), as a fine example of a Desny design, one that was to be highly appreciated and noted for its geometry and architectural proportions. (AP)

Die dem Modernismus entsprechende architektonische Form dieser Stehleuchte (ca. 1930) ist charakteristisch für die Arbeit von La Maison Desny. Die Leuchte ist mit einem verstellbaren Lampenschirm ausgestattet, so dass man das Licht entweder wie bei einem Deckenfluter nach oben richten konnte oder nach unten in den Raum. Die Leuchte war in zahlreichen tonangebenden Zeitschriften abgebildet, so etwa im März 1931 in *Art et Décoration*, und ist ein Beispiel für die ausgezeichneten Entwürfe von Desny, die sehr geschätzt und für ihre geometrischen Formen und architektonischen Proportionen berühmt wurden. (AP)

Clairement influencé par l'architecture moderniste, ce lampadaire (vers 1930) est typique du style de La Maison Desny. Son abat-jour réglable pouvait être orienté soit vers le plafond de manière à créer un éclairage indirect, soit vers le bas si l'on voulait illuminer directement la pièce. Ce modèle fut publié dans de nombreuses revues d'avant-garde, dont *Art et Décoration* (mars 1931), pour illustrer le style Desny. Il était très remarqué et fort apprécié pour ses formes géométriques et ses proportions architecturales. (AP)

la maison desny
floor light

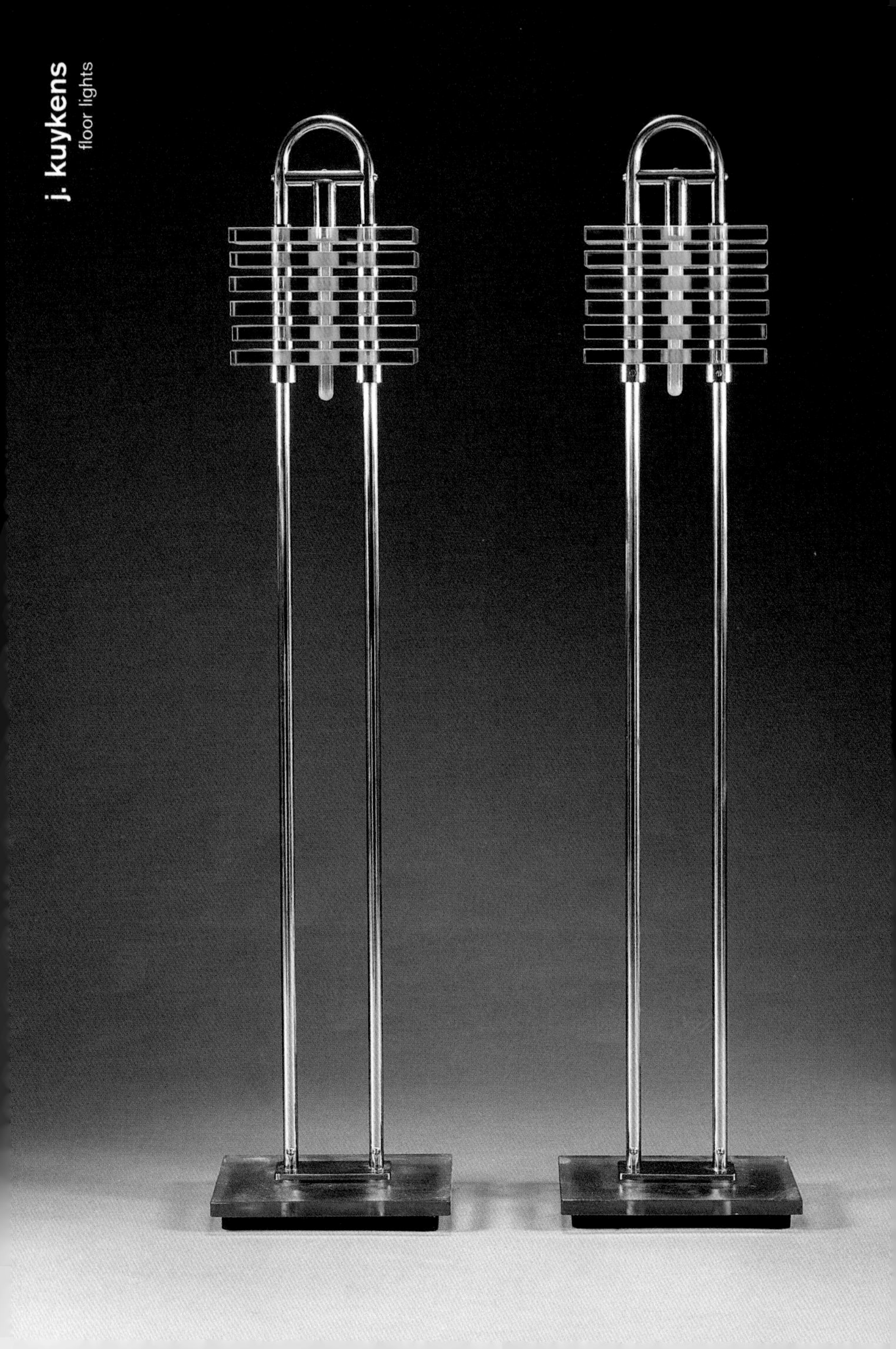

j. kuykens
floor lights

◁ **Floor lights** *c.*1930

Glass base and chrome-plated tubular metal stem with glass diffusers, 175.9 cm high / Sockel aus Glas mit Montierung aus verchromtem Stahlrohr und Diffusoren aus Glas, 175,9 cm hoch / Socle en verre, tige tubulaire en métal chromé, diffuseurs en verre, 175,9 cm de hauteur
The Netherlands

Table light, *c.*1930

Chrome-plated metal base with glass diffusers, 17 cm high / Fuß aus verchromtem Metall mit Diffusoren aus Glas, 17 cm hoch / Base en métal chromé, diffuseurs en verre, 17 cm de hauteur
La Maison Desny, Paris, France

J. Kuykens's floor light (*c.*1930), with its beautiful vertical shape and horizontal layers of frosted glass, echoes the work of modern architects of the period such as Robert Mallet-Stevens. In keeping with the fashionably atmospheric interiors of the day, this striking design did not dazzle the occupier but instead created warm tones to soothe and relax. The elegant Desny table light (*c.*1930) also echoes the architectural style of 1930s Modernists such as Pierre Chareau and his Maison de Verre. Indeed, this light can be seen illustrated in architectural journals, appearing in the most avant-garde interiors of the day. (AP)

In J. Kuykens Stehleuchte (ca. 1930) klingt mit ihrer schönen, vertikalen Form und den horizontalen Mattglasscheiben die Arbeit moderner Architekten der damaligen Zeit an, wie etwa Robert Mallet-Stevens. Im Einklang mit der modisch eleganten Atmosphäre damaliger Innenraumgestaltungen gab diese ungewöhnliche Leuchte kein blendend helles, sondern ein warmes Licht, das beruhigend und entspannend wirkte. Auch die geschmackvolle Tischleuchte (ca. 1930) von Desny bezieht sich auf den architektonischen Stil der Moderne der 1930er Jahre, etwa auf Pierre Chareaus Maison de Verre. Tatsächlich war diese Leuchte in Architekturzeitschriften zusammen mit den avantgardistischsten Interieurs ihrer Zeit abgebildet. (AP)

Avec sa superbe forme élancée et ses strates de verre dépoli, ce lampadaire de J. Kuykens (vers 1930) rappelle l'œuvre d'architectes modernes de l'époque tels que Robert Mallet-Stevens. Loin d'éblouir, il émettait une chaude lumière apaisante qui s'intégrait parfaitement aux intérieurs feutrés alors en vogue. Quant à l'élégante lampe de table signée Desny (vers 1930), elle rappelle aussi l'architecture moderniste des années 1930, en particulier Pierre Chareau et sa Maison de Verre. On la trouve d'ailleurs dans les revues d'architecture de l'époque, associée aux intérieurs les plus avant-gardistes. (AP)

Born in Bruck (now in Slovakia), Jean Perzel initially worked as a glass painter in Munich. In 1910 he moved to Paris where he continued painting glass for various workshops including Gruber. In 1923 he began specializing in the design of lighting for modern-style interiors. He showed his light designs at the Salon d'Automne exhibitions from 1924 and in 1928 won first prize in the Concours d'Éclairage, which was part of the salon of the Société des Décorateurs exhibition. In the 1930s he began designing lighting products, such as these two elegant models, which were intended to reduce glare. (CF/PF)

Der in Bruck (in der heutigen Slowakei) geborene Jean Perzel begann seine Karriere als Glasmaler in München. 1910 zog er nach Paris, wo er weiter als Glasmaler für verschiedene Werkstätten wie die Kunstglaswerstätte Gruber tätig war. Im Jahr 1923 begann er sich auf Leuchtenentwürfe für Innenraumgestaltungen im Modern Style zu spezialisieren. Ab 1924 stellte er seine Entwürfe im Salon d'Automne aus und erhielt 1928 den ersten Preis des Concours d'Eclairage, der Teil des Salon der Société des Décorateurs war. In den 1930er Jahren entwarf er Beleuchtungskörper, die wie diese beiden eleganten Modelle (ca. 1930) so konzipiert waren, dass sie das Blendlicht reduzierten. (CF/PF)

Né à Bruck (aujourd'hui en Slovaquie), Jean Perzel travailla à ses débuts à Munich en tant que peintre sur verre. En 1910, il s'établit à Paris, où il continua à peindre le verre pour plusieurs ateliers, y compris celui de Gruber. En 1923, il commença à se spécialiser dans la création de luminaires destinés à des intérieurs de style moderne. Il exposa ses modèles au Salon d'Automne de 1924 et, en 1928, gagna le premier prix du Concours d'éclairage, qui était organisé dans le cadre du Salon de la Société des Décorateurs. En 1930, il se mit à réaliser des luminaires, dont ces deux élégants modèles, conçus de manière à éviter l'éblouissements. (CF/PF)

Floor light, 1930s

Gilt metal base and shade with vellum-covered shaft terminating in two glass rings, 181,6 cm high / Fuß und Lampenschirm aus vergoldetem Metall, Schaft mit Pergamentverkleidung und zwei Glasringen am oberen Ende, 181,6 cm hoch / Base et abat-jour en métal doré, mât recouvert de vélin et couronné de deux anneaux de verre, 181,6 cm de hauteur
Jean Perzel Luminaires, Paris, France

△ **Model No. 354 ceiling light, c.1930**
Nickel-plated metal mounts with glass panels,
19.75 cm drop / Montierung aus vernickeltem
Metall mit Glasdiffusoren, 19,75 cm lang /
Montures en métal nickelé, plaques de verre,
19,75 cm de hauteur
Jean Perzel Luminaires, Paris, France

▽ *Pages from a Jean Perzel catalog, c.1936 /
Zwei Seiten aus einem Katalog von Jean
Perzel, ca. 1936 / Pages d'un catalogue de
Jean Perzel, vers 1936*

PLAFONNIER Nº 355   JEAN PERZEL   PLAFONNIER Nº 612   JEAN PERZEL

jean perzel

This chic Modernist *torchère* epitomizes the remarkable design output of the Paris-based lighting maestro, Jean Perzel. He was extremely concerned to create designs that would provide a level of light emission that was pleasing to the eye. In order to do this he approached lighting design from an almost scientific perspective and used high-grade white optical glass that was diamond-cut in his own workshops. This floor light (1930s) provides a soft indirect light upward, while at the same time also radiates a gently diffused light downward. (CF/PF)

Der modisch-elegante Deckenfluter verkörpert die eindrucksvolle Entwurfsarbeit des in Paris ansässigen Meisters Jean Perzel. Ihm war besonders wichtig, Beleuchtungskörper zu entwerfen, deren Lichtstrahlung angenehm für das Auge ist. Zu diesem Zweck verfolgte er eine beinahe wissenschaftliche Arbeitsmethode und setzte hochwertiges Opalglas ein, das in seinen eigenen Werkstätten mit dem Diamantschneider bearbeitet wurde. Die Stehleuchte (1930er Jahre) wirft ein weiches, indirektes Licht nach oben, während sie gleichzeitig ein sanftes Streulicht nach unten abstrahlt. (CF/PF)

Cette élégante torchère de style moderniste illustre parfaitement l'œuvre admirable de Jean Perzel, grand virtuose parisien de l'éclairage. Sa grande préoccupation était de créer des modèles capables d'émettre une lumière qui fût agréable pour les yeux. Sa méthode était quasi scientifique : il employait du verre de première qualité qu'il faisait tailler à la manière d'un diamant dans ses propres ateliers. Ce lampadaire (années 1930) illuminait le plafond d'une douce lumière indirecte, tandis qu'une lueur tamisée baignait le reste de la pièce. (CF/PF)

▷ *Model No. 41* floor light, 1930s
Gilt metal base with gilt metal and frosted glass shade, 170.2 cm high / Fuß aus vergoldetem Metall mit Lampenschirm aus vergoldetem Metall und Mattglas, 170,2 cm hoch / Socle en métal émaillé, abat-jour en métal doré et verre dépoli, 170,2 cm de hauteur
Jean Perzel Luminaires, Paris, France

◁ *Contemporary display showing various lights and an illuminated table designed by Jean Perzel, 1930s / Ausstellungsraum mit verschiedenen Leuchten sowie einem beleuchteten Tisch nach Entwurf von Jean Perzel, ca. 1935 / Exposition d'époque présentant divers luminaires conçus par Jean Perzel ainsi qu'une table lumineuse*

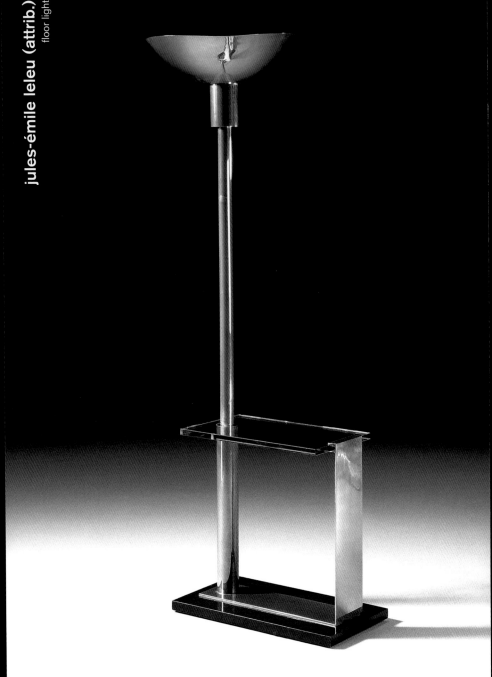

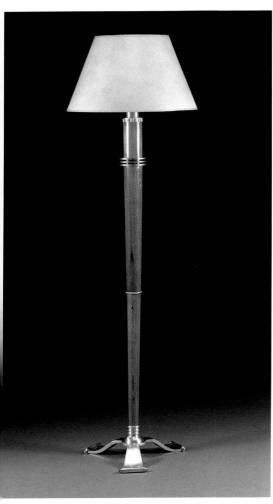

Two floor lights from the same family firm illustrate different sensibilities within French design. The floor light (*c.*1930) ascribed to Jules-Émile Leleu is an archetypal example of French Modernist design. The materials – chrome-plated metal and glass – and the minimalist form perfectly express the style. The other light (*c.*1930) is more in keeping with the rich bourgeois taste that represented the core market for Leleu. A relatively simple silhouette nonetheless leans toward the decorative with such flourishes as the rings near the top of the stem, the scrolled feet, and the use of mahogany. (PG)

Die beiden Stehleuchten, die aus demselben Familienunternehmen stammen, illustrieren unterschiedliche Richtungen im französischen Design ihrer Entstehungszeit. Der Jules-Émile Leleu zugeschriebene Deckenfluter (ca. 1930) ist mit seinen Materialien verchromtes Metall und Glas und seiner minimalistischen Form ein typisches Beispiel für den französischen Modernismus. Dagegen entspricht die Stehleuchte (ca. 1930) mehr dem ornamentalen Geschmack der Bourgeoisie, die im Wesentlichen die Zielgruppe für Leleu repräsentierte. Eine relativ schlichte Silhouette tendiert hier zum Dekorativen mit Verzierungen wie den Ringen am oberen Ende des Leuchtenfußes, den wellenförmigen Sockelfüßen und der Verwendung von Mahagoni. (PG)

Issus de la même entreprise familiale, ces deux lampadaires illustrent les divergences de style qui régnaient parmi les créateurs français. La torchère (vers 1930) attribuée à Jules Leleu est l'exemple parfait du Modernisme français par ses matériaux – verre et métal chromé – et ses lignes minimalistes. Quant à l'autre lampadaire (vers 1930), il reflète les goûts cossus de la bourgeoisie, qui constituait l'essentiel de la clientèle de Leleu. En dépit de sa silhouette assez simple, il est riche en ornements : sa tige en acajou est agrémentée de joncs et le socle décrit une ligne sinueuse. (PG)

◁ **Floor light with integrated table,** **c.1930**
Chrome-plated metal and glass structure on wood base, 175.5 cm high / Konstruktion aus verchromtem Metall und Glas auf Holzsockel, 175,5 cm hoch / Structure en métal chromé et verre, socle en bois, 175,5 cm de hauteur
Leleu Décorateur, Paris, France

Floor light, c.1930
Mahogany and silver-plated bronze base with parchment shade, 162.5 cm high / Fuß aus Mahagoni und versilberter Bronze mit Lampenschirm aus Pergament, 162,5 cm hoch / Socle en acajou et bronze argenté, abat-jour en parchemin, 162,5 cm de hauteur
Leleu Décorateur, Paris, France

Poul Henningsen developed his extensive *PH* lighting range over a period of more than thirty years. During the 1930s he designed many different models including floor lights, piano lights, desk lights and chandeliers. Different colored glass shades were also made available in warm yellow, amber and red hues, and in 1933 socket holders made of Bakelite were introduced. From the early 1930s *PH* lights were increasingly used in private homes rather than solely public and commercial spaces and became so popular in Germany that Louis Poulsen began manufacturing them there as well. (CF/PF)

Poul Henningsen entwickelte seine umfangreiche *PH*-Leuchtenserie in einem Zeitraum von über dreißig Jahren. In den 1930er Jahren entwarf er viele verschiedene Modelle, wie Steh-, Klavier- und Schreibtisch- sowie Deckenleuchten. Auch für die Glasschirme standen nun verschiedene Farben von Bernsteingelb bis zu mehreren Rottönen zur Auswahl, 1933 wurden zudem Lampenfassungen aus Bakelit eingeführt. Seit Anfang der 1930er Jahre wurden die *PH*-Leuchten zunehmend in Privathaushalten statt nur in öffentlichen oder gewerblichen Räumen genutzt. In Deutschland waren die Leuchten so beliebt, dass Louis Poulsen begann, sie auch dort herzustellen. (CF/PF)

Poul Henningsen mit plus de trente ans à réaliser sa vaste gamme de luminaires *PH*. Au cours des années 1930, il en créa plusieurs modèles, y compris des lampadaires, des lampes de piano, des lampes de bureau et des . Ceux-ci étaient assortis d'abat-jour en verre de nuances jaune, ambrée et rouge. Des porte-douille en bakélite furent mis en circulation en 1933. Dès le début des années 1930, les lampes *PH* s'imposèrent dans les maisons particulières comme dans les espaces publics et commerciaux. Elles eurent un tel succès en Allemagne que Louis Poulsen commença à les fabriquer sur place. (CF/PF)

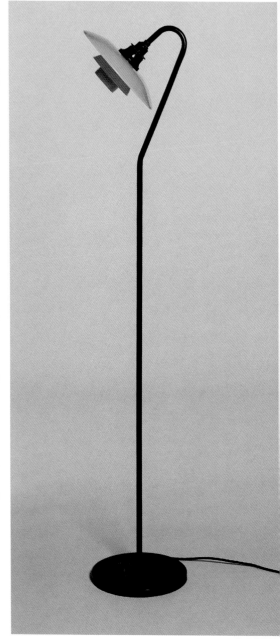

◁◁ *PH* floor light, *c.*1931–1933

Patinated brass base and stem with colored glass shades, 149 cm high / Fuß und Schaft aus patiniertem Messing mit farbigen Lampenschirmen aus Glas, 149 cm hoch / Socle et tige en laiton patiné, abat-jour en verre coloré, 149 cm de hauteur
Louis Poulsen & Co., Copenhagen, Denmark

△ *Model No. PH-3* chandelier, *c.*1931–1933

Patinated brass mounts with opalescent glass shades, 80 cm drop / Montierung aus patiniertem Messing mit Lampenschirmen aus Opalglas, 80 cm lang / Cadre en laiton patiné, abat-jour en verre opalescent, 80 cm de hauteur
Louis Poulsen & Co., Copenhagen, Denmark

◁ *Model No. PH-2* table light, 1931

Patinated brass base and adjustable stem with colored glass shades, 42 cm high / Sockel und verstellbarer Fuß aus patiniertem Messing mit farbigen Lampenschirmen aus Glas, 42 cm hoch / Socle et tige réglable en laiton patiné, abat-jour en verre coloré, 42 cm de hauteur
Louis Poulsen & Co., Copenhagen, Denmark

In 1924 Poul Henningsen designed the first model from his *PH* series for Louis Poulsen. This extensive range of lighting was the result of ten years of scientific study and with its unique system of shades was intended to eliminate glare and produce a soft warm light. According to Henningsen: "The whole trick is not directly illuminating more of a room than is strictly necessary … there has to be a relationship between the directly lit and the unlit areas of a room, plus lighting of such a strength that the reflected light is sufficient to illuminate the unlit areas." (CF/PF)

Im Jahr 1924 entwarf Poul Henningsen das erste Modell seiner *PH*-Leuchtenserie für Louis Poulsen. Die umfangreiche Kollektion war das Ergebnis von zehn Jahren wissenschaftlicher Studien. Mit der einzigartigen Anordnung der Lampenschirme waren die Leuchten so konzipiert, dass sie keinerlei Blendlicht, sondern ein weiches, warmes Licht ausstrahlten. Dazu Henningsen: „Der ganze Trick besteht darin, niemals mehr von einem Raum direkt zu beleuchten als unbedingt notwendig … da muss es ein Verhältnis geben zwischen den direkt beleuchteten und den unbeleuchteten Bereichen eines Zimmers und außerdem einen Lichtstrahl von solcher Stärke, dass das reflektierte Licht ausreicht, um die unbeleuchteten Bereiche zu erhellen." (CF/PF)

En 1924, Poul Henningsen créa le premier modèle de sa gamme *PH* pour Louis Poulsen. Cette vaste série de luminaires, qui était le résultat de dix années de recherches scientifiques, était doté d'un type d'abat-jour unique, censé produire une douce et chaude lumière non éblouissante. Henningsen affirmait que « le secret est de ne pas éclairer la pièce plus qu'il n'est strictement nécessaire. Il est important de créer une relation entre les endroits d'une pièce qui sont éclairées directement, et ceux qui ne le sont pas. L'éclairage doit aussi être assez puissant de manière à ce que la lumière réfléchie puisse aussi éclairer les parties non illuminées ». (CF/PF)

◁ *Cascade* chandelier, *c.*1934
(this version designed in *c.*1960)

Patinated brass mounts with glass shades,
56 cm high / Montierung aus patiniertem
Messing mit Lampenschirmen aus Glas, 56 cm
hoch / Montures en laiton patiné, abat-jour en
verre, 56 cm de hauteur
Louis Poulsen & Co., Copenhagen, Denmark

▷ *PH* hanging light, *c.*1930s

Bronzed metal mounts with glass shades, 41 cm
diameter / Montierung aus bronziertem Metall
und Lampenfassung aus Bakelit mit Lampenschirmen aus Glas, 41 cm Durchmesser /
Montures en métal bronze, porte-douille en
bakélite, abat-jour en verre, 41 cm de diamètre
Louis Poulsen & Co., Copenhagen, Denmark

▽ *German advertisement illustrating* PH *lights,
1930s / Deutsche Werbeanzeige mit* PH-
*Leuchten, 1930er Jahre / Publicité allemande
présentant les lampes* PH, *années 1930*

**Das PH - 3 - Schirme - System
(offene Anordnung) ergibt volle
Lichtausbeute und vermeidet
Blendung!**

**PH - Leuchten sind in allen
Größen zu haben: von 20 bis
85 cm Schirmdurchmesser, mit
Glas und Metallschirmen, weiß
und farbig!**

**Günstige Lichtverteilung /
große Stromersparnis / schöne
edle Formen / verwendbar für
jeden Zweck!**

**Eingeführt in großen Industrie-
u. Handelsbetrieben, in Banken,
Büros, in Gaststätten, Läden,
Ausstellungs- und Sporthallen,
in staatlichen und städtischen
Betrieben, in Privatwohnungen,
Kirchen und Schulen**

**Neuen PH - Katalog D 8 an-
fordern! — Kostenfrei durch:
Deutsche PH-Lampen-Gesell-
schaft m. b. H., Karlsruhe i. B.,
Kaiserstraße 138**

Die aufgeführten Preise beziehen sich auf PH-
Leuchten mit Opal- oder Mattglasschirmen

PH-Wandarm, stehend, Modell 3/2 Rm 65.-,
4/3 Rm 82.-, 5/3 Rm 96.-

PH-Tischleuchte, Modell 3¹/₂ / 2¹/₂ Rm 56.-,
4/3 Rm 70.-, 5/3 Rm 83.-

PH-Hängeleuchte, niedrig hängend, Modell
4/3 Rm 38.-, 5/3 Rm 47.-, 6/3 Rm 99.-

PH-Siebenschirm-Leuchte Rm 190.-
typo canis

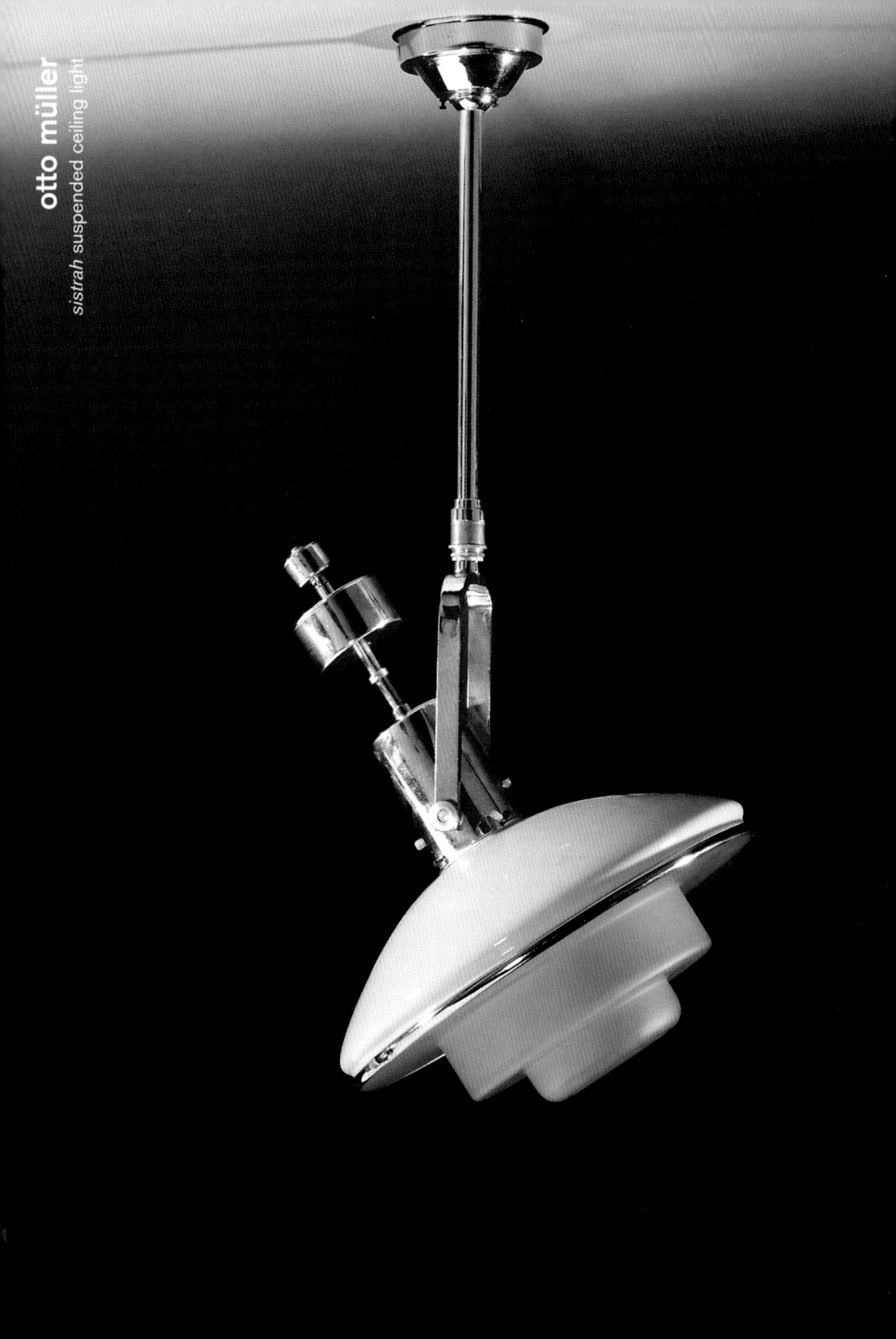

otto müller

sistrah suspended ceiling light

◁ *Sistrah* **adjustable suspended ceiling light, 1931**

Nickel-plated brass mounts with stepped glass shade, 80 cm drop / Montierung aus vernickeltem Messing mit gestuftem Lampenschirm aus Glas, 80 cm lang / Montures en laiton nickelé, abat-jour étagé en verre, 80 cm de hauteur
Müller & Zimmer, Stuttgart, Germany

Model No. P 4.5 Sistrah **hanging light, 1931**

Nickel-plated metal mounts with stepped glass shade, 45 cm diameter / Montierung aus vernickeltem Metall mit gestuftem Lampenschirm aus Glas, 45 cm Durchmesser / Montures en laiton nickelé, abat-jour étagé en verre, 45 cm de diamètre
Müller & Zimmer, Stuttgart Germany (reissued by Sistrah, Stuttgart, Germany)

In 1931 Otto Müller developed his series of *Sistrah* lights, while working at the Technical Institute of Lighting, part of the Institute of Technology in Karlsruhe. The name *Sistrah* derives from the German phrase, "sie strahlt hell" – which can be translated as "she shines brightly". The designs were intended to produce a non-glaring light that could be focused accurately, which meant they were especially suitable for medical environments. Additionally, their stepped, one-piece glass shades were easier to clean than metal shades, thus making them a more hygienic lighting solution. (CF/PF)

Während seiner Tätigkeit am Lichttechnischen Institut, das Teil des Instituts für Technologie der Universität Karlsruhe war, entwickelte Otto Müller 1931 seine Leuchtenserie *Sistrah*. Das Design, dessen Name *Sistrah* von „sie strahlt hell" abgeleitet ist, war so konzipiert, dass die Leuchte ein blendfreies Licht gab, das sich präzise fokussieren ließ, was sie besonders für medizinische Zwecke geeignet machte. Darüber hinaus war der gestufte, aus einem Stück gefertigte Glasschirm leichter zu reinigen als ein Schirm aus Metall und stellte damit eine hygienischere Gestaltungslösung dar. (CF/PF)

En 1931, Otto Müller mit au point sa gamme de lampes *Sistrah* alors qu'il travaillait à l'Institut technique d'éclairage de Institut de Technologie de Karlsruhe. Le nom de *Sistrah* est dérivé de l'expression « Sie strahlt hell », qui signifie « Elle émet une vive lumière ». Ces modèles étaient censés produire une lumière non-éblouissante, pouvant être orientée avec précision et étaient donc parfaitement adaptées à un environnement médical. De plus, leurs abat-jour en verre étagé d'une seule pièce se nettoyaient plus facilement que les modèles en métal et étaient par conséquent plus hygiéniques. (CF/PF)

As the distributor of Poul Henningsen's *PH* lighting range in Germany, Otto Müller decided to produce his own version of these highly successful lights. Manufactured under the *Sistrah* trademark, Müller's designs were the Teutonic equivalent of the *PH* lighting system. The idea behind their design was to make the bulb invisible in order to create a dazzle-free light. The *Model No. T4* table light (1932) is a rarely seen model from *Sistrah* and an elegant Bauhaus-inspired object. As was the case with its Henningsen counterpart, Müller & Zimmer produced many different versions of the *Sistrah* light, for use from desk to ceiling. (AP)

Der für den Vertrieb von Poul Henningsens *PH*-Leuchtenserie in Deutschland zuständige Otto Müller beschloss, seine eigene Version dieses sehr erfolgreichen Leuchtentypus herzustellen. Hinter seinen Entwürfen, die unter dem Markennamen *Sistrah* verkauft wurden, stand die Idee, die Glühbirne unsichtbar zu machen, um ein blendfreies Licht zu erzielen. Die Tischleuchte *Modell Nr. T4* (1932) ist ein seltenes Exemplar aus der *Sistrah*-Fertigung mit einer eleganten, vom Bauhaus inspirierten Gestaltung. Wie bei der *PH* Leuchte von Henningsen produzierte Müller & Zimmer viele verschiedene Versionen des *Sistrah* Modells von Schreibtisch- bis Deckenleuchten. (AP)

Otto Müller, qui distribuait la gamme de lampes *PH* de Poul Henningsen en Allemagne, décida de produire sa propre version de ces modèles très recherchés. Fabriqués sous la marque Sistrah, ils étaient l'équivalent germanique des appareils *PH*. L'idée était de rendre l'ampoule invisible de manière à émettre une lumière non-éblouissante. L'élégant *Modèle n° T4* (1932), d'inspiration Bauhaus, est l'un des moins connus de la gamme Sistrah. Comme son frère jumeau de chez Henningsen, le modèle fut fabriqué par Müller & Zimmer en de nombreuses versions différentes, allant de la lampe de bureau au plafonnier. (AP)

△ *Sistrah* **desk light, *c.*1931**
Nickel-plated metal base and arm with stepped glass shade, 50 cm high, Fuß und Arm aus vernickeltem Metall mit gestuftem Lampenschirm aus Glas, 50 cm hoch, Socle et bras en métal nickelé, abat-jour en verre étagé, 50 cm de hauteur
Müller & Zimmer, Stuttgart, Germany

◁ *Early Müller & Zimmer advertisement showing* Sistrah *hanging lights, 1930s / Werbeanzeige der Firma Müller & Zimmer mit* Sistrah *Hängeleuchten, 1930er Jahre / Réclame d'époque de Müller & Zimmer pour les suspensions* Sistrah, *années 1930*

▷ *Model No. T4 Sistrah* **table light, 1932**
Nickel-plated metal base and stem with stepped glass shade, 45.7 cm high / Fuß und Schaft aus vernickeltem Metall mit gestuftem Lampenschirm aus Glas, 45,7 cm hoch / Socle et fût en métal nickelé, abat-jour en verre étagé, 45,7cm de hauteur
Müller & Zimmer, Stuttgart, Germany (reissued by Sistrah, Stuttgart, Germany)

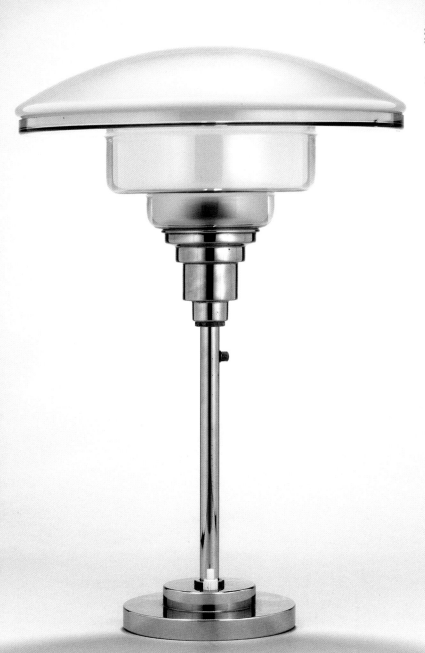

△◁ *Idell* table light, *c.*1933–34

Enameled and chrome-plated metal arm and shade on painted wood base, 47 cm high / Lackierter Holzsockel mit Arm und Lampenschirm aus lackiertem bzw. verchromtem Metall, 47 cm hoch / Bras et abat-jour en métal émaillé et chromé, socle en bois laqué, 47 cm de hauteur
Gebr. Kaiser & Co., Neheim-Hüsten, Germany

△▷ *Model No. 6580 Super* working light, *c.*1932–34

Enameled and chrome-plated metal arms and shades on painted wood base, 58.4 cm high / Lackierter Holzsockel mit Armen und Lampenschirmen aus lackiertem bzw. verchromtem Metall, 58,4 cm hoch / Bras et abat-jour en métal émaillé et chromé, socle en bois laqué, 58,4 cm de hauteur
Gebr. Kaiser & Co., Neheim-Hüsten, Germany

▷ *Gebr. Kaiser & Co. brochure showing a variety of Kaiser Idell lights designed by Christian Dell, c.1935 / Prospekt der Firma Gebr. Kaiser & Co. mit verschiedenen Kaiser Idell Leuchtenmodellen nach Entwurf von Christian Dell, ca. 1935 / Brochure de la firme Kaiser & Co. montrant une sélection de lampes Kaiser Idell créées par Christian Dell, vers 1935*

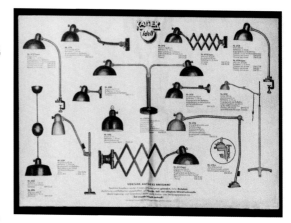

During the 1930s Christian Dell's *Polo*, *Rondella* and *Idell* lighting ranges were manufactured by Bünte & Remmler and Rondella, both in Frankfurt, and Gebr. Kaiser & Co. in Neheim Hüsten, respectively. This remarkable body of work – numbering over 500 designs – was conceived for large-scale industrial production and relied upon the interchangeability of numerous standardized parts. It is a tribute to Dell's extraordinary skills as an industrial designer that his *Idell* range remained in production for over 60 years. (CF/PF)

Während der 1930er Jahre wurden Christian Dells Leuchtenserien *Polo*, *Rondella* und *Idell* von Bünte & Remmler in Frankfurt, Rondella in Oberursel, und Gebr. Kaiser & Co. in Neheim-Hüsten hergestellt. Dells bemerkenswertes Gesamtwerk, das über fünfhundert Entwürfe umfasst, war für die industrielle Massenfertigung konzipiert und stützte sich auf die Austauschbarkeit zahlreicher standardisierter Einzelteile. Es zeugt von Dells außerordentlichen Fähigkeiten als Industriedesigner, dass seine *Idell* Serie mehr als sechzig Jahre lang produziert wurde. (CF/PF)

Pendant les années 1930, les gammes de luminaires *Polo*, *Rondella* et *Idell* conçues par Christian Dell étaient fabriquées respectivement par les firmes Bünte & Remmler et Rondella de Francfort, et l'entreprise Kaiser & Co. de Neheim Hüsten. Cette œuvre très vaste – plus de cinq cents modèles – était destinée à être fabriquée en usine à grande échelle. Les pièces étaient standardisées et interchangeables. La gamme *Idell* continua à être produite pendant plus de soixante ans, preuve s'il en est de l'extraordinaire talent de Dell comme dessinateur industriel. (CF/PF)

Floor light, c.1930
Chrome-plated tubular metal stem with aluminum shade on enameled metal base, 154.9 cm high / Schaft aus verchromtem Stahlrohr mit Lampenschirm aus Aluminium auf lackiertem Metallfuß, 154,9 cm hoch / Fût tubulaire en métal chromé, coiffe en aluminium, socle en métal émaillé, 154,9 cm de hauteur
Bünte & Remmler, Frankfurt/Main, Germany

Model No. 6614 Super Idell wall light, c.1933

Enameled steel and aluminum, 125 cm long (max.) / Konstruktion aus lackiertem Stahl und Aluminium, 125 cm lang (max.) / Acier et aluminium émaillés, 125 cm de longueur maximale
Gebr. Kaiser & Co., Neheim-Hüsten, Germany

Some time around 1933/34 Christian Dell became a designer for the German lighting manufacturers Gebr. Kaiser & Co. in Neheim-Hüsten. He had previously been technical director of the metal workshop at the Weimar Bauhaus (1922–25). While teaching at the Frankfurt School of Applied Arts (1926–33), he had successfully designed modern lighting fixtures. Under the *Kaiser Idell* label he developed a whole range of lights for Gebr. Kaiser & Co., some of which were manufactured and marketed right up to the 1980s. Compared to Dell's 1920s designs for Rondella and Bünte & Remmler, the lights developed for Gebr. Kaiser & Co. have a softer and less stereotypical look. (TB)

Ab ca. 1933/34 war Christian Dell als Entwerfer für den deutschen Leuchtenhersteller Gebr. Kaiser & Co. tätig. Zuvor hatte er sich schon als technischer Leiter der Metallwerkstatt am Bauhaus Weimar (1922–25) und als Dozent an der Frankfurter Kunstgewerbeschule (1926–33) erfolgreich mit dem Entwurf von modernen Beleuchtungskörpern beschäftigt. Unter der Produktbezeichnung *Kaiser Idell* entwickelte er für die Firma Gebr. Kaiser & Co. ein ganzes Programm von Leuchten, die zum Teil bis in die 1980er Jahre erfolgreich produziert und vermarktet wurden. Im Vergleich zu den von Dell in den 1920er Jahren entworfenen Leuchten sind seine späten Modelle in ihrer Gestaltung weicher und weniger stereotyp. (TB)

Vers 1933–1934, Christian Dell entra comme créateur chez Gebr. Kaiser & Co., entreprise allemande de luminaires située à Neheim-Hüsten. Il avait été auparavant directeur technique de l'atelier de ferronnerie du Bauhaus de Weimar (1922–25). Alors qu'il enseignait à l'École des arts appliqués de Francfort (1926–33), il s'était essayé, avec succès, à la conception de luminaires modernes. Sous la marque *Kaiser Idell*, il mit au point toute une gamme de lampes pour Gebr. Kaiser & Co., dont certaines furent fabriquées et commercialisées jusque dans les années 1980. Ces modèles ont un aspect plus doux et moins stéréotypé que ceux qu'il réalisa pour Rondella et Bünte & Remmler dans les années 1920. (TB)

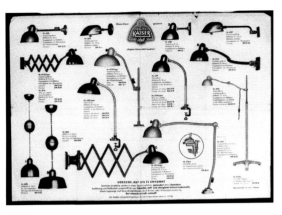

◁ Gebr. Kaiser & Co. brochure showing a variety of Kaiser Idell lights designed by Christian Dell, c.1935 / Prospekt der Firma Gebr. Kaiser & Co. mit verschiedenen Kaiser Idell Leuchtenmodellen nach Entwurf von Christian Dell, ca. 1935 / Brochure de la firme Kaiser & Co. présentant diverses lampes Kaiser Idell conçues par Christian Dell, vers 1935

▽ **Model No. 6631 Luxury Idell desk light, c.1933**

Chrome-plated and enameled metal, 48.5 cm high / Konstruktion aus verchromtem und lackiertem Metall, 48,5 cm hoch / Métal chromé et émaillé, 48,5 cm de hauteur
Gebr. Kaiser & Co., Neheim-Hüsten, Germany

These two table lights, one manufactured in Italy, the other in the United States, highlight the extent to which the Machine Age was an international phenomenon during the 1930s. The *Apparecchio* table light (c.1935) reflects the influence of Italian Futurism, which was itself inspired by the dynamism of mechanization. Similarly, the table light (c.1935) designed by the trail-blazing American industrial designer Walter von Nessen is a celebration of industrial technology, new materials (such as Bakelite), and the soaring skyscrapers that were heralding the dawn of a new and seemingly very modern world. (CF/PF)

Die beiden Tischleuchten, eine davon in Italien, die andere in den Vereinigten Staaten hergestellt, veranschaulichen, in welch hohem Maß das „Maschinenzeitalter" während der 1930er Jahre ein internationales Phänomen darstellte. Die Tischleuchte *Apparecchio* (ca. 1935) spiegelt den Einfluss des italienischen Futurismus wider, der seinerseits von der Dynamik der Mechanisierung inspiriert war. Auf formal ähnliche Weise huldigt die von dem bahnbrechenden Industriedesigner Walter von Nessen entworfene Tischleuchte (ca. 1935) der industriellen Technologie. Neue Materialien (wie Bakelit) und die gestalterische Anlehnung an hoch aufragende Wolkenkratzer verkünden das Erwachen einer neuen und scheinbar sehr modernen Welt. (CF/PF)

Ces deux lampes de table, l'une fabriquée en Italie, l'autre aux États-Unis, illustrent la portée internationale de l'« Ère mécanique » pendant les années 1930. Le modèle *Apparecchio* (vers 1935) est clairement influencé par le Futurisme italien, qui s'inspirait lui-même de l'essor de la mécanisation. De même, le modèle créé par le chef de file de la création industrielle aux États-Unis Walter von Nessen (vers 1935) est une célébration des technologies industrielles, des nouvelles matières (comme la bakélite), et des immenses gratte-ciel qui annonçaient l'avénement d'un monde flambant neuf et très moderne semblait-il. (CF/PF)

Apparecchio (Radiator) table light, **c.1935**

Chrome-plated metal base and finial with rubber shade, 47.6 cm high / Fuß und obere Abschlusskappe aus verchromtem Metall mit Lampenschirm aus Gummi, 47,6 cm hoch / Socle et fleuron en métal chromé, abat-jour en caoutchouc, 47,6 cm de hauteur
Osram, Milan, Italy

▷ **Table light, c.1935**

Aluminum base and mounts with frosted glass shade and Bakelite fittings, 50.8 cm high / Fuß und Montierung aus Aluminium mit Lampenschirm aus Mattglas und Bakelitfassung, 50,8 cm hoch / Socle et montures en aluminium, abat-jour en verre dépoli, parements en bakélite, 50,8 cm de hauteur
Pattyn Products Co., Detroit (MI), USA

Cover of Kurt Versen catalog, late 1930s /
Einband eines Kataloges der Firma Kurt Versen, Ende der 1930er Jahre / Couverture du
catalogue de la Kurt Versen Inc., fin des années
1930

▷ **Model No. M1750 table light, c.1935**

Copper and chrome-plated metal base with
copper and glass shade, 35.9 cm high / Fuß aus
Kupfer und verchromtem Metall mit Lampenschirm aus Kupfer und Glas, 35,9 cm hoch /
Socle en cuivre et métal chromé, abat-jour en
cuivre et verre, 35,9 cm de hauteur
Kurt Versen, New York (NY), USA

After immigrating to the United States in
1930, Kurt Versen began designing and
manufacturing lighting products for use
in commercial spaces and public buildings. Having quickly made a name for
himself, he was commissioned by Howe
& Lescaze to design an indirect lighting
system for their Philadelphia Savings
Fund Society Building (1931). The
M1750 table light (c. 1935) is typical of
Versen's output, which was intended to
meet the growing demand of architects
for contemporary lighting solutions in
keeping with their Modern interiors.
Variations of the *M1750* were also produced with enameled metal bases and
either cork or woven "toyo" shades.
(CF/PF)

Nachdem er 1930 in die Vereinigten
Staaten eingewandert war, begann
Kurt Versen mit der Gestaltung von
Beleuchtungskörpern für gewerbliche
Räume und öffentliche Gebäude. Er
machte sich rasch einen Namen und
wurde 1931 von Howe & Lescaze mit
der Konzeption eines indirekten Beleuchtungssystems für das Gebäude
der Philadelphia Savings Fund Society
beauftragt. Die Tischleuchte *Modell Nr.
1750* (ca. 1935) ist ein typisches Beispiel für Versens Produktion, die dem
wachsenden Bedarf von Architekten
nach zeitgemäßen und zu ihren modernen Interieurs passenden Leuchten entsprechen sollte. Variationen des Modells
M1750 wurden auch mit lackiertem
Metallfuß oder Lampenschirmen aus
Kork oder Webstoff hergestellt. (CF/PF)

Après avoir immigré aux États-Unis en
1930, Kurt Versen se mit à concevoir
et à réaliser des luminaires pour des
espaces commerciaux et des bâtiments
publics. Il devint vite connu et fut chargé par Howe & Lecaze, les propriétaires
de la Philadelphia Savings Fund Society, de mettre au point un éclairage indirect pour leurs bureaux (1931). La
lampe de table *M1750* (vers 1935)
çait en effet de répondre à la demande
croissante d'architectes qui recher-
chaient des luminaires contemporains
assortis à leurs intérieurs modernes.
Plusieurs variantes de la *M1750* furent
produites, certaines dotées d'un pied
en métal émaillé, ou d'un abat-jour
« toyo » en liège ou en tissu. (CF/PF)

Jean-Michel Frank's sophisticated, exclusive and often rather theatrical Art Deco designs were highly sought-after by a wealthy Parisian elite, which included the fashion designer Elsa Schiaparelli. Distinguished by a deep understanding and skillful handling of materials, Frank's lighting products emphasize the formal and expressive potential of the chosen media – from limed oak and vellum to gilt-bronze and green-tinted glass. (CF/PF)

Jean-Michel Franks elegante, exklusive und häufig recht theatralische Entwürfe im Stil des Art Déco waren äußerst begehrt bei der wohlhabenden Pariser Elite, zu der auch die Modeschöpferin Elsa Schiaparelli zählte. Gekennzeichnet durch ein tiefes Verständnis und geschickte Handhabung der Materialien, brachten Franks Leuchtenentwürfe das formale und expressive Potential der ausgesuchten Werkstoffe – von gekalktem Eichenholz und Pergament über vergoldete Bronze bis zu grün getöntem Glas – optimal zur Geltung. (CF/PF)

Les modèles élégants, sophistiqués et souvent assez spectaculaires de style Art Déco que signait Jean-Michel Frank étaient très recherchés par l'élite parisienne, dont la créatrice de mode Elsa Schiaparelli. Frank avait une connaissance approfondie des matières et savait les utiliser au mieux – cela se voit dans ses luminaires, qui exploitent parfaitement les possibilités formelles et expressives de chaque matériau, du chêne cérusé au vélin en passant par le bronze doré et le verre teinté. (CF/PF)

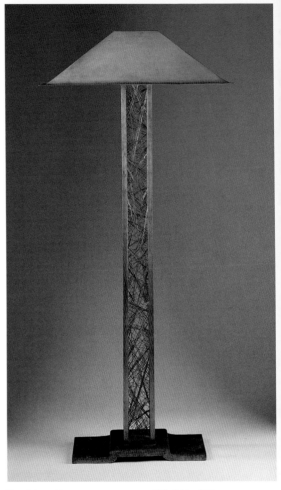

Floor light, *c.*1935
Gilt metal base with vellum shade, 129.5 cm high / Fuß aus vergoldetem Metall mit Lampenschirm aus Pergament, 129,5 cm hoch / Socle en métal doré, abat-jour en vélin, 129,5 cm de hauteur
J.-M. Frank & A. Chanaux, Paris, France

▷ **Table light,** *c.*1935
Bronze and glass base with vellum shade, 56 cm high / Fuß aus Bronze und Glas mit Lampenschirm aus Pergament, 56 cm hoch / Socle en bronze et verre, abat-jour en vélin, 56 cm de hauteur
J.-M. Frank & A. Chanaux, Paris, France

Model No. 1208 Anglepoise task light, c. 1933 – early-production model

Enameled metal base with metal arm and aluminum shade, 90 cm high (max.) / Fuß aus lackiertem Metall mit Metallarm und Schirm aus Aluminium, 90 cm hoch / Socle en métal émaillé, bras métallique, abat-jour en aluminium, 90 cm de hauteur maximale
Herbert Terry & Sons, Redditch, Great Britain

▷ **Model No. 1227 Anglepoise task light, 1934**

Enameled metal base with metal arm and enameled metal shade, 90 cm high (max.) / Fuß aus lackiertem Metall mit Metallarm und Schirm aus Aluminium, 90 cm hoch / Socle en métal émaillé, bras métallique, abat-jour en métal émaillé, 90 cm de hauteur maximale
Herbert Terry & Sons, Redditch, Great Britain

The British automotive engineer George Carwardine specialized in the design of car suspension systems. In 1932 he patented the design of his articulated task light, the *Anglepoise*. This innovative lighting solution, which allowed flexible re-positioning, was based on the constant-tension principle of human limbs, with the light's springs acting in much the same way as human muscles. By balancing a weight against a spring through a linking mechanism, Carwardine was able to ensure that the light remained highly stable and could hold any position over three planes. Hugely influential, the *Anglepoise* was the blueprint for subsequent generations of task lighting. (CF/PF)

Im Jahr 1932 erhielt der britische Kraftfahrzeugingenieur George Carwardine, der auf die Konstruktion von Stoßdämpfern für Autos spezialisiert war, ein Patent für die Konstruktion seiner markanten Arbeitsleuchte mit dem Namen *Anglepoise* (Winkelgleichgewicht). Diese innovative Beleuchtungslösung, die eine flexible Einstellung des Lichtstrahls erlaubte, basierte auf dem Prinzip der Dauerspannung in menschlichen Gliedmaßen, wobei die Spiralfedern der Leuchte ganz ähnlich wie Muskeln funktionieren. Indem Carwardine ein Gewicht mittels Verbindungsmechanismus gegen eine Feder ausbalancierte, gewann die Leuchte ein hohes Maß an Stabilität, so dass sie über drei Ebenen hinweg jede gewünschte Position halten konnte. (CF/PF)

Ingénieur en automobile, George Crawardine était un spécialiste des systèmes de suspension. En 1932, il breveta le fonctionnement de sa lampe de travail articulée, l'*Anglepoise*. Cette innovation, dont on pouvait facilement rectifier la position, s'inspirait du principe de tension permanente des membres humains, dont les muscles étaient ici remplacés par des ressorts. Chaque poids était équilibré par un jeu de ressorts, de sorte que la lampe restait très stable et pouvait maintenir n'importe quelle position à trois niveaux différents. L'*Anglepoise* eut une influence phénoménale et servit de modèle à plusieurs générations de lampes de travail. (CF/PF)

◁ *Luxo L-1* **task light, 1937 (current version)**
Chrome-plated metal arms and mounts and aluminum shade, 113 cm high (max.) – here a later free-standing model / Fuß, Arme und Montierung aus verchromtem Metall mit Lampenschirm aus verchromtem Aluminium, 113 cm hoch (max.) / Bras et montures en métal chromé, abat-jour en aluminium chromé, 113 cm de hauteur maximale Luxo, Oslo, Norway

Publicity photograph showing the Luxo L-1 *task light, 1940s / Werbefoto mit der* Luxo L-1 *Arbeitsleuchte, 1940er Jahre / Photographie publicitaire des années 40 vantant la lampe de travail* Luxo L-1

The Norwegian lighting designer Jacob Jacobsen acquired the Scandinavian manufacturing license for George Carwardine's *Anglepoise* task light of 1934 in 1937. The same year he designed his own task light, the *Luxo L-1*, which incorporated a similar auto-balancing system of springs based on the constant-tension principle of human limbs. There are several variations of this design, including one with an enlarged shade known as the *Panoramic*. Today the original *Luxo L-1* remains in production and to date over 25 million have been sold worldwide. (CF/PF)

Der norwegische Leuchtendesigner Jacob Jacobsen erwarb 1937 die skandinavischen Produktionsrechte für George Carwardines Arbeitsleuchte *Anglepoise* aus dem Jahr 1934. Im selben Jahr konstruierte er die Arbeitsleuchte *Luxo L-1*, die ihr Gleichgewicht durch ein ebenfalls auf dem Prinzip der Dauerspannung beruhendes System von Spiralfedern hielt. Von diesem Design gibt es mehrere Varianten, einschließlich eines Modells mit einem vergrößerten Lampenschirm, das unter dem Namen *Panoramic* vermarktet wurde. Die Original *Luxo L-1* wird bis heute produziert und ist inzwischen weltweit über 25 Millionen mal verkauft worden. (CF/PF)

En 1937, le créateur de luminaires norvégien Jacob Jacobsen acquit la licence de fabrication de la lampe de travail *Anglepoise* de George Carwardine pour toute la Scandinavie. La même année, il mit au point son propre modèle, la *Luxo L-1*, qui était elle aussi maintenue en équilibre grâce à un système de ressorts solidaires imitant le principe de tension permanente des membres humains. Ce modèle existe en plusieurs variantes, dont une dotée d'un abat-jour plus large du nom de *Panoramic*. La *Luxo L-1* d'origine est encore fabriquée aujourd'hui – vingt-cinq millions d'exemplaires s'en sont vendus de par le monde jusqu'à ce jour. (CF/PF)

gio ponti
model no. 0024 hanging light

Gio Ponti believed that it was as much a test of a designer's skill to design luxury goods as it was to design utilitarian ones. He believed that "crystal" was a material eminently suited to the production of objects of "great luxury" and used it accordingly in many of his designs for Fontana Arte. His hanging light of 1931, for example, incorporates light-diffusing disks of tempered glass. This design also reflects Ponti's long-held interest in geometry. Basic geometric forms similarly inspired the *Bilia* table light (1931) with its cone-shaped base supporting a spherical shade almost as if by magic. (CF/PF)

Gio Ponti war davon überzeugt, dass sich die Fähigkeiten eines Designers ebenso in der Gestaltung von Luxusgütern wie in der Gestaltung von einfachen Gebrauchsgegenständen beweise. „Kristall" war für ihn ein Material, das sich ausgezeichnet für „luxuriöse" Objekte eigne, und er setzte es entsprechend häufig bei seinen Entwürfen für Fontana Arte ein. So ist beispielsweise seine Hängeleuchte von 1931 mit lichtstreuenden Scheiben aus gehärtetem Glas ausgestattet. In diesem Entwurf drückt sich zudem Pontis Interesse für Geometrie aus. Geometrische Grundformen inspirierten auch die Gestaltung seiner Tischleuchte *Bilia* (1931), deren kegelförmiger Sockel fast wie durch Magie einen kugelförmigen Lampenschirm trägt. (CF/PF)

Gio Ponti pensait que le talent d'un créateur se mesurait aussi bien à ses objets de luxe qu'à ses créations utilitaires. Selon lui, le cristal se prêtait admirablement à la fabrication d'objets de «grand luxe». Il l'utilisait par conséquent dans un grand nombre de ses créations pour Fontana Arte. Sa suspension de 1931, par exemple, comprend plusieurs disques en verre trempé en guise de diffuseurs. Le modèle reflète, par ailleurs, son indéfectible intérêt pour la géométrie. Celle-ci fut aussi une source d'inspiration pour sa lampe de table *Bilia* (1931), dont le pied conique semble soutenir, comme par magie, l'abat-jour sphérique. (CF/PF)

◁ *Model No. 0024* hanging light, 1931
Chrome-plated metal mounts with opalescent glass panels and concentric glass disks, 53 cm diameter / Montierung aus verchromtem Metall mit Opalglastafeln und konzentrischen Glasscheiben, 53 cm Durchmesser / Montures en métal chromé, plaques de verre opalescent, disques concentriques en verre, 53 cm de diamètre
Fontana Arte, Corsico, Italy

△ *Bilia* table light, 1931
Enameled metal base with frosted glass shade, 43 cm high / Fuß aus lackiertem Metall mit Lampenschirm aus Mattglas, 43 cm hoch / Socle en métal émaillé, abat-jour en verre dépoli, 43 cm de hauteur
Fontana Arte, Corsico, Italy

▷ *Fontana Arte diagram showing the construction of Gio Ponti's* Bilia *table light* / Fontana Arte Diagramm, das die Konstruktion von Gio Pontis Tischleuchte Bilia zeigt / Schéma de Fontana Arte dévoilant la structure de la lampe Bilia de Gio Ponti

◁ **Floor lights, 1930s**

Silver-plated metal bases with glass stems and fabric shades, 172 cm high / Füße aus versilbertem Metall und Glas mit Lampenschirmen aus Stoff, 172 cm hoch / Socles en métal argenté, fûts en ailettes de verre, abat-jour en tissu, 172 cm de hauteur
Fontana Arte, Corsico, Italy

Wall light, 1930s

Glass mount with gilt metal shade, 37,2 cm high / Montierung aus Glas mit Lampenschirm aus vergoldetem Metall, 37,2 cm hoch / Montures en verre, abat-jour en métal doré, 37,2 cm de hauteur
Fontana Arte, Corsico, Italy

Gio Ponti founded Fontana Arte in 1932 as the artistic division of the glassmakers Luigi Fontana & Co. The aim was to produce "originals" – a range of furniture made in glass or crystal for a sophisticated clientele – and to meet an increasing demand for lights designed to the highest standards. Under the artistic direction of Ponti and his associate Pietro Chiesa, the renowned Milanese designer, the company created a series of lights employing sheets of thick glass – a distinctive element of Fontana Arte's early design language. (EK)

Gio Ponti gründete die Firma Fontana Arte im Jahr 1932 als künstlerische Abteilung der Glaswerke Luigi Fontana & Co. Ihr erklärtes Ziel war, „Originale" herzustellen – eine Kollektion von Einrichtungsgegenständen aus Glas oder Kristall für eine anspruchsvolle Klientel – und der wachsenden Nachfrage nach hochwertigen Leuchtenentwürfen zu entsprechen. Unter der künstlerischen Leitung von Ponti und seinem Partner, dem bekannten Mailänder Designer Pietro Chiesa, fertigte die Firma eine Serie von Leuchten mit dicken Glasscheiben – einem charakteristischen Element in Fontana Artes früher Formensprache. (EK)

En 1932, Gio Ponti créa Fontana Arte, département artistique de l'entreprise de verrerie Luigi Fontana & Co. Son objectif était de fabriquer des « originaux » – c'est-à-dire des meubles en verre ou en cristal destinés à une clientèle d'élite – et de répondre à la demande toujours croissante pour des luminaires de très haute qualité. Sous la direction artistique de Ponti et de son associé, le célèbre créateur milanais Pietro Chiesa, l'entreprise mit au point une gamme de luminaires composés d'épaisses plaques de verre – matériau que Fontana Arte utilisait beaucoup à ses débuts. (EK)

pietro chiesa
luminator floor light

As one of the greatest exponents of Italian Art Deco, Pietro Chiesa's work was widely exhibited throughout the 1930s and 1940s. Though sometimes simple in concept, his lighting designs often possessed a striking monumentality, as his best-known light, the *Luminator* floor light (1933), demonstrates particularly well. The elegant fluted form of the *Luminator* introduced into the domestic environment for the first time a type of indirect light that had previously been used only by photographers. (CF/PF)

Die Arbeiten von Pietro Chiesa, einem der hervorragendsten Vertreter des italienischen Art Déco, wurden während der 1920er und 1930er Jahre vielfach ausgestellt. Obgleich in der Konzeption sehr einfach, besaßen seine Leuchtendesigns häufig eine eindrucksvolle Monumentalität, wie seine bekannteste Leuchte, die *Luminator* Stehleuchte (1933), besonders deutlich veranschaulicht. Ihre elegante, flötenartige Form führte eine Art von indirekter Beleuchtung in die häusliche Umgebung ein, die zuvor nur von Berufsfotografen verwendet worden war. (CF/PF)

L'œuvre de Pietro Chiesa, qui était l'un des principaux représentants du style Art Déco italien, fut fréquemment exposée pendant les années 1920 et 1930. En dépit de leur simplicité, ses luminaires étaient souvent impressionnants par leur monumentalité, comme le montre son modèle le plus connu, le lampadaire *Luminator* (1933). Avec son élégante forme évasée, le *Luminator* était le premier luminaire à faire entrer dans l'univers domestique un type d'éclairage indirect jusque-là réservé aux photographes. (CF/PF)

◁◁ *Luminator* floor light, 1933

Enameled tubular brass stem and base,
191,8 cm high / Fuß und Schaft aus lackiertem
Messingrohr, 191,8 cm hoch / Socle en laiton,
fût en tube de laiton émaillé, 191,8 cm de
hauteur
Fontana Arte, Corsico, Italy

△ *Contemporary interior incorporating the
Luminator floor light, as featured in the August
1938 issue of* Domus *magazine / Zeitgenössisches Interieur mit der Stehleuchte* Luminator,
abgebildet in der Zeitschrift Domus, *August
1938 / Intérieur d'époque équipé du* Luminator,
publié dans Domus, *août 1938*

◁ *Fontana Arte advertisement showing the
Luminator floor light, as featured in the July
1937 issue of* Domus *magazine / Werbeanzeige von Fontana Arte mit der Stehleuchte*
Luminator, *erschienen in der Zeitschrift*
Domus, *Juli 1937 / Réclame de Fontana Arte
montrant le* Luminator, *publiée dans* Domus,
juillet 1937

In 1936 the French artist Max Ingrand executed a series of allegorical stained-glass windows which made a lasting impression on Gio Ponti, the founder of Fontana Arte. It has been attributed to Ponti's influence that, 18 years later, Ingrand was made Artistic Director of the company. The asymmetrical element incorporated into the shaft of this c.1938 floor light anticipates Ingrand's postwar designs, while the six-lamp floor light (c.1938), probably designed by Pietro Chiesa, exemplifies Fontana Arte's tendency to reinterpret the mechanical with an artistic "picturesqueness". (EK)

Im Jahr 1936 führte der französische Künstler Max Ingrand eine Serie von allegorischen Buntglasfenstern aus, die einen bleibenden Eindruck bei Gio Ponti, dem Mitbegründer der Firma Fontana Arte, hinterließen. Es wurde denn auch Pontis Einfluss zugeschrieben, dass Ingrand achtzehn Jahre später als künstlerischer Direktor des Unternehmens eingestellt wurde. Das in den Schaft seiner Stehleuchte (ca. 1938) integrierte asymmetrische Element nimmt Ingrands Entwürfe aus der Nachkriegszeit vorweg. Die Pietro Chiesa zugeschriebene, mit sechs Lampenschirmen bestückte Stehleuchte (ca. 1938) ist beispielhaft für die bei Fontana Arte vorherrschende Tendenz, dem Handwerklichen eine künstlerisch-pittoreske Note zu geben. (EK)

En 1936, l'artiste français Max Ingrand réalisa une série de vitraux allégoriques qui firent grande impression sur Gio Ponti, le fondateur de Fontana Arte. Dix-huit ans plus tard, Ingrand fut nommé directeur artistique de l'entreprise, sans doute sous l'influence de Ponti. L'élément asymétrique incorporé au fût de ce lampadaire (vers 1938) anticipe les œuvres qu'Ingrand devait réaliser après la guerre. Quant à la torchère à six bras de lumière (vers 1938), sans doute due à Pietro Chiesa, elle illustre bien le style de Fontana Arte, dont l'esthétique industrielle était souvent égayée d'une note pittoresque. (EK)

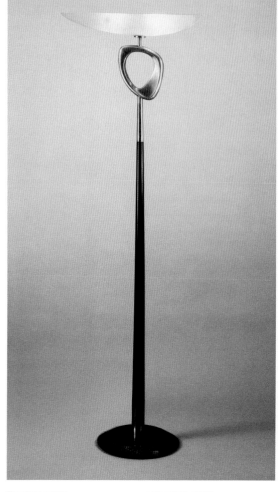

Floor light, c.1938
Bronze base with glass shade, 178 cm high / Bronzefuß mit Lampenschirm aus Glas, 178 cm hoch / Socle en bronze, abat-jour en verre, 178 cm de hauteur
Fontana Arte, Corsico, Italy

▷ **Floor light, c.1938**
Brushed metal base and arms with glass shades, 209 cm high / Fuß und Arme aus mattiertem Metall mit Lampenschirmen aus Glas, 209 cm hoch / Socle et bras en métal brossé, abat-jour en verre, 209 cm de hauteur
Fontana Arte, Corsico, Italy

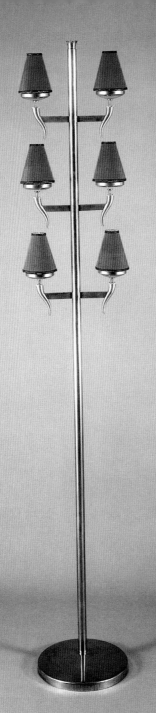

By the 1930s streamlined forms were being used not for functional reasons but to make household products more visually appealing to consumers. The *Executive Model No. 114* desk light (1939) designed by Walter Dorwin Teague is a veritable icon of American Streamlining with its sleek form, elements of which were molded from the new wonder material – Bakelite. Known as "the material of a thousand uses", Bakelite was especially suitable for the manufacture of plastic casings and housings. Like other lights manufactured by the Polaroid Corporation, the *Executive Model No. 114* incorporated the company's patented anti-glare polarizing filters. (CF/PF)

In den 1930er Jahren wurden Stromlinienformen nicht mehr nur aus funktionalen Gesichtspunkten verwendet, sondern auch, um Haushaltsgegenstände und Gebrauchsgüter für die Konsumenten optisch attraktiver zu machen. Die von Walter Dorwin Teague entworfene *Modell Nr. 114 Executive* Schreibtischleuchte (1939) ist mit ihrer eleganten Form, die teilweise aus dem neuen Wundermaterial Bakelit gegossen wurde, eine wahre Ikone des amerikanischen Designs in Stromlinienform. Der als „Material für tausend Verwendungsmöglichkeiten" bekannte Kunststoff Bakelit war besonders gut für die Fertigung von Gehäusen geeignet. Wie andere von der Polaroid Corporation hergestellte Leuchten war auch das *Modell Nr. 114* mit den blendungsfreien Polarisationsfiltern ausgestattet, für die die Firma das Patent besaß. (CF/PF)

Au cours des années 1930, la mode était aux formes épurées, non plus seulement pour des raisons fonctionnelles mais parce que celles-ci plaisaient davantage aux consommateurs. La lampe de bureau *Executive Modèle 114*, conçue par Walter Dorwin Teague, est l'un des plus fameux exemples du « Streamlining » américain. Ses formes effilées étaient en partie modelées en bakélite, ce « matériau aux mille usages » qui se prêtait tout particulièrement à la fabrication de boîtiers et de gainages. À l'instar des autres lampes fabriquées par la Polaroid Corporation, le *Modéle 114* était équipé de filtres polarisants anti-éblouissement brevetés par l'entreprise. (CF/PF)

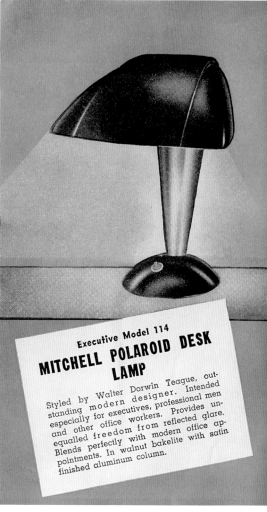

△ *Mitchell Polaroid brochure showing Executive Model No. 114 desk light, early 1940s / Prospekt der Mitchell Polaroid Corp. mit der Modell Nr. 114 Executive Schreibtischleuchte, ca. 1940 / Brochure de Mitchell Polaroid du début des années 1940, présentant la lampe de bureau Executive Modèle 114*

Executive Model No. 114 desk light, 1939

Aluminum stem with Bakelite shade and base, 32.8 cm high / Fuß und Lampenschirm aus Aluminium auf Bakelitsockel, 32,8 cm hoch / Pied en aluminium, abat-jour et socle en bakélite, 32,8 cm de hauteur
Mitchell Manufacturing Company for Polaroid Corporation, Cambridge (MA), USA

In 1932 Edwin Land developed polarizing filters made from a synthetic film-like material. He later founded the Polaroid Corporation in 1937 to develop applications for his newly patented polarizing technology, including sunglasses, car headlamps, cameras and lighting. The resulting *New Student Model No. 100* desk light (c.1939) was specifically marketed as a student's study light and its design has been generally attributed to Walter Dorwin Teague. Like Teague's *Executive* light for Polaroid, the *New Student Model No. 100* has a sleek, streamlined form that epitomizes the American Moderne style. (CF/PF)

Im Jahr 1932 entwickelte Edwin Land Polarisationsfilter aus einem synthetischen, filmartigen Material. 1937 gründete er die Polaroid Corporation und entwickelte Sonnenbrillen, Autoscheinwerfer, Kameras und Beleuchtungskörper auf der Basis seiner inzwischen patentierten Polarisationstechnologie. Die *New Student Modell Nr. 100* Schreibtischleuchte (ca. 1939), deren Design Walter Dorwin Teague zugeschrieben wird, wurde speziell als Arbeitsleuchte für Studenten vermarktet. Ebenso wie Teagues für Polaroid entworfene *Executive* Leuchte hat das *Modell Nr. 100* eine elegante Stromlinienform, die exemplarisch ist für den amerikanischen Moderne style. (CF/PF)

En 1932, Edwin Land fabriqua des filtres polarisants à base d'une mince pellicule synthétique. Par la suite, il fonda, en 1937, la Polaroid Corporation afin de mettre au point des lunettes de soleil, des phares d'automobile, des appareils-photo, des luminaires et autres applications industrielles de cette nouvelle technologie. C'est ainsi que fut inventée la lampe de bureau *Modèle n° 100*, qui s'adressait tout particulièrement aux étudiants, et dont le dessin est généralement attribué à Walter Dorwin Teague. Tout comme le modèle *Executive* fabriqué par Polaroid, le *Modèle n° 100* arbore une élégante forme effilée typique du Modernisme américain. (CF/PF)

Mitchell Polaroid brochure showing New Student Model No. 100 *desk light, early 1940s / Prospekt der Mitchell Polaroid Corp. mit der* New Student Modell Nr. 100 Schreibtischleuchte, *ca. 1940 / Brochure de Mitchell Polaroid présentant la lampe de bureau* New Student Modèle n° 100, *début des années 1940*

▷ **New Student Model No. 100 desk light, c.1939**

Bakelite stem and base with parchment shade, 33 cm high / Sockel und Fuß aus Bakelit mit Lampenschirm aus Pergament, 33 cm hoch / Pied et socle en bakélite, abat-jour en parchemin, 33 cm de hauteur
Mitchell Manufacturing Company for Polaroid Corporation, Cambridge (MA), USA

walter dorwin teague sen. (attrib.)
new student model no. 100 desk light

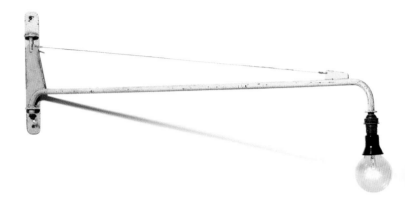

Jib wall light, *c.*1942

Enameled tubular metal construction,
106.6 cm long / Konstruktion aus lackiertem
Metallrohr, 106,6 cm lang / Structure en
tubes de métal émaillé, 106,6 cm de longueur
Les Ateliers Jean Prouvé, Nancy, France

▷ △ *Design drawing of the Jib wall light, c.1942 /
Konstruktionszeichnung der Wandleuchte Jib,
ca. 1942 / Dessin de l'applique murale Jib, vers
1942*

▷ ▽ *The larger version of the Jib wall light /
Die größere Version der Wandleuchte Jib /
Applique murale Jib, grand modèle*

The *Jib* wall light (*c.*1942) by Jean
Prouvé once again concentrates on the
light source: the bulb being exposed,
as in Gerrit Rietveld's designs of the
1920s. Taking its name from the jib of a
sail, the arm of the light can be swung
horizontally in either direction. Prouvé
used these lights in many of his housing
projects, the most famous being for Air
France's offices in Brazzaville, in which
he used the larger *Jib* with an elongated
handle (shown opposite). At over two
meters in length, this wall light was an
impressive interior feature. (AP)

Die *Jib*-Wandleuchte (ca. 1942) von
Jean Prouvé ist eine Konstruktion, die
ganz auf die Lichtquelle ausgerichtet
ist: Wie bei Gerrit Rietvelds Design
der 1920er Jahre steht die freiliegende
Glühbirne im Mittelpunkt. Der Arm der
Leuchte, deren Name von dem engli-
schen Wort für Vorsegel abgeleitet ist,
lässt sich horizontal nach links und
rechts schwingen. Prouvé setzte diese
Leuchten in vielen seiner Innenraumgestaltungen ein, von denen die berühmteste das Air France-Büro in der kongo-
lesischen Hauptstadt Brazzaville war,
wo er die größere *Jib*-Version mit ver-
längertem Arm installierte. Mit über
zwei Metern Länge war diese Wandleuchte ein spektakuläres Ausstattungs-
stück. (AP)

Avec la lampe *Jib* de Jean Prouvé (vers
1942), on retourne à la source de la
lumière, puisque l'ampoule, comme dans
les modèles de Rietveld des années
1920, est apparente. Comme la voile
d'un navire – le mot « jib » en anglais
signifie « foc » – le bras de la lampe peut
pivoter dans les deux sens. On retrouve
ce type e lampe dans de nombreux intérieurs de Prouvé, notamment dans les
bureaux qu'il réalisa pour Air France à
Brazzaville et qu'il équipa du modèle
ci-contre à poignée allongée. Ce modèle, qui faisait plus de deux mètres de
long, était très impressionnant. (AP)

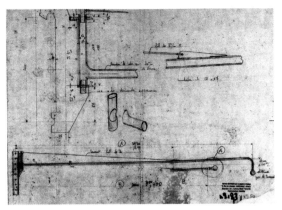

"The thinker-constructor who no longer has an absolute mastery of technique soon loses his ground."

„Ein Designer, der die Technik nicht perfekt beherrscht, verliert bald an Boden."

« Un concepteur qui ne maîtrise pas parfaitement la technique perdra vite pied. »

– Jean Prouvé

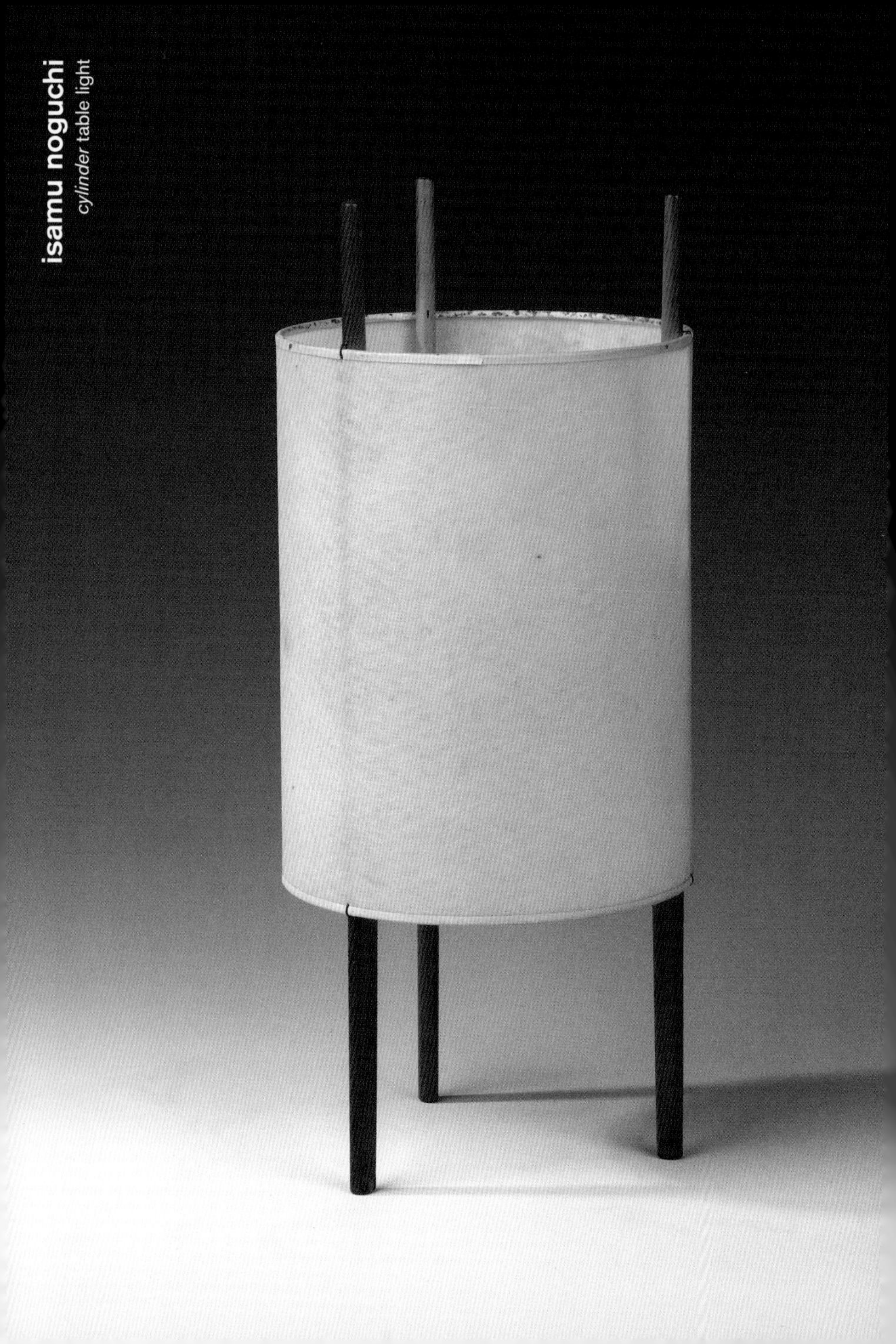
isamu noguchi
cylinder table light

During the early 1940s, the American-Japanese sculptor Isamu Noguchi created a number of illuminated light sculptures known as *Lunars*, which were largely constructed of paper. These were intended for a wealthy clientele and attracted no commercial interest. Around the same time, however, he designed for his sister a table light in aluminum, and in 1944 Knoll Associates put into production a modified version of this light with cherrywood supports and a fiberglass-reinforced polyvinyl shade. This was Noguchi's first product design manufactured by Knoll, but owing to its originality and great sales success it was widely copied. (CF/PF)

Der amerikanisch-japanische Bildhauer Isamu Noguchi schuf Anfang der 1940er Jahre eine Reihe von beleuchteten Skulpturen, die unter der Bezeichnung *Lunars* bekannt wurden und hauptsächlich aus Papier konstruiert waren. Sie waren für eine wohlhabende Klientel gedacht und zogen kein kommerzielles Interesse auf sich. Etwa zur selben Zeit entwarf er für seine Schwester eine Tischleuchte aus Aluminium. 1944 nahm die Einrichtungsfirma Knoll Associates eine leicht abgewandelte Version dieses Entwurfs mit Stützen aus Kirschholz und einem glasfaserverstärkten Lampenschirm aus Polyvinyl in die Produktion auf. Das war Noguchis erstes von Knoll gefertigtes Produktdesign, das aufgrund seiner Originalität und des großen Verkaufserfolgs vielfach kopiert wurde. (CF/PF)

Au début des années 1940, le sculpteur américano-japonais Isamu Noguchi créa plusieurs sculptures lumineuses appelées *Lunars*, fabriquées en grande partie en papier. Celles-ci s'adressaient à une clientèle aisée et ne furent pas commercialisées à grande échelle. Toutefois à peu près à la même époque, il créa pour sa sœur une lampe de table réalisa une version modifiée dotée de pieds en merisier et d'un abat-jour en polyvinyle et fibre de verre. C'était la première fois que Knoll réalisait un modèle de Noguchi, mais en raison de sa grande originalité et de son succès commercial, celui-ci fut abondamment copié. (CF/PF)

◁ *Cylinder* table light, c.1944

Cherrywood supports with fiberglass-reinforced polyvinyl shade, 40.4 cm high / Füße aus Kirschholz mit Lampenschirm aus glasfaserverstärktem Polyvinyl, 40,4 cm hoch / Supports en merisier, abat-jour en polyvinyle armé de fibre de verre, 40,4 cm de hauteur
Knoll Associates, New York (NY), USA (reissued by Vitra Design Museum, Weil/Rhein, Germany)

▷ *Contemporary photograph showing* Isamu Noguchi's *Cylinder* table light, c.1950 / *Zeitgenössisches Interieur mit* Isamu Noguchis *Cylinder* Tischleuchte, ca. 1950 / *Photographie d'époque où l'on peut voir la lampe de table* Cylindre *d'Isamu Noguchi, vers 1950*

"Function … was for me just the beginning. My purpose has always been Art as it relates to life."

„Funktionalität … war für mich nur der Anfang. Mein Ziel war stets die Kunst, die einen Bezug zum Leben hat."

« La fonction… n'était pour moi que le point de départ. Mon objectif a toujours été l'Art dans son rapport avec la vie. »

– Isamu Noguchi

In 1901 the Danish architect Peder Vilhelm Jensen-Klint designed a rustic-style oil-lamp for which he made a simple pleated-paper shade. Soon, making lampshades out of pleated paper became a favorite family pastime and in 1943 his eldest son, Tage Klint, founded a company to commercialize this family hobby. The following year his architect-brother, Kaare, designed his well-known *Fruit* light, which incorporated an innovative "cross-pleated" construction. Simple, sculptural, and relatively inexpensive, the *Fruit* light was highly suitable for use in Modern-Style interiors. (CF/PF)

Im Jahr 1901 entwarf der dänische Architekt Peter Vilhelm Jensen-Klint eine rustikale Ölleuchte, für die er einen einfachen Schirm aus gefaltetem Papier konstruierte. Bald wurde das Herstellen von Lampenschirmen aus Faltpapier zu einer beliebten Freizeitbeschäftigung seiner Familie, und 1943 gründete sein ältester Sohn, Tage Klint, eine Firma, um das Familienhobby kommerziell zu verwerten. Im Jahr darauf entwarf sein Bruder Kaare, ebenfalls Architekt, seine bekannte *Fruit* Hängeleuchte, die sich durch einen innovativen, „über Kreuz" gefalteten Schirm auszeichnete. Schlicht, skulptural und relativ preisgünstig, war die *Fruit* Leuchte sehr geeignet für Wohnräume, die im Modern Style eingerichtet waren. (CF/PF)

En 1901, l'architecte danois Peder Vilhelm Jensen-Klint mit au point une lampe à huile rustique pour laquelle il fabriqua un abat-jour simple en papier plissé. Bientôt, toute sa famille se mit à confectionner des abat-jour à partir de papier plissé et, en 1943, son fils aîné, Tage Klint, fonda une entreprise afin d'exploiter ce passe-temps familial. L'année suivante, son frère Kaare, qui était architecte, conçut sa célèbre lampe *Fruit*, fabriquée selon un système novateur de plis croisés. En raison de sa simplicité, de son aspect sculptural et de son faible coût, le modèle était parfaitement adapté aux intérieurs modernes. (CF/PF)

◁ Gallery in the Rue du Faubourg-Saint-Honoré, Paris, featuring Model No. 101 Fruit hanging lights, c.1955 / Schaufenster einer Galerie in der Pariser Rue du Faubourg-Saint-Honoré, ca. 1955 – mit Kaare Klints Modell Nr. 101 Fruit Hängeleuchten / Vitrine de la rue du Faubourg-Saint-Honoré, Paris, vers 1955, où l'on peut voir plusieurs des suspensions Modèle n°101 Fruit de Kaare Klint

▷ **Model No. 101 Fruit hanging light, 1944**

Hand-pleated paper construction with enameled metal wire fitting, 27 cm, 34 cm or 42 cm diameter / Konstruktion aus handgefaltetem Papier mit Montierung aus lackiertem Metall, 27 cm, 34 cm oder 42 cm Durchmesser / Structure en papier plissé à la main, garnitures en fil de métal émaillé, 27 cm, 34 cm ou 42 cm de diamètre

Le Klint, Odense, Denmark

Although the designer of this extraordinary desk light is unknown, it has been suggested that it might have been the work of the Hungarian-born Art Deco sculptor Gustave Miklós, who was a founder member of the UAM (Union des Artistes Modernes). The *Bolide*'s elegant tear-shaped design could be closed in on itself to create a streamlined, mollusc-like form. Manufactured by La Société Jumo in 1945, the light was a quintessential Machine Age design, which exploited the expressive potential of newly available thermoset plastics. It was available in two colors – black (phenolic plastic – i. e. Bakelite) or white (urea-formaldehyde plastic). (CF/PF)

Auch wenn der Gestalter dieser außergewöhnlichen Schreibtischleuchte unbekannt ist, wird vermutet, dass es sich um eine Arbeit des in Ungarn geborenen Art Déco-Bildhauers Gustave Miklos handelt, Gründungsmitglied der Künstlergruppe UAM (Union des Artistes Modernes). Die elegante, tropfenförmige Konstruktion der *Bolide* Schreibtischleuchte ließ sich zusammenklappen, wodurch sie eine stromlinienförmige, muschelähnliche Gestalt annahm. Die von der Firma La Société Jumo 1945 produzierte Leuchte entsprach vollkommen dem Stil des Maschinenzeitalters und lotete das künstlerische Potential neu entwickelter Kunststoffe aus. Die Leuchte war in zwei Versionen erhältlich: aus schwarzem Bakelit und aus weißem Carbamid-Formaldehyd- Kunststoff. (CF/PF)

On ignore qui est l'auteur de cette extraordinaire lampe de bureau, bien que certains l'attribuent à Gustave Miklos, sculpteur d'origine hongroise qui fut l'un des fondateurs de l'UAM. (Union des artistes modernes). Cet élégant *Bolide* en forme de goutte d'eau pouvait se refermer sur lui-même, ce qui lui donnait l'air d'un coquillage de style *Streamline*. Fabriqué par La Société Jumo en 1945, le modèle est typique de l'esthétique industrielle, laquelle s'intéressait aux tout nouveaux plastiques thermoformés. Il était disponible en deux couleurs : noir (plastique phénolique, c'est à dire bakelite) ou blanc (urée formaldéhyde). (CF/PF)

▽/▷ **Bolide** desk light, 1945

Molded phenolic plastic shade and base with chrome-plated metal and copper arm, 14 cm high (open) / Lampenschirm und Fuß aus Phenoplast-Pressmaterial mit Arm aus verchromtem Metall und Kupfer, 14 cm hoch (geöffnet) / Abat-jour et socle en plastique phénolique (bakélite) moulé, bras en métal et cuivre chromé, 14 cm de hauteur (ouvert) **La Société Jumo**, Brevette, France

Chandelier, 1948

Brass mounts with perforated metal elements and glass shades, 53 cm diameter / Montierung aus Messing mit perforierten Metallelementen und Lampenschirm aus Glas, 53 cm Durchmesser / Montures en laiton, pièces en métal perforé, abat-jour en verre, 53 cm de diamètre
Taito Oy, Helsinki, Finland

▷ **Chandelier, 1948**

Brass mounts with perforated metal elements, 106,8 cm drop / Montierung aus Messing mit perforierten Metallelementen, 106,8 cm lang / Montures en laiton, pièces en métal perforé, 106,8 cm de hauteur
Taito Oy, Helsinki, Finland

In 1918 Paavo Tynell founded his own metalware manufacturing company, Taito Oy, and during the 1920s and 1930s employed a number of talented young designers including Alvar Aalto and Kaj Franck. By the 1940s the firm was producing innovative light fittings designed by Tynell. Inspired by antique crystal chandeliers and traditional Finnish Yuletide *himmeli* mobiles made of straw, these lights were intended to cast interesting shadows and produce a shimmering light effect reminiscent of gaslight or candles. The majority of Tynell's lights were handmade, so production was often limited to a few examples of each design. (CF/PF)

Im Jahr 1918 gründete Paavo Tynell seine eigene Metallwarenfabrik, Taito Oy, die in den 1920er und 1930er Jahre eine Reihe junger, talentierter Designer beschäftigte wie Alvar Aalto und Kaj Franck. Von Anfang der 1940er Jahre an produzierte die Firma auch innovative Beleuchtungskörper, die von Paavo Tynell selbst entworfen wurden. Inspiriert von antiken Kristalllüstern und dem traditionellen finnischen Weihnachtsschmuck, den *himmeli*-Mobiles aus Stroh, waren diese Leuchten so gestaltet, dass sie interessante Schatteneffekte warfen und ein schimmerndes Licht ausstrahlten. Da die Mehrzahl der Leuchten handgefertigt wurde, war deren Herstellung häufig auf nur wenige Exemplare beschränkt. (CF/PF)

En 1918, Paavo Tynell fonda sa propre entreprise de ferronnerie, Taito Oy. Au cours des années 1920 et 1930, il employa plusieurs jeunes talents dont Alvar Aalto et Kaj Franck. Dès le début des années 1940, l'entreprise produisait des luminaires novateurs inventés par Tynell. S'inspirant d'anciens lustres en cristal et de mobiles en paille dont les maisons finlandaises étaient traditionnellement décorées pendant la période de Noël, ces lampes projetaient des ombres intéressantes et émettaient une lumière tremblotante à la manière des bougies et des lampes à gaz. Les lampes de Tynell étaient, pour la plupart, faites à la main, de sorte qu'on ne fabriquait souvent que quelques exemplaires de chaque modèle. (CF/PF)

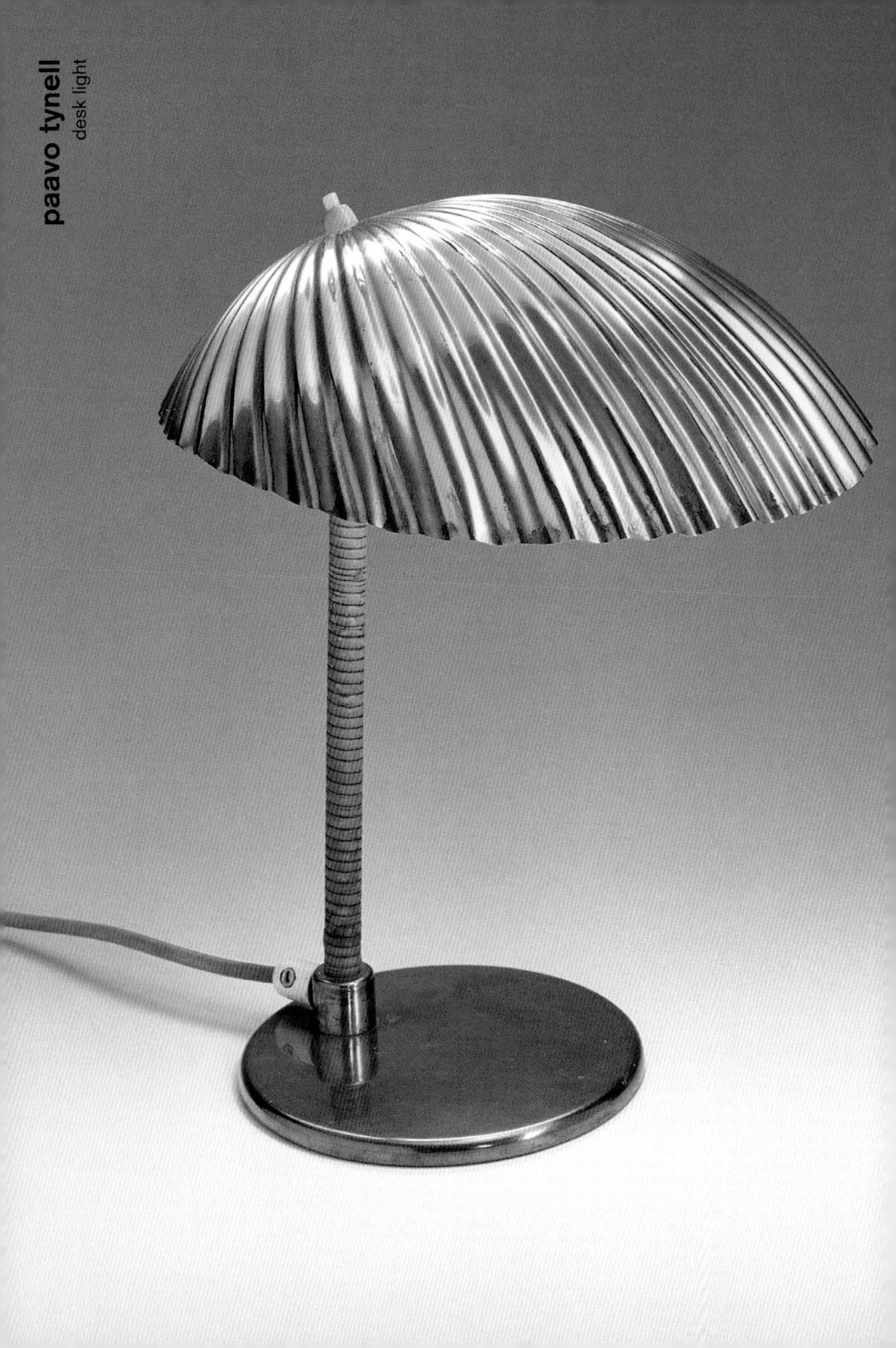

paavo tynell
desk light

Paavo Tynell's work predicted the new sculptural confidence that emerged in Finnish design during the postwar years, which playfully combined superlative craftsmanship with highly refined form. His lighting products, many with perforated shades and sweeping lines, often featured unusual combinations of brass, glass, and leather – a choice of materials that gave his designs an opulent yet elegant appearance. In 1948 Taito Oy began exporting Tynell's light fittings to the United States, where Finland House in New York retailed them. (CF/PF)

Paavo Tynells Entwürfe kündigten das während der Nachkriegsjahre im finnischen Design neu erwachende gestalterische Selbstbewusstsein an, das auf spielerische Weise hervorragendes handwerkliches Können mit äußerst verfeinerten Formen verband. Seine Beleuchtungskörper, viele davon mit perforierten Lampenschirmen und schwungvollen Linien, zeichneten sich häufig durch eine ungewöhnliche Kombination aus Messing, Glas und Leder aus – eine Materialwahl, die den Entwürfen eine opulente und gleichzeitig elegante Erscheinung verlieh. 1948 begann Taito Oy die von Tynell entworfenen Leuchtenmodelle in die Vereinigten Staaten zu importieren, wo sie von Finland House in New York vertrieben wurden. (CF/PF)

L'œuvre de Tynell annonce l'audace sculpturale du design finlandais de l'entre-deux-guerres, qui se distingue par sa maîtrise technique consommée et son grand raffinement formel. Ses luminaires, qu'on reconnaît souvent à leurs abat-jour perforés ainsi qu'à leurs lignes élancées, marient de manière insolite le laiton, le verre et le cuir, d'où leur aspect cossu mais toujours élégant. En 1948, Taito Oy commença à exporter les luminaires de Tynell vers les États-Unis, où ils étaient vendus par la boutique new-yorkaise Finland House. (CF/PF)

◁ **Desk light, 1941**
Brass shade and base with leather-wound stem, 35 cm high / Lampenschirm und Fuß aus Messing mit lederumwickeltem Schaft, 35 cm hoch / Coiffe en forme de coquille et socle en laiton, tige enrubannée de cuir, 35 cm de hauteur
Taito Oy, Helsinki, Finland

△ *Model No. 4305* **desk light, c.1947**
Enameled metal base and shade with chrome-plated metal stem, 30 cm high / Fuß und Lampenschirm aus lackiertem Metall mit Arm aus verchromtem Metall, 30 cm hoch / Socle et abat-jour en métal émaillé, tige en métal chromé, 30 cm de hauteur
Taito Oy, Helsinki, Finland

▷ Model No. 9227 *table light manufactured by* **Taito Oy**, *Helsinki, Finland, c.1950* / Modell Nr. 9227 *Tischleuchte aus der Produktion von* **Taito Oy**, *Helsinki, Finnland, ca.1950* / Lampe de table Modèle n°922 fabriquée par **Taito Oy**, *Helsinki, Finlande, vers 1950*

vico magistretti & mario tedeschi

claritas floor light

◁ *Claritas* floor light, 1946

Enameled metal shade with chrome-plated or enameled metal stem and base, 165 cm high / Lackierter Lampenschirm aus Metall mit Ständer und Fuß aus verchromtem oder lackiertem Metall, 165 cm hoch / Abat-jour en métal émaillé, tige et piétement en métal chromé ou émaillé, 165 cm de hauteur
Reissued by Omikron Design, Milan, Italy

▷ *Claritas* table light, 1946

Enameled base with adjustable enameled aluminium shade and handle, 43 cm high / Fuß aus lackiertem Metall mit verstellbarem Lampenschirm und Griff aus lackiertem Aluminium, 43 cm hoch / Socle en métal émaillé, abat-jour réglable et poignée en aluminium émaillé, 43 cm de hauteur
Italy

The *Claritas* desk light was designed by Vico Magistretti and Mario Tdeschi in 1946. It incorporates a hood-like reflector that can be directionally adjusted using the small handle attached to it. A floor-standing variation of the design was also produced, which was available in a number of different colors. These lights epitomize the stylish yet highly functional nature of postwar design and also predict the innovative and experimental forms that became synonymous with Italian Design in the 1960s and 1970s. (CF/PF)

Die Schreibtischleuchte Claritas wurde 1946 von Vico Magistretti und Mario Tedeschi entworfen. Sie hat einen Blendenförmigen Reflektor, der mittels eines kleinen, daran angebrachten Griffs verstellt werden kann. Eine Stehleuchtenversion des Modells wurde in mehreren Farben produziert. Diese Leuchten verkörpern den eleganten, zugleich aber ausgesprochen funktionalen Stil des Designs der Nachkriegsjahre und lassen bereits die innovativen, experimentellen Formen erahnen, die später für das italienische Design der 1960er und 1970er Jahre standen. (CF/PF)

Vico Magistretti et Mario Tedeschi ont créé en 1946 la lampe de bureau Claritas, équipée d'une poignée qui permet d'en orienter l'abat-jour/capuchon. Elle existait également en version lampadaire, disponible en de multiples coloris différents. Élégante tout en restant fonctionnelle, cette lampe résume les qualités du design italien, dont elle annonce les audaces formelles du tournant des années 1960–1970. (CF/PF)

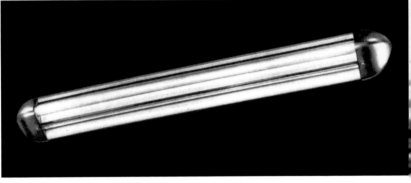

△△ *Model No. 7024 Lytron* **ceiling light, 1948**

Chrome-plated die-cast metal housing with
exposed fluorescent tubes / Gehäuse aus verchromtem Druckgussmetall mit freiliegenden
Leuchtstoffröhren / Boîtier en métal chromé
matricé, tubes fluorescents apparents
Lightolier, Jersey City (NJ), USA

△ *Model No. 7092 Lytron* **ceiling light, 1948**

Chrome-plated die-cast metal housing with
exposed fluorescent tubes / Gehäuse aus verchromtem Druckgussmetall mit freiliegenden
Leuchtstoffröhren / Boîtier en métal chromé
matricé, tubes fluorescents apparents
Lightolier, Jersey City (NJ), USA

The *Lytron* range of ceiling lights (1948)
was a major innovation for the American
lighting manufacturer Lightolier as it featured the early use of newly developed
fluorescent lighting tubes. The *Lytron*'s
streamlined metal housing, which held
the exposed tubes and concealed their
ends, not only looked good but also
allowed plenty of light to be spread in a
room. The range was highly successful
when first introduced and, according
to Lightolier, "became a Levittown standard in the postwar housing boom."
(CF/PF)

Die *Lytron* Deckenleuchten (1948)
waren eine bedeutende Innovation des
amerikanischen Beleuchtungsherstel-
lers Lightolier, da sie ein frühes Beispiel für die Verwendung der neu entwickelten Leuchtstoffröhren darstellten.
Ihr stromlinienförmiges Metallgehäuse,
das die Leuchtstoffröhren sichtbar ließ,
sah nicht nur gut aus, sondern sorgte
auch für eine ausgiebige Lichtverteilung im Raum. Die *Lytron*-Serie war
bei ihrer Markteinführung ein ausge-
sprochener Erfolg und entwickelte
sich, laut Lightolier, „zu einer Standard-
ausstattung im Wohnungsboom der
Nachkriegsjahre." (CF/PF)

Avec ses plafonniers (1948), *Lytron*
était parmi les premières à être équipé
de tubes fluorescents, le fabricant américain de luminaires Lightolier fit figure
de pionnier. Le boîtier en métal du
Lytron maintenait le tube, qui restait
visible, et en cachait les extrémités ;
avec ses formes effilées, il était aussi
agréable à l'œil et diffusait la lumière
dans l'intégralité d'une pièce. La gamme
rencontra un grand succès à son lancement et, selon Lightolier, « on le trouvait
dans toutes les banlieues champignon
d'après-guerre. » (CF/PF)

This highly functional floor light by the American designer Roland Smith incorporates a collapsible music-stand base and a boom-like arm that allows multiple positioning options. As its title suggests, the *Victor* was designed in the period immediately following World War II and its construction reflects the austerity associated with wartime rationing. Shown at the Detroit Institute of Art's "An Exhibition for Modern Living" in 1949, this early "ready-made" light is unusual for its proto-minimalist design. (CF/PF)

Diese höchst funktionale, von dem amerikanischen Designer Roland Smith entworfene Stehleuchte (ca. 1948) besteht aus einem zusammenklappbaren Stativfuß und einem wie ein Mikrofongalgen konstruierten Arm, der sich in zahlreiche Positionen verstellen lässt. Die Leuchte *Victor* entstand kurz nach dem Zweiten Weltkrieg und spiegelt die nüchterne Funktionalität wider, die man mit der Knappheit der Kriegsjahre assoziiert. Dieses frühe Beispiel einer Leuchte im Stil eines „Readymade" war ein ungewöhnliches, protominimalistisches Design und wurde 1949 auf der Ausstellung „An Exhibition for Modern Living" am Detroit Institute of Art gezeigt. (CF/PF)

Ce lampadaire très fonctionnel dessiné par l'Américain Roland Smith emprunte aux pupitres de musique leur pied escamotable et est équipé d'un bras en forme de perche pouvant s'orienter de multiples manières. Comme son nom le laisse entendre, le *Victor* fut inventé juste après la Seconde Guerre mondiale, d'où son style austère influencé par le rationnement. Cette lampe « ready-made » avant l'heure, qu'on pouvait admirer en 1949 à l'exposition intitulée « An Exhibition for Modern Living » à l'Institute of Art de Detroit, frappe par son style proto-minimaliste. (CF/PF)

roland smith
victor floor light

Victor **floor light, c.1948**
Collapsible metal stand and boom-arm, stand 195 cm high / arm 91 cm long / Zusammenklappbarer Stativfuß und Montierung aus Metall, Gestell 195 cm hoch / Arm 91 cm lang / Piétement pliant en métal et bras en forme de perche, 195 cm de hauteur (pied)/ 91 cm de longueur (bras)
James H. Smith & Sons, Chicago (IL), USA

George Nelson referred to the *Bubble* lights as "one of those happy accidents which occur all too infrequently in the designer's experience." With his office needing some large light fixtures, Nelson decided to design his own and began exploring the use of wire constructions that were "cocooned" with a spray-on plastic skin that had been developed for mothballing naval ships. Despite the seeming simplicity of the concept, it took a long time to work out the final production designs. The solution to the lights' assembly lay in the use of special ring connectors, which utilized the tension of the wires to keep the frames together. (CF/PF)

George Nelson bezeichnete die *Bubble*-Leuchten als „einen dieser glücklichen Zufälle, die sich nur allzu selten in der Praxis eines Designers ereignen." Da sein Büro einige große Beleuchtungskörper benötigte, beschloss Nelson, selbst welche zu entwerfen, und begann, mit den Verwendungsmöglichkeiten von Metalldraht zu experimentieren, der mit einer Kokonhaut aus aufgesprühtem, ursprünglich für das Einmotten von Kriegsschiffen entwickeltem Kunststoff versehen war. Trotz der scheinbaren Einfachheit des Konzepts dauerte es lange Zeit, bis das endgültige Produktdesign ausgearbeitet war. Die Lösung für den Zusammenbau der Leuchten lag in der Verwendung spezieller Ringverbindungsteile, die sich die Spannung der Drahtkonstruktion zunutze machten, um den Rahmen zusammenzuhalten. (CF/PF)

George Nelson décrivait les lampes *Bubble* comme « un de ces accidents heureux qui n'arrivent que trop rarement dans la carrière d'un créateur. » Nelson, qui était à la recherche de grands luminaires pour son bureau, décida de les réaliser lui-même à l'aide de structures en fil de fer sur lesquelles il vaporisait une matière inventée pour le conditionnement des cuirassés, qui formait comme une peau en plastique. Malgré la simplicité apparente du concept, les dernières étapes de la production furent laborieuses. On opta finalement pour un système d'anneaux de raccordement, qui utilisaient la tension des cadres en fil de fer pour les maintenir ensemble. (CF/PF)

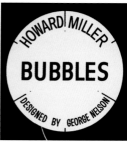

△/▷ *Bubble* **hanging lights, 1947–50**

Translucent vinyl plastic shade with metal rings and mounts, 28 cm diameter (above) and 46 cm diameter (right) / Lampenschirm aus transparentem Vinyl mit Metallmontierung, 28 cm Durchmesser (oben) und 46 cm Durchmesser (rechts) / Abat-jour en vinyle translucide, cadre et anneaux en métal, diamètres de 28 cm (ci-dessus) et 46 cm (ci-contre)
Howard Miller Clock Company, Zeeland (MI), USA

◁ *Howard Miller Clock Company, Bubbles display sign, 1952 / Bubbles-Label der Howard Miller Clock Company, 1952 / Label Bubbles (Howard Miller Clock Company), 1952*

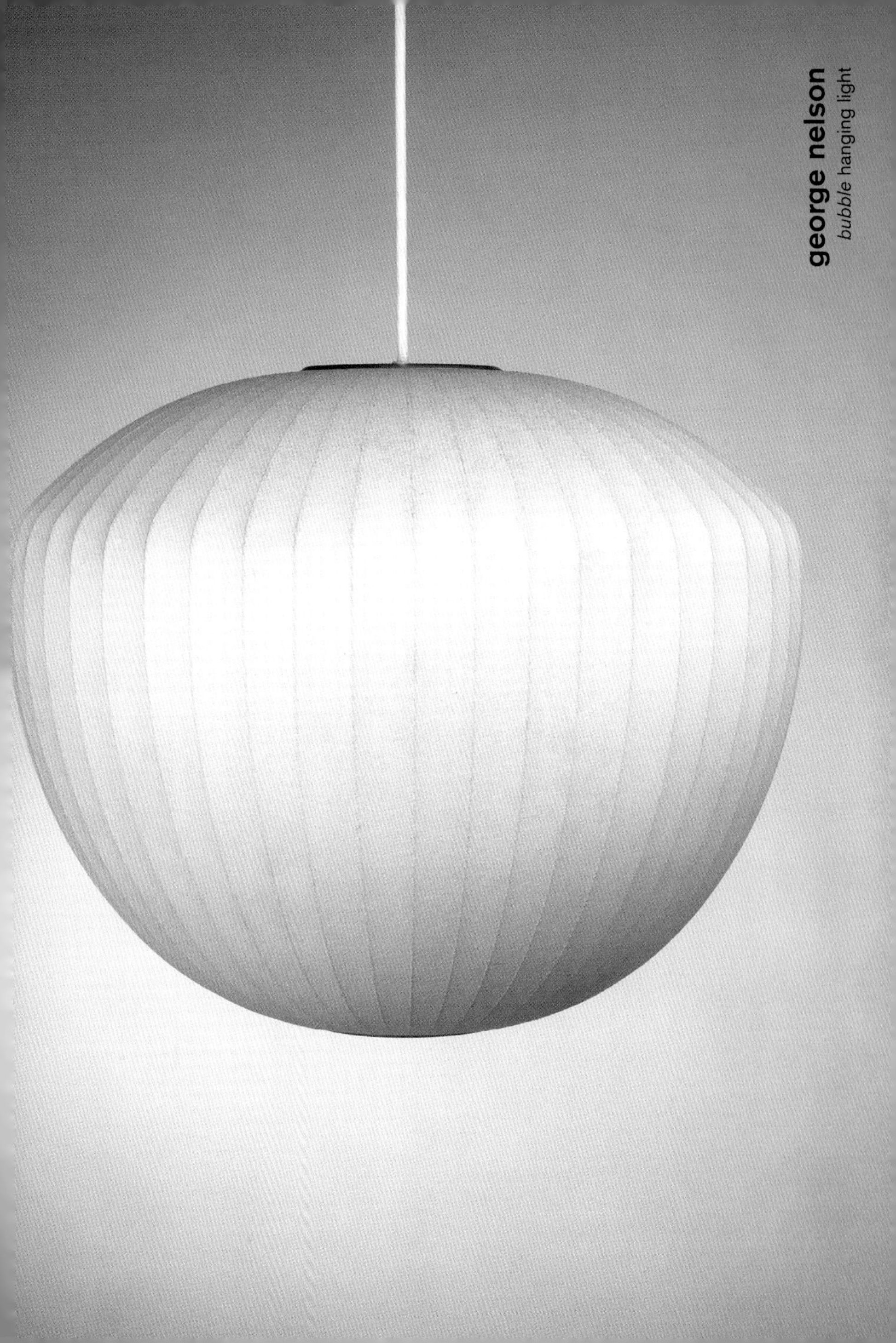

george nelson
bubble hanging light

△ ◁ *Bubble* hanging light, 1947–50

Translucent vinyl plastic shade with metal rings and mounts, 61 cm diameter / Lampenschirm aus transparentem Vinyl auf Metallringen, Montierung aus Metall, 61 cm Durchmesser / Abat-jour en vinyle translucide, cadre et anneaux en métal, 61 cm de diamètre
Howard Miller Clock Company, Zeeland (MI), USA

◁ *Photograph showing the wire construction of the Bubble lights, c.1950 / Fotografie von der Drahtkonstruktion der Bubble-Leuchten, ca. 1950 / Photographie montrant la structure métallique des lampes Bubble, vers 1950*

◁▷ *Bubble* **hanging lights, c.1950**

Translucent vinyl plastic shades with metal rings
and mount, and wood ball fittings, 65 cm high /
Lampenschirme aus transparentem Vinyl auf
Metallringen, Montierung aus Metall mit Holz-
kugeln / Abat-jour en vinyle translucide,
anneaux et montures en métal, billes en bois,
65cm de hauteur
Howard Miller Clock Company, Zeeland (MI),
USA

▷ *Howard Miller Clock Co. advertisment
showing* Bubble *lights, 1950s / Werbeanzeige
der Howard Miller Clock Co. mit* Bubble-*Leuchten, 1950er Jahre / Publicité de la Howard
Miller Clock Co., pour les lampes* Bubble,
années 1950

For those in search of the unusual, George Nelson's trend-starting
concepts begin with clocks, bubble lamps, net lights, ribbon wall,
planters ... and know no limit. For complete free information, write
HOWARD MILLER CLOCK CO., ZEELAND, MICHIGAN

Chandelier, 1946

Hand-blown Murano glass, 67,3 cm drop /
Mundgeblasenes Muranoglas / Verre soufflé
de Murano, 67,3 cm de hauteur
Venini & C., Murano, Italy

▷ **Chandelier, c.1948**

Hand-blown Murano glass, 70 cm drop /
Mundgeblasenes Muranoglas, 70 cm lang /
Verre soufflé de Murano, 70 cm de hauteur
Venini & C., Murano, Italy

Between 1946 and 1950, Gio Ponti designed a number of lights for the renowned Venini glassworks using a Mediterranean palette of intense reds, yellows, blues and greens. Inspired by Venetian antecedents, these color-saturated designs with their twisted stems and frilly, crimped edges exuberantly exploited the age-old skills of the virtuoso glassblowers based in Murano. With a sense of carnival, these chandeliers also emphasized the lightness and transparency of their medium, while expressing Ponti's deeply patriotic love of Italian culture. (CF/PF)

Zwischen 1946 und 1950 entwarf Gio Ponti eine Reihe von Leuchten für die berühmte Glasmanufaktur Venini unter Verwendung einer mediterranen Farbpalette aus intensiven Rot-, Gelb-, Blau- und Grüntönen. Inspiriert von früheren venezianischen Modellen brachten die farbenfrohen Leuchten mit ihren gedrehten Stielen und gekräuselten Rändern die in jahrhundertealter Tradition zur Vollendung gereiften Fertigkeiten der Glaskünstler aus Murano prächtig zur Geltung. Mit ihrer karnevalesken Note betonen diese Kronleuchter außerdem die Leichtigkeit und Transparenz ihres Materials und Pontis tief empfundene patriotische Liebe für die italienische Kultur. (CF/PF)

De 1946 à 1950, Gio Ponti créa pour la célèbre verrerie Venini plusieurs luminaires aux couleurs intenses (rouges, jaunes, bleus et verts) d'inspiration méditerranéenne. Les teintes saturées, les branches recourbées et les rebords finement plissés de ces modèles plein d'exubérance s'inscrivent dans la tradition vénitienne et révèlent pleinement le talent ancestral des souffleurs de verre de Murano. Avec leur petit air de carnaval, ces lustres mettent en valeur la légèreté et la transparence du verre et reflètent l'amour profond que Ponti vouait à la culture italienne. (CF/PF)

Table light, c.1950

Ceramic base with textile shade, 61.3 cm high /
Keramikfuß mit Lampenschirm aus Stoff,
61,3 cm hoch / Pied en céramique, abat-jour
en tissu, 61.3 cm de hauteur
Georges Jouve, Aix-en-Provence, France

The French ceramicist Georges Jouve trained at the École de Boulle in 1929 and later studied painting at the Académie Julian in Paris. Between 1942 and 1944 he lived in the Provençal town of Dieulefit, where he discovered the regional clay nativity figures and dolls known as *santons*. Inspired by this popular art form, he made his own ceramic figures and later turned his attention to the manufacture of ceramic vases, mirror frames, tureens, lighting, etc. Preferring to model clay by hand rather than on a wheel, Jouve created dynamic sculptural forms, such as the base of this table light executed around 1950. (CF/PF)

Der französische Keramiker Georges Jouve absolvierte 1929 eine Ausbildung an der École de Boulle und später ein Studium der Malerei an der Académie Julian in Paris. Zwischen 1942 und 1944 lebte er in der provençalischen Stadt Dieulefit, wo er die regional typischen Weihnachtsfiguren und Puppen aus Ton entdeckte, die so genannten Santons. Inspiriert von diesem volkstümlichen Kunsthandwerk entwarf er seine eigenen Keramikfiguren und wandte sich in der Folge der Fertigung von Vasen, Spiegelrahmen, Terrinen und Leuchten zu. Er zog es vor, den Ton frei mit der Hand statt auf einer Drehscheibe zu modellieren und schuf dynamische, plastisch gestaltete Formen wie den Sockel dieser um 1950 ausgeführten Tischleuchte. (CF/PF)

Le céramiste français Georges Jouve suivit les cours de l'École Boulle en 1929, puis il étudia la peinture à l'Académie Julian à Paris. Entre 1942 et 1944, il vécut à Dieulefit en Provence, où il découvrit les santons – figurines d'argile utilisées dans les scènes de Nativité. Il s'inspira de cet art populaire pour créer, d'abord, ses propres figurines de céramique, puis des vases, des cadres de miroirs, des soupières, des luminaires et autres objets en céramique. Jouve, qui préférait travailler l'argile à la main plutôt qu'au tour, se distinguait par ses formes dynamiques et sculpturales, comme le pied de cette lampe de table, qui date du début des années 1950. (CF/PF)

"It was the shape of the wood that inspired him."

„Es war die Form des Holzes, die ihn inspirierte."

«C'était la forme du bois qui l'inspirait.»

– Odile Noll (Alexandre Noll's daughter)

Table light, 1950s
Carved mahogany base with textile shade, 39.4 cm high / Fuß aus geschnitztem Mahagoni mit Lampenschirm aus Stoff, 39,4 cm hoch / Pied en acajou sculpté, abat-jour en tissu, 39,4 cm de hauteur
Alexandre Noll, Paris, France

Alexandre Noll began working in wood in 1920 and in addition to sculpture also produced exquisitely carved and boldly formed wooden furniture, housewares and lighting. These objects hovered between fine art and utility, and like Noll's works of art were created as one-offs. Noll delighted in exploring the plastic potential of wood, and over his career designed a number of table lights which incorporated mahogany bases in sculptural, organic forms, as in this example from the 1950s. His work is highly prized by collectors today. (CF/PF)

Alexandre Noll begann 1920, Skulpturen aus Holz zu schaffen und fertigte außerdem äußerst kunstvoll geschnitzte und kühn geformte Möbel, Haushaltsgegenstände und Beleuchtungskörper aus Holz. Diese Objekte schwebten zwischen Kunst und Zweckmäßigkeit und waren, wie Nolls bildhauerische Arbeiten, als Unikate angelegt. Mit Begeisterung lotete Noll das plastische Potential von Holz aus und entwarf im Lauf seiner Karriere zahlreiche Tischleuchten wie die hier vorgestellte Leuchte aus den 1950er Jahren, deren skulptural und organisch geformter Fuß aus Mahagoni gearbeitet sind. Seine Arbeiten werden von heutigen Sammlern hoch geschätzt. (CF/PF)

Alexandre Noll commença à travailler le bois en 1920. Hormis ses sculptures, il réalisa aussi des meubles, des articles ménagers et des luminaires aux formes audacieuses et finement sculptées. À mi-chemin entre l'art et l'utilitaire, ces objets étaient, tout comme ses œuvres d'art, créés en un seul exemplaire. Noll adorait explorer les possibilités plastiques du bois et, tout au long de sa carrière, il réalisa plusieurs lampes de tables dotées, comme celle-ci, de pieds en acajou aux formes organiques. Son œuvre est aujourd'hui très recherchée par les collectionneurs. (CF/PF)

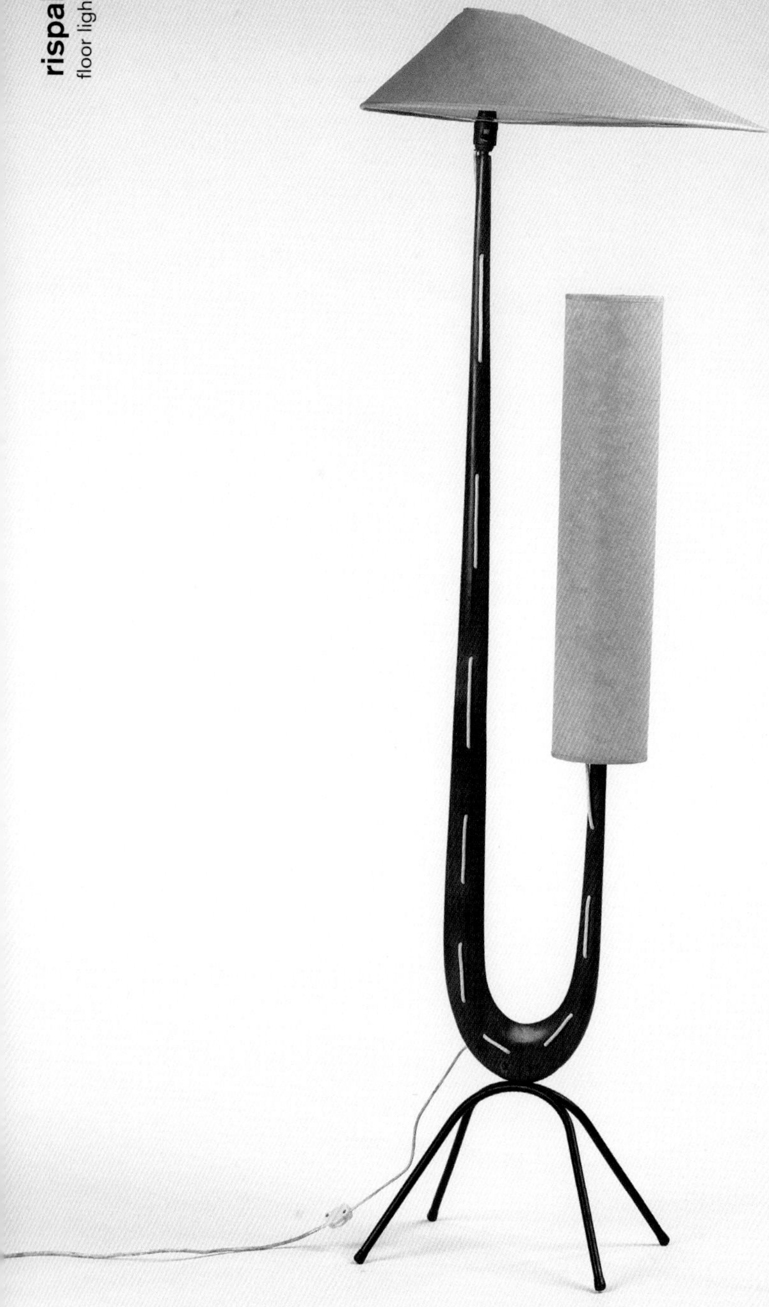

rispal
floor light

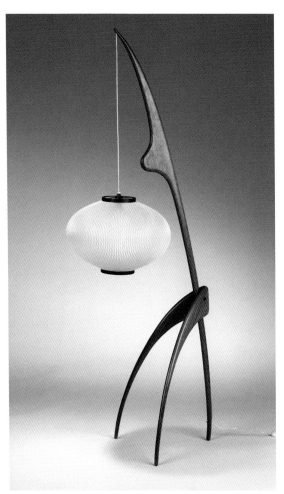

During the early 1950s the French company Rispal produced these two highly sculptural lighting designs. It also manufactured a number of variations of both models, including a light that incorporated a tabletop. These highly expressive floor lights were inspired by contemporary abstract sculpture, especially the work of Hans Arp, and can be seen to work almost as "functional sculpture". With their bold biomorphic forms, these lights were at the cutting-edge of taste in postwar product design. (CF/PF)

Während der frühen 1950er Jahre produzierte die französische Firma Rispal diese beiden stark skulptural gestalteten Leuchten. Außerdem stellte sie eine Reihe von Variationen der beiden Modelle her, beispielsweise eine Version mit integrierter Ablagefläche. Die sehr expressiven Entwürfe waren von zeitgenössischen abstrakten Plastiken inspiriert, insbesondere von den Arbeiten Hans Arps, und lassen sich fast als „funktionale Skulpturen" betrachten. Mit ihrer kühnen, organischen Formgebung gehörten diese Leuchten zur Avantgarde im Produktdesign der Nachkriegszeit. (CF/PF)

Ces deux luminaires aux formes très sculpturales étaient fabriqués au début des années 1950 par l'entreprise française Rispal. Celle-ci les déclinait en plusieurs variantes, dont l'une était équipée d'une tablette. Ces deux modèles très expressifs s'inspiraient de la sculpture abstraite contemporaine, plus particulièrement celle de Hans Arp, si bien qu'on pourrait presque les décrire comme des « sculptures fonctionnelles ». Avec leurs audacieuses formes biomorphiques, ils se situaient à l'avant-garde des tendances de la production de l'époque. (CF/PF)

◁ **Floor light, c.1950**
Walnut base with linen shades, 160 cm high / Fuß aus Walnussholz mit Lampenschirmen aus Leinen, 160 cm hoch / Fût en noyer, abat-jour en lin, 160 cm de haut
Rispal, France

Floor light, 1950
Walnut base with suspended fiberglass bubble shade, 162.5 cm high / Fuß aus Walnussholz mit aufgehängtem Lampenschirm in Kugelform aus Glasfaser, 162,5 cm hoch / Structure en noyer, abat-jour bulle en fibre de verre, 162,5 cm de hauteur
Rispal, France

As its name suggested, the Milan-based lighting company Stilnovo manufactured "new style" designs during the postwar years. Its best-known product from this period is the *Model No. A5011* hanging light designed by Gaetano Scolari in 1950. The height of this light can be easily adjusted using the counter-weighted pulley-like mechanism. Several versions of the design were produced and a number of different color combinations were also made available. Stilnovo later went on to manufacture state-of-the-art lighting by, among others, Joe Colombo, De Pas, D'Urbino, Lomazzi, Cini Boeri Mariani, Gae Aulenti, and Ettore Sottsass. (CF/PF)

Wie der Name suggeriert, produzierte der in Mailand ansässige Leuchtenhersteller Stilnovo während der Nachkriegszeit Leuchten im „neuen Stil". Sein bekanntestes Produkt aus dieser Zeit ist die von Gaetano Scolari 1950 entworfene Hängelampe *Modell Nr. A5011*. Die Hängehöhe dieser Leuchte ließ sich leicht durch einen flaschenzugartigen Mechanismus und ein Ausgleichsgewicht verstellen. Von dieser Leuchte wurden mehrere Versionen produziert, die auch in einer Reihe verschiedener Farbkombinationen erhältlich waren. In späteren Jahren stellte Stilnovo avantgardistische Leuchten nach Entwürfen von Joe Colombo, De Pas, D'Urbino, Lomazzi, Cini Boeri Mariani, Gae Aulenti, Ettore Sottsass und anderen her. (CF/PF)

◁ **Model No. A5011 hanging light, 1950**

Brass mounts and counterweight with enameled metal dome shade and pierced brass diffuser, 61 cm diameter / Montierung und Ausgleichsgewicht aus Messing mit gewölbtem Lampenschirm aus lackiertem Metall und Diffusor aus perforiertem Messing, 61 cm Durchmesser / Monture et contrepoids en laiton, abat-jour arrondi en métal émaillé, diffuseur en laiton perforé, 61 cm de diamètre
Stilnovo, Milan, Italy

▷ **Hanging light, c.1950**

Brass mounts and counterweight with enameled metal dome shade and pierced diffuser, 61 cm diameter / Montierung und Ausgleichsgewicht aus Messing mit gewölbtem Lampenschirm aus lackiertem Metall und perforiertem Diffusor, 61 cm Durchmesser / Monture et contrepoids en laiton, abat-jour arrondi en métal émaillé, diffuseur perforé, 61 cm de diamètre
Stilnovo, Milan, Italy

△ *Contemporary interior incorporating Gaetano Scolari's Model No. A5011 hanging light, as featured in the April 1961 issue of* Domus *magazine / Zeitgenössisches Interieur mit Gaetano Scolaris Hängeleuchte Modell Nr. A5011, abgebildet in der Zeitschrift* Domus, *April 1961 / Vue d'un appartement équipé de la suspension A5011 de Gaetano Scolari publiée dans le magazine* Domus *en avril 1961*

Après la guerre, l'entreprise milanaise d'éclairage Stilnovo se spécialisa, comme son nom l'indique, dans les articles de «style nouveau». Parmi tous les objets qu'elle produisit pendant cette période, on connaît surtout la suspension *Modèle n° A5011* créée en 1950 par Gaetano Scolari. Sa hauteur se réglait facilement grâce à un mécanisme de poulie à contrepoids. Plusieurs versions de ce modèle virent le jour, et il était aussi disponible en de nombreuses combinaisons de couleurs différentes. Par la suite, Stilnovo fabriqua des luminaires ultra-modernes dessinés, entre autres, par Joe Colombo, De Pas, D'Urbino, Lomazzi, Cini Boeri Mariani, Gae Aulenti et Ettore Sottsass. (CF/PF)

mitchell bobrick
table light

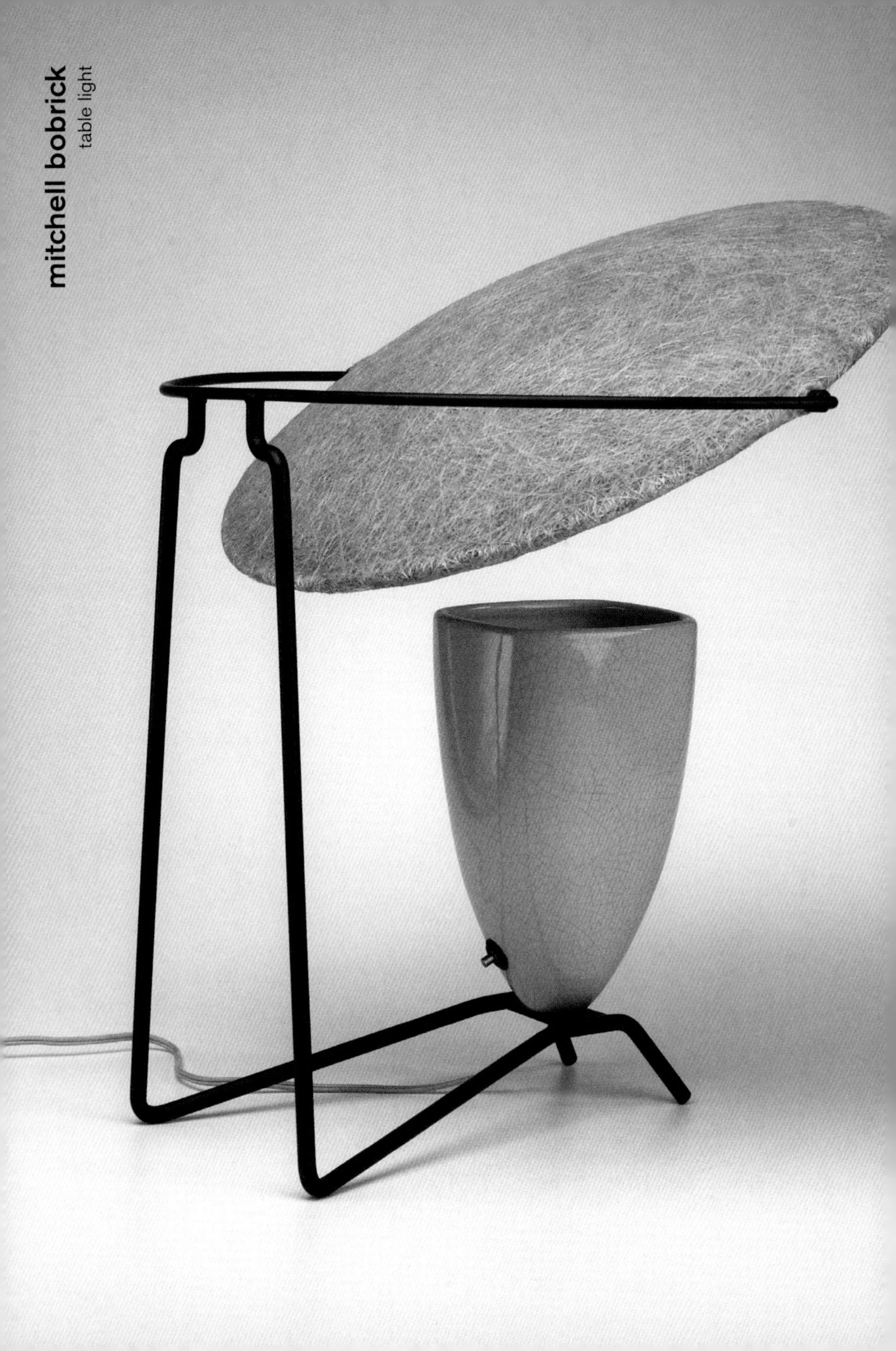

These two lights exemplify the casual elegance of postwar American design. The table light (c.1950) designed by Mitchell Bobrick incorporates an unusual combination of materials – ceramic and fiberglass. He designed a similar floor light in 1949, which also incorporated an adjustable diffuser to give a soft emitted light. Greta Grossman's table light (c.1950) is one of several designs by her that were produced by the Ralph O. Smith Manufacturing Company. Grossman's lights were distinguished by the use of simple, soft-edged forms and then-fashionable contemporary colors – sage green, creamy yellow, smoky plum and coppery brown. (CF/PF)

Diese beiden Leuchten sind exemplarisch für die lässige Eleganz des amerikanischen Designs der Nachkriegszeit. Die von Mitchell Bobrick entworfene Tischleuchte (ca. 1950) weist eine ungewöhnliche Kombination der Werkstoffe Keramik und Glasfaser auf. 1949 hatte er eine ähnliche Stehleuchte entworfen, die ebenfalls mit einem verstellbaren Diffusor ausgestattet war, um ein warmes und weiches Licht abzustrahlen. Greta Grossmans Tischleuchte (ca. 1950) ist einer ihrer zahlreichen Entwürfe, die von der Ralph O. Smith Manufacturing Company hergestellt wurden. Grossmanns Leuchten zeichnen sich durch ihre schlichten, abgerundeten Formen und die damals aktuellen Modefarben aus: Salbeigrün, Zartgelb, Pflaumenblau und Rotbraun. (CF/PF)

Ces deux lampes illustrent bien l'élégante nonchalance du design américain d'après-guerre. Celle de Mitchell Bobrick (vers 1950) marie deux matériaux rarement associés : la céramique et la fibre de verre. En 1949, il réalisa un lampadaire dans le même style (voir pages précédentes), qui était également doté d'un diffuseur réglable permettant d'adoucir la lumière. La lampe de table signée Greta Grossman (vers 1950) est l'un des nombreux modèles qu'elle dessina pour la Ralph O. Smith Manufacturing Company. Les luminaires de Grossman se reconnaissent à leurs formes simples et arrondies et à leurs couleurs à la mode – vert cendré, jaune crème, prune fumé et brun cuivré. (CF/PF)

◁ **Table light,** *c.*1950

Enameled metal frame with ceramic shade and fiberglass diffuser, 43 cm high / Gestell aus lackiertem Metall mit Lampenschirm aus Keramik und Diffusor aus Glasfaser, 43 cm hoch / Cadre en métal émaillé, abat-jour en céramique, diffuseur en fibre de verre, 43 cm de hauteur
Controlight, USA

▷ **Table light,** *c.*1950

Enameled metal frame, shade and diffuser, 35.5 cm high / Montierung, Lampenschirm und Diffusor aus lackiertem Metall, 35,5 cm hoch / Cadre, abat-jour et diffuseur en métal émaillé, 35,5 cm de hauteur
Ralph O. Smith Manufacturing Company, Burbank (CA), USA

In 1950 *Holiday Magazine* approached the eminent designer George Nelson to design an "experiment in living". This resulted in the Holiday House dwelling, which was built on the south shore of Long Island. The interior of the rectangular box-car-like building featured push-button controls for the dimming of lights and intercoms for communication between rooms. This large table light (1950) was designed specifically for the living/dining room and incorporated a parasol-like light reflector. Manufactured by Gotham Lighting – a company founded by Harry Gerstel and Richard Kelly – the design was never put into commercial production. (CF/PF)

Im Jahr 1950 beauftragte das *Holiday Magazine* den bedeutenden Designer George Nelson, ein „Wohnexperiment" zu gestalten. Daraus entstand das so genannte Holiday House, das an der Südküste von Long Island gebaut wurde. Die Innenräume des rechteckigen Gebäudes, das architektonisch eher einem gedeckten Güterwagen ähnelte, waren mit Lichtreglern und Wechselsprechanlagen für die Kommunikation zwischen den Räumen ausgestattet. Die großformatige Tischleuchte (1950) wurde speziell für den Wohn- und Essraum entworfen und hatte einen Reflexionsschirm, der wie ein Sonnenschirm anmutet. Das von Gotham Lighting, einer von Harry Gerstel und Richard Kelly gegründeten Firma, ausgeführte Design wurde nie in die kommerzielle Produktion übernommen. (CF/PF)

En 1950, *Holiday Magazine* demanda au célèbre créateur George Nelson d'imaginer « un mode de vie expérimental ». C'est ainsi que fut construite la « Holiday House » sur la côte sud de Long Island. L'intérieur du bâtiment rectangulaire en forme de fourgon était équipé d'interrupteurs variateurs, ainsi que d'interphones permettant de communiquer d'une pièce à l'autre. Cette imposante lampe de table (1950) était destinée au salon/salle à manger et possédait un réflecteur en forme d'ombrelle. Fabriquée par Gotham Lighting – entreprise fondée par Harry Gerstel et Richard Kelly – elle ne fut jamais commercialisée. (CF/PF)

◁△ **Holiday House table light, 1950**
Enameled aluminum base and shade with
enameled steel supports, 61 cm high / Fuß
und Lampenschirm aus lackiertem Aluminium
mit lackierter Stahlmontierung, 61 cm hoch /
Socle et abat-jour en aluminium émaillé,
supports en acier émaillé, 61 cm de hauteur
Gotham Lighting, New York (NY), USA

◁ *Living/dining room in the Holiday House
showing the table light specially designed for
it by George Nelson, 1950 / Wohn- und Ess-
zimmers im Holiday House mit der speziell hierfür entworfenen Tischleuchte von George
Nelson, 1950 / Salon/salle à manger de la
Holiday House, où l'on peut voir la lampe de
table conçue par George Nelson pour cette
maison expérimentale, 1950*

▷ *Half-Nelson* **table light, c.1955**
Gilded aluminum base with anodized tubular
metal stem and aluminum reflector, 51 cm high /
Fuß aus vergoldetem Aluminium mit eloxierter
Stahlrohrmontierung und Reflektor aus Aluminium, 51 cm hoch / Socle en aluminium doré,
tube de métal anodisé et réflecteur en aluminium, 51 cm de hauteur
Koch & Lowy, Avon (MA), USA

Perhaps George Nelson's most stylish
lighting design, the *Half-Nelson* table
light from c.1955 can be seen as an
evolution of his earlier *Holiday House*
table light (left). The *Half-Nelson* incorporates a cylindrical base that conceals
the light source and an adjustable
saucer-shaped reflector that allows the
light to be efficiently angled. This model
was also available with either a black
enameled or chrome-plated finish. The
well-known lighting manufacturer Koch
& Lowy – a company that made some of
the most progressive mid-century lighting in the United States – produced the
design. (CF/PF)

Man könnte den wohl stilvollsten Leuchtenentwurf von George Nelson, die
Tischleuchte *Half-Nelson* (ca. 1955),
als eine Weiterentwicklung seiner früheren Tischleuchte *Holiday House* betrachten. Das Modell *Half-Nelson* ist
mit einem zylindrischen, die Lichtquelle
verhüllenden Säulenfuß und einem verstellbaren, leicht gewölbten Reflektor
ausgestattet, mit dem der Lichtwinkel
gezielt eingestellt werden kann. Dieses
Design gab es auch in schwarzlackier-
ter oder verchromter Oberflächenaus-
führung. Der namhafte Leuchtenhersteller Koch & Lowy, der einige der
fortschrittlichsten amerikanischen
Leuchten der 1950er Jahre herstellte,
produzierte auch dieses Design.
(CF/PF)

La *Half-Nelson* (vers 1955), qui est
peut-être la plus élégante des œuvres
de Nelson, semble découler de son
modèle antérieur de lampe de table, la
Holiday House. La source de lumière y
est dissimulée dans un socle cylindrique et un réflecteur réglable en forme
de soucoupe permet d'orienter la lumière de manière adéquate. Le modèle
était aussi disponible en version noire
laquée ou chromée. Il était fabriqué par
Koch & Lowy, célèbre fabricant de luminaires américain qui comptait parmi les
plus avant-gardistes de l'époque.
(CF/PF)

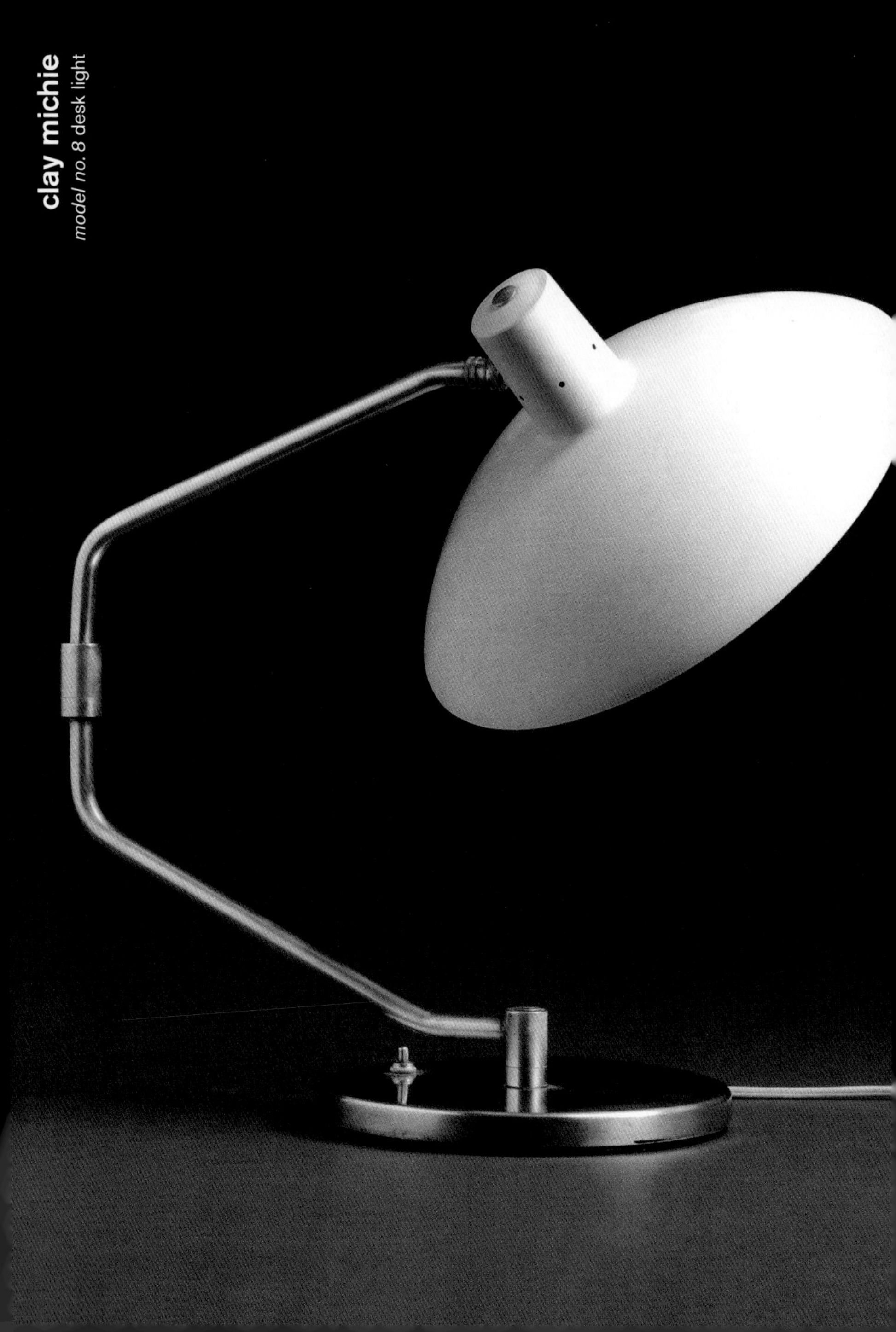

clay michie
model no. 8 desk light

Although best known for its production of avant-garde furniture, Knoll Associates also manufactured this elegant desk light designed in 1950 by Clay Michie. The *Model No. 8* desk light has a pivoting arm that can be rotated through 360 degrees, while its shade can also be angled into a number of positions. Knoll produced variations of the design including a black enameled version and another with a chrome-plated metal base. The company also manufactured a rare floor version. Combining functionality with elegance, Michie's lights complemented the distinctive "Knoll Look" pioneered by Florence Knoll. (CF/PF)

Obgleich am bekanntesten als Hersteller von Avantgarde-Möbeln, fertigte die Firma Knoll Associates auch diese von Clay Michie entworfene elegante Schreibtischleuchte (1950). Die Leuchte mit der Bezeichnung *Modell Nr. 8* hat einen schwenkbaren Arm, der sich um 360 Grad drehen lässt, und auch der Lampenschirm kann in zahlreiche Winkelpositionen gebracht werden. Knoll produzierte von diesem Entwurf einige Varianten, so beispielsweise die abgebildete schwarzlackierte Version und eine weitere mit einem verchromten Metallfuß sowie eine Stehlampe, von der nur einige wenige Exemplare erhalten sind. In der Kombination von Funktionalität mit Eleganz passen Michies Leuchtenentwürfe gut zu dem charakteristischen „Knoll Look", wie er von Florence Knoll geprägt wurde. (CF/PF)

Bien qu'on la connaisse surtout pour les meubles avant-gardistes qu'elle fabriquait, l'entreprise Knoll Associates est aussi à l'origine de cette élégante lampe de bureau signée Clay Michie (1950). Son bras orientable peut pivoter à 360°, tandis que son abat-jour peut s'incliner en plusieurs positions. Knoll fabriquait des variantes de ce modèle, dont une noire émaillée, et une autre dotée d'un socle en métal chromé. Une version lampadaire était aussi disponible quoique plus rare. Les lampes de Michie mariaient fonctionnalité et élégance et s'intégraient parfaitement au « Style Knoll » lancé par Florence Knoll. (CF/PF)

◁ ***Model No. 8* desk light, 1950**
Brass base and adjustable arm with enameled metal shade, 51 cm high / Fuß und verstellbarer Arm aus Messing mit lackiertem Lampenschirm aus Metall, 51 cm hoch / Socle et bras réglable en laiton, abat-jour en métal émaillé, 51 cm de hauteur
Knoll Assoiates, New York (NY), USA

▷ *Black enameled version of the Model No. 8 desk light designed by Clay Michie, 1950 / Schwarz lackierte Version der Schreibtischleuchte Modell Nr. 8 von Clay Michie, 1950 / Lampe de bureau Modèle nº 8 réalisée par Clay Michie, version laquée noire, 1950*

In the early 1950s, Swedish-born Greta Grossman designed a highly successful line of lighting that incorporated cup-shaped and saucer-shaped shades which eliminated glare and could be directionally angled. These two floor lights (c.1950) come from this product range and embody Grossman's belief that modern design was "a growth, progressing out of the needs of contemporary living [rather than] a superimposed style." Her lighting designs were Modern rather than modernistic and were intended to mix easily into different interior schemes. (CF/PF)

In den frühen 1950er Jahren entwarf die in Schweden geborene Designerin Greta Grossman eine höchst erfolgreiche Leuchtenserie, deren Modelle mit Lampenschirmen in Form von Tassen und Untertassen versehen waren, die das Blendlicht eliminierten und deren Strahlungswinkel gezielt eingestellt werden konnte. Zu dieser Serie gehören auch die beiden Stehleuchten (ca. 1950), die Grossmans Überzeugung verkörpern, zeitgenössisches Design sei „[eher] eine Entwicklung, die aus den Bedürfnissen des modernen Lebens erwächst [als] ein aufgesetzter Stil." Ihre Leuchtenentwürfe waren eher modern als modernistisch und sollten sich problemlos mit verschiedenen Einrichtungsprogrammen kombinieren lassen. (CF/PF)

Au début des années 1950, la créatrice d'origine suédoise Greta Grossman mit au point une série de luminaires très réussis, dont les abat-jour en forme de tasses et de soucoupes atténuaient la luminosité et pouvaient s'orienter de diverses manières. Les deux lampadaires ci-contre (vers 1950) font partie de cette série et reflètent la personnalité de Grossman, pour qui le design moderne était « quelque chose qui croît et prend racine dans les besoins de la vie contemporaine, [et non] un style imposé ». De caractère moderne plutôt que moderniste, ses luminaires étaient conçus de manière à se fondre dans des décors de styles variés. (CF/PF)

◁ *Grasshopper* floor light, *c.*1950

Enameled metal base and shade, 127 cm high / Fuß und Lampenschirm aus lackiertem Metall, 127 cm hoch / Piétement et abat-jour en métal émaillé, 127 cm de hauteur
Ralph O. Smith Manufacturing Company, Burbank (CA), USA

Floor light, *c.*1950

Enameled metal base and shade, 127 cm high / Fuß und Lampenschirm aus lackiertem Metall, 127 cm hoch / Piétement et abat-jour en métal émaillé, 127 cm de hauteur
Ralph O. Smith Manufacturing Company, Burbank (CA), USA

▷ **Anywhere table light, 1952**
Enameled tubular metal base with enameled
metal shade and diffuser, 40.5 cm high / Fuß
aus verchromtem Metallrohr mit Lampenschirm
und Diffusor aus lackiertem Metall, 40,5 cm
hoch / Pied tubulaire en métal chromé, abat-jour
et diffuseur en métal émaillé, 40,5 cm de
hauteur
Nessen Studios, New York (NY), USA

Table light, c.1950
Enameled metal base, shade and diffuser with
adjustable metal stem, 51 cm high / Sockel,
Lampenschirm und Diffusor aus lackiertem
Metall mit verstellbarem Metallarm, 51 cm hoch /
Socle, abat-jour et diffuseur en métal émaillé,
tige en métal ajustable, 51 cm de hauteur
Ralph O. Smith Mamufacturing Company,
Burbank (CA), USA

Greta Grossman's table light (*c.*1950)
is a modified version of her *Cobra* light,
which won a "Good Design" award in
June 1950. Its flexible arm allows the
reflector to be easily positioned. With
its signature bullet-shaped shade, this
light belongs to a series of seven lights
that were produced in ten different color
options. Greta von Nessen's well-known
Anywhere light (1952) is a similarly versatile mid-century lighting solution, which
provides a pleasing reflected light. It also
has a pivoting cantilevered base that
allows the light to be used on a table or
hung from a wall or a shelf. (CF/PF)

Greta Grossmans Tischleuchte
(ca. 1950) ist eine modifizierte Version ihrer Leuchte *Cobra*, die 1950
mit dem Preis „Good Design" ausgezeichnet wurde. Mit dem biegsamen
Arm lässt sich der Reflektor mühelos
in jede gewünschte Position bringen.
Die Leuchte gehört zu einer Serie von
sieben Modellen, die jeweils in zehn
verschiedenen Farben produziert wurden. Bei Greta von Nessens bekannter
Leuchte *Anywhere* (1952) handelt es
sich um eine ähnlich vielseitige Gestaltungslösung, die ein angenehm
indirektes Licht ausstrahlt. Mit ihrem
gebogenen Fuß lässt sie sich als Tischleuchte verwenden oder an die Wand
beziehungsweise an ein Regal hängen.
(CF/PF)

Cette lampe de table signée Greta
Grossman (vers 1950) est une version
modifiée de sa lampe *Cobra*, qui remporta un prix « Good Design » en juin
1950. Son bras flexible permettait de
modifier facilement la position du diffuseur. Reconnaissable à son abat-jour en
forme d'obus, elle faisait partie d'une
série de sept modèles disponibles en
dix couleurs différentes. La célèbre
lampe *Anywhere* de Greta von Nessen
(1952) est un autre exemple de ces
luminaires polyvalents du milieu du
siècle. Elle donnait une agréable lumière réfléchie et son socle pivotant en
porte-à-faux permettait de poser la
lampe sur une table ou de l'accrocher
à un mur ou à une étagère. (CF/PF)

gilbert watrous
table light

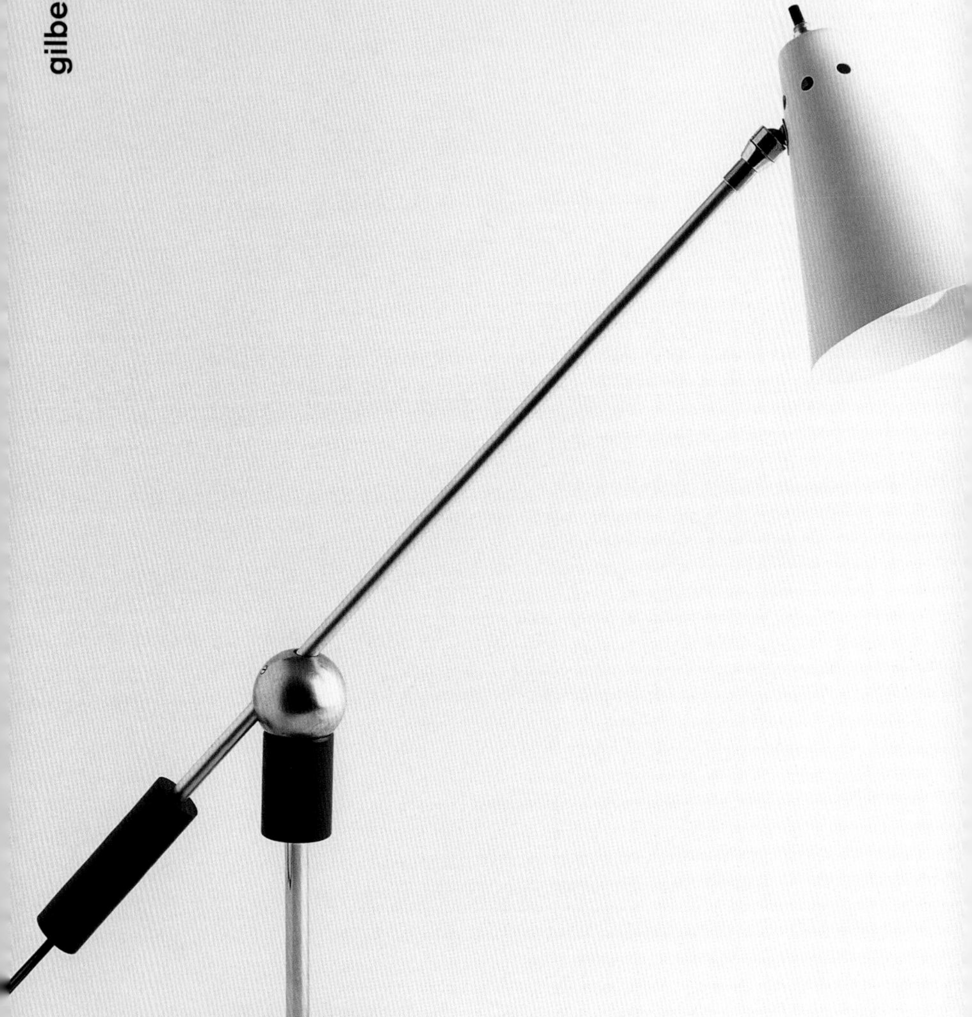

Inspired by Marcel Breuer's comment that he could not find a well-designed modern light that he would put into his own home, the Museum of Modern Art sponsored a low-cost lighting design competition in 1951. The response was phenomenal – over 3,000 entries were received. Gilbert Watrous's floor light, with its tripod base and magnetized steel ball element that allowed secure multi-positioning, was selected as the overall winner. Heifetz subsequently put this light and a number of variations of the design, including table models, into production. (CF/PF)

Angespornt von Marcel Breuers Bemerkung, er könne kein hochwertiges modernes Leuchtendesign für sein eigenes Haus finden, organisierte das Museum of Modern Art im Jahr 1951 einen Wettbewerb für Leuchtendesigner. Die Reaktion auf den Wettbewerb „Low-Cost Lighting" war phänomenal: Über 3 000 Beiträge wurden bei der Jury eingereicht. Die Stehleuchte von Gilbert Watrous mit dem dreibeinigen Fuß und dem Kugelelement aus magnetisiertem Stahl, das den Leuchtenarm in unendlich vielen Positionen sicher im Gleichgewicht hielt, wurde als Gesamtsieger gewählt. Daraufhin nahm die Firma Heifetz diesen Entwurf sowie eine Reihe von Variationen wie das hier gezeigte Tischmodell in ihre Produktion auf. (CF/PF)

En réponse à Marcel Breuer, qui avait déclaré ne pas trouver une seule lampe moderne digne de figurer chez lui, le Museum of Modern Art sponsorisa, en 1951, un concours de création de luminaires. Ce « concours de lampes bon marché » remporta un succès phénoménal – plus de trois mille candidatures furent envoyées. Le premier prix fut décerné au lampadaire de Gilbert Watrous, qui grâce à son piètement tripode et à sa boule d'acier magnétisée, pouvait être orienté de diverses manières sans jamais perdre son équilibre. Le modèle fut par la suite manufacturé par Heifetz, qui en réalisa aussi plusieurs variantes, y compris des lampes de table. (CF/PF)

◁ **Table light, c.1951**
Enameled and chrome-plated metal base with aluminum shade, 56 cm high / Fuß aus lackiertem und verchromtem Metall mit Lampenschirm aus Aluminium, 56 cm hoch / Piétement en métal chromé et émaillé, abat-jour en aluminium, 56 cm de hauteur
Heifetz Manufacturing Co., New York (NY), USA

△◁ *Heifetz Manufacturing Company swing ticket, 1950s / Papieretikett der Heifetz Manufacturing Company, 1950er Jahre / Étiquette de la Heifetz Manufacturing Company, années 1950*

△△ **Table light, 1951**
Metal and enameled metal base with aluminum shade, 66 cm high / Fuß aus lackiertem und verchromtem Metall mit Lampenschirm aus Aluminium, 66 cm hoch / Piétement en métal et métal émaillé, abat-jour en aluminium, 66 cm de hauteur
Heifetz Manufacturing Co., New York (NY), USA

△▷ *Model No. F-1-W* floor light, 1951
Enameled metal base with metal shade, stem 117 cm long, tripod 48 cm high / Lackierter Metallfuß mit Lampenschirm, Armlänge 117 cm, Dreibeinhöhe 48 cm / Piétement tripode en métal émaillé (48 cm de hauteur), abat-jour métallique, 117 cm de longueur (bras)
Heifetz Manufacturing Company, New York (NY), USA

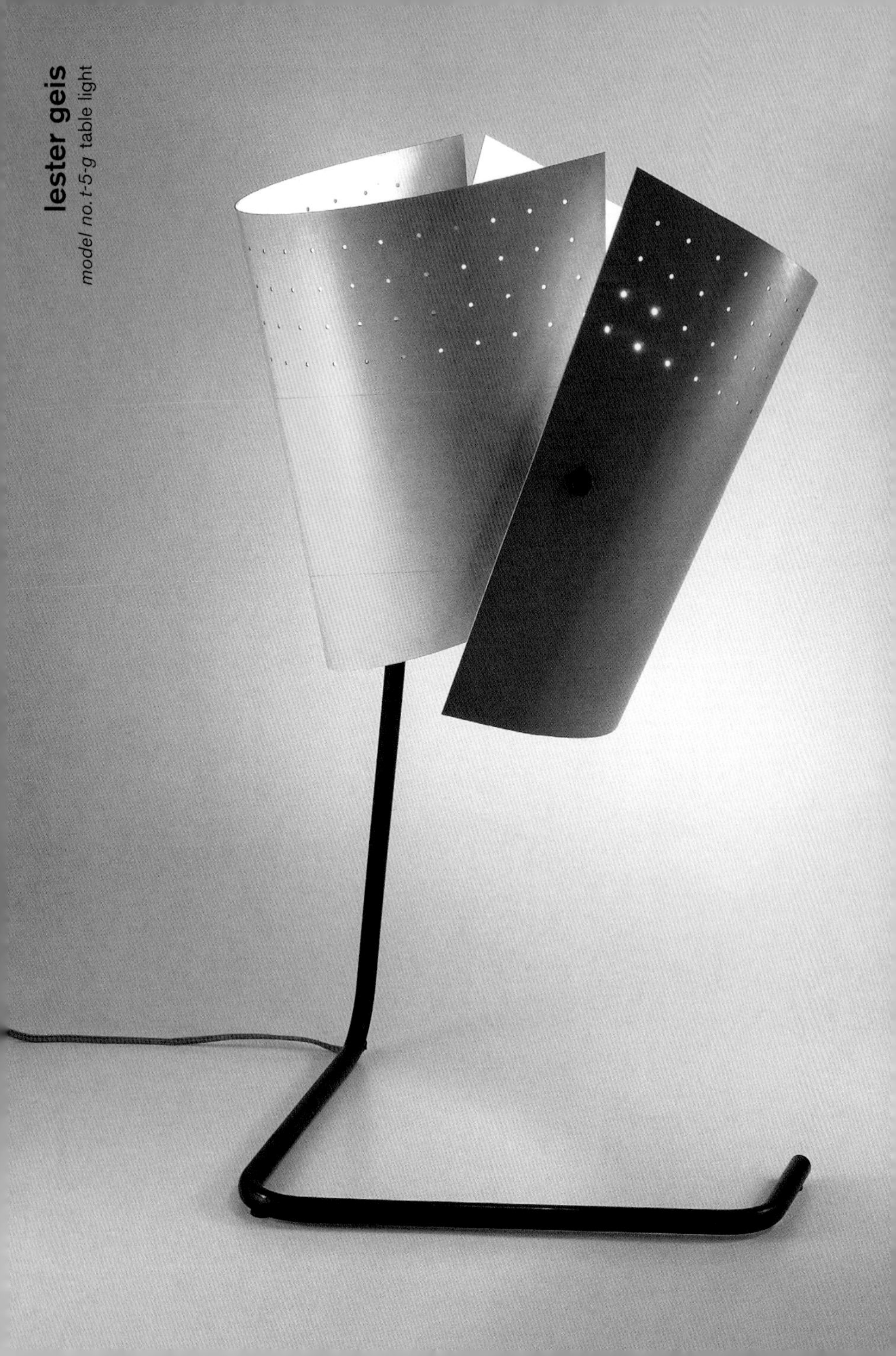

lester geis
model no. t-5-g table light

◁/▷ *Model No. T-5-G* table light, 1951

Enameled brass base with enameled metal
shade, 57 cm high / Fuß aus lackiertem
Messing mit lackiertem Lampenschirm aus
Metall, 57 cm hoch / Pied en laiton émaillé,
abat-jour en métal émaillé, 57 cm de hauteur
Heifetz Manufacturing Co., New York (NY), USA

Lester Geis's *Model No. T-5-G* table
light, designed in 1951, was given an
honorable mention at the Museum of
Modern Art's low-cost lighting competition of the same year. This unusual
design incorporated two perforated
enameled metal shades that had a scis-
sor-like action when they were pivoted
on their mount to either shield or reveal
the light source. The Heifetz Manufacturing Company of New York manufactured this light as well as a further
eight designs, which either won prizes
or received honorable mentions at the
MoMA lighting competition. (CF/PF)

Die von Lester Geis entworfene Tischleuchte *Modell Nr. T-5-G* (1951) erhielt
von der Jury des Wettbewerbs „Low-
Cost Lighting" am Museum of Modern
Art von 1951 eine lobende Erwähnung. Die ungewöhnliche Leuchte ist
mit zwei perforierten Lampenschirmen
aus lackiertem Metall ausgestattet, die
scherenartig agieren, wenn man ihre
Position verstellt, um die Glühbirne
entweder zu verdecken oder sichtbar
werden zu lassen. Die New Yorker
Heifetz Manufacturing Company produzierte diese Leuchte zusammen mit
acht anderen Entwürfen, die bei dem
Leuchtenwettbewerb des Museum of
Modern Art entweder einen Preis oder
eine lobende Erwähnung erhalten
hatten. (CF/PF)

La lampe de table *Modèle n° T-5-G*
de Lester Geis reçut une mention honorable au concours de luminaires organisé en 1951 par le Museum of Modern
Art. Ce modèle insolite était doté de
deux abat-jour en métal perforé qui,
lorsqu'on les faisait pivoter sur leur
pied, glissaient l'un sur l'autre comme
des ciseaux de manière à cacher ou à
révéler la source lumineuse. La Heifetz
Manufacturing Company de New York
fabriqua ce modèle ainsi que huit autres
qui avaient soit gagné un prix, soit reçu
une mention honorable au concours du
MoMA. (CF/PF)

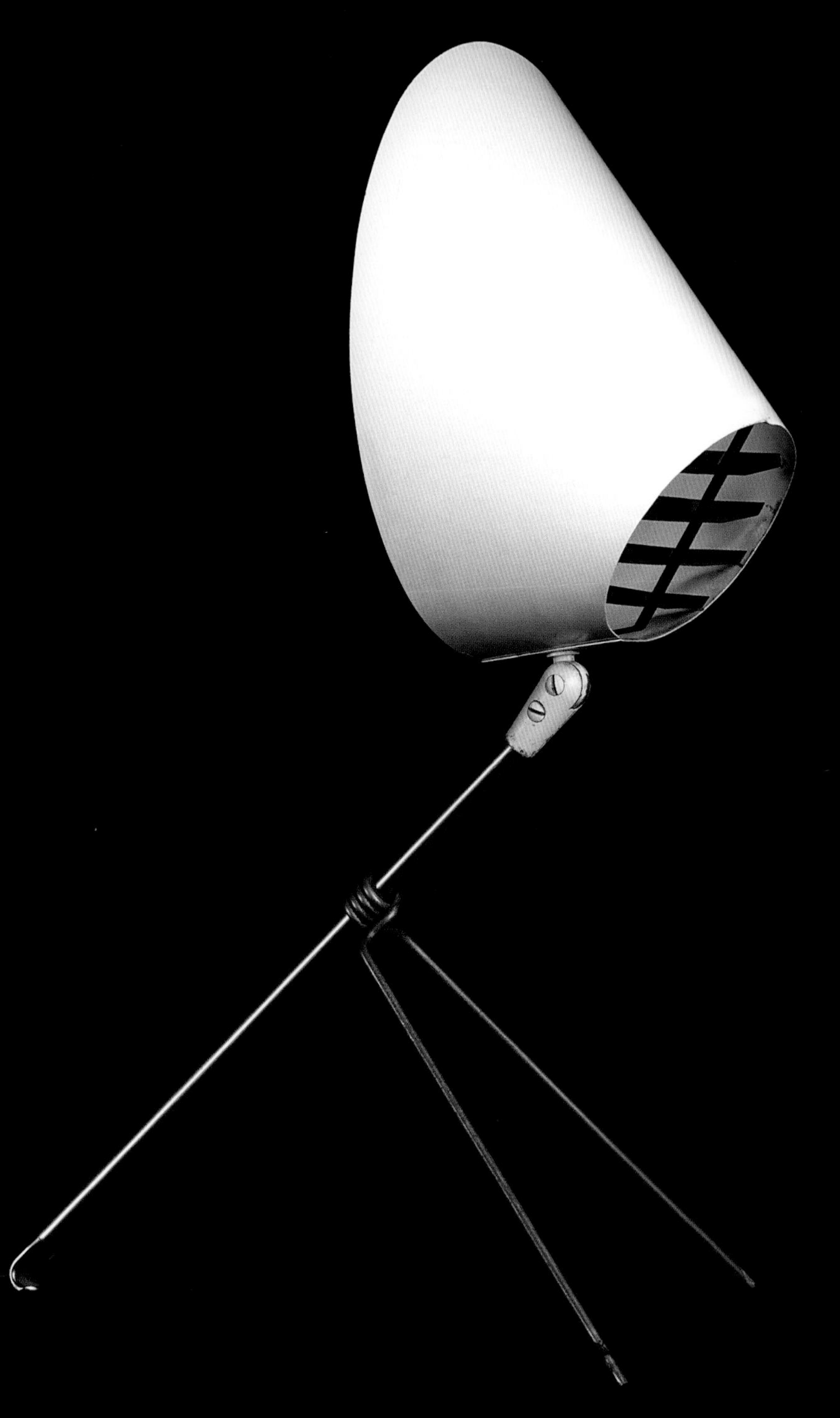

anthony incolia
model no.t-2-i table light

Like the earlier and highly successful Low-Cost Furniture Competition of 1948, the Museum of Modern Art's low-cost lighting competition of 1951 was intended to act as a spur for well-designed products that responded to postwar housing needs. Awarded second prize in the contest, Anthony Incolia's table light ingeniously incorporated a spring-like element that allowed its legs to be positioned along the stem at any point. The light also featured a small hook at the end of its central stem so that it could be hung from a wall or a shelf. (CF/PF)

Wie der vorausgehende und äußerst erfolgreiche Wettbewerb „Low-Cost Furniture", der 1948 durchgeführt wurde, war auch der Wettbewerb „Low-Cost Lighting" am Museum of Modern Art von 1951 als Ansporn für qualitativ hochwertige Designprodukte gedacht, die den Wohnbedürfnissen der Nachkriegsjahre gerecht werden sollten. Anthony Incolias mit dem zweiten Preis ausgezeichnete Tischleuchte (1951) war mit einer raffinierten, federartigen Konstruktion versehen, die es ermöglichte, die Stützhalterung an jeder gewünschten Stelle entlang des Leuchtenfußes zu positionieren. Die Leuchte hatte zudem einen kleinen Haken, so dass man sie an eine Wand oder ein Regalbrett hängen konnte. (CF/PF)

La mission du concours de luminaires organisé en 1951 par le Modern Art Museum était la même que celle du très populaire « Concours de meubles bon marché » de 1948 : encourager la création d'objets de bonne qualité pouvant répondre à la demande en mobilier de ces années d'après-guerre. Le second prix fut décerné à l'ingénieuse lampe de table d'Anthony Incolia, dont les pieds pouvait coulisser le long d'une tige grâce à une pièce en forme de ressort. Un petit crochet situé à l'une des extrémités permettait aussi de l'accrocher à un mur ou à une étagère. (CF/PF)

◁/▽ *Model No. T-2-I* table light, 1951

Metal stem and legs with enameled metal shade and rubber feet, 49.5 cm high / Füße aus Metall mit Gummikappen, lackierter Lampenschirm aus Metall, 49,5 cm hoch / Tige et pieds métalliques, abat-jour en métal émaillé, réceptions en caoutchouc, 49,5 cm de hauteur

Heifetz Manufacturing Co., New York (NY), USA

James Harvey Crate worked as an industrial stylist for General Motors and designed the *Model No. T-3-C* table light for the Museum of Modern Art's low-cost lighting competition of 1951. This dynamic-looking object, which won third prize, has an innovative construction that enables the angle of the reflector to be altered by adjusting the position of the three legs. The floor light designed by A. W. Geller and Marion Geller, which received an honorable mention in the competition, is similarly constructed so that the emitted light is bounced off a saucer-shaped reflector. (CF/PF)

James Harvey Crate, der als Industriedesigner für General Motors arbeitete, entwarf die Tischleuchte *Modell Nr. T-3-C* für den 1951 ausgeschriebenen Wettbewerb „Low-Cost Lighting" am Museum of Modern Art. Bei diesem dynamischen Lichtobjekt, das mit dem dritten Preis ausgezeichnet wurde, handelt es sich um eine innovative Konstruktion, mit der man den Winkel des Reflektors einstellen konnte, indem man die Position der drei Beine veränderte. Die von A. W. Geller und Marion Geller gestaltete Stehleuchte (1951), die beim Wettbewerb eine lobende Erwähnung erhielt, ist ähnlich konstruiert, wobei das ausgestrahlte Licht hier von einem leicht gewölbten Reflektor zurückgeworfen wird. (CF/PF)

James Harvey Crate, qui était styliste industriel chez General Motors, imagina la lampe de table *Modèle n° T-3-C* pour le concours de luminaires organisé par le Museum of Modern Art de 1951. Cet objet à l'allure dynamique remporta le troisième prix – c'était une construction ingénieuse dont on pouvait changer l'angle du réflecteur en modifiant la position des trois pieds. La lampe de table conçue par A. W. Geller et Marion Geller, qui reçut une mention honorable, est élaborée sur le même principe : la lumière émise est renvoyée par un réflecteur en forme de soucoupe. (CF/PF)

◁ **Model No. *T-3-C* table light, 1951**

Stainless steel rods and spun-aluminum base with cork finials and feet and spun-aluminum reflector, 58 cm high / Konstruktion aus Edelstahlstäben mit Korkabschlüssen, Korpus und Reflektor aus Aluminium, 58 cm hoch / Baguettes en inox, socle en aluminium , fleurons et réceptions en liège, réflecteur en aluminium repoussé, 58 cm de hauteur
Heifetz Manufacturing Co., New York (NY), USA

▷ **Floor light, 1951**

Brass and enameled metal base with enameled metal shade and cork feet, 89 cm high / Fuß aus Messing und lackiertem Metall mit lackiertem Metallreflektor und Korkfüßen, 89 cm hoch / Pied en laiton et métal émaillé, abat-jour en métal émaillé, réceptions en liège, 89 cm de hauteur
Heifetz Manufacturing Co., New York (NY), USA

Having received an honorable mention at the Museum of Modern Art's low-cost lighting design competition of 1951, Robert Gage's *Model No. T-6-G* table light was manufactured by Heifetz and retailed through Bloomingdale's department store in New York. This box-like design had four pivoting panels that could be angled to produce an indirect light. When the panels were closed completely, the light functioned as a tabletop uplighter. Like the other prize-winning lights manufactured by Heifetz, *Model No. T-6-G* reflected a new level of confidence and sophistication in American design during the postwar period. (CF/PF)

Nachdem der Beitrag von Robert Gage zum Wettbewerb „Low-Cost Lighting" am Museum of Modern Art von 1951, das *Modell Nr. T-6-G*, eine lobende Erwähnung erhalten hatte, wurde die Tischleuchte von der Firma Heifetz produziert und durch das New Yorker Kaufhaus Bloomingdale vertrieben. Das schachtelartige Design ist mit vier Blendschirmen ausgestattet, die so eingestellt werden können, dass die Leuchte ein indirektes Licht gibt. Wenn die Schirme völlig geschlossen sind, funktioniert die Leuchte als Fluter. Ebenso wie bei anderen auf dem Leuchtenwettbewerb ausgezeichneten und von der Firma Heifetz produzierten Leuchten drückt sich im *Modell Nr. T-6-G* ein neuer Grad an Selbstbewusstsein und Raffinement des amerikanischen Designs der Nachkriegszeit aus. (CF/PF)

Après avoir reçu une mention honorable au concours de luminaires organisé par le Museum of Modern Art en 1951, la lampe de table *Modèle n° T-6-G* de Robert Gage fut manufacturée par Heifetz et vendue au grand magasin new-yorkais Bloomingdale. Ce modèle en forme de boîte était composé de quatre panneaux pivotants dont on pouvait modifier l'angle de manière à obtenir un éclairage indirect. Lorsqu'on fermait complètement les panneaux, le faisceau lumineux était dirigé vers le plafond. Tout comme les autres modèles primés fabriqués par Heifetz, le *Modèle n° T-6-G* illustre le nouveau climat d'optimisme et de sophistication qui régnait dans le monde de design américain après la guerre. (CF/PF)

Model No. T-6-G table light, 1951

Enameled brass base with adjustable Masonite and enameled metal screens, 46 cm high /
Lackierte Messingfüße mit verstellbaren Blendschirmen aus Holzfaserplatten und lackiertem Metall, 46 cm hoch / Piétement en laiton émaillé, panneaux réglables en masonite et métal émaillé, 46 cm de hauteur
Heifetz Manufacturing Co., New York (NY), USA

zahara schatz
table light

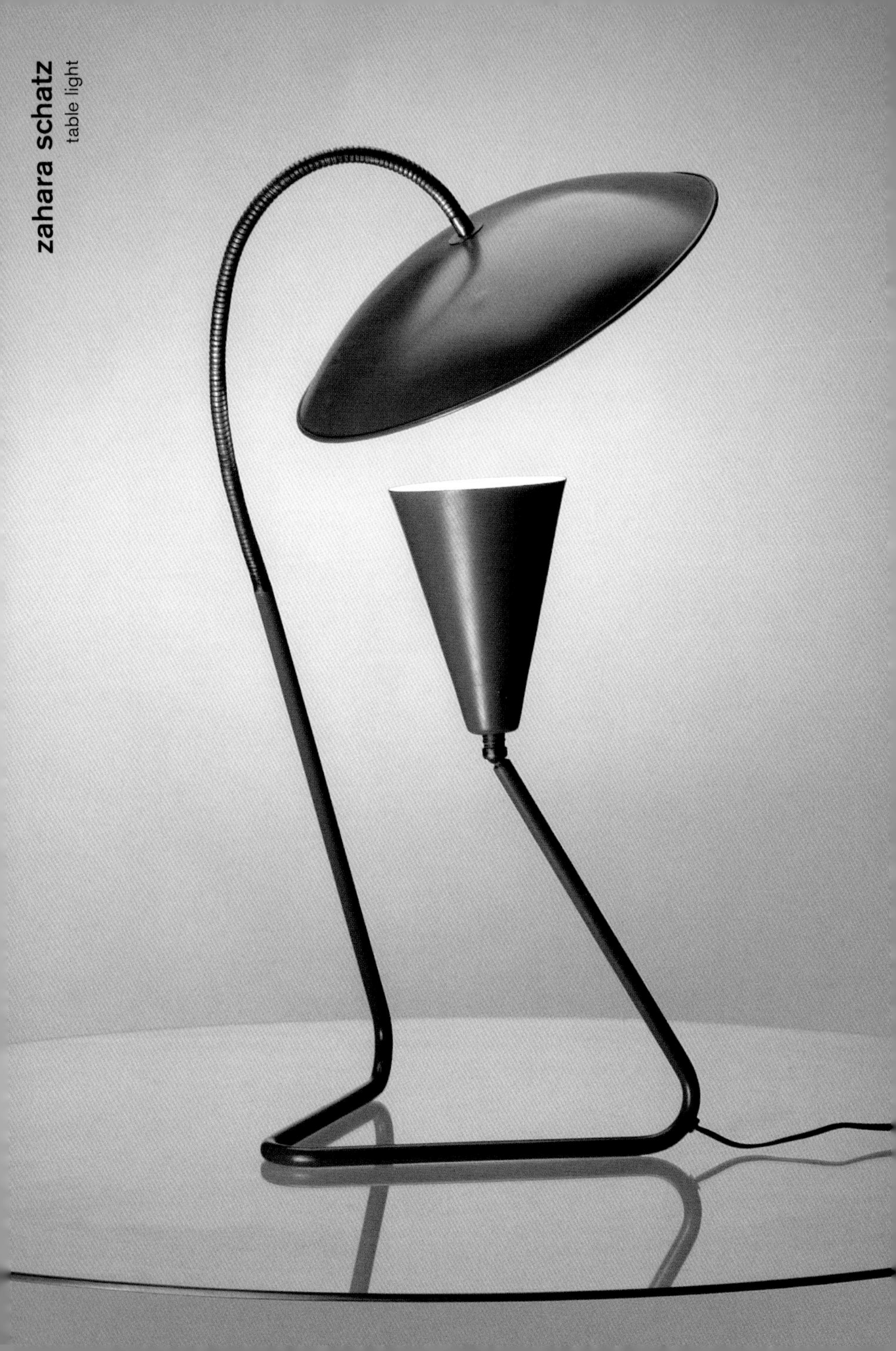

◁ **Table light, 1951**
Metal rod base with articulating metal stem, enameled metal shade and reflector, 68.5 cm high / Fuß aus Stahlrohr mit Gelenkarm aus Metall, Lampenschirm und Reflektor aus lackiertem Metall, 68,5 cm hoch / Base en fin tube métallique, tige métallique articulée, abat-jour et réflecteur en métal émaillé, 68,5 cm de hauteur
Heifetz Manufacturing Co., New York (NY), USA

Model No. T-7-Z **table light, 1951**
African mahogany base with brass arm, painted wood ball adjuster and vellum shade, 49.5 cm high / Fuß aus afrikanischem Mahagoni mit Messingarm, Justierkugel und Pergamentschirm, 49,5 cm hoch / Socle en acajou africain, bras en laiton, ajusteur sphérique en bois peint, abat-jour en vélin, 49,5 cm de hauteur
Heifetz Manufacturing Co., New York (NY), USA

Both these table lights were given an honorable mention at the Museum of Modern Art's low-cost lighting competition of 1951. Zahara Schatz's elegant goose-necked table light features an articulating stem that enables multi-positioning of the reflector, while its cone-like shade can also be adjusted to allow a high degree of lighting direction control. John van Zweinen's *Model No. T-7-Z* table light also provides much directional control through its innovative construction of a tilting shade fixed to an arm that is balanced on a stem by means of a tilting and swiveling device. (CF/PF)

Auch diese beiden Entwürfe erhielten beim Wettbewerb „Low-Cost Lighting" am Museum of Modern Art von 1951 eine lobende Erwähnung der Jury. Die elegante, doppelbogenförmige Tischleuchte von Zahara Schatz besitzt einen flexiblen Gelenkarm, mit dem sich der Reflektor in mehrere Positionen einstellen lässt. Der kegelförmige Lampenschirm wiederum ist so verstellbar, dass die gewünschte Lichtstrahl genau eingestellt werden kann. Auch bei John van Zweinens Tischleuchte *Modell Nr. T-7-Z* lässt sich das Licht gezielt steuern, hier mittels einer innovativen Konstruktion, mit der der schwenkbare Schirm an einem Arm befestigt ist, der durch eine kipp- und drehbare Gelenkmontierung auf dem Fuß austariert wird. (CF/PF)

Ces deux lampes de tables reçurent une mention honorable au concours de luminaires organisé par le Museum of Modern Art en 1951. L'élégant modèle de Zahara Schatz est doté d'une monture flexible en col de cygne permettant d'orienter le réflecteur et d'un abat-jour conique réglable offrant un contrôle optimal du faisceau lumineux. Le *Modèle n° T-7-Z* de John van Zweinen permet lui aussi de diriger le faisceau avec précision : son abat-jour inclinable est fixé à un bras équilibré pouvant pivoter et s'incliner sur son support. (CF/PF)

Otto Kolb designed for himself in Switzerland a remarkable circular glass home which epitomized the postwar International Style. He also designed a number of buildings in the United States, notably the Imre & Maria Horner House in Beverly Shores, Indiana, which was featured in *Arts & Architecture* magazine in October 1952. This flexible table light was designed by the Swissborn architect in the early 1950s and could be easily adjusted into numerous positions. With its stylish nipped-in shade, it can be seen to exemplify the sleek "New Look" of 1950s design. (CF/PF)

Otto Kolb entwarf in seinem Heimatland Schweiz ein bemerkenswertes rundes Glashaus, in dem er selber wohnte und das den International Style der Nachkriegsarchitektur verkörperte. Außerdem gestaltete er eine Reihe von Gebäuden in den Vereinigten Staaten, wobei besonders das im Oktober 1952 in der Zeitschrift *Arts & Architecture* präsentierte Wohnhaus von Imre und Maria Horner in Beverly Shores, Indiana, hervorzuheben ist. Die flexible, in zahlreiche verschiedene Positionen verstellbare Tischleuchte wurde von Kolb Anfang der 1950er Jahre entworfen. Mit ihrem doppelkonischen Lampenschirm ist sie exemplarisch für den raffiniert eleganten „New Look" des Designs der 1950er Jahre. (CF/PF)

Otto Kolb réalisa pour lui-même, en Suisse, une remarquable maison en même du Style International d'après-guerre. Il conçut également un certain nombre de bâtiments aux États-Unis, notamment la résidence d'Imre & Maria Horner située à Beverly Shores, Indiana, qui fit l'objet d'un article dans le magazine *Arts & Architecture* en octobre 1952. L'architecte suisse réalisa cette lampe de table articulée, qui se règle en de nombreuses positions, au début des années 1950. Avec son gracieux abat-jour resserré au milieu, elle incarne le raffinement discret « New Look » des années 1950. (CF/PF)

Table lights, c.1951
Brass rod stem and legs with adjustable connector, enameled metal shade and rubber feet / Fußkonstruktion aus Messingstäben mit Gummischonern, verstellbares Verbindungselement, lackierter Metallschirm / Tige en laiton, pieds coulissants, abat-jour en métal émaillé, réceptions en caoutchouc
USA

Jean-Louis Domecq designed the *Standard* light in 1951 to equip the workstations in his own industrial plant. The light's articulated arm, clamping base and sturdy construction made it ideal for the workshop environment. It proved so successful that in 1953 Domecq established the company Jieldé (the name derived from his initials) to mass-produce both table and floor models with a variety of bases and with one to three arms in different lengths. In 1998 Philippe Belier, Jieldé's current managing director, reinterpreted the *Standard* in the *Loft Courbe* collection featuring curved arms, but that redesigned range is now out of production. (VT)

Jean-Louis Domecq entwarf die *Standard* Leuchte (1951) als Ausstattung für die Arbeitsplätze in seiner eigenen Fabrik. Der Gelenkarm, die Klemmvorrichtung und die robuste Konstruktion machten diese Leuchte zu einer idealen Arbeitsleuchte. Sie erwies sich als so erfolgreich, dass Domecq 1953 die Firma Jieldé (der Name leitet sich von seinen Initialen ab) gründete, um sowohl das Tisch- als auch ein Stehleuchtenmodell industriell zu fertigen. Beide Versionen waren mit unterschiedlichen Füßen und bis zu drei Armen in verschiedenen Längen erhältlich. Philippe Belier, derzeit Vorstandsvorsitzender von Jieldé, entwarf 1998 als Überarbeitung dieses Designs die Kollektion *Loft Courbe*, die Leuchten mit geschwungenen Armen enthielt, inzwischen aber nicht mehr produziert wird. (VT)

Jean-Louis Domecq conçut sa lampe *Standard* pour équiper les postes de travail de sa propre usine. Son bras articulé, son socle à étau et sa facture robuste la rendait idéale pour une utilisation en atelier. Son succès fut tel qu'en 1953, Domecq fonda sa propre entreprise qu'il appela Jieldé (d'après les initiales de son nom) afin de la fabriquer en version lampe de table et lampadaire, avec divers types de socles et jusqu'à trois bras de longueurs différentes. La collection *Loft Courbe*, créée en 1998 par le p.-d.g. actuel de Jieldé, reprend le même modèle de base mais avec un bras courbé. Cette dernière série n'est plus en production actuellement. (VT)

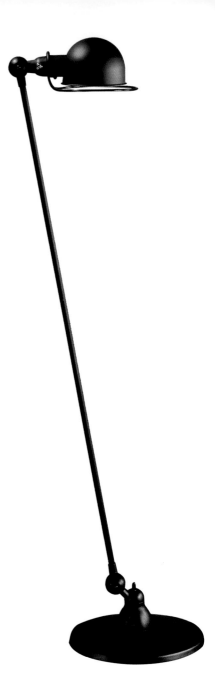

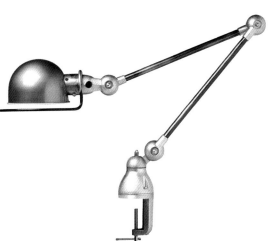

◁◁ *Model No. 1200 Standard*
floor light, 1951

Enameled metal base and shade with adjustable
arm, arm 90 cm long / Fuß und Lampenschirm
aus lackiertem Metall mit verstellbarem Arm,
Armlänge 90 cm / Socle et abat-jour en métal
émaillé, bras réglable de 90 cm de long
Jieldé, Saint-Priest, France

△/◁ *Model No. 1200 Standard*
task lights, 1951

Metal base and shade with adjustable arm,
arm 80 cm long / Fuß und Lampenschirm aus
Metall mit verstellbarem Arm, Armlänge 80 cm /
Socle et abat-jour en métal, bras réglable de
80 cm de long
Jieldé, Saint-Priest, France

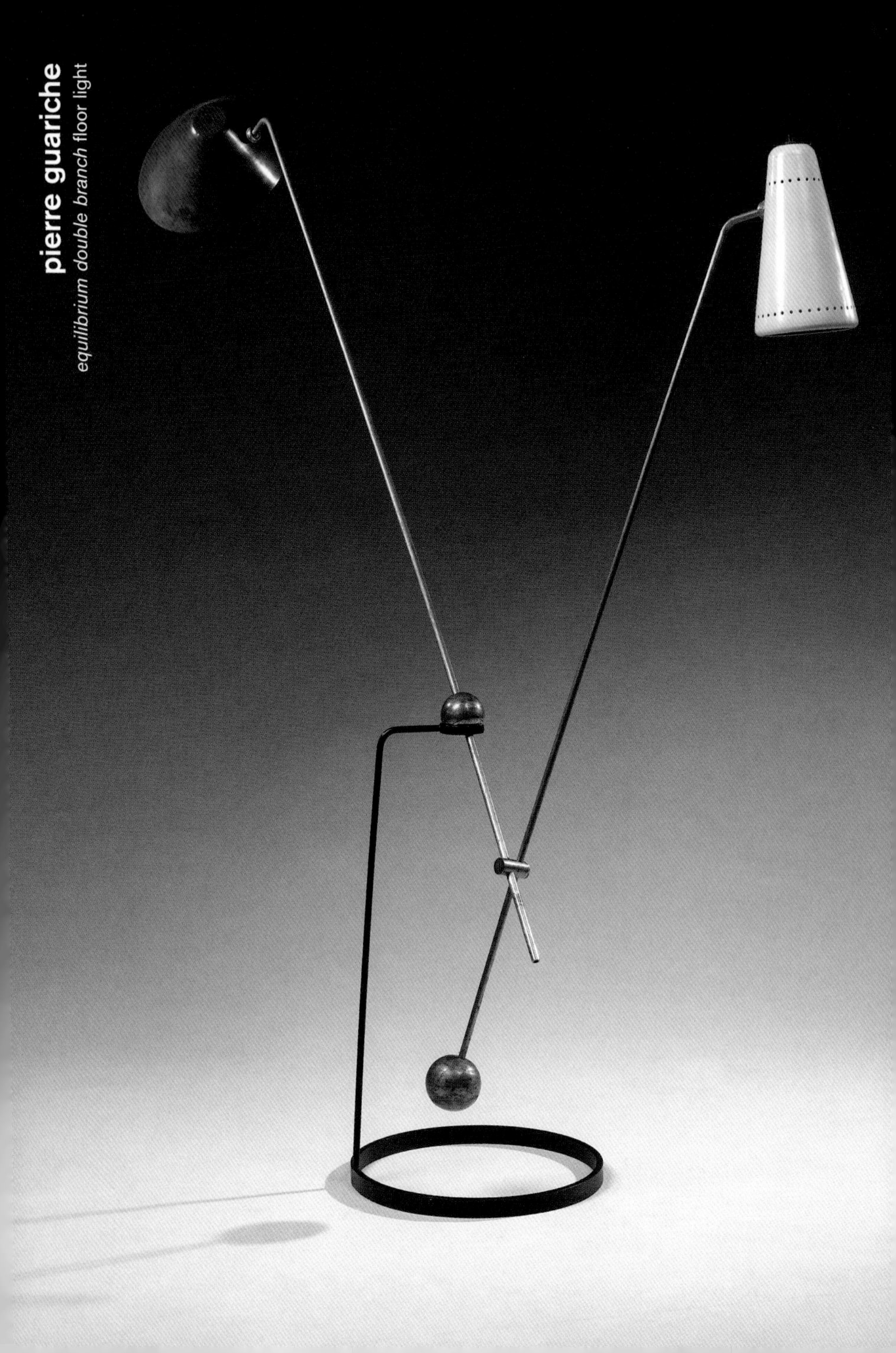

pierre guariche
equilibrium double branch floor light

◁ *Equilibrium Double Branch*
floor light, 1951
Iron base, brass arms and counterweight with
enameled metal shades, 190.5 cm high / Eisenfuß mit Arm und Ausgleichgewicht aus Messing
sowie Lampenschirmen aus lackiertem Metall,
190,5 cm hoch / Socle en fer, bras et contrepoids en laiton, abat-jour en métal émaillé,
190,5 cm de hauteur
Disderot, Boulogne-Billancourt, France

△◁ *Cerf-Volant (Kite)* **floor light, 1952**
Iron base with brass stem with enameled metal
shade and reflector, 200 cm high / Eisenfuß mit
Messingmontierung, Lampenschirm und Reflektor aus lackiertem Metall, 200 cm hoch / Socle
en fer, tige en laiton, abat-jour et réflecteur en
métal émaillé, 200 cm de hauteur
Disderot, Boulogne-Billancourt, France

△▷ *Equilibrium* **floor light, 1951**
Brass base and arm with brass counterweight
and enameled metal shade, 200 cm high / Fuß,
Arm und Ausgleichgewicht aus Messing mit
Lampenschirm aus lackiertem Metall, 200 cm
hoch / Piétement, bras et contrepoids en laiton,
abat-jour en métal émaillé, 200 cm de hauteur
Disderot, Boulogne-Billancourt, France

Pierre Guariche trained at the School of
Decorative Arts in Paris under the pioneering French Modernist René Gabriel.
Subsequently, he developed his own
unique modern style, which has now
become evocative of French 1950s
lighting. Guariche's lights often incorporated a counterbalance to create
perfect harmony – the brass spheres,
which we see on two of these designs,
act as counterweights, and can therefore be moved by the user into almost
any position. (AP)

Pierre Guariche studierte an der Pariser Kunstgewerbeschule bei dem bahnbrechenden französischen Modernisten
René Gabriel. In der Folge entwickelte
er seinen eigenen, außergewöhnlichen
Stil, der inzwischen exemplarisch für
das französische Leuchtendesign der
1950er Jahre ist. Guariches Leuchten
waren häufig mit Ausgleichgewichten
versehen, was ihnen eine ausgezeichnete Balance verlieh. Die Messingku-
geln, die man an zwei der hier abgebildeten Modellen sieht, fungierten als
Gegengewichte, wodurch der Benutzer
die Leuchtquelle in fast jede gewünschte Position bringen konnte. (AP)

Guariche fut formé à l'École des arts
décoratifs de Paris par René Gabriel,
l'un des pionniers du Modernisme
français. Par la suite, il se forgea un
style moderne bien à lui, qu'on associe
aujourd'hui aux luminaires français
des années 1950. Par souci d'harmo-
nie, Pierre Guariche équipait souvent
ses luminaires d'un contrepoids –
les boules de laiton, qu'on peut voir
sur deux des modèles présentés ici,
servent de contrepoids. L'utilisateur
pouvait les déplacer et leur donner
presque n'importe quelle position. (AP)

Suspended ceiling light, 1950s

Brass mounts with opaque glass shade and enameled metal diffuser, 41 cm diameter / Montierung aus Messing mit Lampenschirm aus Opakglas und Diffusor aus lackiertem Metall, 41 cm Durchmesser / Cadre en laiton, abat-jour en verre opaque, diffuseur en métal émaillé, 41 cm de diamètre
Disderot, Boulogne-Billancourt, France

▷ **Floor light, 1950s**

Iron base with plastic and enameled metal shades, 137 cm high / Eisenfuß mit Lampenschirmen aus Plastik und lackiertem Metall, 137 cm hoch / Piétement en fer, abat-jour en plastique et métal émaillé, 137 cm de hauteur
Disderot, Boulogne-Billancourt, France

Pierre Guariche was of a generation of postwar designers who sought an alternative to the opulent traditions of French decorative arts and to the hard chic of French prewar Modernism. He used modest materials that could be pressed into production-line processes to create domestic light fittings that were practical, unfussy and modern, and that could be put into the market place at prices accessible to a reasonably wide public. Pierced, perforated and painted metal is the common distinguishing feature of these two designs from the 1950s. (PG)

Pierre Guariche gehörte zu einer Generation von Nachkriegsdesignern, die eine Alternative suchten, sowohl zur reich verzierten Stiltradition der französischen dekorativen Kunst als auch zu der strengen Eleganz des französischen Vorkriegsmodernismus. Er verwendete einfache, für die Fließbandproduktion geeignete Materialien und schuf damit Wohnraumleuchten, die praktisch, schnörkellos und modern waren und sich zu Preisen verkaufen ließen, die sich ein relativ breites Publikum leisten konnte. Besonderes Merkmal der beiden Entwürfe aus den 1950er Jahren sind die perforierten Lampenschirme aus lackiertem Metall. (PG)

Pierre Guariche appartenait à cette génération de créateurs d'après-guerre qui cherchait une alternative à la traditionnelle opulence des arts décoratifs français, ainsi qu'à l'élégance austère du Modernisme français d'avant-guerre. Ses luminaires, fabriqués à partir de matériaux simples et faciles à assembler à la chaîne, étaient pratiques, modernes et sans façons, et pouvaient être mis sur le marché à des prix relativement abordables. Ces deux modèles ont comme point commun leurs pièces en métal percé, perforé et peint. (PG)

gino sarfatti
model no. 534 table light

Like some exotic magic toadstool, the *Model No. 534* table light appears to be growing from its central stem. Designed in 1951 by Gino Sarfatti, who had an almost maniacal passion for lighting, this whimsical design epitomized the playful exuberance of postwar Italian society, which was emerging as a newly prosperous and culturally influential force. *Model No. 534's* eight multicolored reflecting shades can be tilted into a variety of positions and the arms supporting them can be moved through various angles. (CF/PF)

Wie ein exotisch-magischer Blätterpilz scheint die Tischleuchte *Modell Nr. 534* (1951) von ihrem zentralen Stiel aus zu wachsen. Entworfen von Gino Sarfatti, der eine fast manische Leidenschaft für Beleuchtungskörper hegte, ist dieses eigenwillige Design exemplarisch für den spielerischen Überschwang der italienischen Gesellschaft der Nachkriegszeit, die sich erneut als wohlhabende und kulturell einflussreiche Kraft zu etablieren begann. Die acht verschiedenfarbigen Reflektorschirme können in unterschiedliche Positionen geneigt werden, und die Stützarme lassen sich in mehrere Winkel einstellen. (CF/PF)

Pareille à un champignon exotique, la lampe de table *Modèle n° 534* (1951) semble jaillir comme par magie de sa tige centrale. Conçu par Gino Sarfatti, dont la passion pour les luminaires frisait l'obsession, ce modèle plein de fantaisie reflète le climat de légèreté et d'exubérance qui régnait dans l'Italie d'après-guerre, laquelle était en train de s'imposer comme nouvelle puissance économique et culturelle. Les huit abat-jour multicolores du *Modèle n° 534* peuvent s'incliner dans diverses positions, tout comme les bras qui les soutiennent. (CF/PF)

△/▷ **Model No. 534 table light, 1951**
Enameled metal base, stems and shades, 57 cm high / Fuß, Arme und Lampenschirme aus lackiertem Metall, 57 cm hoch / Socle, tiges et abat-jour en métal émaillé, 57 cm de haut
Arteluce, Milan, Italy

▽ *Contemporary photograph showing the* Model No.534 table light, 1950s / *Zeitgenössisches Interieur mit der Tischleuchte* Modell Nr. 534, *1950er Jahre* / *Photographie d'époque avec la lampe de table* Modèle n°534, *années 1950*

Gino Sarfatti probably designed this unusual wall light in the early 1950s. Certainly, many of his designs included colorful enameled reflectors, such as those used for this model, which could be adjusted in order to angle the emitted light into the required direction. This wall light reveals the strong influence on postwar design of contemporary abstract sculpture – especially the work of Alexander Calder and Hans Arp – and the popularity of amorphous forms during the 1950s. (CF/PF)

Bei dieser ungewöhnlichen Wandleuchte (ca. 1950) handelt es sich vermutlich um einen Entwurf von Gino Sarfatti. Fest steht, dass viele seiner Leuchten wie dieses Modell mit bunt lackierten Metallreflektoren ausgestattet waren. Die Reflektoren waren verstellbar, damit man den Lichtstrahl in die gewünschte Richtung lenken konnte. Diese Wandleuchte offenbart, wie stark das Design der Nachkriegszeit von der zeitgenössischen abstrakten Bildhauerei beeinflusst war – besonders durch die Werke von Alexander Calder und Hans Arp – und wie beliebt amorphe Formen in den 1950er Jahren waren. (CF/PF)

Il semble que Gino Sarfatti ait réalisé cette curieuse applique murale au début des années 1950. Beaucoup de ses modèles étaient équipés de réflecteurs émaillés multicolores, comme ici, que l'on pouvait ajuster afin d'orienter le faisceau lumineux dans telle ou telle direction. Cette applique montre combien les créateurs d'après-guerre étaient influencés par la sculpture contemporaine abstraite – les œuvres d'Alexander Calder et de Hans Arp en particulier – et combien les formes aux contours vagues étaient à la mode dans les années 1950. (CF/PF)

Wall light, c.1950

Adjustable enameled metal reflector with brass arms and additional enameled metal reflectors / Verstellbarer Reflektor aus lackiertem Metall mit Messingarmen und weiteren Reflektoren aus lackiertem Metall / Réflecteur réglable en métal émaillé, tiges en laiton, réflecteurs supplémentaires en métal émaillé
Arteluce, Milan, Italy (attrib.)

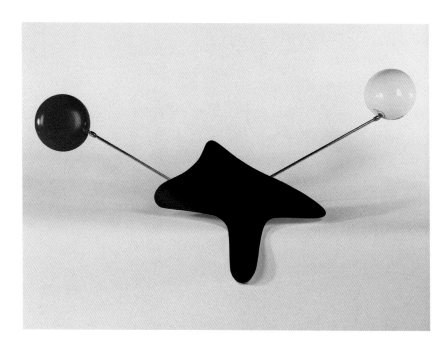

This stylish table light was designed around 1952 by Gino Sarfatti, the maestro of Italian lighting design, and was marketed in the United States by Knoll Associates during the early 1950s. Like the remarkable wall light illustrated overleaf, probably also designed during the 1950s by Sarfatti, this type of ultra-stylish product for the home was central to the "Italian Miracle" – an export-driven economic recovery that hinged on design ingenuity and crafts skills honed over generations in small specialized workshops, rather than on cutting-edge industrial technology and the availability of state-of-the-art production facilities. (CF/PF)

Die stilvolle Tischleuchte (ca. 1952) ist ein Entwurf von Gino Sarfatti, dem Maestro des italienischen Leuchtendesigns, und wurde Anfang der 1950er Jahre in den Vereinigten Staaten über Knoll Associates vertrieben. Wie die vermutlich ebenfalls von Sarfatti gestaltete außergewöhnliche Wandleuchte (1950er Jahre), die auf der nachfolgenden Doppelseite abgebildet ist, war diese Art von ultramodernem Wohnraumdesign ein zentraler Bestandteil des „italienischen Wirtschaftswunders", einer exportorientierten Wirtschaftsleistung, die mehr auf der seit Generationen in kleinen Spezialbetrieben fortentwickelten gestalterischen und handwerklichen Geschicklichkeit als auf den neuesten industriellen Technologien und Produktionsmitteln beruhte. (CF/PF)

Cette élégante lampe de table est (comme la superbe applique murale représentée à la page suivante) l'œuvre du grand créateur italien Gino Sarfatti. Elle était commercialisée aux États-Unis par Knoll Associates au début des années 1950. Ce type de bibelot très sophistiqué joua un rôle primordial dans le « Miracle Italien » – cette renaissance économique fondée sur l'export qui s'appuyait sur l'ingéniosité des créateurs et les savoir-faire ancestraux à défaut de technologies de pointe et d'usines ultra-modernes. (CF/PF)

Table light, *c.*1952

Enameled metal and brass base with enameled metal shades, 28 cm high / Fuß aus lackiertem Metall und Messing mit lackierten Metallschirmen, 28 cm hoch / Socle en laiton et métal émaillé, abat-jour en métal émaillé, 28 cm
Arteluce, Milan, Italy

Arredoluce was one of the most innovative manufacturers of Italian-designed lighting during the 1950s and 1960s. Founded by the industrialist and designer Angelo Lelli, the company was based in Monza and its craftsmen possessed the technical ability to enable designers to create truly avant-garde lighting for the home. During the 1950s the firm produced many light products, the majority of which were distinguished by dynamic and sculptural forms. Among the designers working for Arredoluce at this time were the Castiglioni brothers, Gio Ponti and Ettore Sottsass. (CF/PF)

In den 1950er und 1960er Jahren war Arredoluce einer der innovativsten Hersteller von italienischen Leuchten. Die von dem Industriellen und Designer Angelo Lelli gegründete Firma hatte ihren Sitz in Monza, und ihre Handwerker besaßen die technischen Fertigkeiten, um die wahrhaft avantgardistischen Entwürfe für Wohnraumleuchten der für das Unternehmen tätigen Designer adäquat umzusetzen. In den 1950er Jahren produzierte Arredoluce viele Leuchtenmodelle, die sich durch ihre dynamischen und skulpturalen Formen auszeichneten. Zu den Designern, die damals für die Firma arbeiteten, gehörten die Brüder Castiglioni, Gio Ponti und Ettore Sottsass. (CF/PF)

Arredoluce était l'un des fabricants de luminaires les plus novateurs dans l'Italie des années 1950 et 1960. Fondée par l'industriel et créateur Angelo Lelli, l'entreprise se situait à Monza. Ses artisans possédaient une telle maîtrise technique que les créateurs pouvaient y inventer des luminaires domestiques réellement avant-gardistes. Dans les années 1950, l'entreprise produisit de nombreux luminaires, reconnaissables, pour la plupart, à leurs formes dynamiques et sculpturales. Les frères Castiglioni, Gio Ponti et Ettore Sottsass comptent parmi les créateurs qui travaillaient pour Arredoluce à l'époque. (CF/PF)

▽ **Wall light, _c._1950**

Enameled aluminum reflector with brass mounts / Lackierter Aluminiumreflektor mit Messingmontierung / Réflecteur en aluminium émaillé, montures en laiton
Arredoluce, Monza, Italy

▷ **Suspended ceiling light, 1954**

Enameled metal reflector and shade with brass supports, 89 cm high / Reflektor und Lampenschirm aus lackiertem Metall mit Montierung aus Messing, 89 cm hoch / Réflecteur et abat-jour en métal émaillé, supports en laiton, 89 cm de hauteur
Arredoluce, Monza, Italy

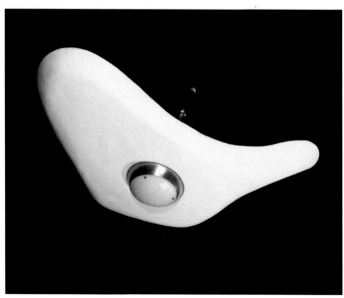

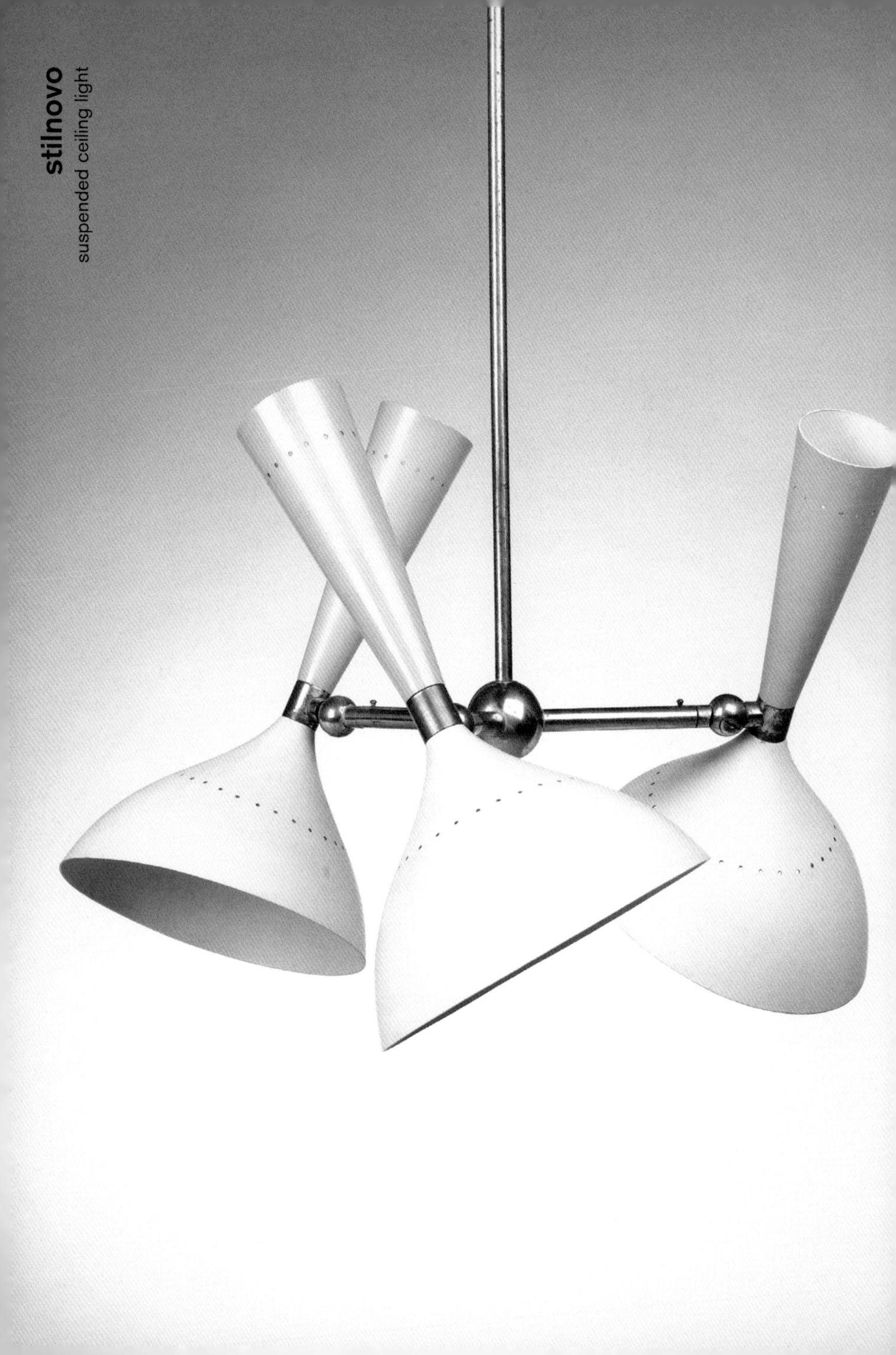

stilnovo
suspended ceiling light

◁ **Suspended ceiling light, 1950s**
Brass mounts with enameled metal shades,
91,5 cm drop / Montierung aus Messing
mit Lampenschirmen aus lackiertem Metall,
91,5 cm lang / Montures en laiton, abat-jour
en métal émaillé, 91,5 cm de hauteur
Stilnovo, Milan, Italy

Desk light, 1950s
Leather and copper base with copper and white
acrylic shade, 44.5 cm high / Sockel und Füße
aus Leder und Kupfer mit Lampenschirm aus
Kupfer und weißem Acryl, 44,5 cm hoch / Socle
en cuir et cuivre, abat-jour en cuivre et acrylique
blanc, 44,5 cm de hauteur
Stilnovo, Milan, Italy

During the 1950s the Italian lighting
manufacturer Stilnovo employed many
leading architects and designers of the
day, including Gaetano Scolari, and
created an abundance of visually striking
lights. With their hourglass forms,
evocative of the "New Look" dresses of
Christian Dior, and their "atomic" spherical details, Stilnovo's works are examples of classic 1950s Italian lighting.
Both of the lights shown here illustrate
Stilnovo's signature materials: brass and
copper. In the succeeding decades,
Stilnovo manufactured even more experimental lighting products designed by,
among others, Joe Colombo and Ettore
Sottsass. (AP)

Während der 1950er Jahre beschäftig-
te der italienische Leuchtenhersteller
Stilnovo viele der damals führenden
Architekten und Designer wie Gaetano
Scolari und produzierte eine Fülle von
eindrucksvollen Leuchten. Mit ihren
Sanduhrformen, die Bezug auf den
„New Look" der Kleider von Christian
Dior nehmen, und ihren kugelförmigen
Gestaltungselementen sind die Arbeiten von Stilnovo beispielhaft für das
klassische italienische Leuchtendesign
der 1950er Jahre. Die beiden hier präsentierten Leuchten sind aus typischen
Stilnovo-Materialien gefertigt: Messing
und Kupfer. In den folgenden Jahrzehnten produzierte Stilnovo noch experi-
mentellere Beleuchtungskörper, entworfen von Designern wie Joe Colombo
und Ettore Sottsass. (AP)

Pendant les années 1950, le fabricant
italien de luminaires Stilnovo travailla
avec plusieurs grands noms du moment,
dont Gaetano Scolari, et réalisa un
grand nombre de modèles superbes.
Avec leurs formes étranglées, qui rappellent les robes « New Look » de Christian Dior, et leurs sphères disposées
« en atome », les produits de Stilnovo
sont des exemples classiques du style
italien des années 1950. Les deux
lampes représentées ici sont faites de
deux matières que Stilnovo utilisait souvent : le laiton et le cuivre. Au cours des
décennies qui suivirent, Stilnovo allait
réaliser des luminaires encore plus
expérimentaux, conçus entre autres par
Joe Colombo et Ettore Sottsass. (AP)

The *Model No. 566* table light from 1956 is a highly progressive design that epitomizes not only Gino Sarfatti's analytical approach to the design of lighting, but also the high manufacturing standards achieved by Arteluce. Patented in 1956, this light has an innovative construction that allowed the light's head to be moved along the whole length of the tilted stem. A similarly rational design is the wall light (opposite). Both this and *Model No. 566* can be described as "essentialist" and exemplify Sarfatti's refined vocabulary of form. (CF/PF)

Bei der Tischleuchte *Modell Nr. 566* (1956) handelt es sich um ein äußerst fortschrittliches Design, das nicht nur Gino Sarfattis eher technischen Zugang zur Gestaltung von Leuchten, sondern auch die von Arteluce erzielten hohen Produktionsstandards verdeutlicht. Die 1956 patentierte Tischleuchte beruht auf einer innovativen Konstruktion, die es ermöglichte, den Lampenkopf über die gesamte Länge des geneigten Fußes zu bewegen. Eine ähnlich rationale Gestaltung weist auch Sarfattis Wandleuchte (1950er Jahre) auf, die sich wie das *Modell Nr. 566* als „elementar" beschreiben lässt und von Sarfattis analytischer Herangehensweise zeugt. (CF/PF)

Très en avance sur son époque, la lampe de table *Modèle n° 566* illustre non seulement la démarche presque mécaniste de Sarfatti, mais aussi la grande qualité des produits Arteluce. Le modèle, qui fut breveté en 1956, est doté d'un système novateur permettant de faire coulisser la tête d'un bout à l'autre de la tige inclinée. L'applique murale, elle aussi signée Sarfatti (années 1950), est tout aussi rationnelle. Chacun de ces deux modèles peut être qualifié d'« essentialiste » et s'inscrit dans la démarche analytique de Sarfatti. (CF/PF)

gino sarfatti
model no. 566 table light

◁ **Wall light, 1950s**
Enameled metal mounts and shade / Montierung und Lampenschirm aus lackiertem Metall / Montures et abat-jour en métal émaillé
Arteluce, Milan, Italy

▷ *Model No. 566* **table light, 1956**
Enameled metal base with chrome-plated tubular metal stem and enameled metal bulb holder, 48 cm high / Fuß und Lampenfassung aus lackiertem Metall mit Arm aus verchromtem Metallrohr, 48 cm hoch / Socle en métal émaillé, pied tubulaire en métal chromé, porte-ampoule en métal émaillé, 48 cm de hauteur
Arteluce, Milan, Italy

▷▷ *Patent drawing of the* Model No. 566 *table light, c.1956 / Patentzeichnung der verstellbaren Tischleuchte* Modell Nr. 566, ca. 1956 / *Dessin du brevet de la lampe de table réglable* Modèle n° 556, vers 1956

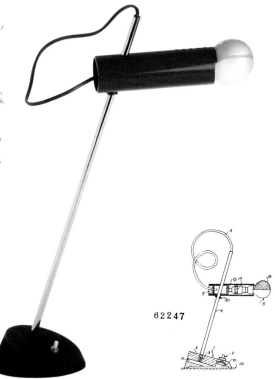

62247

The *Model No.12128 Triennale* floor light (1951) was one of the most popular Italian lights retailed in the United States during the postwar years. Although it was "designed" by Arredoluce – the Italian lighting company established by Angelo Lelli – the floor light was actually manufactured in America by Richards-Morgenthau for the Raymor Corporation. This company was founded by Irving Richards to retail homegrown "good design" alongside imported progressive European products. With their multicolored conical shades, the *Triennale* floor light and the slightly later floor light on the left (*c.*1955) typify the playful nature of much postwar Italian design. (CF/PF)

Die *Modell Nr. 12128 Triennale* Stehleuchte (1951) war eins der populärsten italienischen Leuchtenmodelle, die während der Nachkriegszeit in den Vereinigten Staaten verkauft wurden. Obgleich der Entwurf von der von Angelo Lelli gegründeten italienischen Firma Arredoluce stammt, wurde die Leuchte in den Vereinigten Staaten von der Firma Richards-Morgenthau für die Raymor Corporation hergestellt. Dieses Unternehmen war von Irving Richards ins Leben gerufen worden, um heimisches „gutes Design" neben importierten, fortschrittlichen Artikeln aus Europa zu vertreiben. Mit ihren bunten, kegelförmigen Lampenschirmen sind die *Triennale* Stehleuchte und die Stehleuchte von ca. 1955 typisch für den spielerischen Charakter vieler italienischer Designprodukte der Nachkriegszeit. (CF/PF)

Le lampadaire *Modèle n° 12128 Triennale* (1951) était l'un des modèles italiens vendus aux États-Unis les plus populaires de l'après-guerre. Bien que « créé » par Arredoluce – l'entreprise italienne d'Angelo Lelli – ce lampadaire était en fait fabriqué aux États-Unis par Richards-Morgenthau pour la Raymor Corporation. Cette entreprise avait été fondée par Irving Richards et se spécialisait dans la vente d'articles « *good design* » fabriqués localement et de produits avant-gardistes importés d'Europe. Avec ses abat-jour coniques multicolores, le lampadaire *Triennale* incarne, tout comme l'autre modèle d'Arredoluce (vers 1955), l'esprit ludique du design italien d'après-guerre. (CF/PF)

Floor light, *c.*1955
Metal base, stem and arms with enameled metal shades and enameled metal counterweights, 152 cm high / Fuß, Schaft und Arme aus Metall mit Lampenschirmen und Ausgleichsgewichten aus lackiertem Metall, 152 cm hoch / Socle, tige et bras métalliques, coiffes et contrepoids en métal émaillé, 152 cm de hauteur
Arredoluce, Monza, Italy (manufactured by **Richards-Morgenthau**, New York (NY), USA for **Raymor Corp.**, New York (NY), USA

▷ ***Model No. 12128 Triennale* floor light, 1951**
Brass base, stem and arms with enameled metal shades and enameled metal counterweights, 152 cm high / Fuß, Schaft und Arme aus Messing mit Lampenschirmen und Ausgleichsgewichten aus lackiertem Metall, 152 cm hoch / Socle, tige et bras en laiton, abat-jour et contrepoids en métal émaillé, 152 cm de hauteur
Arredoluce, Monza, Italy (manufactured by **Richards-Morgenthau**, New York (NY), USA for **Raymor Corp.**, New York (NY), USA

These two floor lights share a whimsical, eccentric character that typifies the mid 1950s. Michel Buffet's design from 1953 is functional and well considered. Yet it is also a willful play of slender rods and contrasting cones, and it has a sculptural as well as a practical quality. Boris Lacroix is more usually associated with objects designed in the 1930s and constructed in strict Modernist geometric forms. Here, in c.1954, he has indulged in curving lines for the stems and the asymmetrical shades, and has further played with color in the varied tints of these yellow, gray and lilac shades. (PG)

Den beiden Stehleuchten gemeinsam ist eine spielerische und exzentrische Eigenart, die typisch ist für die Mitte der 1950er Jahre. Michel Buffets Design aus dem Jahr 1953 ist funktional und wohl durchdacht. Aber hier spiegelt sich auch ein bewusstes Spiel mit dem Kontrast von Stab- und Kegelformen, und die Leuchte besitzt neben ihrer praktischen eine durchaus skulpturale Qualität. Boris Lacroix wird in der Regel mit Objekten aus den 1930er Jahren assoziiert, die in den streng geometrischen Formen des Modernismus konstruiert waren. Bei seinem Entwurf von ca. 1954 dagegen erlaubte sich Lacroix die Freiheit geschwungener Formen für die Arme und die asymmetrischen Lampenschirme sowie das Spiel mit den Farben Gelb, Grau und Lila bei der Lackierung der Lampenschirme. (PG)

Ces deux lampadaires arborent le style plein de fantaisie et d'originalité qui est typique du milieu des années 1950. Le modèle de Buffet est fonctionnel et bien étudié : sa forme à la fois sculpturale et pratique joue sur les contrastes entre les cônes et les minces tiges. Lacroix est surtout connu pour ses œuvres des années 1930 aux formes modernistes strictement géométriques. Dans ce lampadaire de 1954, il s'est autorisé quelques courbes dans les tiges et les abat-jour asymétriques, et a joué avec les nuances de jaune, grises et lilas des abat-jour. (PG)

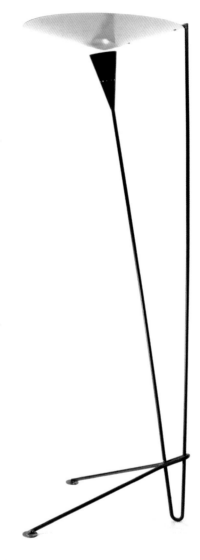

Floor light, 1953

Enameled metal base, shade and reflector, 178 cm high / Fuß, Lampenschirm und Reflektor aus lackiertem Metall, 178 cm hoch / Socle, abat-jour, et réflecteur en métal émaillé, 178 cm de hauteur
Matthieu, France

▷ **Floor light, c.1954**

Iron and enameled tubular steel base with enameled metal shades, 172 cm high / Fuß aus Eisen und lackiertem Stahlrohr mit Lampenschirmen aus lackiertem Metall, 172 cm hoch / Socle en fer et tubes d'acier émaillé, abat-jour en métal émaillé, 172 cm de hauteur
France

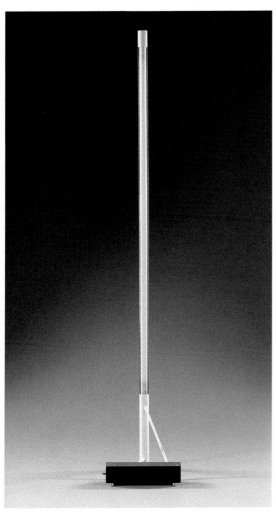

The *Model No. 1063* floor light designed in 1953–54 by Gino Sarfatti is a highly rational solution that pushed the esthetic boundaries of 1950s lighting design with its simple, shaft-like construction. As a highly influential design, it was selected for a Compasso d'Oro in 1954. Sarfatti's table light from *c.*1954 was an equally ingenious design. It features two rotating screens – one translucent and one opaque – that allow an almost infinite number of lighting intensities. The construction of the light is very similar to another design by Sarfatti, the *Model No. 559* table light, which won a Compasso d'Oro in 1954. (CF/PF)

Die Stehleuchte *Modell Nr. 1063* (1953–54) von Gino Sarfatti ist eine äußerst rationale Beleuchtungslösung, die mit ihren einfachen, säulenartigen Formen weit über das Leuchtendesign der 1950er Jahre hinausging. Im Jahr 1954 wurde dieser zukunftsweisende Entwurf mit einem Compasso d'Oro ausgezeichnet. Sarfattis Tischleuchte (ca. 1954) zeichnet sich ebenfalls durch innovatives Design aus: Sie war mit zwei drehbaren Blendschirmen ausgestattet – der eine durchscheinend, der andere opak –, die eine fast unbegrenzte Palette an Lichtstärke- und Helligkeitsgraden boten. Die Konstruktion dieser Leuchte hat große Ähnlichkeit mit Sarfattis Entwurf der Tischleuchte *Modell Nr. 559*, die 1954 ebenfalls mit einem Compasso d'Oro ausgezeichnet wurde. (CF/PF)

Avec sa construction très rationnelle et sa forme simple et longiligne, le lampadaire *Modèle n° 1063* de Gino Sarfatti repoussa les frontières esthétiques des luminaires des années 1950. Modèle très influent, il fut récompensé d'un *Compasso d'Oro* en 1954. La lampe de table, qui est aussi l'œuvre de Sarfatti, est tout aussi ingénieuse : ses deux écrans pivotants – l'un translucide, l'autre opaque – permettent de varier l'intensité lumineuse de manière presque infinie. Par sa conception, elle rappelle beaucoup une autre lampe du même créateur – la lampe de table *Modèle n° 559*, qui gagna un Compasso d'Oro en 1954. (CF/PF)

◁ **Table light, c.1954**
Enameled metal base with translucent plastic and enameled metal shades, 71 cm high /
Lackierter Metallfuß mit Lampenschirmen aus Plastik und lackiertem Metall, 71 cm hoch /
Piétement en métal émaillé, abat-jour en plastique translucide et métal émaillé, 71 cm de hauteur
Arteluce, Milan, Italy

Model No. 1063 floor light, 1953–54
Enameled metal base and mounts with fluorescent tube light, 216 cm high / Fuß und Montierung aus lackiertem Metall mit Leuchtstoffröhre, 216 cm hoch / Socle et montures en métal émaillé, tube fluorescent, 216 cm de hauteur
Arteluce, Milan, Italy

The Castiglioni brothers Achille and Pier Giacomo were perhaps the most influential lighting designers of the 20th century. With their stylish designs, they playfully exploited new forms while at the same time adhering to functionalist principles. Of their many designs, the *Model No. B9 Luminator* floor light of 1955 best reflects their tireless experimentation as well as their objective of "straining to achieve adequate results with minimum means". Importantly, the *Luminator* and the *Tubino* desk light (1951) demonstrated that innovative thinking could revolutionize traditional typologies. Both lights can be seen to have helped pave the way for the later Radical Design Movement in Italy. (CF/PF)

Die Castiglioni-Brüder Achille und Pier Giacomo waren vielleicht die einflussreichsten Leuchtendesigner des 20. Jahrhunderts. Mit ihren stilvollen Entwürfen erkundeten sie auf spielerische Weise neue Möglichkeiten der Formgebung, während sie gleichzeitig funktionalistischen Prinzipien treu blieben. Unter ihren vielen Entwürfen spiegelt wohl am besten die Stehleuchte *Modell Nr. B9 Luminator* (1955) ihre unermüdliche Lust am Experimentieren und ihr Ziel, „sich anzustrengen, um adäquate Resultate mit minimalen Mitteln zu erzielen." Die Stehleuchte *Luminator* sowie die Tischleuchte *Tubino* (1951) demonstrierten, dass durch innovatives Denken traditionelle Typologien grundlegend verändert werden konnten. In diesem Sinne stehen die beiden Leuchten als Wegbereiter für die später in Italien aufkommende Richtung des Radical Design. (CF/PF)

Parmi tous les créateurs de luminaires du XXᵉ siècle, les frères Achille et Pier Giacomo Castiglioni furent peut-être les plus influents. Leurs modèles élégants témoignaient d'une grande recherche formelle tout en restant fidèles aux principes du fonctionnalisme. Le lampadaire *Modèle n° B9 Luminator* de 1955 est sans doute celui qui reflète le mieux leur soif d'expérimentation et leur volonté d' « obtenir des résultats satisfaisants avec un minimum de moyens ». De même que le modèle *Tubino* (1951), il montrait qu'il était possible, en faisant preuve d'inventivité, de bouleverser les typologies traditionnelles. Ces deux lampes ont joué un rôle précurseur dans l'avènement du design radical italien. (CF/PF)

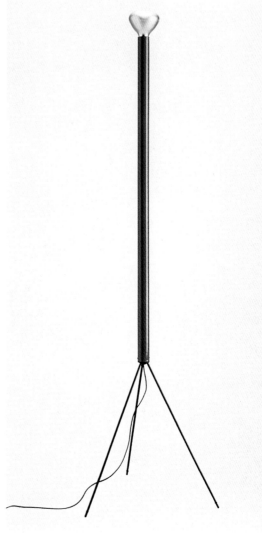

Model No. B9 Luminator floor light, 1955

Enameled metal stem and legs, 189 cm high / Füße und Schaft aus lackiertem Metall, 189 cm hoch / Fût et pieds en métal émaillé, 189 cm de hauteur
Gilardi & Barzaghi, Milan, Italy (later produced by Flos, Bovezzo, Italy)

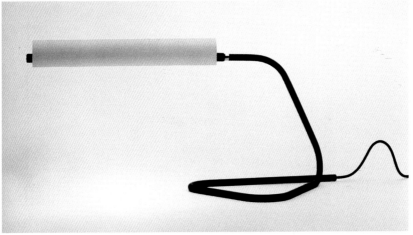

△ Design drawing of Luminator *floor light,*
c.1954 / *Zeichnung der* Luminator *Stehleuchte,*
ca. 1954 / Dessin du lampadaire Luminator,
vers 1954

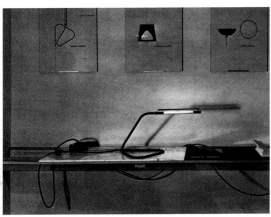

△△ *Tubino* **desk light, 1951**

Enameled metal base with enameled aluminum
shade, 30 cm high / Lackierter Metallfuß mit
lackiertem Lampenschirm aus Aluminium, 30 cm
hoch / Socle en métal émaillé, abat-jour en aluminium émaillé, 30 cm de hauteur
Arredoluce, Monza, Italy (later produced by Flos,
Bovezzo, Italy)

△ Tubino desk light displayed in the lighting
section of the IX. Milan Triennale, 1951 /
Tubino Tischleuchte, ausgestellt bei der neun-
ten Mailänder Triennale, 1951 / La lampe de
bureau Tubino exposée à l'espace luminaire de
la neuvième Triennale de Milan, 1951

Suspended ceiling light, c.1955

Brass mounts with acid-etched glass shade,
57 cm wide / Messingmontierung mit Lampenschirm aus säuregeätztem Glas, 57 cm breit /
Montures en laiton, abat-jour en verre gravé
à l'acide, 57 cm de largeur
Fontana Arte, Corsico, Italy

▷ *Fontana Arte advertisement published in*
Domus *magazine, September 1957 / Werbe-*
anzeige von Fontana Arte in der Zeitschrift
Domus, *September 1957 / Réclame de Fontana*
Arte *publiée dans le magazine* Domus,
Septembre 1957

In the flourishing economic climate of
the 1950s, Fontana Arte's experiments
with new technical processes and
product design left the company in
great need of highly specialized craftsmen. The company enrolled its most
talented apprentices in art and design
polytechnics in order to have a work-
force skilled enough to execute the kind
of decorative forms and complex processing shown in this glass ceiling light
from c.1955. (EK)

Im Klima des wirtschaftlichen Auf-
schwungs der 1950er Jahre brachten
die bei Fontana Arte durchgeführten
Experimente mit neuen technischen
Methoden und Gestaltungskonzepten
einen gesteigerten Bedarf an hoch
spezialisierten Kunsthandwerkern mit
sich. Das Unternehmen schickte deshalb seine talentiertesten Lehrlinge an
Fachhochschulen für Kunst und Design,
damit sie sich qualifizieren konnten, um
so komplexe Fertigungsschritte auszu-
führen, wie sie unter anderem für diese
Deckenleuchte aus Glas von ca. 1955
vonnöten waren. (EK)

Pendant la période de prospérité économique des années 1950, l'entreprise
Fontana Arte était constamment à la
recherche de nouvelles techniques et
de nouveaux modèles, ce qui explique
qu'elle avait besoin d'artisans hautement
qualifiés. Elle embaucha ses meilleurs
apprentis créateurs afin d'avoir à sa
disposition une main d'œuvre assez
habile pour exécuter ses modèles
complexes et sophistiqués, comme
cette suspension en verre (vers 1955).
(EK)

FONTANA ARTE

Dalia suspended ceiling light, 1955

Brass mounts with cut-glass shades, 50 cm
drop / Messingmontierung mit Lampenschirm
aus geschliffenem Glas, 50 cm lang / Montures
en laiton, abat-jour en verre taillé, 50 cm de
hauteur
Fontana Arte, Corsico, Italy

The first model of the *Dalia* ceiling light
was introduced in 1953. In a playful imitation of the dahlia flower on which it is
based, a calyx of cut-glass canopy
shades and brass arms burst from the
suspended frame. With its striking
appearance, this light quickly became
one of Fontana Arte's most popular
products. Throughout the 1950s the
company issued several models of the
Dalia, with variations on the shape,
color and quantity of glass petals. (EK)

Das erste Modell der Deckenleuchte
Dalia kam 1953 auf den Markt. In einer
spielerischen Nachahmung der Dahlien-
blüte, auf der das Design basiert,
strahlen die wie Blütenblätter geformten Lampenschirmpanele sowie die
Messingarme kelchartig von der zentralen Messingmontierung aus. Dieses
auffallende Modell wurde rasch zu einer
der erfolgreichsten Leuchten von Fontana Arte. Während der 1950er Jahre
brachte die Firma mehrere Modelle
der *Dalia* Leuchte heraus, die in Form,
Farbe und Anzahl der Glaspanele
variierten. (EK)

Le premier modèle de la lampe *Dalia* fut
lancé en 1953. Celle-ci est une repré-
sentation ludique d'un dahlia, dont le
calice est formé d'abat-jour incurvés
en verre taillé et de branches de laiton
qui semblent jaillir du cadre suspendu.
Cette superbe lampe devint rapidement l'un des modèles les plus recherchés de Fontana Arte. Tout au long
des années 1950, l'entreprise réalisa
plusieurs versions de la *Dalia*, qui
variaient par leur forme, leur couleur et
le nombre de leurs pétales de verre.
(EK)

▷ **Table light, 1957**

Brass base and shade with glass panels, 60 cm high / Fuß und Lampenschirm aus Messing mit Glaseinsätzen, 60 cm hoch / Socle en laiton, abat-jour en laiton et panneaux de verre, 60 cm de hauteur
Fontana Arte, Corsico, Italy

▽ *Fontana Arte advertisement published in* Domus *magazine, July 1957 / Werbeanzeige von Fontana Arte in der Zeitschrift* Domus, *Juli 1957 / Réclame de Fontana Arte publiée dans le magazine* Domus, *Juillet 1957*

While Fontana Arte continued to experiment with different ways of applying and processing glass, its various departments were gaining in self-confidence, and 1957 saw a reintroduction of materials such as metal and wood into the company's product range. A number of table lights designed during this period also reflect a new geometric style, as illustrated by the complex Constructivist-like structure of this unusual table light designed in 1957. (EK)

Während bei Fontana Arte weiter mit verschiedenen Arten der Glasverarbeitung experimentiert wurde, gewannen auch andere Abteilungen der Firma an Bedeutung, was dazu führte, dass ab 1957 Materialien wie Metall und Holz wieder in die Leuchtenfertigung aufgenommen wurden. Eine Reihe von Tischleuchten, die während dieser Zeit entstanden, spiegeln zudem einen neuartigen geometrischen Stil wider, wie er in der komplexen, konstruktivistisch anmutenden Gestaltung dieser ungewöhnlichen Tischleuchte (1957) anschaulich wird. (EK)

Alors que Fontana Arte poursuivait ses recherches sur le travail du verre, ses divers départements gagnaient en assurance. En 1957, on assista à un retour du métal et du bois dans les productions de l'entreprise. Un grand nombre de lampes de table datant de cette époque arborent également un nouveau type de style géométrique – comme la curieuse et complexe structure ci-dessus (1957), qui évoque l'esthétique constructiviste. (EK)

Luminous Picture wall applique, 1957

Enameled metal fixing plate with brass frame
and reflectors, 41 cm square / Montierung aus
lackiertem Metall mit Rahmen und Reflektoren
aus Messing, 41 x 41 cm / Platine de fixation en
métal émaillé, cadre et réflecteurs en laiton,
41 cm de côté
Arredoluce, Monza, Italy

▽ *Alitalia offices on Fifth Avenue, New York,
designed by Gio Ponti in 1958 / Die 1958 von
Gio Ponti gestaltete Alitalia-Geschäftsstelle
auf der Fifth Avenue in New York / Bureaux
d'Alitalia sur la Cinquième Avenue, New York,
réalisés par Gio Ponti en 1958*

Wall appliques, *c.*1957

Enameled metal fixing plate with gilt-metal
frame and reflectors, 70.5 cm high / Montierung aus lackiertem Metall mit Rahmen und
Reflektoren aus Messing, 70,5 cm hoch /
Platine de fixation en métal émaillé, cadre et
réflecteurs en métal doré, 70,5 cm de hauteur
Arredoluce, Monza, Italy

During the 1950s Gio Ponti explored
"crystal" forms such as diamonds and
hexagons, which he believed were so
perfect they could not be improved. He
incorporated these "finite forms" as well
as squares, rectangles, rhomboids and
circles in a range of wall appliques
(*c.*1957) manufactured by Arredoluce,
which were used in Alitalia's offices in
New York and in the airline's terminal in
Milan. Essentially light sculptures, the
design of these fixtures relates to some
wall lights Ponti had designed earlier
for the Villa Plachart in Caracas, and
became the blueprint for his later *Fato*
wall/table light (1967) manufactured by
Artemide. (CF/PF)

In den 1950er Jahren experimentierte
Gio Ponti mit „Kristallformen" wie
Rhombus und Sechseck, die er für so
vollkommen hielt, dass man sie nicht
verbessern könne. Er setzte diese Formen ebenso wie Quadrate, Rechtecke
und Kreise in einer Serie von Wandapplikationen (ca. 1957) ein, die von
Arredoluce hergestellt und in der New
Yorker Geschäftsstelle von Alitalia und
im Mailänder Terminal der Fluggesell-
schaft installiert wurden. Aus diesen
„Lichtskulpturen", deren Gestaltung
Bezug nimmt auf einige Wandleuchten,
die Ponti zuvor für die Villa Plachart in
Caracas entworfen hatte, entwickelte
er 1967 seine von Artemide produzierte Wand- und Tischleuchte *Fato*.
(CF/PF)

Au cours des années 1950, Gio Ponti
était fasciné par les formes en « cristaux » telles que le losange et l'hexago-
ne. Celles-ci, pensait-il, étaient tellement parfaites qu'il était impossible de
les améliorer. Le carré, le rectangle, le
rhombe, le cercle et d'autres formes
dites « abouties » sont à l'origine d'une
série d'appliques qu'il réalisa pour
Arredoluce (vers 1957) et qui figuraient
dans les bureaux new-yorkais d'Alitalia,
ainsi que dans le terminal de la compagnie à l'aéroport de Milan. Ces lampes,
qui sont de véritables sculptures lumineuses, s'inspirent d'appliques que
Ponti avait conçues pour la Villa Plachart à Caracas. Elles serviront aussi
de modèle aux appliques et lampes de
table *Fato* (1967), qu'il allait créer par
la suite pour Artemide. (CF/PF)

Alvar Aalto was acutely aware of the synthesis between light and space in architectural settings, and it is not surprising therefore that he often designed site-specific fixtures. Many of these were later put into production, as in the case of the floor lights *Model No. A805* (1953–54) and *Model No. A809* (1959): the former was originally created for Helsinki's National Pensions Institute (1952–56), while the latter was created for the house of the French art dealer Louis Carré (1956–59). Both lights had lamellar diffusers constructed of thin strips of enameled metal that filtered the light so as to eliminate all glare. (CF/PF)

Alvar Aalto war sich der Verbindung zwischen Licht und Raum deutlich bewusst. Es ist daher wenig überraschend, dass er häufig für eine bestimmte Umgebung maßgeschneiderte Leuchten entwarf. Viele dieser Modelle wurden später in die serielle Produktion aufgenommen, so die Stehleuchten *Modell Nr. A805* (1953–54) und *Modell Nr. A809* (1959). Erstere wurde ursprünglich für die staatliche Pensionsanstalt in Helsinki konzipiert (1952–56), Letztere für das Haus des französischen Kunsthändlers Louis Carré (1956–59). Beide Leuchten waren mit lamellenförmigen Diffusoren aus dünnen, lackierten Metallstreifen ausgestattet, die das Licht völlig blendfrei filterten. (CF/PF)

Très conscient de la synthèse entre lumière et espace en architecture, Alvar Aalto créait souvent ses luminaires pour des bâtiments spécifiques. Nombre d'entre eux étaient ensuite manufacturés – comme ses lampadaires *Modèle n° A805* (1953–54), conçu à l'origine pour l'Institut national des retraites à Helsinki (1952–56) et *Modèle n° A809* (1959), destiné à la maison du marchand d'art français Louis Carré (1956– 59). Chacun de ces modèles était équipé de minces lamelles de métal émaillé en guise de diffuseurs, qui filtraient et adoucissaient la lumière. (CF/PF)

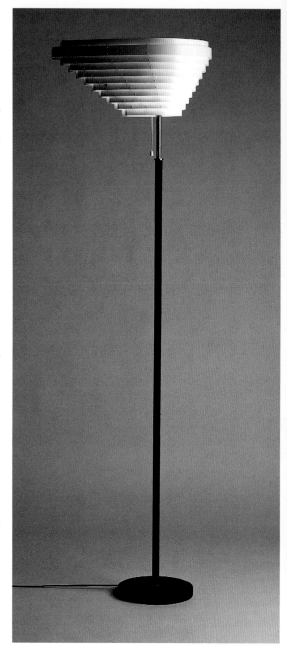

◁◁ *Model No. A805* floor light,
1953–54

Leather-covered stem and brass base with
enameled metal shade, 174 cm high / Leder-
überzogener Schaft auf Messingfuß, Lampenschirm aus lackiertem Metall, 174 cm hoch /
Fût gainé de cuir, socle en laiton, abat-jour en
métal émaillé, 174 cm de hauteur
Artek, Helsinki, Finland

◁ Model No. A809 *floor light in La Maison
Louis Carré, Bazoches-sur-Guyonne, France,
1956–59 / Die Stehleuchte Modell Nr. A809
im Haus des französischen Kunsthändlers
Louis Carré in Bazoches-sur-Guyonne, 1959 /
Lampadaire Modèle n°A809 dans la maison de
Louis Carré à Bazoches-sur-Guyonne, France,
1956–59*

▽ *Detail of* Model No. A809 *floor light, 1959 /
Detail der Stehleuchte Modell Nr. A809, 1959 /
Détail du lampadaire Modèle n°A809, 1959*

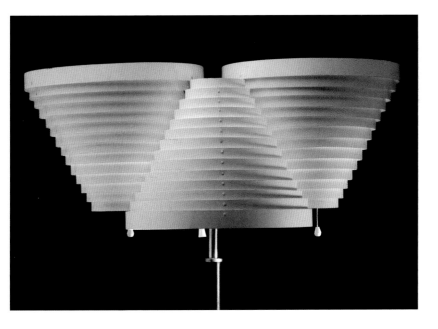

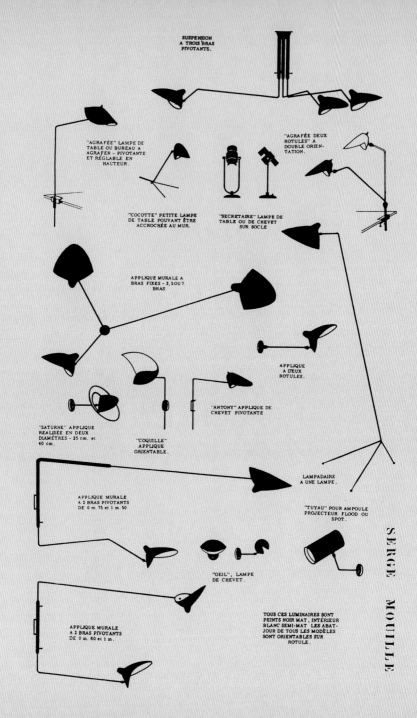

SUSPENSION
A TROIS BRAS
PIVOTANTS.

"AGRAFÉE" LAMPE DE
TABLE OU BUREAU A
AGRAFER - PIVOTANTE
ET RÉGLABLE EN
HAUTEUR.

"AGRAFÉE DEUX
ROTULES" A
DOUBLE ORIEN-
TATION.

"COCOTTE" PETITE LAMPE
DE TABLE POUVANT ÊTRE
ACCROCHÉE AU MUR.

"SECRÉTAIRE" LAMPE DE
TABLE OU DE CHEVET
SUR SOCLE

APPLIQUE MURALE A
BRAS FIXES - 3, 5 OU 7
BRAS

APPLIQUE
A DEUX
ROTULES.

"ANTONY" APPLIQUE DE
CHEVET PIVOTANTE

"SATURNE" APPLIQUE
RÉALISÉE EN DEUX
DIAMÈTRES - 25 cm. et
40 cm.

"COQUILLE"
APPLIQUE
ORIENTABLE.

LAMPADAIRE
A UNE LAMPE.

APPLIQUE MURALE
A 2 BRAS PIVOTANTS
DE 0 m. 75 et 1 m. 50

"TUYAU" POUR AMPOULE
PROJECTEUR FLOOD OU
SPOT.

"OEIL", LAMPE
DE CHEVET.

APPLIQUE MURALE
A 2 BRAS PIVOTANTS
DE 0 m. 60 et 1 m.

TOUS CES LUMINAIRES SONT
PEINTS NOIR MAT, INTÉRIEUR
BLANC SEMI-MAT. LES ABAT-
JOUR DE TOUS LES MODÈLES
SONT ORIENTABLES SUR
ROTULE.

Serge Mouille designed his first proto-type light – the three-arm floor light reproduced overleaf – in 1953 for the decorator and architect Jacques Adnet, who was then director of Süe & Mare's Compagnie des Arts Français (CAF). He subsequently developed a series of elegant lights, which had adjustable black or white enameled metal shades that were supported on slender metal rod stands or arms. Mouille's characteristic *tétine* (teat) shades were the optimum shape for the reflection of light and could be angled in virtually any position. As Mouille noted: "The lamps are like arses or tits; they are made to be touched." (CF/PF)

Serge Mouille entwarf 1953 seinen ersten Leuchtenprototyp – eine drei-armige Stehleuchte – für den Dekora-teur und Architekten Jacques Adnet, den damaligen Direktor der Firma von Süe & Mare, die Compagnie des Arts Français (CAF). In der Folge entwickel-te Mouille eine Serie eleganter Leuch-ten mit verstellbaren Lampenschirmen aus schwarz oder weiß lackiertem Metall, die auf schlanken Metallstäben oder Armen ruhten. Die Form von Mouilles charakteristischen Lampen-schirmen mit dem bezeichnenden Namen *tétine* (Zitze) war optimal für die Lichtreflexion und sie ließen sich praktisch in jede Position einstellen. Dazu Mouille: „Die Leuchten sind wie Ärsche und Titten; sie sind dazu gemacht, berührt zu werden." (CF/PF)

Serge Mouille conçut son premier lumi-naire – un lampadaire à trois branches – en 1953 pour l'architecte décorateur Jacques Adnet, qui était alors directeur de la Compagnie des Arts Français de Süe & Mare. Par la suite, il mit au point une série de lampes élégantes dotées d'abat-jour ajustables en métal émaillé noir ou blanc supportés par de minces pieds en bras métalliques. Mouille affectionnait les abat-jour en forme de tétine, calculés pour réfléchir la lumière de façon optimale et orientables dans pratiquement toutes les positions. Mouille estimait que « les lampes sont comme les culs et les nichons : faites pour être touchées. » (CF/PF)

⊲ *Steph Simon Gallery catalog showing various lights designed by Serge Mouille, 1950s / Seite aus einem Katalog der Steph Simon Galerie mit verschiedenen von Serge Mouille entworfenen Leuchten, 1950er Jahre / Catalogue de la galerie Steph Simon présen-tant diverses lampes réalisées par Serge Mouille, années 1950*

Seven-branch wall light, c.1953
Enameled metal arms and aluminum shades with brass pivot mounts, 167.5 cm long (max.) / Lackierte Metallarme und Lampenschirme aus Aluminium mit Messingdrehgelenken, 167,5 cm Länge (max.) / Bras en métal émaillé, abat-jour en aluminium montés sur rotules en laiton, 167,5 cm de longueur (maximale)
Serge Mouille Workshop, Paris, France (retailed by Steph Simon Gallery, Paris, France)

serge mouille wall light

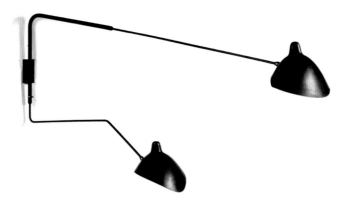

△ *Applique murale* two-arm wall light, c.1953

Enameled metal arms and aluminum shades with brass pivot mounts, 111.7 cm wide / Wandarme aus lackiertem Metall mit Lampenschirmen aus Aluminium und Messingdrehgelenken, 111,7 cm breit / Bras et platine de fixation en métal émaillé, abat-jour en aluminium émaillé, montés sur rotules en laiton, 111,7 cm de largeur **Serge Mouille Workshop**, Paris, France (retailed by Steph Simon Gallery, Paris, France)

▽ ◁ *Lampadaire* floor light, 1953

Enameled metal stem and legs and aluminum shade with brass pivot mount, 160 cm high / Fuß aus lackiertem Metall mit Lampenschirm aus Aluminium und Messingdrehgelenk, 160 cm hoch / Piétement et fût en métal émaillé, abat-jour en aluminium émaillé monté sur rotule en laiton, 160 cm de hauteur **Serge Mouille Workshop**, Paris, France (retailed by Steph Simon Gallery, Paris, France)

▽ ▷ *Three-arm floor light, 1953 – Serge Mouille's first lighting design / Diese dreiarmige Stehleuchte von 1953 ist Serge Mouilles erstes Leuchtendesign / Ce lampadaire à trois branches est le premier luminaire conçu par Serge Mouille, 1953*

△ *Antony* **suspended ceiling /
wall light, c.1953**

Enameled metal stem and aluminum shade with
brass pivot mount, 27 cm high / Montierungen
aus lackiertem Metall mit Lampenschirmen aus
Aluminium und Messingdrehgelenken, 27 cm
hoch / Tige en métal émaillé, abat-jour en aluminium monté sur rotule en laiton, 27 cm de
hauteur
Serge Mouille Workshop, Paris, France (retailed
by Steph Simon Gallery, Paris, France)

◁ *French interior showing* Antony *suspended
ceiling and wall lights, c.1955 / Zeitgenössisches französisches Interieur mit den Decken-/
Wandleuchten* Antony, *ca. 1955 / Photographie d'un intérieur équipé de suspensions/
appliques* Antony, *vers 1955*

While Serge Mouille claimed that "the idea of lighting systems came as a reaction against Italian models, which were beginning to invade the [French] market," he did not mind the diversity that this brought. He did, however, disapprove of Italian designers' penchant for creating lights with complicated forms and combinations of different materials and colors. In contrast, Mouille's range of enameled metal and aluminum lights was positively sombre. Incorporating basic yet highly refined sculptural forms, his lights had a distinctive Parisian stylishness that has undoubtedly ensured their continued popularity among collectors today. (CF/PF)

Wenn Serge Mouille auch einmal erklärte: „Meine Entwürfe für Beleuchtungskörper waren eine Reaktion auf die italienischen Modelle, die anfingen, den [französischen] Markt zu überschwemmen", so hatte er durchaus nichts gegen die stilistische Vielfalt, die das mit sich brachte. Was er jedoch tatsächlich missbilligte, war die Vorliebe vieler italienischer Leuchtendesigner für komplizierte Formen und für Kombinationen verschiedener Materialien und Farben. Im Gegensatz dazu war Mouilles Farbpalette für seine Leuchten aus lackiertem Metall und Aluminium ausgesprochen gedämpft. Mit ihren schlichten und dennoch höchst kunstvoll ausgeführten skulpturalen Formen besaßen seine Leuchten eine ausgeprägt pariserische Eleganz, die zweifellos ein Grund für ihre anhaltende Popularität bei heutigen Sammlern ist. (CF/PF)

Serge Mouillle, qui prétendait s'être tourné vers la création de luminaires « en réaction contre les modèles italiens qui commençaient à envahir le marché [français] », n'avait pourtant rien contre la diversité qu'une telle invasion occasionnait. Il est vrai qu'il n'appréciait guère les formes compliquées et les combinaisons de matières et de couleurs que les créateurs italiens affectionnaient. Ses lampes en aluminium et métal émaillé étaient, par contraste, résolument austères. Avec leurs formes sculpturales dépouillées mais néanmoins très raffinées, ses luminaires avaient une certaine élégance parisienne qui explique sans doute qu'ils soient encore aussi recherchés par les collectionneurs à l'heure actuelle. (CF/PF)

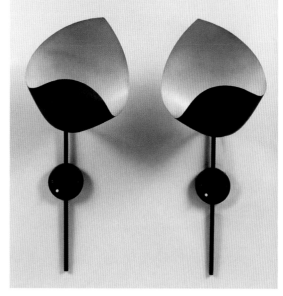

△△ *Saturne* **wall appliques, 1958, commissioned by Louis Sognot**

Enameled metal stem and aluminum shade with brass pivot mount, 25 cm diameter / Lackierter Metallarm mit Lampenschirm aus Aluminium und Messingdrehgelenk, 25 cm Durchmesser / Bras et platine de fixation en métal émaillé, abat-jour en aluminium émaillé monté sur rotule en laiton, 25 cm de diamètre
Louis Sognot, Paris, France

△ *Coquille (Shell)* **wall lights, c.1958**

Enameled metal stem and aluminum shade with brass pivot mount, 58 cm high / Lackierter Metallarm mit Lampenschirm aus Aluminium und Messingdrehgelenk, 58 cm hoch / Bras et platine de fixation en métal émaillé, abat-jour en aluminium émaillé monté sur rotule en laiton, 58 cm de hauteur
Serge Mouille Workshop, Paris, France (retailed by Steph Simon Gallery, Paris, France)

Serge Mouille initially studied as a silversmith at the École des Arts Appliqués in Paris and later established his own studio in 1945. In 1953 he participated in an exhibition at the Musée des Arts Décoratifs, Paris, before collaborating with Louis Sognot on lighting solutions and then going on to become, along with Jean Prouvé, one of the avant-garde designers whose work was shown at the Steph Simon Gallery when it opened in 1956. Incorporating enameled sections of aluminum tubing, Mouille's *Tuyau* range of lighting (c.1953) – including a ceiling version – was perhaps his most rational and predicted his later use of metal cylinders in his totem-like floor lights of the 1960s. (CF/PF)

Serge Mouille absolvierte ursprünglich eine Ausbildung zum Silberschmied an der École des Arts Appliqués in Paris und eröffnete 1945 sein eigenes Atelier. 1953 nahm er an einer Ausstellung im Pariser Kunstgewerbemuseum teil, bevor er begann, zusammen mit Louis Sognot an Gestaltungskonzepten für Leuchten zu arbeiten. Neben Jean Prouvé wurde er zu einem der wichtigsten Avantgarde-Designer. Die Arbeiten beider Designer wurden 1956 bei der Eröffnung der Steph Simon Galerie gezeigt. Mit ihren lackierten Elementen aus Aluminiumrohr waren Mouilles *Tuyau*-Leuchten – einschließlich eines Deckenleuchtenmodells – seine wohl zweckmäßigsten Modelle und nahmen die spätere Verwendung von Metallzylindern für seine totemartigen Stehleuchten der 1960er Jahre vorweg. (CF/PF)

Après des études d'orfèvre à l'École des arts appliqués à Paris, Serge Mouille ouvrit son propre atelier en 1945. Il participa à une exposition au musée des Arts Décoratifs de Paris en 1953, puis réalisa des luminaires en collaboration avec Louis Sognot. Par la suite, ses modèles avant-gardistes furent exposés, comme ceux de Jean Prouvé, à la galerie Steph Simon lorsque celle-ci ouvrit en 1956. Avec ses tronçons de tuyaux d'aluminium émaillé, sa série de lampes *Tuyau* (vers 1953), dont un modèle était décliné en plafonnier, est peut-être la plus rationnelle de ses œuvres. Elle annonce les cylindres métalliques qui figurent dans ses lampadaires en forme de totem des années 1960. (CF/PF)

Tuyau (Pipe) desk light, c.1953
Enameled metal arm and base and aluminum shade with brass pivot mount, 40 cm high / Fuß und Arm aus lackiertem Metall mit Lampenschirm aus Aluminium und Messingdrehgelenk, 40 cm hoch / Bras et socle en métal émaillé, abat-jour en aluminium émaillé monté sur rotule en laiton, 40 cm de hauteur
Serge Mouille Workshop, Paris, France (retailed by Steph Simon Gallery, Paris, France)

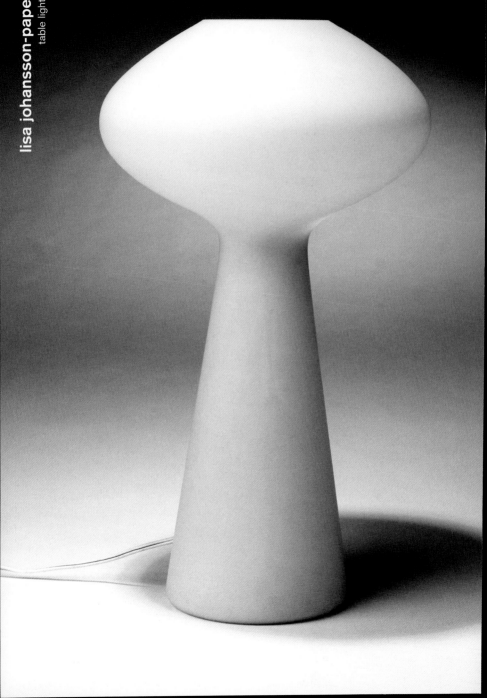

◁ **Table light, 1954**
Mold-blown, sandblasted and acid-etched
glass, 27 cm high / Konstruktion aus formge-
blasenem, sandgestrahltem und säuregeätztem
Glas, 27 cm hoch / Verre pressé soufflé, sablé
et gravé à l'acide, 27 cm de hauteur
Iittala, Iittala, Finland, for Stockmann-Orno,
Kerava, Finland

Sipuli (Onion) **hanging light, 1954**
Mold-blown, sandblasted and acid-etched
glass, 33 cm drop / Lampenschirm aus formge-
blasenem, sandgestrahltem und säuregeätztem
Glas, 33 cm lang / Verre pressé soufflé, sablé et
gravé à l'acide, 33 cm de hauteur
Iittala, Iittala, Finland, for Stockmann-Orno,
Kerava, Finland

Having previously designed furniture for
Stockmann in Helsinki, Lisa Johansson-
Pape began designing lighting for the
department store's sister company,
Stockmann-Orno, around 1947. Her
earliest designs were notable for their
graceful yet simple forms and often
featured pierced metal elements that
allowed the light to shine through. Her
later designs, such as her sandblasted
and etched glass lights from 1954
shown here, were even more sculptural
and were produced for Stockmann-
Orno by the famous Finnish glassworks,
Iittala. In the late 1950s Johansson-
Pape also designed several lights made
of acrylic, which won a number of Milan
Triennale medals. (CF/PF)

Nachdem sie zunächst Möbel für das
Kaufhaus Stockmann in Helsinki entworfen hatte, begann Lisa Johansson-
Pape um das Jahr 1947, Leuchten für
dessen Schwesterfirma Stockmann-
Orno zu gestalten. Ihre frühesten Entwürfe zeichneten sich durch anmutige
und dennoch schlichte Formen aus und
waren häufig mit durchbrochenen
Metallelementen versehen. Ihre späteren Entwürfe, zu denen auch die hier
gezeigten sandgestrahlten und geätzten Glasleuchten (1954) gehören,
waren noch skulpturaler angelegt und
wurden von den berühmten finnischen
Glaswerken Iittala für Stockmann-Orno
hergestellt. Ihre Acrylleuchten aus den
späten 1950er Jahren erhielten etliche
Medaillen auf der Mailänder Triennale.
(CF/PF)

Après avoir dessiné des meubles pour
le grand magasin Stockmann d'Helsinki,
Lisa Johansson-Pape se mit, vers 1947,
à créer des luminaires pour sa compa-
gnie-jumelle Sockmann-Orno. Ses premiers modèles se reconnaissent à leurs
formes simples et gracieuses, et certains comportaient des éléments en
métal ajouré pour laisser passer la
lumière. Ses œuvres plus tardives,
comme les lampes en verre sablé et
gravé représentées ici, étaient encore
plus sculpturales, et étaient fabriquées
pour Stockmann-Orno par la célèbre
verrerie finlandaise Iittala. À la fin des
années 1950, Johansson-Pape réalisa
également plusieurs lampes en acrylique, qui remportèrent des médailles à
la Triennale de Milan. (CF/PF)

◁ **Hanging lights, 1959**

Acrylate and brass construction / Konstruktion aus Acryl und Messing / Structure en polyméthacrylate et laiton
Stockmann-Orno, Kerava, Finland

▷ **Modern Art table light, 1955**

Acrylic base and shade, 40 cm high / Fuß und Lampenschirm aus Acryl, 40 cm hoch / Socle et abat-jour en acrylique, 40 cm de hauteur
Stockmann-Orno, Kerava, Finland
(reissued by Thorn Orno Oy)

Yki Nummi was one of the leading post-war Scandinavian lighting designers. Between 1950 and 1975 he designed many lights for Stockmann-Orno, which were remarkable for their early use of acrylic plastics. His best-known design, the *Modern Art* table light from 1955, which incorporated a section of clear acrylic tubing that functioned as a transparent support for its translucent milkywhite shade, was selected for the permanent collection of the Museum of Modern Art in New York. This design, as well as other lighting by Nummi, exemplifies the highly innovative nature of Finnish design during the 1950s and early 1960s. (CF/PF)

Yki Nummi war einer der führenden skandinavischen Leuchtendesigner der Nachkriegszeit. Zwischen 1950 und 1975 entwarf er zahlreiche Leuchten-modelle für Stockmann-Orno, die wegen ihrer frühen Verwendung des Werkstoffs Acryl bemerkenswert sind. Sein wohl bekanntestes Design, die Tischleuchte *Modern Art* (1955) mit einem Fuß aus transparentem Acryl und einem Lampenschirm aus translu-zentem, milchig-weißem Acryl wurde für die permanente Sammlung des New Yorker Museum of Modern Art ausgewählt. Dieses Modell steht wie andere Leuchten von Nummi exem-plarisch für den sehr neuartigen und fortschrittlichen Charakter des finni-schen Designs der 1950er und frühen 1960er Jahre. (CF/PF)

Yki Nummi était l'un des plus grands créateurs scandinaves d'après-guerre. Entre 1950 et 1975, il conçut de nom-breuses lampes pour Stockmann-Orno avec ceci de particulier qu'elles étaient en plastique acrylique. Sa lampe de table *Art Moderne* (1955) est son œuvre la plus connue : avec son tube en acry-lique transparent servant de support à l'abat-jour blanc translucide, elle fut sélectionnée par le Museum of Modern Art pour figurer dans sa collection per-manente. Comme d'autres modèles imaginés par Nummi, elle offre un bon exemple de la nature très novatrice du design finlandais des années 1950 et 1960. (CF/PF)

Philip Johnson's first major architectural work was The Glass House (1949) – his own home in New Canaan, Connecticut. After its completion, Johnson found that this open-plan pavilion was very difficult to light properly as the glass walls reflected any light source six-fold. In order to overcome this problem he sought the expertise of the lighting consultant Richard Kelly and in 1953 they came up together with a low, three-legged floor light that projected a powerful beam of light upward and then bounced it off a reflector. The light was later modified (c.1954) with the addition of an extra leg to increase stability. (CF/PF)

Philip Johnsons erstes bedeutendes Architekturprojekt war The Glass House, sein eigenes, 1949 gebautes Wohnhaus in New Canaan, Connecticut. Nach dessen Fertigstellung stellte Johnson fest, dass das Innere des pavillonartig und offen angelegten Gebäudes sehr schwierig zu beleuchten war, da sich jede Lichtquelle sechsfach in den Glaswänden spiegelte. Um dieses Problem zu lösen, wandte er sich an den Lichtdesigner Richard Kelly und zusammen entwickelten sie eine niedrige, dreibeinige Stehleuchte (1953), die einen starken Lichtstrahl nach oben warf, der von einem Reflektor als indirektes Licht abgestrahlt wurde. Diese Leuchte wurde etwa 1954 modifiziert, indem sie um ein weiteres Bein ergänzt wurde, was die Stabilität erhöhte. (CF/PF)

La première œuvre importante que réalisa l'architecte Philip Johnson fut sa propre maison à New Canaan dans le Connecticut, la Glass House (1949). Une fois celle-ci terminée, Johnson se rendit compte que ce pavillon ouvert était très difficile à éclairer convenablement, car toute source de lumière se reflétait à l'infini sur les murs de verre. Dans l'espoir de résoudre ce problème, il prit contact avec Richard Kelly, qui était spécialiste en éclairage. Ensemble, ils mirent au point un lampadaire bas à trois pieds qui émettait une forte lumière vers le haut et la faisait « rebondir » sur un réflecteur. Par la suite (vers 1954), on y ajouta un quatrième pied pour le rendre plus stable. (CF/PF)

△ **Floor light (three-legged), 1953**
Bronze base with enameled aluminum shade, 97.3 cm high / Montierung aus Bronze mit Lampenschirm aus lackiertem Aluminium, 97,3 cm hoch / Socle en bronze, abat-jour en aluminium émaillé, 97,3 cm de hauteur
Edison Price, New York (NY), USA

◁ *Interior of The Glass House, New Canaan, Connecticut, c.1953 / Innenraum von The Glass House, New Canaan, Connecticut, ca. 1953 / Intérieur de la Glass House, maison de Philip Johnson à New Canaan, Connecticut, vers 1953*

▷ **Floor light (four-legged), c.1954**
Brass base with enameled aluminum shade, 102 cm high / Montierung aus Messing mit Lampenschirm aus lackiertem Aluminium, 102 cm hoch / Socle en laiton, abat-jour en aluminium émaillé, 102 cm de haut
Edison Price, New York (NY), USA

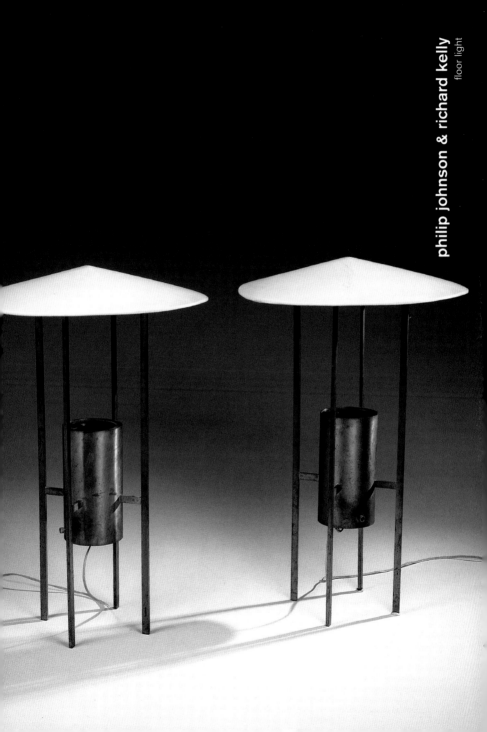

wonderful

things are happening in

lighting!

There's a wonderful **new fashion** in lighting . . . Profile lighting
by Lightolier. Its elements: soft, sculptured silhouettes in dramatic,
elegant combinations of shimmering brass, richly grained walnut, pure linen.
There's a wonderful **new feeling** in lighting . . . an open, airy quality
that makes small rooms seem larger. There's a wonderful **new comfort**
in lighting . . . glare-filtered light that's easy on your eyes, flattering to
your furnishings. Wonderfully **modest prices,** too!

*Today, see Profile and the complete selection of lamps and lighting fixtures
which bear the name Lightolier . . . first in lighting for 50 years.
At better lamp, department, furniture and electrical stores.*

profile by

LIGHTOLIER

Architectural Fixtures • Residential Fixtures • Portable Lamps

JERSEY CITY 5, NEW JERSEY   For a free illustrated brochure write today to   Dept. HG-5

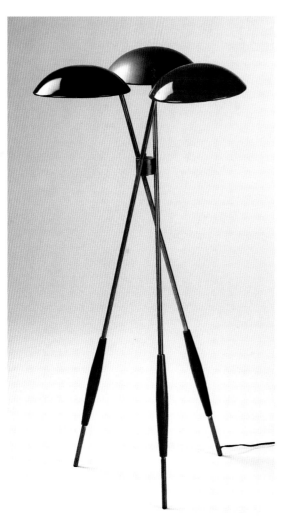

Founded in 1904, the Lightolier Company grew rapidly as a result of its adoption of innovative design and retailing methods – such as its introduction of "Stylebook" catalogs in the 1920s. Guided by its motto "function with style", the company continued to innovate throughout the postwar period. In 1954 it introduced the *Profile* lighting range designed by Gerald Thurston, which comprised floor, desk and table lights that in some cases incorporated glare-filtering plastic diffusers. With their sleek brass and walnut legs, these lights were influenced by Italian styling and as such marked a new level of sophistication in American lighting design. (CF/PF)

Die 1904 gegründete Firma Lightolier wuchs rasch aufgrund ihrer Auswahl innovativer Leuchten und ihrer Vertriebsmethoden – wie die Einführung des „Stylebook" genannten Katalogs im Jahr 1920. Geleitet von dem Motto „Funktion mit Stil" führte das Unternehmen in der Nachkriegszeit weitere Neuerungen ein. Im Jahr 1954 brachte Lightolier die von Gerald Thurston entworfene Lampenserie *Profile* auf den Markt, die aus Steh-, Arbeits- und Tischleuchten bestand. Einige dieser Modelle waren mit Diffusoren aus Kunststoff ausgestattet, die für eine blendfreie Lichtverteilung sorgten. Mit ihren schlanken Beinen aus Messing und Walnussholz waren diese Leuchten deutlich vom italienischen Design beeinflusst und markierten damit einen neuen Grad an modischer Eleganz im amerikanischen Leuchtendesign. (CF/PF)

Fondée en 1904, la compagnie Lightolier savait faire preuve d'innovation, aussi bien dans le style de ses modèles que dans ses techniques de vente – ses catalogues « Stylebook » furent lancés dès les années 1920. Guidée par sa devise « fonction et style », l'entreprise continua à innover après la guerre. La gamme *Profile* conçue par Gerald Thurston, fut lancée en 1954 : elle était composée de lampadaires et de lampes de bureau et de table dont certains modèles étaient équipés de diffuseurs en plastique permettant de réduire l'intensité lumineuse. Avec leurs élégants pieds en laiton et en noyer, elles étaient influencées par le style italien et marquaient l'avènement d'une nouvelle ère de sophistication dans le design américain. (CF/PF)

◁ *Lightolier advertisement showing* Profile *lighting range, 1954 / Werbeanzeige von Lightolier mit der Leuchtenserie* Profile, *1954 / Publicité pour la gamme de luminaires* Profile *de Lightolier, 1954*

Profile floor light, c.1954

Brass and walnut legs with enameled metal shades, 122 cm high / Füße aus Messing und Walnussholz mit lackierten Lampenschirmen aus Metall, 122 cm hoch / Pieds en laiton et noyer, abat-jour en métal émaillé, 122 cm de hauteur
Lightolier , Jersey City (NJ), USA

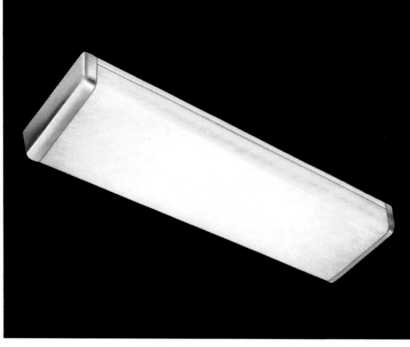

Sightron ceiling light, 1957

Chrome-plated die-cast metal mounts
with extruded acrylic diffuser / Verchromte
Montierung aus Gussmetall mit Diffusor
aus stranggepresstem Acryl / Montures
matricées en métal chromé, diffuseur en
acrylique extrudé
Lightolier, Jersey City (NJ), USA

▷ **Astral Model Nos. 4081 & 4085
(small) suspended ceiling lights, 1954**

Brass arms, stem and mounts / Montierung aus
Messing / Bras, tige et montures en laiton
Lightolier, Jersey City (NJ), USA

The launch of the *Sightron* ceiling light
in 1957 marked another major innovation for the American lighting manufacturer Lightolier. Like the firm's *Optiplex*
lighting system, the *Sightron* was one of
the first fixtures to place fluorescent
tubes behind a single-piece, uniformly
white diffuser in order to shield the light-
source and reduce glare. Importantly,
this design was also the first fluorescent
light unit to incorporate a diffuser made
of extruded acrylic. The *Sightron* was
selected by the Museum of Modern Art
for inclusion in one of its Good Design
exhibitions. (CF/PF)

Die Einführung der *Sightron* Deckenleuchte im Jahr 1957 markierte eine
weitere wichtige Innovation für den
amerikanischen Leuchtenhersteller
Lightolier. Wie das ebenfalls von
Lightolier entwickelte Beleuchtungssystem *Optiplex* war die *Sightron*
Leuchte eines der ersten Modelle, das
Leuchtstoffröhren hinter einem ein-
teiligen, durchgängig weißen Diffusor
verbarg, um das Blendlicht zu reduzieren. Darüber hinaus wurde bei dieser
Röhrenleuchte auch erstmalig ein
Diffusor aus stranggepresstem Acryl
eingesetzt. Die *Sightron* Leuchte wurde
von den Kuratoren des Museum of
Modern Art als Beitrag zu einer ihrer
„Good Design"-Ausstellungen gewählt.
(CF/PF)

Le lancement du plafonnier *Sightron*
en 1957 représente un pas en avant
important pour le fabricant américain
de luminaires Lightolier. À l'instar de
son modèle *Optiplex*, le *Sightron* était
l'un des premiers appareils à posséder
un tube fluorescent caché derrière un
diffuseur blanc d'une seule pièce, qui
en diminuait la luminosité. C'était aussi
le premier luminaire fluorescent à être
équipé d'un diffuseur en acrylique extrudé, ce qui représentait une innovation
importante. Le *Sightron* fut sélectionné
par le Museum of Modern Art pour
figurer dans l'une de ses expositions
« Good Design ». (CF/PF)

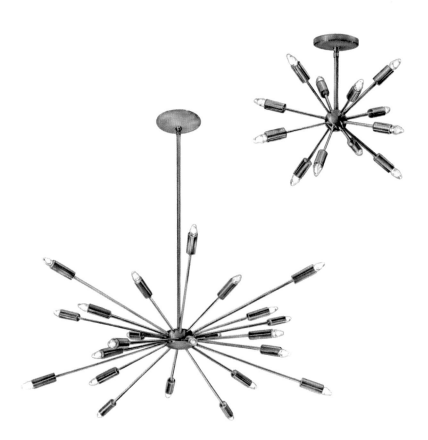

In 1954 Lightolier launched the *Astral* lighting range, which comprised four different models – *Astral, Skyrocket, Sparkler* and *Mobile* – that were available in a variety of sizes. The two most popular lights from the range were the *Astral* and the *Skyrocket.* According to the 1954 Lightolier catalog, these products were inspired by Italian design, but as some of the first Sputnik-type lights to be produced in the United States they were themselves highly influential both at home and abroad. Although the *Astral* range was discontinued around 1959, it inspired many replicas in the 1960s and 1970s. (CF/PF)

Im Jahr 1954 brachte Lightolier die *Astral* Leuchtenserie auf den Markt. Sie bestand aus vier verschiedenen Modellen, die in mehreren Größen erhältlich waren: *Astral, Skyrocket, Sparkler* und *Mobile.* Die beiden beliebtesten Designs aus dieser Serie waren die Modelle *Astral* und *Skyrocket.* Dem Lightolier-Katalog von 1954 gemäß waren diese Leuchten vom italienischen Design inspiriert, doch sie selbst waren als einige der ersten futuristischen Leuchten, die in den Vereinigten Staaten produziert wurden, sowohl im eigenen Land als auch im Ausland richtungsweisend. Obgleich die Produktion der Serie um 1959 eingestellt wurde, gab es in den 1960er und 1970er Jahren zahlreiche Reproduktionen dieses Designs. (CF/PF)

En 1954, Lightolier lança la gamme *Astral,* qui était composée de quatre modèles différents – l'*Atral,* le *Skyrocket,* le *Sparkler* et le *Mobile* – dont chacun était disponible en plusieurs formats. Le catalogue Lightolier de 1954 note qu'ils étaient inspirés par le design italien, mais ils étaient aussi parmi les premiers luminaires américains à adopter le style Spoutnik et furent par conséquent eux-mêmes abondamment imités, aux États-Unis comme á l'étranger. La fabrication de série *Astral* fut interrompue en 1959, ce qui ne l'empêcha pas d'être largement copiée pendant les années 1960 et 1970. (CF/PF)

Frequently misattributed to the French designer Pierre Paulin, these elegant table lights from 1955 were actually designed by Louis Christiaan Kalff, the art director of the Philips Laboratory in Eindhoven, The Netherlands. Obviously influenced by Italian styling, the dynamic forms of the lights epitomize the "New Look" of the 1950s. Their innovative shade construction with a light bulb piercing the middle provides an interesting decorative effect and a useful division of light when illuminated. In 1958 Kalff organized an important multimedia presentation at the Exposition Universelle et Internationale de Bruxelles that showcased the latest developments in electronics and engineering. (CF/PF)

Bei den eleganten Tischleuchten (1955), die häufig fälschlich dem französischen Designer Pierre Paulin zugeschrieben wurden, handelt es sich um Entwürfe von Louis Christiaan Kalff, dem damaligen künstlerischen Leiter der Firma Philips im holländischen Eindhoven. Die offensichtlich vom zeitgenössischen italienischen Design beeinflussten dynamischen Formen der Leuchten sind beispielhaft für den „New Look" der 1950er Jahre. Ihre innovative Lampenschirmkonstruktion mit einer die Mitte durchstoßenden Glühbirne sorgt für einen interessanten Effekt und eine praktische Lichtverteilung. Im Jahr 1958 organisierte Kalff eine wichtige Multimedia-Präsentation auf der Weltausstellung in Brüssel, in der die neuesten Entwicklungen auf dem Gebiet der Elektronik und industriellen Technologie vorgestellt wurden. (CF/PF)

Souvent attribuées à tort au créateur français Pierre Paulin, ces élégantes lampes de table (1955) sont en fait l'œuvre de Louis Christiaan Kalff, qui était directeur artistique au Laboratoire Philipe d'Eindhoven, aux Pays-Bas. Puisant aux sources du style italien, ces lampes arborent une ligne dynamique typique du « New Look » des années 1950. Leurs abat-jour novateurs sont percés en leur centre de manière à laisser passer l'ampoule, ce qui créait un effet intéressant et une bonne répartition de la lumière lorsque les lampes étaient allumées. En 1958, Kalff organisa une importante conférence multimédia à l'Exposition universelle et internationale de Bruxelles, afin de présenter les toutes dernières découvertes en électronique et en technologie. (CF/PF)

Table light, 1955
Enameled metal shade on brass base, 43 cm high / Lackierter Lampenschirm aus Metall auf Messingfuß, 43 cm hoch / Abat-jour en métal émaillé, pied en laiton, 43 cm de hauteur
Philips, Eindhoven, The Netherlands

Table light, 1955
Enameled metal shade on brass base, 43 cm high / Lackierter Lampenschirm aus Metall auf Messingfuß, 43 cm hoch / Abat-jour en métal émaillé, pied en laiton, 43 cm de hauteur
Philips, Eindhoven, The Netherlands

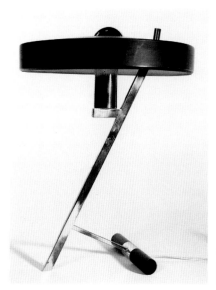

Oscar Torlasco designed a number of lights for the Milan-based lighting manufacturer Lumi, including this adjustable task light from 1955. With its streamlined, bullet-shaped shade and stylish combination of brass and matt-black enamel, the *Lumi* was an innovative and highly functional lighting solution – its height could be adjusted along virtually the full length of the stem, while its ball and socket connector allowed the shade to be flexibly positioned throughout 360 degrees. The optical glass diffuser also ensured that the glare of the light source was effectively eliminated. (CF/PF)

Oscar Torlasco entwarf eine Reihe von Leuchten für den in Mailand ansässigen Leuchtenhersteller Lumi, zu der auch diese verstellbare Arbeitsleuchte (1955) zählt. Mit ihrem stromlinienförmigen und wie eine Patrone gestalteten Lampenschirm und der eleganten Kombination von Messing und mattschwarzer Lackierung stellte die *Lumi* Leuchte eine innovative und äußerst funktionale Beleuchtungslösung dar. Sie war praktisch über die gesamte Länge des Schafts in der Höhe verstellbar, während sich der Lampenschirm durch ein Kugelgelenk um 360 Grad drehen ließ. Darüber hinaus sorgte der Diffusor aus optischem Glas für eine blendfreie Lichtstreuung. (CF/PF)

Oscar Torlasco dessina un certain nombre de lampes pour le fabricant milanais Lumi, notamment cette lampe de travail réglable (1955). Avec ses lignes fuselées, son abat-jour en forme d'obus et son élégante combinaison de laiton et d'émail noir mat, la Lumi était novatrice et très fonctionnelle. On pouvait régler la hauteur en faisant coulisser le porte-ampoule tout au long de la tige, et une rotule permettait de faire pivoter l'abat-jour à 360°. Quant au diffuseur en verre optique, il atténuait efficacement la luminosité. (CF/PF)

oscar torlasco
lumi task light

Lumi task light, 1961

Brass and enameled metal base and shade with optical glass diffuser, 37 cm high / Fuß und Lampenschirm aus Messing und lackiertem Metall mit Diffusor aus optischem Glas, 37 cm hoch / Socle et abat-jour en laiton et métal émaillé, diffuseur en verre optique, 37 cm de hauteur
Lumi, Milan, Italy

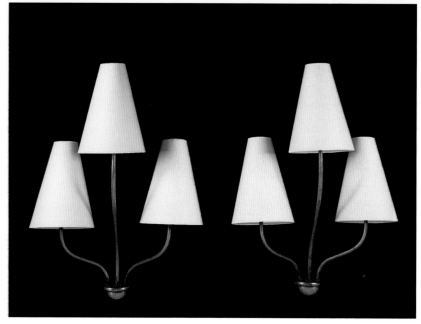

These wall lights by Jean Royère illustrate the designer's skill at creating elegant and graceful lighting for the French interiors of the late 1940s and early 1950s. The wall lights below are from the *Corbeille* series, which adopted square-sectioned metalwork as its signature. These particular lights were part of a commission for a property in Beirut, a city that contains many of Royère's interiors, and where he opened an office in 1947, not leaving until 1972, when he stopped working completely. (AP)

Die Wandleuchten nach Entwürfen von Jean Royère offenbaren das Talent des Designers, dessen Kreationen eleganter und anmutiger Leuchten für die französischen Innenräume der 1940er und 1950er Jahre so typisch waren. Die Wandleuchten aus der Serie *Corbeille* (1950er Jahre) besitzen als besonderes Kennzeichen aus Vierkantstäben zusammengesetzte Metallmontierungen. Diese Leuchten waren ursprünglich für ein von Royère eingerichtetes Wohnhaus in Beirut konzipiert, einer Stadt, in der es viele von ihm gestaltete Interieurs gab. 1947 hatte Royère hier ein eigenes Büro eröffnet, das er erst 1972 aufgab, als er in den Ruhestand ging. (AP)

Ces appliques illustrent bien le talent de Jean Royère, dont on pouvait admirer dans de nombreux intérieurs français de la fin des années 1940 et du début des années 1950. Les appliques que l'on voit en bas appartiennent à la série *Corbeille*, reconnaissable à ses ferronneries de section carrée. Ces modèles faisaient partie d'une commande pour une propriété située à Beyrouth. Royère réalisa beaucoup d'intérieurs dans cette ville, où il ouvrit d'ailleurs un bureau en 1947. Il y resta jusqu'en 1972, date à laquelle il prit définitivement sa retraite. (AP)

◁△ *Entrance hall of the Maison de Pontault-Combault with furniture and lighting designed by Jean Royère, c.1958 / Eingangshalle im Maison de Pontault-Combault mit Möbeln und Leuchten von Jean Royère, ca. 1958 / Hall d'entrée de la Maison de Pontault-Combault, mobilier et luminaires de Jean Royère, vers 1958*

◁▽ **Wall lights, *c.*1955**
Gilt metal mounts with parchment shades, 48.2 cm high / Montierungen aus vergoldetem Metall mit Lampenschirmen aus Pergament, 48,2 cm hoch / Montures en métal doré, abat-jour en parchemin, 48,2 cm de hauteur
Jean Royère, Paris, France

▽ ***Corbeille* wall lights, 1950s**
Gilt metal mounts with parchment shades, 45.7 cm high / Montierungen aus vergoldetem Metall mit Lampenschirmen aus Pergament, 45,7 cm hoch / Montures en métal doré, abat-jour en parchemin, 45,7 cm de hauteur
Jean Royère, Paris, France

The rare, fantastical and flamboyant *Liane* series of lights (*c.*1959) by Jean Royère is perhaps his most extravagant and freeform set of designs. The iron rods of the *Liane* were twisted and turned like spaghetti to create wall lights, floor lights, and wall murals where the light creeps along the surface like a vine. The original period interior photographed below shows the *Liane* wall light as well as the floor light, coupled with the equally striking Royère *Ours Polaire* (Polar Bear) sofa and armchairs. (AP)

Bei den seltenen, ungewöhnlich bizarr und phantasievoll gestalteten *Liane*-Leuchten (ca. 1959) handelt es sich vielleicht um die extravagantesten und von allen historischen Vorbildern am weitesten befreiten Entwürfen von Jean Royère. Die gebogenen und verdrehten schmiedeeisernen Konstruktionselemente der *Liane* Wand- und Stehleuchten, an denen die Lampenschirme wie Weinreben hängen, wirken wie die Ranken einer Kletterpflanze. Das zeitgenössische Interieur zeigt die *Liane* Steh- und Wandleuchte in Verbindung mit der ebenfalls von Royère entworfenen Polstergarnitur *Ours Polaire* (Polarbär), deren Design ebenso ungewöhnlich ist wie das der Leuchten. (AP)

Insolites et spectaculaires, les lampadaires, appliques et lampes murales de la série *Liane* (vers 1959) comptent parmi les œuvres les plus extravagantes et les plus libres de Royère. Leurs tiges de fer étaient courbées et retournées comme des spaghettis, ce qui leur donnait l'allure aspect de plantes grimpantes. On peut voir l'applique murale et le lampadaire sur cette photo d'époque, de même que les étonnants canapé et fauteuils de la gamme *Ours Polaire*, elle aussi conçue par Royère. (AP)

Living room in Paris designed by Jean Royère featuring Liane *floor and wall lights, 1962 / Wohnzimmer in einer von Jean Royère eingerichteten Pariser Wohnung mit der Steh- und Wandleuchte* Liane, *1962 / Salle de séjour parisienne conçue par Jean Royère, 1962, où l'on peut voir le lampadaire et l'applique murale* Liane

▷ ***Liane* floor light, *c.*1959**

Wrought-iron construction with paper shades, 213 cm high / Konstruktion aus Schmiedeeisen mit Lampenschirmen aus Papier, 213 cm hoch / Structure en fer forgé, abat-jour en papier, 213 cm de hauteur
Jean Royère, Paris, France

Moon Phases table light, c.1955

Silk-screen printed and enameled brass base with parchment shade trimmed with twine, 61 cm high / Fuß aus lackiertem Messing, im Siebdruckverfahren bedruckt, Lampenschirm aus Pergament mit Kordeleinfassung, 61 cm hoch / Socle en laiton émaillé et sérigraphié, abat-jour en parchemin brodé de ficelle, 61 cm de hauteur
Fornasetti, Milan, Italy

▷ *Fornasetti interior showing silk-screen printed table light / Fornasetti-Interieur mit einer im Siebdruckverfahren dekorierten Tischleuchte / Intérieur réalisé par Fornasetti où l'on peut voir une lampe de table sérigraphiée*

Reviving the rich Italian decorative tradition of *trompe l'œil*, Piero Fornasetti loved illusionistic ornament, especially if it had a Surrealist quality. As he noted: "I want to free my inspiration from the limitations of the usual." Fornasetti designed over 85 different silk-screened decorative motifs – patterned marble, moon phases, pansies, shells, daggers, snakes, architectural motifs, newsprint, butterflies, etc. – for his light bases, which came in a range of standard sizes and shapes. His *Blackamoor* floor light (c.1955), however, was his most quirky design and placed him well and truly within the anti-Rationalist camp of postwar Italian design. (CF/PF)

Piero Fornasetti, der die alte italienische Tradition der *Trompe-l'œil*-Malerei in seinen Arbeiten wiederbelebte, verwendete mit besonderer Vorliebe illusionistische Ornamente, speziell solche mit einer surrealistischen Note. Für die von ihm entworfenen Leuchtenfüße und -sockel, kreierte Fornasetti über 85 verschiedene, im Seidensiebdruckverfahren gefertigte Dekormotive: Marmor, Mondphasen, Stiefmütterchen, Muscheln, Dolche, Schlangen, architektonische Motive, Zeitungspapier, Schmetterlinge etc. Sein eigenwilligstes Design jedoch war die Stehleuchte *Blackamoor* (Mohr) von ca. 1955, die ihm eindeutig einen Platz im Lager der Anti-Rationalisten unter den italienischen Designern der Nachkriegszeit zuwies. (CF/PF)

Fornasetti aimait les riches trompe-l'œil de la tradition italienne, surtout lorsqu'ils avaient une dimension surréaliste. « Je veux libérer mon imagination des frontières de l'habituel », déclarait-il. Il réalisa, pour ses socles de lampes de tailles et de formes variées, plus de quatre-vingt-cinq sérigraphies différentes – marbrures, quartiers de lune, pensées, coquillages, poignards, serpents, détails architecturaux, papier journal, papillons, etc. Son lampadaire *Tête de Maure* (vers 1955), qui est la plus originale de ses œuvres, proclamait haut et fort son appartenance à la branche anti-rationaliste du design italien d'après-guerre. (CF/PF)

piero fornasetti

piero

◁◁ **Floor lights, 1950s**

Silk-screen printed metal base with parchment
shade, 155 cm high / Säulensockel aus Metall,
im Siebdruckverfahren bedruckt, Lampenschirme aus Pergament, 155 cm hoch / Socle
en métal sérigraphié, abat-jour en parchemin,
155 de hauteur
Fornasetti, Milan, Italy

◁ *Blackamoor* **floor light, c.1955**

Silk-screen printed metal base supporting
glazed ceramic bust terminating in candelabra
with crystal drops, 153 cm high / Säulensockel
aus Metall, im Siebdruckverfahren bedruckt, mit
Büste aus glasierter Keramik und Kandelaber
mit Kristallprismen, 153 cm hoch / Socle en
métal sérigraphié, surmonté d'un buste en
céramique vernissée et d'un candélabre à
pendeloques de cristal, 153 cm de hauteur
Fornasetti, Milan, Italy

▽ **Table light bases, 1950s**

Silk-screen printed metal bases with brass
mounts / Metall, im Siebdruckverfahren
bedruckt mit Messingmontierungen / Socle
en métal sérigraphié, montures en laiton
Fornasetti, Milan, Italy

The *AJ* wall, table and floor lights (1957) were specially designed by Arne Jacobsen for his International Style masterwork – the SAS Royal Hotel, Copenhagen (1956–61). Synthesizing the strong rectilinear esthetic of the building with the more organic formal vocabulary of the well-known *Swan* and *Egg* chairs that were also designed for the project, these lights had an egg-shaped base, a slender sloping stem and a visor-like shade, which could be adjusted to alter the direction of the light. This latter feature enabled a hotel guest to read in bed using an *AJ* table light without disturbing his or her roommate. (CF/PF)

Die *AJ*-Serie mit Wand-, Tisch- und Stehleuchten (1957) wurde von Arne Jacobsen speziell für sein Meisterwerk im International Style – das SAS Terminal mit zugehörigem Royal Hotel in Kopenhagen (1956–61) – entworfen. Wie in einer Synthese zwischen der kraftvollen, rechtwinkligen Ästhetik des Gebäudes und der eher organischen Formensprache der ebenfalls für dieses Projekt entstandenen berühmten Stühle *Swan* und *Egg* sind diese Leuchten mit einem eiförmigen Fuß, einem schlanken Schaft und einem visierartigen Lampenschirm ausgestattet, den man in die jeweils gewünschte Richtung verstellen kann. Durch diese Konstruktion konnte ein Hotelgast im Schein der *AJ*-Tischleuchte lesen, ohne seinen Zimmergenossen zu stören. (CF/PF)

Les appliques, lampes de table et lampadaires *AJ* (1957) furent spécialement créés par Arne Jacobsen pour son chef d'œuvre de Style International – l'hôtel Royal de la SAS à Copenhague (1957). Ces lampes, qui réunissent l'esthétique rectiligne de l'hôtel et les formes plus organiques des célèbres fauteuils *Cygne* et *Œuf*, conçus pour le même bâtiment, sont dotées d'un socle ovale, d'une tige légèrement inclinée et d'un abat-jour en visière, qui pouvait se régler de façon à orienter le faisceau lumineux. Grâce à ce mécanisme, les clients de l'hôtel pouvaient lire au lit sans déranger leur compagnon de chambre. (CF/PF)

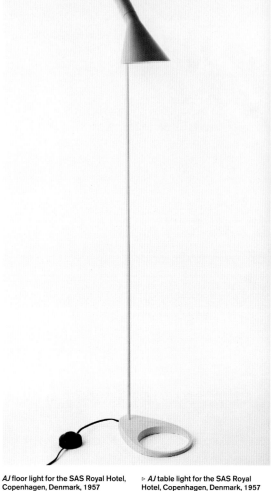

AJ floor light for the SAS Royal Hotel, Copenhagen, Denmark, 1957

Enameled tubular metal stem, cast-iron base and aluminum shade, 130 cm high / Lackierter Fuß aus Gusseisen, Schaft aus Metallrohr und Lampenschirm aus Aluminium, 130 cm hoch / Tige en tube de métal émaillé, socle en fonte, abat-jour en aluminium, 130 cm de hauteur
Louis Poulsen Lighting, Copenhagen, Denmark

▷ **AJ table light for the SAS Royal Hotel, Copenhagen, Denmark, 1957**

Enameled tubular metal stem, cast-iron base and aluminum shade, 56 cm high / Lackierter Fuß aus Gusseisen, Arm aus Metallrohr und Lampenschirm aus Aluminium, 55 cm hoch / Tige en tube de métal émaillé, socle en fonte, abat-jour en aluminium, 56 cm de hauteur
Louis Poulsen Lighting, Copenhagen, Denmark

In 1957 the architect Charles Gjerrild asked Poul Henningsen to design an economical yet decorative light for his Adventist Church at Skodsborg Hydro. The resulting design, the *PH Louvre* (1957) was cheaper to manufacture than Henningsen's earlier *PH Spiral* light (1942) because of its simpler construction, which comprised thirteen concentric metal shades set on a simple four-ribbed frame. Originally the shades were enameled pale orange so as to give a warm glow. Introduced a year later, the *PH Snowball* had a similar construction, but was decreased in diameter and used only eight shades, making it suitable for smaller spaces. (CF/PF)

Im Jahr 1957 bat der Architekt Charles Gjerrild Poul Henningsen, eine sparsame und dennoch dekorative Beleuchtung für die von ihm realisierte Adventisten-Kirche in Skodsborg Hydro zu entwerfen. Die daraus resultierende Leuchte *PH Louvre* (1957) war in der Herstellung billiger als Henningsens frühere Hängeleuchte *Spirale* (1942). Das lag an der einfacheren Konstruktion, die aus dreizehn konzentrisch angeordneten Metallschirmen auf einem einfachen, aus vier Längsrippen gebildeten Rahmen bestand. Ursprünglich waren die Lampenschirme in einem blassen Orange lackiert, so dass sie ein warmes Licht abstrahlten. Die ein Jahr später auf den Markt gebrachte Hängeleuchte *PH Schneeball* (1958) war ähnlich konstruiert, hatte aber einen geringeren Durchmesser und nur acht Lampenschirme, so dass sie auch für kleinere Räume geeignet war. (CF/PF)

En 1957, l'architecte Charles Gjerrild demanda à Poul Henningsen d'inventer une lampe peu coûteuse mais néanmoins décorative pour son église adventiste de Skodsborg Hydro. C'est ainsi que fut créé le modèle *Louvre* (1957), lequel, avec ses treize lamelles métalliques concentriques fixées à un cadre à quatre arceaux, était plus simple, et par conséquent moins chère à fabriquer que son modèle *Spirale* de 1942. À l'origine, les abat-jour étaient émaillés en orangé pâle pour diffuser une lumière chaleureuse. Lancée un an plus tard, la *Snowball* (Boule de Neige, 1958) était construite selon le même principe, mais son diamètre était plus petit et elle ne comptait que huit lames abat-jour, ce qui la rendait parfaite pour les espaces plus exigus. (CF/PF)

△ **PH Louvre hanging light, 1957**
Enameled aluminum reflectors with chrome-plated brass frame, 65 cm high / Lackierter Aluminiumschirm mit verchromter Messingmontierung, 65 cm hoch / Abat-jour en lames d'aluminium émaillé, cadre en laiton chromé, 65 cm de hauteur
Louis Poulsen Lighting, Copenhagen, Denmark

▷ **PH Snowball hanging light, 1958 (new model 1982)**
Enameled aluminum reflectors with chrome-plated aluminum frame, 39 cm high / Lackierter Aluminiumschirm mit verchromter Messingmontierung, 39 cm hoch / Abat-jour en aluminium émaillé, cadre en aluminium chromé, 39 cm de hauteur
Louis Poulsen Lighting, Copenhagen, Denmark

◁ PH Louvre *lights in the Adventist Church, Skodsborg Hydro, Denmark /* PH Louvre-*Leuchten in der Adventisten-Kirche in Skodsborg Hydro, Dänemark /* Suspensions Louvre *dans l'Église adventiste de Skodsborg Hydro, Danemark*

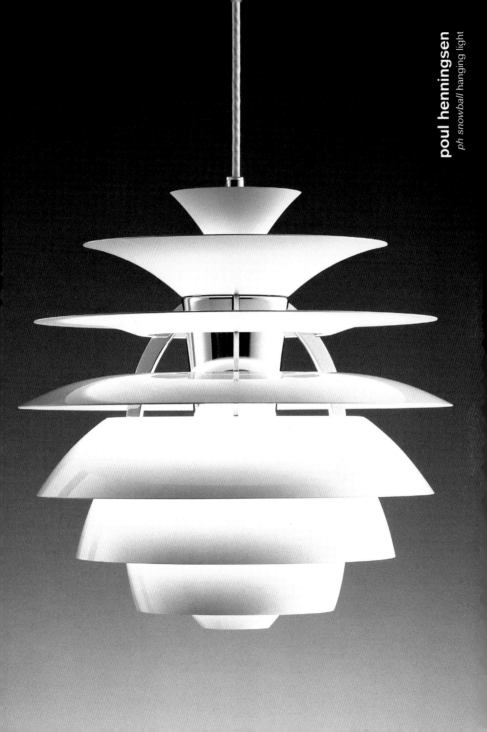

Page from Den Permanente *catalogue showing
the* PH Artichoke *hanging light, c.1960 / Seite
aus einem* Den Permanente *Katalog mit der
Hängeleuchte* PH Artichoke, *ca. 1960 /
Page du catalogue* Den Permanente *(Louis
Poulsen) où l'on peut voir la suspension* Artichaut, *vers 1960*

Of all the lights designed by Poul Henningsen, the *PH Artichoke* (1957) best
displays his ability to create poetic yet
functional forms. The architects Eva and
Nils Koppel originally commissioned the
light for the Langelinie Pavilion in
Copenhagen and it would appear from
a few surviving rough sketches that its
basic design was conceived very quickly. The *PH Artichoke*'s glare-eliminating
construction fulfilled Henningsen's long-
held objective of making his seven-
shade *PH* hanging light (1926–27) into
a free-leaved, pine-cone-like fixture.
Available in reduced sizes for domestic
use, the light's fragmented, overlapping
flaps set at different angles give it a
spectacular decorative effect. (CF/PF)

Von allen seinen Entwürfen offenbart
die Hängeleuchte *PH Artischocke*
(1957) am deutlichsten Poul Henningsens Fähigkeit, poetische und gleichzeitig funktionale Formen zu kreieren.
Ursprünglich wurde die Leuchte von
den Architekten Eva und Nils Koppel in
Auftrag gegeben, und zwar als Beleuchtung für den Langelinie Pavillon in
Kopenhagen. Die wenigen erhaltenen
Skizzen vermitteln den Eindruck, als sei
das Gestaltungskonzept sehr rasch
entstanden. Mit der blendfreien Konstruktion führte Henningsen seine ursprüngliche *PH*-Leuchte von 1926–27
zu einem freier gestalteten und wie ein
Tannenzapfen strukturierten Entwurf.
Die Leuchte hat durch die in unterschiedlichen Winkeln angeordneten
Lamellen eine sehr dekorative Wirkung.
(CF/PF)

De toutes les lampes de Poul Henningsen, l'*Artichaut* (1957) est celle qui dit
le mieux sa capacité à concilier poésie
et fonctionnalité. Elle avait été comman-
dée par les architectes Eva et Nils
Koppel pour le Pavillon Langelinie de
Copenhague, et les quelques croquis
sommaires qui sont parvenus jusqu'à
nous laissent à penser qu'elle fut
conçue très rapidement, du moins dans
ses grandes lignes. Depuis longtemps,
Henningsen avait rêvé de transformer
sa lampe *PH* à sept lames abat-jour en
une structure à feuilles détachées,
évoquant une pomme de pin. La lampe
était aussi disponible en formats plus
petits et plus adaptés à un usage
domestique. Ses pans fragmentés qui
se chevauchaient à des angles différents lui donnaient un aspect très décoratif et spectaculaire. (CF/PF)

△ **PH Artichoke** hanging light, 1957

Brushed copper, stainless steel or enameled metal leaves with chrome-plated steel frame, 58 cm, 65 cm or 72 cm high / Lamellen aus mattiertem Kupfer, rostfreiem Stahl oder lackiertem Metall mit verchromter Stahlmontierung, 58 cm, 65 cm, oder 72 cm hoch / Lamelles en cuivre brossé, inox ou métal émaillé, cadre en acier chromé, 58 cm, 65 cm ou 72 cm de hauteur
Louis Poulsen Lighting, Copenhagen, Denmark

◁ *The Langelinie Pavilion, Copenhagen 1959 – featuring* PH Artichoke *and* PH Plate *hanging lights, 1957 and 1958 / Der Langelinie Pavillon, Kopenhagen, 1959 – mit den von Poul Henningsen 1957 bzw. 1958 entworfenen Hängeleuchten* PH Artichoke *und* PH Plate */ Le Pavillon Langelinie, Copenhague, 1959, où l'on peut voir les lampes* Artichaut *et* Assiette, *créées respectivement en 1957 et 1958*

isamu noguchi

model no. 33s-bb3 akari floor light

On a trip to Japan in 1951, Isamu Noguchi was asked by the Mayor of Gifu to help revive the area's traditional paper lantern industry, which was being threatened by the popularity of cheaper mass-produced silk lanterns. Traditionally, the folding Japanese *chochin* lanterns utilized *washi* paper (made from the inner bark of mulberry trees) and structural ribs made of bamboo known as *higo*. While this type of lantern was normally illuminated by candle, Noguchi ingeniously decided to integrate the paper shades with electrical fittings. He called the resulting lights *Akari* – the Japanese word for light. (CF/PF)

Während einer Japanreise im Jahr 1951 wurde Isamu Noguchi von dem Bürgermeister von Gifu um Hilfe für die Wiederbelebung der traditionellen Papierlaternenindustrie der Region gebeten, die durch die Popularität billigerer Massenartikel aus Seide gefährdet war. Traditionell fertigte man die gefalteten japanischen *Chochin*-Laternen aus *Washi*-Papier, das aus der Innenrinde von Maulbeerbäumen gewonnen wird, sowie aus einer Rahmenkonstruktion aus Bambus, *Higo* genannt. Während diese Laternen früher von Kerzen erleuchtet wurden, hatte Noguchi die Idee, die Papierschirme mit elektrischen Lampen auszustatten. Er gab dem fertigen Design den Namen *Akari* – das japanische Wort für Licht. (CF/PF)

Lors d'un voyage au Japon en 1951, Isamu Noguchi rencontra le maire de Gifu, qui lui demanda de faire quelque chose pour relancer l'industrie locale traditionnelle des lanternes en papier. Celles-ci étaient en effet menacées par la production en série de lanternes en soie, qui coûtaient moins cher et remportaient par conséquent un vif succès. Traditionnellement, les lampes *Chochin* (lanternes japonaises pliables) étaient faites de papier *Washi*, fabriqué à partir de l'écorce interne du mûrier, et d'un type de bambou appelé *Higo*, qui servait à confectionner les nervures structurales. Ces lanternes fonctionnaient généralement à la bougie, mais Noguchi décida d'en équiper les abat-jour en papier d'ampoules électriques. Il donna aux lampes ainsi créées le nom d'*Akari*, qui, en japonais, signifie lumière. (CF/PF)

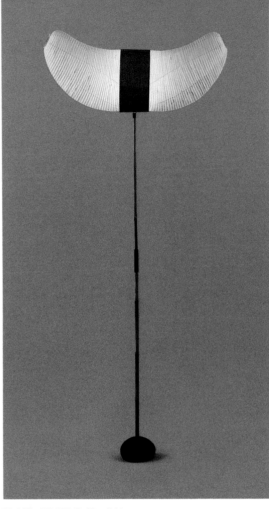

Model No. 33S-BB3 *Akari* floor light, 1960

Bamboo stem and cast-iron base with mulberry-bark paper and bamboo shade, 165 cm high (approx.) / Fuß aus Gusseisen, Schaft aus Bambus mit Lampenschirm aus Maulbeerbaumrinde und Bambus, ca. 165 cm hoch / Tige en bambou, socle en fonte, abat-jour en papier d'écorce de mûrier sur une âme de bambou, 165 cm de hauteur environ.
Ozeki & Co., Gifu, Japan for Akari Associates, Long Island City (NY), USA

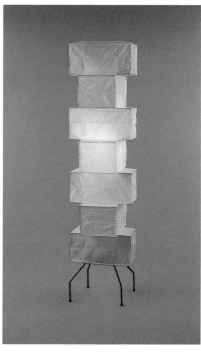

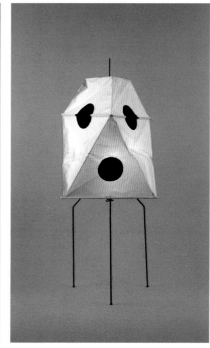

**Model No. UF4-L10 Akari floor light,
1950s**

Enameled metal rod supports with mulberry-bark
paper shade, 193 cm high / Füße und Rahmen
aus lackiertem Metall mit Lampenschirm aus
Maulbeerbaumrinde, 193 cm hoch / Structure
en baguette de métal émaillé, abat-jour en
papier d'écorce de mûrier, 193 cm de hauteur
Ozeki & Co., Gifu, Japan for Akari Associates,
Long Island City (NY), USA

**Model No. UF3-Q Akari floor light,
1950s**

Enameled metal rod supports with mulberry-bark
paper shade, 145 cm high / Füße und Rahmen
aus lackiertem Metall mit Lampenschirm aus
Maulbeerbaumrinde, 145 cm hoch / Structure
en baguette de métal émaillé, abat-jour en
papier d'écorce de mûrier, 145 cm de hauteur
Ozeki & Co., Gifu, Japan for Akari Associates,
Long Island City (NY), USA

Isamu Noguchi began designing his
extensive range of *Akari* lights in 1951
and over the next 35 years he added
new designs annually – each one
possessing a strong sculptural quality
that was reminiscent of his earlier *Lunar*
light sculptures. Increasingly, the forms
of Noguchi's *Akari* lights became less
rigid and symmetrical, as evidenced his
Model No. UF3-Q floor light (1950s)
and his monumental spiral hanging lights
from the mid-1960s. Referring to these
designs, Noguchi wrote: "Function…
was for me just the beginning. My purpose has always been Art as it relates to
life." (CF/PF)

Isamu Noguchi begann 1951 mit der
Gestaltung seiner umfangreichen Kollektion von *Akari*-Leuchten und fügte
ihr im Lauf der folgenden fünfund-
dreißig Jahre jährlich ein neues Modell
hinzu. Ein jedes zeugt von einer kraftvollen skulpturalen Qualität, die an seine früheren *Lunar*-Lichtskulpturen erinnert. Noguchis *Akari*-Leuchten wurden
mit der Zeit formal weniger streng und
symmetrisch, wie man an seiner Stehleuchte *Modell Nr. UF3-Q* (1950er
Jahre) und seinen monumentalen, spiralförmig gestalteten Hängeleuchten
der 1960er Jahre erkennen kann. In
Bezug auf diese Entwürfe schrieb
Noguchi: „Funktion … war für mich
bloß der Anfang. Mein Ziel ist immer
die Kunst gewesen, in ihrer Wechsel-
beziehung zum Leben." (CF/PF)

Ayant démarré sa vaste série *Akari* en
1951, Isamu Noguchi y ajouta chaque
année, pendant les trente-cinq ans qui
suivirent, de nouveaux modèles, dont
l'aspect n'était pas sans rappeler ses
sculptures lumineuses appelées *Lunar*.
Au fil du temps, leurs formes devinrent
de moins en moins rigides et symé-
triques, comme le montrent le lampadaire *Modèle N° UF3-Q* ci-dessus et les
monumentales suspensions en spirale
que Noguchi réalisa au milieu des
années 1960. « Pour moi, » écrivit-il à
leur sujet, « la fonction n'était que le
point de départ. Mon objectif a toujours
été l'Art dans son rapport avec la vie. »
(CF/PF)

isamu noguchi
akari lights

◁◁ *Chuey House in Los Angeles (CA), photographed by Julius Shulman – featuring Akari floor lights, 1956 / Akari-Leuchten im Chuey House in Los Angeles, fotografiert von Julius Shulman, 1956 / Lampes Akari dans la Maison Chuey à Los Angeles, Californie, photographiée par Julius Shulman, 1956*

△ *Isamu Noguchi at the Ozeki Factory working on an Akari light, Gifu, Japan, 1978 / Isamu Noguchi in der Ozeki-Fabrik bei der Arbeit an einer Akari-Leuchte, Gifu, Japan, 1978 / Isamu Noguchi en train de fabriquer une lampe Akari à l'usine Ozeki, Gifu, Japon, 1978*

◁ *Akari publicity photo, c.1953 / Werbefoto für Akari-Leuchten, ca. 1953 / Photographie publicitaire pour les lampes Akari, vers 1953*

Among the most forward-looking lighting designs to come out of Italy during the 1950s, Ettore Sottsass's hanging lights were manufactured by Arredoluce – a progressive company founded immediately after World War II by the designer-entrepreneur Angelo Lelli. The hanging light seen here comes from a series of stylishly playful lights that incorporated suspended enameled metal reflectors in order to provide a soft, indirect light. Similarly sculptural in form, through not by Sottsass, the Arredoluce floor light opposite can be seen as an early example of "contesting" design, in that it broke all notions of what a floor light was traditionally meant to look like. (CF/PF)

Zu den fortschrittlichsten Leuchten-entwürfen, die in den 1950er Jahren aus Italien kamen, gehören die von Ettore Sottsass entworfenen Hänge-leuchten. Sie wurden von Arredoluce produziert, einer unmittelbar nach dem Zweiten Weltkrieg von dem Designer und Industriellen Angelo Lelli gegründeten Leuchtenfirma. Die Hängeleuchte (1956–57) stammt aus einer Serie von spielerisch eleganten Leuchten, die mit eingehängten Reflektoren aus lackiertem Metall bestückt waren, welche für ein warmes, indirektes Licht sorgten. Die – obgleich nicht von Ettore Sottsass entworfene – in der Formgebung ähnlich plastisch gestaltete Steh-leuchte (1958) der Firma Arredoluce lässt sich als ein frühes Beispiel für ein „kontroverses" Design betrachten, da sie sämtliche tradierten Vorstellungen davon, wie eine Stehleuchte aussehen sollte, verwarf. (CF/PF)

Ce lampadaire et cette suspension signés Ettore Sottsass comptent parmi les luminaires les plus en avance sur leur temps à avoir été fabriqués en Italie pendant les années 1950. Ils étaient réalisés par Arredoluce, entreprise progressiste fondée au sortir de la Seconde Guerre mondiale par le créateur et entrepreneur Angelo Lelli. La suspension ci-contre (1956–57) appartient à une série de lampes ludiques et élégantes qui produisaient une douce lumière indirecte grâce à leurs réflecteurs en métal émaillé. Le lampadaire (1958), dont la forme est tout aussi graphique, est peut-être l'un des premiers exemples de design « contestataire » – il remettait en effet en question toute idée pré-établie de ce à quoi un lampadaire devait ressembler. (CF/PF)

▵ **Hanging light, 1956–57**
Enameled metal mounts and shades, 101 cm drop / Montierung und Lampenschirme aus lackiertem Metall, 101 cm lang / Montures et abat-jour en métal émaillé, 101 cm de hauteur
Arredoluce, Monza, Italy

▷ *Hanging light designed by Ettore Sottsass, c.1956–57* / Hängeleuchte von Ettore Sottsass, ca. 1956–57 / Suspension d' Ettore Sottsass, vers 1956–57

▷▷ **Floor light, 1958**
Marble base and steel frame with glass diffusers, 216 cm high / Marmorfuß und Stahlrahmen mit Glasdiffusoren, 216 cm hoch / Socle en marbre, cadre en acier, diffuseurs en verre, 216 cm de hauteur
Arredoluce, Monza, Italy

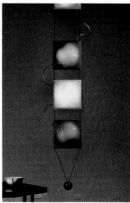

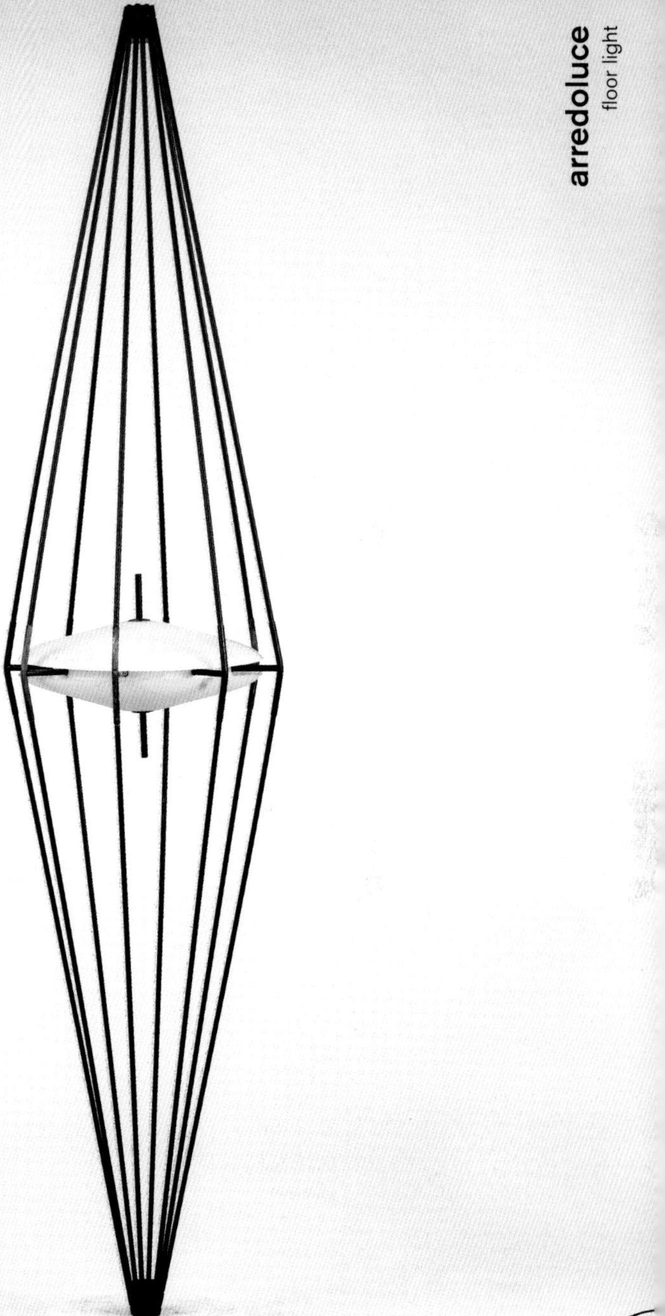

arredoluce
floor light

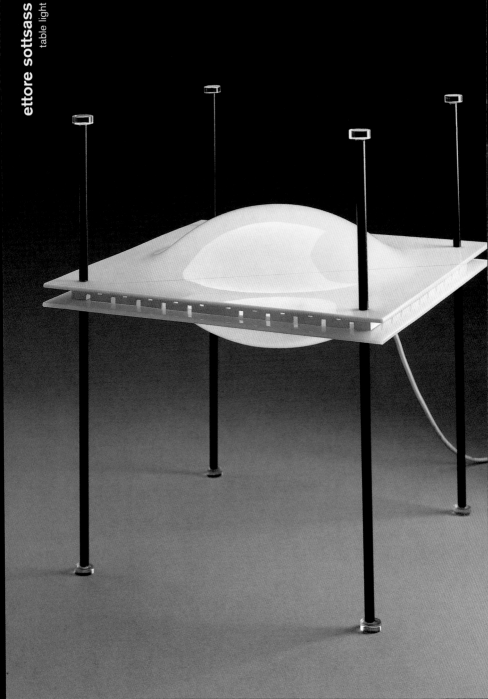

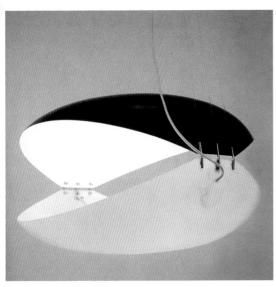

Both these lights by Ettore Sottsass can be seen as precursors of the Italian Radical Design Movement of the late 1960s, and ultimately of Post-Modernism. Their sculptural yet functional forms were influenced by Sottsass's interest in Constructivist sculpture and innovative materials applications. The table light (1957) could be inverted so as to produce an alternative lighting effect, while its acrylic feet glowed from the light emitted from its translucent diffusers. The hanging light (1958) was also functionally innovative in that it could be angled in various positions through the adjustment of its wires. (CF/PF)

Beide Leuchten nach Entwürfen von Ettore Sottsass lassen sich als Vorläufer des im Italien der 1960er Jahre aufkommenden Radical Design und letztendlich sogar der Postmoderne betrachten. Ihre skulpturalen und gleichzeitig funktionalen Formen waren von Sottsass' Interesse an der Bildhauerei der Konstruktivisten und seiner Begeisterung für neue Werkstoffe beeinflusst. Die Tischleuchte (1957) kann umgedreht werden, wodurch ein alternativer Beleuchtungseffekt erzielt wird. Die kleinen, transparenten Acrylscheiben, die oben und unten an den vier Leuchtenfüßen angebracht sind, reflektieren das abgegebene Licht und fangen ihrerseits an zu leuchten. Auch die Hängeleuchte (1958) war für die damalige Zeit in ihrer Funktion innovativ, da man sie durch das Verstellen ihrer Drahtseilaufhängung in verschiedene Positionen bringen kann. (CF/PF)

Chacun de ces deux luminaires signés Ettore Sottsass annonce le mouvement du Design Radical italien de la fin des années 1960, voire le Post-Modernisme. Leur forme sculpturale mais néanmoins fonctionnelle était influencée par la sculpture constructiviste et les nouvelles matières, aux quelles Sottsass s'intéressait vivement. La lampe de table (1957) pouvait être retournée si l'on souhaitait un éclairage différent, et la lumière émise par ses diffuseurs translucides faisait luire ses pieds en acrylique. Quant à la suspension (1958), elle est tout aussi novatrice dans son fonctionnement : on pouvait l'incliner de diverses façons en ajustant ses fils métalliques. (CF/PF)

◁ **Table light, 1957**
Enameled metal uprights with clear acrylic disk feet/finials supporting a two-part domed acrylic shade, 35 cm high / Füße aus lackiertem Metall mit transparenten Acrylscheiben als oberer und unterer Abschluss, zweiteiliger Lampenschirm aus gelbem Acryl, 35 cm hoch / Montants en métal émaillé, pieds et fleurons circulaires en acrylique transparent, abat-jour acrylique incurvé en deux parties, 35 cm de hauteur
Arredoluce, Monza, Italy

△ **Hanging light, 1958**
Enameled metal and plastic shade with suspension wires / Lampenschirm aus lackiertem Metall und Plastik mit Drahtseilaufhängung / Abat-jour en métal émaillé, abat-jour en plastique, fils métalliques de suspension
Arredoluce, Monza, Italy

▷ *Contemporary publicity photograph showing hanging light designed by Ettore Sottsass, c.1958 / Zeitgenössisches Werbefoto mit Hängeleuchten von Ettore Sottsass, ca. 1958 / Photographie publicitaire d'époque où l'on peut voir la suspension d'Ettore Sottsass, vers 1958*

Lantern Series hanging light, c.1958

Plastic construction, 61 cm diameter / Plastik-konstruktion, 61 cm Durchmesser / Strcuture en plastique, 61 cm de diamètre
Howard Miller Clock Company, Zeeland (MI), USA

▷ **Lantern Series table light, c.1958**

Walnut base with plastic shade, 74 cm high / Fuß aus Walnussholz mit Lampenschirm aus Plastik, 74 cm hoch / Base en noyer, abat-jour en plastique, 74 cm de hauteur
Howard Miller Clock Company, Zeeland (MI), USA

The *Lantern Series* (c.1958) designed by George Nelson anticipated the fashion in the 1960s for plastic origami-like lighting products. This product range was based on the use of either folded plastic (as shown here) or molded, bubble-like plastic lampshades. The series was produced by the Howard Miller Clock Company, which also manufactured Nelson's earlier and more commercially successful *Bubble* lights (1947–50), and included several different table models with sculptural wooden bases. The *Lantern Series* exemplifies Nelson's approach to lighting design through the innovative use of materials, bold forms and functional practicality. (CF/PF)

Die von George Nelson entworfenen *Lantern Series* Leuchten (ca. 1958) boten einen Vorgeschmack auf die in den 1960er Jahren in Mode kommenden origamiartigen Beleuchtungen aus Plastik. Die Serie basierte auf dem Einsatz von Lampenschirmen, die entweder aus gefaltetem Plastik oder aus blasenartiger Presskunststoffmasse gefertigt waren. Sie wurde von der Howard Miller Clock Company produziert, die auch Nelsons frühere *Bubble*-Leuchten (1947–50) herstellte, und enthielt mehrere Tischmodelle mit plastisch gestalteten Füßen aus Holz. Die *Lantern Series* Leuchten sind ein anschauliches Beispiel für Nelsons Leuchtendesign, das sich durch innovative Materialauswahl, markante Formen und funktionale Zweckmäßigkeit auszeichnet. (CF/PF)

La gamme *Lantern Series* conçue par George Nelson (vers 1958) était un avant-goût des luminaires en plastique en forme d'origami qui allaient faire fureur pendant les années 1960. Les abat-jour de ces lampes étaient en plastique qui était soit plié en accordéon (comme ici), soit moulé en forme de boule. La série était fabriquée par la Howard Miller Clock Company, qui manufacturait également la gamme *Bubble*, créée quelques années auparavant (1947–50) et qui rencontrait plus de succès. Elle comprenait aussi plusieurs modèles de lampes de table aux socles en bois très dessinés. La *Lantern Series* illustre bien la démarche de Nelson, qui recourrait volontiers à des matières et à des formes audacieuses dans ses luminaires, sans jamais négliger les qualités pratiques. (CF/PF)

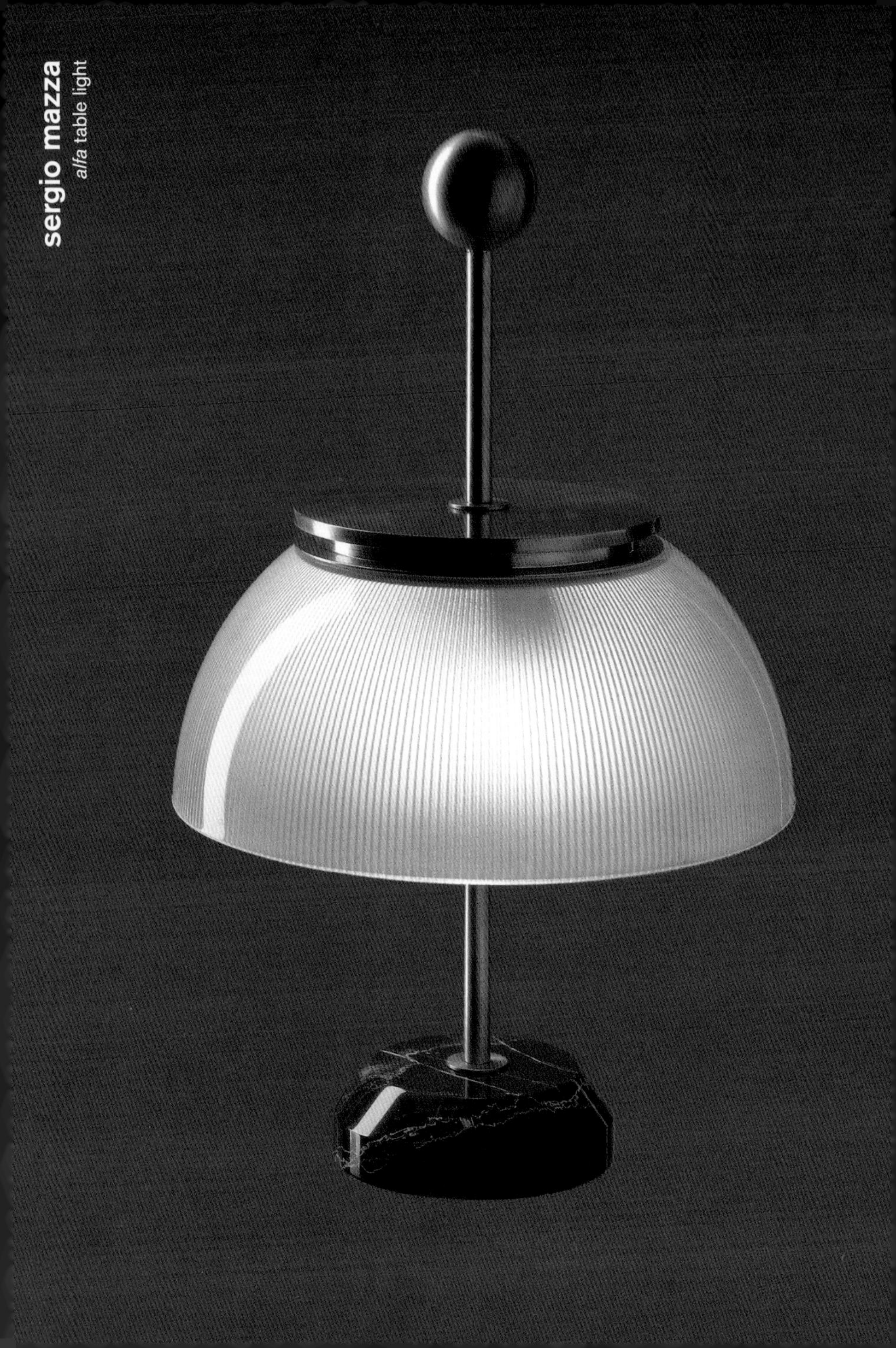
sergio mazza
alfa table light

◁ *Alfa* **table light, 1959**

Nickel-plated metal stem and marble base with crystal glass shade, 48 cm high / Vernickelter Metallfuß auf Marmorsockel mit Lampenschirm aus Kristallglas, 48 cm hoch / Pied en métal nickelé sur socle en marbre, abat-jour en cristal, 48 cm de hauteur
Artemide, Pregnana Milanese, Italy

Artemide publicity photograph showing the Alfa table light, c.1960 / Werbefoto von Artemide mit der Tischleuchte Alfa, ca. 1960 / Photographie publicitaire d'Artémide où l'on peut voir la lampe de table Alfa, vers 1960

Sergio Mazza's *Alfa* table light (1959) reflects the widespread rejection of "cold" rationalism in Italian postwar design (and possibly its associations with the Mussolini era) in favor of a return to more bourgeois values. Incorporating luxury materials such as marble and crystal, this diminutive design was a modern reworking of the traditional boudoir light. Expressing nostalgia for the warm domesticity of a bygone age, the *Alfa* table light was the first lighting product manufactured by Artemide. (CF/PF)

Die von Sergio Mazza entworfene Tischleuchte *Alfa* (1959) reflektiert die im italienischen Design der Nachkriegszeit weitverbreitete Abneigung gegen eine „kalte" Rationalität (und möglicherweise deren Assoziation mit der Mussolini-Ära) zugunsten einer Rückkehr zu eher bürgerlichen Werten. In der Verwendung edler Materialien wie Marmor und Kristallglas war dieses kleinformatige Design eine moderne Interpretation einer traditionellen Boudoir-Leuchte. Die von Nostalgie und behaglicher Wohnatmosphäre einer vergangenen Zeit geprägte Tischleuchte *Alfa* war das erste von Artemide produzierte Leuchtendesign. (CF/PF)

La lampe *Alfa* de Sergio Mazza (1959) s'inscrivait dans le vaste mouvement de rejet à l'encontre du côté « froidement » rationaliste du design italien d'après-guerre (peut-être du fait de ses associations avec l'ère mussolinienne). Elle semblait au contraire prôner le retour à des valeurs plus bourgeoises. Avec ses matériaux précieux de luxe comme le marbre et le cristal, ce minuscule modèle était une version moderne de la traditionnelle lampe de boudoir. Premier luminaire à être fabriqué par Artemide, la lampe de table *Alfa* évoquait avec nostalgie la chaleureuse ambiance des maisons d'antan. (CF/PF)

Although Lightolier did not invent the first pole light, the company certainly advanced this type of lighting when it introduced the *Lytespan* system in 1959. The *Lytespan* was the first pole light to incorporate interchangeable lighting elements and could be installed either from ceiling to floor or table to ceiling without the use of tools. Up to ten 75-watt lights could be installed on either side of the electrified pole and a large variety of shades, tables and planters were available, allowing a high degree of customization. By turning the *Lytespan* sideways and modifying the design, Lightolier went on to invent track lighting. (CF/PF)

Zwar hat Lightolier die zwischen Boden und Decke spannbaren Ständerleuchten nicht erfunden, aber das Unternehmen hat die Verbreitung dieses im Original „Pole Light" genannten Leuchtentyps mit der Einführung des *Lytespan*-Systems im Jahr 1959 zweifellos gefördert. Es war das erste System dieses Typs, das ohne Einsatz von Werkzeug installiert werden konnte. An beiden Seiten des stromführenden Ständers konnten jeweils bis zu zehn 75-Watt-Lampen angebracht werden. Außerdem stand eine Vielzahl verschiedener Lampenschirme, integrierter Tische und Anbringungselemente zur Auswahl. In einer Modifizierung des *Lytespan*-Designs erfand Lightolier später das Leuchtschienensystem. (CF/PF)

Bien que la colonne lumineuse n'ait pas été inventée par Lightolier, l'entreprise en perfectionna considérablement le principe lorsqu'elle lança, en 1959, l'appareil *Lytespan*. Celui-ci était la première colonne lumineuse à être équipée de lampes interchangeables, et se fixait sans outil entre le sol et le plafond (on pouvait aussi le poser sur une table). Jusqu'à dix lampes de 75 W pouvaient être disposées de part et d'autre de la colonne électrifiée. Un grand choix d'abat-jour, de tablettes et de pots de fleurs étaient aussi disponibles, de sorte que la colonne était facile à personnaliser. Lightolier n'eut qu'à basculer l'appareil sur le côté et à le modifier légèrement pour inventer l'éclairage sur rail. (CF/PF)

Lytespan pole lights, 1959
Enameled metal and chrome-plated metal or brass adjustable pole and light units / Konstruktion aus lackiertem Metall und verchromtem Metall oder Messing / étal émaillé, métal ou laiton chromé
Lightolier, Jersey City (NJ), USA

▷ Lightolier "Mix, Match and Move" advertisement showing Lytespan pole lighting system, 1959 / „Mix, Match and Move" Werbeanzeige der Firma Lightolier für das Lytespan-Ständerleuchtensystem, 1959 / Réclame «Mix, Match and Move» de Lightolier présentant le mât lumineux Lytespan, 1959

YTESPAN By LIGHTOLIER

Mix, Match and Move

r the first time
u can have
ERSONALLY
signed lighting

Lights you can arrange and re-arrange

With your own choice of elements

To serve your minute-to-minute needs

To suit your own taste and decor

FLOOR-TO-CEILING UNITS go up in instant without tools, plug in like amp.

FURNITURE-TO-CEILING UNITS d on table tops, desks, bookcases, adboards. Save floor space, drama-e decor.

ADD AS MANY LIGHTING UNITS ND ACCESSORIES AS YOU WANT Colorful new ad-a-lyte "spots," in- ect torchiere reflectors, stylized al "chimneys," smart porcelain nters, bedside and chairside walnut ys.

MIX direct, indirect and general light- ing units to achieve the perfect com- bination for *your* needs. Use up to ten 75 watt units on each column.

MATCH or contrast colors to suit your own taste ... sophisticated white & black ... beige & brown for neutral blending ... the formal look of white & brass ... and a dozen other color combinations.

MOVE any lighting element, anytime, anywhere, with a flick of your finger! Move it to *any position* along the full length of the column, *on both sides!* ...Move spots on any-position swivels ... Move entire Lytespan unit to another part of your room in seconds.

A WEALTH OF COMMERCIAL USES TOO

Starting from a 1957 prototype designed by Hans Scharoun, in 1959 Günter Ssymmank – at that time Scharoun's assistant at the Technical University of Berlin – developed the *Integra* floor light, now manufactured under the name of *Ssymmank* by the firm Mawa Design. Ssymmank's version retained the original spiral base that enabled the whole light to be moved from side to side. He replaced the glass reflector and shade of the original with an organic arrangement of petal shapes in polycarbonate, at that time a highly innovative material. The movable "petals" can be opened and closed and easily exchanged for others of a different color. (TB)

Ausgehend von einem Prototypen von Hans Scharoun (1957) entwickelte Günter Ssymmank – zur damaligen Zeit Assistent von Scharoun an der Technischen Universität Berlin – 1959 die *Integra* Stehleuchte, die heute unter der Bezeichnung *Ssymmank* von der Firma Mawa Design produziert wird. Ssymmank übernahm bei seinem Entwurf den spiralförmig konstruierten Leuchtenfuß, durch den die gesamte Leuchte bei Berührung in Schwingung versetzt werden kann. Den gläsernen Reflektor und Lampenschirm des Prototyps ersetzte er durch eine organische, blütenförmige Konstruktion aus dem damals neuartigen Werkstoff Polycarbonat. Die beweglichen Blätter der „Blüte" lassen sich öffnen, schließen und leicht gegen andersfarbige austauschen. (TB)

C'est en s'inspirant d'un prototype dessiné en 1957 par Hans Scharoun (dont il était l'assistant à l'Université technique de Berlin-Charlottenburg, que Günter Ssymmank inventa le lampadaire *Integra*, aujourd'hui commercialisé sous le nom de *Ssymmank* par Mawa Design. Ssymmank a conservé, du prototype, le socle en spirale qui autorise une rotation complète du lampadaire. En revanche, il a préféré, au verre de l'abat-jour d'origine, le polycarbonate, matière alors toute nouvelle, dont il assemblé des « pétales » pour former une fleur, que l'on peut ouvrir ou refermer à volonté. Les pétales amovibles permettent aussi d'en changer aisément la couleur. (TB)

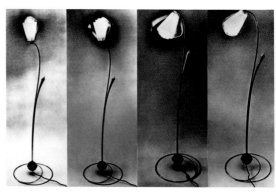

△△ *Detail of the shade of the* Model No. sy1 Ssymannk (Integra) *floor light / Detail des Leuchtenschirms der* Modell Nr. sy1 Ssymmank (Integra) *Stehleuchte / Détail de l'abat-jour du lampadaire* Modèle n°sy1 Ssymmank (Integra)

△ *Prototype of the* Ssymannk (Integra) *floor light after a design by Hans Scharoun, 1957 / Prototyp der* Ssymannk (Integra) *Stehleuchte nach Entwurf von Hans Scharoun, 1957 / Prototype du lampadaire* Ssymmank (Integra) *d'après un dessin de Hans Scharoun, 1957*

▷ **Model No. sy1 Ssymmank (Integra) floor light, 1959**

Chromium-plated metal base and stem with interchangeable colored nylon shade elements, 140 cm high / Fuß und Schaft aus verchromtem Metall mit austauschbaren Lampenschirmelementen aus farbigem Nylon, 140 cm hoch / Socle et tige en métal chromé, abat-jour à pièces interchangeables en nylon coloré, 140 cm de hauteur
Integra, Berlin, Germany (reissued by Mawa Design, Langerwisch, Germany)

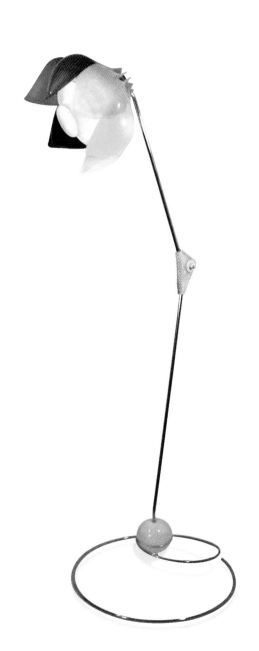

Model No. Sch1 Schliephacke floor light, 1959–60

Cast-iron base with matt aluminum stand and polished anodized aluminum shade, 165 cm high / Sockel aus schwarzem Gusseisen, Schaft und verstellbarer Arm aus mattiertem Aluminium, Lampenschirm aus poliertem und eloxiertem Aluminium, 165 cm hoch / Socle en fonte, pied en aluminium mat, abat-jour en aluminium anodisé poli, 165 cm de hauteur
Wilhelm Noack, Berlin, Germany (reissued by Mawa Design, Langerwisch, Germany)

The *Schliephacke* floor light, designed in 1959–60 by the architect and designer Fridtjof Schliephacke for the Eichkamp student hall of residence in Berlin, is striking for its functional design, clearly following in the Bauhaus tradition. The multipurpose light was intended to meet the students' every need: easy to operate, it provided both direct and indirect lighting. It was also intended to be inexpensive, but in fact production costs proved too high and these lights were not installed at the hall of residence. Schliephacke also worked with, among others, Vassili Luckhardt and was a close associate of Ludwig Mies van der Rohe. (TB)

Die *Schliephacke* Stehleuchte, ursprünglich 1959–60 von dem Architekten und Designer Fridtjof Schliephacke für das Studentenwohnheim Berlin-Eichkamp entworfen, überzeugt durch ihre funktionale Formgebung, die eindeutig in der Bauhaus-Tradition steht. Die multifunktionale Leuchte sollte alle Anforderungen der Studenten (direkte und indirekte Beleuchtung) erfüllen, leicht zu handhaben und preiswert sein. Die zu hohen Herstellungskosten verhinderten jedoch den Einsatz der Leuchte in dem Studentenwohnheim. Schliephacke arbeitete u. a. mit Wassili Luckhardt zusammen und stand auch in engem persönlichem Kontakt zu Ludwig Mies van der Rohe. (TB)

Imaginé à l'origine en 1959–60 par l'architecte et créateur Fridtjof Schliephacke pour le foyer d'étudiants d'Eichkamp à Berlin, le lampadaire *Schliephacke* étonne par son style fonctionnel, qui s'inscrit clairement dans la lignée du Bauhaus. Ce luminaire polyvalent était censé répondre à tous les besoins des étudiants. Il émettait un éclairage direct et indirect, était facile à actionner et, du moins en théorie, bon marché. Il s'avéra toutefois coûteux à fabriquer, si bien qu'il ne fut finalement pas installé dans le foyer d'étudiants. Schliephacke travaillait aussi avec Wassili Luckhardt, entre autres, et était un proche associé de Ludwig Mies van der Rohe. (TB)

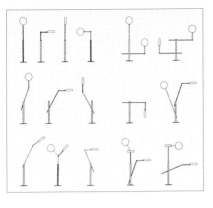

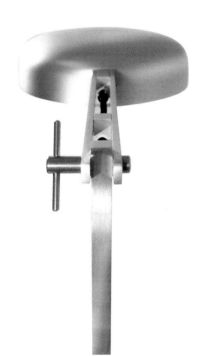

fridtjof schliephacke

model no. sch1 schliephacke floor light

△ ◁ *Drawing showing the different settings for the* Model No. Sch1 Schliephacke *floor light / Zeichnung der verschiedenen Positionsmöglichkeiten der* Modell Nr. Sch1 Schliephacke *Stehleuchte / Dessin montrant les différentes positions que peut prendre le lampadaire* Modèle n°. Sch1 Schliephacke

◁/△▷ *Alternative view and detail of the* Model No. Sch1 Schliephacke *floor light / Die* Modell Nr. Sch1 Schliephacke *Stehleuchte aus einer anderen Perspektive und im Ausschnitt / Lampadaire* Modèle n° Sch1 Schliephacke, *vu sous un autre angle, et détail du même modèle*

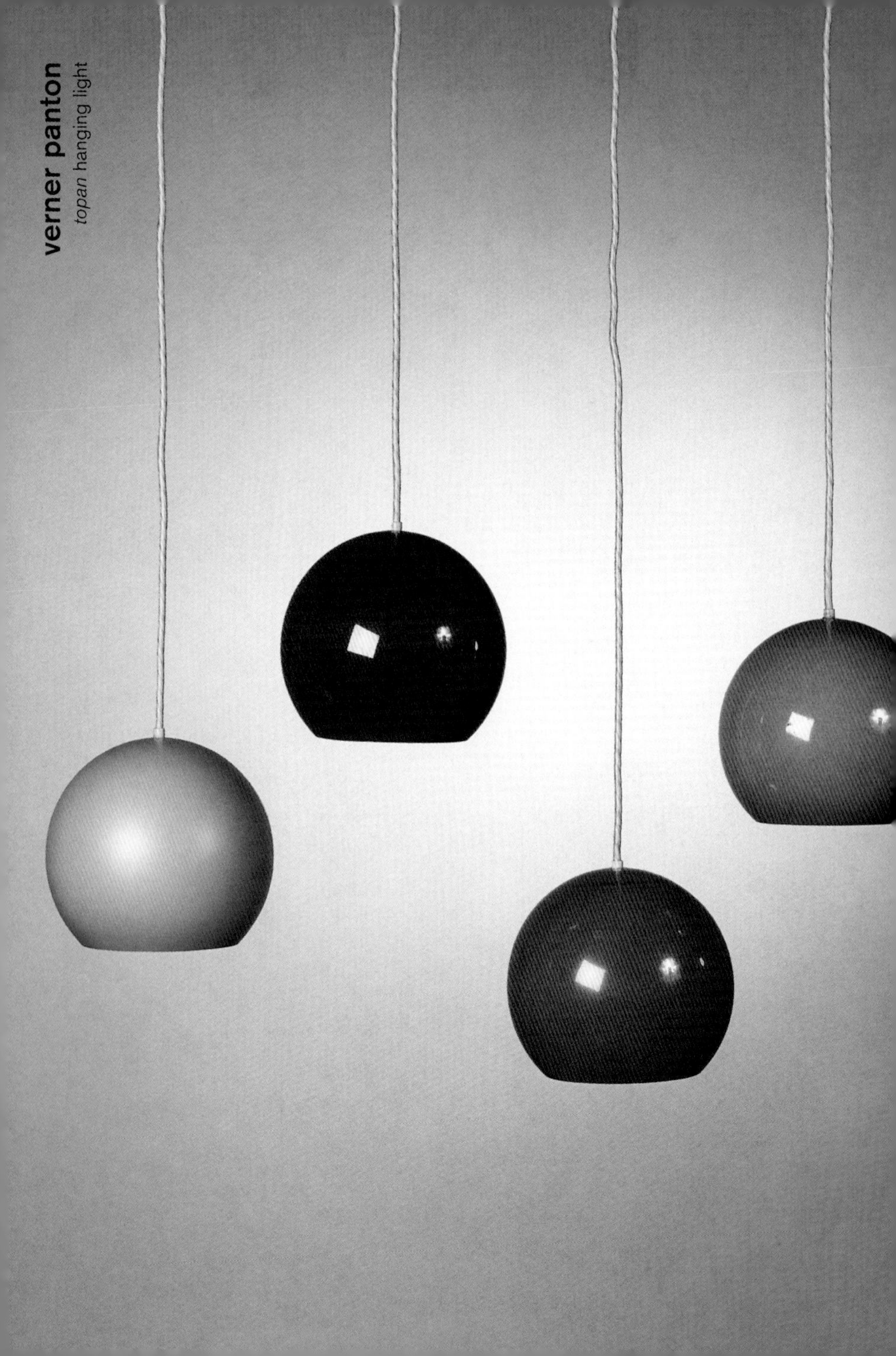

verner panton
topan hanging light

> "My pieces try to be versatile and accessible to all classes of buyer."
>
> „Meine Objekte wollen vielseitig und für alle Käuferschichten zugänglich sein."
>
> « J'essaye d'offrir des créations variées et accessibles au plus grande nombre. »

– Verner Panton

◁ *Topan* **hanging light, 1959**

Enameled metal shade, 21 cm diameter /
Lampenschirm aus lackiertem Metall, 21 cm
Durchmesser / Abat-jour globes en métal
émaillé, 21 cm de diamètre
Louis Poulsen Lighting, Copenhagen, Denmark

*Contemporary publicity photograph showing
Topan hanging lights, c.1960 / Zeitgenössisches Werbefoto für Topan-Hängeleuchten,
ca. 1960 / Photographie publicitaire montrant
des suspensions Topan, vers 1960*

Having been designed specifically for the Scandinavian exhibition stand at the Cologne Furniture Fair, the *Topan* hanging light (1959) became Verner Panton's first lighting design to be put into mass-production. With its simple spherical form, the *Topan* had a universal appeal that enabled it to be used in a wide variety of interior settings. The light was meant to be suspended low down to reduce glare and could also be hung in clusters. Initially it was produced only in polished aluminum, but in the 1960s Louis Poulsen began manufacturing it in vibrant colors. (CF/PF)

Nachdem sie speziell für den skandinavischen Ausstellungsstand auf der Kölner Möbelmesse entworfen worden war, wurde die Hängeleuchte *Topan* (1959) als erstes Leuchtenmodell von Verner Panton in die Massenfertigung aufgenommen. Mit ihrer schlichten Kugelform fand die Leuchte *Topan* allgemein Anklang und konnte in einer Vielzahl unterschiedlich gestalteter Wohnräume verwendet werden. Die Leuchte sollte relativ tief gehängt werden, um das Blendlicht zu reduzieren, und ließ sich auch in Gruppen installieren. Ursprünglich war sie nur in poliertem Aluminium erhältlich, doch in den 1960er Jahren begann Louis Poulsen, sie in einer Auswahl kräftiger Farben herzustellen. (CF/PF)

Réalisée tout spécialement pour la section scandinave du Salon de meuble de Cologne, la suspension *Topan* (1959) fut l'un des premiers modèles de Verner Panton à faire l'objet d'une production de masse. Sa simple forme sphérique plaisait à tout le monde et s'intégrait à toutes sortes d'intérieurs. La *Topan* était censée être placée assez bas de manière à en atténuer la luminosité, et pouvait être installée par groupes de plusieurs. Au départ, elle était uniquement disponible en aluminium poli, jusqu'à ce que Louis Poulsen commence à la fabriquer en couleurs vives à la fin des années 1960. (CF/PF)

△ The Castiglioni brothers introducing their
new range of "Cocoon" spray-on plastic lights
to Marcel Breuer, c.1960 / Die Brüder
Castiglioni präsentieren Marcel Breuer ihre
neuen „Cocoon"-Glasfaserhaut-Leuchten, ca.
1960 / Les frères Castiglioni montrant leur
nouvelle gamme de luminaires en plastique
projeté « Cocoon » à Marcel Breuer, vers 1960

Taraxacum hanging light, 1960
Metal wire frame with "Cocoon" spray-on plastic
coating, 60 cm diameter / „Cocoon"-Glasfaser-
haut auf Montierung aus Metalldraht, 60 cm
Durchmesser / Membrane en plastique projeté
« Cocoon » sur structure en fil métallique, 60 cm
de diamètre
Flos, Bovezzo, Italy

**"I define the enterprise
of industrial design as the
result of a creativity that is
truly collective."**

**„Ich definiere Industrie-
design als das schöpfe-
rische Ergebnis einer
Kollektive."**

**« Je dèfinis cette entre-
prise qu'est le design
industriel comme
l'aboutissement d'une
créativité authentique-
ment collective. »**

– Achille Castiglioni

Viscontea hanging light, 1960
Metal wire frame with "Cocoon" spray-on
plastic coating, 36.8 cm high / "Cocoon"-Glas-
faserhaut auf Montierung aus Metalldraht,
36,8 cm hoch / Membrane en plastique projeté
«Cocoon» sur structure en fil métallique,
36,8 cm de haut
Flos, Bovezzo, Italy

During the postwar years a new kind of
self-skinning spray-on plastic known as
"Cocoon" was developed in the United
States for the mothballing of naval ves-
sels. Arturo Eisenkeil from Merano
imported this state-of-the-art material
into Italy and began searching for commercial applications for it. In 1959 he
co-founded, with Dino Gavina and
Cesare Cassina, a new company
named Flos to produce light fixtures uti-
lizing the material. This led to the Castiglioni brothers designing their series of
"Cocoon" lights, issued by Flos and
including the *Viscontea* (1960), the
Taraxacum (1960) and the *Gatto*
(1962). (CF/PF)

In den Nachkriegsjahren wurde in den
USA unter dem Namen „Cocoon"
(Kokon) ein neuartiger Kunststoff für
das Einmotten von Schiffen entwickelt,
der nach dem Aufspritzen eine kokon-
artige Schicht bildete. Arturo Eisenkeil
aus Meran importierte diesen Werkstoff
nach Italien und versuchte dafür kommerzielle Anwendungen zu finden.
1959 gründete er gemeinsam mit Dino
Gavina und Cesare Cassina die Firma
Flos zur Herstellung von Beleuchtungskörpern aus diesem Material. Später
kam es zur Zusammenarbeit mit den
Castiglioni-Brüdern, die für Flos die
„Cocoon"-Leuchten *Viscontea* (1960),
Taraxacum (1960) und *Gatto* (1962)
entwarfen. (CF/PF)

Après-guerre, un nouveau type de plastique à projeter armé de fibre de verre
appelé «Cocoon» fut mis au point aux
États-Unis pour mettre sous protection
des navires de guerre déclassés. Arturo Eisenkeil, de Merano, importa ce
matériau d'avant-garde en Italie et commença à en rechercher des applications commerciales. En 1959, avec
Dino Gavina et Cesare Cassina, il
fonda une nouvelle société, Flos, pour
produire des luminaires à partir de ce
matériau, ce qui amena les frères Castiglioni à concevoir la série de lampes
«Cocoon», éditée par Flos, dont la
Viscontea (1960), la *Taraxacum* (1960)
et la *Gatto* (1962). (CF/PF)

The Castiglioni brothers' "Cocoon" lights were the first European lighting products to use this new self-skinning plastic and helped to establish Flos as a truly innovative lighting company. Like the *Taraxacum* (1960) and the *Viscontea* (1960) hanging lights, the *Gatto* table light (1962) has a form that is reminiscent of a seedpod, while its textural surface is evocative of the protective silky envelopes secreted by insects. The light below (1960) is a rare elongated version of the *Taraxacum*. (CF/PF)

Die „Cocoon"-Leuchten der Brüder Castiglioni waren die ersten europäischen Beleuchtungskörper, für die die neu entwickelte „Cocoon"-Glasfaserhaut verwendet wurde. Sie trugen dazu bei, dass sich Flos als innovativer Beleuchtungsproduzent etablieren konnte. Wie die Hängeleuchten *Taraxacum* (1960) und *Viscontea* (1960) erinnert auch die Tischleuchte *Gatto* (1962) in der Form an eine Samenkapsel, während ihre Oberflächenstruktur an einen aus Insektensekreten gesponnenen, schützenden Seidenkokon denken lässt. Bei der unten abgebildeten Leuchte (1960) handelt es sich um eine seltene längliche Version der *Taraxacum* Hängeleuchte. (CF/PF)

Les lampes « Cocoon » des frères Castiglioni furent les premières en Europe à utiliser ce nouveau plastique à peau intégrée et ont contribué à faire de Flos un éditeur de luminaires novateur. Comme les suspensions *Taraxacum* (1960) et *Viscontea* (1960), la lampe de table *Gatto* (1962) a la forme d'une gousse, tandis que sa texture évoque les soyeuses enveloppes de protection secrétées par certains insectes. La lampe du bas (1960) est une rare version allongée de la *Taraxacum*. (CF/PF)

▵▵ **Gatto table light, 1962**
Metal wire frame with "Cocoon" spray-on plastic coating, 30.5 cm high / „Cocoon"-Glasfaserhaut auf Montierung aus Metalldraht, 30,5 cm hoch / Membrane en plastique projeté « Cocoon » sur structure en fil métallique, 30,5 cm de haut
Flos, Bovezzo, Italy

▵ **Hanging light, 1960**
Metal wire frame with "Cocoon" spray-on plastic coating, 38.1 cm high / „Cocoon"-Glasfaserhaut auf Montierung aus Metalldraht, 38,1 cm hoch / Membrane en plastique projeté « Cocoon » sur structure en fil métallique, 38,1 cm de haut
Flos, Bovezzo, Italy

▷ *Interior of a house on Long Island designed by Marcel Breuer incorporating "Cocoon" lights / Interieur eines von Marcel Breuer gestalteten Hauses auf Long Island mit "Cocoon"-Leuchten / Interieur d'une maison de Long Island conçue par Marcel Breuer, éclairée par les lampes « Cocoon »*

With their geometric mould-blown glass elements and graphic outlines, Tapio Wirkkala's *Model No. K2–134* (1960) and *Model No. 66–051* lights (1961) both exemplify his belief that "No one has ever invented new forms. It's only a question of the way in which line and shape are used." *Model No. K2–134* was intended to be used in conjunction with three angular incandescent opal light bulbs that Wirkkala had designed for Airam in 1959. In fact, virtually all of Wirkkala's lighting products were designed as part of a modular system, so that by varying the combination of fixture components and light bulbs it was possible to create many different configurations. (CF/PF)

Mit ihren geometrischen Elementen aus formgeblasenem Glas und ihren grafischen Silhouetten stehen Tapio Wirkkalas Hängeleuchten *Modell Nr. K2–134* (1960) und *Nr. 66–051* (1961) als Ausdruck seiner Überzeugung, dass es niemals gelingt, neue Formen zu erfinden: „Es geht immer nur darum, wie die Formen zusammengesetzt werden." Als Leuchtmittel für das *Modell Nr. K2–134* waren drei, in der Form eckige, opale Glühbirnen vorgesehen, die Wirkkala 1959 für die Firma Airam entworfen hatte. Praktisch alle Beleuchtungskörper von Wirkkala gehörten zu einem modularen System, das die Kombination verschiedener Leuchtenelemente und Glühbirnen ermöglichte und dadurch sehr variantenreich war. (CF/PF)

Par leurs éléments géométriques en verre soufflé-moulé et leur allure graphique, les modèles *n° K2–134* (1960) et *n° 66–051* (1961) de Tapio Wirkkala illustrent une de ses affirmations : « Personne n'a jamais inventé de formes nouvelles. C'est seulement une question d'utilisation de la ligne et de la forme. » Le *Modèle n° K2–134* utilisait trois ampoules opalescentes triangulaires dessinées par Wirkkala pour Airam en 1959. En fait, pratiquement tous les luminaires de Wirkkala ont été conçus comme des éléments d'un système modulaire qui permettait, en combinant composants et ampoules, de créer de multiples configurations. (CF/PF)

△ **Model No. 66–051 hanging light, 1961**

Mould-blown smoked outer glass shade with opalescent inner glass shade, 30 cm high / Äußerer Lampenschirm aus formgeblasenem Rauchglas mit innerem Lampenschirm aus Opalglas, 30 cm hoch / Abat-jour extérieur en verre fumé soufflé-moulé et verre intérieur opalescent, 30 cm de haut
Iittala, Helsinki, Finland, for Stockmann, Helsinki, Finland

◁ **WIR light bulbs with original packaging, 1959**

Opalescent glass light bulbs with paper packaging / Opale Glühbirnen mit Originalverpackung / Ampoules opalescentes, conditionnement en carton d'origine
Airam Electric, Helsinki, Finland

▷ **Model No. K2–134 hanging light, 1960**

Enameled copper mount with glass shade, 25 cm drop / Montierung aus lackiertem Kupfer mit Lampenschirm aus Glas, 25 cm lang / Monture en cuivre émaillé, abat-jour en verre, 25 cm de haut
Iittala, Helsinki, Finland, for Idman, Mäntsälä, Finland

tapio wirkkala

model no. k2-134 hanging light

Conceived in 1961 and put into production by the manufacturer Flos in
1964, the Castiglioni brothers' *Splügen
Bräu* hanging light is an object of surprising beauty. The undulations of the
polished spun-aluminum construction
animate the light that falls on it. The
shade becomes a curiously elusive form;
its edges seem to melt and it appears
liquid, like mercury. This sophisticated
effect is achieved, as one might expect
from the thoughtful Castiglioni brothers,
in the simplest of ways. (PG)

Die 1961 entworfene und ab 1964
von der Firma Flos hergestellte Hängeleuchte *Splügen Bräu* der Brüder
Castiglioni ist ein Objekt von verblüffen-
der Schönheit. Die Wellenlinien auf
dem Lampenschirm aus poliertem Aluminium verleihen dem reflektierten Licht
den Eindruck von gleißender Flüchtig-
keit. Die Konturen des Lampenschirms
schmelzen förmlich und verflüssigen
sich gleichsam wie Quecksilber. Dieser
beeindruckende Effekt wird, wie von
den Brüdern Castiglioni nicht anders
zu erwarten, mit einfachsten Mitteln erzielt. (PG)

Conçue en 1961 et mise en production par le fabricant Flos en 1964, la
suspension *Splügen Bräu* des frères
Castiglioni est un objet d'une surpre-
nante beauté. Les ondulations de
l'aluminium filé animent la lumière qui
s'y accroche. La forme devient curieu-
sement floue, ses contours semblent
s'estomper et elle semble adopter un
état liquide, qui rappelle le mercure.
Cet effet sophistiqué est atteint par
les moyens les plus simples, comme
on pouvait s'y attendre de la part des
habiles frères Castiglioni. (PG)

Inspired by a wartime invention for an egg timer/light "made out of a cocktail shaker, old tins and things", Edward Craven Walker spent several years developing a new kind of liquid-and-wax filled light. His first light, the *Astro* was launched in 1963, and was followed by a large number of other models made by his company, Crestworth (which was later renamed Mathmos and still manufactures his designs in the original factory in Poole, Dorset.) Around 1965, the Lava Manufacturing Corp. of Chicago acquired the US rights to produce Crestworth designs and subsequently coined the "Lava Lite" name. Walker's lights enjoyed huge commercial success and helped to bring the Psychedelic Movement into mainstream consciousness. (CF/PF)

Inspiriert von einer in der Kriegszeit erfundenen Apparatur, die Eieruhr und Leuchte zugleich und „aus einem Cocktailshaker, Blechdosen und anderem Zeugs" zusammengebaut war, verbrachte Edward Craven Walker mehrere Jahre damit, eine neuartige Leuchte zu entwickeln, die mit einer Flüssigkeit und Wachs gefüllt war. Seine erste Leuchte *Astro* kam 1963 auf den Markt, gefolgt von zahlreichen anderen Modellen, die seine Firma Crestworth herstellte. (Bis zum heutigen Tag werden seine Entwürfe in der alten Fabrik der später zu Mathmos umbenannten Firma in Poole, Dorset, gefertigt.) Um 1965 erwarb die Lava Manufacturing Corp. of Chicago die US-Produktionsrechte für die Crestworth-Modelle und prägte in der Folge den Namen „Lava Lite". Walkers Leuchten waren kommerziell ungeheuer erfolgreich und trugen dazu bei, dass die psychedelische Bewegung ins allgemeine Bewusstsein drang. (CF/PF)

Inspiré par une invention datant de la Seconde Guerre mondiale d'une lampe/minuterie à œufs « faite d'un shaker à cocktails, de vieux trucs de récupération,» Edward Craven Walker consacra plusieurs années à la mise au point de cire liquide. Son premier luminaire, le *Astro*, fut lancé en 1963, puis suivi par un grand nombre d'autres modèles fabriqués par sa société, Crestworth (qui prit plus tard le nom de Mathmos et réalise toujours ses projets dans l'usine d'origine de Poole, Dorset). Vers 1965, la Lava Manufacturing Corp. de Chicago acquit les droits de fabrication des modèles Crestworth pour les États-Unis et déposa par la suite le nom de *Lava Light*. Les lampes de Walker ont connu un énorme succès et ont contribué à faire connaître le mouvement psychédique auprès du grand public. (CF/PF)

"If you buy my lamp, you won't need to buy drugs."

„Wer meine Leuchten kauft, braucht keine Drogen."

« Si vous achetez mes lampes, vous n'aurez pas besoin de drogues.»

– Edward C. Walker

▽ *Lava lights produced by Crestworth, late 1960s / „Lava"-Leuchten aus der Produktion von Crestworth, Ende der 1960er Jahre / Lampes Lava produites par Crestworth, fin des années 1960*

▷ *Astro* **lava light, 1963**

Copper holder with glass bottle filled with wax and colored water, 43.5 cm high / Fuß und Kappe aus Kupfer, mit Wachs und gefärbtem Wasser gefüllte Glasflasche, 43,5 cm hoch / Support en cuivre, bouteille en verre remplie de cire et d'eau colorée, 43,5 cm de haut
Crestworth, Dorset, Great Britain (reissued by Mathmos, London, Great Britain)

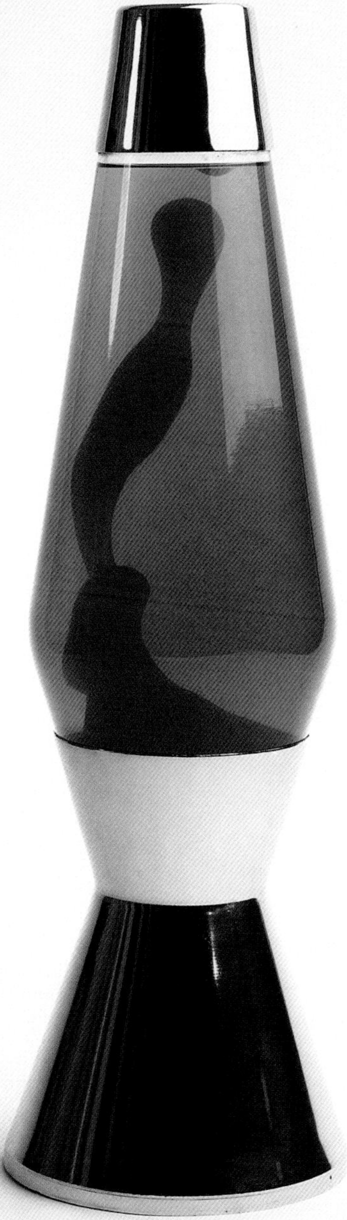

edward c. walker
astro lava light

The Castiglioni brothers are universally recognized as talented innovators of contemporary lighting. In this case, the idea that a car headlamp could be used as a light source led to the creation of the contemporary lighting industry's most famous ready-made. All the components – from the transformer to the electric cable – are exposed in their original form, thus eschewing any form of "shell" and giving validity and expression to the original esthetics of the individual, anonymous, non-designer components. Like many other projects by the Castiglionis, this light (1962) combines functionality, irony, and an understanding of the zeitgeist. (SC)

Die Brüder Castiglioni sind als begabte Neuerer des zeitgenössischen Leuchtendesigns international anerkannt. Im vorliegenden Beispiel hat die Idee, einen Autoscheinwerfer als Lichtquelle zu verwenden, das berühmteste Readymade der heutigen Beleuchtungsindustrie hervorgebracht. Alle Bestandteile – vom Transformator bis zum Stromkabel – bleiben in ihrer eigentlichen Form sichtbar, jede „Hülle" wird vermieden, wodurch die ursprüngliche Ästhetik der einzelnen, anonymen, von keinem Designer gestalteten Komponenten zur Geltung kommt. Wie viele andere Projekte der Brüder Castiglioni verbindet auch diese Leuchte (1962) Funktionalität mit Ironie und Sinn für den Zeitgeist. (SC)

Les frères Castiglioni sont universellement reconnus pour être d'immenses et talentueux novateurs dans le domaine de l'éclairage contemporain. Ici, l'idée qu'un phare de voiture puisse servir de source lumineuse a débouché sur l'un des plus célèbres *ready-made* de l'industrie du luminaire du XXᵉ siècle. Tous les composants – du transformateur au câble d'alimentation – sont utilisés sous leur forme d'origine. L'absence d'une quelconque protection rend à leur esthétique de composants anonymes toute sa validité et son expressivité. Comme beaucoup d'autres projets des Castiglioni, ce lampadaire (1962) combine fonctionnalisme, ironie et une grande sensibilité à l'esprit du temps. (SC)

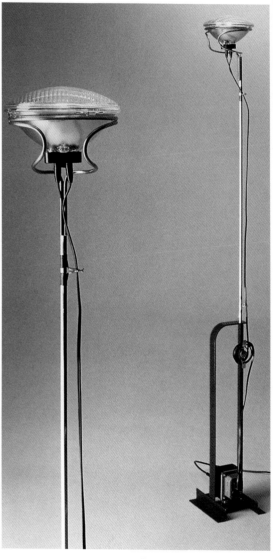

Toio uplighter, 1962

Enameled metal base, chrome-plated stem, 200 cm high (max.) / Fuß aus lackiertem Metall, Schaft aus verchromten Metall, 200 cm hoch (max.) / Socle en métal laqué, tige chromée, 200 cm de haut (max.)
Flos, Bovezzo, Italy

Gian Luigi Banfi, Lodovico Barbiano di Belgiojoso, Enrico Peressutti and Ernesto Nathan Rogers founded the Milan-based BBPR design studio in 1932. After World War II, the practice played an important role in the promotion of Rationalism in both architecture and design. The *Ro* table light (1962) was originally designed for the offices of Olivetti and was one of Artemide's first collaborations with consultant designers. Also available in a floor version known as the *Talia* (1962), the *Ro* light embodied the group's belief in "Design as a union of utility and beauty." (CF/PF)

1932 gründeten Gian Luigi Banfi, Lodovico Barbiano di Belgiojoso, Enrico Peressutti und Ernesto Nathan Rogers in Mailand das Architektur- und Designbüro BBPR. Nach dem Zweiten Weltkrieg führten nicht zuletzt praktische Anforderungen zur Durchsetzung des Rationalismus sowohl in der Architektur als auch im Design. Die Tischleuchte *Ro* (1962) wurde ursprünglich für die Büros der Firma Olivetti entworfen und war eine der ersten Kooperationen zwischen Artemide und einem unabhängigen Designstudio. Bei der *Ro* Tischleuchte und ihrer Stehleuchten-Version *Talia* (1962) wird deutlich sichtbar, dass das Studio BBPR „Design als Einheit von Funktion und Schönheit" verstand. (CF/PF)

Gian Luigi Banfi, Lodovico Barbiano di Belgiojoso, Enrico Peressutti et Ernesto Nathan Rogers fondèrent le studio de design milanais BBPR en 1932. Après la Seconde Guerre mondiale, celui-ci joua un rôle important dans la promotion du Rationalisme aussi bien en architecture qu'en design. La lampe de table *Ro* (1962) avait été conçue à l'origine pour les bureaux d'Olivetti et constituait l'une des premières collaborations d'Artemide avec des designers consultants. Également disponible en version lampadaire, le *Talia* (1962), la *Ro* incarnait la conviction du groupe : « Le design est l'union de l'utile et du beau. » (CF/PF)

studio bbpr
ro table light and *talia* floor light

▽ *Ro* table light, 1962

Chromed metal base with enameled metal shade and crystal diffusers, 42 cm high / Fuß aus verchromtem Metall, Lampenschirm aus lackiertem Metall, Diffusoren aus Kristallglas, 42 cm hoch / Pied en métal chromé, abat-jour en métal laqué, diffuseurs en cristal, 42 cm de haut
Artemide, Pregnana Milanese, Italy

▷ *Talia* floor light, 1962

Chromed metal base with enameled metal shade and crystal diffusers / Fuß aus verchromtem Metall, Lampenschirm aus lackiertem Metall, Diffusoren aus Kristallglas / Pied en métal chromé, abat-jour en métal laqué, diffuseurs en cristal
Artemide, Pregnana Milanese, Italy

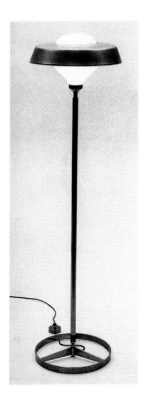

The Castiglioni brothers' ingenious *Taccia* table light (1962) incorporates three main elements – a fluted aluminum column that houses an incandescent light bulb and ventilation openings, a rotating clear-glass parabolic bowl, and a curved spun-aluminum reflector. Providing a soft, diffused light that can be directed by turning the "light bowl" through 360 degrees, the *Taccia* is a simple yet ingenious lighting solution that illustrates the Castiglionis' desire to "achieve adequate results with minimum means." By combining an overtly industrial esthetic with a column-like form, the *Taccia* anticipates the ironic classical vocabulary of Post-Modernism. (CF/PF)

Die Tischleuchte *Taccia* (1962) der Brüder Castiglioni vereint drei Elemente zu einem kunstvollen Design: eine gerippte Säule aus Aluminium, in der eine Glühbirne und Lüftungsöffnungen untergebracht sind, eine drehbare, parabolisch geformte Schale aus transparentem Glas und einen konischen Reflektor aus Aluminium. Mit ihrem weichen und gedämpften Lichtschein, der durch Schwenken der „Lichtschale" um 360 Grad beliebig ausgerichtet werden kann, ist die *Taccia* Leuchte ein einfacher und zugleich kunstvoller Beleuchtungskörper. Durch die Kombination einer unverhohlen industriellen Ästhetik mit einer klassisch anmutenden Säule nimmt die *Taccia* Leuchte die ironische Formensprache der Postmoderne vorweg. (CF/PF)

L'ingénieuse lampe de table des frères Castiglioni, *Taccia* (1962), se compose de trois éléments principaux : une colonne cannelée en aluminium contenant une ampoule à incandescence et des ouvertures de ventilation, une vasque parabolique mobile en verre clair et un réflecteur incurvé en aluminium moulé. Offrant une lumière diffuse et délicate, orientable en tournant la « coupe de lumière » à 360°, la *Taccia* est une solution aussi simple qu'ingénieuse. En combinant une esthétique franchement industrielle à une forme de colonne, la *Taccia* préfigure le vocabulaire classique ironique du postmodernisme. (CF/PF)

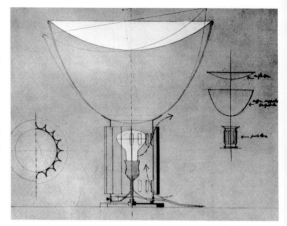

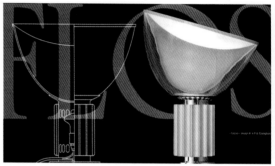

"We consider it the Mercedes of lamps, a symbol of success."

„Für uns ist sie der Mercedes unter den Leuchten, ein Symbol des Erfolgs."

« Pour nous, c'est la Mercedes des lampes, un symbole de succès. »

– Achille & Pier Giacomo Castiglioni

▷ *Taccia* table light, 1962

Steel and enameled aluminum base with glass shade, 58.4 cm high / Fuß aus Stahl und lackiertem Aluminium, Lampenschirm aus Glas, 58,4 cm hoch / Base en acier et aluminium émaillé, diffuseur en verre, 58,4 cm de haut
Flos, Bovezzo, Italy

△△ Design drawing of the Taccia table light, c.1958–62 / Konstruktionszeichnung der Tischleuchte Taccia, ca. 1958–62 / Dessin de la lampe de table Taccia, vers 1958–62

△ Flos advertisement for the Taccia table light, c.1962 / Werbeanzeige von Flos für die Tischleuchte Taccia, ca. 1962 / Publicité Flos pour la lampe Taccia, vers 1962

achille & pier giacomo castiglioni
taccia table light

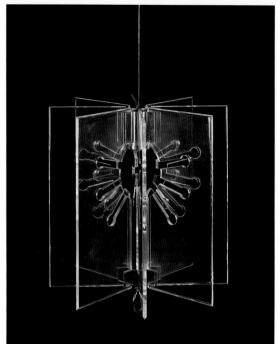

Pierced rectangular acrylic plates radiating from chrome-plated brass fitting / Gestanzte Acryl-Platten, strahlenförmig um die verchromte Messingmontierung angeordnet / Plaques rectangulaires d'acrylique découpé rayonnant à partir d'une monture en laiton chromé
Arteluce, Milan, Italy

▷ Model No. 281 Acrilica table light, 1962

Enameled metal base with clear acrylic diffuser, 23 cm high / Fuß aus lackiertem Metall mit Diffusor aus transparentem Acryl, 23 cm hoch / Base en métal laqué, diffuseur en acrylique transparent, 23 cm de haut
O Luce, Milan, Italy

In 1952 the architect Franca Helg joined Franco Albini's studio in Milan and the two subsequently collaborated on a number of design projects, including the Model No. 524 hanging/table light (1962). This product was one of the first lights to incorporate elements made of acrylic and in doing so it anticipated the material's widespread use in lighting design over the coming years. While the Model No. 524 hanging/table light encapsulates the optimistic spirit of the Space Age 1960s, it also reflects the legacy of Italian Rationalism and Albini's fascination with Functionalist geometry. (CF/PF)

1952 trat die Architektin Franca Helg in Franco Albinis Mailänder Designbüro ein. Beide arbeiteten in der Folge gemeinsam an mehreren Projekten. Unter anderem entwickelten sie die Hänge-/Tischleuchte Modell Nr. 524 (1962), eine der ersten Leuchten der Designgeschichte mit Acrylelementen, und nahmen damit die spätere Beliebtheit dieses Materials im Beleuchtungsdesign vorweg. Dieses Leuchtendesign verkörpert den optimistischen Geist des beginnenden Weltraumfahrtzeitalters in den 1960er Jahren und lässt zugleich deutlich das Vermächtnis des italienischen Rationalismus sowie Albinis Begeisterung für funktionelle Geometrie erkennen. (CF/PF)

En 1952, l'architecte Franca Helg entre à l'agence de Franco Albini à Milan et tous deux collaborent à un certain nombre de projets de design, dont la suspension/lampe de table Modèle n° 524 (1962). Ce produit fut l'un des premiers luminaires à intégrer des composants en acrylique et annonce l'usage répandu de ce matériau dans les appareils d'éclairage des années qui suivirent. Si le Modèle n° 524 incarne l'esprit optimiste des années 1960, il reflète également un legs du rationalisme italien et la fascination d'Albini pour la géométrie fonctionnelle. (CF/PF)

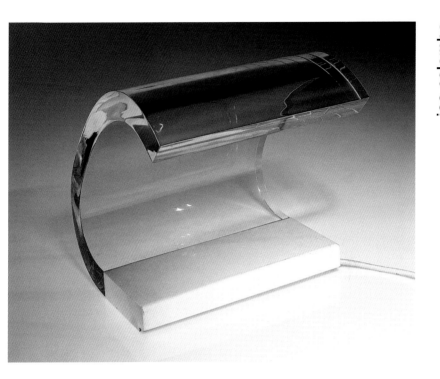

The interiors that Joe Colombo designed for a Sardinian hotel in 1962
included ceiling fixtures made of acrylic
prisms that diffracted light. With his
brother Gianni, Colombo proceeded to
evolve this idea in the design of the
Acrilica table light (1962). Awarded a
gold medal at the XIII Milan Triennale
in 1964, this elegant design can be
seen as the culmination of Colombo's
studies into the thermoplastic and optical properties of PMMA (polymethyl
methacrylate). Easily molded using heat
and pressure, the acrylic is formed into
a C-shape that elegantly reveals the
material's ability to carry light even
round bends.
(CF/PF)

1962 entwarf Joe Colombo die Innen-
ausstattung für ein Hotel in Sardinien.
Dazu gehörten auch Deckenleuchten
mit Acrylprismen, die das Licht brachen.
Gemeinsam mit seinem Bruder Gianni
entwickelte Colombo diese Idee bei
der Tischleuchte *Acrilica* (1962) weiter.
Das elegante Design der bei der XIII.
Triennale in Mailand 1964 mit einer
Goldmedaille ausgezeichneten Leuchte
bildet den Höhepunkt von Colombos
Beschäftigung mit den thermoplasti-
schen und optischen Eigenschaften
von Polymethylmethacrylat. Das unter
Hitze und Druck leicht formbare Acryl
ist hier zu einem C gebogen, wodurch
die Eigenschaft dieses Werkstoffes,
Licht lenken zu können, deutlich wird.
(CF/PF)

Les aménagements intérieurs conçus
par Joe Colombo pour un hôtel sarde
en 1962 comprenaient des suspensions faites de prismes d'acrylique qui
diffractaient la lumière. Avec son frère
Gianni, Colombo fit évoluer cette idée
dans le projet de lampe de table *Acrilica* (1962). Médaille d'or à la XIIIᵉ Triennale de Milan en 1964, cette lampe
élégante peut être considérée comme
l'aboutissement des recherches de
Colombo sur les propriétés thermo-
plastiques et optiques du PMMA
(polyméthacrylate de méthyle). Facile à
mouler en utilisant la chaleur et la pression, l'acrylique prend ici une forme en
« C » qui montre la capacité de ce matériau à conduire la lumière même dans
ses parties coudées. (CF/PF)

Playfully subverting convention, this design transforms the ceiling light into a freestanding floor unit. Inspired by street lighting, the *Arco* floor light (1962) was originally intended for dining areas – hence the reason why the arched stem is positioned some eight feet above its base, allowing sufficient room for a table and chairs. Included in the 1972 "Italy: The New Domestic Landscape" exhibition at the Museum of Modern Art in New York, it has three separate height adjustments and can be moved relatively easily by inserting a broomstick through the hole provided in the marble base. (CF/PF)

Bei diesem Entwurf wurde eine Deckenleuchte durch spielerischen Umgang mit Konventionen in eine frei stehende Bodenleuchte verwandelt. Die Stehleuchte *Arco* (1962) erinnert an Straßenlaternen und war ursprünglich für den Essbereich vorgesehen – die Lichtquelle ist bis zu 2,5 m über dem Fuß positioniert und ermöglicht die Nutzung über einer Essgruppe mit Tisch und Stühlen. Sie ist dreifach ausziehbar und kann mit einem Besenstiel, der durch das Loch im Marmorfuß gesteckt wird, relativ leicht transportiert werden. 1972 wurde die Leuchte in die Ausstellung „Italy: The New Domestic Landscape" im Museum of Modern Art in New York aufgenommen. (CF/PF)

Se jouant des conventions avec humour, ce projet résulte de la transformation d'une suspension en lampadaire. Inspiré de l'éclairage urbain, le lampadaire *Arco* (1962) était à l'origine destiné aux zones de repas, d'où le positionnement de la source lumineuse à quelque 2,40 m de la base pour permettre de placer une table et des sièges. Présenté en 1972 à l'exposition du Museum of Modern Art de New York « Italy : The New Domestic Landscape », il bénéficie d'un triple réglage en hauteur et se déplace relativement facilement grâce au trou ménagé dans sa base de marbre. (CF/PF)

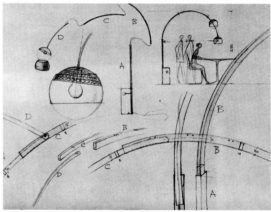

△△ *Stendig showroom with Arco floor light, c.1965 / Ausstellungsraum des New Yorker Kaufhauses Stendig mit Stehleuchte Arco, ca. 1965 / Intérieur du magasin Stendig à New York, présentant le lampadaire Arco, vers 1965*

△ *Design drawing of Arco floor light, c.1962 / Entwurfszeichnung der Arco Stehleuchte, ca. 1962 / Dessins de conception du lampadaire Arco, vers 1962*

▷ **Arco floor light, 1962**
Carrara marble base with satin-finished stainless steel telescopic stem and polished aluminum reflector, 250 cm high (max.) / Fuß aus Carraramarmor mit ausziehbarem Arm aus mattiertem rostfreiem Stahl, Reflektor aus poliertem Aluminium, 250 cm hoch (max.) / Base en marbre de Carrare, tige télescopique en acier inoxydable satiné, réflecteur en aluminium poli, 250 cm de haut (max.)
Flos, Bovezzo, Italy

The entrepreneur/designer Angelo Lelli created numerous lighting products that were manufactured by his own company, Arredoluce. His range of low-voltage, high-intensity mini spotlights incorporating magnetic spherical shades were among the first of their kind and are perhaps his most significant achievement. The standardized "eyeball" shades of the three models shown here (1962–63) allow easy yet accurate angling of the light. Arredoluce also manufactured a number of other lighting designs incorporating this novel feature, including a wall-mounted version known as the *Lexico* (c.1963). (CF/PF)

Der Unternehmer und Designer Angelo Lelli entwarf zahlreiche Beleuchtungskörper für seine eigene Firma, den Leuchtenhersteller Arredoluce. Seine Niedervolt-Ministrahler mit kugelförmigen, magnetischen Schirmen gehörten zu den ersten ihrer Art und sind sein vielleicht bedeutendster Beitrag zum Beleuchtungsdesign. Die standardisierten „Augapfel"-Lampenschirme der hier abgebildeten Modelle (1962–63) erlauben eine einfache und dabei sehr genaue Ausrichtung des Lichts. Arredoluce hat dieses neue Element auch in einer Serie weiterer Leuchten verwendet, so unter anderem bei der Wandleuchte *Lexico* (ca. 1963). (CF/PF)

L'industriel et designer Angelo Lelli conçut de nombreux luminaires fabriqués par sa propre société, Arredoluce. Sa gamme de mini-spots basse tension était dotée d'abat-jour sphériques aimantés, parmi les premiers du genre. Ils constituent peut-être sa réussite la plus significative. Les abat-jour « globes oculaires » des trois modèles présentés ici (1962–63) permettent une orientation facile et précise du faisceau. Arredoluce a également fabriqué un certain nombre d'autres modèles intégrant ce dispositif, dont une version d'applique appelée *Lexico* (vers 1963). (CF/PF)

Mini spotlight showing the metal "eye-like" shade disconnected from the magnetized base / Ministrahler mit „Augapfel"-Lampenschirm außerhalb der magnetisierten Halterung / Mini spotlight montrant l'abat-jour métallique « globe oculaire » séparé de sa base aimantée

▷ **Columnar mini spotlight, height-adjustable mini spotlight and *Contrast* mini spotlight, 1962–63**

Enameled metal bases housing transformers with magnetic adjustable metal shades, 27.3, 40 and 24.8 cm high / Füße aus lackiertem Metall, darin installierte Transformatoren mit magnetischen, verstellbaren Metalllampenschirmen, 27,3, 40 und 24,8 cm hoch / Bases en métal laqué contenant les transformateurs, abat-jour métalliques réglables aimantés, 27,3, 40 et 24,8 cm de haut
Arredoluce, Monza, Italy

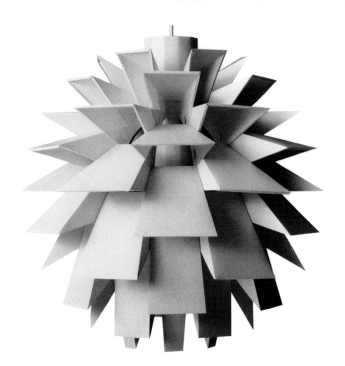

Norm 69 hanging light, 1969

Self-assembly plastic sheet construction,
51 cm diameter / Konstruktion aus Plastikteilen
zur Selbstmontage, 51 cm Durchmesser /
Structure en feuilles de plastique à assembler
soi-même, 51 cm de diamètre.
Normann Copenhagen, Copenhagen, Denmark

▷ **Skyflyer hanging light, 1960**

Opaque acrylic shade with suspension chains,
50 and 70 cm diameter / Lampenschirm aus
opakem Acryl an Metallketten, 50 und 70 cm
Durchmesser / Abat-jour en acrylique opaque,
chaînettes de suspension, 50 et 70 cm de
diamètre
Stockmann-Orno, Kerava, Finland (reissued
by Adelta, Dinslaken, Germany)

The *Norm 69* hanging light (1969) is made up of 69 pieces of thin plastic sheet that can be put together like a puzzle without having to use any tools or glue. It is sold in flat-pack form and when constructed it gives a warm, non-dazzling light. Although similarly sculptural, the *Skyflyer* hanging light (1960) comprises a simpler two-piece shade made of molded opaque acrylic. This design was also known as *Lokki*, meaning "seagull" in Finnish, and certainly when hung together as a group the lights can give the appearance of a flock of birds. (CF/PF)

Die Hängeleuchte *Norm 69* (1969) besteht aus 69 Einzelteilen aus dünnem Plastik, die ohne Werkzeug oder Kleber wie ein Puzzle zusammengefügt werden können. Sie wird flach verpackt geliefert und gibt ein warmes, blendfreies Licht. Die Hängeleuchte *Skyflyer* (1960) ist zwar ähnlich skulptural angelegt, hat aber einen einfacheren zweiteiligen Lampenschirm aus gepresstem, opakem Acryl. Diese Leuchte wurde auch unter dem Namen *Lokki* bekannt, dem finnischen Wort für „Möwe". Wenn mehrere Leuchten gruppiert aufgehängt werden, wirken sie tatsächlich wie ein Vogelschwarm. (CF/PF)

La suspension *Norm 69* (1969) se compose de soixante-neuf pièces découpées dans une feuille de plastique mince qui s'assemblent comme un puzzle, sans outil ni colle. Vendue à plat, elle diffuse une fois montée une lumière chaude, non éblouissante. Également sculpturale, la suspension *Skyflyer* (1960) se compose d'un abat-jour en deux parties en acrylique opaque appelé *Lokki* («mouette» en finnois), car suspendu à plusieurs exemplaires, il peut faire penser à un vol d'oiseaux. (CF/PF)

**Lightspan track lighting system,
1963–64**

Electrified track with moveable aluminum cylinder shades, various sizes / Stromschiene mit beweglichen zylindrischen Lampenschirmen aus Aluminium, verschiedene Größen / Rail électrifié à spots cylindriques mobiles en aluminium, diverses tailles
Lightolier, Fall River (MA), USA

▷ Page from Lightolier catalog featuring the different track heads of the Lightspan *track lighting system, c.1965 / Seite aus einem Katalog von Lightolier mit den verschiedenen Strahlern des Leuchtschienensystems* Lightspan, ca. 1965 / Page de catalogue Lightolier *présentant les différents types de spots du système d'éclairage par rail* Lightspan, vers 1965

Lightolier began developing the world's first track lighting system in 1963. The design utilized the idea behind their earlier *Lytespan* pole light (an electrified column with interchangeable lighting elements), turning it onto its side to create the firm's most influential lighting design ever. Track lighting is now ubiquitous in public and commercial interiors, but *Lightspan* was originally marketed as providing "theatrical lighting" for the home. It is a tribute to Lightolier's then principal designer, Kingsley Chan, that the majority of the company's track head fittings remain compatible today with the system he developed over 40 years ago. (CF/PF)

Lightolier begann 1963 mit der Entwicklung des weltweit ersten Leuchtschienensystems und setzte dabei die Grundidee der früheren Ständerleuchten *Lytespan* (einer Stromsäule mit austauschbaren Beleuchtungselementen) nun in der Waagerechten um. Das neue Beleuchtungssystem ist in seiner Wirkung unübertroffen. Obwohl *Lightspan* anfänglich als „Theaterbeleuchtung" für den Wohnbereich beworben wurde, sind Leuchtschienensysteme heute in öffentlichen und kommerziellen Räumen allgegenwärtig. Die meisten von Lightolier hergestellten Beleuchtungskörper sind bis heute mit dem vor vierzig Jahren entwickelten System kompatibel – eine Verneigung vor dem damaligen Chef-Designer der Firma, Kingsley Chan. (CF/PF)

Lightolier commença à mettre au point les premiers systèmes de rails d'éclairage en 1963. Ce projet faisait appel à une idée déjà présente dans leur lampadaire *Lytespan* (une colonne électrifiée à éléments d'éclairage interchangeables), dont la mise à l'horizontale donna naissance au modèle le plus influent jamais réalisé par la firme. L'éclairage par rail est aujourd'hui omniprésent dans les lieux aussi bien publics que privés, mais *Lightspan* fut au départ commercialisé pour apporter un « éclairage théâtral » dans la maison. Hommage à Kingsley Chan, directeur du design de Lightolier à époque : la majorité des accessoires proposés aujourd'hui par la firme restent compatibles avec le système mis au point il y a plus de 40 ans. (CF/PF)

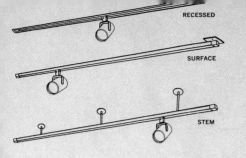

RECESSED

SURFACE

STEM

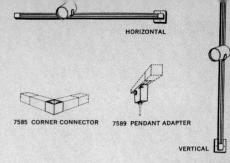

HORIZONTAL

7585 CORNER CONNECTOR   7589 PENDANT ADAPTER

VERTICAL

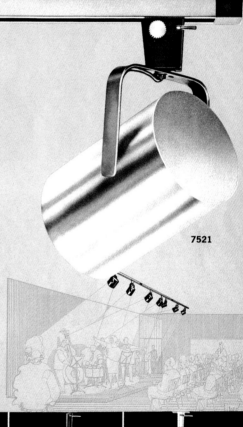

7500 4' track unit, satin anodized aluminum.

7501 8' track unit, satin anodized aluminum.

7530 Satin white. Dia. 6⅛", body length 5¾". 150 W. PAR-38/3 (side prong) bulb, spot or flood.

7521 Sat. alum., satin black. Dia. 6⅛", body length 8¼". 150 W. PAR-38 or R-40 bulbs, spot or flood.

7522 Satin aluminum, satin black. Dia. 2", body length 7". 30, 50, 75, 150 or 300 watt R and 150 watt PAR-38 bulbs. (Shown w/7587 shield.)

7527 Satin aluminum, satin black. Dia. 3", length 7½". 30 or 50 watt R-20 bulbs.

7538 Satin white, with louver. Dia. 6", length 8⅝". 150 W. PAR-38 and 150 or 300 W. R-40 bulbs.

7550 Same as 7520, canopy mounting.

7551 Same as 7521, canopy mounting.

7552 Same as 7522, canopy mounting.

7557 Same as 7527, canopy mounting.

7558 Same as 7538, canopy mounting.

7583 Canopy mounting kit. White. Includes mounting plate (attaches to 3" and 4" octagonal outlet boxes) and two cover halves.

7585 Corner connector. Silver gray. 90° joiner for surface or stem mounted Lytespan track units.

7589 Pendant adapter. Silver gray. Supports decorative Lightolier pendant fixtures suspended on cord, tubing or chain.

9504 Same as 7527, satin white finish.

7581 4' recessed housing. White.

NOTE: For complete information on recessed and stem mounting Lytespan accessories as well as other Lytespots and accessories, consult Brochure No. 40A.

7521

7530

7522 (w/7587 shield)

7527
7519

9504
7518

7538

In 1967 Joe Colombo won a Compasso d'Oro and an A.I.D. International Design Award for his *Spider* lighting system (1965). The range is based on a single enameled reflector made of pressed sheet metal that can be mounted onto a variety of supports, from table and floor bases to clamp and ceiling fixtures, to meet different lighting requirements. The system utilizes an innovative plastic joint that allows the horizontal spotlight to be rotated, height-adjusted and tilted. The *Spider* lights, which are intended for both domestic and office environments, exemplify Colombo's career-long search for dynamic and multi-functional product solutions. (CF/PF)

1967 wurde Joe Colombo für sein Leuchtensystem *Spider* (1965) mit einem Compasso d'Oro und einem A.I.D. International Design Award ausgezeichnet. Basierend auf einem einzelnen Reflektor aus lackiertem, gepresstem Blech, der mit verschiedensten Ständern und Füßen für Tisch- und Stehleuchten oder auch mit Klemmvorrichtungen kombiniert werden kann und sich sogar zur Deckenmontage eignet, erfüllt dieses Leuchtensystem die unterschiedlichsten Bedürfnisse. Durch die Verwendung eines neuartigen Gelenks aus Kunststoff ist der horizontale Strahler drehbar, höhenverstellbar und schwenkbar. Die *Spider* Leuchten sind sowohl für den Wohnwie für den Bürobereich vorgesehen und veranschaulichen Colombos ständige Suche nach dynamischen und multifunktionalen Produktlösungen. (CF/PF)

En 1967, Joe Colombo remporte un Compasso d'Oro et un A.I.D. International Design Award pour le système *Spider* (1965). La gamme repose sur un réflecteur émaillé unique, constitué d'une feuille de métal embouti et monté sur divers supports pour créer des lampes, des lampadaires, des suspensions et des lampes à pince, répondant à divers besoins d'éclairage. Le système utilise un joint en plastique d'un type nouveau qui permet d'orienter le réflecteur horizontalement, en hauteur et d'en modifier l'inclinaison. Les *Spider*, conçues pour des usages domestiques ou de bureau, illustrent les recherches que Colombo mena tout au long de sa carrière pour trouver des solutions dynamiques et multifonctionnelles. (CF/PF)

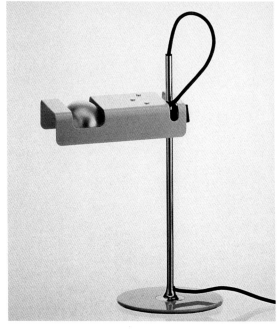

Model No. 291 Spider table light, 1965
Enameled metal base with chrome-plated tubular metal stem and enameled metal shade with Melamine fitting, 40 cm high / Fuß aus lackiertem Metall und verchromtem Metallrohr, Lampenschirm aus lackiertem Metall mit Melaminmontierung, 40 cm hoch / Base en métal laqué, tige métallique tubulaire chromée, réflecteur en métal laqué, accessoires en mélamine, 40 cm de haut
O Luce, Milan, Italy

▷ Joe Colombo's apartment, 1965 / Joe Colombo's Privatwohnung, 1965 / Appartement de Joe Colombo, 1965

▽ Design sketch for Spring floor light, c.1965 – a variation of the Spider light / Entwurfszeichnung für die Stehleuchte Spring, ca. 1965 – eine Variation der Leuchte Spider / Dessin du lampadaire Spring, vers 1965 – une variation de la lampe Spider

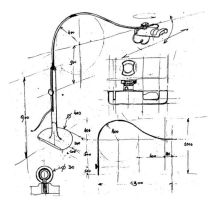

The *Coupé* series of lights (1967) designed by Joe Colombo were conceived as a variant of his *Spider* lighting range (1965) and as such utilized the same bases and stems. An ingenious plastic joint fitting enables the stove-enameled semi-cylindrical shade to be tilted, rotated and height-adjusted along the slender chromed stem. In 1968 the *Coupé* series won an International Design Award from the American Institute of Interior Designers in Chicago. As part of this innovative range, Joe Colombo also designed several variations that had hemispherical rather than semi-cylindrical shades. (CF/PF)

Die von Joe Colombo entworfene Leuchtenserie *Coupé* (1967) war als eine Variante seines Beleuchtungssystems *Spider* (1965) konzipiert und hat identische Füße und Schäfte. Ein ausgeklügeltes Plastikgelenk ermöglicht es, den einbrennlackierten, halb zylindrischen Lampenschirm zu schwenken, zu drehen und entlang des schlanken verchromten Schaftes in der Höhe zu verstellen. 1968 wurden die *Coupé* Leuchten vom American Institute of Interior Designers in Chicago mit einem International Design Award ausgezeichnet. Im Zusammenhang mit diesem innovativen Leuchtensystem entwarf Joe Colombo weitere Varianten mit halbkugelförmigen Lampenschirmen anstelle der halb zylindrischen. (CF/PF)

La série de luminaires *Coupé* (1967) de Joe Colombo, variante de sa gamme *Spider* (1965), utilise les mêmes socles et tiges. Un ingénieux joint de plastique permet à l'abat-jour semi-cylindrique émaillé à chaud de s'incliner, de pivoter et de se régler en hauteur le long d'une fine tige chromée. En 1968, la série *Coupé* a remporté l'International Design Award de l'American Institute of Interior Designers de Chicago. Dans le cadre de cette série novatrice, Colombo dessina également plusieurs variantes à abat-jour hémisphérique. (CF/PF)

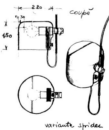

Model no. 2202 coupé table light, 1967

Enameled metal base and shade with chrome-plated metal stem and Melamine fittings, 40 cm high / Fuß und Schirm aus lackiertem Metall mit Schaft aus verchromtem Metall und Melaminmontierung, 40 cm hoch / Socle et abat-jour en métal émaillé, tige de métal chromé, accessoires en Mélamine, 40 cm de haut
O Luce, Milan, Italy

◁ Design sketch for the shade of the *Coupé* light, c.1967 / Entwurfszeichnung für den Lampenschirm der Leuchte *Coupé*, ca. 1967 / Croquis de conception de l'abat-jour de la lampe *Coupé*, vers 1967

▷ **Model no. 3321 Coupé floor light, 1967**

Enameled metal base and shade with chromed metal stem and Melamine fittings, 140 cm high / Fuß und Lampenschirm aus lackiertem Metall mit Schaft aus verchromtem Metall und Melaminmontierung, 140 cm hoch / Socle et abat-jour en métal émaillé, tige de métal chromé, accessoires en Mélamine, 140 cm haut
O Luce, Milan, Italy

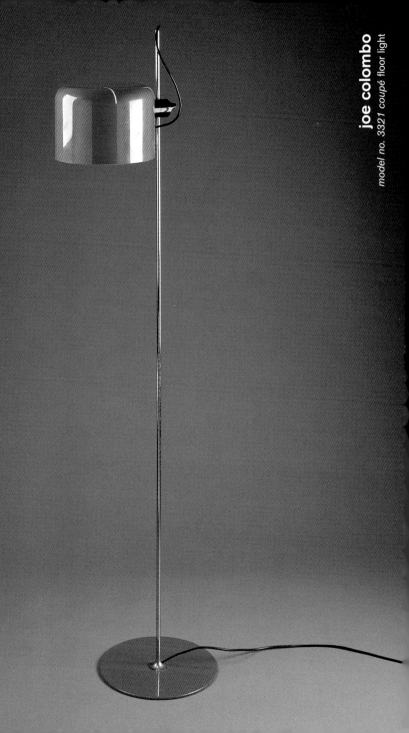

The concept behind these table lights can be traced to an earlier model that Joe Colombo designed almost jokingly in 1964. Featuring an opalescent plastic cylinder and a rotating black shield of Ebanil, it was pocked with holes of graduated sizes, allowing the user to vary the amount of light emitted by selecting the size of the holes. The multiple-hole feature proved too costly to manufacture, however, and the two-part plastic light went into final production with just a single hole in its colored swiveling screen, with each model number offering a different size of hole. (CF/PF)

Die Grundidee dieser Tischleuchten findet sich bereits in einem früheren Modell, einem nicht ganz ernst gemeinten Entwurf Joe Colombos aus dem Jahr 1964. Dabei war ein Zylinder aus opalweißem Kunststoff von einem drehbaren schwarzen Lampenschirm aus Ebanil mit Löchern in unterschiedlichen Größen umgeben. Durch Verschieben der Löcher ließ sich der Lichtstrahl steuern. Der durchlöcherte Außenschirm erwies sich jedoch als zu kostspielig für die Produktion, und so wurde das zweiteilige Kunststofflicht schließlich mit nur einem Loch im farbigen Drehschirm hergestellt, das bei jedem Modell eine andere Größe hat. (CF/PF)

Le concept de ces lampes de table vient d'un précédent modèle dessiné presque par jeu par Joe Colombo en 1964. Il se composait d'un cylindre en plastique opalescent et d'une gaine de protection rotative en Ebanil noire percée de découpes de dimensions diverses permettant de varier le volume de lumière émise en sélectionnant ces ouvertures. Ce projet se révéla trop coûteux à fabriquer et l'écran de protection coloré du modèle définitif ne possédait qu'une seule découpe, chaque référence en proposant une de forme différente. (CF/PF)

"Furnishings will disappear… the habitat will be everywhere."

„Traditionelle Möbel werden verschwinden … der Lebensraum wird überall sein."

« Le mobilier va disparaître … l'habitat sera partout. »

– Joe Colombo

◁ Model Nos. 4088/5, 4008/5 and 4024/5 table lights, 1964–65
Opalescent methacrylate inner cylinders with rotating Moplen outer shields, 15.5 cm diameter / Innenzylinder aus opalweißem Methacrylat mit drehbaren Außenschirmen aus Moplen, 15,5 cm Durchmesser / Cylindre interne en méthacrylate opalescent et gaine de protection rotative en Moplen, 15,5 cm diamètre de Kartell, Noviglio, Italy

▷ Contemporary promotional photograph showing Joe Colombo's prototype swivel-screen table light designed in 1964 / Zeitgenössisches Werbefoto mit dem Prototyp der 1964 von Joe Colombo entworfenen Tischleuchte mit Drehschirm / Photographie de promotion de l'époque montrant le prototype de la lampe de table à écran pivotant, conçue en 1964

△ *Model No. 2DM Fun* hanging light, 1964

Chrome-plated metal frame with shell disks, 61 cm drop / Verchromte Metallmontierung mit Muschelplättchen, 61 cm lang / Structure en métal chromé, disques en nacre, 61 cm de haut
J. Lüber, Basel, Switzerland

▷ *Model No. 1TM Fun* table light, 1964

Chrome-plated metal frame with shell disks, 43.2 cm high / Verchromte Metallmontierung mit Muschelplättchen, 43,2 cm hoch / Structure en métal chromé, disques en nacre, 43,2 cm de haut
J. Lüber, Basel, Switzerland

▷▷ *Model No. 1STM Fun* floor light, 1964

Chrome-plated metal frame with shell disks, 119.4 cm high / Verchromte Metallmontierung mit Muschelplättchen, 119,4 cm hoch / Structure en métal chromé, disques en nacre, 119,4 cm de haut
J. Lüber, Basel, Switzerland

Verner Panton was adept at developing variations on a theme. He saw the possibilities of exploiting the characteristics of natural materials and made disks for a range of lights from slices of shell. Semi-translucent and lustrous, when hung from chains and clustered around a light source the shell shimmered and gave a special magic to the light. The *Fun* shell range (1964) included hanging, floor and table lights, the disks either forming a mass or suspended from two or three concentric rings that were stepped down and outward to create the effect of an iridescent cascade. (PG)

Verner Panton verstand es meisterhaft, ein Thema zu variieren. Er erkannte die Einsatzmöglichkeiten natürlicher Werkstoffe und ließ für eine Leuchtenserie scheibenförmige Plättchen aus Muscheln fertigen. Die halbdurchscheinenden und glänzenden Muschelplättchen schimmern, wenn sie an Ketten hängend um eine Lichtquelle angeordnet sind, und verleihen dem Licht eine ganz besondere Magie. Die Muschelleuchtenserie *Fun* (1964) umfasst Hängeleuchten sowie Steh- und Tischleuchten. Dabei sind die Plättchen entweder zu einer Traube angeordnet oder hängen an zwei oder drei konzentrischen Ringen, die von oben nach unten größer werdend eine Treppe bilden und wie eine schillernde Kaskade wirken. (PG)

Verner Panton aimait développer des variations sur un même thème. Partant des possibilités d'exploitation des caractéristiques des matériaux naturels, il fit réaliser des disques en nacre pour une série de luminaires. Accrochés à des chaînettes et regroupés autour d'une source lumineuse, ces disques semi-translucides et satinés étincelaient et diffusaient une lumière magique. La gamme *Fun* (1964) comprend des suspensions, des lampadaires et des lampes de table, les disques étant soit regroupés en une masse, soit suspendus à deux ou trois anneaux concentriques, étagés en cercles de diamètre croissant pour donner l'impression d'une cascade iridescente. (PG)

verner panton
model no. 1stm fun floor light

"By experimenting with lighting … I try to show new ways to encourage people to use their fantasy and make their surroundings more exciting."

„Durch das Experimentieren mit Beleuchtung … versuche ich neue Möglichkeiten aufzuzeigen und die Menschen zu ermuntern, ihre Fantasie einzusetzen und ihre Umgebung aufregender zu gestalten."

«Par mes expérimentations dans le domaine de l'éclairage … j'essaye de montrer de nouvelles voies, d'encourager les gens à utiliser leur imagination, à rendre leur environnement plus stimulant.»

– Verner Panton

◁ *Model No. 4DM Fun* **hanging light, 1964**
Painted wood support, shell disks, chrome-plated metal chains, 110 cm drop / Deckenplatte aus lackiertem Holz, Muschelplättchen, verchromte Metallketten, 110 cm lang / Support en bois peint, disques en nacre, chaînes en métal chromé, 110 cm de hauteur
J. Lüber, Basel, Switzerland

△ *Page from* Mobilia *showing* Model No.12DM Fun *hanging light in a Verner Panton interior, March 1975 / Abbildung aus der Zeitschrift* Mobilia *mit einem Interieur von Verner Panton und Hängeleuchte Modell Nr. 12DM Fun, März 1975 / Page de* Mobilia *présentant un interieur de Verner Panton avec sa suspension Modèle n° 12DM Fun, mars 1975*

With the variant models of his *Fun* hanging lights, Verner Panton anticipated in 1964 the dramatic designs that were to establish Spanish architect-designer Paco Rabanne as one of the great innovators in Paris couture. Rabanne achieved instant celebrity with his integration of metal and plastic disks in clothing and jewelry. His models, clad in a kind of chain mail or in garments and adornments of colored plastic disks, became a defining image of the late 1960s. Panton had yet again proved himself a visionary. (PG)

Mit den Varianten seiner Hängeleuchten *Fun* nahm Verner Panton 1964 die aufsehenerregenden Kreationen vorweg, die den spanischen Architekten und Designer Paco Rabanne zu einem der großen Neuerer der Pariser Modeszene machen sollten. Rabanne gelangte über Nacht zu Berühmtheit, als er kleine Scheiben aus Metall und Kunststoff zu Kleidern und Schmuck verarbeitete. Seine mit einer Art Kettenhemd oder mit Kleidern und Accessoires aus bunten Plastikscheiben bekleideten Mannequins wurden zum Inbegriff der ausgehenden 1960er Jahre. Panton hatte sich damit erneut als Visionär erwiesen. (PG)

Les variantes des suspensions *Fun* de Verner Panton préfiguraient, en 1964, les créations spectaculaires qui allaient faire du designer-architecte Paco Rabanne l'un des grands rénovateurs de la haute couture parisienne. Rabanne atteignit instantanément à la célébrité en utilisant des pastilles de plastique et des crochets métalliques pour élaborer des vêtements et des bijoux. Ses mannequins revêtus de ces cotes de maille nouvelle manière et de parures colorées en disques de plastique sont une icône de la fin des années 1960. Panton avait montré une fois de plus qu'il était un authentique visionnaire. (PG)

design line
tranquil table light

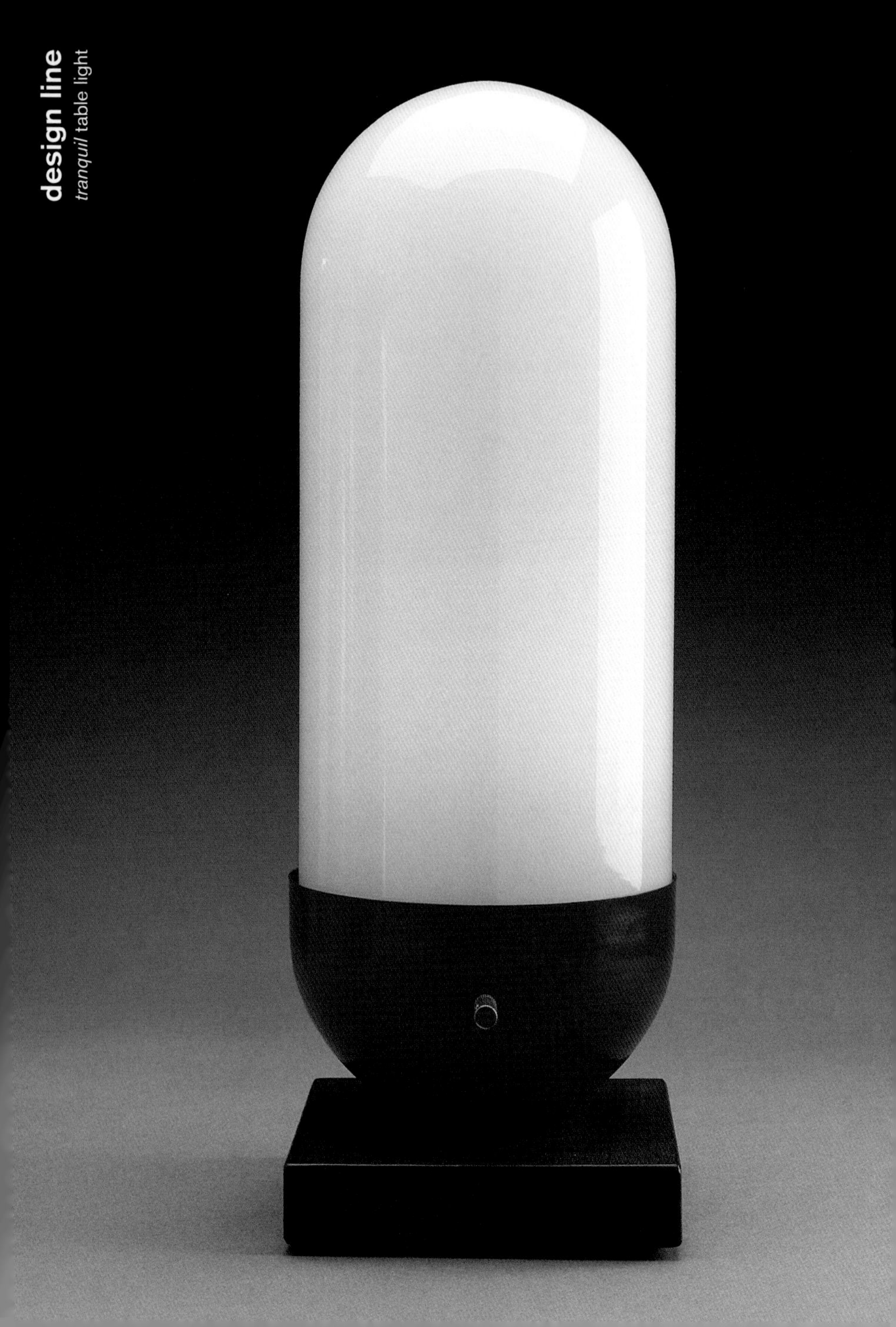

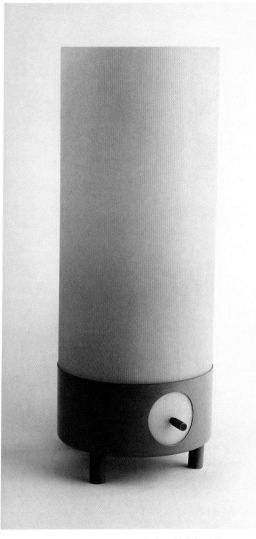

The title and form of the *Tranquil* table light (1966) make reference to the increasing use of tranquilizers in the United States during the 1960s. In so doing, it can be seen as an early and rare example of radical American design and as an important precursor of Studio D. A.'s colorful, pill-shaped *Pillola* table/floor lights of 1968. The *Limelite* table light (1965) was also manufactured by Design Line and, as a low-cost product with a highly rational construction, was selected for an Excellence in Design award by the Pasadena Art Museum in the mid-1960s. (CF/PF)

Name und Form der Tischleuchte *Tranquil* (1966) nehmen Bezug auf den in den 1960er Jahren in den USA deutlich gestiegenen Konsum von Tranquilizern. Die Leuchte ist ein frühes und seltenes Beispiel für das amerikanische Radical Design und kann als bedeutende Vorläuferin der vom Studio D. A. gestalteten, farbenfrohen Tisch-/Stehleuchten *Pillola* in Pillenform aus dem Jahr 1968 gelten. Auch die Tischleuchte *Limelite* (1965) wurde von Design Line gefertigt und Mitte der 1960er Jahre als preisgünstiges Produkt in besonders funktionaler Ausführung vom Art Museum in Pasadena mit einem Excellence in Design Award ausgezeichnet. (CF/PF)

Le nom et la forme de la lampe de table *Tranquil* (1966) font référence à l'usage grandissant des tranquillisants aux États-Unis au cours des années 1960. De ce fait, elle peut être considérée comme un précoce et rare exemple de design radical américain et un important précurseur des *Pillola*, les lampes de table et de sol colorées en forme de pilules lancées par Studio D. A. en 1968. La lampe de table *Limelite* (1965), également fabriquée par Design Line selon des principes de montage très rationnels permettant un prix réduit, fut sélectionnée pour un «Excellence in Design Award» du Pasadena Art Museum au milieu des années 1960. (CF/PF)

◁ *Tranquil* **table light, 1966**
Wood and enameled metal base with opaque acrylic diffuser / Fuß aus Holz und lackiertem Metall mit Diffusor aus opakem Acryl / Pied en métal laqué et bois, diffuseur en acrylique opaque
Design Line, El Segundo (CA), USA

Limelite **table light, 1965**
Enameled metal base with opaque acrylic diffuser, 33.5 cm high / Fuß aus lackiertem Metall mit Diffusor aus opakem Acryl, 33,5 cm hoch / Pied en métal lacqué et bois, diffuseur en acrylique opaque, 33,5 cm de haut
Design Line, El Segundo (CA), USA

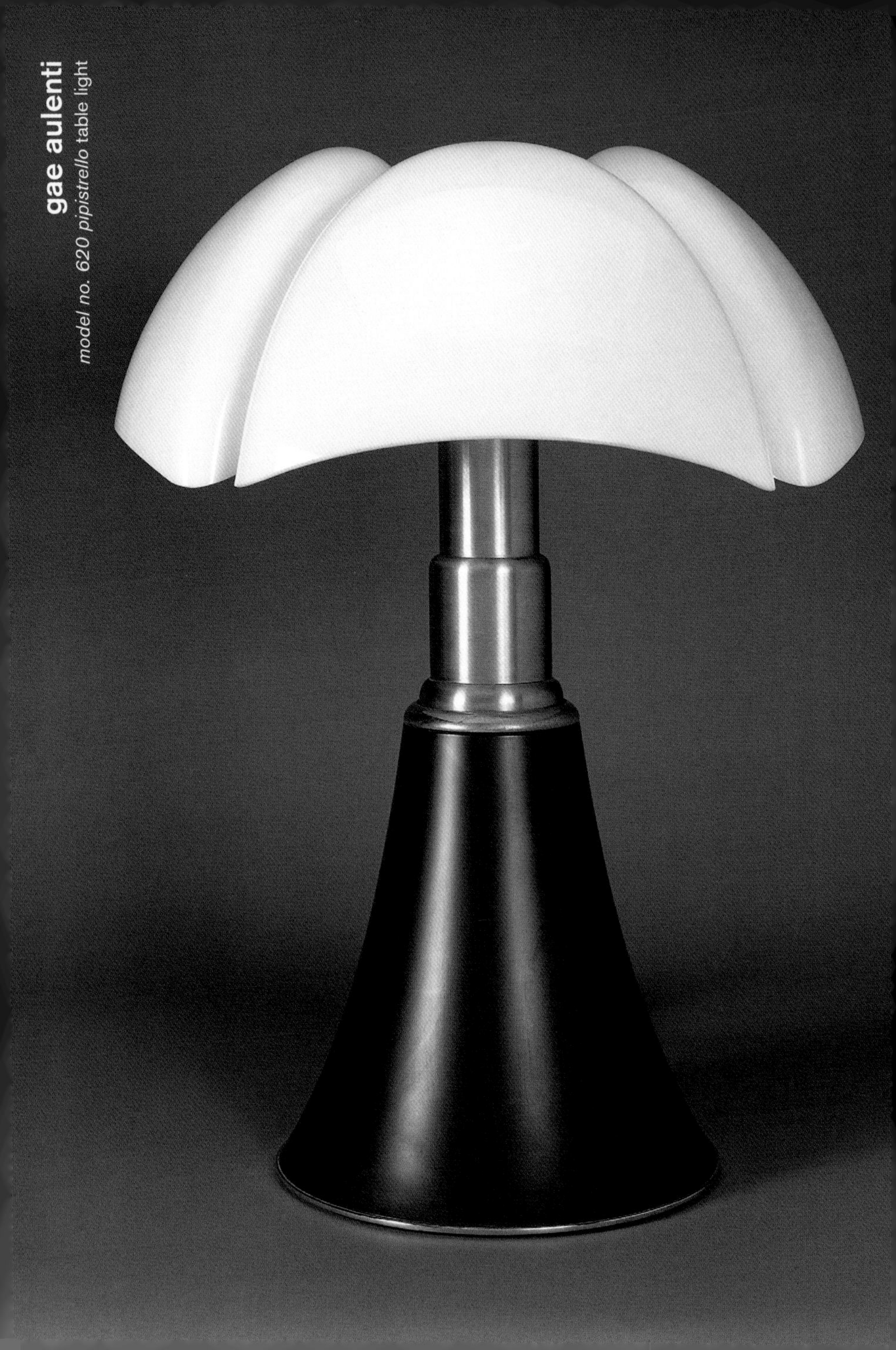

gae aulenti

model no. 620 pipistrello table light

"I never thought of lamps in terms of technical lighting or like a machine for making light, but like forms in a harmonious relationship with the context for which they are created."

„Ich habe Leuchten nie als Technik gesehen oder als eine Maschine zur Herstellung von Licht, sondern als Formen, die mit dem Kontext, für den sie geschaffen werden, harmonieren."

«Je n'ai jamais pensé aux luminaires en termes d'éclairage technique ou de machine à éclairer, mais de formes, dans une relation harmonieuse avec le contexte pour lequel ils sont créés.»

– Gae Aulenti

◁ *Model No. 620 Pipistrello* table light, 1965–66
Enameled aluminum base, stainless-steel telescopic shaft, acrylic shade, 86 cm high (max.) / Fuß aus lackiertem Aluminium, Teleskopschaft aus Edelstahl, Lampenschirm aus Acryl, 86 cm hoch (max.) / Pied en aluminium laqué, colonne télescopique en acier inoxydable, abat-jour en acrylique, 86 cm de haut (max.)
Martinelli Luce, Lucca, Italy

▷ *Paris interior designed by Gae Aulenti, c.1965 / Von Gae Aulenti gestaltetes Pariser Interieur, ca. 1965 / Intérieur à Paris conçu par Gae Aulenti; vers 1965*

The *Pipistrello* table light was created in the mid-1960s and achieved considerable success. It acquired immediate status as a fashionable item to set in a contemporary interior and featured in countless chic living rooms in Milan, Paris, London and elsewhere through the late 1960s and 1970s. The name refers to the batwing outline of the segmented opaline acrylic shade. The flared metal base incorporates a telescopic steel stem, allowing the light to be lowered or raised and hence positioned either on furniture or the floor. (PG)

Die Mitte der 1960er Jahre entworfene Tischleuchte *Pipistrello* fand sofort großen Anklang und entwickelte sich schnell zu einem Ausstattungsobjekt, das bis in die 1970er Jahre zahllose moderne Wohnzimmer in Mailand, Paris, London und anderen Städten zierte. Ihr Name bezieht sich auf die an Fledermausflügel erinnernde Silhouette des opalweißen Acryllampenschirms. Der nach unten hin konisch erweiterte Metallfuß enthält einen Teleskopschaft aus Edelstahl, wodurch die Leuchte ausgezogen oder gesenkt werden kann und sich daher für die Aufstellung sowohl auf Möbeln als auch auf dem Boden eignet. (PG)

La lampe de table *Pipistrello*, créée au milieu des années 1960, connut un succès considérable. Objet élégant, elle s'imposa immédiatement comme un symbole de classe indispensable dans un intérieur contemporain et figura dans d'innombrables séjour chics de Milan, Paris, Londres et ailleurs, tout au long des années 1960 et 1970. Son nom – chauve-souris – lui vient des contours de l'abat-jour segmenté en acrylique. Le pied évasé enserre une colonne télescopique en acier qui permet de lever ou baisser la lampe et ainsi, de l'utiliser posée sur un meuble ou au sol. (PG)

Many designers have taken the lightness and luminosity of clouds as an inspiration for the creation of light fittings. In these two cases we are dealing with two quite different personalities. Roberto Lucci collaborated in the 1960s with the architect and artist Marcello Pietrantoni, and it seems that they both chose the cloud form because of its expressiveness. In the case of Superstudio, a sketch shows that the design for the light (1968) came from the idea of simply cutting through a section of cloud-shaped tubing – a brilliant method that produced a result that was not unlike the *Nuvola* light (1966). (SC)

Viele Designer haben sich von der Leichtigkeit und der strahlenden Helligkeit von Wolken zu Beleuchtungskörpern inspirieren lassen. Bei den hier vorgestellten Beispielen begegnet man zwei sehr unterschiedliche Designerpersönlichkeiten. Roberto Lucci arbeitete in den 1960er Jahren mit dem Architekten und Künstler Marcello Pietrantoni zusammen, und beide wählten die Wolkenform wegen ihrer Ausdruckskraft. Im Fall der Leuchte von Superstudio (1968) geht aus einer Entwurfszeichnung hervor, dass das Modell auf der einfachen Idee basierte, einen Ausschnitt aus einer wolkenförmigen Röhre zu verwenden – ein brillanter Einfall, dessen Ergebnis jedoch der Leuchte *Nuvola* (1966) nicht unähnlich ist. (SC)

De nombreux designers se sont inspirés de la légèreté et de la luminosité des nuages pour créer des luminaires. Ces deux exemples sont signés de deux personnalités assez différentes. Roberto Lucci a travaillé dans les années 1960 avec l'architecte et artiste Marcello Pietrantoni et il semble que tous deux ont choisi la forme du nuage pour son expressivité. Dans le cas de Superstudio, un croquis montre que le projet (1968) était venu de l'idée de couper en biais un tube en forme de nuage, méthode inattendue qui aboutit à un résultat assez peu éloigné de la lampe *Nuvola* (1966). (SC)

Nuvola **ceiling/wall light, 1966**

White acrylic body, wooden fixing frame, 153 cm (max.) / Leuchtenkörper aus weißem Acryl, Montierung aus Holz, 153 cm (max.) / Corps en acrylique blanc, armature de fixation en bois, 153 cm (max.)
Stilnovo, Lainate, Italy

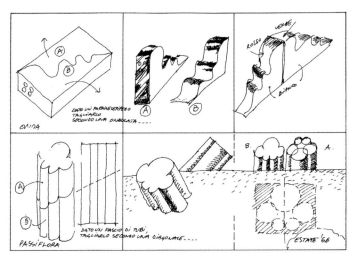

▽ *Passiflora* **floor/wall light, 1968**

Opalescent colored methacrylate construction,
28 cm high / Konstruktion aus farbigem,
opalisierendem Methacrylat, 28 cm hoch /
Corps en méthacrylate opalescent de couleur,
28 cm de haut
Poltronova, Montale, Italy

△ *Design drawing for the* Passiflora *floor/wall
light, c.1968 / Entwurfszeichnung für die
Steh-/ Wandleuchte* Passiflora, ca. 1968 /
Croquis pour la lampe Passiflora, vers 1968

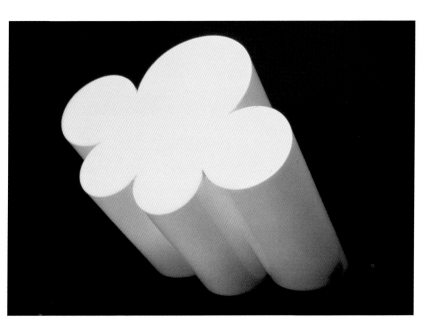

Gae Aulenti tended to favor pure geometric forms and most of her light designs of the 1960s are of an austere construction. They nonetheless have an insistent sculptural presence and a quality beyond the practical. The *Locus Solus* floor light (1964) is more playful in concept. Its particular character derives from two features – the choice of color and the slightly bent stem, which combine to suggest a curious quasi-organic form that has emerged from the floor. The green acrylic shapes of the light (*c.*1969) manufactured by the Rome-based company, New Lamp, recall underwater fronds. (PG)

Gae Aulenti bevorzugte unverfälschte geometrische Formen, und die meisten ihrer Leuchtenentwürfe aus den 1960er Jahren zeichnet eine gewisse Strenge aus. Dennoch besitzen sie jenseits aller Zweckmäßigkeit auch eine skulpturale Präsenz. Die Stehleuchte *Locus Solus* (1964) zeigt ein eher spielerisches Konzept in der Kombination aus Farbgebung und dem schlangenähnlich geformten Arm, der an eine organische Gestalt denken lässt, die aus dem Boden wächst. Die grünen Acrylformen der von New Lamp in Rom hergestellten Tischleuchte (ca. 1969) hingegen erinnern an die Blätter von Wasserpflanzen. (PG)

Gae Aulenti privilégie souvent les formes géométriques pures et la plupart de ses luminaires des années 1960 sont de construction austère. Ils possèdent néanmoins une présence et une qualité sculpturale qui va bien au-delà du simple aspect pratique. La lampe de sol *Locus Solus* (1964) est de conception plus ludique. Son caractère particulier tient à deux éléments : le choix de la couleur et la tige sinueuse, forme bizarre, quasi organique qui semble jaillir du sol. Les découpes étranges des plaques d'acrylique du modèle (vers 1969) fabriqué par la société romaine New Lamp, évoquent les fonds sous-marins. (PG)

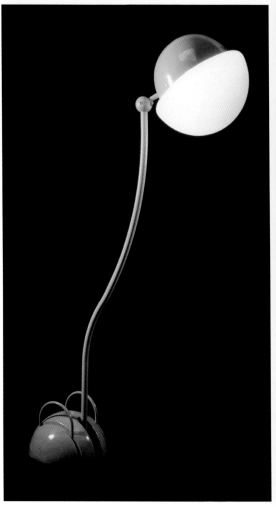

Locus Solus floor light, 1964

Enameled metal base, stem and head with opalescent diffuser, 200 cm high / Fuß, Arm und Leuchtenkopf aus lackiertem Metall mit opalem Diffusor, 200 cm hoch / Pied en métal émaillé, tige et tête à diffuseur opalescent, 200 cm de haut
Poltronova, Montale, Italy

▷ **Table light, c. 1969**

Chrome-plated metal base with acrylic diffusers / Fuß aus verchromtem Metall mit Diffusoren aus Acryl / Base en métal chromé, diffuseurs en acrylique
New Lamp, Rome, Italy

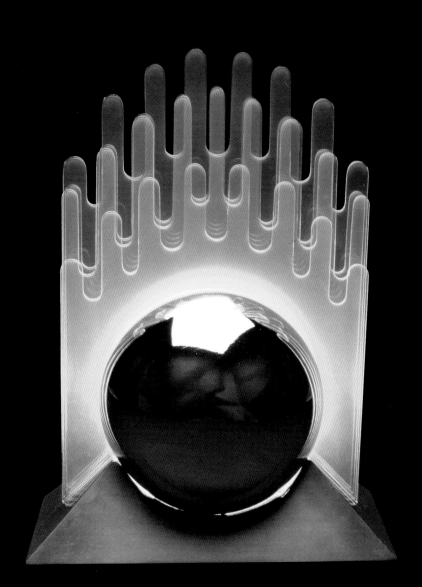

▷ *Bulb* table light, 1966
Polished chrome-plated metal base with hand-blown glass shade, 30 cm high / Fuß aus glänzend verchromtem Metall mit Lampenschirm aus mundgeblasenem Glas, 30 cm hoch / Pied en métal chromé poli, corps en verre soufflé, 30 cm de haut
Ingo Maurer, Munich, Germany

◁ *Range of lighting products designed by Ingo Maurer and others for Design M, c.1970 / Beleuchtungskörper nach Entwürfen von Ingo Maurer und anderen für Design M, ca. 1970 / Gamme de luminaires créés par Ingo Maurer et d'autres pour Design M, vers 1970*

In 1966 Ingo Maurer set up his Design M studio in Munich, laying the foundations for the lighting manufacturer Ingo Maurer GmbH, which began life in 1973. Maurer's first lighting design, the *Bulb* table light (1966), pays homage to Thomas Alva Edison's first commercial light bulb. Its shape shows the influence of the American Pop culture that Maurer had experienced in the early 1960s. The light, in the form of an outsized bulb in chrome-plated metal and hand-blown glass, recalls the inordinately large versions of everyday objects created by the American Pop artist Claes Oldenburg. (TB)

Ingo Maurer gründete 1966 in München das Atelier Design M, aus dem 1973 die Leuchtenfirma Ingo Maurer GmbH hervorging. Maurers erster Leuchtenentwurf, die Tischleuchte *Bulb* (1966), ist eine Hommage an Thomas Alva Edisons erste kommerziell vertriebene Glühleuchte unter dem Einfluss der Pop-Kultur, die Maurer Anfang der 1960er Jahre in Amerika kennen gelernt hatte. Die Leuchte in Form einer überdimensionalen Glühbirne aus verchromten Metall und mundgeblasenem Glas erinnert an die vergrößerten Alltagsobjekte des amerikanischen Pop-Art-Künstlers Claes Oldenburg. (TB)

C'est en 1966 que Ingo Maurer créa le studio Design M à Munich, embryon de l'entreprise de fabrication de luminaires Ingo Maurer GmbH, fondée en 1973. La première création de Maurer, la lampe de table *Bulb* (1966), rend hommage à l'invention par Thomas Alva Edison de l'ampoule électrique. Sa forme montre l'influence de la culture pop américaine découverte par le designer au début des années 1960. La lampe, en forme d'ampoule surdimensionnée, en verre soufflé et métal chromé, rappelle les versions agrandies d'objets quotidiens créées par l'artiste pop américain Claes Oldenburg. (TB)

Jay Monroe invented a sturdy, high-intensity desk light specifically for students and in 1957 established the Tensor Corp. to manufacture and distribute it. This version, probably from the early 1960s, has a heatproof flock-coated shade. Another version, the *Model No. 6500*, was produced with a wider, flared shade. Although the *Tensor* was widely used as a dorm light in colleges, it could not compete with later and more stylish lighting solutions, such as Michael Lax's *Lytegem*. American business schools later used the case study of the Tensor Corp. to demonstrate that even with a great product, a company can flounder through poor management. (CF/PF)

Jay Monroe konstruierte speziell für Studenten eine robuste und lichtstarke Schreibtischleuchte, zu deren Produktion und Vertrieb er 1957 die Tensor Corp. gründete. Die hier abgebildete Version (ca. 1960) hat einen Lampenschirm, der mit einem hitzebeständigen Flockenmaterial beschichtet ist. Eine andere Version, das *Modell Nr. 6500*, besaß einen etwas breiteren, kelchförmigen Lampenschirm. Obwohl die Leuchte *Tensor* in den Studentenwohnheimen der amerikanischen Colleges weit verbreitet war, konnte sie mit späteren Designlösungen wie der Leuchte *Lytegem* (1965) von Michael Lax nicht konkurrieren. An amerikanischen Universitäten galt die Tensor Corp. später als Fallbeispiel für eine Firma mit einem guten Produkt, aber schlechtem Management. (CF/PF)

Jay Monroe conçut spécialement cette solide lampe de bureau basse tension pour les étudiants et fonda en 1957 la Tensor Corp. pour la fabriquer et la distribuer. Cette version, qui date probablement du début des années 1960, possède un réflecteur floqué résistant à la chaleur. Une autre version, baptisée *Modèle n° 6500*, possédait un réflecteur plus large et évasé. Bien que la *Tensor* ait été beaucoup utilisée dans les dortoirs de collèges, elle ne pouvait concurrencer des solutions plus sophistiquées comme la *Lytegem* de Michael Lax. Les écoles de gestion américaines utilisèrent par la suite le cas de la Tensor Corp. pour prouver que même avec un excellent produit, une entreprise pouvait échouer à cause d'un mauvais management. (CF/PF)

◁ **Tensor student light, c.1960**
Enameled metal base housing transformer with enameled tubular metal arms and flock-coated metal shade, 51 cm high (max.) / Metallfuß mit eingebautem Transformator, Arme aus lackiertem Stahlrohr mit Lampenschirm aus beflocktem Metall, 51 cm hoch (max.) / Socle en métal laqué abritant le transformateur, bras en tube métallique laqué, réflecteur en métal floqué, 51 cm de haut (max.)
Tensor Corp., Brooklyn (NY), USA

▷ *Lightolier advertisement showing the* Lytegem *versus the* Tensor *student light, 1960s / Werbeanzeige von Lightolier mit Gegenüberstellung der Leseleuchten* Lytegem *und* Tensor, *1960er Jahre / Annonce de Lightolier montrant la* Lytegem *face à la* Tensor, *années 1960*

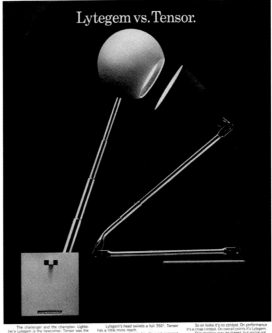

Lytegem vs. Tensor.

◁ ***Lytegem* mini spotlight, 1965**
Polycarbonate base with telescopic arm and
stamped metal shade, 38.1 cm high (max.) /
Fuß aus Polycarbonat mit Teleskoparm, Lampenschirm aus gepresstem Metall, 38,1 cm
hoch (max.) / Base en polycarbonate, bras
télescopique, réflecteur en métal embouti,
38,1 cm de haut (max.)
Lightolier, Fall River (MA), USA (limited re-
edition, 2004)

Lytegem *mini spotlight with packaging,
c.1965 / Minispot* Lytegem *mit Originalverpackung, ca. 1965 / Mini-spot* Lytegem *et
son emballage, vers 1965*

The *Lytegem* mini spotlight, which
Michael Lax designed for Lightolier in
1965, was one of the first lighting products to introduce high-intensity low-voltage lighting into the domestic environment. High-intensity lighting had
previously been deployed chiefly in
workshops and garages. In close collaboration with Lightolier's engineers,
Lax developed this compact light for the
home using a cube-like base that
housed the transformer, a swiveling
telescopic arm and a light-shielding,
spherical shade. Available in a range of
muted tones, the *Lytegem* combined
American no-nonsense practicality with
the Scandinavian flair for form, texture
and color. (CF/PF)

Der von Michael Lax 1965 für Lightolier
entworfene Minispot *Lytegem* gehörte
zu den ersten Beleuchtungskörpern,
durch die die lichtintensive Niedervolt-
technologie in den Wohnbereich eingeführt wurden. Bis dahin war diese Art
von Lichttechnik vor allem in Werkstätten und Garagen eingesetzt worden.
Lax entwickelte die kompakte Leuchte
in enger Zusammenarbeit mit den
Technikern von Lightolier. Das Design
besteht aus einem würfelförmigen Fuß
mit integriertem Transformator, einem
schwenkbaren Teleskoparm sowie
einem kugelförmigen Lampenschirm
und wurde in mehreren gedeckten Farben angeboten. Die *Lytegem* Leuchte
kombiniert amerikanische Zweckmäßigkeit mit skandinavischem Gespür für
Form, Material und Farbe. (CF/PF)

Le spot *Lytegem* dessiné par Michael
Lax pour Lightolier en 1965 a été l'un
des premiers produits d'éclairage à
faire appel à l'alimentation basse tension haute intensité dans l'environnement de la maison. Ce type d'éclairage
était utilisé auparavant dans les ateliers
et les garages. En étroite collaboration
avec les ingénieurs de Lightolier, Lax
mit au point ce modèle compact pour
la maison. Le socle cubique dissimulait
le transformateur, le bras télescopique
était orientable et un réflecteur sphérique protégeait l'ampoule. Proposée
dans plusieurs couleurs sourdes, la
Lytegem combinait le sens pratique
américain et le goût scandinave des
formes, des textures et des couleurs.
(CF/PF)

Realizing the benefits of a bedside light with easily regulated brightness, Vico Magistretti designed the diminutive *Eclisse* in 1965–66. The light is made up of three hemispheres – one acts as a base, another as a shade, and the third controls the amount of light by functioning as an eyelid-like shield. As with other lighting designs by Magistretti, the play of light accentuates the juxtaposition of the simple geometric forms used. Although small in scale the *Eclisse* has a strong sculptural presence and became one of the designer's best-known products, winning a Compasso d'Oro award in 1967. (CF/PF)

Nach Auffassung von Vico Magistretti sollte gerade bei Nachttischleuchten die Lichtstärke leicht regulierbar sein. In diesem Sinne gestaltete er 1965–66 die kleine Nachttischleuchte *Eclisse*. Die Leuchte besteht aus drei Halbkugeln, von denen je eine als Fuß und als Lampenschirm fungiert, während die dritte wie ein Augenlid zur Lichtregulierung funktioniert. Wie bei anderen Leuchtenentwürfen von Magistretti unterstützt das Lichtspiel das Zusammenwirken der einfachen geometrischen Formen. Trotz ihrer geringen Größe besitzt die *Eclisse* Leuchte eine starke skulpturale Präsenz und ist einer der bekanntesten Entwürfe Magistrettis. Sie wurde 1967 mit einem Compasso d'Oro ausgezeichnet. (CF/PF)

Comprenant l'intérêt d'une lampe de chevet d'intensité facilement règlable, Vico Magistretti dessina la toute petite *Eclisse* en 1965–66. Elle se compose de trois parties hémisphériques : l'une est sa base, l'autre son réflecteur, la troisième contrôle la quantité de lumière en se fermant comme une paupière. Comme dans d'autres luminaires de Magistretti, le jeu de la lumière accentue l'effet de juxtaposition de formes géométriques simples. Bien que de petite échelle, l'*Eclisse* possède une authentique présence sculpturale. Après avoir remporté un Compasso d'Oro en 1967, elle est devenue l'un des créations les plus connues de ce designer. (CF/PF)

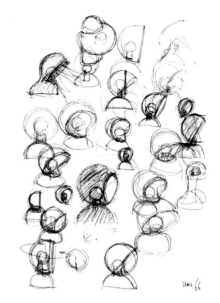

△△ *Sketch of the* Eclisse *bedside light, 1966 / Entwurfsskizzen der Nachttischleuchte* Eclisse, *1966 / Croquis de la lampe de chevet* Eclisse, *1966*

△ *Artemide publicity photograph of the* Eclisse *bedside light, c.1966 / Werbefoto von Artemide mit Nachttischleuchte* Eclisse, *ca. 1966 / Photographie publicitaire Artemide de la lampe de chevet* Eclisse, *vers 1966*

▷ ***Eclisse* bedside light, 1965–66**

Enameled aluminum base and shades, 18 cm high / Fuß und Lampenschirme aus lackiertem Aluminium, 18 cm hoch / Base et réflecteurs en aluminium laqué, 18 cm de haut
Artemide, Pregnana Milanese, Italy

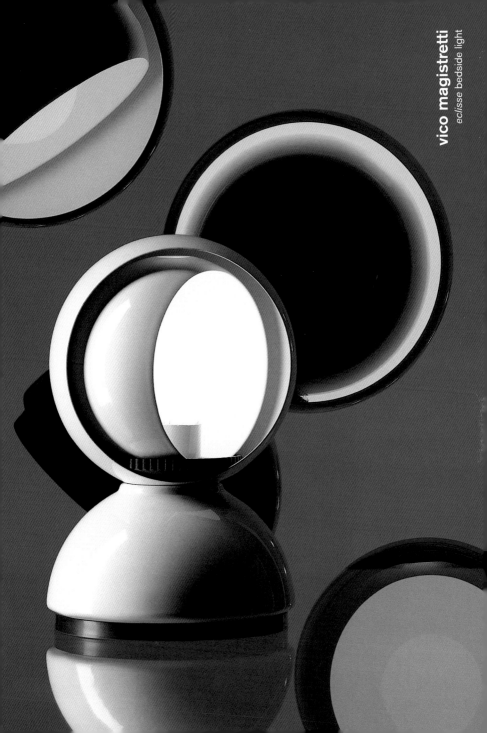

Named after the loveable "Peanuts" character, the form of the *Snoopy* light (1967) was inspired by the cartoon dog's protruding nose. Although humorous, this perfectly balanced design is also quite rational in its construction. Having enjoyed throughout his long career products that were imbued with wit as well as stylish functionalism, Achille Castiglioni noted: "There has to be irony both in design and in the objects … I see around me a professional disease of taking everything too seriously. One of my secrets is to joke all the time." (CF/PF)

Die Form der nach der liebenswerten „Peanuts"-Figur benannten Tischleuchte *Snoopy* (1967) ist der markanten Nase des Comic-Hundes nachempfunden. Trotz des humorvollen Bezuges ist dieser ausgewogene Entwurf in der Konstruktion durchaus zweckmäßig. Achille Castiglioni, dessen Kreationen sich ebenso durch Witz wie durch Stil und Funktionalität auszeichnen, meinte einmal: „Eine gewisse Ironie muss sowohl im Design wie in den Objekten zu finden sein … Ich stelle in meiner Umgebung eine Berufskrankheit fest, die darin besteht, dass alles zu ernst genommen wird. Eines meiner Geheimnisse ist es, dauernd Witze zu machen." (CF/PF)

La forme de la lampe *Snoopy* (1967) s'inspire du nez proéminent du célèbre chien de bande dessinée auquel elle doit son nom. Bien qu'humoristique, ce modèle parfaitement équilibré reste assez rationnel dans sa conception. Ayant imaginé pendant toute sa longue carrière des produits spirituels et d'un fonctionnalisme élégant, Achille Castiglioni faisait remarquer : « Il doit y avoir de l'ironie à la fois dans le design et les objets … Je constate autour de moi la maladie professionnelle de prendre tout trop au sérieux. L'un de mes secrets est de plaisanter tout le temps. » (CF/PF)

◁ *Snoopy* **table light, 1967**
Marble base with enameled metal or glass shade resting on glass disk, 37 cm high / Marmorfuß mit auf einer Glasscheibe aufliegendem Lampenschirm aus lackiertem Metall oder Glas, 37 cm hoch / Pied en marbre, abat-jour en verre ou métal, sur un disque de verre, 37 cm de haut
Flos, Bovezzo, Italy

Contemporary photograph showing disassembled components of Snoopy table light, *c.1967 / Zeitgenössische Photographie mit den zerlegten Komponenten der Tischleuchte* Snoopy, *ca. 1967 / Photographie contemporaine des pièces composant la lampe de table* Snoopy, *vers 1967*

angelo mangiarotti
lesbo table light

> ▷ *Artemide publicity photograph of* Lesbo
> *table light, c.1967 / Werbefoto von Artemide
> mit Tischleuchte* Lesbo, ca. 1967 / Photogra-
> phie publicitaire Artemide pour la lampe de
> table Lesbo, vers 1967

▽ *Lesbo* table light, 1966–67

Chrome-plated metal base with hand-blown
glass diffuser, 37 cm high / Fuß aus verchromtem Metall mit Diffusor aus mundgeblasenem
Glas, 37 cm hoch / Socle en métal chromé,
diffuseur en verre soufflé, 37 cm de haut
Artemide, Pregnana Milanese, Italy

One of the great philosophical protagonists of Italian design and architecture, Angelo Mangiarotti named these two organic table lights (1966–67) after the Greek island of Lesbos and its 7th-century BC poetess, Sappho. The graduated opaque shading of the diffusers conceals the light source, helping to reflect the light upwards. Both lights emit a soft glow that accentuates the intrinsic qualities of the hand-blown Murano glass. The mushroom-like form of these highly sculptural designs was a recurring theme in Mangiarotti's work. (CF/PF)

Angelo Mangiarotti, einer der großen Philosophen des italienischen Designs und der Architektur, benannte seine beiden organischen Tischleuchten (1966–67) nach der griechischen Insel Lesbos und der Dichterin Sappho, die im 7. Jahrhundert v. Chr. dort lebte. Die Lichtquelle ist jeweils hinter einem Lampenschirm mit abgestuft opaker Schattierung verborgen, der das Licht nach oben hin reflektiert. Beide Leuchten verbreiten ein weiches Licht, das die Eigenschaften des mundgeblasenen Muranoglases besonders gut zur Geltung kommen lässt. Die Pilzform dieser skulpturalen Modelle taucht in Mangiarottis Werk immer wieder auf. (CF/PF)

Un des grands philosophes du design et de l'architecture italiens, Angelo Mangiarotti, a nommé ces deux lampes de table (1966–67) de forme organique d'après l'île grecque de Lesbos et la poétesse du VIIᵉ siècle av.-J-C., Sappho. L'effet d'ombre gradué des diffuseurs dissimule la source lumineuse et contribue à diriger la lumière vers le haut. Les deux lampes émettent un halo subtil qui accentue la qualité intrinsèque du verre soufflé de Murano. La forme en champignon de ces modèles hautement sculpturaux constitue un thème récurrent dans l'œuvre de Mangiarotti. (CF/PF)

angelo mangiarotti *Saffo* table light

Saffo table light, 1966–67

Chrome-plated metal base with hand-blown smoked glass diffuser, 34 cm high / Fuß aus verchromtem Metall mit Diffusor aus mundgeblasenem Rauchglas, 34 cm hoch / Socle en métal chromé, diffuseur en verre soufflé fumé, 34 cm de haut
Artemide, Pregnana Milanese, Italy

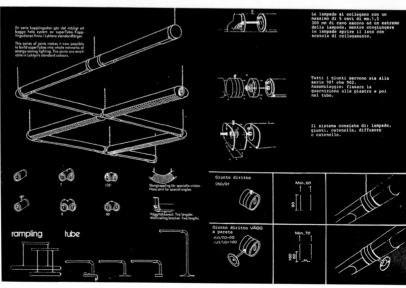

En serie kopplingsdon gör det möjligt att bygga hela system av supertube. Kopplingsdonen finns i Lyktans standardfärger.

This series of joints makes it now possible to build super Tubes into whole networks of energy-saving lighting. The joints are available in Lyktan's standard colours.

Le lampade si collegano con un massimo di 5 cavi di mm. 1,5 300 mm di cavo escono ad un estremo della lampada, mentre congiungere le lampade aprire il lato con scatola di collegamento.

Tutti i giunti servono sia alla serie 901 che 902. Assemblaggio: fissare la guarnizione alla piastra e poi nel tubo.

Il sistema consiste di: lampade, giunti, catenelle, diffusore o catenelle.

T
135°

X
90°

Slangkoppling för speciella vinklar.
Hose joint for special angles.

Vägg/takkonsol. Två längder.
Wall/ceiling bracket. Two lengths.

rampling   tube

Giunto diritto
950/01

Giunto diritto VÄGG
a parete
950/02-60
950/02-100

Min.60

Min.70

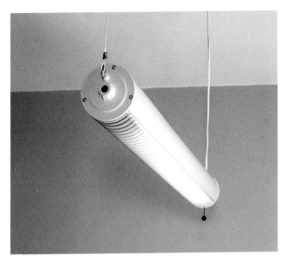

Anders Pehrson's *Supertube* lighting system (c.1967) was designed to reduce energy consumption. It comprises extruded aluminum tubes, housing low-wattage fluorescent bulbs, that can be connected into a simple network by means of rigid elbows, flexible plastic joints or multi-directional couplings. Available in ten colors, the tubes can be suspended by chains or mounted directly onto ceilings and walls. They can also be used individually with a single 40-watt tube. As a lighting system that can be infinitely extended with the addition of extra elements, the revolutionary *Supertube* is especially suitable for large, open-plan spaces. (CF/PF)

Anders Pehrson ging es bei seinem Leuchtensystem *Supertube* (ca. 1967) um eine Reduzierung des Stromverbrauchs. Er verwendete dazu Niedrigwatt-Leuchtstofflampen, die in Röhren aus stranggepresstem Aluminium montiert waren. Die Röhren können mittels starren bzw. flexiblen Verbindungsstücken bzw. T-Verbindern aus Kunststoff zu einem einfachen System zusammengesetzt werden. Sie sind in zehn verschiedenen Farben erhältlich und können an Ketten herabgehängt oder direkt an Decken und Wänden montiert werden. Einzeln sind sie mit einer 40-Watt-Leuchtstoffröhre zu verwenden. Mit zusätzlichen Elementen beliebig erweiterbar, eignet sich das revolutionäre *Supertube* System besonders für Großraumbüros. (CF/PF)

Le système *Supertube* (vers 1967) d'Anders Pehrson a été conçu pour réduire la consommation d'énergie. Il se compose de tubes d'aluminium extrudé, accueillant des lampes fluorescentes basse tension, connectables en réseau grâce à des coudes rigides, des joints en plastique souple ou des manchons d'accouplement multidirectionnels. Proposés en dix coloris, ces tubes se suspendent par des chaînes ou s'intègrent directement aux plafonds ou aux murs. Ils peuvent également être utilisés séparément, équipés d'un tube de 40 watts. Système d'éclairage extensible à l'infini par l'adjonction d'éléments supplémentaires, ce *Supertube* révolutionnaire est bien adapté aux plateaux en open-space. (CF/PF)

anders pehrson
supertube lighting system

△△ ***Supertube*** **lighting system, c.1967**
Enameled extruded aluminum tubes with various metal and plastic connectors, various sizes / Röhren aus lackiertem stranggepresstem Aluminium mit Verbindungsstücken aus Metall und Kunststoff, unterschiedliche Größen / Tubes métalliques en aluminium extrudé laqué, divers connecteurs métalliques et plastiques, différentes tailles
Ateljé Lyktan, Åhus, Sweden

◁/ △ *Diagram and photographs of* Supertube *lighting system in situ / Schematischer Bauplan des Leuchtensystems* Supertube *und Anwendungsbeispiele / Schéma du système d'éclairage* Supertube *et photographies in situ*

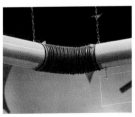

Giancarlo Mattiolo was one of a number of Italian designers who have explored ways to achieve a discreet ambient light source in which one is not conscious of the bulb. In the *Nesso* table light (1962) Mattiolo exploits the idea of diffusing light through colored plastic. He thereby avoids assaulting the eye with the specific intensity of the bulb. The partial transparency of the material spreads an even glow, whilst the choice of colors of the plastic gives warmth to this luminosity. (PG)

Giancarlo Mattiolo gehörte zu jenen italienischen Designern, die nach Möglichkeiten suchten, eine diskrete, stimmungsvolle Beleuchtung zu schaffen und dabei die Glühbirne nach Möglichkeit unsichtbar zu machen. Mit seiner Tischleuchte *Nesso* (1962) verwirklichte er die Idee, künstliches Licht durch farbigen Kunststoff zu leiten und so die Augen vor dem aggressiven Licht der Glühbirnen zu schützen. Der teilweise lichtdurchlässige, eingefärbte ABS-Kunststoff der *Nesso* Leuchte sorgt für eine gleichmäßige und gemütliche Beleuchtung. (PG)

Giancarlo Mattiolo fut l'un des designers italiens qui explorèrent de nouveaux modes d'obtention d'une lumière d'ambiance discrète, avec des luminaires qui faisaient oublier la présence d'une ampoule. Dans la lampe de table *Nesso* (1962), il exploite l'idée de diffusion de la lumière à travers un plastique coloré. Il évite que l'œil soit agressé par l'intensité de l'ampoule. La transparence partielle du matériau diffuse une lueur uniforme, tandis que le choix des couleurs du plastique assure une lumière chaleureuse. (PG)

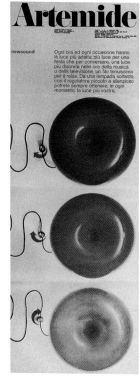

△△ *Nesso* table light, 1962

ABS base and shade, 54 cm diameter / Fuß und Lampenschirm aus ABS-Kunststoff, 54 cm Durchmesser / Pied et abat-jour en ABS, 54 cm de diamètre
Artemide, Pregnana Milanese, Italy

△ *Artemide publicity photograph showing the* Nesso *table light, c. 1962 / Werbefoto von Artemide mit Tischleuchte* Nesso*, ca. 1962 / Annonce publicitaire Artemide présentant la lampe de table* Nesso*, vers 1962*

◁ *Artemide catalog featuring the* Nesso *table light, c. 1962 / Werbeseite aus einem Katalog von Artemide mit Tischleuchte* Nesso*, ca. 1962 / Catalogue Artemide présentant la lampe de table* Nesso*, vers 1962*

MT floor light, 1969
Enameled aluminum construction, 47 cm high /
Konstruktion aus lackiertem Aluminium, 47 cm
hoch / Structure en aluminium laqué, 47 cm de
haut
Sirrah, Imola, Italy

Giancarlo Mattiolo's *MT* floor light (1969) is designed to sit on the ground and to radiate light at floor level. One small central bulb casts a light that is reflected and channeled between the numerous fins. The effect is unusual, subtle and seductive. This clean, sculptural and highly effective design was featured in the important "Italy: The New Domestic Landscape" exhibition held in 1972 at the Museum of Modern Art in New York, where it was presented, appropriately, within the section devoted to "Objects selected for their formal and technical means." (PG)

Die Bodenleuchte *MT* (1969) von Giancarlo Mattiolo ist so konzipiert, dass sie auf dem Boden aufgestellt ihr Licht nach allen Richtungen gleichmäßig verteilt. Von einer kleinen Glühbirne in der Mitte ausgehend breitet sich das Licht, reflektiert von einem Lamellenkranz, strahlenförmig aus. Die Wirkung ist verblüffend – raffiniert und verführerisch. Dieses klare, skulpturale und sehr wirkungsvolle Modell wurde 1972 vom Museum of Modern Art in New York in dessen spektakuläre Ausstellung „Italy: The New Domestic Landscape" aufgenommen und als eines der „Objekte, die aufgrund ihrer formalen und technischen Mittel ausgewählt wurden", präsentiert. (PG)

La lampe *MT* (1969) de Giancarlo Mattiolo est conçue pour être posée au sol et diffuser la lumière à ce niveau. Une petite ampoule centrale projette une lumière qui est réfléchie et canalisée par de multiples ailettes. L'effet est inhabituel, subtil et séduisant. Ce luminaire, de conception sculpturale et précise, figura dans l'importante exposition organisée par le Museum of Modern Art de New York en 1972 « Italy : The New Domestic Landscape », où il était à juste tire présenté dans la section consacrée aux « Objets sélectionnés pour leurs moyens formels et techniques ». (PG)

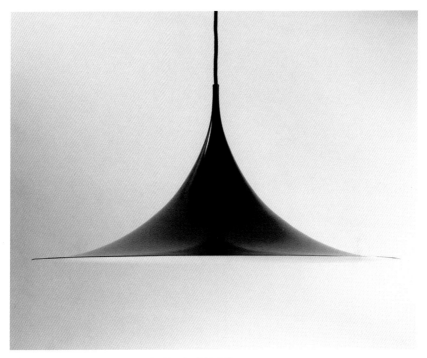

◁ Archival photograph of interior showing the
Semi hanging light, c.1970 / Zeitgenössisches
Interieur mit Hängeleuchte Semi, ca. 1970 /
Photographie d'archive d'un intérieur équipé
de la suspension Semi, vers 1970

Semi hanging light, 1967
Enameled metal shade, small: 38 cm diameter,
large: 60 cm diameter / Lampenschirm aus
lackiertem Metall, klein: 38 cm Durchmesser,
groß: 60 cm Durchmesser / Abat-jour en métal
laqué, petit modèle : 38 cm de diamètre, grand
modèle : 60 cm de diamètre
Fog & Morup, Aalestrup, Denmark

The elegant *Semi* hanging light (1967)
by the architect duo Claus Bonderup
and Torsten Thorup can be seen as an
evolution of the highly stylized tulip
forms that gained popularity in the mid-
1950s. Like Eero Saarinen's earlier
Tulip chair (1955–56) and Nils Landberg's *Tulipen* glasses from the mid-
1950s, the *Semi* light has an extremely
refined and attenuated organic form.
Particularly suitable for illuminating dining tables, Bonderup and Thorup's
design graced many European interiors
in the 1960s and 1970s, especially in
Scandinavia. The *Semi* was available in
various sizes and colors, including
white, chocolate brown and black. (AP)

Die vom Architektenduo Claus Bonderup und Torsten Thorup entworfene elegante Hängeleuchte *Semi* (1967) ist
eine Weiterentwicklung der stark stilisierten Tulpenformen, die Mitte der
1950er Jahre populär wurden. Wie der
einbeinige Plastikstuhl *Tulip* (1955–56)
von Eero Saarinen und Nils Landbergs
Tulpengläser aus der Mitte der 1950er
Jahre weist auch die Leuchte *Semi* eine
bis zum Äußersten abstrahierte und
reduzierte Form auf. Die vor allem zur
Ausleuchtung des Esstisches geeignete Leuchte schmückte in den 1960er
und 1970er Jahren viele europäische
Inneneinrichtungen, vor allem in Skan-
dinavien. Die Leuchte gab es in verschiedenen Größen und Farben, unter
anderem in Weiß, Schokoladenbraun
und Schwarz. (AP)

L'élégante suspension *Semi* (1967) du
duo d'architectes formé par Claus
Bonderup et Torsten Thorup, peut être
considérée comme une évolution de la
forme de tulipe stylisée très à la mode
au milieu des années 1950. Comme la
chaise *Tulip* d'Eero Saarinen datant de
1955–56 et les verres *Tulipen* de Nils
Landberg de cette même période, la
Semi présentait une forme organique
extrêmement raffinée et épurée. Particulièrement adaptée à l'éclairage des
tables de salles à manger, elle fut très
à la mode en Europes et plus spécialement en Scandinavie, dans les années
1960 et 1970. La *Semi* était proposée
en diverses dimensions et couleurs,
dont le blanc, le brun chocolat et le
noir. (AP)

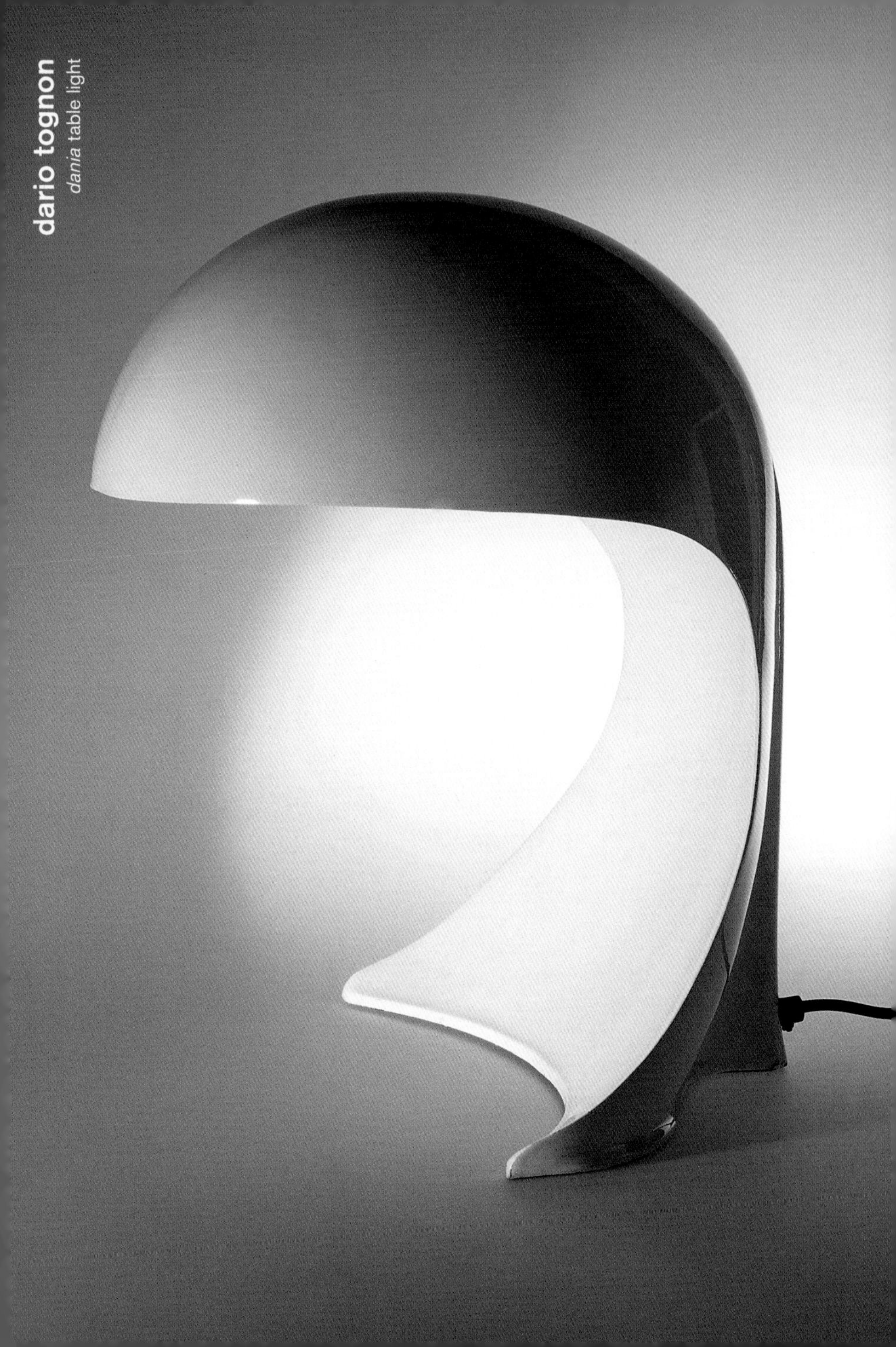

dario tognon
dania table light

One of the central goals of Modern design has been the realization of single-material, single-piece constructions – the idea being that design unity makes manufacturing much more efficient. Both these lighting products could be said to achieve this ideal with their unified constructions. Dario Tognon's *Dania* (1969) rises in an elegant cobra-like sweep of cast aluminum, while Vico Magistretti's *Dalú* (1965) innovatively translates the cantilever into ABS. This latter diminutive yet elegant design can be seen as the lighting equivalent of Verner Panton's groundbreaking single-form, single-material plastic *Panton* chair of 1959–60. (CF/PF)

Ein Ziel der modernen Formgebung war die Umsetzung von Gebrauchsgegenständen, die aus einem einzigen Werkstoff und in einem Stück gefertigt werden konnten, was die Produktion dieser Objekte effizienter machen sollte. Die hier gezeigten Leuchten erfüllten diesen Anspruch: Dario Tognons Tischleuchte *Dania* (1969) in Form einer stilisierten Kobra ist in einem Stück aus Aluminium gegossen. Vico Magistrettis kleine, aber elegante Tischleuchte *Dalú* (1965) aus ABS-Kunststoff übertrug die bahnbrechenden Konstruktionsprinzipien des *Panton* Stuhls (1959–60 von Verner Panton entworfen) – der erste Freischwinger, der in einem Stück aus Kunststoff produziert wurde – auf einen Beleuchtungskörper. (CF/PF)

◁ **Dania table light, 1969**
Enameled cast-aluminum construction, 41 cm high / Konstruktion aus lackiertem Gussaluminium, 41 cm hoch / Fabrication en aluminium moulé et laqué, 41 cm de haut
Artemide, Pregnana Milanese, Italy

△ **Dalú table light, 1965**
ABS construction with cable-management spring, 26 cm high / Konstruktion aus ABS-Kunststoff mit Kabelaufzug, 26 cm hoch / Structure en ABS avec ressort d'enroulement du cordon, 26 cm de haut
Artemide, Pregnana Milanese, Italy

▷ *Design drawing of the Dalú table light, c.1965 / Entwurfszeichnung der Tischleuchte Dalú, ca. 1965 / Dessins de conception de la lampe de table Dalú, vers 1965*

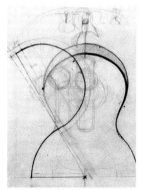

L'un des grands objectifs du Mouvement moderne fut de créer des produits d'une seule pièce et dans un seul matériau, l'idée étant que l'unité de conception rendait la fabrication plus rationnelle et économique. On peut dire que ces deux lampes atteignirent ce but. La *Dania* (1969) de Dario Tognon dresse son élégante courbe d'aluminium moulé, à la façon d'un cobra, tandis que la *Dalú* (1965) de Vico Magistretti développe un audacieux porte-à-faux en ABS. Cette dernière, de petite taille, peut être considérée comme l'équivalent dans le domaine du luminaire, de la fameuse chaise révolutionnaire en un seul matériau, la *Panton* de Verner Panton (1959–60). (CF/PF)

Vico Magistretti's *Telegono* table light (1968) is related to his smaller *Eclisse* bedside light (1965–66) in that it also uses a hemispherical eyelid-like shield to regulate the emitted light. In the *Telegono*, however, this feature is made of opalescent plastic rather than enameled metal as in the earlier *Eclisse*. Available in white, red, black or orange, the *Telegono* employs simple geometric forms to create a strong graphic profile. It was also one of the earliest consumer products to be made of ABS. Artemide also produced a variation of this table light that incorporates a white tray for pens and other items. (CF/PF)

Vico Magistrettis Tischleuchte *Telegono* (1968) ähnelt in der Konstruktion seiner kleineren Nachtischleuchte *Eclisse* (1965–66). Beide Leuchten sind mit einem halbkugelförmigen Lampenschirm ausgestattet, der wie ein Augenlid funktioniert und so die Lichtstärke reguliert. Bei der *Telegono* Leuchte besteht dieser Lampenschirm jedoch nicht aus Metall, sondern aus milchig weißem Kunststoff. Aufgrund ihrer einfachen geometrischen Formgebung erzielt die in Weiß, Rot, Schwarz oder Orange produzierte Leuchte, bei der es sich um eines der frühsten aus ABS-Kunststoff produzierten Konsumgüter handelt, eine starke Präsenz im Raum. Die Firma Artemide produzierte auch eine Variation dieser Leuchte, die mit einer Ablage für Stifte und Ähnliches ausgestattet war. (CF/PF)

La lampe de table *Telegono* (1968) de Vico Magistretti n'est pas sans lien avec sa lampe de chevet, plus petite, *Eclisse* (1965–66) qui fait également appel à une occultation hémisphérique en forme de paupière pour moduler l'éclairage. Dans la *Telegono*, cependant, cet écran est en plastique opalescent et non en métal laqué. Proposée en blanc, rouge, noir et orange, la *Telegono* utilise des formes géométriques simples pour atteindre à un profil très graphique. Ce fut également l'un des premiers produits de grande consommation réalisés en ABS. Artemide en produisait aussi une variante blanche, à vide-poches pour crayons et petits objets. (CF/PF)

△△ *Vico Magistretti working in his studio with the* Telegono, *c.1968 / Vico Magistretti in seinem Büro mit der Tischleuchte* Telegono, *ca. 1968 / Vico Magistretti au travail dans son studio avec la lampe* Telegono, *vers 1968*

△ *Office with* Telegono *table lights, c.1969 / Büro mit Tischleuchten* Telegono, *ca. 1969 / Bureau équipé de lampes Telegono, vers 1969*

▷ ***Telegono* table light, 1968**
ABS Marbon Cycolac plastic base and reflector, 40 cm high / Fuß und Reflektor aus ABS-Marbon-Cycolac, 40 cm hoch / Pied et réflecteur en ABS Marbon Cycolac, 40 cm de haut
Artemide, Pregnana Milanese, Italy

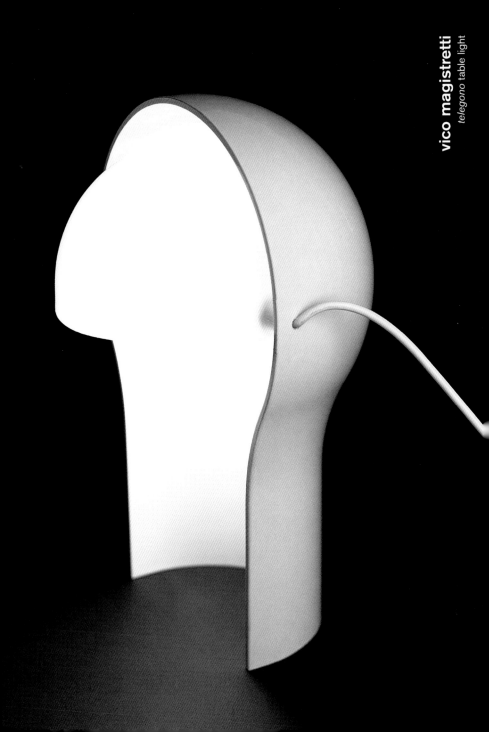

The innovative wave-like form of Vico Magistretti's *Chimera* light (1966) provides the design with its own self-supporting structure. Magistretti later exploited the structural potential of serpentine shapes in molded plastics in the design of furniture, most famously in his *Selene* chair (1969) and *Gaudí* chair (1970). The elegant and undulating single-form acrylic structure of the *Chimera* diffuses and softens the emitted light, while also lending the design a strong sculptural identity. (CF/PF)

Dank ihrer innovativen wellenartigen Formgebung kommen die von Vico Magistretti entworfene Stehleuchte *Chimera* (1966) und ihre kleine Schwester, die Tischleuchte *Mezzochimera* (1966), ohne zusätzliche Stütz- oder Rahmenmontierung aus. Später setzte Magistretti das Potential von solchermaßen profilierten Kunststoffen auch für die Konstruktion von Möbeln ein. Die bekanntesten Beispiele hierfür sind die von ihm entworfenen Stühle *Selene* (1969) und *Gaudí* (1970). Die elegant aus einem einzigen Stück Acryl geformte *Chimera* Leuchte strahlt ein weich gestreutes Licht aus und besitzt eine starke skulpturale Ausstrahlung. (CF/PF)

D'esprit nouveau, la forme en vague de la *Chimera* (1966) de Vico Magistretti est en soi une structure autonome. Magistretti explora plus tard le potentiel structurel des formes sinueuses en plastique moulé dans le mobilier, en particulier dans ses célèbres sièges *Selene* (1969) et *Gaudí* (1970). L'élégante forme ondulée en acrylique moulé d'une seule pièce de la *Chimera* diffuse une lumière douce, tout en affirmant sa forte identité sculpturale. (CF/PF)

vico magistretti
chimera floor light

◁ **Mezzochimera** table light, 1966

Molded opaque acrylic diffuser on enameled metal base, 78 cm high / Diffusor aus gebogenem, opakem Acryl auf Fuß aus lackiertem Metall, 78 cm hoch / Diffuseur en acrylique moulé opaque, sur base métallique laqué, 78 cm de haut
Artemide, Pregnana Milanese, Italy

▽ ◁ *Design sketch of the Chimera light, c.1966 / Entwurfszeichnung der Leuchte Chimera, ca. 1966 / Croquis de conception du lampadaire Chimera, vers 1966*

▽ **Chimera** floor light, 1966

Molded opaque acrylic diffuser on enameled metal base, 180 cm high / Diffusor aus gebogenem, opakem Acryl auf Fuß aus lackiertem Metall, 180 cm hoch / Diffusour en acrylique moulé opaque, sur base métallique laquée, 180 cm de haut
Artemide, Pregnana Milanese, Italy

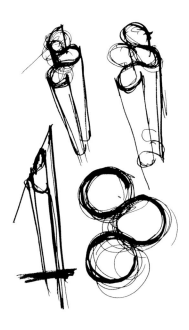

Mario Bellini is one of the most distinguished Italian designers of industrial and domestic products. Always inventive and highly versatile, his design solutions are characterized by a sophisticated sense of form and proportion, a classical restraint, an innate respect for the properties of the materials used and a commitment to practicality. His *Chiara* floor light (1964) for Flos effectively sculpts a single, flat sheet of steel into a column and diffusing hood. (PG)

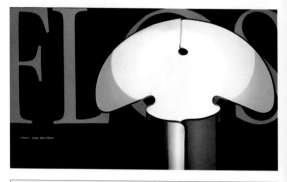

Mario Bellini zählt zu den profiliertesten italienischen Entwerfern im Bereich des Industrie- und Produktdesigns. Die stets innovativen und vielseitig einsetzbaren Produktlösungen zeugen von seinem ausgeprägten Sinn für Formen und Proportionen, seiner Begeisterung für klassische Eleganz, aber auch von Materialgerechtigkeit und Funktionalität. Bei der Stehleuchte *Chiara* (1964), die er für den italienischen Leuchtenhersteller Flos entwarf, gelang es Bellini, aus einem einzigen Stück Stahlblech einen säulenartigen Leuchtenfuß mit integrierter Diffusorhaube zu formen. (PG)

Mario Bellini est l'un des plus remarquables designers italiens de produits industriels et domestiques. Toujours inventives, très variées, ses créations se caractérisent par un sens sophistiqué de la forme et des proportions, une retenue classique, un respect inné pour les propriétés des matériaux utilisés et un souci de praticité. Son lampadaire *Chiara* (1964), pour Flos, est la mise en forme efficace et sculpturale d'une unique feuille d'acier. (PG)

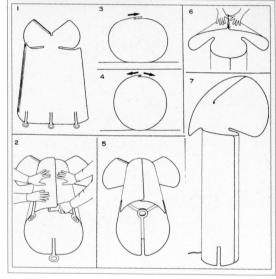

△△ *Flos's advertisement for the* Chiara *floor light, c.1964 / Werbeanzeige von Flos mit Stehleuchte* Chiara, *ca. 1964 / Annonce publicitaire Flos pour le lampadaire* Chiara, *vers 1968*

△ *Diagram showing the construction of the* Chiara *floor light / Schematischer Bauplan für die Stehleuchte* Chiara / *Croquis d'étude technique pour le lampadaire* Chiara

▷ **Chiara floor light, 1964**

Stainless-steel sheet-metal construction with enameled interior, 145 cm high / Konstruktion aus Edelstahl mit lackiertem Innenraum, 145 cm hoch / Structure en feuille d'acier inoxydable, intérieur laqué, 145 cm de haut
Flos, Bovezzo, Italy

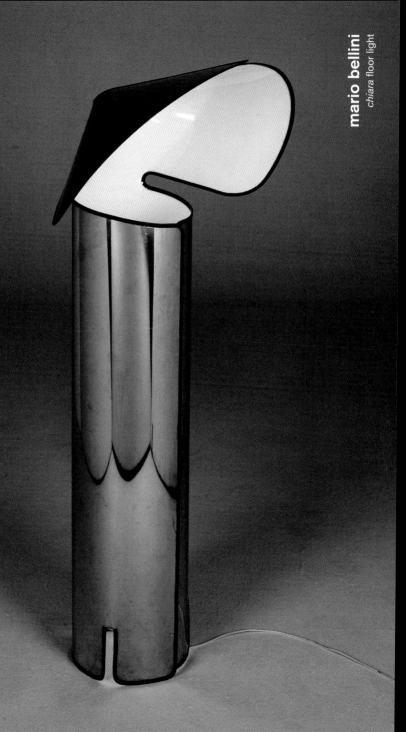

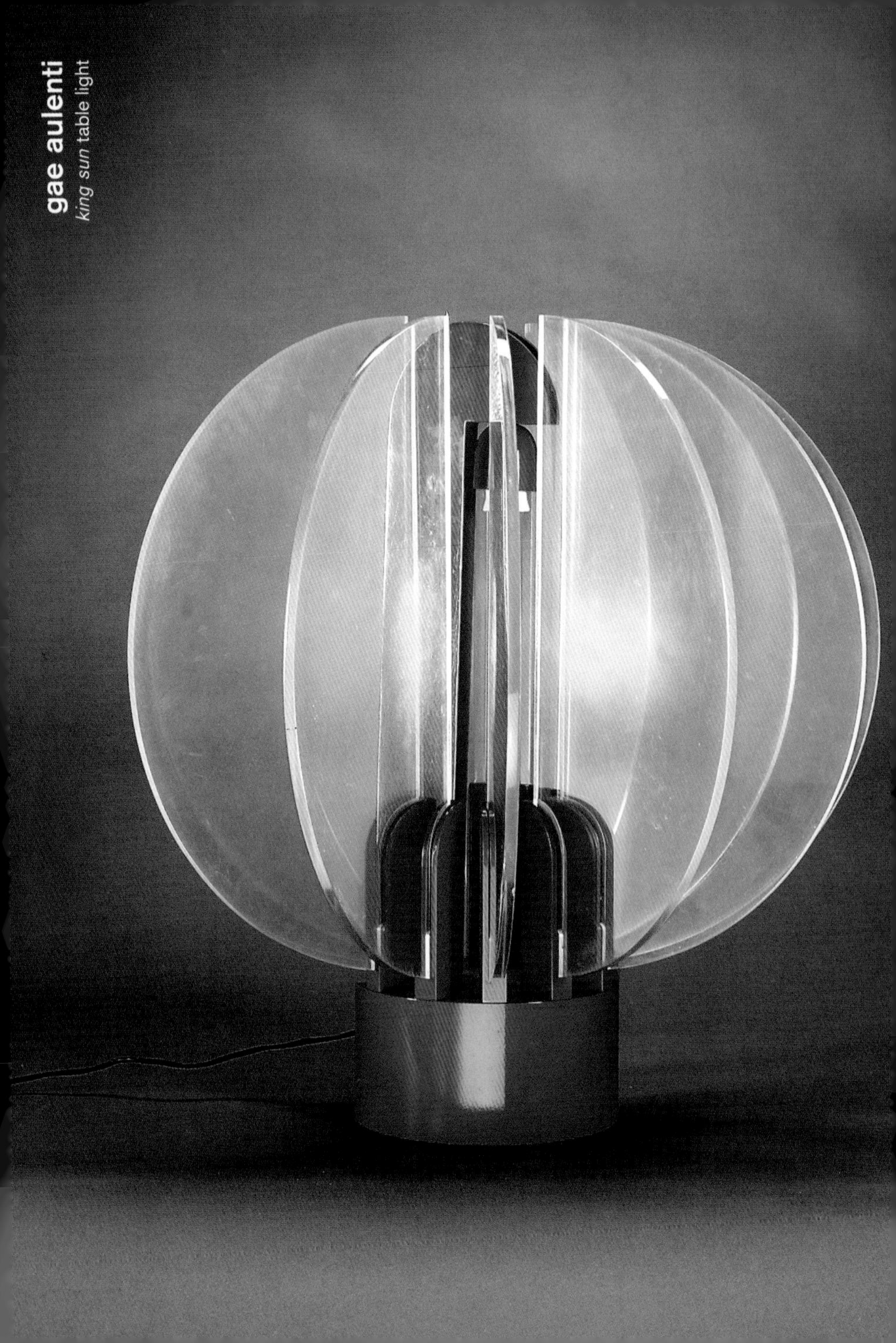

gae aulenti
king sun table light

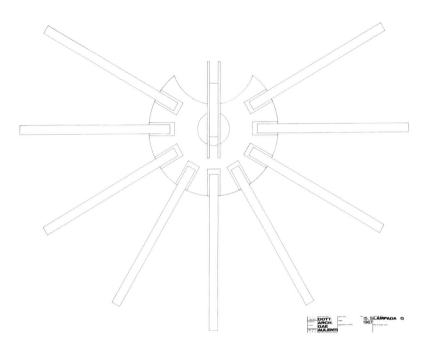

◁ **King Sun table light, 1967**
Enameled metal base with transparent acrylic fins, 72.1 cm high / Fuß aus lackiertem Metall mit transparenten, halbkreisförmigen Acrylscheiben, 72,1 cm hoch / Pied en métal laqué, ailettes en acrylique transparent, 72,1 cm de haut
Kartell, Noviglio, Italy

Design drawing of the King Sun table light, c.1967 / Entwurfszeichnung der Tischleuchte King Sun, ca. 1967 / Esquisse pour la lampe de table King Sun, vers 1967

This imposing light (1967) comprises a series of transparent acrylic fins slotted into an orange-red enameled metal base. The fins radiate from the center, where they contain and conceal the light source that refracts outwards through them. The design might be interpreted as a stylized sun, as its effect when illuminated is of a radiant ball. The bright color situates this design in the age of Pop, just as the use of acrylic sheets calls to mind contemporaneous experiments by avant-garde sculptors. (PG)

Die beeindruckende Tischleuchte *King Sun* (1967) von Gae Aulenti besteht aus einer Reihe von transparenten, halbkreisförmigen Acrylscheiben, die in einem Fuß aus orangerot lackiertem Metall stecken. Die konzentrisch angeordneten Scheiben verdecken die Lichtquelle in der Mitte und leiten das Licht nach außen. Im eingeschalteten Zustand ergibt sich so der Eindruck einer leuchtenden Kugel, die an eine stilisierte Sonne erinnert. Die knallige Farbgebung des Fußes ist typisch für das Design der Pop-Ära, ebenso lässt die Verwendung von Acrylglas an die Experimente zeitgenössischer Avantgarde-Bildhauer denken. (PG)

Cette lampe imposante (1967) est constituée d'ailettes en acrylique glissées dans une base en métal laqué rouge orangé. Elles diffusent la lumière à partir du centre où se dissimule la source lumineuse. L'ensemble peut être interprété comme un soleil stylisé. Une fois allumée, la lampe fait penser à une boule de lumière. Sa couleur vive situe ce projet dans la période Pop, de même que les feuilles d'acrylique rappellent les expérimentations contemporaines de sculpteurs d'avant-garde. (PG)

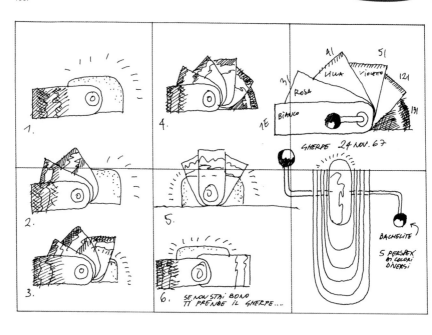

Gherpe floor light, 1967

Translucent curved strips of Plexiglas mounted on a chrome-plated metal frame, adjustable dimensions, 43 cm high (max.) / Transparente, gebogene Plexiglasstreifen auf verchromtem Metallgestell, Größe verstellbar, 43 cm hoch (max.) / Bandes d'acrylique Perspex translucide montées sur une structure chromée, dimensions réglables, 43 cm de haut (max.)
Poltronova, Montale, Italy

▽ Sketch of the Gherpe floor light, c.1967 / Skizze der Bodenleuchte Gherpe, ca. 1967 / Croquis de la lampe à poser Gherpe, vers 1967

Throughout the 1960s and 1970s, the Italian company Poltronova manufactured many of its products according to the precepts of "radical" design. This included a number of lights by Superstudio. Among these, the *Gherpe* floor light from 1967 (the name of a kind of imaginary monster that frightens children) reflects the group's interest in the possible mutations that can arise from repeating the same component in an object, in this case the plastic elements with which the product is transformed and the light intensity adjusted. The repeated element in the *Polaris* series (1969) is the classic white glass sphere that derives from the Bauhaus. (SC)

In den 1960er und 1970er Jahren produzierte die italienische Firma Poltronova viele Entwürfe von Vertretern des Radical Designs, darunter auch mehrere Modelle von Superstudio. In der Leuchte *Gherpe* aus dem Jahr 1969 (der Name stammt von einer Art Ungeheuer, das Kindern Angst einjagt) äußert sich das Interesse der Designgruppe an Variationen, die durch die mehrfache Verwendung ein und desselben Bestandteils in einem Objekt entstehen können. In diesem Modell sind es die Kunststoffstreifen, durch die das Produkt verändert und die Lichtintensität gesteuert werden kann. Bei der Leuchtenserie *Polaris* (1969) stellt die vom Bauhaus-Design abgeleitete klassische weiße Glaskugel das Wiederholungselement dar. (SC)

Tout au long des années 1960 et 1970, la société italienne Poltronova a fabriqué de nombreux modèles conçus par des acteurs du design « radical », dont un certain nombre de luminaires pour Superstudio. Parmi ceux-ci, la lampe *Gherpe* de 1967 (du nom d'un monstre imaginaire qui effraie les enfants) reflète l'intérêt du groupe pour les mutations que peut provoquer la répétition du même composant dans un objet, en l'occurrence des bandeaux de plastique qui permettent de transformer l'aspect de la lampe et de régler l'intensité de l'éclairage. L'élément répétitif de la série *Polaris* (1969) est le classique globe de verre dérivé du Bauhaus. (SC)

△ *Poltronova photograph of Polaris floor lights, c.1969 / Werbefoto von Poltronova mit Stehleuchten Polaris, ca. 1969 / Photographie publicitaire Poltronova pour le lampadaire Polaris, vers 1969*

▷ *Polaris* **table light, 1969**

Marble base, chrome-plated metal frame and spherical glass diffusers, 48 cm high / Sockel aus Marmor, Fuß aus verchromtem Metall, kugelförmige Diffusoren aus Glas, 48 cm hoch / Socle en marbre, structure en métal chromé et diffuseurs sphériques en verre, 48 cm de haut
Poltronova, Montale, Italy

Cespuglio table light, 1968

Satin-finished aluminum base with colored acrylic diffusers, 34 cm high / Fuß aus mattiertem Aluminium mit Diffusoren aus farbigem Acryl, 34 cm hoch / Pied en aluminium satiné, diffuseurs en acrylique de couleur, 34 cm de haut
Harvey Guzzini DH (Design House), Recanati, Italy

Ennio Lucini's *Cespuglio* table light (1968) ranks among the most stunning Italian Pop designs of the late 1960s. Its hauntingly beautiful light effect is achieved through the use of jagged sheets of acrylic. In Italian *cespuglio* means "bush," and certainly this light appears to have been plucked from some psychedelic sci-fi landscape. Available in milky white, yellow, red or green, the *Cespuglio* is a highly innovative composition with a diagrammatic quality that produces a strong sense of three-dimensionality. This type of provocative and experimental product came to define the "golden age" of Italian design between 1968 and 1973. (CF/PF)

Ennio Lucini's Tischleuchte *Cespuglio* (1968) zählt zu den beeindruckendsten Entwürfen des italienischen Pop-Designs der späten 1960er Jahre. Durch die Verwendung von gezackten Acrylscheiben erstrahlt die Leuchte in magischem Licht. Das italienische Wort *cespuglio* bedeutet „Busch", und die Leuchte erweckt tatsächlich den Eindruck, als stamme sie aus einer psychedelischen Science-Fiction-Landschaft. Es handelt sich um einen äußerst innovativen Entwurf, dessen Konturen für eine starke, dreidimensionale Wirkung sorgen. Diese Art von provokativen und zugleich experimentellen Produkten sollte für das „goldene Zeitalter" des italienischen Designs zwischen 1968 und 1973 bestimmend werden. (CF/PF)

La *Cespuglio* (1968) d'Ennio Lucini compte parmi les plus étonnantes créations italiennes pop de la fin des années 1960. Elle est constituée de feuilles d'acrylique déchiquetées à leur extrémité qui offrent d'étranges et magnifiques effets d'éclairage. En italien, *cespuglio* signifie « buisson » et cette lampe semble en effet avoir été cueillie dans une végétation de science-fiction. Disponible en blanc, jaune, rouge ou vert, ce modèle très original présente une qualité graphique qui renforce le sentiment de tridimensionnalité. Ce type de produit provocateur et expérimental illustre « l'âge d'or » du design italien entre 1968 et 1973. (CF/PF)

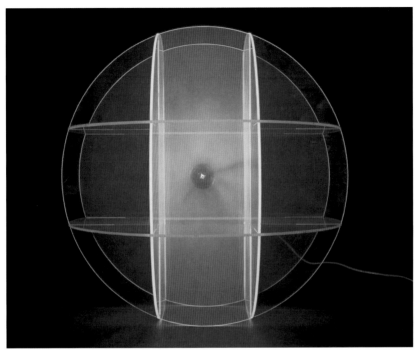

Quasar table light, 1969
Fluorescent methacrylate construction,
80 cm high / Konstruktion aus fluoreszieren-
dem Methacrylat, 80 cm hoch / Structure en
méthacrylate fluorescent, 80 cm de haut
New Lamp, Rome, Italy

Innovations in design are frequently
fueled by advances in technology, and
this Italian light of the late 1960s represents an imaginative response to the
availability of translucent acrylic in large
sheet form. This material shares certain
characteristics with glass, but without
being fragile and thus potentially haz-
ardous. It also has its own distinctive
way of transmitting light, which appears
to pass through it slower than through
glass, allowing it to glow and even fluo-
resce in seemingly magical ways. (PG)

Innovationen im Design werden häufig
von technischem Fortschritt vorange-
trieben. So ist bei der Konstruktion dieser italienischen Leuchte aus den späten 1960er Jahren nach Entwurf von
Gianfranco Fini der damals neu entwickelte Werkstoff Acryl in Plattenform
auf sehr fantasievolle Weise eingesetzt
worden. Acryl hat mit dem Werkstoff
Glas einige Gemeinsamkeiten, ist aber
weniger leicht zerbrechlich und stellt
damit eine kleinere Gefahrenquelle dar.
Überdies wird künstliches Licht von
Acryl anders gebrochen als durch Glas.
Das Licht scheint sich langsamer aus-
zubreiten und verbreitet zudem einen
geheimnisvoll anmutenden, fluoreszie-
renden Schein. (PG)

Les innovations en matière de design
se nourrissent fréquemment de progrès
technologiques et cette lampe italienne
qui date de la fin des années 1960
offre une réponse pleine d'imagination
à l'apparition d'acrylique translucide
en feuilles de grandes dimensions.
Ce matériau partage certaines caractéristiques avec le verre, mais sans sa
fragilité ni sa dangerosité éventuelle.
Il possède également une manière
particulière de transmettre la lumière,
qui semble le parcourir plus lentement
que le verre, créant des effets de
rayonnement et même de fluorescence
qui peuvent paraître magiques. (PG)

The *Rimorchiatore* table light (1967) takes its name from the trailers that can be hitched behind cars to tow a load. It is a highly stylized interpretation of this idea and uses a series of crisp geometric forms serving a variety of functions. Aulenti's fondness for such forms is also evident in the *Ruspa* (1967) – a characteristic Aulenti exercise in pure geometry. Cast in metal, this is at once a substantial object and a sophisticated sculptural concept, in which segmented three-quarter hemispheres serve as shades above the quarter segments that constitute the base. (PG)

Die Tischleuchte *Rimorchiatore* (1967) nach Entwurf von Gae Aulenti in Form eines stark abstrahierten Schleppdampfers ist aus unterschiedlichen, rein geometrischen Körpern zusammengesetzt, die jeweils unterschiedliche Funktionen übernehmen. Aulentis Vorliebe für die geometrische Formgebung kommt auch in ihrer Schreibtischleuchte *Ruspa* (1967) zum Ausdruck. Bei dieser aus Metall produzierten Leuchte handelt es sich um einen markanten Entwurf, der auf einem ausgeklügelten skulpturalen Konzept beruht: Der Lampenschirm ist in Form einer Dreiviertelkugel konstruiert, das „herausgeschnittene" Einviertelkugelsegment bildet den Leuchtenfuß. (PG)

La *Rimorchiatore* (1967) de Gae Aulenti tire son nom des navires remorqueurs à vapeur, dont elle est une interprétation très stylisée. Conjuguant différentes formes géométriques aux lignes dynamiques, elle offre plusieurs fonctions différentes. Le goût d'Aulenti pour ce type de forme est tout aussi évident dans la *Ruspa* (1967), un exercice de pure géométrie caractéristique de son style. En métal moulé, c'est à la fois un objet important et un concept de sculpture sophistiqué dans lequel des formes aux trois-quarts hémisphériques servent d'abat-jour au-dessus du quatrième segment qui constitue la base. (PG)

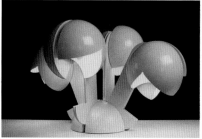

△△ *Ruspa* **desk light, 1967**

Enameled metal base and shades, 58 cm high / Füße und Lampenschirme aus lackiertem Metall, 58 cm hoch / Pied et réflecteurs en métal laqué, 58 cm de haut
Martinelli Luce, Lucca, Italy

△ *Ruspa* **table light, 1969**

Enameled metal base and shades, 55.9 cm high / Fuß und Lampenschirme aus lackiertem Metall, 55,9 cm hoch / Pied et réflecteurs en métal laqué, 55,9 cm de haut
Martinelli Luce, Lucca, Italy

▷ *Rimorchiatore* **table light, 1967**

Enameled cast metal base, opaline blown-glass diffusers, transparent blown glass vase and ashtray, 40 cm high / Fuß aus lackiertem Gussmetall, Diffusor aus mundgeblasenem Opalglas, Vase und Aschenbecher aus transparentem, mundgeblasenem Glas, 40 cm hoch / Base en métal moulé émaillé, diffuseurs en verre soufflé opalescent, vase et cendrier en verre soufflé transparent, 40 cm de haut
Fontana Arte, Corsico, Italy

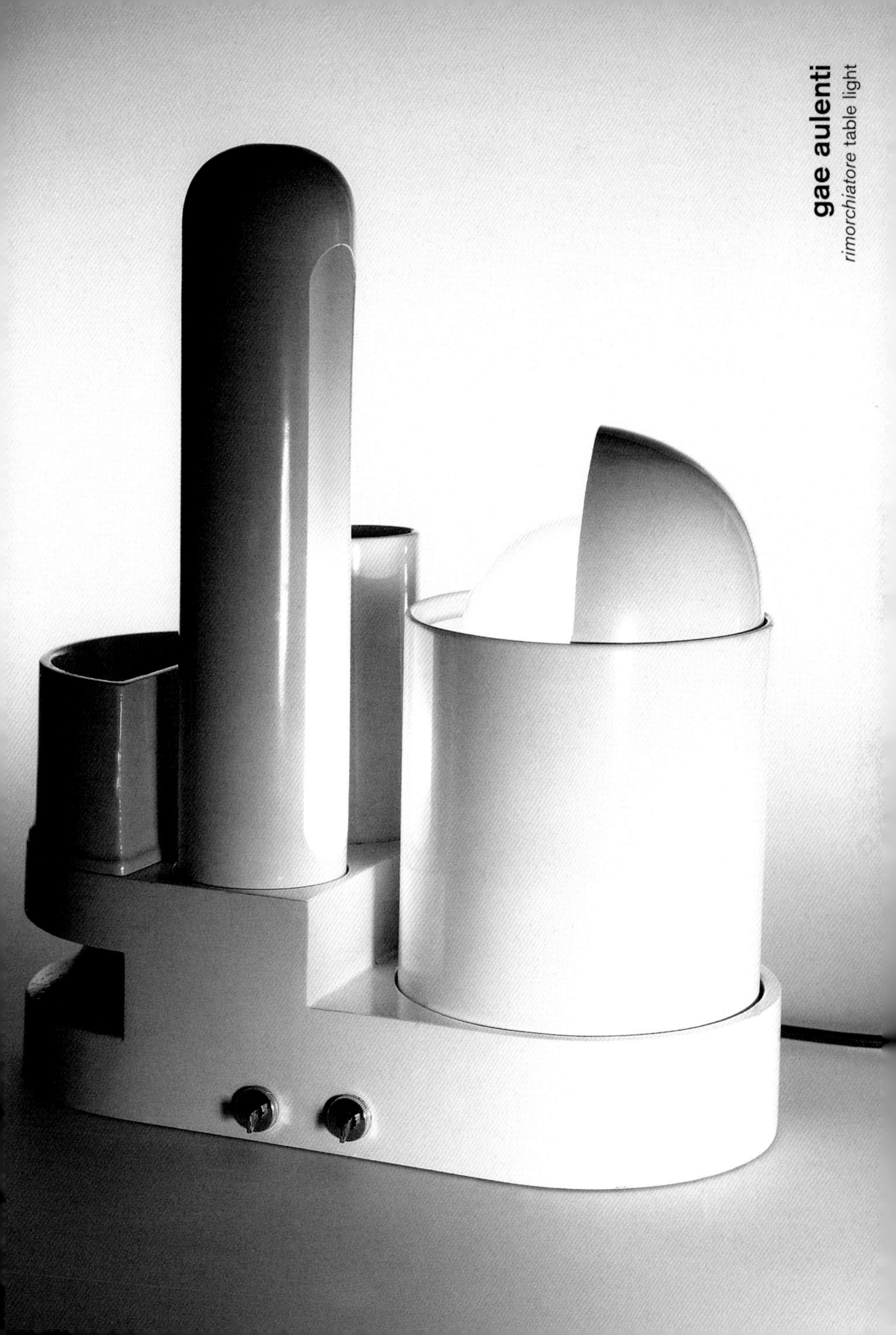

gae aulenti
rimorchiatore table light

With its functional adaptability, esthetic purity and novel forms, the *Flash* lighting system (1968) exemplifies the remarkably forward-looking nature of Joe Colombo's work. The *Flash*'s reflector was originally designed as a horizontal spotlight and with its narrow horizontal slit was inspired by a camera flash unit. The table version featured a dimmer switch on the reflector's stem. The *Flash* system also comprised a series of specially designed mounts and bases that enabled the reflector to be used as a clamp light, desk light, floor light and wall light. (CF/PF)

Mit seiner anpassungsfähigen Funktionalität, seiner ästhetischen Klarheit und neuartigen Formgebung ist das Leuchtensystem *Flash* (1968) beispielhaft für das bemerkenswert fortschrittliche Werk Joe Colombos. Der Reflektor der *Flash* Leuchten, dessen Formgebung von einem alten Blitzlicht inspiriert wurde, war mit seiner schlitzartigen Öffnung ursprünglich nur für die horizontale Nutzung gedacht. Das Leuchtensystem umfasste eine Reihe von speziell entwickelten Montierungen und Leuchtenfüßen, mit deren Hilfe man die Grundversion auch in eine Klemm-, Schreibtisch-, Steh- oder Wandleuchte verwandeln konnte. Die aufrecht stehende Tischversion war zudem mit einem Dimmer ausgestattet. (CF/PF)

Par sa souplesse fonctionnelle, sa pureté esthétique et la nouveauté de ses formes, le système *Flash* (1968) illustre la nature remarquablement novatrice des travaux de Joe Colombo. Le réflecteur *Flash* était à l'origine conçu pour être un spot horizontal dont l'étroite ouverture en forme de fente s'inspirait d'un flash d'appareil photo. La version de table possède un variateur rhéostatique monté sur la tige métallique. Le système *Flash* comprenait également une série de montures et de bases permettant d'utiliser le réflecteur comme lampe à pincer, lampe de bureau, lampadaire et applique. (CF/PF)

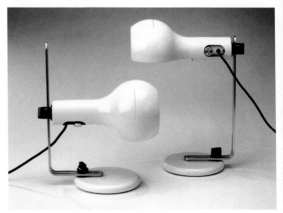

△ **Flash table light, 1968**

Enameled metal base with enameled metal shade and plastic fittings, 38.1 cm high / Füße und Lampenschirme aus lackiertem Metall mit Montierungen aus Kunststoff, 38,1 cm hoch / Base et réflecteur en métal laqué, raccords plastiques, 38,1 cm de haut
O Luce, Milan, Italy

◁ Flash *table light, 1968 – early edition / Tischleuchte* Flash, *1968 – frühe Version / Lampe de table* Flash, *1968 – une des premières éditions*

▷ **Model No. 2206 flash table light, 1968 – re-edition**

Coated aluminum base with sandblasted glass shade, 29 cm high / Fuß aus beschichtetem Aluminium mit Lampenschirm aus sandgestrahltem Glas, 29 cm hoch / Base en aluminium revêtu de plastique, réflecteur en verre sablé, 29 cm de haut
O Luce, Milan, Italy

The *Periscopio* features a flexible plastic joint that enables the light to be placed in virtually any position. It has neither shade nor reflector and the bulb is half-covered with a reflective surface to prevent glare and to increase the intensity of the beam. As well as the classic 1966 *Periscopio*, Stilnovo also produced later variations, including a modified desk light (1968) and a floor light. In 1972, the *Periscopio* was included in the legendary exhibition "Italy: The New Domestic Landscape" at the Museum of Modern Art in New York. (TB)

Die Leuchte *Periscopio* lässt sich durch ein flexibles Kunststoffgelenk in nahezu jede Position bringen. Sie besitzt weder einen Lampenschirm noch einen Reflektor, ihre Glühbirne ist parallel zur Längsachse zur Hälfte verspiegelt, schützt so vor Blendung und verstärkt zusätzlich die Lichtintensität. Neben der klassischen *Periscopio* Leuchte aus dem Jahr 1966 baute Stilnovo später Varianten der Leuchte, darunter eine modifizierte Schreibtischleuchte (1968) sowie eine Stehleuchte. Die *Periscopio* war 1972 in der legendären Ausstellung „Italy: The New Domestic Landscape" im New Yorker Museum of Modern Art vertreten. (TB)

La *Periscopio* est conçue à partir d'un flexible en plastique souple qui permet de l'orienter dans pratiquement toutes les positions. Elle ne possède ni abatjour ni réflecteur mais son ampoule est à moitié recouverte d'un film réflechissant qui diminue l'éblouissement et concentre l'intensité du faisceau lumineux. Stilnovo en produisit ultérieurement d'autres versions, dont une lampe de bureau modifiée (1968) et un lampadaire. En 1972, la *Periscopio* fit partie de la légendaire exposition « Italy : The New Domestic Landscape » du Museum of Modern Art de New York. (TB)

◁ *Periscopio* **desk light, 1968**
Enameled metal and plastic base with rubber joint, 47 cm high (max.) / Fuß aus lackiertem Metall mit flexiblem Kunststoffgelenk, 47 cm hoch (max.) / Pied en métal laqué, flexible en plastique, 47 cm de haut (max.)
Stilnovo, Lainate, Italy

▷ *Photograph showing the full movement of the Periscopio adjustable desk light (this version from 1966) / Foto der verstellbaren Schreibtischleuchte Periscopio mit Darstellung des gesamten Bewegungsradius (Version von 1966) / Photographie montrant les mouvements possibles de la lampe de bureau réglable Periscopio (version de 1966)*

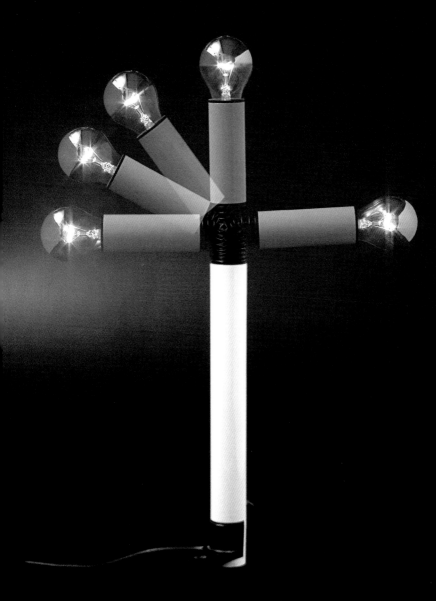

The *Tenagli* floor light, designed in 1969 by Francesco Buzzi Ceriani, is a typical example of the futuristic Pop designs of the late 1960s. Influenced by manned space flight and the first moon landing in the same year, Ceriani gave the light a spherical lampshade, reminiscent of a space helmet with a visor. The two halves of the shade can be set at different angles, allowing variable amounts of light to radiate, thereby creating different effects in a room. The light was manufactured in various heights, first by Francesconi and later by Bieffeplast. (TB)

Die Stehleuchte *Tenagli* (1969), entworfen von dem Designer Francesco Buzzi Ceriani, ist ein typisches Beispiel für das futuristische Pop-Design der späten 1960er Jahre. Beeinflusst von bemannten Flügen in den Weltraum und der ersten Mondlandung im gleichen Jahr, entwarf Ceriani die Leuchte mit dem visierförmigen Lampenschirm in Kugelform. Der Öffnungswinkel der beiden Lampenschirmhälften ist variabel. Je nach Einstellung dringt mehr oder weniger Licht nach außen, wodurch unterschiedliche Lichtwirkungen im Raum entstehen. Die Leuchte wurde zunächst von Francesconi und später von Bieffeplast in unterschiedlichen Höhenvarianten produziert. (TB)

Le lampadaire *Tenagli* conçu en 1969 par Francesco Buzzi Ceriani est un exemple typique des créations Pop futuristes de la fin des années 1960. Influencé par le vol habité par l'homme et le premier alunissage la même année, Ceriani donna à son luminaire un réflecteur sphérique, rappelant un casque de cosmonaute et sa visière. Ses deux moitiés peuvent être positionnées à des angles différents, ce qui permet de contrôler la quantité de lumière émise, et donc de générer différents effets lumineux. Ce lampadaire fut fabriqué de différentes hauteurs, par Francesconi d'abord, puis par Bieffeplast. (TB)

Tenagli floor light, 1969

Enameled metal base and shades, 203 cm high / Fuß und Lampenschirm aus lackiertem Metall, 203 cm hoch / Pied et réflecteurs en métal laqué, 203 cm de haut
Fratelli Francesconi, Roncadelle, Italy (reissued by Bieffeplast, Caselle di Selvazzano, Italy)

The Italian architecture and design cooperative Superstudio was founded in Florence in 1966 by Adolfo Natalini, Cristiano Toraldo di Francia, Roberto and Alessandro Magris, and Piero Frassinelli. Superstudio saw itself as a protest movement against the established architecture and design of the postwar years, which was largely based on the values of the Bauhaus and the International Style. It was part of the anti-design movement, which sought to create a contrast with the "Good Design" of the 1950s and early 1960s. The resemblance of the 1968 *Olook* hanging light to an astronaut's helmet rather than a well-designed piece of lighting equipment is entirely deliberate and very much in keeping with the Superstudio philosophy. (TB)

Die italienische Architektur- und Designkooperative Superstudio wurde 1966 in Florenz von Adolfo Natalini, Cristiano Toraldo di Francia, Roberto und Alessandro Magris sowie Piero Frassinelli gegründet. Superstudio verstand sich als Protestbewegung gegen die etablierte Architektur und das Design der Nachkriegsjahre, das weitgehend auf den Werten des Bauhauses sowie des Internationalen Stils beruhte. Superstudio war Teil der Anti-Design-Bewegung, die im Kontrast zu dem „Guten Design" der 1950er und frühen 1960er Jahre stand. Dass die Hängeleuchte *Olook* (1968) weniger wie eine elegant gestaltete Leuchte wirkt, dafür aber in ihrer Formgebung an einen Astronautenhelm erinnert, ist durchaus gewollt und entspricht der Philosophie von Superstudio. (TB)

L'agence coopérative d'architecture et de design italienne Superstudio fut fondée à Florence en 1966 par Adolfo Natalini, Cristiano Toraldo di Francia, Roberto et Alessandro Magris et Piero Frassinelli. Le Superstudio se voyait comme un mouvement de protestation contre l'architecture et le design établis des années de l'après-guerre, reposant en grande partie sur les valeurs du Bauhaus et du Style international. Il fit partie du mouvement de l'Anti-Design qui cultivait l'opposition au *Good Design* des années 1950 et du début des années 1960. La ressemblance entre la suspension *Olook* (1968) et un casque de cosmonaute est délibérée, tout à fait dans l'esprit de la philosophie de Superstudio. (TB)

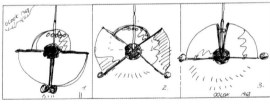

△△ **Olook** hanging light, 1968

Chrome-plated metal mounts with enameled metal shades, 76 cm diameter / Montierungen aus verchromtem Metall mit Lampenschirmen aus lackiertem Metall, 76 cm Durchmesser / Montures en métal chromé et abat-jour en métal laqué, 76 cm de diamètre
Poltronova, Montale, Italy

△ *Sketch of* Olook *hanging light, 1968 / Entwurfszeichnung der Hängeleuchte* Olook, *1968 / Croquis de la suspension* Olook, *1968*

cesare casati & emanuele ponzio

pillola table/floor lights

The vivdly colored *Pillola* lights (1968) were conceived for use in a group, rather as if they were indeed pills that had spilled from a pharmacist's bottle. They are archetypal Pop objects – a domestic design that takes a known form and re-creates it, vastly over-scaled and serving an alternative function. Cesare Casati and Emanuele Ponzio (working as Studio D. A.) have drawn directly on the work of Andy Warhol and Claes Oldenburg, two artists who were instrumental in defining the Pop idea of recontextualizing the banal object and challenging our perceptions. (PG)

Die knallig bunten Leuchten *Pillola* (1968) waren dafür gedacht, in Gruppen aufgestellt zu werden, so als seien es tatsächlich Pillen, die gerade aus einer Tablettendose gefallen sind. Es handelt sich um klassische Pop-Design-Objekte – Gebrauchsgegenstände des alltäglichen Lebens, die auf einer wohlbekannten Form beruhen, diese überdimensional vergrößern und mit einer neuen Funktion belegen. Cesare Casati und Emanuele Ponzio (zusammen gründeten sie das Studio D.A.) wurden bei ihren Entwürfen stark von den Arbeiten der Pop Art Künstler Andy Warhol und Claes Oldenburg beeinflusst, die in ihrem Werk banale Alltagsobjekte in einen neuen Kontext gestellt haben. (PG)

De couleurs vives, les lampes *Pillola* (1968) furent conçues pour une utilisation groupée, un peu comme des gélules tombées d'un flacon de médicaments. Ce sont des objets pop archétypiques, des créations pour la maison qui empruntent une forme connue, la recréent, la redimensionnent pour servir à une autre fonction. Cesare Casati et Emanuele Ponzio (associés sous le nom de Studio D. A.) se sont directement inspirés des œuvres d'Andy Warhol et de Claes Oldenburg, deux artistes qui ont joué un rôle fondamental dans la définition de l'idée pop de recontextualisation des objets banals pour remettre en question nos perceptions. (PG)

◁/▽ *Pillola* **table/floor lights, 1968**
ABS and acrylic construction, 55 cm high /
Konstruktion aus ABS-Kunststoff und Acryl,
55 cm hoch / Corps en ABS et acrylique,
55 cm de haut
Ponteur, Bergamo, Italy

Poltronova publicity photograph showing Sanremo floor light with Mies chairs, c.1969 / Werbefoto der Firma Poltronova mit Stehleuchte Sanremo und Stühlen Mies, ca. 1969 / Photographie publicitaire de Poltronova montrant le lampadaire Sanremo et des sièges Mies, vers 1969

▷ **Sanremo floor light, 1968**

Enameled metal base with enameled aluminum stem and acrylic diffusers, 238.7 cm high / Fuß aus lackiertem Metall mit Schaft aus eloxiertem Aluminium und Diffusoren aus Acryl, 238,7 cm hoch / Pied en métal laqué, fût en aluminium anodisé, diffuseurs en acrylique, 238,7 cm de haut
Poltronova, Montale, Italy

The work of the Italian radical design group Archizoom Associati drew references from popular culture while also mocking the pretensions of "Good Design." Like Archizoom's famous faux leopardskin-covered *Safari* seating unit, designed the same year, the *Sanremo* floor light (1968) playfully incorporates a symbolic element of kitsch in its reference to a palm-tree. The acrylic fronds of this remarkable "tree" light glow at their edges when the light source is turned on, creating an out-of-this-world and subversive rendition of popular imagery. As with their other products, Archizoom's *Sanremo* pointed the way forward to a glamorous new era in design. (CF/PF)

Das Werk der italienischen Designergruppe Archizoom bezog Anregungen aus der Popkultur und ironisierte dabei gleichzeitig die Wertvorstellungen des „Guten Designs". Wie bei Archizooms berühmter mit Leopardenfell-Imitat bezogener Sitzlandschaft *Safari*, die im gleichen Jahr entstand, besitzt die in Form einer Palme gestaltete Stehleuchte *Sanremo* (1968) eine scheinbar kitschige Ausstrahlung. Die Acrylwedel dieses „Baumes" leuchten an ihren Kanten, sobald der Strom eingeschaltet wird, und schaffen so eine außerirdische Atmosphäre, welche die normalen Sehgewohnheiten auf den Kopf stellt. Wie alle Entwürfe von Archizoom war die *Sanremo* Leuchte richtungsweisend und ebnete den Weg für ein glamouröses Design-Zeitalter. (CF/PF)

Les travaux du groupe italien de design radical Archizoom Associati tiraient leurs références de la culture populaire tout en se moquant des prétentions du *Good Design*. Comme les fameux sièges *Safari* d'Archizoom recouverts de faux léopard, conçus la même année, le *Sanremo* (1968) intègre avec humour un élément kitsch symbolique : une référence au palmier. L'arête des palmettes en acrylique de ce remarquable lampadaire-arbre scintille lorsque la source lumineuse est activée, créant une interprétation subversive et quasi surnaturelle d'une image populaire. Comme les autres créations d'Archizoom, le *Sanremo* annonçait pour le design une ère nouvelle, plus sensible au charme. (CF/PF)

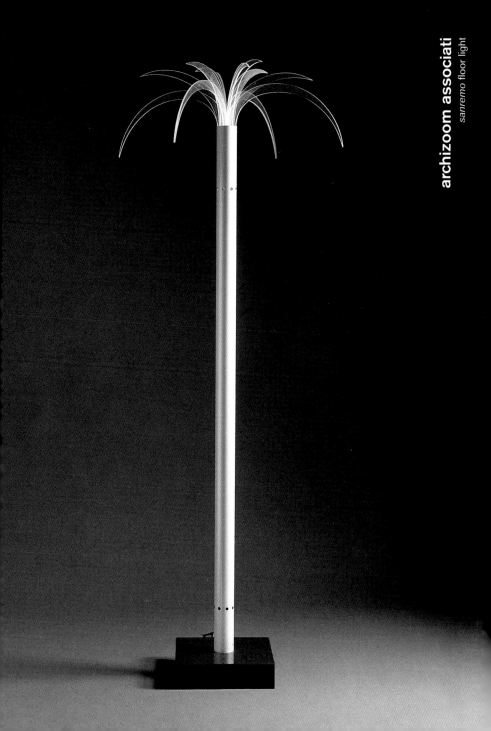

archizoom associati
sanremo floor light

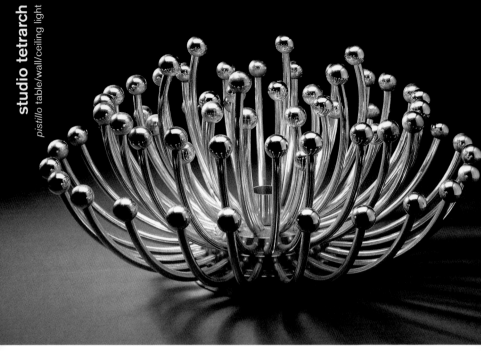

Pistillo table/wall/ceiling light, 1969
Chromed ABS construction, 32 cm high /
Konstruktion aus verchromtem ABS-Kunststoff,
32 cm hoch / Structure en ABS chromé, 32 cm
de haut
Valenti, Cusago, Italy

Studio Tetrarch's *Pistillo* (1969) takes its form and its name from the cluster of pistils at the heart of a flower. In nature each stem carries the pollen that will be spread by insect or wind. In this clever concept the stems and their spherical tips are of chromed or gilded ABS plastic and the highly reflective surfaces serve to multiply and spread the modest light emitted by the one small bulb at the center. The design team responsible for the *Pistillo* has borrowed conceptually as well as formally from nature. (PG)

Form und Name der vom Studio Tetrarch entworfenen Leuchte *Pistillo* (1969) sind den Stempeln im Kelch einer Blüte nachempfunden. In der Natur ist der Stempel Träger des Pollenstaubs, der durch Insekten oder den Wind verbreitet wird. In diesem Entwurf sind die Stempel mit ihren kugelförmigen Enden aus verchromtem oder vergoldetem ABS-Kunststoff gefertigt, und die stark spiegelnden Oberflächen dienen dazu, das von einer einzigen kleinen Glühbirne in der Mitte ausgehende spärliche Licht zu verstärken und zu streuen. Das Designerteam, das für die *Pistillo* Leuchte verantwortlich zeichnet, hat sowohl das Konzept als auch ihre Form der Natur entliehen. (PG)

La *Pistillo* (1969) du Studio Tetrarch tire sa forme et son nom du pistil de la fleur, dans lequel chaque étamine porte le pollen qui sera dispersé par un insecte ou le vent. Dans le cadre de ce concept habile, les étamines et leurs extrémités sphériques sont en plastique ABS chromé ou doré et les surfaces très réfléchissantes multiplient et diffusent la modeste puissance lumineuse de la petite ampoule présente au centre. L'équipe responsable de la *Pistillo* s'est ainsi inspirée formellement et conceptuellement de la nature. (PG)

△ *Original packaging for the* Pistillino *light
(1969), a smaller version of the* Pistillo */ Originalverpackung der Leuchte* Pistillino *(1969),
einer kleineren Version der* Pistillo */ Conditionnement d'origine de la* Pistillino *(1969), version
réduite de la* Pistillo

▽ *Pistillo* **table/wall/ceiling light, 1969**

Gilded ABS construction, 32 cm high / Konstruktion aus vergoldetem ABS-Kunststoff,
32 cm hoch / Structure en ABS doré, 32 cm
de haut
Valenti, Cusago, Italy

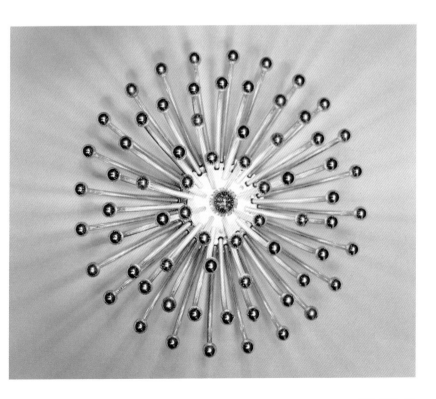

gio ponti
fato wall light

The *Fato* wall light (1965) is based on the rectangular and polygonal wall lights designed as early as 1954 for Gio Ponti's Villa Planchart in Caracas and used again in various interiors, including his proposed Feal house for the 1957 Milan Triennale and the Alitalia offices in New York in 1958. While these early models were made by Arredoluce, the August 1967 issue of *Domus* introduced the wall light illustrated here as a "new" Artemide product intended for serial manufacture. The *Polsino* table lights (1968) exemplify Ponti's ongoing experimentation with lightness, versatility and portability. (VT)

Die Wandleuchte *Fato* (1965) basiert auf den vier- bzw. mehreckigen Wandleuchten, die Gio Ponti bereits 1954 für die Villa Planchart in Caracas entworfen hatte und später in unterschiedlichen Innenräumen immer wieder verwendete, unter anderem auch in seinem Feal-Haus-Modell für die Mailänder Triennale 1957 und im New Yorker Büro von Alitalia 1958. Während die frühen Leuchten von Arredoluce hergestellt wurden, stellte die Zeitschrift *Domus* im August 1967 die hier gezeigte Wandleuchte als „neues" Produkt von Artemide vor. Die Tischleuchten *Polsino* (1968) waren das Ergebnis von Pontis ständigem Bemühen, leichte, vielseitige und tragbare Produkte zu gestalten. (VT)

La lampe *Fato* (1965) s'inspire des appliques rectangulaires et polygonales créées dès 1954 par Gio Ponti pour la villa Planchart à Caracas et utilisées dans de nombreux intérieurs, dont la maison Feal présentée à la Triennale de Milan de 1957 ou les bureaux new-yorkais d'Alitalia en 1958. Alors que ces premiers modèles avaient été fabriqués par Arredoluce, le numéro d'août 1967 de *Domus* présentait l'applique montrée ici comme un « nouveau » produit dont Artemide envisageait la production en série. Les lampes de table *Polsino* (1968) illustrent les expérimentations constantes de Ponti dans le domaine de la légèreté, de la polyvalence et de la mobilité. (VT)

▵▵ **Fato wall light, 1965**
Enameled, welded steel frame and screens, 35.6 cm high / Rahmen und Blenden aus lackiertem, verschweißtem Stahl, 35,6 cm hoch / Cadre et écrans en acier laqué soudé, 35,6 cm de haut
Artemide, Pregnana Milanese, Italy

▵ *Artemide publicity photograph showing* **Fato** *wall light in use* / *Werbefoto von Artemide mit Wandleuchte* Fato / *Photographie publicitaire Artemide montrant l'applique* Fato *en situation*

▷ **Polsino table lights, 1968**
Chrome-plated mounts with plastic diffusers, 38.1 cm high (max.) / Montierungen aus verchromtem Metall mit Diffusoren aus Kunststoff, 38,1 cm hoch (max.) / Support chromé et diffuseurs en plastique, 38,1 cm de haut (max.)
Harvey Guzzini DH (Design House), Recanati, Italy

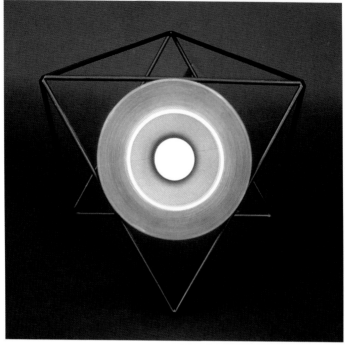

▵ *Poliedra* **lighting system, 1969**

Enameled metal frame and mount with
methacrylate shade / Rahmen aus lackiertem
Metall, Montierung und Lampenschirm aus
Methacrylat / Structure et montures en métal
laqué, abat-jour en méthacrylate
Harvey Guzzini DH (Design House), Recanati,
Italy

▷ *Poliedra* **lighting system, 1969**

Chrome-plated metal frame and mounts with
methacrylate shades / Rahmen aus verchromtem Metall, Montierungen und Lampenschirme
aus Methacrylat / Structure et montures en
métal chromé, abat-jour en méthacrylate
Harvey Guzzini DH (Design House), Recanati,
Italy

Felice Ragazzo was formally trained in
woodworking, and the *Poliedra* lighting
system (1969) stands out as his only
lighting design. Yet it is a perfect example of his devotion to geometry. When
the *Poliedra* – Guzzini's first lighting
system – was exhibited at the 1970
"Eurodomus" exhibition, *Domus* pro-
claimed it a happy solution to modular
lighting. These dramatic, innovative
lights were inspired by theatrical truss-
es, but are infinitely more versatile. The
building blocks for the system are four,
five and eight-faceted units that can be
stacked and joined, while the lights are
clipped onto the sides. (VT)

Felice Ragazzo ist ausgebildeter Möbel-
tischler. Bei dem Leuchtensystem
Poliedra (1969), das seine Vorliebe für
geometrische Formen zeigt, handelt es
sich um sein bislang einziges Leuchtendesign. Als das *Poliedra* System –
das erste von Guzzini produzierte
Leuchtensystem – 1970 in der Ausstellung „Eurodomus" präsentiert wurde,
bezeichnete es die Zeitschrift *Domus*
als gelungene Lösung im Bereich der
Modulleuchten. Das aufregende und
innovative System wurde von Theater-
gerüsten inspiriert, ist in seiner Anwendung jedoch wesentlich vielseitiger. Es
besteht aus vier-, fünf- oder achtseiti-
gen Modulen, die miteinander verbunden werden können. Die Leuchten werden seitlich zwischen das Gestänge
geklemmt. (VT)

Felice Ragazzo était ébéniste de formation, et le système d'éclairage *Poliedra* (1969) fut sa seule création de
luminaire. C'est cependant un parfait
exemple de sa passion de la géométrie. Lorsque le *Poliedra* – premier système d'éclairage édité par Guzzini – fut
présenté à l'exposition «Eurodomus»
en 1970, *Domus* l'annonça comme une
ingénieuse formule d'éclairage modulaire. Ces lampes spectaculaires et
innovantes s'inspiraient des praticables
de théâtre tout en étant beaucoup plus
souples d'utilisation. Les composants
du système sont des éléments à quatre,
cinq et huit facettes qui peuvent être
empilés et assemblés, tandis que les
lampes s'accrochent sur les côtés.
(VT)

felice ragazzo

poliedra lighting system

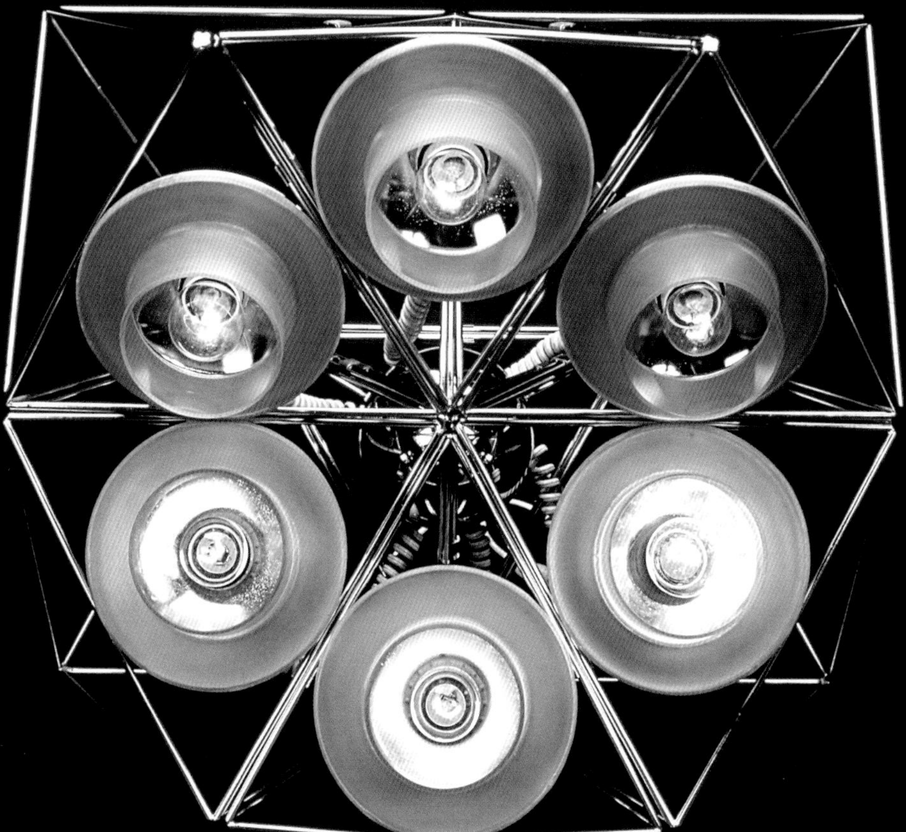

Not since the heroism of early Modernism, when Eileen Gray made a light that consisted of little more than a tube bulb supported by the most minimal metal mounts, have we seen an idea as reductivist in its esthetic as Nanda Vigo's *Linea* floor light (1969). The simplicity of the form is so extreme as to become a powerful statement of faith. Vigo has used polished stainless steel, hard, cold and highly reflective – a perfect choice of material for the cool refinement of this light. (PG)

Seit den heroischen Anfangstagen des Modernismus, als Eileen Gray eine Leuchte schuf, die aus kaum mehr als einer Neonröhre und einer absolut minimalistischen Metallmontierung bestand, wurde keine Leuchte mehr erdacht, die in ihrer Ästhetik so puristisch ist wie die Stehleuchte *Linea* (1969) von Nanda Vigo. Die Einfachheit der Formgebung ist ins Extrem gesteigert und wird dadurch zu einem eindrucksvollen Designbekenntnis. Vigo verwendete polierten Edelstahl, der hart und kalt ist und stark spiegelt – das ideale Material für die kühle Perfektion dieser Leuchte. (PG)

On n'avait pas vu d'approche esthétique aussi minimaliste que celle du lampadaire *Linea* (1969) de Nanda Vigo, depuis les débuts héroïques du modernisme et un luminaire d'Eileen Gray tout juste constitué d'un néon sur des montures de métal très sommaires. La simplicité de cette forme est si extrême qu'elle en devient presque un acte de foi. Vigo a utilisé l'acier inoxydable poli, un matériau dur, froid et hautement réfléchissant, parfaitement adapté au raffinement glacé de ce luminaire. (PG)

Linea floor light, 1969
Stainless-steel base and stem with fluorescent tube, 183 cm high / Fuß und Schaft aus Edelstahl mit Leuchtstoffröhre, 183 cm hoch / Pied et corps en acier inoxydable, tube fluorescent, 183 cm de haut
Arredoluce, Monza, Italy

▷ **Floor light, 1960s**
Stainless-steel base and stem with fluorescent tube / Fuß und Schaft aus Edelstahl mit Leuchtstoffröhre / Pied et corps en acier inoxydable, tube fluorescent
Arredoluce, Monza, Italy (attrib.)

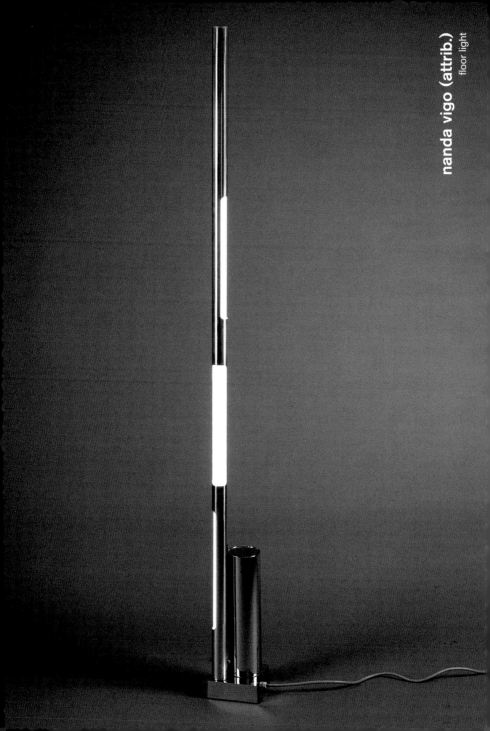

◁ *Model No. 167* hanging light, 1967
PVC sheet construction, 37 cm diameter /
Lampenschirm aus PVC, 37 cm Durchmesser /
Structure en PVC, 37 cm de diamètre
Le Klint, Odense, Denmark

Model No. 169 hanging light, 1969
PVC sheet construction, 47 cm diameter /
Lampenschirm aus PVC, 47 cm Durchmesser /
Structure en PVC, 47 cm de diamètre
Le Klint, Odense, Denmark

While still a student at the Royal Danish Academy of Fine Arts, Poul Christiansen began developing a hand-folded lightshade that incorporated sine curves. In 1967 he presented his design to Le Klint – a Danish manufacturer already well known for its hand-pleated paper light shades. The company's director, Jan Klint, immediately saw its potential and put the *Model No. 167* (1967) into production. Christiansen went on to add a new sine curve hanging light to the Le Klint range on an annual basis, with the model numbers referring to the year of design – i.e., *Model No. 169* was designed in 1969. (CF/PF)

Schon als Student an der Königlichen Dänischen Akademie der Künste hatte Poul Christiansen damit begonnen, einen handgefalteten, auf Sinuskurven basierenden Lampenschirm zu entwickeln. 1967 stellte er seinen Entwurf dem dänischen Hersteller Le Klint vor, der sich mit solchen Papierschirmen bereits einen Namen gemacht hatte. Der Firmenchef Jan Klint erkannte sofort das Potenzial von Christiansens Idee und nahm das *Modell Nr. 167* (1967) in seine Produktion auf. Jedes Jahr gestaltete Christiansen eine neue Sinuskurvenleuchte für Le Klint, wobei sich die Modellnummern jeweils auf das Entstehungsjahr des Entwurfs beziehen. Das *Modell Nr. 169* entstand demnach 1969. (CF/PF)

Tandis qu'il était encore étudiant à l'Académie royale des Beaux-Arts, Poul Christiansen commença à étudier un abat-jour en papier plié à courbes sinusoïdales. En 1967, il présenta son projet à Le Klint, un fabricant danois déjà connu pour ses abat-jour en papier plissé. Le directeur – Jan Klint – en comprit immédiatement le potentiel et lança la fabrication du *Modèle n° 167* (1967). Christiansen ajouta chaque année quelques nouveaux modèles à courbes sinusoïdales à cette gamme, l'année du modèle renvoyant à l'année de conception : le *Modèle n° 1969* a ainsi été dessiné en 1969. (CF/PF)

◁ *Mezzoracolo* table light, 1970

Enameled metal base with opal glass globe,
68 cm high / Fuß aus lackiertem Metall mit
kugelförmigem Lampenschirm aus Opalglas,
68 cm hoch / Pied en métal laqué, globe
en verre opalescent, 68 cm de haut
Artemide, Pregnana Milanese, Italy

▽ *Contemporary interior with* Mezzoracolo
*table light, c.1972 / Zeitgenössisches Interieur
mit Tischleuchte* Mezzoracolo, *ca. 1972 /
Intérieur contemporain avec la lampe de table*
Mezzoracolo, *vers 1972*

▷ *Oracolo* floor light, 1968

Enameled metal base with opal glass globe,
139.7 cm high / Fuß aus lackiertem Metall mit
kugelförmigem Lampenschirm aus Opalglas,
139,7cm hoch / Pied en métal laqué, globe en
verre opalescent, 139,7 cm de haut
Artemide, Pregnana Milanese, Italy

With her characteristic architectural instinct, Gae Aulenti has developed, in the *Oracolo* (1968) and its smaller *Mezzoracolo* counterpart (1970), lights that exude a sense of structural solidity. A white glass sphere sits atop a cylindrical column of enameled metal. The shape is not far removed from that of the bulb that is contained within this sturdy and practical light. Italian design of the 1960s and 1970s comprised numerous strands, from the practical to the poetic and the political. Aulenti's work, however, is seemingly without agenda. It is design that engages with function and with pure form. (PG)

Mit dem für sie typischen Instinkt der Architektin hat Gae Aulenti mit der Stehleuchte *Oracolo* (1968) und ihrem kleineren Gegenstück, der Tischleuchte *Mezzoracolo* (1970), Entwürfe vorgelegt, die in ihrer Ausführung sehr solide wirken. Auf einer zylindrischen Säule aus lackiertem Metall sitzt eine weiße Glaskugel. Die Form lehnt sich stark an die Glühbirne an, die im Inneren dieser massiven und praktischen Leuchte untergebracht ist. Das italienische Design der 1960er und 1970er Jahre umfasste viele Strömungen und war einmal praktisch, dann wieder poetisch oder politisch ausgerichtet. Die Arbeiten von Aulenti scheinen hingegen keine bestimmten Absichten zu verfolgen. Ihr geht es ausschließlich um Form und Funktion. (PG)

Grâce à son instinct architectural très personnel, Gae Aulenti a mis au point, avec l'*Oracolo* (1968) et son pendant plus petit, la *Mezzoracolo* (1970), des lampes qui dégagent une impression de puissance structurelle. La sphère en verre blanc est posée au sommet d'une colonne cylindrique en métal laqué. La forme de ce luminaire robuste et pratique n'est pas très éloignée de celle de l'ampoule qu'il contient. Le design italien des années 1960 et 1970 comprenait de nombreuses tendances, du pratique au politique en passant par le poétique. Le travail d'Aulenti, cependant, semble à part. C'est le design confronté à la fonction et à la forme pure. (PG)

gae aulenti
oracolo floor light

Boalum table/floor/wall light, 1969

Flexible PVC diffuser with metal rings enclosing strand of 25 light bulbs, 200 cm long / 25 miteinander verbundene Torpedolämpchen, umhüllt von Diffusor aus flexiblem PVC mit Metallringen, 200 cm lang / Diffuseur souple flexible en PVC à anneaux métalliques protégeant un cordon avec 25 ampoules, 200 cm de long
Artemide, Pregnana Milanese, Italy

From 1952 onwards Livio Castiglioni worked independently from his brothers and specialized in designing lighting and electronics. His snake-like *Boalum* (1969), designed with Gianfranco Frattini, was inspired by the flexible tube of a vacuum cleaner. Made from a PVC tube strengthened with metal rings and containing a bead-like strand of 25 light bulbs, the *Boalum* can be used as a table, floor or wall light. It is a quintessential Pop design that not only allows user interaction – it can be arranged in an infinite number of shapes – but also challenges preconceptions of what a light should look like. (CF/PF)

Ab 1952 arbeitete Livio Castiglioni unabhängig von seinen Brüdern und spezialisierte sich auf das Entwerfen von Beleuchtungskörpern und Elektrowaren. Seine gemeinsam mit Gianfranco Frattini entworfene, schlangenförmige Leuchte *Boalum* (1969) war inspiriert von dem flexiblen Schlauch eines Staubsaugers. Sie besteht aus einem mit Metallringen verstärkten PVC-Schlauch, in dem ein Draht mit 25 aneinander gereihten kleinen Lampen untergebracht ist. Diese Leuchte ist der Inbegriff des Pop-Designs: Die Benutzer können damit interagieren und sie auf jede nur erdenkliche Weise immer wieder neu arrangieren. Zugleich stellt sie die Vorstellungen darüber, wie eine Leuchte auszusehen hat, völlig auf den Kopf. (CF/PF)

À partir de 1952, Livio Castiglioni se sépara de ses frères pour se spécialiser dans la conception de luminaires et d'appareils électroniques. Sa lampe *Boalum* (1969) de forme serpentine, conçue avec Gianfranco Frattini, s'inspirait du tuyau flexible d'un aspirateur. Composée d'un tube de PVC renforcé d'anneaux de métal qui abrite une sorte de collier avec 25 ampoules, elle peut servir de lampe de table, de sol ou d'applique. C'est un modèle pop par essence qui non seulement permet l'interaction de l'utilisateur – elle peut prendre une infinité de formes – mais remet aussi en question a priori sur ce à quoi doit ressembler une lampe. (CF/PF)

△ ◁ The Boalum *light in a contemporary interior,*
Domus, *March 1972 / Leuchte* Bolaum *in einem
zeitgenössischen Interieur,* Domus, *März 1972 /*
Boalum *dans un intérieur contemporain,*
Domus, *mars 1972*

△ *Photographs showing the assembly of the*
Boalum *light, c.1970 / Fotos mit Anleitung
zum Zusammenbau der Leuchte* Boalum *, ca.
1970 / Photographies de l'assemblage de la*
Boalum, *vers 1970*

◁ *Design drawing of the* Boalum *light from the*
Artemide *catalog, 1970 / Konstruktionszeichnung der Leuchte* Boalum *aus einem Katalog
von* Artemide, *1970 / Dessin de conception de
la* Boalum *dans le catalogue* Artemide, *1970*

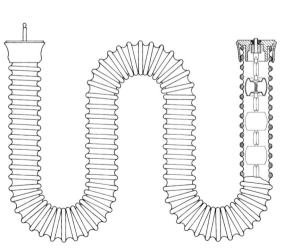

Verner Panton's *SP2* and *SP3* hanging lights (1969) are part of the *Spiral-Lampen* range of designs that were the product of his close collaboration with manufacturer J. Lüber of Switzerland. While Danish designers are generally associated with understatement and a respect for traditional materials, Panton developed an opposite, exploratory visual language that involved the radical exploitation of new materials, notably plastics, and a fearless use of color. These lights are designed to shimmer and to provoke a spirit of fun – they are more for dancing than for reading. (PG)

Verner Pantons Hängeleuchten *SP2* und *SP3* (1969) gehören zur *Spiral-Lampen*-Serie, die aus seiner engen Zusammenarbeit mit dem Schweizer Hersteller J. Lüber hervorging. Während man den dänischen Designern eher Understatement und den Hang zu traditionellen Materialien zuschreibt, entwickelte Panton eine völlig konträre, experimentelle Formensprache, die sich mit der radikalen Verwendung von neuen Werkstoffen, insbesondere Kunststoffen, und dem unerschrockenen Einsatz von Farben verband. Diese Leuchten sollen strahlen und Lebenslust wecken – sie sind mehr fürs Tanzen als fürs Lesen gedacht. (PG)

Les suspensions *SP2* et *SP3* (1969) de Verner Panton font partie de la gamme *Spiral-Lampen* produite en collaboration étroite avec le fabricant suisse J. Lüber. Si l'on associe généralement les designers danois à la discrétion et au respect des matériaux traditionnels, Panton mit au point un langage visuel exploratoire opposé, à partir d'une exploitation radicale des matériaux nouveaux, en particulier des plastiques, et d'un recours sans timidité aucune à la couleur. Faits pour danser plus que pour lire, ces luminaires sont conçus pour créer des effets scintillants et provoquer une excitation joyeuse. (PG)

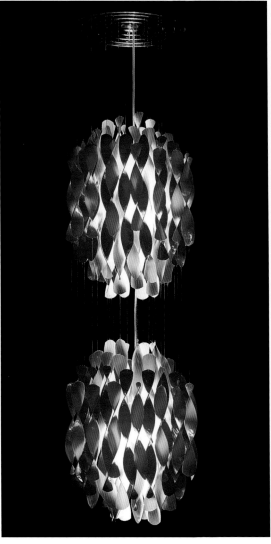

Model No. SP2 Spiral-Lampe hanging light, 1969

Chrome-plated ceiling plate with plastic spiral elements in various colors attached with nylon threads, 150 cm high, 48 cm diameter / Verchromte Deckenplatte mit Spiralelementen aus verschiedenfarbigem Kunststoff, mit Nylonfäden montiert, 150 cm hoch, 48 cm Durchmesser / Rosace en métal chromé, éléments en spirales de plastique de couleurs variées reliés par des fils de nylon, 150 cm de haut, 48 cm de diamètre
J. Lüber, Basel, Switzerland

▷ *Lobby of the Varna Restaurant designed by Verner Panton in Aarhus, Denmark, 1971 – showing* Model No. SP3 Spiral-Lampe *hanging lights / Lobby des Restaurants Varna in Aarhus, Dänemark, gestaltet von Verner Panton, mit* Modell Nr. SP3 Spiral-Lampe, 1971 */ Salon d'accueil du restaurant Varna conçu par Verner Panton à Aarhus, Danemark, éclairé par des suspensions* Modèle n° SP3 Spiral-Lampe, 1971

With the light source hidden behind a dense mass of colored plastic spheres, which consequently lend their tint to the light emanating from within, the 1969 *Kugel-Lampen (Ball Lamp)* range is a variation on a distinctive Verner Panton theme. There is a festive quality to the design, a sense of fun and youthfulness characteristic of the Pop sensibility that Panton explored and expressed so effectively. There is also something appealing in the soft, organic look of this and other Panton lights, an anti-Modernist challenge that found its cinematic expression in certain of the sets for *Barbarella*. (PG)

Mit ihrer hinter einer dichten Masse von farbigen Plastikkugeln verborgenen Lichtquelle und der vom Farbton der Kugeln bestimmten Tönung des Lichts stellt Verner Pantons *Kugel-Lampen*-Serie (1969) die Variation eines für ihn typischen Themas dar. Die Modelle strahlen das Lebensgefühl der Pop-Ära mit der für sie charakteristischen Lebensfreude und Jugendlichkeit aus, die Panton so gut nachzuempfinden und in Szene zu setzen verstand. Die weiche, organische Formgebung dieser und anderer Leuchten von Panton ist durchaus gewollt und kann als anti-modernistisches Statement verstanden werden, das seinen filmischen Ausdruck in einigen Filmsets für *Barbarella* fand. (PG)

verner panton
kugel-lampe typ f and typ h hanging lights

Kugel-Lampe TYP F hanging light, 1969

Plastic ceiling rose with nylon thread and plastic Cellidor spheres, 44 cm diameter / Deckenrosette aus Kunststoff mit Nylonfäden und Kugeln aus Cellidor-Kunststoff, 44 cm Durchmesser / Rosace de plafond en plastique, fils de nylon et sphères en plastique Cellidor, 44 cm diamètre
J. Lüber, Basel, Switzerland

▷ **Kugel-Lampe TYP H hanging light, 1969**

Metal mounts with nylon thread and plastic Cellidor spheres, 44 cm diameter / Metallmontierung mit Nylonfäden und Kugeln aus Cellidor-Kunststoff, 44 cm Durchmesser / Montures en métal, fils de nylon, sphères en plastique Cellidor, 44 cm de diamètre
J. Lüber, Basel, Switzerland

◁ *Publicity photograph showing a variation of the* Kugel-Lampe, *c.1970 / Werbefoto mit einer Variante der* Kugel-Lampe, *ca. 1970 / Photographie publicitaire présentant une variante de* Kugel-Lampe, *vers 1970*

Avec sa source lumineuse dissimulée au sein d'une masse de sphères en plastique de couleur qui teintent la lumière diffusée, la gamme des *Kugel-Lampen* (lampes-boules) de 1969 est une variante sur un thème cher à Verner Panton. On y trouve ce design festif, ce sens du plaisir et de la jeunesse caractéristiques de la sensibilité pop qu'il explora et exprima avec tant d'efficacité. Tout aussi séduisante est l'allure organique, pleine de douceur de cette lampe et d'autres modèles de Panton, défis antimodernistes qui trouvèrent leur expression cinématographique dans certains des décors de *Barbarella*. (PG)

Designed in 1969, Panton's *VP Globe* hanging light was a quintessential product of the 1960s. The globe form and Space-Age character of the design owe much to the legacy of the *Apollo* missions that proved so rich a source of imagery in all areas of design from the mid-1960s. The acrylic sphere – in itself a clever innovation – contains a series of shallow chromed and enameled reflector disks that cleverly multiply and diffuse the light. Originally produced for the "Visiona 2" exhibition at the 1970 Cologne Furniture Fair, the *VP Globe* was later modified for serial production. This later design was known as the *Panto Lamp*. (PG)

Verner Pantons 1969 entworfene Hängeleuchte *VP Globe* ist eine Designikone der 1960er Jahre. Die Kugelform und das Space-Age-Design sind eindeutig beeinflusst von den *Apollo*-Missionen, die ab Mitte der 1960er Jahre die Formensprache der gesamten Designwelt so sehr bereicherten. Die Acrylkugel, an sich schon eine intelligente Innovation, enthält eine Reihe von leicht gewölbten, verchromten und lackierten Reflektorscheiben, die das Licht vervielfachen und streuen. Die ursprünglich für die Ausstellung „Visiona 2" auf der Kölner Möbelmesse 1970 produzierte Leuchte wurde später für die Serienfertigung modifiziert. Dieses spätere Modell ist als *Panto Lamp* bekannt geworden. (PG).

Dessinée en 1969, la suspension *VP Globe* de Verner Panton est un produit qui résume les années 1970. Sa forme de globe et le caractère spatial de sa conception doivent beaucoup aux missions Apollo qui constituèrent une riche source iconographique pour le design du milieu des années 1960. La sphère en acrylique – en soi une brillante nouveauté – contient une série de disques réflecteurs concaves, laqués et chromés, qui diffractent judicieusement la lumière. Produite à l'origine pour l'exposition « Visiona 2 » à la Foire du meuble de Cologne de 1970, la *VP Globe* fut ultérieurement modifiée pour la production en série. Ce dernier modèle était connu sous le nom de *Panto Lamp*. (PG)

△△ **VP Globe** hanging light, 1969

Acrylic sphere with chrome-plated and enameled metal reflector disks and fittings, 50 or 60 cm diameter / Acrylkugel mit Reflektorscheiben und Montierungen aus verchromtem und lackiertem Metall, 50 oder 60 cm Durchmesser / Sphère en acrylique, disques réflecteurs et pièces de montage en métal laqué et chromé, 50 ou 60 cm de diamètre
Louis Poulsen Lighting, Copenhagen, Denmark

△ *Fritz Hansen publicity photograph showing 1-2-3 Series chairs with VP Globe hanging light, 1970s / Werbefoto der Firma Fritz Hansen mit Stühlen aus der Serie* System 1-2-3 *und Hängeleuchte* VP Globe, *1970er Jahre / Publicité Fritz Hansen montrant les sièges de la gamme* System 1-2-3 *accompagnés de la suspension* VP Globe, *années 1970*

▷ *Panto Lamp* hanging light, 1977

Acrylic sphere with chrome-plated and enameled metal reflector disks and fittings, 50 cm diameter / Acrylkugel mit Reflektorscheiben und Montierungen aus verchromtem und lackiertem Metall, 50 cm Durchmesser / Sphère en acrylique, disques réflecteurs et pièces de montage en métal laqué et chromé, 50 cm de diamètre
Louis Poulsen Lighting, Copenhagen, Denmark

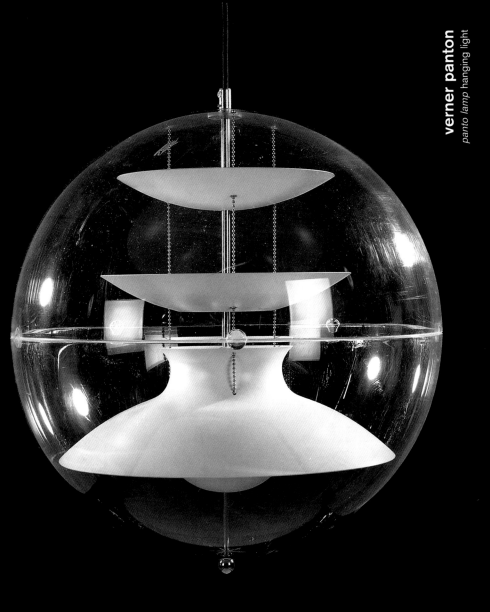

Sergio Asti's *Profiterole* light (1968) and Guy de Rougement's *Nuage* light (1970) are typical examples of Pop Design. The *Profiterole*, shaped like a huge bowl filled with that indulgent confection, is made of fiberglass. The upper and lower sections of the light, which can be used as either a table or a floor light, are held together by a black rubber ring. Guy de Rougemont's aptly named *Nuage* (Cloud), which hovers on the boundaries between a functional lamp and an *objet d'art* that also provides artificial light, was produced only in a limited edition of ten copies. (TB)

Sowohl die Leuchte *Profiterole* von Sergio Asti (1968) als auch die Leuchte *Nuage* (1970) von Guy de Rougemont sind typische Beispiele des Pop-Designs. Die *Profiterole* Leuchte in Form einer riesigen, mit italienischen Profiteroles gefüllten Schüssel besteht aus Fiberglas. Ober- und Unterteil der Konstruktion, die sowohl als Tisch- wie auch als Bodenleuchte verwendet werden kann, sind durch einen schwarzen Gummiring miteinander verbunden. De Rougemonts Entwurf *Nuage* in Form einer leuchtenden Wolke ist nur in einer limitierten Auflage von zehn Exemplaren angefertigt worden. Mit verschwimmen die Grenzen zwischen einer funktionalen Leuchte und einem beleuchtenden Kunstobjekt. (TB)

La *Profiterole* de Sergio Asti (1968) et le *Nuage* de Guy de Rougemont (1970) sont des exemples typiques de Pop Design. *Profiterole*, en forme de coupe remplie de profiteroles à l'italienne, est en fibre de verre. Les deux parties, supérieure et inférieure, de la lampe, qui peut être posée sur une table ou au sol, sont maintenues ensemble par un anneau en caoutchouc noir. La lampe *Nuage* de Guy de Rougemont, qui hésite entre la lampe fonctionnelle et l'objet d'art qui émettrait un éclairage, n'a été produite qu'en édition limitée à dix exemplaires. (TB)

Model No. 640 *Profiterole* table/floor light, 1968

Fiberglass with black rubber ring, 60 cm diameter / Konstruktion aus Fiberglas mit schwarzem Gummiring, 60 cm Durchmesser / Fibre de verre, anneau de caoutchouc noir, 60 cm de diamètre
Martinelli Luce, Lucca, Italy

▷ ***Nuage* table/floor light, 1970**

Plastic construction, 50.9 cm high / Konstruktion aus Kunststoff, 50,9 cm hoch / Structure en plastique, 50,9 cm de haut
Galerie Xiane et Eric Germain, Paris, France (produced in a limited edition of 10)

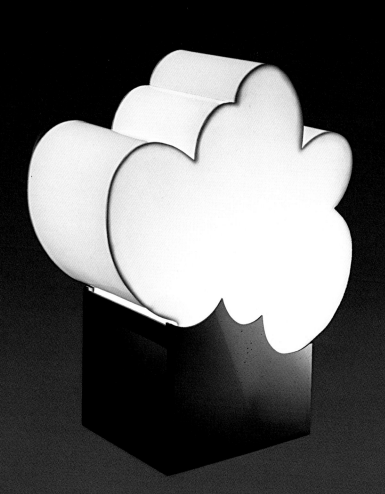

For years the *Model No. 12919 Cobra*
table light (1962) was misattributed to
Gio Ponti. It was in fact designed by
Angelo Lelli, founder of Arredoluce, the
company that manufactured the *Cobra*.
As in Lelli's innovative range of mini
spotlights, the *Cobra* features a spherical magnetic adjustable shade, which
permits easy yet accurate angling of the
light. The transfomer housed in its base
also allows it to be used with low-voltage, high-intensity tungsten-filament
bulbs. This unusual and highly sculptural product was featured in *Domus* magazine in 1965. (CF/PF)

Die Tischleuchte *Modell Nr. 12919
Cobra* (1962) wurde lange Zeit fälschlich Gio Ponti zugeschrieben. Tatsächlich stammt der Entwurf zu dieser
Leuchte von Angelo Lelli, von dessen
Firma Arredoluce sie auch gefertigt
wurde. Wie die innovative Serie seiner
Ministrahler ist dieses Modell mit einem
beweglichen, magnetischen Kugel-
schirm ausgestattet, so dass der Lichtstrahl exakt ausgerichtet werden kann.
Der im Fuß untergebrachte Transformator ermöglicht die Verwendung von
Niedervolt-Wolframbirnen mit hoher
Leuchtkraft. 1965 wurde diese ungewöhnliche und ausgesprochen skulpturale Leuchte in der Zeitschrift *Domus*
vorgestellt. (CF/PF)

Pendant des années, la lampe *Modèle
n° 12919 Cobra* (1962) fut attribuée
à tort à Gio Ponti. Elle avait en fait été
dessinée par Angelo Lelli, fondateur
d'Arredoluce, la société qui fabriquait
ce modèle. Comme les lampes de sa
très novatrice gamme de mini-spots, la
Cobra dispose d'un abat-jour sphérique
aimanté qui autorise un réglage facile
et précis de l'orientation du faisceau.
Le transformateur dissimulé dans le
socle lui permet d'utiliser des lampes
basse tension à filament de tungstène.
Ce produit inhabituel et très sculptural
a été présenté dans le magazine
Domus en 1965. (CF/PF)

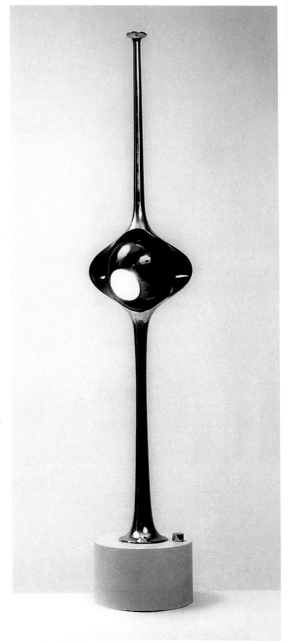

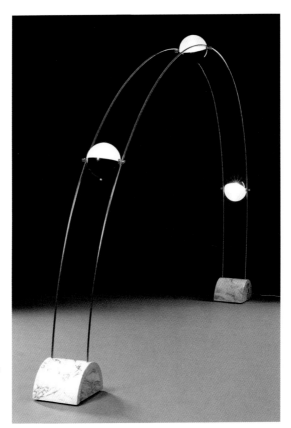

◁ **Model No. 12919 Cobra table light, 1962**

Enameled metal base housing transformer with chrome-plated brass stem and magnetic adjustable metal shade, 62 cm high / Fuß aus lackiertem Metall mit eingebautem Transformator, Schaft aus verchromtem Messing mit verstellbarem, magnetischem Lampenschirm aus Metall, 62 cm hoch / Base en métal laqué contenant le transformateur, tige en laiton chromé, abat-jour métallique aimanté réglable, 62 cm de haut
Arredoluce, Monza, Italy

▷ **Ponte floor light, 1971**

Marble bases with chrome-plated metal mounts and Lexan plastic diffusers, 380 cm wide (max.) / Füße aus Marmor mit Bogenarmen aus verchromtem Metall und Diffusoren aus Lexan-Kunststoff, 380 cm breit (max.) / Bases en marbre, arcs en métal chromé, diffuseurs en plastique Lexan, 380 cm de large (max.)
Sormani, Arosio, Italy

The Gruppo ARDITI studio's sculptural *Ponte* floor light (1971) epitomizes the contesting nature of early 1970s Italian design. The light, whose name means "bridge," functions more as a *presenza* (presence) than as a functional lighting solution. The height of the arch can be adjusted by moving the marble bases either closer together or further apart. By offering a measure of user interaction, the *Ponte* has a *grado di libertà* (degree of liberty) that is further enhanced by its spherical plastic diffusers, which can be pivoted in order to provide flexible light positioning. (CF/PF)

In der skulpturalen Stehleuchte *Ponte* (1971) der Gruppo ARDITI kommen die unterschiedlichen Ansätze im italienischen Design der 1970er Jahre deutlich zum Ausdruck. Das „Brücke" benannte Modell hat mehr von einer *presenza* (Präsenz) als von einem funktionellen Beleuchtungskörper. Die Höhe des Bogens variiert, je nachdem, in welcher Entfernung voneinander man die beiden Marmorfüße aufstellt. Die *Ponte* Leuchte erlaubt ihrem Besitzer also einen gewissen *grado di libertà* (Spielraum), der durch die drehbaren, kugelförmigen Kunststoffdiffusoren und die damit verbundene Möglichkeit, den Lichtstrahl nach Belieben auszurichten, noch vergrößert wird. (CF/PF)

Sculptural, le lampadaire *Ponte* (1971) de Gruppo ARDITI incarne la nature contestataire du design italien du début des années 1970. Ce projet – dont le nom signifie *le pont* – fonctionne davantage comme une « présence » que comme une solution d'éclairage fonctionnel. La hauteur de l'arc peut être modifiée en rapprochant ou éloignant les bases en marbre. Grâce à cette interaction, le *Ponte* offrait un *grado di libertà* (degré de liberté) renforcé par ses diffuseurs sphériques en plastique, qui pouvaient pivoter pour moduler l'orientation des faisceaux lumineux. (CF/PF)

achille castiglioni & pio manzù
parentesi suspended pole light

Throughout his long career, Achille Castiglioni proved himself arguably the most intelligent creator of lights of the past 50 years. The *Parentesi* (1970), developed from an idea first explored by Pio Manzù, well exemplifies Castiglioni's particular genius at finding new possibilities for lighting design while employing the utmost economy of means. The *Parentesi* allows total flexibility of height and angle, using the simple device of a spot in a pivoting mount held by a sliding bracket on a taut vertical wire. The kit comprises just seven pieces. (PG)

Im Lauf seiner langen Karriere hat Achille Castiglioni bewiesen, dass er als intelligentester Leuchtendesigner der letzten fünfzig Jahre gelten kann. Die Leuchte *Parentesi* (1969), die auf einer Idee von Pio Manzù aufbaut, ist ein gutes Beispiel für sein besonderes Talent als Designer neuartiger Beleuchtungskörper, die er aus einfachsten Materialien und Formen entwickelte. Die *Parentesi* Leuchte erlaubt vollkommene Flexibilität in Bezug auf Höhe und Neigung und kommt dabei mit einem einfachen Strahler in einer drehbaren Fassung aus, die von einer höhenverstellbaren Montierung an einem vertikal gespannten Draht gehalten wird. Der gesamte Bausatz besteht aus nur sieben Teilen. (PG)

Tout au long de sa carrière, Achille Castiglioni s'est montré probablement le plus brillant créateur de luminaires de ces cinquante dernières années. La *Parentesi* (1970), mise au point à partir d'une idée initialement explorée par Pio Manzù, illustre bien son génie particulier pour trouver de nouvelles formules d'éclairage dans la plus grande économie de moyens. La *Parentesi* permet une souplesse totale d'inclinaison et de hauteur grâce à un simple spot fixé à une monture pivotante, retenu par une fixation en forme de parenthèse coulissant sur un fil vertical tendu. L'ensemble compte sept pièces seulement. (PG)

Flos advertisement featuring the Parentesi *light, c.1972 / Werbeanzeige von Flos für die Leuchte* Parentesi, *ca. 1972 / Annonce publicitaire Flos pour la lampe* Parentesi, *vers 1972*

▷ *Parentesi* **suspended pole light, 1970**

Steel cable, enameled metal tube with elastomer head, 400 cm long (cable max.) / Drahtseil, Rohr aus lackiertem Metall mit Leuchtenfassung aus Elastomer, 400 cm lang (Seil max.) / Câble d'acier, tube de métal laqué, tête en élastomère, 400 cm de long (câble max.)
Flos, Bovezzo, Italy

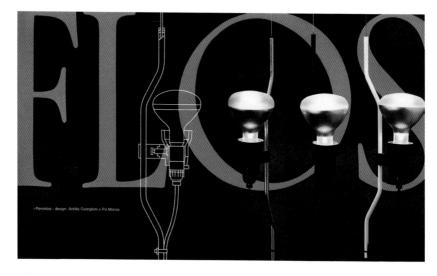

-Parentesi- design: Achille Castiglioni e Pio Manzù

Available in either a black or white enameled finish, the *Alogena* (1970) was among the first lighting products intended for domestic use that incorporated a halogen bulb. Designed as a system, the *Alogena* came either in floor, wall or ceiling versions and featured a height-adjustable diffuser that could be tilted into the required direction. Now marketed by O Luce under the name *Colombo*, it was a High-Tech functional design that reflected its designer's futuristic vision for flexible, multi-purpose living environments. (CF/PF)

Die mit schwarzer oder weißer Lackierung erhältlichen Leuchten *Alogena* (1970) gehörten zu den ersten Beleuchtungskörpern für den Wohnbereich, die mit einer Halogenlampe bestückt waren. Das System bestand ursprünglich aus Boden-, Wand- und Deckenleuchten, die mit einem in Höhe und Richtung verstellbaren Diffusor ausgestattet waren. In ihrem funktionalen Hightech-Design kommt Joe Colombos futuristische Vision von flexiblen Mehrzweckwohnräumen zum Ausdruck. Heute wird das Programm von O Luce unter dem Namen *Colombo* vertrieben. (CF/PF)

Proposée en finition laquée noire ou blanche, la lampe *Alogena* (1970) est l'un des premiers appareils d'éclairage domestique utilisant une ampoule halogène. Conçue comme un système, l'*Alogena* existait en lampadaire, applique ou suspension et bénéficiait d'un diffuseur à hauteur réglable inclinable dans la direction voulue. Aujourd'hui commercialisée par O Luce sous le nom de *Colombo*, sa conception fonctionnelle et son esprit high-tech illustrent la vision futuriste de son designer qui imaginait des cadres de vie totalement modulables. (CF/PF)

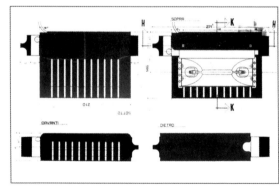

△△ **Model no. 761 Alogena wall light, 1970**

Enameled metal mount with chrome-plated metal stem and enameled metal diffuser, 40 cm high / Montierung aus lackiertem Metall mit Schaft aus verchromtem Stahlrohr, Diffusor aus lackiertem Metall, 40 cm hoch / Monture en métal laqué, tige en métal chromé, diffuseur en métal laqué, 40 cm de haut
O Luce, Milan, Italy

△ *Design drawing of the* Alogena *light, c.1970 / Konstruktionszeichnung der Leuchte* Alogena, *ca. 1970 / Dessin de conception de la lampe* Alogena, *vers 1970*

***Alogena* suspended ceiling light, 1970**

Enameled metal mount with chrome-plated
metal stem and enameled metal diffuser, 60 or
90 cm drop / Montierung aus lackiertem Metall
mit Schaft aus verchromtem Stahlrohr, Diffusor
aus lackiertem Metall, 60 oder 90 cm lang /
Monture en métal laqué, tige en métal chromé,
diffuseur en métal laqué, 60 ou 90 cm de
hauteur
O Luce, Milan, Italy

In 1969 Max Sauze designed a monumental lighting fixture for the Palais des Congrès in Aix-en-Provence. The *Cassiopé* (c.1970) represents a smaller version of that fixture, and of the 20 lights Sauze designed was the largest to go into production. Jean-Pierre Vitrac's *Lampe Fleur* (1970), also sculptural, was originally designed as a low-cost plastic light for the garden. Each petal element was wired individually, allowing them to be lit (or not), as desired. The petals could be configured vertically, at a 45° angle or even layered horizontally, one on top of each other. Verre Lumière manufactured the light in metal rather than in the plastic that Vitrac had originally intended. (VT)

1969 entwarf Max Sauze für das Palais des Congrès in Aix-en-Provence einen monumentalen Beleuchtungskörper. Die Hängeleuchte *Cassiopé* (ca. 1970) ist eine kleinere Version davon, jedoch die größte der von Sauze gestalteten zwanzig Leuchten, die in Serie produziert wurden. Jean-Pierre Vitracs ebenfalls skulpturale Tisch- und Stehleuchte *Lampe Fleur* (1970) war eigentlich als billige Kunststoffleuchte für den Garten gedacht. Die Blütenelemente waren einzeln verkabelt, so dass sie nach Belieben ein- bzw. ausgeschaltet werden konnten. Die Blütenblätter konnten vertikal in einem Winkel von 45° oder sogar horizontal übereinander angeordnet werden. Verre Lumière fertigte die Leuchte jedoch aus Metall statt aus dem von Vitrac vorgesehenen Kunststoff. (VT)

Lampe Fleur table/floor light, 1970
Chrome-plated metal base and shades, 121,9 cm high / Fuß und Lampenschirme aus verchromtem Metall, 121,9 cm hoch / Pied et abat-jour en métal chromé, 121, 9 cm de haut
Verre Lumière, Paris, France

▷ Lampe Fleur *table/floor light partially closed* / Tisch-/Stehleuchte Lampe Fleur, *teilweise geschlossen* / La lampe à poser Lampe Fleur, *partiellement refermée*

◁ *Cassiopé* **hanging light, c. 1970**
Aluminum, 63.5 cm drop / Konstruktion aus Aluminium, 63,5 cm lang / Structure en aluminium, 63,5 cm de haut
Self-Production and later manufactured by Atrow (Atelier Robert Weil), Aix-en-Provence, France

En 1969, Max Sauze avait conçu un énorme lustre pour le Palais des congrès d'Aix-en-Provence. La *Cassiopée* (vers 1970) en est une version réduite, et la plus importante des vingt luminaires dessinés par ce designer à avoir été éditée. La *Lampe Fleur* (1970) de Jean-Pierre Vitrac, également sculpturale, fut au départ conçue pour être fabriquée en plastique et était destinée au jardin. Chaque « pétale » pouvait s'allumer individuellement et prendre une position verticale, à 45° ou même horizontale. Verre Lumière préféra fabriquer ce modèle en métal. (VT)

isao hosoe
hebi table light

While searching for new ideas and materials in the late 1960s, the Japanese designer Isao Hosoe was looking around an electrical goods shop in Milan when he came across a new type of flexible tube. The tube, designed to be used to carry electrical cables, was the inspiration for his *Hebi* table light (1970). Like a snake, the light winds its way upward to a reflector which can be turned through 360° for absolute flexibility. Since 1970, the *Hebi* has been manufactured by the Italian company Valenti, and so far more than 200,000 examples have been sold worldwide. (TB)

Auf der Suche nach neuen Ideen und Werkstoffen stieß der japanische Designer Isao Hosoe Ende der 1960er Jahre in einem Mailänder Elektrowarengeschäft auf neuartige flexible Röhren für Elektroinstallationen, von denen er sich zu seiner Tischleuchte *Hebi* (1970) – seinem nach eigenen Angaben wohl bekanntesten Entwurf – inspirieren ließ. Wie eine Schlange windet sich die Leuchte in die Höhe und ist durch ihren um 360° drehbaren Reflektor in ihrer Handhabung absolut flexibel. Die *Hebi* Leuchte wird seit 1970 von der italienischen Firma Valenti produziert, und bislang sind mehr als 200 000 Exemplare weltweit verkauft worden. (TB)

Tout en cherchant des idées et des matériaux nouveaux à la fin des années 1960, le designer japonais Isao Hosoe découvrit par hasard chez un électricien milanais un nouveau type de tube souple. Conçu pour protéger des câbles électriques, il est la source d'inspiration de sa lampe de table *Hebi* (1970). Tel un serpent, elle se dresse pour se terminer par un réflecteur qui pivote à 360°. Depuis 1970, la *Hebi* est fabriquée par la société italienne Valenti et plus de deux cent mille exemplaires en ont été vendus dans le monde. (TB)

"*Hebi* was born from a kind of ready-made, functional assembly operation, from already existing elements."

„Die *Hebi* ist als eine Art Readymade in einem funktionalen Montagevorgang aus vorhandenen Elementen entstanden."

« *Hebi* est née d'une sorte de ready-made, d'une opération d'assemblage fonctionnel d'éléments existants. »

– Isao Hosoe

Drawing of the Hebi *table light, by Milo Manara, c.1970 / Tischleuchte* Hebi, *gezeichnet von Milo Manara, ca. 1970 / Dessin de la lampe de table* Hebi, *par Milo Manara, vers 1970*

▷ ***Hebi* table light, 1970**

Flexible techno-polymer covered arm with revolving aluminum reflector, 70 cm high (max.) / Flexibler, mit Technopolymer überzogener Arm, drehbarer Reflektor aus lackiertem Aluminium, 70 cm hoch (max.) / Bras souple gainé de techno polymère, réflecteur pivotant en aluminium laqué, 70 cm de haut (max.)
Valenti, Cusago, Italy

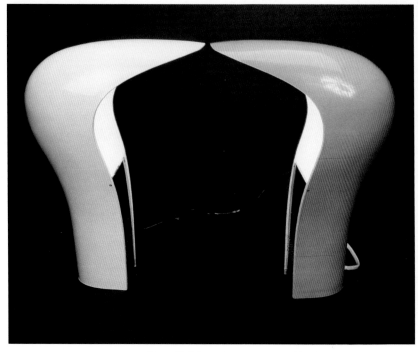

Pelota table light, 1970

ABS construction, 33 cm high / Konstruktion
aus ABS-Kunststoff, 33 cm hoch / Corps en
ABS, 33 cm de haut
Lamperti, Robbiate, Italy

▷ **Model No. 615 table light, 1970**

Enameled metal base and shade, 30.5 cm high /
Fuß und Lampenschirm aus lackiertem Metall,
30,5 cm hoch / Base et abat-jour en métal
laqué, 30,5 cm de haut
Martinelli Luce, Lucca, Italy

As its name suggests, the *Pelota* table light (1970) was inspired by the wooden or woven-reed scoops used in the traditional Basque ball game. Made of injection-molded ABS, Studio D. A.'s design was mass-produced at low cost and widely distributed in the United States, where literally thousands were sold. In contrast, Elio Martinelli's *Model No. 615* table light (1970), which shares a similar cantilevered form, was a much more expensive product to manufacture. While not as well known as his *Serpente* (1965) or *Cobra* (1968) table lights, the *Model No. 615* is an elegant product solution whose design is unmistakably Italian. (CF/PF)

Die Tischleuchte *Pelota* (1970) wurde, wie schon der Name sagt, von dem traditionellen baskischen Ballspiel bzw. den dazugehörigen Holz- oder Korbschlägern inspiriert. Die vom Studio D. A. entworfene, aus Spritzguss-ABS-Kunststoff gefertigte Leuchte war ein kostengünstiges Massenprodukt, das in den Vereinigten Staaten große Verbreitung fand und in vielen tausend Exemplaren verkauft wurde. Elio Martinellis Tischleuchte *Modell Nr. 615* (1970), die eine ähnliche Kragform aufweist, war hingegen ein sehr viel kostspieliger herzustellendes Produkt. Auch wenn sie nicht so bekannt wurde wie seine Tischleuchten *Serpente* (1965) oder *Cobra* (1968), ist *Modell Nr. 615* eine elegante Erscheinung mit unverkennbar italienischer Provenienz. (CF/PF)

Comme son nom le suggère, la lampe de table *Pelota* (1970) s'inspire des chisteras d'osier tressé ou de bois de la pelote basque. Fabriquée en ABS moulé par injection, cette création de Studio D. A. fut produite en grande série à bas prix et vendue à des milliers d'exemplaires aux États-Unis. Par contraste, le *Modèle n° 615* (1970) de lampe de table d'Elio Martinelli, qui présente de même une forme en porte-à-faux, était beaucoup plus coûteuse à réaliser. Bien que moins connu que ses lampes de table *Serpente* (1965) ou *Cobra* (1968), le *Modèle n° 615* est un produit élégant au design incontestablement italien. (CF/PF)

nanda vigo
golden gate floor light

These two designs from 1970 are of a striking simplicity. Yet both have an insistent presence. Somehow they seem closer to the work of certain minimalist sculptors than to the principles of Functionalism from which they might at first glance be presumed to derive. They date from a period in which Carl André, Dan Flavin and Donald Judd were investigating the symbolic potential of sculptures reduced to the most basic of components – fluorescent strips, bricks, metal blocks or boxes. It is perhaps relevant that each light has a name with a conceptual, architectural association – *Golden Gate* and *Utopia*. (PG)

Diese beiden Leuchtenmodelle aus dem Jahr 1970 sind von bestechender Einfachheit und besitzen dennoch eine starke Präsenz. In gewisser Weise scheinen sie dem Werk bestimmter minimalistischer Bildhauer näher zu stehen als den Prinzipien des Funktionalismus, dem man sie vielleicht auf den ersten Blick zuschreiben möchte. Sie stammen aus einer Zeit, in der Carl André, Dan Flavin und Donald Judd das symbolische Potenzial von auf das absolut Wesentliche – Leuchtstoffröhren, Ziegel, Metallblöcke oder -gehäuse – reduzierten Skulpturen auszuloten versuchten. Es kommt vielleicht nicht von ungefähr, dass beide Leuchten Namen tragen, die an architektonische Konzepte denken lassen: *Golden Gate* und *Utopia*. (PG)

Ces deux modèles de l'année 1970 sont d'une simplicité frappante, tout en affirmant une présence marquée. D'une certaine façon, ils semblent plus proches de l'œuvre de certains sculpteurs minimalistes que des principes fonctionnalistes auxquels, au premier regard, il devraient pourtant se rattacher. Ils datent d'une période pendant laquelle Carl André, Dan Flavin et Donald Judd étudiaient le potentiel symbolique de sculptures réduites à leurs composants les plus essentiels – tubes fluorescents, briques, dalles ou boîtes de métal. Il n'est pas inintéressant de noter que chaque lampe possède un nom à connotation architecturale et conceptuelle : *Golden Gate* et *Utopia*. (PG)

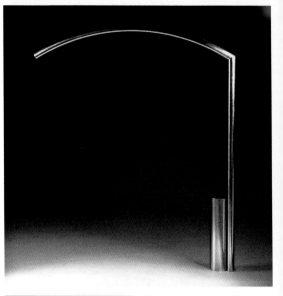

Golden Gate floor light, 1970
Chrome-plated tubular metal stem and arm enclosing fluorescent tube with weighted base housing transformer, 241 cm high / Schaft und Arm aus verchromtem Metallrohr, integrierte Leuchtstoffröhre, beschwerter Fuß mit Transformator, 241 cm hoch / Support tubulaire et bras en métal chromé, contenant un tube fluorescent, base lestée contenant le transformateur, 241 cm de haut
Arredoluce, Monza, Italy

◁ *Arredoluce publicity photograph of* Golden Gate *floor light, c.1970 / Werbefoto von Arredoluce mit Stehleuchte* Golden Gate, *ca. 1970 / Photographie publicitaire Arredoluce du lampadaire* Golden Gate, *vers 1970*

▷ **Utopia table light, 1970**
Tubular stainless-steel frame encasing fluorescent tubes on stainless-steel feet, 50 cm high / Rahmen aus Edelstahl mit eingefassten Leuchtstoffröhren auf Füßen aus Edelstahl, 50 cm hoch / Cadre tubulaire en acier inoxydable contenant des tubes fluorescents, pieds en acier inoxydable, 50 cm de haut
Arredoluce, Monza, Italy

nanda vigo
utopia table light

ettore sottsass
cometa floor light

"My idea … is … to design keeping as near as possible to the anthropological state of things, which, in turn, is to be as near as possible to the need a society has for an image of itself."

„Meine Vorstellung … ist … mich im Design so eng wie möglich an das anthropologische Wesen der Gegenstände zu halten und damit dem Bedürfnis der Gesellschaft nach einem Bild von sich selbst so nahe wie möglich zu kommen."

«Mon idée … est de rester aussi près que possible de l'état anthropologique des choses, qui, à son tour, est aussi près que possible du besoin d'une société d'avoir une image de soi.»

– Ettore Sottsass

▷ *Cometa* floor light, 1970
Methacrylate diffuser on enameled metal base, 210 cm high / Diffusor aus Methacrylat auf Fuß aus lackiertem Metall, 210 cm hoch / Diffuseur en méthacrylate sur base en métal laqué, 210 cm de haut
Poltronova, Montale, Italy

◁ *Interior showing* Cometa *floor light, c.1970 / Interieur mit Stehleuchte* Cometa*, ca. 1970 / Intérieur montrant le lampadaire* Cometa*, vers 1970*

Ettore Sottsass is more than a designer. He is a thinker, a philosopher and an influential *agent provocateur*. While he has proved himself exceptionally skillful in creating objects that perfectly serve their prime practical function – in the case of the *Cometa* floor light (1970), to offer various lighting options within a room – he is acutely conscious of the possibility of investing designs with an extra dimension, as metaphors for existence. It is Sottsass the shaman who has created this modern totem and endowed it with a special, quasi-mystical aura. (PG)

Ettore Sottsass ist mehr als ein Designer. Er ist Denker, Philosoph und einflussreicher *agent provocateur* zugleich. Obwohl er es außerordentlich gut versteht, Objekte zu schaffen, die ihren primären praktischen Zweck perfekt erfüllen – etwa mehrere Beleuchtungsvarianten in einem Raum zu ermöglichen, wie im Fall der Stehleuchte *Cometa* (1970) –, ist ihm immer daran gelegen, seinen Entwürfen eine zusätzliche Dimension zu geben, sie als existenzielle Metaphern zu gestalten. Es ist Sottsass der Schamane, der diesen modernen Totem geschaffen und ihm eine eigene, gewissermaßen mystische Aura verliehen hat. (PG)

Ettore Sottsass est plus qu'un designer. C'est un penseur, un philosophe et un influent «agent provocateur». S'il s'est révélé extrêmement talentueux dans la création d'objets répondant à leur fonction pratique primaire – pour le lampadaire *Cometa* (1970), offrir différents modes d'éclairage – il s'attache à investir ses projets d'une dimension supplémentaire, qui est une métaphore de son existence. Ainsi, c'est Sottsass le chaman qui a créé ce totem moderne et lui a insufflé une aura particulière, quasi mystique. (PG)

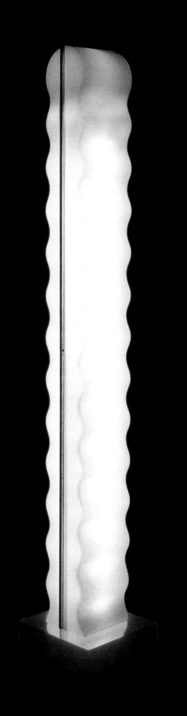

Inventing new forms for traditional objects and finding design solutions that also have a distinct presence as totemic artifacts seems to come naturally to the talented and inspired Ettore Sottsass. He breathes a lyrical quality into the things he creates, each one hinting at ideas way beyond the mere serving of a practical function. At a lighting conference in which he participated in the 1970s, others addressed the technical aspects of light design. Sottsass's approach was first to reflect on the mystery and magic of light itself. (PG)

Dem talentierten und ideenreichen Ettore Sottsass scheint es leicht zu fallen, traditionelle Objekte in neue Formen zu kleiden und Designlösungen zu finden, die zugleich eine starke skupturale Präsenz besitzen. Er verleiht den Dingen, die er schafft, eine emotionale Ausstrahlung, die auf weit über die praktische Funktion hinausgehende Ideen verweist. Während die anderen Teilnehmer einer einschlägigen Fachkonferenz in den 1970er Jahren über die technischen Aspekte des Beleuchtungsdesigns sprachen, war es Sottsass wichtiger, zunächst über das Geheimnis und den Zauber des Lichts zu reflektieren. (PG)

Inventer des formes nouvelles pour des objets traditionnels et des solutions conceptuelles qui assurent une présence forte à des artefacts totémiques semble être naturel chez le talentueux et très inspiré Ettore Sottsass. Il insuffle une qualité lyrique à ce qu'il crée, chaque objet illustrant des idées qui vont bien au-delà de la simple réponse à une fonction pratique. Lors d'une conférence sur l'éclairage à laquelle il participait dans les années 1970, alors que d'autres traitaient des aspects pratiques du design de luminaires, son approche consistait surtout à ètudier le mystère et la magie de la lumière elle-même. (PG)

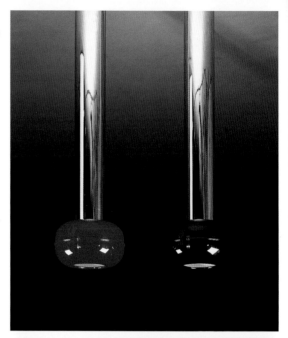

△△ *Mefistole* ceiling light, 1970

Chrome-plated tubular metal stem with enameled metal shade, 109.5 cm high / Montierung aus verchromtem Metallrohr mit Lampenschirm aus lackiertem Metall, 109,5 cm hoch / Tige tubulaire chromée et abat-jour en métal laqué, 109,5 cm de haut
Stilnovo, Lainate, Italy

△ *Bruco* floor/table light, 1970

Chrome-plated metal frame with methacrylate shade enclosing fluorescent tube, 12 cm high / Montierung aus verchromtem Metall, Lampenschirm aus Methacrylat mit innen liegender Leuchtstoffröhre, 12 cm hoch / Structure en métal chromé, cache en méthacrylate sur tube fluorescent, 12 cm de haut
Design Centre (Poltronova), Agliana, Italy

***Bruco* ceiling light, 1970**

Chrome-plated metal frame with methacrylate
shade enclosing fluorescent tube, 103 cm drop /
Montierung aus verchromtem Metall, Lampenschirm aus Methacrylat mit innen liegender
Leuchtstoffröhre, 103 cm lang / Structure en
métal chromé, cache en méthacrylate sur tube
fluorescent, 103 cm de haut
Design Centre (Poltronova), Agliana, Italy

▽ *Interior showing Ettore Sottsass's* Mobili
Grigi *collection for Poltronova, including* Bruco
*lights, 1970 / Zeitgenössisches Interieur mit
Möbeln aus der von Ettore Sottsass für Poltro-
nova entworfenen* Mobili Grigi *Kollektion und*
Bruco *Leuchten, 1970 / Intérieur contemporain
équipé des* Mobili Grigi *d'Ettore Sottsass pour
Poltronova, et des luminaires* Bruco, *1970*

Gaetano Pesce was and remains a willfully provocative voice in Italian design. He sees the subversion of convention as an expression of freedom and as something to explore. Pesce has experimented with materials and forms. His designs are among the most exuberant and challenging to emerge from the Anti-Design movement. Ever playful, while passionately committed to his ideas, he has turned his attention to the *Moloch* floor light (1970–71) and to the question of scale. Rather than redesign a successful existing concept, he has simply scaled it up to four times the originally intended size, turning the conventional into the disconcerting. (PG)

Gaetano Pesce war und bleibt eine bewusst provokante Stimme in der italienischen Design-Szene. Konventionen aufzubrechen, ist für ihn Ausdruck der Freiheit und der Neugierde des Entdeckens. Er experimentierte mit Werkstoffen und Formen und seine Entwürfe zählen zum Überschwänglichsten und Provokantesten, das aus der Anti-Design-Bewegung hervorgegangen ist. Spielerisch, dabei immer leidenschaftlich seine Ideen verfolgend, wendete er bei der Stehleuchte *Moloch* (1970–71) seine Aufmerksamkeit der Frage der Dimension zu. Statt ein erfolgreiches Konzept zu überarbeiten, vergrößerte er es einfach auf das Vierfache seiner ursprünglichen Dimension und entwickelte damit aus dem Konventionellen etwas Verwirrendes. (PG)

Gaetano Pesce fut et reste l'une des voix les plus insolentes du design italien. Il voyait, dans la subversion des conventions, l'expression de la liberté et d'une authentique curiosité. Il s'est livré à des nombreuses expérimentations sur les matériaux et les formes, et ses créations figurent parmi les plus exubérantes et les plus audacieuses du mouvement de l'Anti-Design. Toujours ludique, passionnément engagé dans la défense de ses idées, il s'intéresse, avec à la lampe *Moloch* (1970–71), au problème de l'échelle. Plutôt que de redessiner un produit existant et réussi, il l'a simplement agrandi à quatre fois ses dimensions d'origine, conférant à cet objet conventionnel une présence déconcertante. (PG)

Contemporary interior with "oversized" Moloch *floor light, 1970s / Zeitgenössisches Interieur mit „überdimensionaler" Stehleuchte* Moloch, *1970er Jahre / Intérieur contemporain, montrant la lampe géante* Moloch, *années 1970*

▷ *Moloch* floor light, 1970–71

Enameled metal base and shade with metal arms. Arms: 230 and 312 cm long / Fuß und Lampenschirm aus lackiertem Metall, Gelenkarme aus Metall. Arme: 230 und 312 cm lang / Socle et abat-jour en métal laqué avec bras en métal. Bras : 230 et 312 cm de large **Bracciodiferro**, Genoa, Italy

Best known for their iconic inflatable *Blow* chair, Jonathan de Pas, Donato d'Urbino & Paolo Lomazzi have consistently designed flexible yet stylish product solutions for over four decades. Their *Multipla* lighting range (1970), which included table, floor, wall and ceiling options, incorporated a dish-like reflector that could be horizontally angled on its chrome-plated frame, which itself could be vertically adjusted to enable multi-directional light positioning. Like other lighting products manufactured by Stilnovo, the *Multipla* is functionally innovative while also possessing a high object integrity derived from the exquisite detailing of its engineering.
(CF/PF)

Jonathan de Pas, Donato d'Urbino und Paolo Lomazzi, die vor allem durch ihren zur Design-Ikone avancierten aufblasbaren Sessel *Blow* berühmt wurden, haben mehr als vier Jahrzehnte lang flexible und dennoch stilvolle Produktlösungen vorgelegt. Ihre Beleuchtungsserie *Multipla* (1970), bestehend aus Tisch-, Steh-, Wand- und Hängeleuchten, umfasst einen tellerähnlichen Reflektor, der auf einem verchromten Rahmengestell horizontal gedreht werden kann. Das Gestell selbst ist vertikal verschiebbar, sodass der Lichtstrahl vielfältig ausgerichtet werden kann. Wie so manches von Stilnovo hergestellte Produkt ist auch die *Multipla* funktional innovativ und erfüllt durch die hohe Qualität der technischen Ausführung alle Ansprüche an die Designintegrität. (CF/PF)

Surtout connus pour leur célèbre siège gonflable *Blow*, Jonathan de Pas, Donato d'Urbino et Paolo Lomazzi proposent avec constance depuis plus de quarante ans des créations à la fois de style brillant et d'utilisation ingénieuse. Leur gamme de luminaires *Multipla* (1970), qui regroupe des versions pour table, sol, murs et plafond, comporte un réflecteur en forme d'assiette qui peut être placé à l'horizontale sur son support chromé, lui-même réglable à la verticale pour offrir de multiples possibilités d'orientation. Comme d'autres luminaires fabriqués par Stilnovo, la *Multipla* est fonctionnellement innovante tout en constituant un objet de grand intérêt, marqué par le raffinement exceptionnel de sa fabrication. (CF/PF)

Multipla table light, 1970
Chrome-plated metal frame with enameled metal reflector, 51 cm diameter / Rahmengestell aus verchromtem Metall mit Reflektor aus lackiertem Metall, 51 cm Durchmesser / Structure en métal chromé, réflecteur en métal laqué, 51 cm de diamètre
Stilnovo, Lainate, Italy

◁ **Multipla floor light, 1970**
Chrome-plated metal frame with enameled metal reflector on enameled tubular metal stem and base, 160 cm high / Montierung aus verchromtem Metall mit Reflektor, Schaft und Fuß aus lackiertem Metall, 160 cm hoch / Structure en métal chromé, réflecteur et pied en métal laqué, 160 cm de haut
Stilnovo, Lainate, Italy

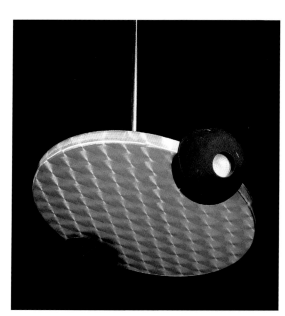

Yonel Lébovici began his career in 1959 with the Société Nationale de Constructions Aéronautiques du Sud-Est (an aircraft manufacturer). He later studied industrial design at the Conservatoire des Arts et Métiers in Paris. In 1972 he opened his own gallery, Formes et Couleurs, which retailed his idiosyncratic space-age Pop designs. Lighting creations such as his *Soucoupe* range of floor, table and ceiling lights owed much in constructional terms to his earlier work in the aeronautics industry. Lébovici's handmade "functional sculpture" lighting designs became highly prized in the mid-1970s by a small and wealthy clientele. (CF/PF)

Yonel Lébovici begann seine Karriere 1959 bei dem Flugzeugbau-Unternehmen Société Nationale de Constructions Aéronautiques du Sud-Est. Später studierte er Industriedesign am Conservatoire des Arts et Métiers in Paris. 1972 eröffnete er die Galerie Formes et Couleurs, in der er seine exzentrischen, ganz dem Pop-Design des Raumfahrtzeitalters verschriebenen Schöpfungen verkaufte. Konstruktionstechnisch profitierten Lébovicis Beleuchtungskreationen, wie seine aus Steh-, Tisch- und Hängeleuchten bestehende *Soucoupe*-Serie, deutlich von seinen Erfahrungen in der Flugzeugindustrie. Seine handgefertigten „funktional-skulpturalen" Beleuchtungskörper erzielten Mitte der 1970er Jahre bei einer kleinen, vermögenden Klientel sehr hohe Preise. (CF/PF)

Yonel Lébovici débuta sa carrière en 1959 auprès de la Société nationale de constructions aéronautiques du Sud-Est. Il étudia par la suite le design au Conservatoire national des arts et métiers à Paris. En 1972, il ouvrit sa propre galerie, Formes et Couleurs, qui distribuait ses créations très personnelles de luminaires pop, comme la gamme *Soucoupe* (lampes de sol, de table et suspensions), qui devaient beaucoup, en termes de conception, à son passage dans l'industrie aéronautique. Ses luminaires – « sculptures fonctionnelles » – fabriqués à la main étaient très appréciés, au milieu des années 1970, par une petite clientèle aisée. (CF/PF)

Soucoupe **ceiling light, 1978**
Polished aluminum construction with enameled metal transformer and shade for halogen bulb, 57 x 50 cm / Konstruktion aus poliertem Aluminium mit Transformator und Lampenschirm aus lackiertem Metall und Halogenlampe, 57 x 50 cm / Fabrication en aluminium poli, transformateur en métal laqué et abat-jour pour ampoule halogène, 57 x 50 cm
Yonel Lébovici, France

▷ *Soucoupe* **floor light, 1970**
Polished aluminum construction, 200 cm high / Konstruktion aus poliertem Aluminium, 200 cm hoch / Fabrication en aluminium poli, 200 cm de haut
Yonel Lébovici, France

After studying aeronautics, in the mid-1960s Yonel Lébovici turned his attention to sculpture. In 1978 he began working with aluminum and created several oversized and out-of-context lighting products that blurred the boundaries between art and design. By super-sizing trivial objects of everyday life – a safety pin or an electrical plug – he not only subverted their function but also playfully transformed their meaning. As a "Sculpteur de la Lumière," Lébovici exhibited his work in art galleries rather than stores and his iconic lighting designs were manufactured in limited editions. (CF/PF)

Nach einer Ausbildung zum Luftfahrttechniker wandte Yonel Lébovici Mitte der 1960er Jahre sein Interesse der Skulptur zu. Ab 1978 arbeitete er mit Aluminium und schuf mehrere andere Kontexten entnommene, überdimensionale Beleuchtungskörper, bei denen sich die Grenze zwischen Design und Kunst verwischte. Durch extreme Vergrößerung von trivialen Alltagsobjekten – einer Sicherheitsnadel oder einem Stromstecker – stellte er nicht nur ihre Funktion auf den Kopf, sondern veränderte auch auf spielerische Weise das, wofür sie stehen. Als „Sculpteur de la Lumière" präsentierte Lébovici seine Arbeiten eher in Kunstgalerien als in Verkaufsräumen, und dementsprechend wurden seine ikonhaften Beleuchtungskörper auch in nur kleinen, limitierten Auflagen gefertigt. (CF/PF)

Après avoir étudié la construction aéronautique au milieu des années 1960, Yonel Lébovici s'intéressa à la sculpture. En 1978, il commença à travailler l'aluminium et créa plusieurs luminaires surdimensionnés et hors contexte qui brouillaient les frontières entre le design et les arts plastiques. En surdimensionnant des objets quotidiens – une épingle de nourrice ou une fiche électrique – non seulement il détournait leur fonction mais il transformait leur sens avec humour. «Sculpteur de la lumière», Lébovici exposait ses œuvres dans des galeries d'art plutôt que dans des magasins et ses créations n'étaient fabriquées qu'en éditions très limitées. (CF/PF)

Fiche Mâle floor light, c.1970

Polished aluminum body enclosing two fluorescent tubes, 36.2 cm / Konstruktion aus poliertem Aluminium mit zwei Leuchtstoffröhren, 36,2 cm / Corps en aluminium poli, contenant deux tubes fluorescents, 36,2 cm de long
Yonel Lébovici, France

▷ **L'Épingle floor light, 1975**

Chrome-plated metal construction concealing fluorescent tube, 198 cm high / Konstruktion aus verchromtem Metall mit Leuchtstoffröhre, 198 cm hoch / Corps en métal chromé, tube fluorescent, 198 cm de haut
Yonel Lébovici, France

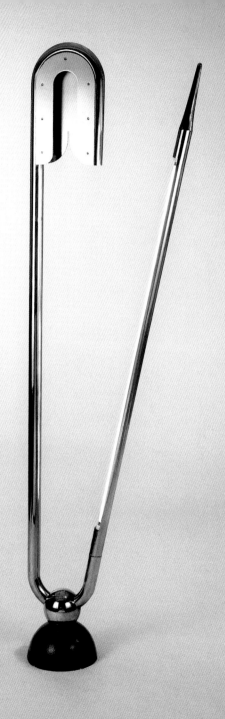

yonel lébovici
l'épingle floor light

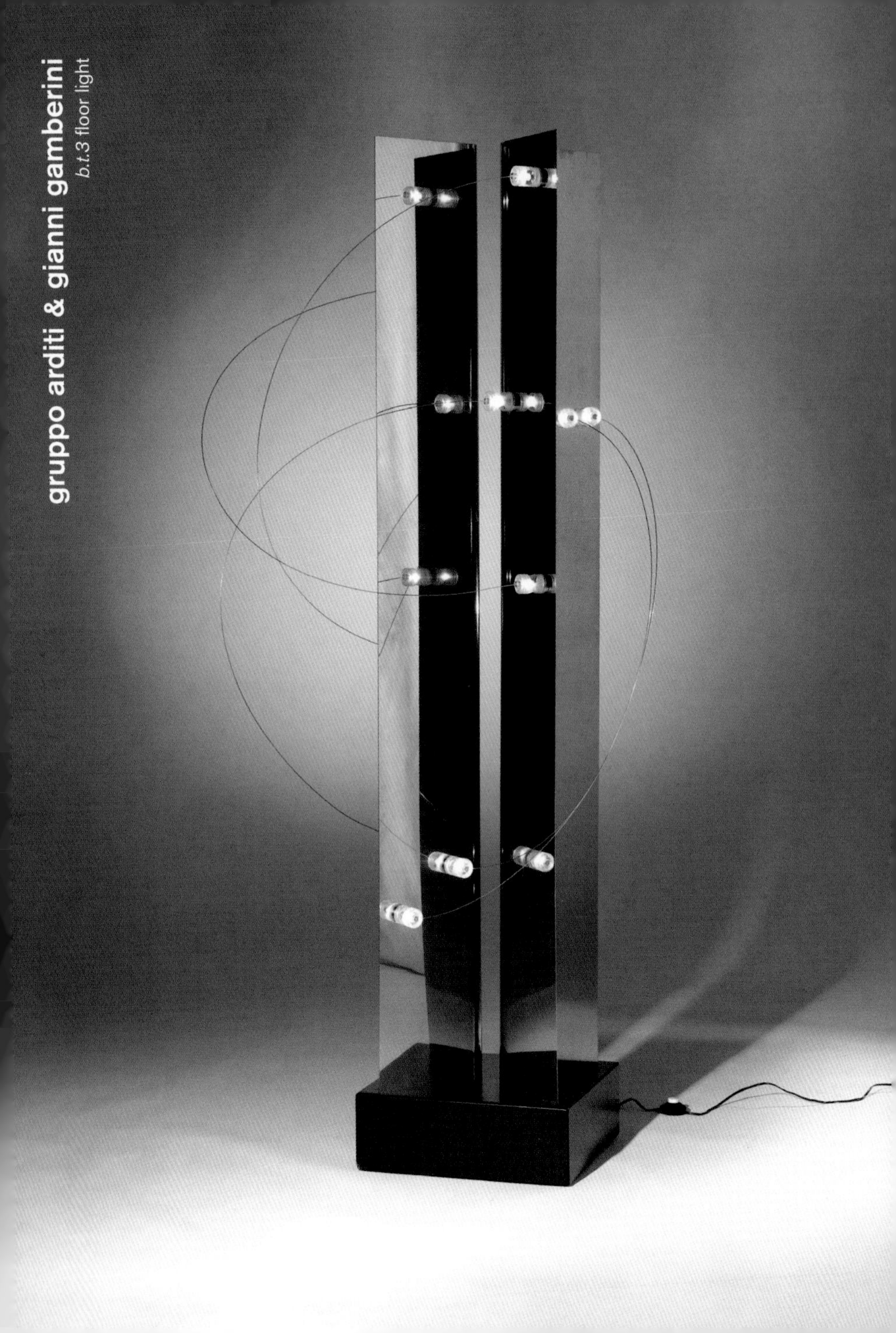

gruppo arditi & gianni gamberini
b.t.3 floor light

◁ *B.T.3* floor light, 1971

Painted wood base, stainless-steel columns and steel wires with magnetic nylon bulb housings, 230 cm high / Fuß aus bemaltem Holz, Säulen aus Edelstahl, Stahldrähte und Nylongehäuse mit Magneten, 230 cm hoch / Socle en bois peint, colonnes et fils d'acier, douilles d'ampoules en nylon magnétisé, 230 cm de haut Nucleo – a division of **Sormani**, Arosio, Italy

B.T.2 table light, 1971

Stainless-steel base and steel wires with magnetic nylon bulb housings, 25 x 25 cm (base) / Fuß aus Edelstahl, Stahldrähte und Nylongehäuse mit Magneten, 25 x 25 cm (Fuß) / Socle en acier, douilles d'ampoules en nylon magnétisé, 25 x 25 cm (base) Nucleo – a division of **Sormani**, Arosio, Italy

These remarkable and highly interactive light sculptures (1971) were the outcome of a working collaboration between Gianni Gamberini and the Florentine Radical Design group ARDITI (Associazione Reazionaria Designers Italiani Totalmente Integrati), whose members included Alessandro Mazzoni delle Stelle, Duccio Trassinelli and Elisabetta Scheggi. The low-voltage bulbs are held in magnetized nylon mounts and switch on only when they make contact with the stainless steel of the stem or base. As Mazzoni delle Stelle explained, "Light has always fascinated man: being able to play with it, almost touch it, embroidering shadows." (CF/PF)

Diese bemerkenswerten und stark interaktiven Lichtskulpturen (1971) gingen aus einer Zusammenarbeit zwischen Gianni Gamberini und der dem Radical Design angehörenden Florentiner Gruppe ARDITI (Associazione Reazionaria Designers Italiani Totalmente Integrati) hervor, zu deren Mitgliedern Alessandro Mazzoni delle Stelle, Duccio Trassinelli und Elisabetta Scheggi gehörten. Die Niedervoltbirnen befinden sich in mit Magneten ausgestatteten Nylongehäusen und schalten sich nur ein, wenn sie mit dem Edelstahl der Säule bzw. des Fußes in Berührung kommen. Wie Mazzoni delle Stelle erklärte, habe „Licht den Menschen immer fasziniert, da man damit spielen, es beinahe berühren und damit Schatten werfen kann". (CF/PF)

Ces sculptures lumineuses (1971) à la fois remarquables et très interactives sont l'aboutissement d'une collaboration entre Gianni Gamberini et le groupe florentin de design radical ARDITI (Associazione Reazionaria Designers Italiani Totalmente Integrati) dont faisaient partie Alessandro Mazzoni delle Stelle, Duccio Trassinelli et Elisabetta Scheggi. Les ampoules basse tension, insérées dans des montures en nylon couronnées par un aimant, ne s'allument que lorsqu'elles entrent en contact avec l'acier inoxydable de la tige ou de la base. Comme l'expliquait Mazzoni delle Stelle : « La lumière a toujours fasciné l'homme : pouvoir jouer avec elle, la toucher presque, broder des ombres ». (CF/PF)

Big Flower Pot hanging light, c.1971
Enameled and silk-screen printed metal shade
and reflector, 34 cm high / Lampenschirm und
Reflektor aus lackiertem, siebbedrucktem Metall,
34 cm hoch / Abat-jour et réflecteur en métal
laqué et sérigraphié, 34 cm de haut
Louis Poulsen Lighting, Copenhagen, Denmark

▷ *Verner Panton interior with* Big Flower Pot
hanging lights, Mobilia, *March 1975 / Interieur
nach Entwurf von Verner Panton mit Hängeleuchten* Big Flower Pot, Mobilia, *März 1975 /
Intérieur de Verner Panton, montrant les suspensions* Big Flower Pot, Mobilia, *mars 1975*

Verner Panton has taken his *Flower
Pot* light of 1968 one stage further in
this large hanging version (*c.*1971). The
two hemispheres are a blank canvas
onto which he prints a simple pattern of
swirling lines. The motif reflects various
art movements of the preceding years.
It contains echoes of Op and Kinetic
Art, and the colors and sensual lines
call to mind the psychedelic graphics
that enjoyed such popularity in the late
1960s. Panton was very much in tune
with fashion as well as with the practical issues of lighting design. (PG)

Bei der großen Version seiner Hängeleuchte *Flower Pot* (ca. 1971) ging
Verner Panton noch einen Schritt über
seinen früheren Entwurf von 1968 hinaus. Beide Halbkugeln bestehen aus
weißer Leinwand mit einem einfachen
Muster aus Wellenlinien. In diesem
Motiv finden sich mehrere Kunstströ-
mungen der vorangegangenen Jahre
wieder. Es enthält Anklänge an die Op
Art und die kinetische Kunst, während
die Farben und sinnlichen Linien an die
Ende der 1960er Jahre so beliebten
psychedelischen Formen erinnern. Panton war sowohl in Bezug auf modische
Strömungen als auch auf die praktischen Seiten des Leuchtendesigns
immer auf der Höhe der Zeit. (PG)

Avec cette grande suspension (vers
1971), Verner Panton a poussé encore
plus loin le concept de sa célèbre
lampe *Flower Pot* de 1968. Les deux
hémisphères sont pour lui une sorte
de toile vierge sur laquelle il imprime
un motif de lignes ondulées, dont le
style renvoie à différents mouvements
artistiques des années précédentes,
comme l'Op Art et l'art cinétique, tandis que les couleurs et les lignes sen-
suelles rappellent le style psychédé-
lique extrêmement populaire à la fin
des années 1960. Panton était aussi
sensible à la mode qu'aux enjeux pratiques de la conception de luminaires.
(PG)

Although relatively small, the *Sinus* table light (1972) commands the totemic presence so characteristic of Sottsass's large-scale designs. With its bold, undulating outline, the design also possesses a strong graphic quality, while its row of silvered light bulbs are evocative of glamorous Hollywood dressing rooms. Designed to be used either vertically or horizontally, the *Sinus* is constructed of (the then) state-of-the-art injection-molded ABS. This diminutive yet perfectly formed light reflects not only Sottsass's interest in the iconography of popular culture, but also his skillful handling of new materials and production techniques. (CF/PF)

Obwohl Ettore Sottsass' Tischleuchte *Sinus* (1972) relativ klein ist, zeichnet sie sich wie seine größeren Entwürfe durch eine ausgeprägt skulpturale Präsenz aus. Die gewagte Wellenform verstärkt diesen Eindruck, während die verspiegelten Glühbirnen an den Glamour von Hollywood-Garderoben erinnern. Die *Sinus* Leuchte kann sowohl liegend als auch stehend aufgestellt werden und ist aus dem (damals) völlig neuartigen Spritzguss-ABS-Kunststoff hergestellt. Die kleine, aber perfekt geformte Leuchte veranschaulicht nicht nur Sottsass' Interesse an der Ikonografie der Popkultur, sondern auch seinen gekonnten Einsatz von neuen Materialien und Fertigungstechniken. (CF/PF)

Bien que relativement petite, la lampe de table *Sinus* (1972) possède la présence totémique si caractéristique des projets à plus grande échelle de Sottsass. Par son audacieux contour ondulé, ce modèle présente une forte qualité graphique, tandis que sa rangée d'ampoules argentées évoque les loges d'actrices d'Hollywood. Conçue pour être utilisée aussi bien horizontalement que verticalement, la *Sinus* est en ABS moulé par injection, technique d'avant-garde à l'époque. Cette petite lampe de formes parfaites reflète non seulement l'intérêt de Sottsass pour l'iconographie de la culture populaire, mais aussi sa grande maîtrise des matériaux et des modes de production nouveaux. (CF/PF)

Sinus table light, 1972
ABS body with silvered light bulbs, 32.5 cm / Leuchtenkörper aus ABS-Kunststoff mit verspiegelten Glühbirnen, 32,5 cm / Corps en ABS, ampoules argentées, 32,5 cm
Stilnovo, Lainate, Italy

Achille Castiglioni's *Noce (Nut)* floor light, designed in 1972, can also be used as a table or wall light. With its robust, watertight, die-cast aluminum shell and sturdy pressed-glass diffuser, the *Noce* is extremely hardwearing and can be used outdoors. Two bulbs fixed to a mounting plate inside the shell provide direct and diffused light. By turning an external knob, the angle of the mounting plate can be adjusted to cast light in different directions to produce varied effects. Since 1972, *Noce* has been kept in uninterrupted production by the Italian lighting manufacturer Flos. (TB)

Die Bodenleuchte *Noce (Nuss)*, 1972 von Achille Castiglioni entworfen, kann auch als Tisch- oder Wandleuchte benutzt werden. Ihr robustes, wasserdichtes Gehäuse aus Gussaluminium und starkem Pressglas macht die Leuchte extrem unempfindlich und lässt ihren Gebrauch im Freien zu. In ihrem Inneren bilden zwei Glühbirnen, die auf einer Trägerplatte befestigt sind, die Lichtquelle für direktes und diffuses Licht. Der Winkel der Trägerplatte lässt sich von außen mit einem Drehknopf verstellen. Auf diese Weise kann das Licht gelenkt und die Lichtwirkung somit je nach Wunsch verändert werden. Seit 1972 befindet sich die *Noce* Leuchte ohne Unterbrechung in Produktion des italienischen Leuchtenherstellers Flos. (TB)

La lampe *Noce (Noix)* d'Achille Castiglioni, conçue en 1972, peut s'utiliser aussi bien sur une table et au sol qu'en applique. Grâce à sa robuste coque en fonte d'aluminium et son diffuseur en verre moulé, elle est extrêmement résistante et peut même servir à l'extérieur. Deux ampoules fixées sur une monture donnent un éclairage direct et diffus. Une bouton situé à l'extérieur de la coque permet de faire pivoter la monture afin de diriger la lumière dans différentes directions pour obtenir divers effets. La *Noce* est produite sans interruption par le fabricant italien Flos depuis 1972. (TB)

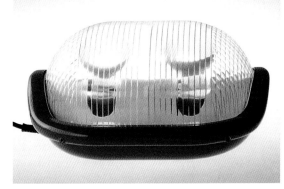

Noce floor/table/wall light, 1972

Enameled die-cast aluminum body with clear pressed-glass diffuser, 18.5 cm high / Gehäuse aus lackiertem Druckgussaluminium mit Diffusor aus klarem Pressglas, 18,5 cm hoch / Corps en fonte d'aluminium, diffuseur en verre clair moulé, 18,5 cm de haut
Flos, Bovezzo, Italy

The *Manzoni 14* table light (1971) was the first of a series of experimental products conceived in the 1970s outside the limitations of "Good Design." It took its name from the (then) address of Ettore Sottsass's Milan studio. George Sowden was at that time working in the office-equipment industry, designing mechanical calculators for Olivetti. His *Star Lamp* (1972) was produced as a one-off for an exhibition. Like the *Manzoni 14*, it combined brightly colored plastic with sculptural form to create a powerful Anti-Design statement, which anticipated the arrival of Post-Modernism in the applied arts. (CF/PF)

Die Tischleuchte *Manzoni 14* (1971) war die erste in einer Reihe von experimentellen Produkten, die in den 1970er Jahren die Grenzen des „Guten Designs" sprengten. Ihr Name bezieht sich auf die damalige Adresse des Mailänder Büros von Ettore Sottsass. George Sowden arbeitete zu dieser Zeit in der Büromaschinenindustrie und entwarf Rechenmaschinen für Olivetti. Seine Tisch-/Stehleuchte *Star Lamp* (1972) wurde als Einzelstück für eine Ausstellung gefertigt. Wie die *Manzoni 14* Leuchte brachte sie durch ihre Kombination von buntem Kunststoff mit einer skulpturalen Form den Standpunkt des Anti-Designs überzeugend zum Ausdruck und kündigte bereits die Postmoderne in der angewandten Kunst an. (CF/PF)

La lampe de table *Manzoni 14* (1971) a été la première d'une série de productions expérimentales conçues dans les années 1970 en réaction aux contraintes du *Good Design*. Son nom correspond à l'adresse du studio milanais d'Ettore Sottsass. George Sowden travaillait alors à la conception de machines à calculer mécaniques pour Olivetti. Sa *Star Lamp* (1972) fut produite à un unique exemplaire pour une exposition. Comme la *Manzoni 14*, elle combinait un plastique de couleur vive et une forme sculpturale dans une approche anti-design qui annonçait l'arrivée du postmodernisme dans les arts appliqués. (CF/PF)

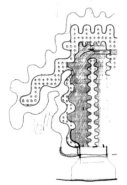

Star Lamp table/floor light, 1972

Painted wood base with methacrylate diffusor, 100 cm high (approx.) / Fuß aus lackiertem Holz mit Diffusor aus Methacrylat, 100 cm hoch (ca.) / Pied en bois peint, diffuseur en méthacrylate, 100 cm de haut (environ)
Self-production – one-off design

▷ *Manzoni 14* table light, 1971

Enameled metal base with acrylic and vacuum-formed polystyrene diffusers and U-shaped fluorescent tube, 61 cm high / Fuß aus lackiertem Metall, Diffusor aus Acryl und vakuumgeformtem Polystyrol, U-förmige Leuchtstoffröhre, 61 cm hoch / Base en métal laqué, diffuseurs en acrylique et polystyrène formé sous vide, tube fluorescent en U, 61 cm de haut
Self-production (later manufactured in a limited edition of 30 by **Planula**, Agliana, Italy)

◁ *Design drawing for Manzoni 14 table light, c.1971 / Entwurfszeichnung der Tischleuchte* Manzoni 14, *ca. 1971 / Croquis de la conception pour la lampe de table* Manzoni 14, *vers 1971*

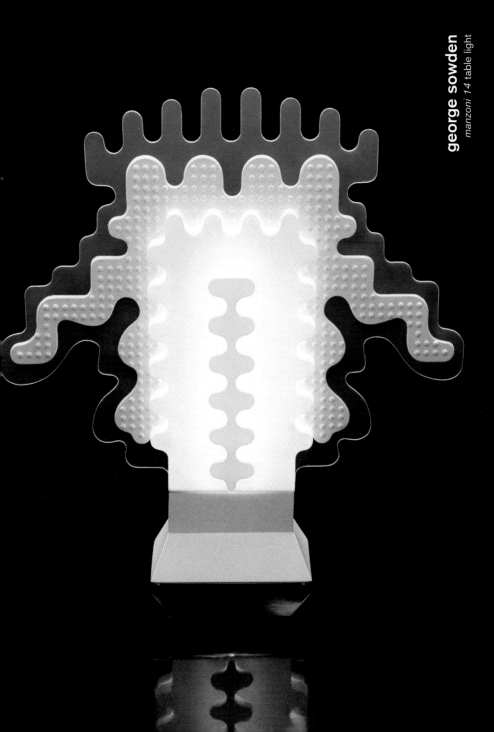

Gae Aulenti conceived the *Pileo* floor light (1972) for Artemide, one of the most prominent Italian manufacturers of modern lighting. Artemide is one of numerous firms based in and around Milan that have benefited from close and open-minded collaboration with designers and made the city a Mecca for imaginative design. The forms of the *Pileo* are geometrically pure and are cut from two basic shapes – the cylinder and the sphere. The distinctive and clever feature of the design is the idea of a shade that pivots like a helmet visor and allows various options in directing the light. (PG)

Gae Aulenti gestaltete die Stehleuchte *Pileo* (1972) für Artemide, einen der prominentesten italienischen Hersteller von modernen Beleuchtungskörpern. Artemide gehört zu den zahlreichen in und um Mailand angesiedelten Firmen, die von ihrer engen und sehr aufgeschlossenen Zusammenarbeit mit Designern profitiert und die Stadt zu einem Mekka des kreativen Designs gemacht haben. Die Gestalt der *Pileo* ist reine Geometrie, zusammengesetzt aus den Grundformen Zylinder und Kugel. Das Besondere an dieser Leuchte ist ihr ausgeklügelter Lampenschirm, der sich wie ein Visier aufklappen lässt, so dass der Lichtstrahl in unterschiedliche Richtungen gelenkt werden kann. (PG)

Gae Aulenti a conçu le lampadaire *Pileo* (1972) pour Artemide, l'un des plus importants fabricants italiens de luminaires modernes. Artemide est l'une de ces nombreuses entreprises basées à Milan ou dans les environs qui ont bénéficié d'une collaboration intelligente et ouverte avec les designers et ont fait de cette ville une Mecque du design créatif. Les formes de la *Pileo* sont géométriquement pures et découpées dans deux figures de base, le cylindre et la sphère. L'élément le plus remarquable est l'abat-jour qui pivote comme une visière de casque et permet diverses orientations de la lumière. (PG)

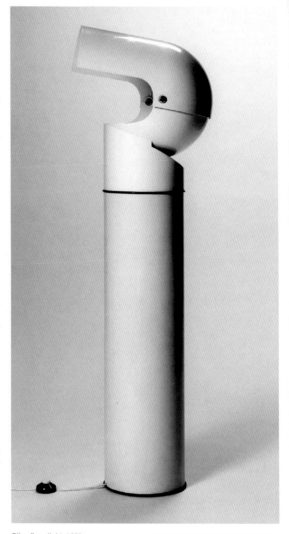

***Pileo* floor light, 1972**

Enameled metal base and hinged visor on ABS stand with rubber fittings, 140 cm high / Fuß und klappbarer Lampenschirm aus lackiertem Metall auf Fuß aus ABS-Kunststoff mit Montierung aus Gummi, 140 cm hoch / Corps en métal laqué, visière articulée sur pied en ABS, joint caoutchouc, 140 cm de haut
Artemide, Pregnana Milanese, Italy

▷ *Fiell Gallery in New King's Road, London, 1990, showing Pileino table light designed by Gae Aulenti in 1972 / Galerie Fiell in der Londoner New King's Road, 1990, mit Tischleuchte Pileino nach Entwurf von Gae Aulenti aus dem Jahr 1972 / La galerie Fiell, New King's Road à Londres en 1990, présentant la lampe de table Pileino dessinée par Gae Aulenti in 1972*

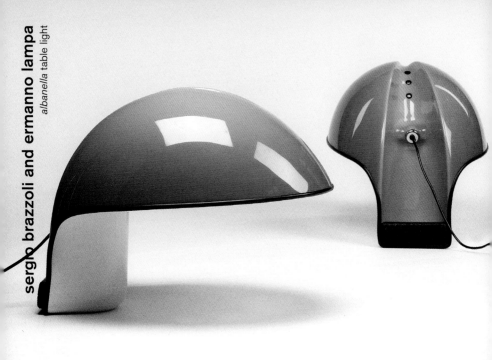

Albanella table light, 1972

Metal base with plastic body and rubber trim, 50.8 cm high / Sockel aus Metall mit Leuchtenkörper aus Kunststoff und Einfassung aus Gummi, 50,8 cm hoch / Base en métal, corps en plastique, bordure en caoutchouc, 50,8 cm de haut
Harvey Guzzini DH (Design House), Recanati, Italy

▷ **Alba floor light, 1972**

Metal base with plastic body and rubber trim, 192 cm high / Sockel aus Metall mit Leuchtenkörper aus Kunststoff und Einfassung aus Gummi, 192 cm hoch / Base en métal, corps en plastique, bordure en caoutchouc, 192 cm de haut
Harvey Guzzini DH (Design House), Recanati, Italy

The *Albanella* light (1972) is a deceptively simple design, an intelligently conceived sculptural form in which the bowed sheet that serves as the base melts into the curves of the domed shade. White on one side, black or colored on the other, the outside visibly becomes the inside within this series of multi-directional curves. Sergio Brazzoli and Ermanno Lampa created this design, in its low and high versions, for the firm of Harvey Guzzini – one of the most progressive manufacturers of industrially designed lighting products in Italy. (PG)

Das Design der Leuchte *Albanella* (1972) wirkt trügerisch einfach. Dabei handelt es sich jedoch um einen äußerst ausgeklügelten, skulpturalen Entwurf, bei dem das gebogene Blech, das als Fuß dient, in die Rundungen des kuppelförmigen Lampenschirms übergeht. Sie ist auf der einen Seite weiß und auf der anderen schwarz oder farbig, wobei das Äußere mit dem Richtungswechsel der Kurven sichtbar zum Inneren wird. Sergio Brazzoli und Ermanno Lampa kreierten diese Leuchte in einer niedrigen und in einer hohen Version für den Leuchtenproduzenten Harvey Guzzini – einen der progressivsten italienischen Herstellern von industriell entworfenen Leuchtkörpern. (PG)

La lampe *Albanella* (1972) est un modèle trompeusement simple, une forme sculpturale habile dans laquelle la forme en arc qui sert de base épouse les courbes de l'abat-jour en coupole. Blanc d'un côté, noir ou coloré de l'autre, l'extérieur se transforme en intérieur dans un jeu de courbes multidirectionnelles. Sergio Brazzoli et Ermanno Lampa ont créé ce modèle, en version basse et haute, pour Harvey Guzzini, l'un des fabricants italiens d'appareils d'éclairages de conception industrielle les plus novateurs. (PG)

richard sapper
tizio task light

In Italian the word *tizio* means "fellow" or "chap," and certainly Richard Sapper's iconic task light (1972) has an endearing yet masculine character. With its blatantly high-tech rhetoric, the *Tizio* enjoyed huge popularity in the 1980s as a must-have Matt Black "designer" object. Its commercial success, however, did not rest on stylistic grounds alone. With its tilting head and exquisitely counterbalanced arms that carry the low-voltage current, the *Tizio* achieved an important technical breakthrough. In recognition of this, the design was awarded a Compasso d'Oro in 1979. A smaller and a larger version of the light were introduced in the early 1990s. (CF/PF)

Das italienische Wort *tizio* bedeutet „Kamerad" oder „Kumpel", und Richard Sappers ikonenhafte Arbeitsleuchte hat zweifellos etwas Sympathisches und zugleich Maskulines an sich. Mit ihrer demonstrativ zur Schau gestellten Hightech-Formensprache war die *Tizio* Leuchte in den 1980er Jahren ein außerordentlich beliebtes Designobjekt, das „man haben musste". Der kommerzielle Erfolg beruhte allerdings nicht nur auf formalen Gründen. Mit ihrem neigbaren Leuchtenkopf und den außergewöhnlichen Armen mit Gegengewichten, über die der Niederspannungs-Strom geleitet wird, erzielte die Leuchte einen bedeutenden technischen Durchbruch, der 1979 mit einem Compasso d'Oro ausgezeichnet wurde. Anfang der 1990er Jahre kam die Leuchte in einer kleineren sowie einer größeren Version auf den Markt. (CF/PF)

En Italien, *tizio* signifie « type » et cette lampe de table icônique de Richard Sapper possède certainement un caractère masculin. Par sa rhétorique ouvertement high-tech, la *Tizio* (1972) a connu une immense popularité dans les années 1980. C'était l'objet signé noir et chic qu'il fallait absolument posséder. Son succès commercial ne repose cependant pas sur de simples raisons stylistiques. Avec sa tête inclinable et ses bras délicatement équilibrés qui conduisent le courant électrique basse tension, la *Tizio* représentait une avancée technologique importante qui lui valut un Compasso d'Oro en 1979. Une version plus petite et une autre, plus grande, furent lancées au début des années 1990. (CF/PF)

◁ *Tizio* task light, 1972
Enameled aluminum base and arms, head with plastic fittings, 120 cm high / Fuß und Arme aus lackiertem Aluminium, Kopf und Montierungen aus Kunststoff, 120 cm hoch / Pied et bras en aluminium laqué, coiffe et pièces de montage en plastique, 120 cm de haut
Artemide, Pregnana Milanese, Italy

Detail of *Tizio* task light / Detailansichten der Arbeitsleuchte *Tizio* / Détail de la lampe de table tizio

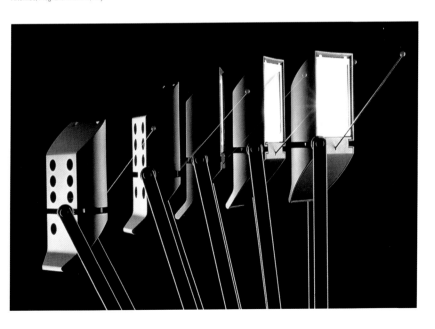

shiro kuramata
k-series oba-q floor lights

"My intuition comes from
my subconscious memory."

„Ich beziehe meine Intuition
aus meiner unterbewussten
Erinnerung."

«Mon intuition vient de la
mémoire de mon incon-
scient.»

– Shiro Kuramata

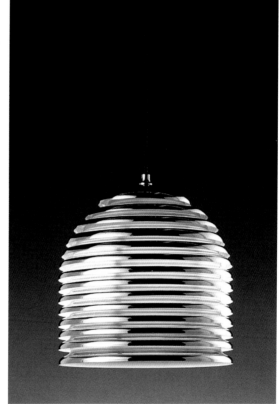

◁ *K-Series Oba-Q* floor lights, 1972
Molded sheets of opalescent methacrylate,
45, 70 or 80 cm high / Gepresste opalweiße
Methacrylatfolie, 45, 70 oder 80 cm hoch /
Feuilles de méthacrylate moulé opalescent,
45, 70 ou 80 cm de haut
Yamagiwa, Tokyo, Japan

▷ *Saturno* hanging light, 1972
Spun metal construction, 29 cm high / Kon-
struktion aus gedrehtem Metall, 29 cm hoch /
Structure en métal filé, 29 cm de haut
Yamagiwa, Tokyo, Japan

Produced by Yamagiwa, the renowned Japanese lighting manufacturer, both these lights are excellent examples of progressive Japanese design from the 1970s. The *K-Series* floor lights (1972) designed by Shiro Kuramata are manufactured from a single sheet of white acrylic that appears to defy gravity. Available in three different sizes, no two lights are exactly alike as each is shaped individually by hand by four specially trained craftsmen. The *Saturno* hanging light (1972) by Kazuo Motozawa shares a similar sculptural poetry with its ribbed shade, which reflects and scatters the light. In 1972 the *Saturno* won an iF award. (CF/PF)

Die von dem renommierten japanischen Leuchtenhersteller Yamagiwa produzierten Entwürfe sind hervorragende Beispiele für das progressive japanische Design der 1970er Jahre. Die Bodenleuchten aus der *K-Serie* (1972) nach Entwurf von Shiro Kuramata werden aus einer einzigen weißen Acrylfolie hergestellt und scheinen der Schwerkraft zu trotzen. Keine dieser in drei Größen erhältlichen Leuchten gleicht der anderen, da jedes Stück manuell gefertigt wird. Die Hängeleuchte *Saturno* (1972) von Kazuo Motozawa strahlt mit ihrem gerippten Lampenschirm, der das Licht reflektiert und streut, eine ähnlich skulpturale Poesie aus. 1972 wurde die Leuchte mit einem iF-Preis ausgezeichnet. (CF/PF)

Éditées par Yamagiwa, le célèbre fabricant de luminaires japonais, ces deux lampes sont d'excellents exemples des avancées du design japonais dans les années 1970. La *K-Series* (1972) conçue par Shiro Kuramata, fabriquée à partir d'une seule feuille d'acrylique blanc, semble défier la gravité. Disponible en trois tailles, chaque modèle est différent puisque fabriqué à la main par quatre artisans spécialement formés. Dans le même esprit poétique, la suspension *Saturno* (1972) de Kazuo Motozawa a une surface cannelée qui reflète et disperse la lumière. En 1972, la *Saturno* a remporté un prix iF. (CF/PF)

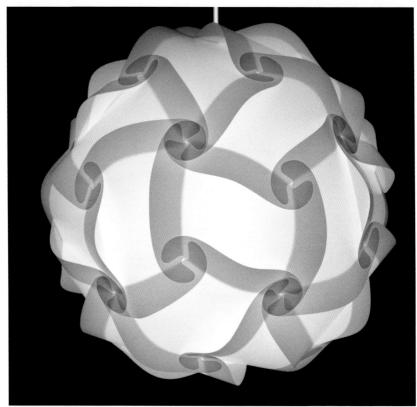

◁ **IQ hanging light, 1972**

PVC sheet self-assembly construction, various sizes depending on configuration / Konstruktion aus PVC-Folie zur Selbstmontage, verschiedene Größen je nach Zusammenstellung / Feuille de PVC à assembler, diverses tailles selon configuration
Kilkenny Illuminations, Kilkenny, Ireland (later reissued by Holger Strøm, Birkerød, Denmark)

◁▽ *Two configurations of the IQ hanging light, 1972 / Zwei Montagebeispiele der Hängeleuchte IQ, 1972 / Deux variations de la suspension IQ, 1972*

△ **Model No. 172 Giant Sinus** hanging **light, 1972**

Hand-folded PVC sheet construction, 85 cm diameter / Konstruktion aus handgefalteter PVC-Folie, 85 cm Durchmesser / Structure en feuille de PVC mise en forme à la main, 85 cm de diamètre
Le Klint, Odense, Denmark

The Latin word *sinus* means "curve" or "fold" and is therefore a highly appropriate name for Poul Christiansen's hanging light (1972), which is made up of PVC sheets cut and folded into sculptural sine curves. Holger Strøm's *IQ* lighting system (1972) shares a similar mathematical approach to form, being constructed of identical interlocking quadrilateral pieces of PVC sheet. The elements can be configured into many different shapes and sizes requiring no supporting frame. As the *IQ* of the name implies, however, the assembly of this puzzle-like light and its many variations poses something of an intellectual challenge! (CF/PF)

Das lateinische Wort *sinus* bedeutet „Kurve" oder „Falte" und ist damit ein sehr passender Name für Poul Christiansens Hängeleuchte (1972). Sie besteht aus PVC-Folienstreifen, die plastische Sinuskurven bilden. Holger Strøm hat bei seinen Hängeleuchten *IQ* (1972) eine ähnlich mathematische Formgebung gefunden und dafür gleich große, ineinander greifende PVC-Vierecke verwendet. Die Elemente können ohne Stützrahmen zu vielen verschiedenen Formen und Größen zusammengesteckt werden. Wie das *IQ* im Namen andeutet, stellt das Zusammensetzen der Einzelteile dieser Puzzle-Leuchte mit ihren vielfältigen Variationsmöglichkeiten durchaus eine intelektuelle Herausforderung dar! (CF/PF)

Le terme latin *sinus,* qui signifie « courbe » ou « pli », convient bien à cette suspension (1972) de Poul Christiansen, faite de feuilles de PVC découpées et pliées selon des courbes sculpturales. Le système d'éclairage *IQ* (1972) d'Holger Strøm, présente la même approche formelle mathématique. Il est également constitué de morceaux rectangulaires de feuilles de PVC imbriqués. Tous ces éléments, qui n'ont pas besoin de structure de soutien, sont configurables de multiples façons. Comme l'implique son nom *IQ* (QI), l'assemblage de cette lampepuzzle et de ses nombreuses variantes représente cependant un certain défi intellectuel. (CF/PF)

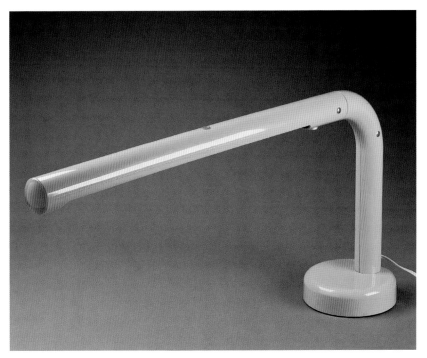

◁ *Office interior showing the* Tube *desk light,
c.1975 / Büro mit Schreibtischleuchten* Tube,
ca. 1975 / Bureau équipé des lampes Tube,
vers 1975

Tube desk light, 1973

Enameled tubular metal construction with
plastic fittings, 39 cm high, 78 cm long /
Konstruktion aus lackierten Metallrohren mit
Plastikfassungen, 39 cm hoch, 78 cm lang /
Structure en tube métallique laqué, pièces de
montage en plastique, 39 cm de haut, 78 cm
de long
Ateljé Lyktan, Åhus, Sweden

Anders Pehrson transformed the small
Swedish lighting company, Lyktan, after
he took the helm in 1964. He created
elegant, functional lighting products that
were constructed from a small number
of standardized components and could
easily be assembled on a production
line. He actively promoted the firm's
range through international trade fairs
and rapidly established such models as
the *Tube* desk light (1973) as popular
classics. The bright color enamel finish
is a post-Pop feature typical of its era.
(PG)

Als Anders Pehrson 1964 die Leitung
des kleinen schwedischen Leuchtenproduzenten Lyktan übernahm, trieb er
Neuerungen im Unternehmen voran.
Aus wenigen genormten Bauteilen
kreierte er elegante, funktionale Beleuchtungskörper, die sich gut zur
Serienfertigung eigneten. Durch aktive
Werbung für die Produktpalette der
Firma auf internationalen Messen konnte er Modelle wie die hier gezeigte
Schreibtischleuchte *Tube* (1973) sehr
bald als beliebte Klassiker etablieren.
Die grelle Lackierung ist typisch für
die Post-Pop-Ära. (PG)

C'est Anders Pehrson qui transforma la
petite société de fabrication de luminaires suédoise Lyktan, après en avoir pris
la tête en 1964. Il créa des lampes
fonctionnelles et élégantes montées
à partir d'un nombre réduit de pièces
standardisées et facilement assembla-
bles à la chaîne. Il fit activement la promotion de sa production dans les foires
internationales et sut faire, de modèles
comme la lampe de bureau *Tube*
(1973), des classiques très populaires.
La finition laquée de couleur vive est
une note pop tout à fait typique de
l'époque. (PG)

Sculptural yet functional, the *Area* lights (1974) are perhaps Mario Bellini's most poetic product designs. The standardized reflector, which is made of a synthetic textile-like paper, appears like a gigantic floating handkerchief and provides a soft romantic light. Its elegant free-form shape contrasts strongly with the strict geometry and hard-edged esthetic of the contemporaneous High-Tech style. In these lights Bellini has begun exploring a more emotionally seductive language of design, which in later decades became a preoccupation among Europe's avant-garde designers. The *Area* collection received a Compasso d'Oro mention in 1979. (CF/PF)

Bei der skulpturalen und doch funktionalen Leuchtenserie *Area* (1974) handelt es sich vielleicht um Mario Bellinis poetischstes Produktdesign. Der bei allen *Area* Leuchten baugleiche Reflektor aus synthetischem, textilähnlichem Papier wirkt wie ein riesiges schwebendes Taschentuch und erzeugt ein weiches, romantisches Licht. Seine elegante Freiform bildet einen deutlichen Kontrast zur strengen Geometrie und kantigen Ästhetik des Hightech-Stils der Zeit. Bellini hat bei diesen Leuchten eine die Gefühle ansprechende Designsprache erprobt, die später zu einer Vorliebe der europäischen Design-Avantgarde wurde. Die *Area* Serie erhielt 1979 eine besondere Erwähnung beim Compasso d'oro. (CF/PF)

Sculpturales mais fonctionnelles, les lampes *Area* (1974) figurent sans doute parmi les créations les plus poétiques de Mario Bellini. Le réflecteur standardisé, fabriqué dans un matériau synthétique semblable à du papier, fait penser à un gigantesque mouchoir flottant et fournit une lumière douce et romantique. Sa forme libre et élégante contraste fortement avec la stricte géométrie et les angles vifs du style high-tech d'alors. Dans ces lampes, Bellini commençait à explorer un langage plus émotionnel et plus séduisant qui, au cours de la décennie suivante, fut au centre des préoccupations des designers de l'avant-garde européenne. La collection *Area* obtint une mention au Compasso d'Oro de 1979. (CF/PF)

◁ *Area Curvea* table light, 1974

Enameled tubular metal stem with cast-iron base, fiberglass-reinforced paper reflector and plastic fittings, 82 cm high / Schaft aus lackiertem Metallrohr mit Fuß aus Gusseisen, Reflektor aus glasfaserverstärktem Papier mit Montierung aus Kunststoff, 82 cm hoch / Tige tubulaire en métal laqué, base en fonte, réflecteur en papier renforcé de fibre de verre et pièces de montage en plastique, 82 cm de haut

Artemide, Pregnana Milanese, Italy

Area floor, table and hanging lights, 1974

Enameled metal mounts with fiberglass-reinforced paper reflectors and plastic fittings, 50 x 50 cm (shade) / Montierung aus lackiertem Metall mit Reflektor aus glasfaserverstärktem Papier und Armaturen mit Montierung aus Kunststoff, 50 x 50 cm (Schirm) / Tige tubulaire en métal laqué, base en fonte, réflecteur en papier renforcé de fibre de verre et pièces de montage en plastique, 50 x 50 cm (abat-jour)

Artemide, Pregnana Milanese, Italy

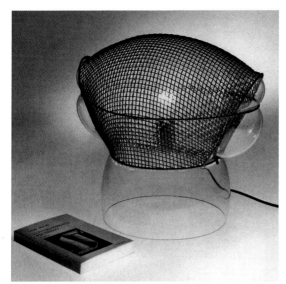

Gae Aulenti has adapted the features of the exterior storm light, protected by a wire cage, to the design of the *Patroclo* table light (1975). The single bulb is contained within the swollen form of the clear shade, itself contained within a wire cage. This creates a graphic pattern of squares and lozenges that if scaled up to architectural proportions would be worthy of Buckminster Fuller or Norman Foster. The cage-work grid has the clever effect of breaking the light source up into a pattern of small bright specks as it falls on nearby surfaces. (PG)

Für den Entwurf der Tischleuchte *Patroclo* (1975) hat sich Gae Aulenti metallverstärkte Sturmlampen zum Vorbild genommen. Die einzige Glühbirne ist in der bauchigen Form des transparenten Lampenschirms untergebracht, der wiederum von einem Drahtkäfig umgeben ist. Dadurch entsteht ein grafisches Muster aus Quadraten und Rhomben, das bei entsprechender Vergrößerung den architektonischen Proportionen eines Buckminster Fuller oder eines Norman Foster entspräche. Durch das filigrane Gitternetz wird das Licht gebrochen und wirft ein Muster von kleinen hellen Rauten auf die umgebenden Flächen. (PG)

Gae Aulenti a adapté le principe de la lampe-tempête protégée par une grille en fil de fer à sa lampe de table *Patroclo* (1975). L'ampoule unique est contenue dans une forme bombée en verre transparent, elle-même prise dans une cage protectrice. Cette disposition crée un motif graphique de carrés et de losanges qui, projeté à une échelle architecturale, évoquerait des réalisations de Buckminster Fuller ou de Norman Foster. La grille diffracte la lumière en une multitude de petites taches brillantes autour de la lampe. (PG)

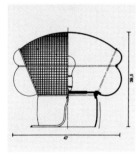

◁ *Patroclo* **table light, 1975**
Clear glass shade enclosed in wire cage, 39.5 cm high / Lampenschirm aus transparentem Glas, umgeben von einem Drahtkäfig, 39,5 cm hoch / Abat-jour en verre transparent dans une cage de fil métallique, 39,5 cm de haut
Artemide, Pregnana Milanese, Italy

△ Alcinoo *table light designed by Gae Aulenti for Artemide, 1975 / Tischleuchte Alcinoo nach Entwurf von Gae Aulenti für Artemide, 1975 / Lampe de table Alcinoo conçue par Gae Aulenti pour Artemide, 1975*

△△/△ *Artemide photograph and diagram of the* Patroclo *table light / Werbefoto von Artemide und Diagramm der Tischleuchte* Patroclo */ Photographie Artemide et schéma de la lampe de table* Patroclo

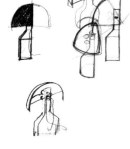

◁ ***Atollo*** **table light, 1977**
Enameled metal base and reflector, 70 cm high
(largest version) / Fuß und Reflektor aus lackiertem Metall, 70 cm hoch (größte Version) / Pied
et réflecteur en métal laqué, 70 cm de haut
(plus grande version)
O Luce, Milan, Italy

◁△ *Design sketch of the* Atollo *table light,*
c.1977 / Entwurfsskizze der Tischleuchte
Atollo, ca. 1977 / Croquis de conception de
la lampe de table Atollo, *vers 1977*

△ *Opaline glass version of the* Atollo *table light*
in various sizes / Opalglas-Variante der Tisch-
leuchte Atollo *in verschiedenen Größen /*
Version en verre opalin de la lampe de table
Atollo *dans différentes dimensions*

The *Atollo* table light (1977) is one of
Vico Magistretti's best-known products
and in many ways can be seen as a
summary of his approach to design –
to explore "the very essence of the
object, looking at usual things with an
unusual eye." The *Atollo*'s strong elemental quality is derived from three
Euclidean forms, the hemisphere, cylinder and cone, whose arrangement
traces the abstract outline of a traditional table light. It is as much this underlying symbolism as its bold sculptural
form that makes the design so visually
engaging. Available in black or white
and in three different sizes, the *Atollo*
was awarded a Compasso d'Oro in
1979. (CF/PF)

Die Tischleuchte *Atollo* (1977) gehört
zu den bekanntesten Entwürfen von
Vico Magistretti und bringt in mehrfa-
cher Hinsicht seine Design-Auffassung
zum Ausdruck, „dem Wesen des Ob-
jekts" auf den Grund zu gehen, indem
man „gewöhnliche Alltagsgegenstände
aus einem ungewöhnlichen Blickwinkel
betrachtet". Die *Atollo* Leuchte bezieht
ihre Wirkung aus dem Zusammenspiel
von drei euklidischen Formen – Halbku-
gel, Zylinder und Kegel –, deren Anordnung die abstrakte Kontur einer traditionellen Tischleuchte nachzeichnet.
Ihre Attraktivität ist ebenso in diesem
Symbolismus wie in ihrer kühnen skulpturalen Form begründet. Die Leuchte
wurde 1979 mit einem Compasso
d'Oro ausgezeichnet. (CF/PF)

La lampe de table *Atollo* (1977) est
l'une de créations les plus célèbres
de Vico Magistretti et, à de nombreux
égards, peut être considérée comme
un résumé de son approche du design :
explorer « l'essence même de l'objet,
regarder les choses habituelles avec
un œil neuf. » La forte présence de
l'*Atollo* est due à trois formes eucli-
diennes, la demi-sphère, le cylindre
et le cône, dont la disposition reprend
le contour stylisé d'une lampe traditionnelle. C'est autant ce symbolisme
sous-jacent que sa puissance sculpturale qui rendent cette création si séduisante. Proposée en noir ou en blanc et
en trois tailles différentes, l'*Atollo* reçut
un Compasso d'Oro en 1971. (CF/PF)

△ Pin-Spot *track lighting head with wire mesh*
diffuser / Strahler Pin-Spot *mit Blendschutz-*
Diffusor aus Drahtgitter / Spot Pin-Spot *à tête*
équipée d'un diffuseur en maillage métallique

▷ *Diagram showing rotating colored filter disk /*
Diagramm mit Darstellung der drehbaren Farb-
filterscheibe / Schéma montrant la rotation du
disque de filtres de couleur

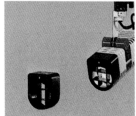

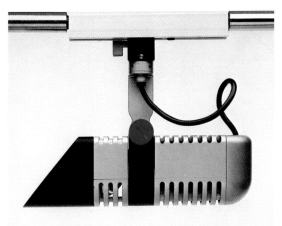

Pin-Spot track lighting system, 1977

Thermoplastic body with aluminum reflector,
34 cm high / Gehäuse aus thermoplastischem
Kunststoff mit Reflektor aus Aluminium, 34 cm
hoch / Corps en thermoplastique, réflecteur en
aluminium, 34 cm de haut
Erco, Lüdenscheid, Germany

Roger Tallon studied electrical engineering in Paris and in 1953 joined the French design consultancy Technès, where he was manager of research from 1960 onwards. He applied his High-Tech design language to trains, televisions, typewriters, furniture, wristwatches and, of course, lighting systems. His *Pin-Spot* system (1977) for Erco was hugely influential with its use of halogen lamps and large reflectors. This low-voltage spotlight could be rotated in all directions and slid easily along the track. It came with a variety of accessories, including a thermoplastic shield, a rotating colored filter disk and an anti-glare wire mesh diffuser. (CF/PF)

Roger Tallon studierte in Paris Elektrotechnik und trat 1953 in das französische Designbüro Technès ein, wo er von 1960 an die Forschungsabteilung leitete. Er gestaltete Züge, Fernsehgeräte, Schreibmaschinen, Möbel, Armbanduhren und natürlich auch Leuchtensysteme in der für ihn typischen Hightech-Designsprache. Für sein für Erco entworfenes Leuchtschienensystem *Pin-Spot* (1977) verwendete er Halogenlampen und große Reflektoren und übte damit einen immensen Einfluss auf die Entwicklungen im Beleuchtungssektor aus. Der Niedervolt-Strahler konnte in alle Richtungen gedreht werden und ließ sich auf der Stromschiene leicht verschieben. Er wurde mit umfangreichem Zubehör ausgeliefert, unter anderem mit einer Blende aus thermoplastischem Kunststoff, einer drehbaren Farbfilterscheibe und einem Blendschutz-Diffusor aus Drahtgitter. (CF/PF)

Après des études d'ingénieur en électricité à Paris, Roger Tallon rejoignit en 1953 l'agence de design Technès, dont il dirigea le bureau de recherche à partir de 1960. Il appliqua son langage de conception high-tech à des trains, des téléviseurs, des machines à écrire, des meubles, des montres et, bien entendu, des systèmes d'éclairage. Son système *Pin-Spot* (1977) pour Erco a exercé une énorme influence par son utilisation d'ampoules halogènes et de grands réflecteurs. Ce spot basse tension pouvait pivoter dans toutes les directions et coulisser facilement sur son rail. Il était livré avec divers accessoires dont un écran en thermoplastique, un filtre en forme de disque rotatif de couleur et un diffuseur en treillis métallique anti-éblouissement. (CF/PF)

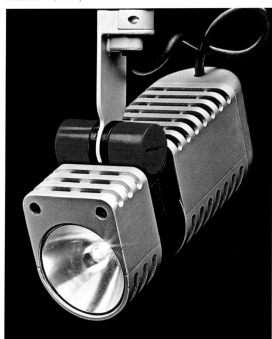

Valigia table light, 1977

Enameled sheet and metal tube construction, 33.5 cm high / Konstruktion aus lackiertem Blech und Stahlrohr, 33,5 cm hoch / Tôle émaillée et tube métallique, 33,5 cm de haut Stilnovo, Lainate, Italy

▷ **_Svincolo_ floor light, 1979**

Laminated plastic base and column, chrome-plated steel braces, red and white neon tubes, 180 cm high (approx.) / Fuß und Schaft aus Laminat, verchromte Stahlstreben, rote und weiße Neonröhren, 180 cm hoch (ca.) / Base et colonne en lamifié plastique, supports en acier chromé, tubes néon rouge et blanc, 180 cm de haut (environ)
Studio Alchimia, Milan, Italy

Within the space of just a few years Ettore Sottsass moved from a contained irony, expressed through objects that were still plausible, to the heights of expressive freedom, which began with Studio Alchimia and continued with Memphis. A possible link between the two is the inspiration Sottsass derives from his extensive travels. This is obvious in the form of the table light *Valigia* ("suitcase") from 1977, but with regard to the floor light *Svincolo* (1979) it is necessary to explain to a non-Italian public that the word evokes motorway approaches and exits where streetlights are high overhead. More than a light fitting, this is a monument to travel and the traveler and was produced for Studio Alchimia's first Bauhaus collection. (SC)

Innerhalb nur weniger Jahre entwickelte sich der verhalten ironische Designstil von Ettore Sottsass zu völliger künstlerischer Freiheit – eine Entwicklung, die mit seiner Zusammenarbeit mit Studio Alchimia begann und in der Gruppe Memphis ihre Fortsetzung fand. Für die beiden hier gezeigten Modelle bezog Sottsass seine Inspiration aus Reisen. Im Fall der Tischleuchte *Valigia* („Koffer") von 1977 ist dies schon aus der Form ersichtlich, während die Stehleuchte *Svincolo* (1979) außerhalb von Italien nicht ohne die Information auskommt, dass ihr Name an die hohen Straßenlampen der italienischen Autobahnausfahrten erinnert. Dieses Modell aus der ersten Bauhaus-Kollektion von Alchimia ist ein Denkmal für das Reisen und die Reisenden. (SC)

En l'espace de quelques années seulement, Ettore Sottsass évolua d'une ironie contenue, exprimée dans des objets qui restaient encore plausibles, jusqu'aux sommets de la liberté d'expression. Ce mouvement, initié avec le Studio Alchimia, se poursuivit avec Memphis. Le lien possible entre les deux tient peut-être aux nombreux voyages de l'architecte. C'est évident dans la forme de la *Valigia* (« valise ») de 1977, mais pour le *Svincolo* (1979), il est nécessaire d'expliquer que ce mot italien désigne les bretelles d'accès aux autoroutes éclairées par d'immenses lampadaires. Plus qu'un appareil d'éclairage, il s'agit d'un monument au voyage et au voyageur, qui faisait partie de la première collection Bauhaus du Studio Alchimia. (SC)

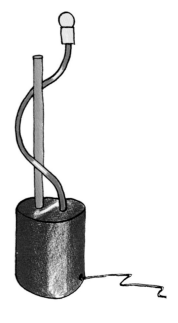

Sinerpica table/floor light, 1978

Enameled metal base, tubular metal stem and support, 75 cm high/ Fuß aus lackiertem Metall, Schaft und Stütze aus Stahlrohr, 75 cm hoch / Pied en métal laqué, tige et support en tube métallique, 75 cm de haut
Studio Alchimia, Milan, Italy

Drawing of Sinerpica *table/floor light, c.1979 / Skizze der Tisch-/Stehleuchte* Sinerpica, *ca. 1979 / Dessin de la lampe de table/lampadaire* Sinerpica, *vers 1979*

Before his own career gained momentum, Michele De Lucchi worked alongside Ettore Sottsass, assimilating the latter's Pop tendencies and injecting them with a certain degree of sarcasm. When Alessandro Guerriero's Studio Alchymia (later Alchimia) invited him to contribute to its *Bauhaus* collection, he sketched some humorous designs, including this virtually useless light (1978) with its purely decorative bulb. The name *Sinerpica* is a joke in Italian; it means "she climbs up", referring to the light's vague resemblance to a climbing plant. De Lucchi would soon abandon the *Sinerpica*'s pastel patterns and Disneyesque shapes for more sedate and commercial "Good Design." (SC)

Bevor er selbst Karriere machte, arbeitete Michele De Lucchi an der Seite von Ettore Sottsass, dessen Tendenz zur Pop Art er aufgriff und mit einem gewissen Sarkasmus versetzte. Als er von Alchymia (später Alchimia), dem Designbüro Alessandro Guerrieros, gebeten wurde, etwas für dessen Bauhaus-Kollektion zu gestalten, fertigte er einige humorvolle Entwürfe an, zu denen auch diese praktisch nutzlose Leuchte (1978) mit ihrer ausschließlich dekorativen Glühbirne gehörte. Der italienische Name *Sinerpica* ist scherzhaft gemeint und bedeutet „sie klettert hinauf". Bald danach begann De Lucchi, sich dem ernsteren und kommerziell orientierten „Guten Design" zuzuwenden. (SC)

Avant de s'affirmer dans sa propre carrière, Michele De Lucchi avait travaillé auprès de Ettore Sottsass, dont il avait assimilé le goût pour les tendances pop, mais repris par lui non sans un certain degré de moquerie. Lorsque Alessandro Guerriero du Studio Alchymia (plus tard Alchimia) l'invita à contribuer à la collection Bauhaus, il dessina quelques modèles pleins d'humour, dont cet lampe pratiquement sans usage précis (1978), à l'ampoule purement décorative. Le nom de *Sinerpica* est un trait d'humour. En italien, il signifie «elle grimpe». De Lucchi allait bientôt abandonner ces formes à la Disney et les motifs pastels de la *Sinerpica* pour un *Good Design* plus posé et plus commercial. (SC)

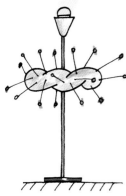

Drawing of Sinvola *table light, c.1979 / Skizze der Tischleuchte* Sinvola, *ca. 1979 / Dessin de la lampe de table* Sinvola, *vers 1979*

Sinvola table light, 1979

Enameled metal base and tubular metal support with padded cushion and hat-pins, 63 cm high / Fuß aus lackiertem Metall, Schaft aus lackiertem Stahlrohr, wattiertes Kissen mit Hutnadeln, 63 cm hoch / Socle en metal émaillée, structure en tube métallique laqué, coussin rembourré, épingles à cheveux, 63 cm de haut
Studio Alchimia, Milan, Italy

The *Sinerpica* table/floor light (1978) and the *Sinvola* table light (1979) were the first objects designed by Michele De Lucchi for Studio Alchimia. Like all the Bauhaus I and II collection pieces, the *Sinvola* mocks the kind of design where function has been completely distorted or deliberately disregarded. The product conceals an essential uselessness, and the desire to create a characteristic and memorable image prevails over the need to resolve a lighting problem. Much criticized by the Italian design establishment when it first appeared, this object now holds its value in the decorative arts collectors' market. (SC)

Bei der Tisch-/Stehleuchte *Sinerpica* (1978) und der Tischleuchte *Sinvola* (1979) handelt es sich um die ersten von Michele De Lucchi für das Studio Alchimia entworfenen Objekte. Wie alle Stücke der Bauhaus-Kollektionen I und II ahmt die *Sinvola* Leuchte jene Art von Design auf ironische Weise nach, bei dem die Funktion völlig entstellt oder bewusst außer Acht gelassen wird. Hier verschleiert der Gesamteindruck die grundlegende Nutzlosigkeit des Produkts, und es geht viel mehr darum, ein typisches und einprägsames Bild zu erzeugen als ein Beleuchtungsproblem zu lösen. Das italienische Design-Establishment reagierte auf dieses Modell mit heftiger Kritik, dennoch hat es heute als Sammlerobjekte seinen Wert. (SC)

Les lampes *Sinerpica* (1978) et *Sinvola* (1979) sont les premiers objets conçus par Michele De Lucchi pour Studio Alchimia. Comme tous les modèles des collections Bauhaus I et II, la *Sinvola* se moque du design fonctionnel en usant de la distorsion ou de la négligence totale de la fonction. Le produit ne peut cacher son inutilité fondamentale. Le désir de créer une image forte et mémorable prévaut sur le besoin de résoudre un problème d'éclairage. Très critiqués par l'establishment du design italien lors de leur apparition, cet objet a conservé sa valeur sur le marché des collectionneurs d'arts décoratifs. (SC)

One of Achille Castiglioni's best-known designs, the *Gibigiana* table light (1980) is named after the Italian term for a flash of light reflected by a mirror. This title precisely describes the constructional principle of the design, which uses a moveable circular mirrored element to angle and reflect the light emitted from the small halogen bulb housed inside its cone-like body. A lever that runs along the spine of the design controls the intensity of the light. Like a scientific instrument, the *Gibigiana* is a highly engineered object that offers absolute precision. (CF/PF)

Die Tischleuchte *Gibigiana* (1980) zählt zu Achille Castiglionis bekanntesten Entwürfen und hat ihren Namen von dem italienischen Ausdruck für einen Lichtblitz, der von einem Spiegel reflektiert wird. Der Name beschreibt exakt das Konstruktionsprinzip der Leuchte, bei der ein runder, beweglicher Spiegel dazu dient, das Licht, das von einer kleinen Halogenlampe im kegelförmigen Körper entweicht, zu streuen und zu reflektieren. Die Lichtintensität kann mit einem Schieberegler auf der Rückseite der Leuchte abgestuft werden. Die *Gibigiana* Leuchte ist ein technisch sehr ausgereiftes Objekt mit der absoluten Präzision eines wissenschaftlichen Instruments. (CF/PF)

Une des créations les plus célèbres d'Achille Castiglioni, la lampe de table *Gibigiana* (1980), tire son nom d'un terme italien utilisé pour parler d'un éclair de flash reflété par un miroir. Cette dénomination décrit avec précision le principe de construction de ce modèle, qui fait appel à un élément mobile à miroir circulaire pour diriger et refléter la lumière émise par une petite ampoule halogène logée dans le corps conique. Le petit levier qui coulisse au dos contrôle l'intensité de la lumière. Tel un instrument scientifique, la *Gibigiana* est un objet d'une précision absolue. (CF/PF)

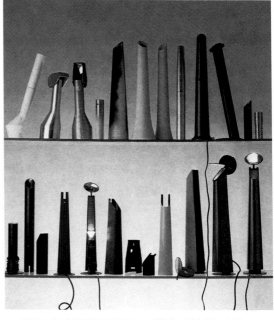

▷ *Gibigiana* **table light, 1980**

Enameled aluminum body with plastic fittings, mirrored reflector, 52 cm high / Leuchtenkörper aus Aluminium mit Montierungen aus Kunststoff, Reflektor mit Spiegel, 52 cm hoch / Corps en aluminium émaillé, pièces de montage en plastique, réflecteur à miroir, 52 cm de haut Flos, Bovezzo, Italy

△ *Prototypes of the* Gibigiana *table light, c.1980 / Prototypen der Tischleuchte* Gibigiana, *ca. 1980 / Prototypes de la lampe de table* Gibigiana, *vers 1980*

◁ *Detail of* Gibigiana *table light showing mirrored reflector / Detail der Tischleuchte* Gibigiana: *Reflektor mit Spiegel / Détail de la lampe de table* Gibigiana *montrant le réflecteur à miroir*

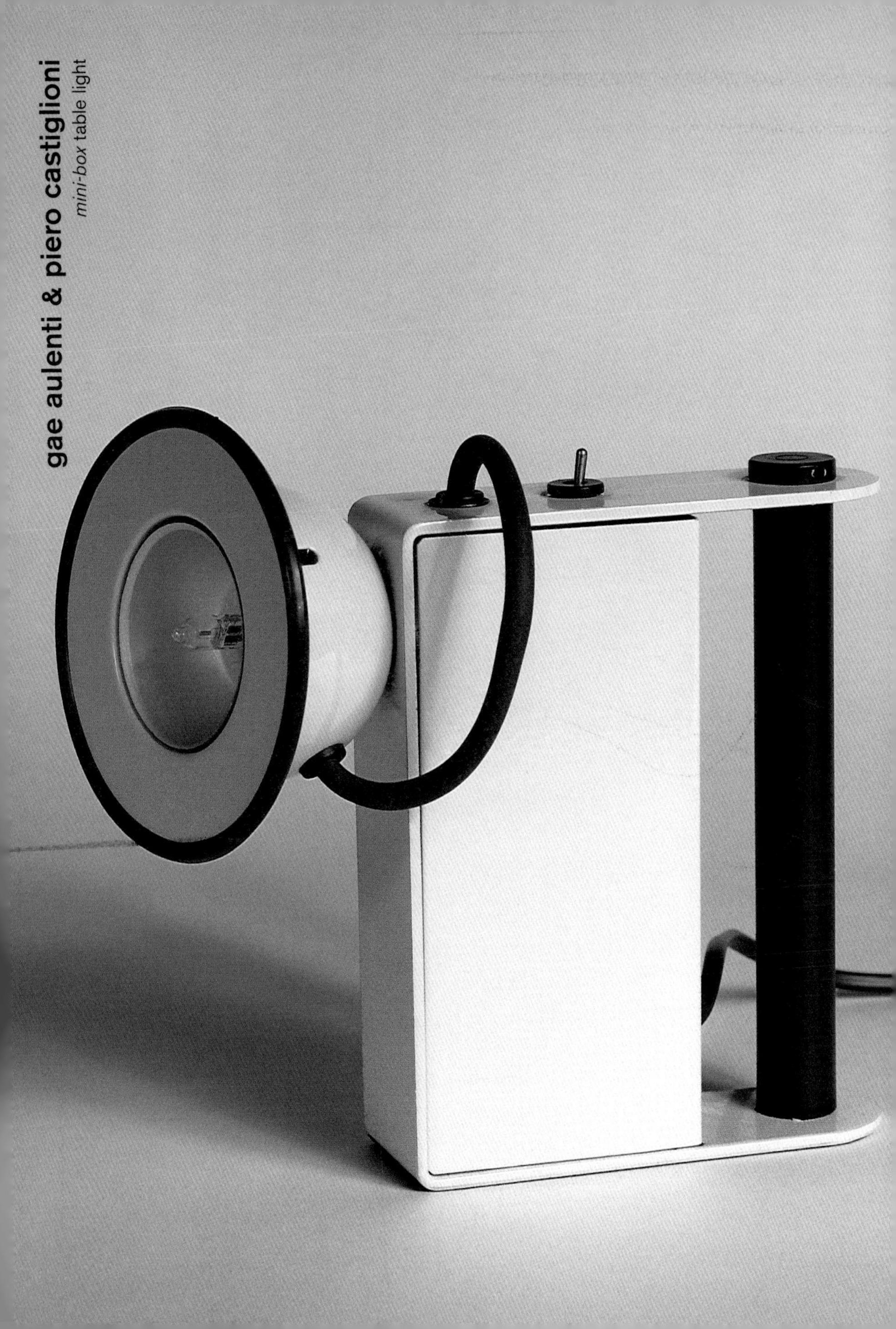

gae aulenti & piero castiglioni
mini-box table light

impugnatura in ferro laccato grigio/verde h cm 16

magnete per attacco e rotazione della calotta

trasformatore

guarnizione in gomma

riflettore

alogena 20 W - 12 V

In their *Mini-Box* table light (1980), Gae Aulenti and Piero Castiglioni have created a tough, efficient-looking object. The robust handle invites you to use this light, with its intense single halogen bulb, as a torch. The clearly visible switch and deliberately exposed wire add to the character of the piece, emphasizing the notion that it is designed for a practical purpose rather than as a formal, sculptural exercise or to amuse the eye. The *Mini-Box* range included low-voltage table, wall, ceiling and track lights. (PG)

Mit ihrer tragbaren Tischleuchte *Mini-Box* (1980) haben Gae Aulenti und Piero Castiglioni ein strenges, effizient aussehendes Objekt geschaffen. Der robuste Griff fordert dazu auf, diese Leuchte mit ihrer starken Halogenlampe in die Hand zu nehmen und wie eine Taschenlampe zu verwenden. Der deutlich sichtbare Schalter und das bewusst heraushängende Stromkabel unterstützen diesen Charakter und verweisen auf ihren praktischen Zweck. Die Serie der *Mini-Box* Leuchten umfasste mit Niedervoltlampen bestückte Tisch-, Wand- und Deckenleuchten sowie Strahler. (PG)

La *Mini-Box* (1980) de Gae Aulenti et Piero Castiglioni est un objet robuste d'aspect efficace, doté d'une puissante ampoule halogène. Sa solide poignée invite à l'utiliser comme une torche. L'interrupteur bien visible et le câble électrique laissé volontairement apparent confirment le caractère utilitaire de cet objet plutôt que l'idée d'un simple exercice de sculpture pour le plaisir. La gamme de luminaires basse tension *Mini-Box* comprenait des lampes de table, des appliques, de plafonniers et cette torche. (PG)

◁ *Mini-Box* table light, 1980

Enameled metal base housing transformer with adjustable magnetized reflector and halogen bulb, 16 cm high / Gehäuse aus lackiertem Metall mit integriertem Transformator, verstellbarer magnetischer Reflektor mit Halogenlampe, 16 cm hoch / Base en métal laqué contenant un transformateur, réflecteur aimanté réglable, ampoule halogène, 16 cm de haut
Stilnovo, Lainate, Italy

△ Diagram of Mini-Box lights published in Domus magazine, c.1981 / Diagramm der Mini-Box *Leuchten, veröffentlicht in der Zeitschrift* Domus, ca. 1981 / Plans de lampes Mini-Box *publiés dans le magazine* Domus, vers 1981

"Any man-made object … cannot but allude to its relationship with the city, the place where human conditions are found."

„Jedes von Menschenhand gefertigte Objekt … hat zwangsläufig einen Bezug zu der Stadt, dem Ort, wo Menschen wohnen."

«Tout objet fabriqué par l'homme est lié à la ville, siège de la condition humaine.»

– Gae Aulenti

Italian architect-designer Michele De Lucchi was one of the founding associates of the Memphis project. His *Oceanic* table light (1981) might be described as the spiritual sibling of Ettore Sottsass's *Tahiti* (1981). For these two lights appear to share an attractive and engaging naivety of style. Yet they are sophisticated, questioning objects. Both are vaguely anthropomophic, wittily evoking highly stylized cartoon animal forms. And they seem to have been constructed with enameled toy-box bricks; or were they made with pieces of confectionary, lollipops and candy sticks? (PG)

Der italienische Architekt und Designer Michele De Lucchi war einer der Mitbegründer des Memphis-Projekts. Seine Tischleuchte *Oceanic* (1981) und Ettore Sottsass' Leuchtenentwurf *Tahiti* (1981) könnten als wesensverwandt beschrieben werden. Beiden Leuchten gemeinsam ist ihr einnehmend naiver Stil. Zugleich handelt es sich um raffinierte, Fragen aufwerfende Objekte. Durch ihre witzigen, wenn auch stark stilisierten Anklänge an Comic-Tiergestalten wirken sie vage anthropomorph. Und sie sehen aus, als wären sie aus lackierten Bauklötzen zusammengesetzt worden. Oder bestehen sie gar aus Süßigkeiten wie Lutschbonbons und Zuckerstangen? (PG)

L'architecte-designer italien Michele De Lucchi fut l'un des membres fondateurs de la groupe Memphis. Sa lampe de table *Oceanic* (1981) est parente par l'esprit de la *Tahiti* (1981) de Ettore Sottsass. Ces deux lampes semblent en effet partager une même naïveté de style, plein, d'allant. Ce sont néanmoins des objets sophistiqués qui interpellent. Tous deux sont vaguement anthropomorphiques, évoquant avec humour des animaux de dessin animé stylisés. Ont-ils été fabriqués avec des briques de jeux d'enfants peintes de couleurs vives, avec des bonbons ou des sucettes ? (PG)

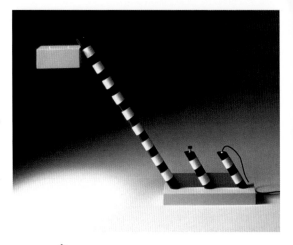

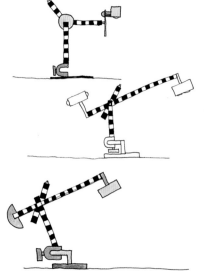

△△ *Oceanic* **table light, 1981**

Enameled metal construction, 40.5 cm high / Konstruktion aus lackiertem Metall, 40,5 cm hoch / Lampe en métal émaillé, 40,5 cm de haut **Memphis**, Pregnana Milanese, Italy

△ *Design drawing of variations of the* Oceanic *table light, c.1981 / Entwurfskizze von Varianten der Tischleuchte* Oceanic, *ca. 1981 / Dessin de conception de variantes de la lampe de table* Oceanic, *vers 1981*

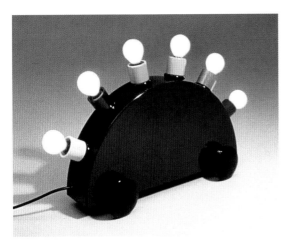

The French architect-designer Martine Bedin studied in Paris and later in Florence, where in 1978 she met Adolfo Natalini and began working in his design office, Superstudio. With this strong connection to the Radical Design movement in Italy, it is not surprising that Bedin became a member of the Memphis design group when it first erupted onto the design scene in 1981. The same year her whimsical *Super* table/floor light was included in the group's first collection. This playful polchromatic design invited user interaction with its moveable wheels and countered expectations of what a table light should look like. (CF/PF)

Die französische Architektin und Designerin Martine Bedin studierte zuerst in Paris und später in Florenz, wo sie 1978 Adolfo Natalini kennen lernte und in dessen Designbüro Superstudio eintrat. Angesichts dieser engen Verbindung zur Bewegung des Radical Design in Italien überrascht es nicht, dass sich Martine Bedin der Designergruppe Memphis anschloss, als diese 1981 in der Szene schlagartig bekannt wurde. Im selben Jahr wurde ihre ungewöhnliche Tisch-/Bodenleuchte *Super* in die erste Kollektion der Gruppe aufgenommen. Dieses Modell forderte mit seinen beweglichen Rädern zur Interaktion auf und widersprach allen Erwartungen an das Aussehen einer traditionellen Leuchte. (CF/PF)

L'architecte et designer française Martine Bedin a étudié à Paris et à Florence, où elle a rencontré en 1978 Adolfo Natalini puis a commencé à travailler dans son agence de design, Superstudio. Très liée au mouvement du Design radical italien, il n'est pas surprenant qu'elle soit devenue membre du groupe Memphis dès son apparition en 1981. La même année, sa très personnelle lampe de table/de sol *Super* faisait partie de la première collection du groupe. Ce modèle ludique et polychrome invite son utilisateur à l'interaction grâce à ses roues qui fonctionnent réellement. Il est à l'opposé de ce que l'on pourrait attendre d'une lampe de table classique. (CF/PF)

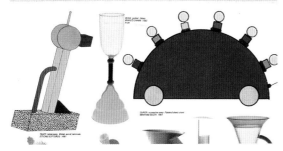

△△ *Super* **table/floor light, 1981**
Enameled sheet steel (later fiberglass) with rubber wheels, 50 cm high / Lackiertes Stahlblech (später Fiberglas) mit Gummirädern, 50 cm hoch / Tôle d'acier laquée (puis fibre de verre), roues en caoutchouc, 50 cm de haut
Memphis, Pregnana Milanese, Italy

△ *Pamphlet for the Memphis exhibition held at the Boilerhouse, Victoria & Albert Museum, London, 1982 / Ausstellungsprospekt der Gruppe Memphis, Boilerhouse, Victoria & Albert Museum, London, 1982 / Prospectus de l'exposition Memphis à la Boilerhouse, Victoria & Albert Museum, Londres, 1982*

▷ *Tahiti* **table light, 1981**
Laminated plastic and enameled metal con-
struction, 60 cm high / Konstruktion aus Kunst-
stofflaminat und lackiertem Metall, 60 cm hoch /
Plastique stratifié et métal laqué, 60 cm de haut
Memphis, Pregnana Milanese, Italy

◁ *Design drawing of the* Tahiti *table light
with variations by Ettore Sottsass, c.1981 /
Entwurfszeichnung der Tischleuchte* Tahiti
*mit Varianten von Ettore Sottsass, ca. 1981 /
Dessin de la lampe de table* Tahiti *et de ses
variantes par Ettore Sottsass, vers 1981*

The *Tahiti* table light (1981) featured
in the first, ground-breaking collection
issued by Ettore Sottsass and his associates under the brand name of Memphis. The project was a willful assault
on notions of "good taste" and "perfect"
form. The designs were challenging and
ironic and drew deliberately on kitsch
and vernacular sources. *Tahiti* has a jok-
iness that is anti-chic, anti-fashion, anti-
pretension. "We are all sure that Memphis furniture will soon go out of style,"
wrote Sottsass provocatively. Yet, as a
philosophical position, Memphis has
proved an indelible aspect of recent
design history. (PG)

Die Tischleuchte *Tahiti* (1981) war Teil
der ersten, richtungsweisenden Kollektion, mit der Ettore Sottsass und seine
Freunde unter dem Markennamen
Memphis in Erscheinung traten. Das
Projekt war ein gezielter Angriff auf
das, was als „guter Geschmack" oder
„perfekte" Form galt. Die Entwürfe der
Designer von Memphis waren provo-
kant und ironisch, und sie setzten ganz
bewusst Kitsch und volkstümliche Elemente ein. Die *Tahiti* Leuchte wendet
sich scherzhaft gegen Schick, Mode-
bewusstsein und Snobismus. „Wir sind
alle davon überzeugt, dass die Mem-
phis-Möbel bald aus der Mode sein
werden", schrieb Sottsass. Als philo-
sophischer Standpunkt wurde Memphis jedoch zu einem unvergesslichen
Aspekt der Designgeschichte. (PG)

La lampe de table *Tahiti* (1981) a
figuré dans la première collection-
événement éditée par Ettore Sottsass
et ses associés sous le nom de marque de Memphis. Le projet était une
attaque délibérée contre le « bon goût »
et la forme « parfaite ». Les projets
étaient audacieux et ironiques et ten-
daient délibérément vers le kitsch et le
vernaculaire. *Tahiti* est une plaisanterie
anti-chic, anti-mode, anti-snob. « Nous
sommes sûrs que le mobilier Memphis
sera bientôt démodé », écrivait Sottsass
pour provoquer. Néanmoins, en tant
que position philosophique, Memphis
s'est révélé un épisode incontournable
de la récente histoire du design. (PG)

ettore sottsass
tahiti table light

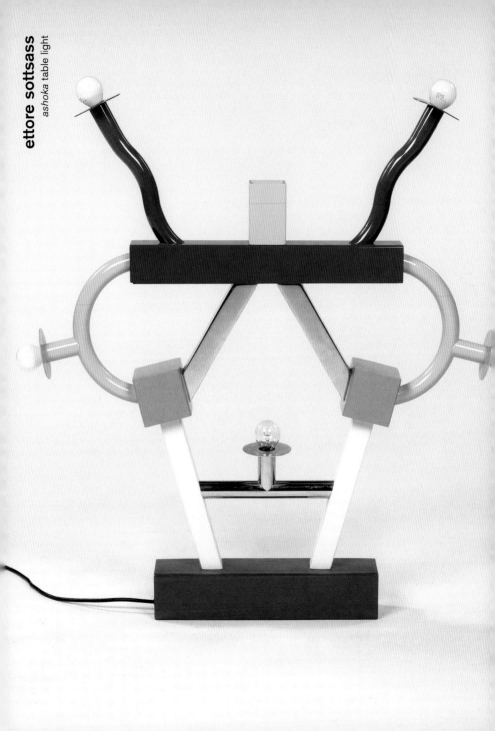

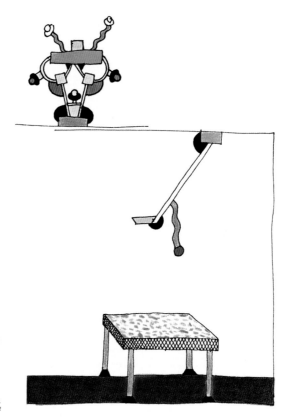

◁ *Ashoka* **table light, 1981**

Enameled and chrome-plated metal construction, 87 cm high / Konstruktion aus lackiertem
und verchromtem Metall, 87 cm hoch / Structure en métal laqué et chromé, 87 cm de haut
Memphis, Pregnana Milanese, Italy

▷ *Design drawing showing the* Ashoka table
light *and other Memphis designs, c.1981 /
Entwurfszeichnung der Tischleuchte* Ashoka
*und anderer Objekte von Studio Memphis, ca.
1981 / Dessin de la lampe de table* Ashoka *et
autres objets du studio Memphis, vers 1981*

The *Ashoka* table light (1981) is characteristic of the unsettling products
made by the Memphis studio. The name
Memphis itself was purposely ambigu-
ous, referring to the American city, and
songs by Chuck Berry and Bob Dylan,
while evoking a mystical ancient Egypt.
Ettore Sottsass was tilting at the rigidity
of Modernists who sought a fixed solution to any design question. For him,
questioning was a way of life. Sottsass
regarded the designer's role as a process of making travel notes, of suggest-
ing temporary possibilities, "momentary
and provisional figures that can be
envisaged during the great, mad, super-
senseless journey of History." (PG)

Die Tischleuchte *Ashoka* (1981) ist
typisch für das irritierende Design des
Studio Memphis. Der Name Memphis
war mit Absicht zweideutig und nahm
Bezug auf die gleichnamige amerikanische Stadt sowie auf Songs von
Chuck Berry und Bob Dylan, erinnerte
aber auch an das mystische alte Ägypten. Ettore Sottsass lief Sturm gegen
die Rigidität der Modernisten, die für
jede Designfrage eine vorgefertigte
Lösung parat hatten. Fragen zu stellen,
war für ihn Teil seines Selbstverständ-
nisses. Er betrachtete den Designer als
einen Reisenden, der seine Eindrücke
notiert und temporäre Möglichkeiten
anbietet – „flüchtige und vorläufige Formen, die sich im Lauf der großen, ver-
rückten, supersinnlosen Reise der
Geschichte ausdenken lassen". (PG)

La lampe de table *Ashoka* (1981)
est caractéristique des produits déran-
geants du studio Memphis. Le nom de
Memphis, lui-même ambigu, renvoyait à
la fois à la ville américaine, à des chan-
sons de Chuck Berry et de Bob Dylan,
et à l'ancienne Égypte mystique. Ettore
Sottsass fustigeait la rigidité du modernisme qui recherchait une solution dé-
terminée à n'importe quel problème de
design. Pour lui, remettre les choses
en cause était une façon de vivre. Il
considérait le rôle du designer comme
un processus de notes de voyage, ou
la suggestion de possibilités temporai-
res : « des figures momentanées et pro-
visoires qui peuvent s'envisager tout
au long du parcours immense, fou et
insensé, de l'Histoire ». (PG)

"All my creations look like small architecture."

„Alle meine Entwürfe wirken wie kleine Architekturen."

« Toutes mes créations ont l'air de petites architectures. »

– Ettore Sottsass

Pausania desk/table light, 1982

Metal and plastic resin construction, 43.3 x 43 cm / Konstruktion aus Metall und Kunstharz, 43,3 x 43 cm / Structure en métal et résine plastique, 43,3 x 43 cm
Artemide, Pregnana Milanese, Italy

▷ **Callimaco** uplighter, 1982

Enameled metal construction with halogen bulb, 200 cm high / Konstruktion aus lackiertem Metall mit Halogenlampe, 200 cm hoch / Structure en métal laqué, ampoule halogène, 200 cm de haut
Artemide, Pregnana Milanese, Italy

After designing various objects for Studio Alchimia, freely inspired by his love of Pop Art, Ettore Sottsass established the Memphis research group in 1981. One of the group's supporters was Ernesto Gismondi, the founder of Artemide. For this company, Sottsass designed lighting that, although influenced by the Memphis style, was more mindful of industrial requirements. The *Callimaco* (1982) is a powerful "luminator," a type of uplighter devised in the 1930s, which incorporates a dimmer to regulate brightness, while the *Pausania* (1982) is an architectural interpretation of the traditional desk light. (SC)

Nachdem Ettore Sottsass verschiedene Objekte, die von seiner Liebe zur Pop Art inspiriert waren, für das Studio Alchimia entworfen hatte, gründete er 1981 die Designergruppe Memphis. Zu den Förderern der Gruppe zählte unter anderen Ernesto Gismondi, der Gründer von Artemide. Sottsass entwarf für dessen Firma Beleuchtungskörper, die zwar stilistisch von Memphis beeinflusst waren, aber doch mehr Rücksicht auf die Anforderungen der Industrie nahmen. Die Leuchte *Callimaco* (1982) ist eine Art Deckenfluter im Stil der 1930er Jahre, ausgestattet mit einem Dimmer zur Regulierung der Lichtstärke. Die Leuchte *Pausania* (1982) stellt hingegen eine architektonische Interpretation der traditionellen Schreibtischleuchte dar. (SC)

Après avoir créé divers objets librement inspirés par son amour du Pop Art pour le Studio Alchimia, Ettore Sottsass fonda le groupe de recherches Memphis en 1981 dont l'un des soutiens était Ernesto Gismondi, fondateur d'Artemide. Pour cette société, Sottsass dessina un luminaire qui, bien qu'influencé par le style Memphis, prenait mieux en compte les contraintes industrielles. Le *Callimaco* (1982) est un type de lampadaire à éclairage indirect mis au point dans les années 1930, équipé d'un régulateur d'intensité, tandis que la *Pausania* (1982) est une interprétation architecturale de la lampe de bureau traditionnelle. (SC)

"I cannot see any borderline between art and design."

„Ich kann zwischen Kunst und Design keine Grenze sehen."

«Je ne peux pas distinguer de frontière entre l'art et le design.»

– Ingo Maurer

◁/▷ *Ya Ya Ho* lighting system, 1982–84
Plastic, metal, ceramic and glass construction, 1,000 cm long (max.) / Konstruktion aus Kunststoff, Metall, Keramik, Porzellan, Glas, 1 000 cm lang (max.) / Système en plastique, métal, céramique, porcelaine et verre, 1 000 cm long (max.)
Ingo Maurer, Munich, Germany

The idea for the *Ya Ya Ho* low-voltage halogen lighting system (1982–84) first occurred to Ingo Maurer one New Year's Eve in Haiti. In a small village square, he came across bulbs with no holders soldered straight onto an electric cable extending from house to house right across the square. Inspired by this extremely simple but highly dangerous arrangement, Maurer and his team developed the much-copied *Ya Ya Ho* system. Presented for the first time at the international lighting exhibition "Euroluce" in Milan in 1984, *Ya Ya Ho* caused an immediate sensation. (TB)

Die Idee zu dem Niedervolt-Halogen-Sytem *Ya Ya Ho* (1982–84) kam Ingo Maurer während einer Sylvesternacht auf Haiti: Auf einem kleinen Dorfplatz entdeckte er Glühbirnen, die ohne Fassung an stromführende Kabel gelötet waren, die wiederum von Haus zu Haus quer über den Platz gespannt waren. Inspiriert von dieser sehr einfachen, aber auch gefährlichen Beleuchtung entwickelten Maurer und sein Team das oft kopierte *Ya Ya Ho* Halogen-System auf Niedervoltbasis. 1984 erstmals auf der „Euroluce" in Mailand der Öffentlichkeit vorgestellt, sorgte das System unmittelbar für Furore. (TB)

L'idée du système d'éclairage halogène basse tension *Ya Ya Ho* (1982–84) vint à Ingo Maurer un soir de nouvel an à Haïti. Sur une petite place de village, il tomba sur une guirlande d'ampoules soudées directement, sans support, sur un câble électrique courant de maison en maison. Inspiré par ce principe extrêmement simple et très dangereux, il mit au point avec son équipe le système *Ya Ya Ho*, si souvent copié. Présenté pour la première fois au salon international du luminaire «Euroluce» à Milan en 1984, il fit sensation. (TB)

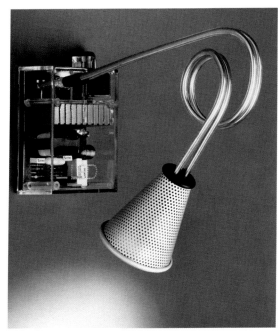

The *LED* table light (1983) designed by Roberto Lucci and Paolo Orlandini in fact uses a halogen bulb as its main illuminant, but takes its name from the light-emitting diode (LED) incorporated within the transparent plastic base housing the transformer. This single LED gives a constant marker-like glow so that the on/off switch of the light, which was originally intended for bedside use, can be found easily in the dark. Innovative from both a technical and an esthetic standpoint, the *LED* table and wall lights also employ two-part bendable stems made of copper cable sheathed in PVC. (CF/PF)

Bei der von Roberto Lucci und Paolo Orlandini entworfenen Tischleuchte *LED* (1983) ist zwar eine Halogenlampe die eigentliche Lichtquelle, dennoch beruht ihr Name auf der Leuchtdiode (LED) in dem transparenten Plastikfuß, der den Transformator enthält. Diese einzelne LED leuchtet konstant wie ein Positionslicht, so dass der An- und Ausschalter der ursprünglich als Nachttischlampe vorgesehenen Leuchte im Dunkeln leicht zu finden ist. Die sowohl aus technischer wie aus ästhetischer Sicht innovativen *LED* Tisch- und Wandleuchten besitzen einen extrem flexiblen Arm, der aus zwei parallel laufenden, mit PVC verkleideten Kupferkabeln gefertigt ist. (CF/PF)

La lampe de table *LED* (1983) conçue par Roberto Lucci et Paolo Orlandini utilise en fait comme source lumineuse principale une ampoule halogène, mais tire son nom de la diode lumineuse (LED) intégrée dans le socle en plastique transparent qui contient le transformateur. Cette LED unique reste allumée en permanence pour que l'on puisse facilement trouver l'interrupteur de cette lampe originellement prévue pour un chevet. Novateurs sur le plan à la fois technique et esthétique, ces modèles *LED* sont tous deux dotés de tiges flexibles en câble de cuivre gainé de PVC. (CF/PF)

roberto lucci & paolo orlandini
led wall and table lights

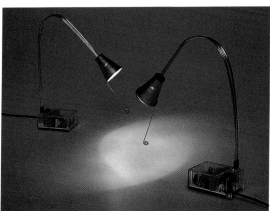

◁/△ **LED table light, 1983**

Transparent methacrylate base housing transformer and LED with self-supporting PVC-sheathed copper cable stem, anodized aluminum shade and halogen bulb, 44 cm high (approx.) / Fuß aus transparentem Methacrylat mit eingebautem Transformator und LED, Arm aus selbsttragendem, PVC-verkleideten Kupferkabel, Lampenschirm aus eloxiertem Aluminium mit Halogenlampe, 44 cm hoch (ca.) / Socle en méthacrylate transparent

contenant le transformateur et LED, câble autoporteur en cuivre gainé de PVC, abat-jour en aluminium anodisé, ampoule halogène, 44 cm de haut (environ)
Segno, Parabiago, Italy

△△ LED wall light designed by Roberto Lucci and Paolo Orlandini for Segno, 1983 / Wandleuchte LED, entworfen von Roberto Lucci und Paolo Orlandini für Segno, 1983 / Applique LED conçue par Roberto Lucci et Paolo Orlandini pour Segno, 1983

RHa 2 task light, 1981–84

Thermoplastic base, elbow and shade with aluminum arm and stem, 26–52 cm high / Fuß, Winkelstück und Lampenschirm aus Thermoplast mit Armen aus Aluminium, 26–52 cm hoch / Socle, réflecteur et coude en thermoplastique, tige et bras en aluminium, 26–52 cm de haut

Tecnolumen, Bremen, Germany

"Good design means as little design as possible."

„Gutes Design bedeutet so wenig Design wie möglich."

« Le *Good Design* signifie aussi peu de design que possible. »

– Dieter Rams

Dieter Rams is widely acknowledged as having set the standard in industrial design in postwar Germany. He worked very closely with manufacturers, notably the firm of Braun, on product development and championed, with a renewed rigor and refinement, the principles first defined in the 1920s at the Bauhaus: truth to materials and purity of form. He has here collaborated with Andreas Hackbarth to design an adjustable and functional work light (1981– 84) that is understated and faultlessly proportioned. (PG)

Dieter Rams gilt allgemein als der Mann, der im Industriedesign Nachkriegsdeutschlands neue Maßstäbe setzte. Er arbeitete bei der Produktentwicklung sehr eng mit den Herstellern zusammen, insbesondere mit der Firma Braun, und propagierte die Wiedereinsetzung der in den 1920er Jahren definierten und nun verfeinerten und noch strenger angewendeten Gestaltungsprinzipien der Bauhaus-Bewegung: Materialtreue und Reinheit der Form. Mit dem hier gezeigten, in Zusammenarbeit mit Andreas Hackbarth entstandenen Modell hat er eine verstellbare und funktionale Arbeitsleuchte (1981–84) geschaffen, die sich durch Understatement und perfekte Proportionen auszeichnet. (PG)

Dieter Rams est l'un des pères reconnus des standards du design industriel de l'Allemagne d'après-guerre. Il a collaboré étroitement avec les fabricants, en particulier Braun, pour développer ses produits, défendant avec un raffinement et une vigueur sans cesse renouvelés les principes définis dès les années 1920 au Bauhaus : vérité des matériaux et pureté de formes. Ici, il a travaillé avec Andreas Hackbarth au dessin de cette lampe de travail (1981–84) réglable et fonctionnelle, d'une grande retenue et de proportions impeccables. (PG)

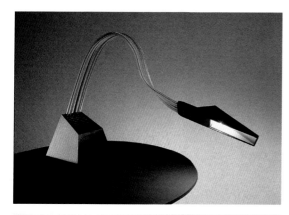

The *Nastro* light (1983) is a clever and good-looking light that adapts an existing product to a new function. Alberto Fraser was working as a designer in a word-processor research center. He became fascinated by the beauty and potential of the multi-colored, co-extruded coaxial cables that spilled forth from the disembodied computers around him. He developed a simple co-extrusion that incorporated electrical and mechanical elements and used this as the basis of a flexible table light – an elegant by-product of the computer age. (PG)

Die Tischleuchte *Nastro* (1983) hat ein intelligentes und optisch ansprechendes Design, bei dem ein vorhandenes Produkt für eine neue Funktion adaptiert wurde. Alberto Fraser arbeitete als Designer in einem Forschungszentrum für Textverarbeitungssysteme und war fasziniert von der Schönheit und dem Potential der bunten, aus einem Stück gefertigten Koaxial-Kabel, die aus den offenen Computern herausquollen. Darauf aufbauend entwickelte er ein einfaches, transparentes Koaxial-Kabel, das sowohl die stromführenden Kupferdrähte als auch ein Verfestigungselement aufnimmt, und konstruierte daraus als elegantes Nebenprodukt des Computerzeitalters eine Tischleuchte mit flexiblem Arm. (PG)

La lampe de table *Nastro* (1983) est une lampe intelligente et de belle allure, qui adapte un produit existant à une fonction nouvelle. Alberto Fraser, designer dans un centre de recherche sur les ordinateurs, était fasciné par la beauté et le potentiel des câbles coaxiaux multicolores jaillissant des appareils démontés. Il mit au point un procédé simple de co-extrusion intégrant des éléments électriques et mécaniques, et l'utilisa pour créer cette lampe de table flexible, élégant produit dérivé de l'ère des ordinateurs. (PG)

alberto fraser
nastro table light

Nastro table light, 1983
Polycarbonate base and head with cabling and structural elements embedded in extruded PVC stem, 21 cm (stem), 14 cm (base) / Fuß und Leuchtenkopf aus Polykarbonat, stranggepresstes PVC mit integrierten stromführenden Kabeln und Verfestigungselement, 21 cm (Arm), 14 cm (Fuß) / Socle et tête en polycarbonate, câblage et éléments structurels noyés dans une tige en PVC extrudé, 21 cm (tige), 14 cm (socle)
Stilnovo, Lainate, Italy

Peter Shire first came to international prominence in the early 1980s, when he began working with Memphis, designing Post-Modern furniture and ceramics that Ettore Sottsass found "fresh, witty and full of information for the future." His polychromatic *Olympia* floor light was specially designed for use in the athletes' village during the Los Angeles Summer Olympics held in 1984. This quirky design epitomizes Shire's remarkable ability to synthesis craft, design and art into humorous yet contesting objects. As he notes, "Mystical absurdism, amazing, astounding phenomena on a human scale … the way we love and hate industrial things … is what interests me." (CF/PF)

Peter Shire wurde Anfang der 1980er Jahre als Designer international bekannt, als seine Zusammenarbeit mit der Gruppe Memphis begann und er postmoderne Möbel und Keramiken entwarf, die Ettore Sottsass mit „frisch, witzig und zukunftsweisend" beschrieb. Die mehrfarbige Stehleuchte *Olympia* entstand für das Olympische Dorf der Sommerspiele 1984 in Los Angeles. Das verspielte Design veranschaulicht Shires bemerkenswerte Fähigkeit, aus der Synthese von Handwerk, Design und Kunst humorvolle und gleichzeitig richtungsweisende Objekte entstehen zu lassen. Ihn interessiere, so schreibt er, „mystische Absurdität, erstaunliche, überraschende Phänomene auf einer menschlichen Ebene … die Art, wie wir industrielle Gegenstände lieben und hassen". (CF/PF)

Peter Shire fit une percée internationale au début des années 1980 lorsqu'il commença à travailler avec Memphis, concevant des meubles et des céramiques postmodernes que Ettore Sottsass jugea « frais, drôles et pleins d'informations sur le futur. » Son lampadaire polychrome *Olympia* fut spécialement conçu pour le village olympique lors des Jeux Olympiques d'été de Los Angeles en 1984. Ce modèle sinueux illustre la remarquable capacité de Shire à synthétiser l'artisanat, le design et l'art dans des objets à la fois humoristiques et contestataires. Comme il le précise : « absurdité, mystique, phénomènes étonnants, abasourdissants à l'échelle humaine… la façon dont nous aimons et haïssons les objets industriels… est ce qui m'intéresse ». (CF/PF)

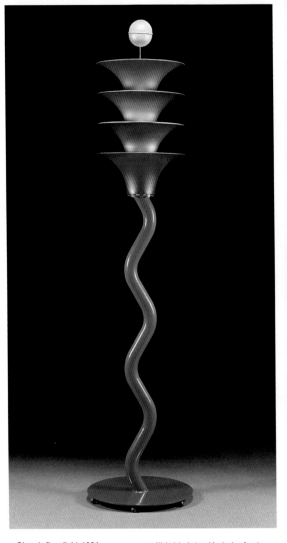

△ *Olympia* **floor light, 1984**

Enameled metal and aluminum construction, 274.3 cm high / Konstruktion aus lackiertem Metall und Aluminium, 274,3 cm hoch / Structure en métal laqué et aluminium, 274,3 cm de haut
USA

▷ *Nightclub, designed for the Los Angeles Summer Olympics by Peter Shire, 1984 / Von Peter Shire gestalteter Nachtclub für die Sommerolympiade in Los Angeles, 1984 / Night-club conçu par Peter Shire pour les Jeux Olympiques d'été à Los Angeles, 1984*

◁ ***Tree* floor lights, 1983–84**

Enameled weighted steel bases with flexible tubular steel arms and halogen bulbs, small: 170 cm high, large: 220 cm high / Füße aus lackiertem Metall mit Armen aus flexiblem Stahlrohr und Halogenlampen, klein: 170 cm hoch, groß: 220 cm hoch / Bases lestées en acier émaillé, bras en tube d'acier flexible, ampoules halogènes, petit modèle : 170 cm de haut, grand modèle : 220 cm de haut
One-Off, London, Great Britain (variation manufactured by Zeus, Milan, Italy)

▷ ***Mira* floor light, 1983**

Enameled tubular metal construction with rotating aluminum head, 66, 63.5 and 38 cm long (length of arms) / Konstruktion aus lackiertem Stahlrohr mit drehbarem Leuchtenkopf aus Aluminium, 66, 63,5 und 38 cm lang (Armlänge) / Fabrication en tube métallique, tête rotative en aluminium, 66, 63,5 et 38 cm long (longueur des bras)
Programmaluce, Milan, Italy

Ron Arad's *Tree* floor lights (1983– 84) demonstrate how a group of British-based designers – Arad, Tom Dixon and André Dubreuil amongst them – created works in metal and found objects, dubbed "salvage design." Using parts from various discarded objects of the day, the *Tree* light, with its flexible hose and welded frame, anticipated Arad's designs of the late 1980s, which also included his *Scaffold* furniture and hand-beaten stainless-steel pieces. In comparison, Mario Arnaboldi's Modernistic *Mira* floor light (1983) epitomizes the 1980s Matt Black style, which was an evolution of the earlier 1970s High-Tech look. (AP)

Die Stehleuchten *Tree* (1983–84) von Ron Arad sind typisch für die aus Metall und „Fundstücken" geschaffenen, als „salvage design" bezeichneten Werke einer britischen Designergruppe, zu der neben Arad auch Tom Dixon und André Dubreuil gehörten. Arad verwendete für seine Entwürfe Teile von ausrangierten Alltagsobjekten. Arads *Tree* Leuchten nehmen Ende der 1980er Jahre entstandene Designs vorweg, so seine *Scaffold* Möbel aus Baugerüst-Elementen oder seine handgeschmiedeten Stahlobjekte. Mario Arnaboldis modernistische Stehleuchte *Mira* (1983) ist dagegen typisch für den Matt-Schwarz-Stil der 1980er Jahre, der eine elegante Weiterentwicklung des Hightech-Looks der 1970er Jahre darstellt. (AP)

Les lampadaires *Tree* (1983–84) de Ron Arad illustrent le travail d'un groupe de designers britanniques – Arad, Tom Dixon et le Français André Dubreuil, entre autres – qui se retrouvèrent autour du « design sauvage » d'œuvres en métal et divers objets de récupération. Utilisant des morceaux d'objets mis au rebut, la *Tree*, à flexibles et structure soudée, annonce les créations d'Arad de la fin des années 1980, dont le mobilier *Scaffold* et des pièces d'acier inoxydable mises en forme à la main. Par comparaison, le lampadaire moderniste *Mira* (1983) de Mario Arnaboldi illustre le style « noir-mat » des années 1980 qui était une évolution stylistique du high-tech du début des années 1970. (AP)

mario arnaboldi
mira floor light

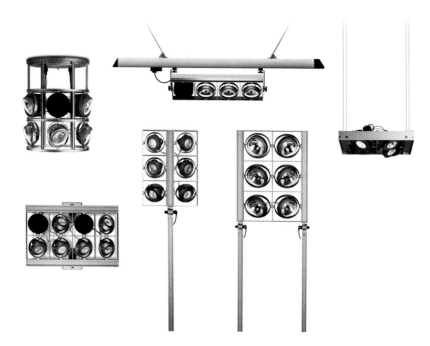

Cestello lighting system, 1985
Die-cast aluminum mounts with adjustable gimbals and aluminum reflectors, various heights / Montierung aus Druckgussaluminium mit verstellbaren Drehgelenken und Reflektoren aus Aluminium, verschiedene Höhen / Monture en fonte d'aluminium, réflecteurs en aluminium à compas réglables, diverses hauteurs
iGuzzini Illuminazione, Recanati, Italy

▷ **Cylindrical Cestello ceiling light, 1985**
Die-cast aluminum mounts with adjustable gimbals and aluminum reflectors, 53 cm high / Montierung aus Druckgussaluminium mit verstellbaren Drehgelenken und Reflektoren aus Aluminium, 53 cm hoch / Monture en fonte d'aluminium, réflecteurs en aluminium à compas réglables, 53 cm de haut
iGuzzini Illuminazione, Recanati, Italy

Originally designed for the interiors of the Palazzo Grassi in Venice, the *Cestello* lighting system (1985) was conceived specifically to meet exhibition requirements and as such has been used in numerous museums and art galleries around the world – it even illuminates Leonardo da Vinci's *Last Supper*. Although the *Cestello* shape has been variously copied over the last 20 years, Aulenti notes that "no one has been able to reproduce the performance levels of the real thing." In recognition of its flexibility, design integrity and superlative performance, the *Cestello* lighting system was awarded a Compasso d'Oro in 1995. (CF/PF)

Das ursprünglich für die Innenbeleuchtung des Palazzo Grassi in Venedig entworfene Leuchtensystem *Cestello* (1985) wurde so konzipiert, dass es den Anforderungen an Ausstellungsbeleuchtungen gerecht wurde, und kam daher auch in Museen und Kunstgalerien weltweit zum Einsatz – es rückt sogar Leonardo da Vincis *Letztes Abendmahl* ins rechte Licht. Obwohl die typische *Cestello* Form im Lauf der letzten zwanzig Jahre mehrfach kopiert wurde, war nach Gae Aulenti „niemand in der Lage, das Leistungsniveau des Originals zu reproduzieren". Für seine Flexibilität, sein originelles Design und seine außergewöhnliche Leistungsfähigkeit wurde das *Cestello* Beleuchtungssystem 1995 mit einem Compasso d'Oro ausgezeichnet. (CF/PF)

Conçu à l'origine pour l'intérieur du Palazzo Grassi à Venise, le système *Cestello* (1985) devait spécifiquement répondre aux nécessités des expositions et a été depuis utilisé dans de nombreux musées et galeries d'art du monde entier (il éclaire même *La Cène* de Léonard de Vinci). Bien que la forme du *Cestello* ait été souvent copiée au cours de ces vingt dernières années, Aulenti a fait remarquer que « personne n'a été capable de reproduire le niveau de performances de l'original ». En reconnaissance de sa souplesse, de son intégrité de conception et de ses remarquables performances, le système a reçu un Compasso d'Oro en 1995. (CF/PF)

"Geometry is balance."

„Geometrie bedeutet Ausgewogenheit."

« La géométrie est équilibre. »

– Mario Botta

◁ *Shogun* **table light, 1986**
Enameled metal construction with revolving per-forated sheet-metal diffusers, 59.5 cm high / Konstruktion aus lackiertem Metall mit drehba-ren Diffusoren aus gelochtem Stahlblech, 59,5 cm hoch / Structure en métal laqué, diffuseurs pivotants en plaques de métal perforé, 59,5 cm de haut
Artemide, Pregnana Milanese, Italy

▷ *Shogun* **floor light, 1986**
Enameled metal construction with revolving per-forated sheet-metal diffusers, 197 cm high / Konstruktion aus lackiertem Metall mit drehba-ren Diffusoren aus gelochtem Stahlblech, 197 cm hoch / Structure en métal laqué, diffuseurs pivotants en plaques de métal perforé, 197 cm de haut
Artemide, Pregnana Milanese, Italy

The Swiss architect-designer Mario Botta is renowned for his use of striking geometric forms. His *Shogun* lights (1986) reflect his belief that lighting should create an atmosphere through its use of shadows. He also considers it important for a light to look good even when it is not switched on. As he notes, "A lamp … is an object that creates light when there is none, so it has to be a visible artifact with a function, an image … that's why I started designing lamps which are people. *Shogun* is a person. He has a head, body and feet, plus a navel." (CF/PF)

Der Schweizer Architekt und Designer Mario Botta ist bekannt für seine streng geometrische Formensprache. In den Leuchten *Shogun* (1986) kommt seine Überzeugung zum Ausdruck, dass Licht mithilfe von Schatten eine stim-mungsvolle Atmosphäre erzeugen soll-te. Außerdem muss eine Leuchte für ihn auch in ausgeschaltetem Zustand überzeugen: „Eine Leuchte … ist ein Objekt, das Licht erzeugt, wenn keines vorhanden ist, sie muss also ein sicht-barer Gegenstand mit einer Funktion sein, ein Bildnis … deshalb habe ich angefangen, Leuchten wie Menschen zu gestalten. *Shogun* ist eine Person mit Kopf, Körper und Füßen und mit einem Bauchnabel." (CF/PF)

L'architecte-designer suisse Mario Botta est réputé pour mettre en œuvre de puissantes formes géométriques. Ses lampes *Shogun* (1986) reflètent sa conviction qu'un luminaire doit créer une atmosphère par la maîtrise des ombres. Il pense également qu'il est important qu'une lampe soit belle même éteinte. Il fait remarquer : «Une lampe … est un objet qui crée la lumière lorsqu'il n'y en a pas, aussi doit-elle être un artéfact visible doté d'une fonction, d'une image … c'est pourquoi j'ai commencé à dessiner des lampes qui sont des êtres. *Shogun* est une personne. Elle a une tête, un corps, des pieds et un nombril. » (CF/PF)

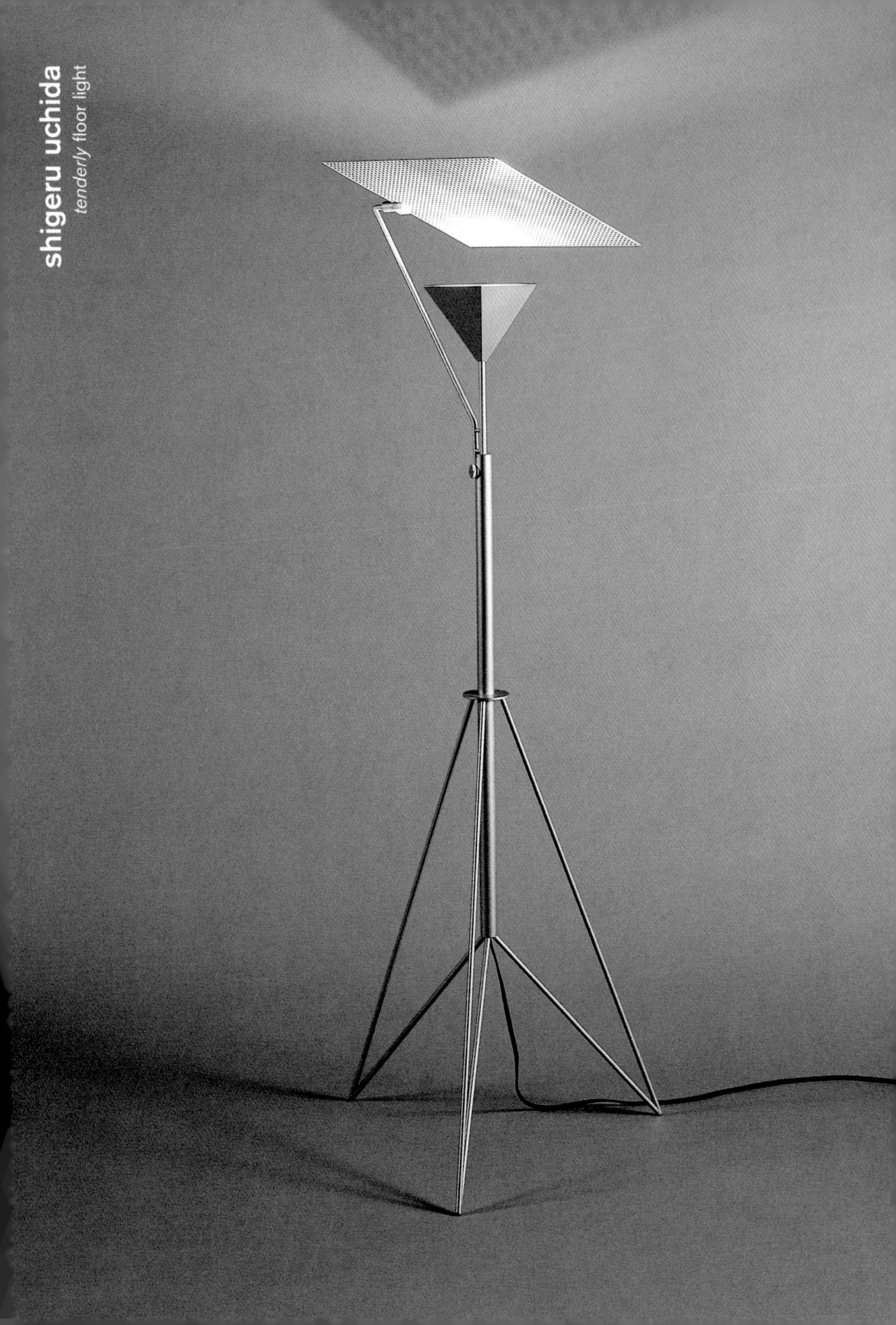

shigeru uchida
tenderly floor light

◁ ***Tenderly* floor light, 1985**

Melamine-coated steel and aluminum construction, 136.8 cm high / Konstruktion aus melaminbeschichtetem Stahl und Aluminium, 136,8 cm hoch / Fabrication en aluminium et acier mélaminé, 136,8 cm de haut Chairs, Tokyo, Japan (reissued by Yamagiwa, Tokyo, Japan)

***Umeda Stand* table light, 1986**

Molded rubber base with glass diffuser, small: 28 cm high, large: 42 cm high / Fuß aus Formgummi mit Diffusor aus Glas, klein: 28 cm hoch, groß: 42 cm hoch / Base en caoutchouc moulé, diffuseur en verre, petit modèle : 28 cm de haut, grand modèle : 42 cm de haut Yamagiwa, Tokyo, Japan

Shigeru Uchida and Masanori Umeda have both synthesized Eastern and Western cultures in the design of these lights. Uchida's *Tenderly* floor light (1985) foregrounds the relationship between object and space, while also exploiting the poetic qualities of industrial materials – in this case wire mesh. It is based on "the image of Japanese men holding up their sun visors to see who is good-looking." Masanori Umeda, who had previously produced furniture designs for Memphis, designed the *Umeda Stand* light in 1986. Sharing the lyrical quality of the *Tenderly*, it offers a quintessential example of Japanese Post-Modernism. The light received an iF Product Design Award in 1987. (CF/PF)

Shigeru Uchida und Masanori Umeda haben im Design dieser beiden Leuchten die östliche und die westliche Kultur miteinander verschmolzen. Uchidas Stehleuchte *Tenderly* (1985) stellt die Beziehung zwischen Objekt und Raum in den Vordergrund. Sein Entwurf beruht auf „dem Bild japanischer Männer, die die Sonnenblenden auf ihren Brillen hochklappen, um zu schauen, wer gut aussieht". Masanori Umeda, der zuvor bereits Möbel für Memphis entworfen hatte, schuf 1986 die Tischleuchte *Umeda Stand.* Wie die *Tenderly* Leuchte besitzt sie eine lyrische Qualität und ist ein typisches Beispiel für den japanischen Postmodernismus. 1987 wurde die Leuchte mit einem iF Product Design Award ausgezeichnet. (CF/PF)

Shigeru Uchida et Masanori Umeda marient les cultures occidentales et orientales dans la conception de ces lampes. Le lampadaire *Tenderly* d'Uchida (1985) explore les relations entre l'objet et l'espace tout en exploitant les qualités poétiques des matériaux industriels, en l'occurrence le treillis métallique. Il etait inspiré par « l'image de Japonais levant leur visière pour regarder une belle passante ». Masanori Umeda, qui avait auparavant réalisé des projets de meubles pour Memphis, a conçu la lampe *Umeda Stand* en 1986. Partageant les qualités lyriques de la *Tenderly*, elle est un des exemples typiques du postmodernisme japonais. Elle a reçu un iF Product Design Award en 1987. (CF/PF)

One of the great maestros of Italian product design, Mario Bellini has designed innovative lighting for Flos, Artemide and Erco. His work has consistently been exemplified by a strong unity of design, combining form and function with an understanding of human needs. His *Eclipse* track lighting (1986) was conceived as a completely modular and interchangeable system, making it highly adaptable. Like the lenses on a professional camera, the light heads – spotlights, floodlights and wall-washers – can easily be changed to suit a wide variety of tasks, from art exhibitions to shop displays. (CF/PF)

Mario Bellini, einer der großen Meister des italienischen Produktdesigns, hat für Flos, Artemide und Erco eine Vielzahl von innovativen Beleuchtungskörpern entwickelt. Seine Entwürfe zeichnen sich durch ein konstant hohes Niveau aus und kombinieren Form und Funktion mit den Bedürfnissen der Benutzer. Bellinis Leuchtschienensystem *Eclipse* (1986) ist modular aufgebaut und mit seinen austauschbaren Elementen höchst anpassungsfähig. Die Leuchtenköpfe – Punktstrahler, Scheinwerfer und Wandfluter – können so leicht wie ein Kameraobjektiv ausgewechselt werden, wodurch das System vielfältig einsetzbar ist – von Kunstausstellungen bis hin zu Schaufensterauslagen. (CF/PF)

Mario Bellini, l'un des grands maîtres du design produit italien, a conçu des lampes particulièrement innovantes pour Flos, Artemide et Erco. Son travail de conception est toujours marqué par une réflexion soutenue, qui combine forme et fonction dans la compréhension des besoins de l'utilisateur. Son système d'éclairage *Eclipse* (1986) est conçu comme un système entièrement modulaire et interchangeable, qui le rend particulièrement adaptable. Comme les lentilles d'un appareil-photo, la partie projecteur – spot, *flood* ou *wall-washer* – peut facilement être changée pour répondre à différentes utilisations, de l'exposition d'art à la vitrine de magasin. (CF/PF)

◁ *Eclipse* track lighting system, 1986
Enameled cast-aluminum housing and bracket with reflector and safety-glass diffuser, various sizes / Gehäuse und Bügel aus lackiertem Gussaluminium mit Reflektor und Diffusor aus Sicherheitsglas, verschiedene Größen / Corps et fixation en fonte d'aluminium laquée, réflecteur et diffuseur à protection en verre de sécurité, dimensions diverses
Erco, Lüdenscheid, Germany

△△/△ Eclipse *low-voltage halogen spotlights / Niedervolt-Halogenstrahler des Leuchtschienensystems* Eclipse / *Spots halogènes basse tension* Eclipse

▷ Eclipse *metal floodlight / Scheinwerfer aus Metall des Leuchtenschienensystems* Eclipse / *Lampe flood en métal* Eclipse

The appeal of the *Costanza* lights (1985–86), designed by Paolo Rizzato, lies in their look of timeless elegance and the absence of trendy trimmings. While the forms are classic, the materials are avant-garde. The silk-screen-printed polycarbonate shades are washable and therefore easy to clean. Height-adjustable, telescopic aluminum bases add to the versatility of the *Costanza* table and floor lights. Instead of a traditional switch, a slender rod placed at an angle under the shade turns the light on and off and in some versions serves as a dimming device. (TB)

Die Attraktivität der von Paolo Rizzato entworfenen Leuchtenserie *Costanza* (1985–86), liegt in ihrer zeitlosen Eleganz, die ohne irgendein modisches Beiwerk auskommt. Während die Formgebung eher klassisch anmutet, sind die verwendeten Werkstoffe avantdistisch: Die Lampenschirme aus siebbedrucktem Polykarbonat sind abwaschbar und daher leicht zu reinigen. Bei der *Costanza* Tisch- und Bodenleuchte sorgen die höhenverstellbaren teleskopartigen Leuchtenfüße aus Aluminium für Variabilität. Anstelle eines traditionellen Schalters dient ein dünner Stab, der schräg unter dem Schirm herausragt, als Ein- und Ausschalter und bei einigen Versionen der Leuchte zusätzlich als Sensor-Dimmer. (TB)

La séduction des lampes *Costanza* créées par Paolo Rizzato en 1985–86 tient à leur élégance intemporelle et leur absence totale de références à la mode. Si les formes restent classiques, les matériaux sont d'avant-garde. Les abat-jour, en polycarbonate sérigraphié lavable, sont faciles à nettoyer. Hauteur réglable et, pied télescopique en aluminium renforcent la polyvalence de ces modèles. Fixée sous l'abat-jour, une fine tige inclinée fait office d'interrupteur et sert, dans certaines versions, de rhéostat à commande sensorielle. (TB)

Costanza hanging light, 1986

Silk-screened polycarbonate shade with opaque chromed steel counterweight, 40 cm diameter / Lampenschirm aus siebbedrucktem Polykarbonat mit Gegengewicht aus matt verchromtem Stahl, 40 cm Durchmesser / Abat-jour en polycarbonate sérigraphié, contrepoids en acier chromé mat, 40 cm de diamètre
Luceplan, Milan, Italy

▷△ Components for the Constanza *table light /*
Bestandteile der Tischleuchte Costanza /
Composants de la lampe de table Constanza

▷ Costanza table light, 1986

Enameled or powder-coated aluminum base with silk-screened polycarbonate shade, 110 cm high (max.) / Fuß aus lackiertem oder pulverbeschichtetem Aluminium mit Lampenschirm aus siebbedrucktem Polykarbonat, 110 cm hoch (max.) / Pied en aluminium laqué ou peinte par poudrage, abat-jour en polycarbonate sérigraphié, 110 cm de haut (max.)
Luceplan, Milan, Italy

▷▷ Costanza floor light, 1985

Enameled or powder-coated aluminum base with silk-screened polycarbonate shade, 160 cm high (max.) / Fuß aus lackiertem oder pulverbeschichtetem Aluminium mit Lampenschirm aus siebbedrucktem Polykarbonat, 160 cm hoch (max.) / Pied en aluminium laqué ou peinte par poudrage, abat-jour en polycarbonate sérigraphié, 160 cm de haut (max.)
Luceplan, Milan, Italy

michele de lucchi & giancarlo fassina
tolomeo task light

Among the most commercially successful lighting designs of the last 50 years, the *Tolomeo* task light (1987) designed by Michele De Lucchi and Giancarlo Fassina won a coveted Compasso d'Oro award in 1989. Anticipating the recent obsession with all things aluminum, the light's polished aluminum cantilevered arm enables easy positioning, while its anodized aluminum diffuser rotates in all directions, allowing a remarkable level of adjustment. During the 1990s two smaller versions were introduced, the *Tolomeo Mini* (1991) and the *Tolomeo Micro* (1999–2000), as well as a model designed to be used with VDU terminals, the *Tolomeo Video* (1991). (CF/PF)

Die von Michele De Lucchi und Giancarlo Fassina entworfene Arbeitsleuchte *Tolomeo* (1987) gehört zu den meistverkauften Beleuchtungskörpern der letzten fünfzig Jahre. 1989 wurde sie mit dem begehrten Compasso d'Oro ausgezeichnet. Ihr Erfolg nahm die bis heute anhaltende Begeisterung für den Werkstoff Aluminium im Wohnraumdesign vorweg. Durch die ausrichtbaren Arme aus poliertem Aluminium und den in alle Richtungen verstellbaren Lampenschirm aus eloxiertem Aluminium kann die Leuchte außerordentlich gut den jeweiligen Bedürfnissen angepasst werden. In den 1990er Jahren kamen zwei kleinere Versionen auf den Markt, die *Tolomeo Mini* (1991) und die *Tolomeo Micro* (1999–2000), sowie ein besonders für Bildschirmarbeitsplätze geeignetes Modell, die *Tolomeo Video* (1991). (CF/PF)

L'un des luminaires ayant le plus grand succès commercial au cours de ces cinquante dernières années est la *Tolomeo* (1987), conçue par Michele De Lucchi et Giancarlo Fassina, qui a remporté le très convoité Compasso d'Oro en 1989. Annonçant l'obsession actuelle pour tout ce qui est en aluminium, les bras en aluminium poli et en porte-à-faux autorisent de multiple positions, tandis que le diffuseur pivote dans n'importe quelle direction, permettant une remarquable précision de réglage. Dans les années 1990, deux versions plus petites furent introduites, la *Tolomeo Mini* (1991) et la *Tolomeo Micro* (1999–2000) ainsi qu'un modèle conçu pour être placé près des écrans d'ordinateurs, la *Tolomeo Video* (1991). (CF/PF)

◁ *Tolomeo* task light, 1987

Powder-coated aluminum base, polished aluminum arms and mounts with matt anodized aluminum, 123 cm high (max.) / Fuß aus pulverbeschichtetem Aluminium, Arme und Montierung aus poliertem Aluminium, Lampenschirm aus matt eloxiertem Aluminium, 123 cm hoch (max.) / Socle en aluminium peint par poudrage, bras et pièces de montage en aluminium poli, diffuseur en aluminium anodisé, 123 cm de haut (max.)
Artemide, Pregnana Milanese, Italy

△ *Tolomeo Terra, Tolomeo Lettura, Tolomeo Stelo Terra & Tolomeo Micro Terra* floor lights, 1987–2001

Polished aluminum bases and arms with matt anodized aluminum diffusers and polished aluminum fittings, 151–226 cm high / Füße, Arme und Montierungen aus poliertem Aluminium, Lampenschirme aus matt eloxiertem Aluminium, 151–226 cm hoch / Socles et tiges en aluminium poli, diffuseur en aluminium anodisé et pièces de montage en aluminium poli, 151–226 cm de haut
Artemide, Pregnana Milanese, Italy

▷ *Tolomeo Micro Faretto* wall light, 2000

Polished aluminum mounts with matt anodized aluminum diffuser, 23 cm high / Lampenschirm aus matt eloxiertem Aluminium mit Montierung aus poliertem Aluminium, 23 cm hoch / Monture en aluminium poli, diffuseur en aluminium anodisé, 23 cm de haut
Artemide, Pregnana Milanese, Italy

The 1987 *Lola* floor light, designed by Alberto Meda and Paolo Rizzato and manufactured by Luceplan in Milan, is the ultimate High-Tech product made from innovative materials. The telescopic, height-adjustable, carbon-fiber stem is supported by a flexible polyurethane tripod base, which cushions any impact. This serves to protect the delicate 300 W lamp, held by a Y-shaped thermoplastic polyester head. In 1989, the *Lola* was awarded a Compasso d'Oro. Since 2001, the stem of *Lola*, which is also available as a wall light, is made of aluminum and marketed under the name *Lola 2001*. (TB)

Die Stehleuchte *Lola* (1987), von Alberto Meda und Paolo Rizzato entworfen und von der Mailänder Firma Luceplan hergestellt, ist ein absolutes High-Tech-Produkt, gefertigt aus innovativen Materialien. Der teleskopartig höhenverstellbare Schaft aus Kohlenstoffgewebe wird von einem federnden Dreifuß aus Polyurethan getragen, der Stöße abfängt, und so das empfindliche 300-W-Leuchtmittel schützt, dessen Fassung von einem Y-förmigen Aufsatz aus thermoplastischem Polyester gehalten wird. 1989 wurde die *Lola* Leuchte mit einem Compasso d'Oro ausgezeichnet. Seit 2001 wird der Schaft der *Lola*, die auch als Wandleuchte erhältlich ist, aus Aluminium produziert und unter der Produktbezeichnung *Lola 2001* vertrieben. (TB)

Le lampadaire *Lola* (1987), conçu par Alberto Meda et Paolo Rizzato et fabriqué par Luceplan à Milan, est le nec plus ultra des luminaires hightech réalisés en matériaux nouveaux. La tige télescopique en fibre de carbone, réglable en hauteur, est soutenue par un tripode en polyuréthane souple, qui amortit tout choc éventuel, pour protéger le délicat réflecteur de 300 W, maintenu par une tête en polyester thermoplastique en forme de Y. En 1989, *Lola* a reçu un Compasso d'Oro. Depuis 2001, la tige de *Lola*, qui est disponible aussi comme applique, est réalisée en aluminium et commercialisée sous le nom de *Lola 2001*. (TB)

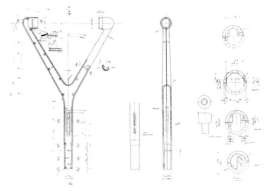

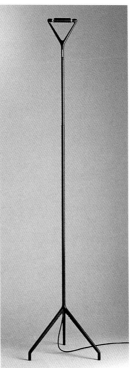

◁ **Lola floor light, 1987**
Carbon-fiber telescopic stem with thermoplastic polyester head and micro-perforated metal reflector on flexible polyurethane tripod base, 200 cm high (max.) / Teleskopschaft aus Kohlenstofffaser mit Leuchtkopf aus thermoplastischem Polyester und Reflektor aus mikroperforiertem Metall auf Stativ aus flexiblem Polyurethan, 200 cm hoch (max.) / Tige télescopique en fibre de carbone, tête en polyester thermoplastique et réflecteur métallique à micro-perforations sur tripode en polyuréthane souple, 200 cm de haut (max.)
Luceplan, Milan, Italy

△ *Design drawing of* Lola *floor light, c.1987 / Konstruktionszeichnung der Stehleuchte* Lola, *ca. 1987 / Dessin de conception du lampadaire* Lola, *vers 1987*

▷ **Lola wall light, 2001**
Micro-perforated metal reflector with anti-UV Pyrex protection glass and self-extinguishing ABS wall attachment, 25 cm high / Reflektor aus mikroperforiertem Metall mit Schutzglas aus Pyrex gegen UV-Strahlen, Wandhalter aus nichtbrennbarem ABS-Kunststoff, 25 cm hoch / Réflecteur de métal à micro-perforations, verre de protection anti UV en Pyrex, fixation murale en ABS apyre, 25 cm de haut
Luceplan, Milan, Italy

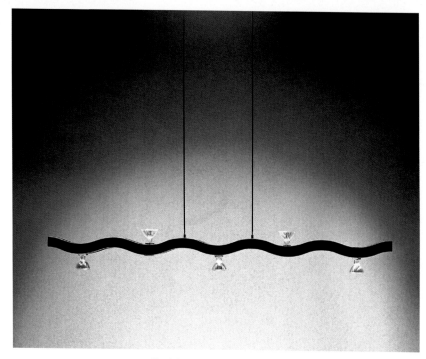

Nessie hanging light, 1985

Aluminum construction suspended on wires, 100 cm wide / An Drähten herabhängende Aluminiumkonstruktion, 100 cm breit / Structure en aluminium, suspension par câbles métalliques, 100 cm de large
Stilnovo, Lainate, Italy (reissued by Lumina Italia, Arluno, Italy)

▷ **Taraxacum hanging light, 1988**

Polished aluminum body with 60 clear light-bulbs, 80 cm diameter / Leuchtenkörper aus poliertem Aluminium mit 60 transparenten Glühbirnen, 80 cm Durchmesser / Corps en aluminium poli, 60 ampoules transparentes, 80 cm de diamètre
Flos, Bovezzo, Italy

These two lights share the principle of exposing the bulbs as key elements of the design. Both are little more than mountings that acquire their sculptural quality once bulbs are fitted into place. In the case of the *Nessie* hanging light (1985), the undulations of the linear horizontal mount add a fashionable, date-specific note of graphic indulgence, softening the austerity of line. Achille Castiglioni's *Taraxacum* (1988) resembles a bouquet of sparkling flowers as the clustered bulbs shimmer with their direct and reflected light. (PG)

Beide Leuchten werden von einem Gestaltungsprinzip geprägt, das auf der Sichtbarkeit der Glühbirnen basiert. Beide stellen kaum mehr als Montierungen dar, die erst mit dem Einsetzen der Glühbirnen skulpturale Qualitäten erlangen. Die Hängeleuchte *Nessie* (1985) erhält durch die Wellenform der horizontalen Montierung noch eine modische, zeitspezifische Note grafischer Prägung, die der kargen Linie eine gewisse Anmut verleiht. Achille Castiglionis Hängeleuchte *Taraxacum* (1988) ähnelt einem Strauß funkelnder Blumen, wenn die rundum dicht nebeneinander angeordneten Glühbirnen mit ihrem direkten und reflektierten Licht erstrahlen. (PG)

Ces deux luminaires partagent un principe identique : faire des ampoules nues et apparentes l'élément clé de la conception. Tous deux ne sont guère plus que des montures qui acquièrent leur vérité sculpturale une fois les ampoules en place. Dans le cas de la *Nessie* (1985), les ondulations de la monture horizontale ajoutent une note élégante de style graphique spécifiquement daté, qui adoucit l'austérité de la ligne. Lorsque les ampoules brillent de tout leur éclat, direct et indirect, la *Taraxacum* d'Achille Castiglioni (1988) fait penser à un bouquet de fleurs étincelantes. (PG)

One of Philippe Starck's most commercially successful products, the horn-shaped *Ará* table light (1988), was named after his daughter. This classic Starck design incorporates bold sweeping lines that give it a highly distinctive sculptural presence. Like so many of Starck's product solutions, the *Ará* also has a strong sense of character. Its tilting head allows the light source to be directed upwards or downwards, while the point of its horn is curved so that it fits the hand. A quintessential 1980s design, the *Ará* is one of the most enduring status symbols from this designer-obsessed decade. (CF/PF)

Die hornförmige Tischleuchte *Ará* (1988) gehört zu Philippe Starcks meistverkauften Produkten und ist nach seiner Tochter benannt. Die Linien dieses klassischen Starck-Designs sind kühn geschwungen und verleihen dem Modell eine ausgeprägt skulpturale Präsenz. Wie viele Produktlösungen von Starck wirkt auch dieser Entwurf sehr eigenwillig. Durch ihren beweglichen Kopf kann die Lichtquelle nach oben oder nach unten gerichtet werden. Die *Ará* Leuchte verkörpert den Stil der 1980er Jahre und erfreut sich als Statussymbol aus diesem so designverliebten Jahrzehnt nach wie vor großer Beliebtheit. (CF/PF)

L'un des plus grands succès commerciaux de Philippe Starck, la lampe de table *Ará* en forme de corne (1988), porte le nom de sa fille. Ce dessin classique, aux lignes enlevées et audacieuses, affirme une remarquable présence sculpturale. Comme tant des réalisations de ce designer, elle possède aussi un caractère affirmé. Sa tête inclinable permet de diriger le flux lumineux vers le haut ou le bas, tandis que la pointe de sa corne est incurvée pour s'adapter à la main. Objet emblématique des années 1980, la lampe *Ará* est l'un des « indispensables » les plus durables de ces années obsédées de design. (CF/PF)

◁ *Royalton Hotel in New York with lights designed by Philippe Starck, 1988 / Royalton Hotel in New York mit Leuchten von Philippe Starck, 1988 / Royalton Hotel à New York avec lampes conçues par Philippe Starck, 1988*

△△ *Philippe Starck with a pair of* Arà *table lights, c.1988 / Philippe Starck mit Tischleuchten* Arà, *ca. 1988 / Philippe Starck tenant deux lampes de table* Arà, *vers 1988*

△ ***Ará* table light, 1988**

Chrome-plated steel base and stem with die-cast metal alloy head, 56.5 cm high / Fuß und Arm aus verchromtem Stahl, Leuchtenkopf aus gegossener Metalllegierung, 56,5 cm hoch / Base et tige en acier chromé, tête en alliage moulé, 56,5 cm de haut
Flos, Bovezzo, Italy

Luigi I chandelier, 1989

Brass mounts with hand-blown glass elements, 60 cm diameter / Konstruktion aus mundgeblasenen Glas-Elementen auf Messingmontierung, 60 cm Durchmesser / Lustre avec des éléments en verre soufflé et montures en laiton, 60 cm de diamètre
Driade, Fossadello di Caorso, Italy

▷ **Yola floor and table lights, 1989**

Enameled metal bases with polypropylene sheet diffusers and plastic fittings, 155 and 66 cm high / Füße aus lackiertem Metall mit Diffusoren aus Polypropylenfolie und Montierungen aus Kunststoff, 155 und 66 cm hoch / Bases en métal émaillé, diffuseurs en feuille de polypropylène, pièces de montage en plastique, 155 and 66 cm de haut
Alva Lighting, London, Great Britain

Born in Czechoslovkia, Bořek Šipek eventually settled in The Netherlands, where he cultivated his reputation as a fine architect and designer. Drawing upon the Bohemian and Tzigane (Hungarian gypsy) cultures and upon the Baroque style, particularly for his designs in glass, he valued traditional craftsmanship in their manufacture. These ideals, combined with his relationship with Driade, led to a variety of furniture and lighting designs, including the *Luigi* family (1989), which is part of Driade's "Follies" collection. Given a simple brief by Driade, Šipek created a bright and exuberant chandelier of writhing and twisting stylized floral forms. (VT)

Der in der Tschechoslowakei geborene Bořek Šipek ließ sich später in den Niederlanden nieder und wurde dort zu einem renommierten Architekten und Designer. Besonders seine Glasarbeiten, bei deren Herstellung er sich gerne auf das alte böhmische Glasbläserhandwerk stützte, waren inspiriert von der Kultur Böhmens und der ungarischen Roma sowie vom Barock. Aus diesen Idealen und seiner Zusammenarbeit mit Driade gingen zahlreiche Möbel und Beleuchtungskörper hervor, so die Leuchtenserie *Luigi* (1989), die Teil der Kollektion *Follies* von Driade sind. Aus der knappen Auftragsbeschreibung, die Šipek von Driade erhielt, machte er einen strahlenden, sinnlichen Kronleuchter mit gewundenen und verflochtenen floralen Formen. (VT)

Né en Tchécoslovaquie, Bořek Šipek s'est installé aux Pays-Bas où il a bâti sa réputation d'architecte et de designer. S'appuyant sur les cultures bohémiennes et tziganes et le style baroque, en particulier dans ses réalisations en verre, il accorde également beaucoup d'importance au travail artisanal. Ces idéaux, combinés à une relation suivie avec Driade, ont donné naissance à de multiples meubles et luminaires, dont la gamme *Luigi* (1989) qui fait partie de la collection *Follies* de Driade. À partir d'un simple cahier des charges du fabricant, Šipek a créé ce lustre exubérant et étincelant, composé de formes florales stylisées entremêlées. (VT)

The *Yola* floor and table lights (1989) are among Jack Woolley's first lighting designs and are still made by the London-based manufacturing company he established with David Edgerley in 2000. Radiating a soft ambient light, they have a remarkably straightforward construction – a cornet of parchment-like polypropylene sheet resting on a simple metal base – that gives them a strong and visually appealing sculptural presence. Easy to assemble and inexpensive to manufacture, the *Yola* lights (also known as *Hal*) have an unpretentiousness and simplicity that meshes with our increasingly nomadic lives. (CF/PF)

Die Steh- und Tischleuchten *Yola* (1989) gehören zu Jack Woolleys ersten Leuchtenentwürfen und werden heute von der Londoner Beleuchtungsfirma gefertigt, die er 2000 zusammen mit David Edgerley gründete. Die Leuchten strahlen ein weiches, stimmungsvolles Licht aus und sind ungewöhnlich einfach konstruiert. Eine spitze Tüte aus pergamentartiger Polypropylenfolie, die auf einem einfachen Metallfuß ruht, verleiht ihnen ein stark skulpturales und ansprechendes Aussehen. Die leicht und kostengünstig herzustellenden *Yola* Leuchten (auch bekannt unter dem Namen *Hal*) sind unprätentiös und einfach. Sie passen damit zu unserer zunehmend nomadischen Lebensweise. (CF/PF)

Le lampadaire et la lampe de table *Yola* (1989) font partie des premiers travaux de Jack Woolley dans ce domaine. Ils sont encore fabriqués par l'entreprise londonienne qu'il a créée avec David Edgerley en 2000. Diffusant une douce lumière d'ambiance, ils bénéficient d'une conception remarquablement simple – un cornet en feuille de polypropylène style parchemin reposant sur une simple base de métal – qui assure une présence visuelle sculpturale, séduisante et puissante. Faciles à monter et économiques à réaliser, ces lampes *Yola* (appelées aussi *Hal*) sont d'une simplicité et d'une absence de prétention accordées à nos existences de plus en plus nomades. (CF/PF)

Detail of the Titania *light's diffuser / Detail des
Diffusors der Hängeleuchte* Titania */ Détail du
diffuseur de la suspension* Titania

Named after Shakespeare's Queen of
the Fairies, the *Titania* hanging light
(1989) indeed appears to hover in mid-
air, being suspended on two height-
adjustable nylon strands that are almost
invisible. The curious elliptical, rib-like
elements have polycarbonate filters
that are available in a number of interchangeable colors – yellow, green, blue,
violet and red – so that the light can be
used to create different visual effects,
from a single band of color to a rain-
bow-like spectrum. Above all else, this
remarkable light demonstrates the
extent to which technical innovation
can lead to new esthetic possibilities.
(CF/PF)

Nach Shakespeares Königin der Elfen
benannt, scheint die an fast unsichtba-
ren, höhenverstellbaren Nylonfäden angebrachte Hängeleuchte *Titania* (1989)
tatsächlich in der Luft zu schweben.
Die seltsamen elliptischen Rippenele-
mente haben austauschbare Polykar-
bonatfilter in den Farben Gelb, Grün,
Blau, Violett und Rot, mit denen das
Aussehen der Leuchte von einfarbig
verändert werden kann. Vor allem aber
demonstriert diese bemerkenswerte
Leuchte, in welchem Ausmaß technische Innovationen neue ästhetische
Möglichkeiten eröffnen. (CF/PF)

Comme Titania, la reine des fées de
Shakespeare dans *Le Songe d'une
nuit d'été*, cette suspension (1989)
accrochée par deux câbles invisibles
en nylon de longeur réglable, semble
flotter dans les airs. Les curieux
éléments elliptiques, qui évoquent une
cage thoracique, sont dotés de filtres
de polycarbonate de couleurs interchangeables – jaune, vert, bleu, violet
et rouge – qui génèrent divers effets
visuels, du simple bandeau de lumière
au spectre de l'arc-en-ciel. Mais par-
dessus tout, cette suspension remarquable prouve à quel point l'innovation
technique peut faire naître de nouvelles
possibilités esthétiques. (CF/PF)

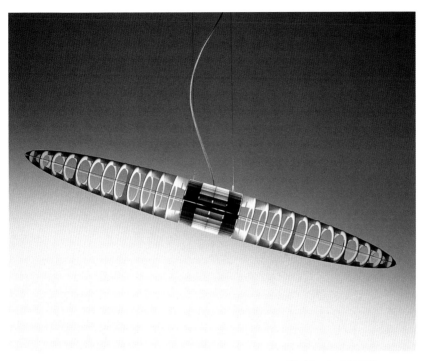

Titania hanging light, 1989

Aluminum lamellae construction with interchangeable polycarbonate filters and nylon
suspension wires, 70 cm long / Lamellenge-
häuse aus Aluminium mit austauschbaren Poly-
karbonatfiltern und Nylonaufhängung, 70 cm
lang / Suspension en lamelles d'aluminium
anodisé avec filtres interchangeables en polycarbonate et câbles en nylon, 70 cm de long
Luceplan, Milan, Italy

◁ Titania *floor light designed by Alberto Meda
and Paolo Rizzato in 1995 / Stehleuchte*
Titania, *entworfen von Alberto Meda und
Paolo Rizzato, 1995 / Lampadaire* Titania
*conçu par Alberto Meda et Paolo Rizzato
en 1995*

One from the Heart (1989), a halogen table light, is one of Ingo Maurer's ground-breaking designs of the 1980s. It was one of the first lights to be fitted with Touch Tronic, the transformer-sensor-dimmer system developed by Maurer himself. A quick touch turns the light on and off, while more prolonged contact produces a gradual dimming effect. Situated above the heart-shaped, red plastic reflector is a small, adjustable glass mirror to direct the light in the desired position. The inspiration for *One from the Heart* came to Maurer on a sudden impulse and he rapidly developed the light from a sketch. (TB)

Die Halogen-Tischleuchte *One from the Heart* (1989) gehört zu den bahnbrechenden Entwürfen von Ingo Maurer aus den 1980er Jahren. Sie war eine der ersten Leuchten, die mit dem von Maurer selbst entwickelten Transformator-Sensor-Dimmer Touch Tronic ausgestattet war. Durch eine kurze Berührung wird das Licht ein- und ausgeschaltet, eine längere Berührung ermöglicht stufenloses Dimmen. Über dem herzförmigen, roten Reflektor aus Kunststoff ist ein kleiner, verstellbarer Glasspiegel angebracht, mit dem das Licht in die gewünschte Richtung gelenkt werden kann. Maurer zeichnete die Leuchte einem Impuls folgend und entwickelte sie dann rasch zur Serienreife weiter. (TB)

One from the Heart (1989), lampe de table halogène, est l'une des créations historiques d'Ingo Maurer pour les années 1980. Ce fut l'un des premiers luminaires équipés du système Touch Tronic, transformateur-rhéostat-capteur développé par Maurer lui-même. Un simple toucher allume ou éteint la lampe, tandis qu'un contact prolongé déclenche un effet de variation progressif. Au-dessus du réflecteur en plastique rouge en forme de cœur, se trouve un petit miroir réglable qui oriente la lumière selon l'angle souhaité. L'inspiration de ce modèle vint brusquement à Maurer, qui le mit très rapidement au point à partir d'un simple croquis. (TB)

One from the Heart table light, 1989

Metal, plastic, adjustable glass mirror, 95 cm high / Metall, Kunststoff, verstellbarer Glasspiegel, 95 cm hoch / Métal, plastique, miroir en verre orientable, 95 cm de haut
Ingo Maurer, Munich, Germany

When Ingo Maurer designed *Bulb Bulb* in 1980, he used a similar form to that of his very first creation, the 1966 *Bulb* table light. *Bulb Bulb* is shaped like an outsize light bulb made of injection molded plastic. Different colored bulbs can be used to vary the appearance of the light. *Bulb Bulb*'s slightly kitschy look is completely intentional. Maurer himself talks about having fun mixing Pop with kitsch. Although the hanging light was designed for the American market and is also manufactured under license in the USA, *Bulb Bulb* has enjoyed great success in Europe. (TB)

Beim Entwurf seiner Hänge-/Stehleuchte *Bulb Bulb* (1980) griff der deutsche Leuchtendesigner Ingo Maurer formal auf seinen ersten Leuchtenentwurf, die Tischleuchte *Bulb* (1966), zurück. Die *Bulb Bulb* Leuchte in Form einer über-dimensionalen Glühbirne besteht aus spritzgussgeformtem Kunststoff. Durch den Einsatz von farbigen Glühbirnen lässt sich ihr Erscheinungsbild verän-dern. Das leicht kitschige Auftreten der *Bulb Bulb* Leuchte ist dabei durchaus gewollt. Maurer selbst spricht von einer Mischung aus romantischem Pop und Kitsch, die Spaß machen soll. Obwohl die Leuchte zunächst nur für den ame-rikanischen Markt gedacht und dort auch im Auftrag produziert wurde, wurde sie auch in Europa zu einem großen Erfolg. (TB)

Lorsque Ingo Maurer dessina la *Bulb Bulb* en 1980, il reprit une forme simi-laire à celle de sa lampe de table *Bulb* de 1966. *Bulb Bulb* a la forme d'une ampoule classique surdimensionnée en plastique moulé par injection. Diffé-rentes ampoules de couleur peuvent être utilisées pour faire varier l'aspect de la lumière produite. L'allure légère-ment kitsch est entièrement volontaire. Maurer lui-même a parlé de son plaisir à mélanger pop et kitsch. Bien que la suspension ait été conçue pour le marché américain et soit aussi fabri-quée sous licence aux États-Unis, *Bulb Bulb* a connu un grand succès en Europe. (TB)

ingo maurer
bulb bulb hanging/floor light

△△ **Bulb Bulb** hanging/floor light, **1980**

Plastic with a silver or yellow threaded element, 60 cm long / Kunststoff mit silberner oder gelber Schraubfassung, 60 cm lang / Plastique avec « pas de vis » argenté ou jaune, 60 cm long Ingo Maurer, Munich, Germany

△ *Publicity photograph for the* Bulb Bulb *hanging/floor light, c.1980 / Werbefoto der Hänge-/ Stehleuchte* Bulb Bulb, *ca. 1980 / Photographie publicitaire pour la suspension/ lampe à poser* Bulb Bulb, *vers 1980*

"*Bulb Bulb* is fun. Pop and Kitsch."

„*Bulb Bulb* ist Spaß. Pop und Kitsch."

« *Bulb Bulb* est amusante. Pop et Kitsch. »

– Ingo Maurer

The most striking feature of the *Portia* desk and floor lights (1990), designed by the Japanese architect Kunihide Oshinomi, is their radical minimalist design. The lights' enameled aluminum construction, available in red, green, black or white, is devoid of any superfluous decoration and achieves its effect merely through carefully balanced proportions and bold colors. *Portia* lights use fluorescent tubes and the arms can be turned left or right through an angle of 45°. The manufacturer, Yamagiwa Corp., produces lighting to its own designs and distributes lights from leading European and American producers to the Japanese market. (TB)

Die Schreibtisch- und Stehleuchten *Portia* (1990), entworfen von dem japanischen Architekten Kunihide Oshinomi, überzeugen durch ihr radikal minimalistisches Design. Die in Rot, Grün, Schwarz und Weiß produzierten Aluminiumgehäuse der Leuchten verzichten auf jede Art von unnötigem Dekor und wirken allein durch ihre ausgewogenen Proportionen und kräftigen Farben. Die Arme der *Portia* Leuchte lassen sich nach rechts und links um jeweils 45° drehen, als Leuchtmittel fungiert eine Leuchtstoffröhre. Die Yamagiwa Corp. produziert Leuchten nach eigenen Entwürfen, vertreibt gleichzeitig aber auch Leuchten führender europäischer und amerikanischer Hersteller auf dem japanischen Markt. (TB)

Lampadaire ou lampe de table, la *Portia* (1990), conçue par l'architecte japonais Kunihide Oshinomi, convainc par son design minimaliste radical. La structure en aluminium se passe de tout décor inutile et s'impose par ses proportions équilibrées et ses couleurs vives (rouge, vert, noir ou blanc). Le bras de la *Portia* peut pivoter à 45° vers la gauche ou la droite, la source lumineuse étant un tube fluorescent. Yamagiwa produit des luminaires conçus par ses propres équipes mais distribue aussi des créations de grands designers européens et américains sur le marché japonais. (TB)

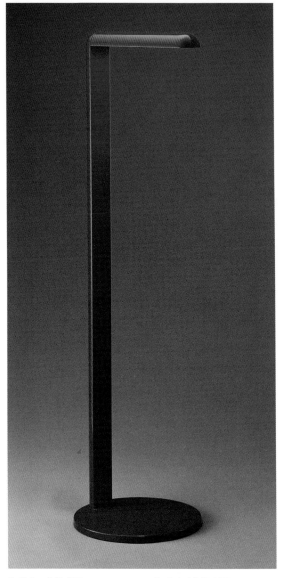

Portia floor light, 1990

Enameled aluminum construction, 125 cm high / Konstruktion aus lackiertem Aluminium, 125 cm hoch / Structure en aluminium laqué, 125 cm de haut
Yamagiwa, Tokyo, Japan

▷ **Portia desk light, 1990**

Enameled aluminum construction, 38.5 cm high / Konstruktion aus lackiertem Aluminium, 38,5 cm hoch / Structure en aluminium laqué, 38,5 cm de haut
Yamagiwa, Tokyo, Japan

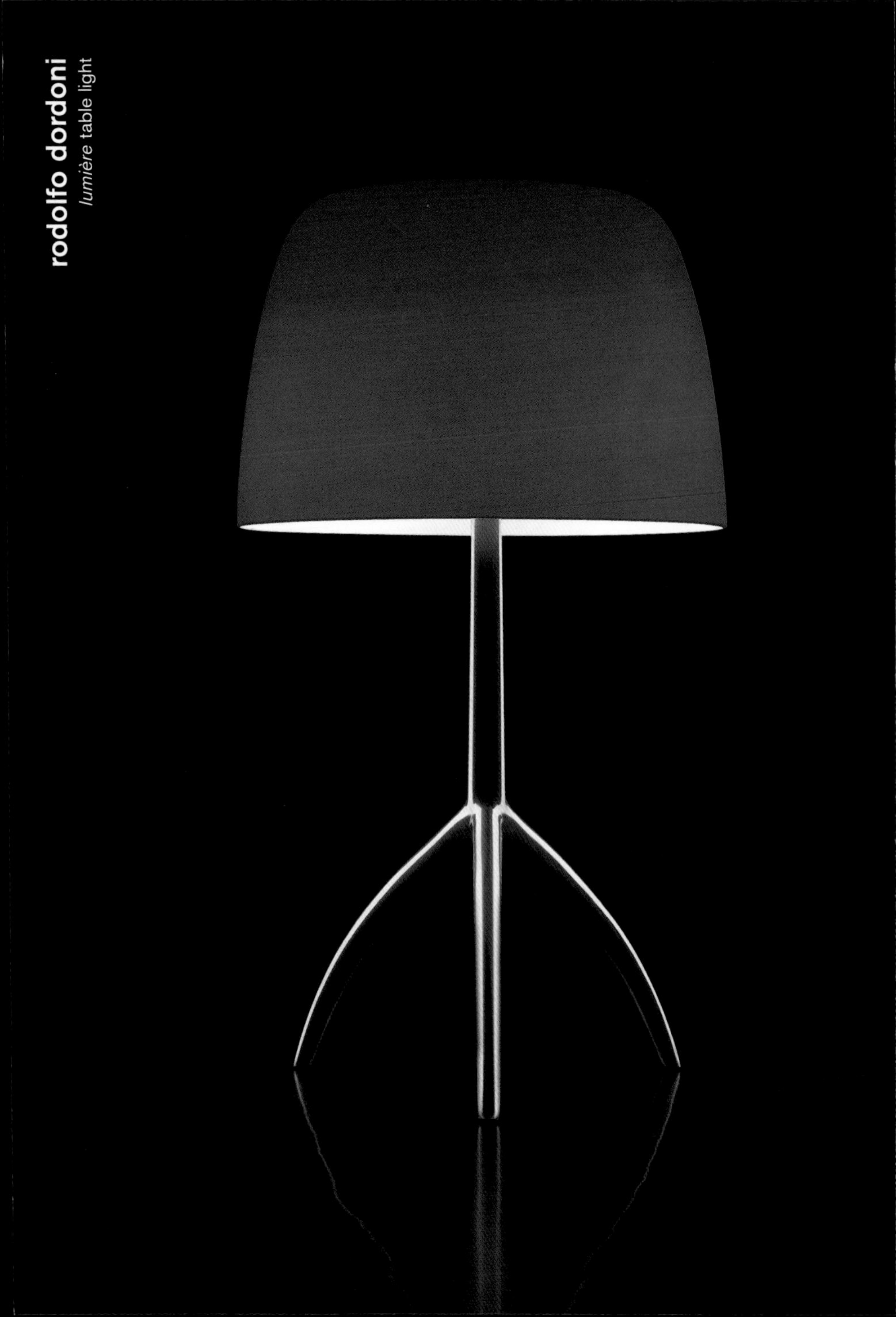
rodolfo dordoni
lumière table light

◁ ***Lumière* table light, 1990**
Polished aluminum base and blown glass shade, 45 cm high / Fuß aus poliertem Aluminium, Lampenschirm aus mundgeblasenem Glas, 45 cm hoch / Pied en aluminium poli et abat-jour en verre soufflé, 45 cm de haut
Foscarini, Marcon, Italy

***Musa (Calliope, Talia, Melpomen* and *Polinnia)* hanging lights, 1994**
Enameled metal, blown and sheet glass, 180 cm drop (max.) / Lackiertes Metall, mundgeblasenes Glas und Tafelglas, 180 cm lang (max.) / Métal laqué, verre soufflé et feuille de verre, 180 cm de haut, hors tout (max.)
Artemide, Pregnana Milanese, Italy

Rodolfo Dordoni served as artistic director of Foscarini from 1988 to 1993 and during that time created the sleek, futuristic *Lumière* table light (1990), which began as a quick sketch and became a best-selling model. Thirteen years after its introduction, Foscarini produced a *Lumière Oro* limited edition in gold-plated metal with a white glass shade with gold-leaf inclusions. The *Musa* family of lights (1994) comprises three glass forms in different combinations, creating seven models, each named after a muse. The wavy suspension rods and bright colors make the lights a playful accent in domestic interiors. (VT)

Rodolfo Dordoni war von 1988 bis 1993 Art Director bei Foscarini. Während dieser Zeit entwarf er unter anderem die elegante, futuristische Tischleuchte *Lumière* (1990), die sich zu einem absoluten Verkaufserfolg entwickelte. 13 Jahre nach ihrer Einführung legte Foscarini die Leuchte als *Lumière Oro* in einer limitierten Edition aus vergoldetem Metall mit einem Lampenschirm aus weißem Glas mit Blattgold-Einschlüssen noch einmal auf. Die Leuchtenserie *Musa* (1994) umfasst drei Glaskörper, die in verschiedenen Kombinationen sieben Modelle ergeben. Jedes davon ist nach einer Muse benannt. Durch die leichte Wellenform der Aufhängung und die helle Farbgebung setzen die Leuchten einen verspielten Akzent. (VT)

Rodolfo Dordoni a été directeur artistique de Foscarini de 1988 à 1993 et c'est au cours de cette période qu'il a créé la futuriste et très épurée lampe de table *Lumière* (1990). Élaborée à partie d'un croquis rapide, elle est devenue un best-seller. Treize ans après son lancement, Foscarini a réalisé une *Lumière Oro*, édition limitée en métal doré à abat-jour blanc orné d'inclusions de feuille d'or. La ligne *Musa* (1994) comprend trois formes de verreries dont les différentes combinaisons permettent de créer sept modèles, chacun portant le nom d'une muse. Le fil de suspension ondulé et les couleurs vives enrichissent l'intérieur de la maison de leurs accents lumineux et ludiques. (VT)

Miss Sissi (1990) is a sassy little table light that became one of Philippe Starck's greatest commercial successes. Made of an injection-molded polycarbonate, this affordable design is easy to mass-produce and is offered in seven translucent colors that make it look almost good enough to eat. Although essentially a High-Tech industrial product, Starck has cleverly given it a human touch by adding faux-stitched detailing, which evokes the image of handcrafted leatherwork. Like so many of Starck's designs, this diminutive light has been christened with a name that is intended to imbue it with personality. (CF/PF)

Die flotte kleine Tischleuchte Miss Sissi (1990) gehört zu den größten Verkaufserfolgen von Philippe Starck. Das aus spritzgegossenem Polykarbonat gefertigte, ausgezeichnet für die Massenproduktion geeignete und damit erschwingliche Modell wird in sieben durchscheinenden Farben angeboten. Obwohl es sich im Wesentlichen um ein Produkt der Hightech-Industrie handelt, hat Starck seinem Entwurf durch imitierte Stiche, die an handgenähtes Leder erinnern, eine menschliche Komponente verliehen. Wie so viele Kreationen von Starck hat auch diese kleine Leuchte einen Namen, der ihr eine eigene Persönlichkeit geben soll. (CF/PF)

Miss Sissi (1990) est une petite lampe de table culottée, devenue l'un des plus grands succès commerciaux de Philippe Starck. Fabriquée, en polycarbonate moulé par injection, ce modèle économique, facile à produire en série, est proposé en sept couleurs translucides qui lui donnent un air presque appétissant. Bien qu'il s'agisse essentiellement d'un produit industriel de haute technologie, Starck lui a conféré une touche d'humanité en lui ajoutant une fausse piqûre qui évoque le souvenir des abat-jour en cuir. Comme nombre des créations de ce designer, cette petite lampe a reçu un nom qui veut lui donner encore plus de personnalité. (CF/PF)

△△ Flos photograph advertising Miss Sissi table lights / Werbefoto von Flos mit Tischleuchten Miss Sissi / Photographie publicitaire Flos montrant des lampes de table Miss Sissi

△ Range of Miss Sissi table lights in different colors / Tischleuchten Miss Sissi in verschiedenen Farben / Gamme des lampes de table Miss Sissi en différentes couleurs

▷ **Miss Sissi table light, 1990**
Colored, injection-molded polycarbonate construction with weighted base, 28.4 cm high / Konstruktion aus spritzgegossenem, farbigem Polykarbonat, Fuß mit eingelegtem Bleigewicht, 28,4 cm hoch / Fabrication en polycarbonate moulé par injection et teinté dans la masse, base lestée, 28,4 cm de haut
Flos, Bovezzo, Italy

In 1993 Gijs Bakker and Renny Ramakers founded Droog Design to promote innovative contemporary design
by "unknowns." For over a decade,
Droog products have challenged our
perceptions of what objects should look
like or be made of, while also offering
us a wry take on the world of con-
sumerism – in Dutch the word *droog*
actually means "dry," as in a sense of
humor. Tejo Remy's *Milkbottle* hanging
light (1991), for example, not only sub-
verts the function of a dozen humble
milk bottles, but also elevates their
value and status through illumination
and by giving them an icy-looking frosted finish. (CF/PF)

1993 gründeten Gijs Bakker und Renny
Ramakers Droog Design, um innovatives, aktuelles Design von „unbekann-
ten Designern" zu fördern. Mehr als
zehn Jahre lang stellte Droog Design
die Vorstellungen darüber in Frage,
wie Objekte auszusehen haben oder
woraus sie hergestellt sein sollten.
Zugleich öffneten die holländischen Designer uns die Augen durch ihren ironischen Blick auf die Konsumgesellschaft
– das holländische Wort „droog" bedeutet „trocken", und steht für ihren
wahrlich trockenen Humor. Tejo Remy
zum Beispiel stellt bei seiner Hängeleuchte *Milkbottle* (1991) nicht nur die
Funktion von einem Dutzend beschei-
dener Milchflaschen auf den Kopf, er
erhöht zudem ihren Wert und Status,
indem er sie beleuchtet und ihnen ein
frostig wirkendes, mattiertes Finish
gibt. (CF/PF)

En 1993, Gijs Bakker et Renny Ramakers fondèrent Droog Design pour promouvoir un design contemporain novateur signé par des « inconnus ». Depuis
plus de dix ans, les créations Droog
remettent en cause nos perceptions de
l'apparence et des matériaux de fabrication de nos objets, tout en proposant un regard distancié sur le monde
de la consommation (en néerlandais,
droog signifie *sec* comme dans le
sens d'humour sec). La suspension
Milkbottle de Tejo Remy (1991) par
exemple, non seulement détourne la
fonction d'une douzaine de modestes
bouteilles de lait, mais transforme leur
valeur et leur statut par leur illumination
et leur finition dépoli, comme givrée.
(CF/PF)

***Milkbottle* hanging light, 1991**

Sandblasted milk bottle diffusers with metal
caps, 310 cm drop / Diffusoren aus sandgestrahlten Milchflaschen mit Metallverschlüssen,
310 cm lang / Bouteilles de lait en verre dépoli,
capsules métalliques, 310 cm de haut
DMD, Amsterdam, The Netherlands, for **Droog
Design**, Amsterdam, The Netherlands

santiago calatrava
onidia table light

Spanish architect-engineer Santiago Calatrava has here conceived floor and table light variations (1990 and 1992) on a theme for Italian manufacturer Artemide. Calatrava is known for his Expressionist tendency and has infused these graphically simple and attenuated forms with character. Just as fashion demands change, so the ongoing convention of minimalism is here given a new twist and the suggestion of a fresh approach. The form of the fluid, organic two-branch base is repeated in reduced scale to support the two styles of shade, one giving a focused, the other a diffused light. (PG)

Der spanische Architekt und Techniker Santiago Calatrava hat hier für den italienischen Leuchtenhersteller Artemide sowohl eine Steh- als auch eine Tischleuchte (1990 und 1992) entworfen, die ein Thema variieren. Calatrava ist für seine expressionistische Tendenz bekannt und hat den grafisch einfachen und gemäßigten Formen einen eigenen Charakter verliehen. Ganz so, wie die Mode nach Veränderung verlangt, wird der aktuelle Minimalismus bei diesen Leuchten anders interpretiert und ein neuer Zugang angeregt. Die Form des fließenden, zweiteiligen organischen Fußes kehrt verkleinert in den Stützen der beiden unterschiedlichen Lampenschirme wieder, die für direktes oder für diffuses Licht sorgen. (PG)

L'architecte et ingénieur espagnol Santiago Calatrava a conçu plusieurs variantes d'un lampadaire-lampe de table- (1990 et 1992) sur un même thème pour le fabricant italien Artemide. Calatrava, connu pour son style expressionniste, a su donner du caractère à des formes élancées, d'un style graphique épuré. De même que la mode aime le changement, la convention du minimalisme trouve ici une nouvelle orientation qui suggère le renouvellement d'une approche. La forme fluide et organique du pied à deux branches se retrouve à échelle réduite pour soutenir les deux types d'abat-jour proposés, l'un donnant une lumière concentrée, l'autre diffuse. (PG)

Onidia table light, 1992

Color-coated metal base with thermoplastic head, 45 cm high / Fuß aus lackiertem Metall mit Leuchtenkopf aus Thermoplast, 45 cm hoch / Base en métal teinté dans la masse avec tête en thermoplastique, 45 cm de haut
Artemide, Pregnana Milanese, Italy

▷ **Montjuic floor light, 1990**

Sand-blasted glass diffuser and synthetic resin base, 190 cm high / Diffusor aus sandgestrahltem Glas mit Fuß aus Kunstharz, 190 cm hoch / Diffuseur en verre sablé et base en résine synthétique, 190 cm de haut
Artemide, Pregnana Milanese, Italy

◁ *Artemide publicity photograph of* Montjuic *floor light, 1990 / Werbefoto von Artemide mit Stehleuchte* Montjuic, *1990 / Photographie publicitaire Artemide du lampadaire* Montjuic, *1990*

Ferruccio Laviani's *Orbital* (1992) is one of the most commercially successful floor lights of the 1990s. Referring to the biomorphic forms so popular in the 1950s, the shape of its eye-catching polychromatic diffusers give the design a strong retro esthetic. Made of sandblasted Murano glass, these colorful elements produce a soft atmospheric light. Already being hailed as a "design classic" in certain quarters, the *Orbital* is included in the New York Museum of Modern Art's permanent design collection. More recently Laviani has designed lighting for Kartell, including the *Take* table light (2003) and the *Easy* hanging light (2003). (CF/PF)

Die Leuchte *Orbital* (1992) von Ferruccio Laviani ist eine der kommerziell erfolgreichsten Stehleuchten der 1990er Jahre. Die Formgebung der auffallenden mehrfarbigen Diffusoren verweist auf die in den 1950er Jahren so beliebten biomorphen Formen und gibt dem Modell eine deutlich retro-ästhetische Komponente. Von den aus sandgestrahltem Muranoglas gefertigten bunten Glaselementen geht ein weiches, stimmungsvolles Licht aus. Die von manchen bereits als „Design-klassiker" gepriesene *Orbital* Leuchte hat in die ständige Designsammlung des New Yorker Museum of Modern Art Eingang gefunden. In neuerer Zeit hat Laviani Beleuchtungskörper für die Firma Kartell entworfen, darunter die Tischleuchte *Take* (2003) und die Hängeleuchte *Easy* (2003). (CF/PF)

L'*Orbital* (1992) de Ferruccio Laviani a été l'un des lampadaires les plus vendus des années 1990. Renvoyant aux formes biomorphiques si populaires dans les années 1950, ses diffuseurs polychromes un peu tapageurs confirment son esthétique nettement rétro. Fabriqués en verre de Murano sablé, ces éléments colorés diffusent une lumière délicate. Déjà salué comme un « classique du design » par certains, l'*Orbital* est présent dans la collection permanente de design du Museum of Modern Art de New York. Plus récemment, Laviano a conçu des luminaires pour Kartell, dont la lampe de table *Take* (2003) et la suspension *Easy* (2003). (CF/PF)

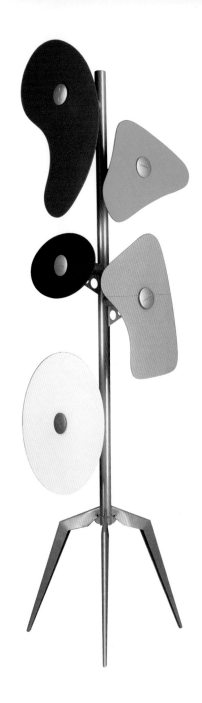

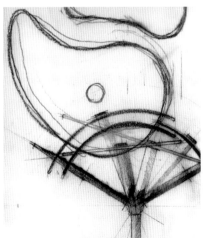

◁◁ ***Orbital* floor light, 1992**
Aluminum base with sandblasted glass diffusers, 170 cm high / Fuß aus Aluminium mit Diffusoren aus sandgestrahltem Glas, 170 cm hoch / Structure en aluminium, diffuseurs en verre sablé teinté, 170 cm de haut
Foscarini, Marcon, Italy

△ *White* Orbital *floor light in interior setting, 1990s / Zeitgenössisches Interieur mit Stehleuchte* Orbital *in weißer Ausführung, 1990er Jahre / Lampadaire* Orbital *blanc dans un intérieur, années 1990*

◁ *Design sketch for the* Orbital *floor light, c.1992 / Entwurfsskizze für die Stehleuchte* Orbital, *ca. 1992 / Croquis de conception pour le lampadaire* Orbital, *vers 1992*

Isao Hosoe's work testifies to an enduring fascination with abstracted animal forms. The *Hebi* table light from 1970 immediately suggests a coiled snake, while the *Vola* hanging light from c.1996 has bird-like wings that rise and fall as the light is switched on and off. The *Heron* light (1994) is his most accomplished design in this vein, however, with a graceful form and smooth, dignified movements that perfectly capture its fish-spearing namesake. At the same time a highly functional work light, the *Heron* contains a pantograph mechanism that keeps its head parallel to the desk surface. (QC)

Bei Isao Hosoes Arbeiten wird seine Begeisterung für abstrahierte Formen aus der Tierwelt sichtbar. Bei der Tischleuchte *Hebi* aus dem Jahr 1970 denkt man sofort an eine eingerollte Schlange, und die Hängeleuchte *Vola* (ca. 1996) hat vogelähnliche Schwingen, die sich beim Einschalten der Lampe heben und beim Ausschalten wieder senken. Sein ausgereiftestes Werk dieser Art ist jedoch die Schreibtischleuchte *Heron* (1994) mit ihrer eleganten Form und den geschmeidigen Bewegungen, in denen ein Reiher als fischfangender Namensgeber perfekt eingefangen ist. Sie ist zudem ein äußerst funktionales Arbeitslicht, dessen Pantograf-Mechanismus den Leuchtenkopf parallel zur Tischfläche hält, wenn der Leuchtenarm verstellt wird. (QC)

L'œuvre d'Isao Hosoe témoigne de son indéfectible fascination pour les formes animales stylisées. La lampe de table *Hebi* (1970), suggère à première vue un serpent dressé, tandis que la suspension *Vola* (vers 1996) possède des ailes qui s'élèvent et s'abaissent lorsque la lampe s'allume ou s'éteint. La *Heron* (1994) reste cependant sa création la plus accomplie dans cette veine : sa forme gracieuse et ses mouvements majestueux et posés expriment littéralement son nom. Elle reste néanmoins une lampe très fonctionnelle. Un pantographe permet de maintenir la tête d'éclairage parallèle à la surface du bureau. (QC)

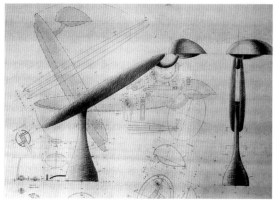

▵▵ *Heron* **desk light, 1994**
Fiberglass-reinforced nylon body with aluminum reflector, 64 cm high (max.) / Leuchtenkörper aus glasfaserverstärktem Nylon mit Reflektor aus Aluminium, 64 cm hoch (max.) / Corps en nylon renforcé de fibre de verre avec réflecteur en aluminium, 64 cm de haut (max.)
Luxo, Oslo, Norway

▵ *Design drawing of* Heron desk light, c.1994 / *Konstruktionszeichnung der Schreibtischleuchte* Heron, ca. 1994 / *Dessin de conception de la lampe de bureau* Heron, vers 1994

Components of the Bap *task light /*
Bestandteile der Arbeitsleuchte Bap */*
Composants de la lampe de travail Bap

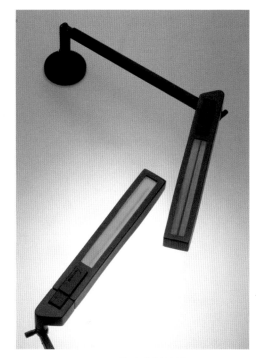

***Bap* task light, 1992**

ABS and polycarbonate base, aluminum arm
and polycarbonate head, 80 cm (max.) / Fuß
aus ABS-Kunststoff und Polykarbonat, Arm
aus Aluminium, Leuchtenkopf aus Polykarbonat,
80 cm (max.) / Base en ABS et polycarbonate,
bras en aluminium, tête en polycarbonate,
80 cm (max.)
Luceplan, Milan, Italy

The collaboration of Alberto Meda and
Paolo Rizzato has been a fertile one,
producing a range of classics from the
Lola floor light (1987) to the *Titania*
hanging light (1989). In the sphere of
task lighting, too, the *Bap* light (1992)
was prefigured by their *Berenice* light
of 1985 and has since been joined by
their *Fortebraccio* light of 1998. Wearing its workplace colors of black or
gray, the *Bap* light was designed to
eliminate the dazzle caused by interfer-
ence with office computer screens. Its
adjustable arm was also painstakingly
engineered to glide as smoothly as "a
mouse across a menu." (QC)

Die Zusammenarbeit von Alberto Meda
und Paolo Rizzato war sehr fruchtbar
und brachte eine Reihe von Klassikern des Beleuchtungsdesigns hervor,
von der Stehleuchte *Lola* (1987) bis
zur Hängeleuchte *Titania* (1989). Im
Bereich der Arbeitsleuchten hatte die
Leuchte *Bap* (1992) einen Vorläufer
in der *Berenice* von 1985 und einen
Nachfolger in der *Fortebraccio* von
1998. Die in Schwarz oder Grau ausgeführte *Bap* Leuchte sollte die Blend-
wirkung am Bildschirmarbeitsplatz ver-
hindern. Auch der verstellbare Arm ist
technisch sehr ausgereift und lässt sich
leicht wie „die Maus über ein Menü"
bewegen. (QC)

La collaboration entre Alberto Meda
et Paolo Rizzato a été fertile. Elle a
abouti à toute une gamme de classiques, du lampadaire *Lola* (1987) à la
suspension *Titania* (1989). Dans le
domaine des lampes de bureau, la *Bap*
(1992) avait été préfigurée en 1985
par leur *Berenice* et a été rejointe depuis par la *Fortebraccio* de 1998. Ha-
billée de ses couleurs de travail, noir
ou gris, la *Bap* a été conçue pour éviter l'éblouissement provoqué par les
interférences avec les écrans d'ordina-
teur. Son bras réglable est spécifiquement conçu pour glisser aussi doucement qu' « une souris sur un menu ».
(QC)

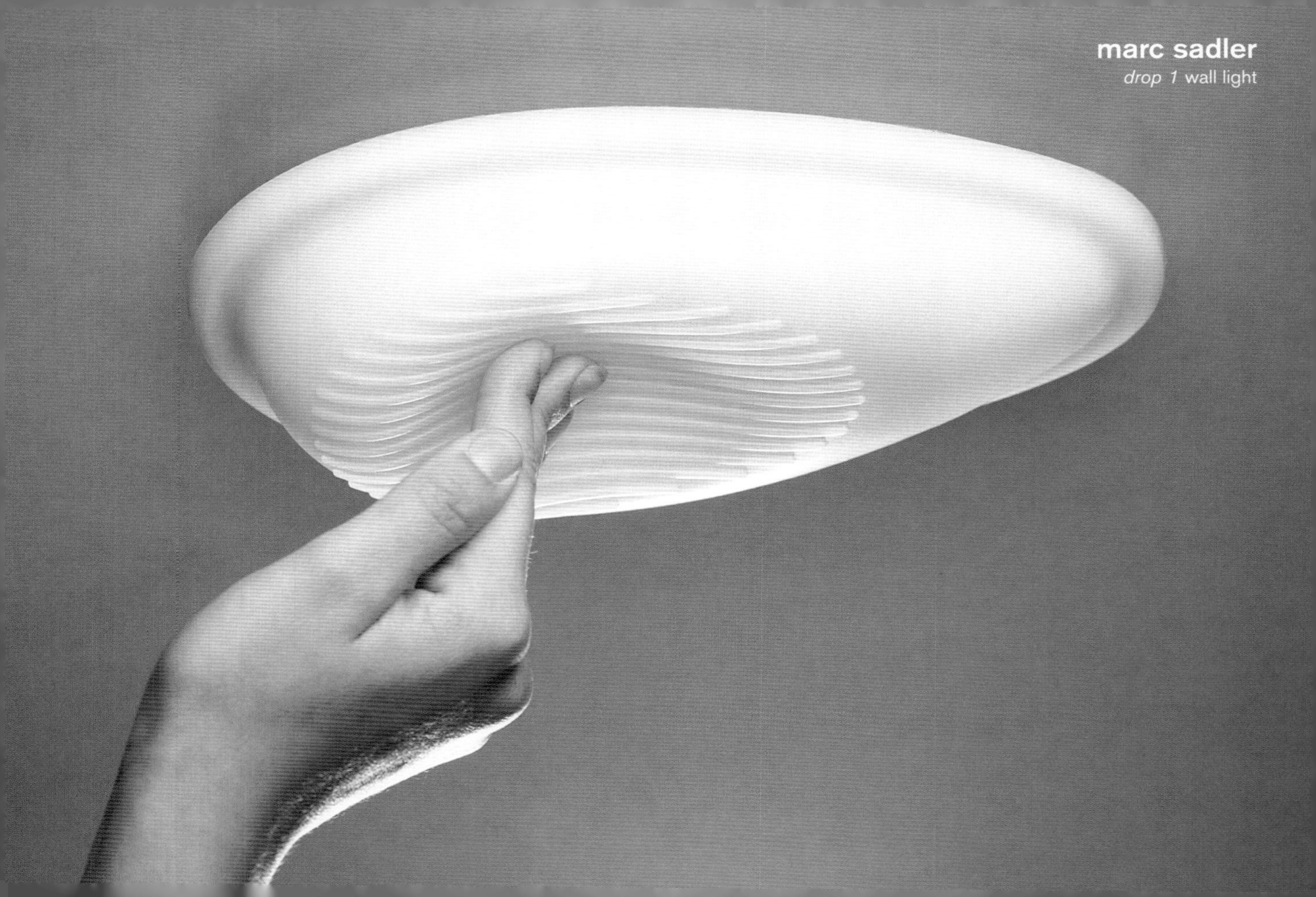

marc sadler

drop 1 wall light

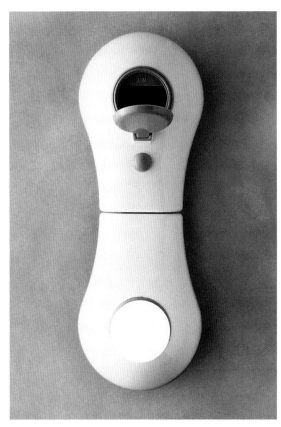

Since the 1960s Austrian-born designer Marc Sadler has specialized in groundbreaking plastic products – notably for the sports sector. Now based in Milan, he has designed a number of technically innovative lights, including the Compasso d'Oro-winning *Drop I* and *Drop II* (1993), which incorporate flexible, injection-molded silicone-elastomer diffusers that fit snugly over their polycarbonate wall mounts, making them highly suitable for bathroom usage. His *Train-Train* lighting system (1996), also for washrooms, comprises modular components that fit together like box cars. For Sadler, functional considerations are paramount. As he admits, "esthetics are the last thing I worry about." (CF/PF)

Der in Österreich geborene Marc Sadler ist seit den 1960er Jahren auf neuartige Kunststoffprodukte spezialisiert – insbesondere für den Sportsektor. Heute lebt und arbeitet er in Mailand und hat mehrere technisch innovative Leuchten entworfen, zu denen auch die mit dem Compasso d'Oro ausgezeichneten Modelle *Drop I* und *Drop II* (1993) gehören. Mit ihren Diffusoren aus flexiblem Spritzguss-Silikonelastomer sind diese Leuchten prädestiniert für den Einsatz im Badezimmer. Sadlers ebenfalls für Waschräume vorgesehenes Beleuchtungssystem *Train-Train* (1996) umfasst Module, die wie Waggons an eine Lokomotive gekoppelt werden können. Für Sadler stehen funktionale Erwägungen an erster Stelle, und er sagt selbst, dass die „Ästhetik das letzte ist, worüber ich mir Gedanken mache". (CF/PF)

Depuis les années 1960, le designer d'origine autrichienne Marc Sadler s'est spécialisé dans des produits révolutionnaires en plastique, en particulier dans le secteur du sport. Aujourd'hui installé à Milan, il a conçu une série de luminaires technologiquement innovants, notamment les *Drop I* et *Drop II* (1993) qui ont remporté un Compasso d'Oro. Ils sont dotés de diffuseurs souples en silicone élastomère moulé par injection, qui permet de les utiliser dans une salle de bains. Son système d'éclairage *Train-Train* (1996), également pour pièces humides, comprend des éléments modulaires qui se connectent comme des wagons. Pour Sadler, les considérations fonctionnelles sont essentielles : « L'esthétique est la dernière chose dont je me soucie. » (CF/PF)

△/▷ *Train-Train* **wall light, 1996**
Chrome-plated or color-coated injection-molded plastic modular components, 9.9 cm wide, 17 cm long / Module aus verchromtem oder lackiertem Kunststoffspritzguss, 9,9 cm breit, 17 cm lang / Composants modulaires en plastique moulé par injection chromés ou teintés dans la masse, 9,9 cm de large, 17 cm de long
Flos, Bovezzo, Italy

◁ *Drop* **wall light, 1993**
Lexan polycarbonate wall mounts with injection-molded silicone-elastomer diffuser, 24.6 cm high / Wandmontierung aus Lexan Polykarbonat mit Diffusor aus Spritzguss-Silikonelastomer, 24,6 cm hoch / Monture murale en polycarbonate Lexan, diffuseur en silicone élastomère moulé par injection, 24,6 cm de haut
Arteluce Milan, Italy (reissued by **Flos**, Bovezzo, Italy)

The *Light Lite* hanging light (1992) and the *Walla Walla* wall light (1994), both designed by Philippe Starck and produced by the Italian lighting manufacturer Flos, are made of thermo-formed plastic. Both have the advantage of light weight and a large selection of color variations. Starck developed *Light Lite* specially for use with energy-saving fluorescent bulbs (CFLs). The teardrop inserts on the shade come in three interchangeable colors. Meanwhile, *Walla Walla* comes with four different colored filters to create changes of mood. (TB)

Die Hängeleuchte *Light Lite* (1992) und die Wandleuchte *Walla Walla* (1994), beide entworfen von Philippe Starck und produziert von der italienischen Leuchtenfirma Flos, sind aus thermoplastisch geformtem Kunststoff gefertigt. Beide Leuchten überzeugen durch ihr leichtes Gewicht und die große Auswahl an farblichen Varianten. Die *Light Lite* Leuchte ist von Starck speziell für den Gebrauch von energiesparenden Leuchtstofflampen entwickelt worden. Die tropfenförmigen Einsätze ihres Lampenschirms, die es in drei unterschiedlichen Farben gibt, lassen sich austauschen. Bei der *Walla Walla* Leuchte sorgen dagegen vier farblich unterschiedliche Filter für Abwechslung. (TB)

La suspension *Light Lite* (1992) et l'applique *Walla Walla* (1994), signées Philippe Starck et produites par le fabriquant italien Flos, sont en plastique thermoformé. Légères, toutes deux offrent un large choix de coloris. Starck a spécialement mis au point la *Light Lite* pour les nouvelles ampoules fluorescentes à consommation réduite. Les inserts en forme de larmes sur l'abat-jour sont de trois couleurs interchangeables. La *Walla Walla* est proposée avec quatre filtres de couleurs différentes pour modifier les ambiances. (TB)

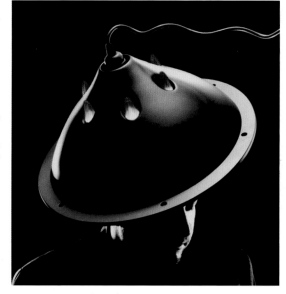

▵▵ **Light Lite** hanging light, 1992

Serigraphed and thermoplastic shade with plastic inserts, 43 cm diameter / Lampenschirm aus siebbedrucktem und thermoplastischem Kunststoff mit Kunststoffeinsätzen, 43 cm Durchmesser / Abat-jour en thermoplastique sérigraphié, avec inserts plastiques, 43 cm de diamètre
Flos, Bovezzo, Italy

▵ *Philippe Starck wearing* Light Lite *hanging light, c.1992 / Philippe Starck mit Hängeleuchte* Light Lite, *ca. 1992 / Philippe Starck avec la suspension* Light Lite *vers 1992*

▷ **Walla Walla** wall light, 1994

Thermoplastic mounts and diffuser, 37 cm high / Lampenschirm und Diffusor aus Thermoplast, 37 cm hoch / Abat-jour et diffuseur en thermoplastique, 37 cm de haut
Flos, Bovezzo, Italy

Growing up in Australia, rather than in Europe or America, ensured that Marc Newson came to the design profession with a fresh eye that was unsullied by Modernist or Post-Modernist polemical baggage. Instead, he has drawn inspiration from the colorful Space Age products, imported into Australia from Italy, that he encountered in his youth – most notably designs by Joe Colombo. His elegant *Helice* floor light (1993) combines futuristic sci-fi connotations with beautiful geometric proportions that perfectly balance the base and head at different ends of its conical, tapering aluminum stem. (CF/PF)

Marc Newson wuchs nicht in Europa oder Amerika, sondern in Australien auf und kam mit einem unbefangenen und noch nicht von der modernistischen oder postmodernistischen Polemik getrübten Blick zum Design. Stattdessen bezog er seine Inspiration aus den bunten Space-Age-Produkten seiner Jugend, die aus Italien importiert worden waren, insbesondere Arbeiten Joe Colombos. Seine elegante Stehleuchte *Helice* (1993) verbindet futuristische Science-Fiction-Formen mit ansprechenden geometrischen Proportionen, die den an den beiden Enden des konisch verjüngten Aluminiumstabes sitzenden Fuß und Kopf der Leuchte in perfekte Balance bringen. (CF/PF)

Le fait d''avoir grandi en Australie et non en Europe ou aux États-Unis, a certainement donné à Marc Newson un regard neuf, non contaminé par les polémiques modernistes ou postmodernistes. Il tire plutôt son inspiration des produits de l'ère de la conquête spatiale, importés d'Italie en Australie, qu'il découvrit dans sa jeunesse, en particulier les œuvres de Joe Colombo. Son élégant lampadaire *Helice* (1993), combine des connotations de science-fiction et de superbes proportions qui équilibrent à la perfection les rapports entre la base et la tête fixées à chaque extrémité d'une tige d'aluminium profilée. (CF/PF)

▽/▷ ▽▽ *Detail and design drawing of* Helice *floor light, c.1993 / Detailansicht und Entwurfszeichnung der Stehleuchte* Helice, *ca. 1993 / Détail et dessin de la conception du lampadaire* Helice, *vers 1993*

▷▽ *Marc Newson with* Helice *floor light / Marc Newson mit Stehleuchte* Helice / *Marc Newson posant derrière le lampadaire* Helice

▷ ***Helice* floor light, 1993**

Aluminum base, stem and head, 190 cm high / Fuß, Schaft und Leuchtenkopf aus Aluminium, 190 cm hoch / Pied, tige et tête en aluminium, 190 cm de haut
Flos, Bovezzo, Italy

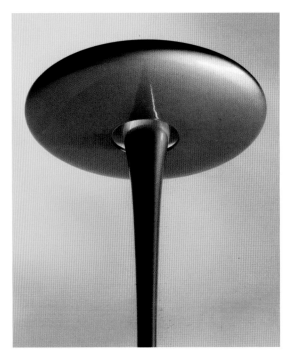

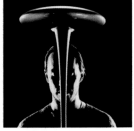

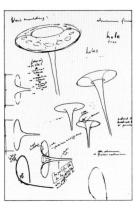

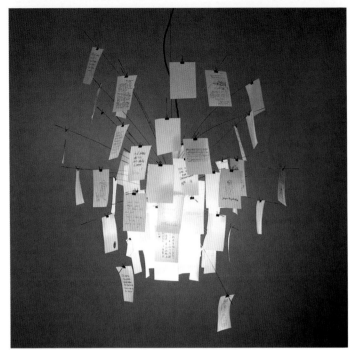

Zettel'z 6 chandelier, 1998

Stainless-steel, heat-resistant satin-frosted glass and Japanese paper construction, 60 cm diameter (approx.) / Edelstahl, hitzebeständiges mattiertes Glas, Japanpapier, 60 cm Durchmesser (ca.) / Acier inoxydable, verre satiné résistant à la chaleur, papier Japon, 60 cm de diamètre (environ)
Ingo Maurer, Munich, Germany

▷ **Porca Miseria! chandelier, 1994**

Stainless-steel, porcelain and metal construction, 110 x 150 cm (approx.) / Edelstahl, Porzellan, Metall, 110 x 150 cm (ca.) / Acier inoxydable, porcelaine, métal, 110 x 150 cm (environ)
Ingo Maurer, Munich, Germany

There is nothing that Ingo Maurer cannot use for his lights. His *Zettel'z 6* chandelier (Zettel means "slip of paper"), designed in 1998, comprises metal rods radiating from the central lighting element. Attached to these are scraps of rice paper with poems, messages and aphorisms, held in place by paperclips. Blank sheets can also be supplied so that owners can add their own notes. The 1994 chandelier *Porca Miseria!* ("Damn It!"), which looks like an explosion in a china cabinet, is similarly constructed. Shards of white porcelain and pieces of cutlery are mounted on the ends of metal rods. (TB)

Es gibt keinen Gegenstand, den Ingo Maurer nicht für eine seiner Leuchten benutzen kann. Bei der Hängeleuchte *Zettel'z 6* (1998) sind um den zentralen Lichtkörper strahlenförmig Metallstäbe angeordnet, an denen mit Gedichten, Notizen und Aphorismen bedruckte Notizzettel aus Japanpapier von Büroklemmen gehalten werden. Wahlweise stehen auch unbedruckte Blätter zur Verfügung, die man mit eigenen Texten oder Zeichnungen versehen kann. Die Hängeleuchte *Porca Miseria!* (1994), die an eine Explosion im Geschirrschrank erinnert, ist ähnlich konstruiert. An den Enden ihrer Metallstäbe sind zerschlagene Geschirrteile aus weißem Porzellan sowie Besteckteile montiert. (TB)

Aucun matériau n'échappe à Ingo Maurer. Son lustre *Zettel'z 6* (Zettel signifie «morceau de papier» en allemand), conçu en 1998, se compose de fils métalliques rayonnant à partir d'un élément d'éclairage central. À leur extrémité sont aussi fixés de petits bouts de papier de riz imprimés de poèmes, messages et aphorismes divers, tenus en place par des pinces. Des feuilles blanches sont fournies pour que l'acheteur puisse ajouter ses propres réflexions. Le lustre de 1994 *Porca Miseria!* («Misère de misère!»), qui fait penser à l'explosion d'un service de porcelaine, est élaboré de façon similaire. Les morceaux de porcelaine blanche et de ménagère sont aussi montés sur des tiges de métal. (TB)

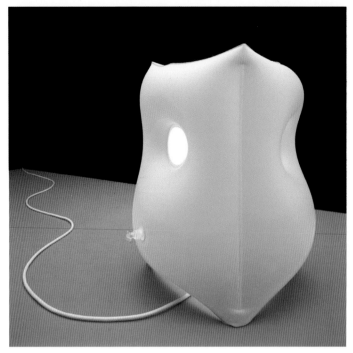

Inflatable table light, 1996

Inflatable PVC construction, 45 cm high / Konstruktion aus aufblasbarem PVC, 45 cm hoch / Structure en PVC gonflable, 45 cm de haut
Inflate Design, London, Great Britain

"Design is about creatively exploiting constraint."

„Design bedeutet, Zwänge kreativ zu nützen."

« Le design est l'art d'exploiter la contrainte. »

– Inflate Design

Inflate Design launched its first collection of inflatable household products at the "100% Design" exhibition in London in 1995. The following year Nick Crosbie, one of the group's founders, designed this table light (1996) made of inflatable PVC – a material not generally associated with lighting design but which has an inherent translucence that produces a pleasingly soft diffused light. Cheap to produce and distribute, this eye-catching design is very affordable and is available in blue, cream, white or yellow. (CF/PF)

Inflate Design stellte ihre erste Kollektion von aufblasbaren Haushaltsprodukten 1995 bei der Ausstellung „100% Design" in London vor. Im Jahr darauf entwarf Nick Crosbie, Mitbegründer der Gruppe, eine Tischleuchte (1996) aus aufblasbarem PVC – einem Material, das man im Leuchtendesign im Allgemeinen nicht erwartet, obwohl es durchscheinend ist und ein angenehm weiches, diffuses Licht erzeugt. Dieses sowohl in der Produktion wie im Vertrieb kostengünstige Produkt ist ein Blickfang und zu sehr moderaten Preisen in Blau, Creme, Weiß und Gelb erhältlich. (CF/PF)

Inflate Design a lancé sa première collection de produits gonflables pour la maison lors de l'exposition « 100% Design » organisée à Londres en 1995. L'année suivante, Nick Crosbie, l'un des fondateurs du groupe, a conçu cette lampe de table (1996) en PVC gonflable, matériau rarement associé aux luminaires mais offrant une translucidité qui produit une agréable lumière diffuse. Aussi économique à fabriquer qu'à distribuer, cette création séduisante est vendue à un prix très abordable en bleu, crème, blanc ou jaune. (CF/PF)

UFO hanging light, 1996

Inflatable PVC construction, 45 cm diameter /
Konstruktion aus aufblasbarem PVC, 45 cm
Durchmesser / Structure en PVC gonflable, 45
cm de diamètre
Inflate Design, London, Great Britain

This playful inflatable hanging light alludes to the sci-fi world of space-ships and little green men. Sold in flat-pack form, it is made from sheets of PVC (polyvinylchloride) that are high-frequency welded. As Inflate Design explains, "We specialize in developing projects around old, under-exploited manufacturing processes ... our priority is coming up with something new." Available in white, cream, yellow, orange or blue, the inexpensive *UFO* hanging light (1996) has a youthful neo-Pop quality. It reflects the group's love of surprising solutions containing an inherent transience and expendability. (CF/PF)

Diese lustige aufblasbare Hängeleuch-te spielt auf die Science-Fiction-Welt der Raumschiffe und kleinen grünen Männchen an. Sie ist aus hochfre-quenzverschweißter PVC-Folie (Poly-vinylchlorid) gefertigt und wird flach verpackt verkauft. Laut eigener Aus-sage spezialisiert sich Inflate Design darauf, „ausgehend von alten, zu wenig genutzten Handwerksprozessen Pro-jekte zu entwickeln ... mit der Priorität, etwas Neues hervorzubringen". Die in Weiß, Creme, Gelb, Orange oder Blau erhältliche, preisgünstige Hängeleuchte *UFO* (1996) hat eine jugendliche Neo-Pop-Ausstrahlung. Sie macht die Vor-liebe der Gruppe für überraschende Lösungen deutlich, die nicht für die Ewigkeit gemacht sind. (CF/PF)

Cette suspension gonflable ludique fait allusion à l'univers de science-fiction des vaisseaux spatiaux et des petits hommes verts. Vendue à plat, elle est faite de feuilles de PVC (chlorure de polyvinyle) soudées à haute fréquence. Comme l'explique Inflate Design, « Nous sommes spécialisés dans la mise au point de projets autour de processus de fabrication anciens et sous-exploi-tés... notre priorité est d'arriver à quel-que chose de nouveau ». Proposée en blanc, crème, jaune, orange ou bleu, cette suspension *UFO* (1996), bon marché possède un esprit neo-Pop juvénile. Elle reflète l'amour du groupe pour les solutions surprenantes et plutôt éphémères. (CF/PF)

Part of Artemide's groundbreaking *Metamorfosi* collection, the *Esperia* table light (1996) and the *Antinoo* floor light (1996) incorporate the company's patented light-control system that allows the user to regulate the color and intensity of the emitted light to suit the environment. Both lights have rotating diffusers, which take the form of a four-leaf clover and house four separate halogen bulbs as well as a microprocessor, a remote-control sensor, parabolic deflectors and colored glass filters. With their ability to create approximately 12 million different color gradations, these products provide a remarkable degree of atmospheric mood control. (CF/PF)

Die Tischleuchte *Esperia* (1996) und die Stehleuchte *Antinoo* (1996), beide zur bahnbrechenden Kollektion *Metamorfosi* von Artemide gehörend, verwenden das patentierte Lichtsteuersystem der Firma, mit dem der Benutzer die Farbe und Intensität des Lichtstrahls der Umgebung anpassen kann. Beide Leuchten haben einen drehbaren Diffusor in Form eines vierblättrigen Kleeblatts, in dem vier Halogenlampen sowie ein Mikroprozessor, ein Empfangssensor für die Fernsteuerung, Parabolreflektoren und Farbfilter aus Glas untergebracht sind. Mit dieser Technologie können rund 12 Millionen verschiedene Farbschattierungen erzielt werden. Dabei entstehen ein bemerkenswertes Maß an unterschiedlichen Lichtstimmungen. (CF/PF)

Éléments de la collection révolutionnaire d'Artemide *Metamorfosi*, la lampe de table *Esperia* (1996) et le lampadaire *Antinoo* (1996) sont dotées du système de contrôle d'éclairage breveté qui permet à l'utilisateur de modifier la couleur et l'intensité de la lumière émise en fonction de l'environnement. Les deux modèles possèdent des diffuseurs rotatifs en forme de trèfle à quatre feuilles, quatre ampoules halogènes indépendantes, ainsi qu'un microprocesseur, un capteur de télécommande, des déflecteurs paraboliques et des filtres en verre de couleur. Capables de créer environ douze millions de nuances différentes, ces luminaires apportent un remarquable degré de contrôle de l'ambiance lumineuse. (CF/PF)

△△ ***Esperia* table light, 1996**

Enameled and perforated steel construction, 26 cm high / Konstruktion aus lackiertem und perforiertem Stahl, 26 cm hoch / Structure an acier laqué perforé, 26 cm de haut
Artemide, Pregnana Milanese, Italy
△ Esperia *table light in use* / Tischleuchte Esperia *in Betrieb* / Lampe de table Esperia *en fonctionnement*

▷ ***Antinoo* floor light, 1996**

Enameled steel base and stem with aluminum diffuser, 180 cm high / Fuß und Schaft aus lackiertem Metall mit Diffusor aus Aluminium, 180 cm hoch / Socle et tige en acier laqué avec diffuseur en aluminium, 180 cm de haut
Artemide, Pregnana Milanese, Italy

Guglielmo Berchicci studied architecture at the Politecnico di Milano and subsequently established his own design practice in Milan. His work is inspired by both the simplicity and complexity of nature on micro and macro levels. He is fascinated by the spirituality of forms that have evolved in nature as well as by natural systems, including the chaos theory. His *E.T.A. (Extra-Terrestrial Angel)* lights of 1997 have an organic globularity that gives them an engaging zoomorphism. (CF/PF)

Guglielmo Berchicci studierte am Politecnico di Milano Architektur und eröffnete später in Mailand ein Designbüro. Seine Arbeit ist von der Einfachheit und ebenso von der Komplexität der Natur auf dem Mikro- und auf der Makroebene inspiriert. Die Spiritualität von Formen, die in der Natur entstanden sind, fasziniert ihn ebenso wie natürliche Systeme, etwa die Chaostheorie. Seine 1997 entstandenen Leuchten *E.T.A. (Extra-Terrestrial Angel),* wirken durch ihre organische Kugelform faszinierend zoomorph. (CF/PF)

Guglielmo Berchicci a étudié l'architecture au Politecnico de Milan puis a fondé son agence de design dans la même ville. Son œuvre s'inspire de la simplicité et de la complexité de la nature, aux niveaux aussi bien microque macroscopiques. Il est fasciné par la spiritualité des formes qui ont évolué dans la nature et par les systèmes naturels, notamment la théorie du Chaos. Ses lampes *E.T.A. (Extra Terrestrial Angles)* de 1997, présentent une forme globulaire organique qui les tire vers un zoomorphisme séduisant. (CF/PF)

▽ **E.T.A. floor light, 1997**

Molded fiberglass construction, 200 cm high / Konstruktion aus geformtem Fiberglas, 200 cm hoch / Structure en fibre de verre moulée, 200 cm de haut
Kundalini, Milan, Italy

▽▷ **E.T.A. Baby table light, 1997**

Molded fiberglass construction, 45 cm high / Konstruktion aus geformtem Fiberglas, 45 cm hoch / Structure en fibre de verre moulée, 45 cm de haut
Kundalini, Milan, Italy

▷ **E.T.A. SAT hanging light, 1997**

Molded fiberglass construction, 54 cm high / Konstruktion aus geformtem Fiberglas, 54 cm hoch / Structure en fibre de verre moulée, 54 cm de haut
Kundalini, Milan, Italy

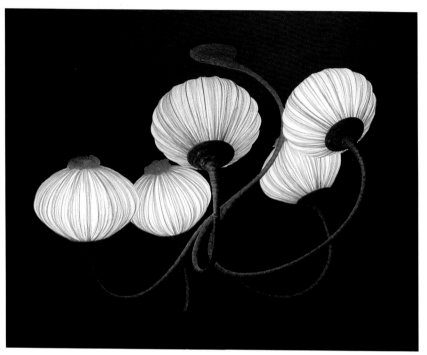

◁ *Morning Glory* **floor light, 1994**

Metal frame with resin-coated silk diffuser, 212 cm high / Metallgestell mit Diffusor aus harzbeschichteter Seide, 212 cm hoch / Structure métallique, diffuseur en soie enduite de résine, 212 cm de haut
Aqua Creations, Tel Aviv, Israel

Five Palms **chandelier, 1997**

Tubular metal branches hand-wrapped with organza and resin-coated silk diffusers, 103 x 89 cm / Arme aus Metallrohr, von Hand umwickelt mit Organza, Diffusor aus harzbeschichteter Seide, 103 x 89 cm / Branches tubulaires en métal gainé à la main d'organza, diffuseurs en soie enduite de résine, 103 x 89 cm
Aqua Creations, Tel Aviv, Israel

For over a decade Ayala Serfaty has sculpted beautiful lights inspired by forms from the natural world – jellyfish, shells, coral, seedpods and flowers. These remarkable lights are created out of resin-coated silk, which yields both a wonderful sense of tactility and a suffused, colored light that is appealingly warm. Serfaty's designs are patiently fabricated by hand by skilled craftspeople in her own company, Aqua Creations, run with the help of her photographer husband, Albi. She describes the resulting products as "gentle but firm, soft and yet very much defined." (CF/PF)

Seit mehr als zehn Jahren gestaltet Ayala Serfaty ansprechende Leuchten, die von Naturformen inspiriert sind – Quallen, Muscheln, Korallen, Samenhülsen und Blumen. Diese bemerkenswerten Leuchten werden aus harzbeschichteter Seide hergestellt, die wunderbar taktil ist und ein angenehm warmes, gedämpftes Licht in verschiedenen Farben durchscheinen lässt. Ayala Serfatys Leuchten werden von den kunstfertigen Handwerkern ihrer Firma Aqua Creations, die sie gemeinsam mit ihrem Ehemann Albi, einem Fotografen, leitet, einzeln angefertigt. Sie beschreibt ihre Produkte als „sanft, aber fest, weich, und doch sehr definiert". (CF/PF)

Depuis plus d'une décennie, Ayala Serfaty sculpte de merveilleux luminaires inspirés de formes naturelles : méduses, coquillages, coraux, algues et fleurs. Ses remarquables créations sont en soie enduite de résine, ce qui leur donne un toucher merveilleux et contribue à un éclairage délicat, d'une attirante chaleur. Elle gère la société Aqua Creations en compagnie de son mari photographe, Albi. Elle décrit ses créations comme « délicates mais fortement présentes, douces et très précises à la fois. » (CF/PF)

Le Perroquet spotlight system, 1998

Die-cast aluminum and thermoplastic construction with Fresnel lenses and colored glass filters, various heights / Konstruktion aus Druckgussaluminium und Thermoplast mit Fresnel-Linse und farbigen Glasfiltern, verschiedene Abmessungen / Structure en fonte d'aluminium et thermoplastique, lentilles de Fresnel et filtres en verre coloré, diverses hauteurs
iGuzzini Illuminazione, Recanati, Italy

Lingotto wall light, 1990

Die-cast aluminum body with safety-glass reflector, reflector: 33 cm depth / Konstruktion aus Druckgussaluminium mit Schutzglasreflektor, Reflektor: 33 cm tief / Structure en fonte d'aluminium, réflecteur en verre de sécurité, réflecteur: 33 cm de profondeur
iGuzzini Illuminazione, Recanati, Italy

Renzo Piano's *Lingotto* wall light (1990) can throw a strong flood of light upwards or downwards. It is a robust product with a high degree of technical sophistication and shares the industrialized esthetic that typifies Piano's wonderfully inventive architecture. Beautifully engineered, the *Le Perroquet* system (1998), designed by Piano's office, features spotlights with dimmable transformers, which can be horizontally rotated through 360° degrees and vertically tilted by 100° to allow very precise light positioning. More like an "optical instrument" than a traditional track lighting system, *Le Perroquet* won a Compasso d'Oro award in 1998. (CF/PF)

Die Wandleuchte *Lingotto* (1990) von Renzo Piano richtet ihren Lichtstrahl nach oben oder unten. Sie ist ein robustes, technisch ausgereiftes Produkt, das sich durch die gleiche industrialisierte Ästhetik auszeichnet wie Pianos einfallsreiche Architektur. Die Strahler des hoch entwickelten, von Pianos Büro entworfenen Systems *Le Perroquet* (1998) sind mit einem dimmbaren Transformator ausgestattet und können horizontal um 360° gedreht und vertikal um 100° geneigt werden, was eine sehr präzise Positionierung des Lichts ermöglicht. 1998 wurden die *Le Perroquet* Strahler, die eher wie „optische Instrumente" als wie Bestandteile eines traditionellen Leuchtschienensystems wirken, mit einem Compasso d'Oro ausgezeichnet. (CF/PF)

L'applique *Lingotto* de Renzo Piano (1990) projette un puissant flux de lumière vers le haut ou le bas. C'est un produit robuste d'une grande sophistication technique qui renvoie à l'esthétique industrielle typique de l'architecture merveilleusement inventive de son auteur. D'une réalisation technique impeccable, le système *Le Perroquet* (1998), conçu par l'agence de Piano, se compose de spots à transformateurs rhéostatés, qui peuvent pivoter horizontalement à 360° et s'incliner verticalement à 100° pour permettre un positionnement très précis du rayon lumineux. Davantage « instrument d'optique » que système d'éclairage par rail traditionnel, *Le Perroquet* a remporté un Compasso d'Oro en 1998. (CF/PF)

knud holscher
quinta spotlight system

◁ **Quinta spotlight system, 1993**
Powder-coated cast-aluminum mounts and
housing with safety-glass lens, 21.8 cm drop /
Montierung und Gehäuse aus pulverbeschichtetem Gussaluminium mit Sicherheitsglaslinse,
21,8 cm lang / Monture et habillage en fonte
d'aluminium peints par poudrage, lentilles en
verre de sécurité, 21,8 cm de haut
Erco, Lüdenscheid, Germany

▷ **Stella spotlight, 1999**
Powder-coated cast-aluminum mounts and
housing with safety-glass lens, 31.3 cm drop /
Montierung und Gehäuse aus pulverbeschichtetem Aluminiumguss mit Sicherheitsglaslinse,
31,3 cm lang / Monture et habillage en fonte
d'aluminium peints par poudrage, lentilles en
verre de sécurité, 31,3 cm de haut
Erco, Lüdenscheid, Germany

Founded in 1934, Erco continues to
manufacture some of the most innovative architectural lighting. Its product
line is founded on the concept of "Light,
not luminaries" and on the belief that
light is the fourth dimension of architecture. The company's lighting ranges,
such as the *Quinta* (1993) and *Stella*
(1999), are distinguished by a logical
approach to design in which variously
sized housings, lamp options, optical
systems and accessories can be combined to create a plethora of tailored
options. Mainly used in contract and
public settings, Erco's state-of-the-art
products are renowned for their superlative engineering and technological
simplification. (CF/PF)

Die 1934 gegründete Firma Erco gehört bis heute zu den innovativsten
Herstellern im Bereich der Architektur-
beleuchtung. Ihre Produktlinie basiert
auf der Unternehmensphilosophie „Licht
statt Leuchten" und auf der Überzeugung, dass Licht die vierte Dimension
der Architektur sei. Ercos Produktse-
rien, darunter die Systeme *Quinta*
(1993) und *Stella* (1999), sind nach
dem Prinzip der Logik gestaltet, sodass
unterschiedliche Gehäusegrößen und
Zubehörteile zu einer Vielzahl von maß-
geschneiderten Lösungen kombiniert
werden können. Die Produkte von Erco
verwenden die aktuellsten Technologien und sind berühmt für ihre außergewöhnliche Präzision und einfache
Bedienbarkeit. (CF/PF)

Fondée en 1934, Erco propose pério-
diquement certains des appareils
d'éclairage les plus novateurs du
moment. Sa ligne de produits repose
sur le concept « De la lumière, pas des
luminaires » et sur la conviction que la
lumière est la quatrième dimension de
l'architecture. Ses produits, comme les
systèmes *Quinta* (1993) et *Stella*
(1999) se distinguent par une approche logique du design dans lequel
spots, choix de sources lumineuses,
systèmes optiques et accessoires se
combinent pour créer une pléthore de
solutions sur mesure. Utilisés surtout
dans des équipements publics ou dans
l'immobilier commercial, les produits
d'avant-garde d'Erco sont renommés
pour leur réalisation de haute qualité et
leur approche technologique. (CF/PF)

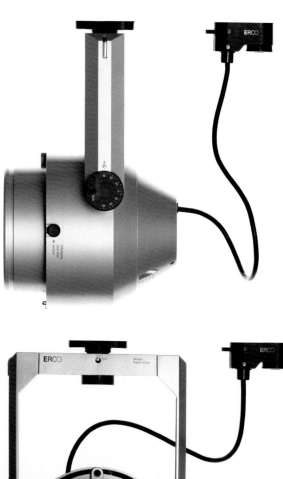

Lightcast recessed downlight, 1997

Thermoplastic and cast-aluminium housing and fittings, 14–17cm diameter / Gehäuse und Montierung aus Thermoplast und Gussaluminium, 14–17 cm Durchmesser / Boîtiers et pièces de montage en thermoplastique et fonte d'aluminium, 14–17 cm de diamètre
Erco, Lüdenscheid, Germany

▷ Lightcast *recessed downlight in situ /*
Anwendungsbeispiel für die Deckeneinbau-
leuchte Lightcast / *Le système* Lightcast *en*
fonctionnement

The *Lightcast* recessed downlights (1997) set new standards of quality for recessed spotlights when first introduced by Erco in 1997. Developed using sophisticated computer programs, the extensive *Lightcast* range was designed specifically for use with energy-efficient compact fluorescent lamps. Incorporating Erco's "darklight" technology, the range uses reflector cut-off angles of between 30° and 50°, degrees, ensuring the best balance between horizontal and vertical illumination, and thereby providing the optimum comfort level of brightness. With such unobtrusive yet technically sophisticated solutions now available, it is no wonder that many designers now feel free to explore the more expressive and sculptural side of lighting. (CF/PF)

Mit der Deckeneinbauleuchte *Lightcast* (1997) hat Erco neue Maßstäbe für diese Art der Beleuchtung gesetzt. Die vielfältige *Lightcast* Serie wurde speziell für die Verwendung mit energiesparenden Kompakt-Leuchtstofflampen entworfen und setzt die von Erco entwickelte „Darklight"-Technik um. Abblendwinkel zwischen 30° und 50° ermöglichen eine optimale Ausgewogenheit von horizontaler und vertikaler Beleuchtung und sorgen für maximalen Sehkomfort. Angesichts der Tatsache, dass so unauffällige und zugleich technisch ausgereifte Lösungen auf dem Markt sind, verwundert es nicht, dass sich viele der heutigen Designer den expressiven und skulpturalen Seiten des Beleuchtungsdesigns zuwenden. (CF/PF)

Mise au point grâce à des logiciels sophistiqués, la *Lightcast* (1997) a imposé de nouveaux critères de qualité pour les spots encastrés lors de son lancement par Erco en 1997. Cette vaste gamme a été spécialement conçue pour recevoir des ampoules compactes fluorescentes basse consommation d'énergie et utiliser la technologie «Darklight» de Erco. Les angles de fermeture du réflecteur, de 30° à 50°, assurent un équilibre optimal entre l'illumination verticale et horizontale, donc le meilleur confort d'éclairage possible. À travers des solutions aussi discrètes que techniquement sophistiquées, les designers actuels jouissent d'une nouvelle liberté pour explorer les aspects les plus expressifs et sculpturaux de l'éclairage. (CF/PF)

◁ *Ciros* **suspended ceiling light, 1995**
Aluminum body with PMMA upper diffuser,
inner specular polycarbonate reflector, lower
frosted glass ring and metal mounts, 45 or
49 cm diameter / Leuchtenkörper aus Aluminium mit Diffusor aus PMMA oben, Spiegel-
reflektor aus Polykarbonat innen, Ring aus
Mattglas unten und Montierungen aus Metall,
45 oder 49 cm Durchmesser / Corps en aluminium, diffuseur supérieur en PMMA, réflecteur intérieur spéculaire en polycarbonate,
anneau inférieur en verre dépoli et monture
métallique, 45 ou 49 cm de diamètre
Zumtobel Staff, Dornbirn, Austria

▷ *Claris* **lighting system, 1997–98**
Enameled or anodised aluminum, 127 cm long /
Konstruktion aus lackiertem oder eloxiertem
Aluminium, 127 cm lang / Structure en alumi-
nium laqué ou anodisé, 127 cm de long
Zumtobel Staff, Dornbirn, Austria

In 1980 Ettore Sottsass founded
Sottsass Associati with two younger
disciples, Marco Zanini and Matteo
Thun. Over the following years the
partnership expanded as new members
joined. Since 1988, this influential
Milan-based interdisciplinary studio has
designed various lighting products for
the Austrian manufacturer Zumtobel
Staff, with the *Ciros* suspended ceiling
light (1995) being one of the best-
known. Like so much of the studio's
output, the *Ciros* (which also exists
in a wire-suspended version) reflects
Sottsass Associati's distinctive signature style, characterized by bold forms
and dynamic graphic lines. (CF/PF)

1980 gründete Ettore Sottsass mit
zwei jüngeren Kollegen, Marco Zanini
und Matteo Thun, die Firma Sottsass
Associati. In den nächsten Jahren ex-
pandierte das Unternehmen und bekam
neue Teilhaber. Seit 1988 hat dieses
einflussreiche interdisziplinäre Studio
mit Sitz in Mailand verschiedene Beleuchtungskörper für den österreichischen Hersteller Zumtobel Staff entworfen, von denen die Deckenleuchte
Ciros (1995) zu den bekanntesten
zählt. Wie viele andere Entwürfe des
Studios trägt die *Ciros* Leuchte, die
es auch mit Kabelaufhängung gibt,
deutlich die von mutigen Formen und
dynamischen grafischen Konturen
bestimmte Handschrift der Sottsass
Associati. (CF/PF)

C'est en 1980 qu'Ettore Sottsass
fonda Sottsass Associati avec deux
de ses jeunes disciples, Marco Zanini
et Matteo Thun. Ce partenariat s'ouvrit
par la suite à de nouveaux membres.
Depuis 1988, cette influente agence
interdisciplinaire milanaise a conçu
divers appareils d'éclairage pour le fabricant autrichien Zumtobel Staff, dont
la suspension *Ciros* (1995) est l'un
des plus connus. Comme une grande
partie de la production de l'agence, la
Ciros (qui existe également en suspension par câble) reflète le style spéci-
fique de Sottsass Associati, caractérisé
par des formes audacieuses et un graphisme dynamique. (CF/PF)

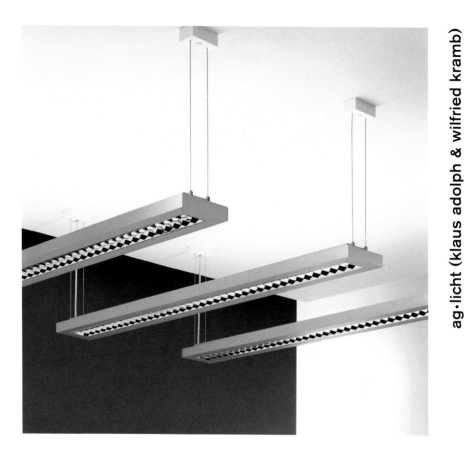

The *Claris* lighting system (1997–98) was originally developed by ag·Licht for the German Federal Government's Press and Information Office in Berlin. Since 1999 it has also been marketed by the Austrian lighting manufacturer Zumtobel Staff. The system is striking for its clear, geometric formal language. Reduction to absolute essentials combined with high-class materials and state-of-the-art technology makes *Claris* the ideal lighting system for Modern public architecture. Since 1996, ag·Licht, headed by the two designers and lighting planners Klaus Adolph and Wilfried Kramb, has been successfully engaged in designing lighting schemes and products for the lighting industry. (TB)

Das Leuchtensystem *Claris* (1997–98), ursprünglich von der ag·Licht für das Presse- und Informationsamt der Bundesregierung in Berlin entwickelt und seit 1999 im Programm des österreichischen Leuchtenherstellers Zumtobel Staff, überzeugt durch seine klare, geometrische Formensprache. Die Reduktion auf das Wesentliche in Kombination mit hochwertigen Materialien und modernster Lichttechnik macht es zum idealen Beleuchtungssystem für moderne Architektur im öffentlichen Raum. Die ag·Licht, betrieben von den beiden Designern und Lichtplanern Klaus Adolph und Wilfried Kramp, beschäftigt sich seit 1996 erfolgreich mit der Planung von Tages- und Kunstlicht sowie mit Produktentwicklung im Bereich der Leuchtenindustrie. (TB)

Le système *Claris* (1997–98) fut mis au point à l'origine par ag·Licht pour le service d'information du Gouvernement fédéral allemand à Berlin. Depuis 1999, il a également été commercialisé par le fabricant autrichien Zumtobel Staff. C'est un projet frappant par la clarté de son langage géométrique. La réduction à l'essentiel absolu combinée à des matériaux de haute qualité et à une technologie d'avant-garde font de *Claris* le système d'éclairage idéal pour l'architecture d'aujourd'hui. Depuis 1996, ag·Licht, dirigée par les deux designers et ingénieurs en éclairage Klaus Adolph et Wilfried Kramb, a réalisé avec succès des systèmes et des produits pour l'industrie du luminaire. (TB)

Like a flower, the *Solar Bud* outdoor light (1995–98) gets its energy from the sun and therefore does not require cabling – the bane of outdoor lighting. The solar energy is collected by a polycrystalline silicon photovoltaic cell and then stored in two rechargeable batteries. At sunset the energy accumulated throughout the day powers the energy-efficient LEDs, with 13 to 15 hours of sunlight yielding roughly five hours of illumination. Although the light emitted is not strong, the *Solar Bud*, which spikes into the ground, is useful as a glowing marker in a garden or along a path. (CF/PF)

Wie eine Blume erhält die Außenleuchte *Solar Bud* (1995–98) ihre Energie von der Sonne und braucht daher keine Verkabelung, die ohnehin der Untergang jeder Außenbeleuchtung ist. Die Sonnenenergie wird von einer fotovoltaischen Zelle aus polykristallinem Silikon aufgenommen und in zwei wiederaufladbaren Batterien gespeichert. Die während des Tages gesammelte Energie versorgt bei Einbruch der Dunkelheit die energiesparenden LEDs, wobei 13 bis 15 Sonnenstunden etwa fünf Stunden Beleuchtung ergeben. Die Lichtemission ist zwar nicht stark, aber als Begrenzungslicht in einem Garten oder entlang eines Pfades ist die *Solar Bud* Leuchte, die man einfach in den Boden spießt, sehr brauchbar. (CF/PF)

Telle une fleur, le *Solar Bud* (1995–98) tire son énergie du soleil et n'a donc pas besoin de cordon d'alimentation, solution idéale pour un appareil d'éclairage extérieur. L'énergie solaire est collectée pendant la journée par une cellule photovoltaïque à cristaux de silicone puis accumulée dans deux batteries rechargeables. Lorsque le soleil se couche, elle alimente des diodes lumineuses. Treize à quinze heures d'exposition au soleil fournissent environ cinq heures d'éclairage. Bien que l'éclairage émis ne soit pas puissant, le *Solar Bud*, qui se plante dans le sol, peut servir à délimiter un chemin ou animer un jardin. (CF/PF)

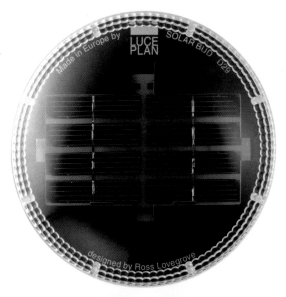

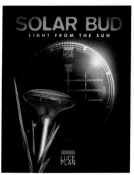

△△ *The diffuser of the Solar Bud outdoor light showing photovoltaic cell / Diffusor der Außenleuchte* Solar Bud *mit sichtbarer fotovoltaischer Zelle / Le diffuseur de la lampe d'extérieur* Solar Bud *et ses cellules photovoltaïques*

△ *Luceplan brochure and publicity photograph of the* Solar Bud *outdoor light, 1998 / Broschüre und Werbefoto von Luceplan mit Außenleuchte* Solar Bud*, 1998 / Brochure et photographie publicitaire Luceplan de la lampe d'extérieur* Solar Bud*, 1998*

▷ *Solar Bud* outdoor light, 1995–98
Tubular anodized aluminum stem with UV-resistant methacrylate head housing photovoltaic cell, nickel cadmium batteries and LED light source, 37 cm high / Schaft aus eloxiertem Aluminiumrohr und Leuchtenkopf aus UV-lichtbeständigem Methacrylat mit fotovoltaischer Zelle, Nickel-Cadmium-Batterien und LED-Lichtquelle, 37 cm hoch / Tige tubulaire en aluminium anodisé, tête en méthacrylate anti-UV à cellules photovoltaïques, batteries au cadmium de nickel, éclairage par diodes, 37 cm de haut
Luceplan, Milan, Italy

◁ Pod Lens *outdoor lights in their natural habitat / Außenleuchten* Pod Lens *im Garten / Lampes d'extérieur* Pod Lens *dans leur environnement naturel*

Pod Lens outdoor light, 1998

Molded polycarbonate diffuser with prismatic internal sides and over-molded lens, 28.5 cm long (diffuser) / Diffusor aus Spritzguss-Polykarbonat mit prismatischer Innenseite und aufgedruckter Linse, 28,5 cm lang (Diffusor) / Diffuseur en polycarbonate moulé à faces intérieures prismatiques et lentilles surmoulées, 28,5 cm de long (diffuseur)
Luceplan, Milan, Italy

Employing the same plastic-molding technology used to make car taillights, Ross Lovegrove's *Pod Lens* outdoor light (1998) can be festooned around a garden to accentuate trees and plants. It uses either normal incandescent bulbs or energy-efficient compact fluorescent bulbs, while its UV-resistant polycarbonate diffuser has over-molded walls to ensure that they are kept completely waterproof. The *Pod Lens* range, which is available in sage green, sandy yellow, terracotta red and silver/gray also includes floor and wall-mounted versions. (CF/PF)

Ross Lovegroves Außenleuchte *Pod Lens* (1998) wird mit demselben Kunststoff-Spritzgießverfahren hergestellt, das auch bei Autoscheinwerfern Verwendung findet. Sie kann im Garten als Girlande zur Akzentuierung von Bäumen und Pflanzen aufgehängt werden und ist mit normalen Glühlampen oder energiesparenden Kompakt-Leuchtstofflampen einsetzbar. Der gegen UV-Licht unempfindliche Diffusor ist durch seine aus einem Stück gegossene Wandung vollkommen wasserdicht. Die *Pod Lens* Serie ist in den Farben Salbei, Sand, Terrakotta und Grau erhältlich und umfasst auch eine Steh- und eine Wandleuchtenversion. (CF/PF)

Réalisée à partir de la même technologie que celle du moulage des phares en plastique pour automobiles, la *Pod Lens* (1998) de Ross Lovegrove est une lampe d'extérieur à suspendre en guirlande autour d'un jardin ou dans un arbre. Elle utilise soit des ampoules à incandescence soit des lampes fluorescentes économiques. Son diffuseur en polycarbonate anti-UV est par ailleurs entièrement étanche à l'humidité. La gamme des *Pod Lens*, proposées en verre sauge, jaune sable, rouge terre cuite et gris argent, comprend également des versions lampadaire et applique. (CF/PF)

Technically inventive, Alberto Meda and Paolo Rizzato's *Fortebraccio* (1998) was the first task/table light with a halogen bulb and no transformer that could be handled safely. Its comfortable polycarbonate handle-like grip and innovative central elbow-like joint, which enables the articulated arm to rotate both horizontally and vertically, provides the user with a high degree of directional light control. Although inspired by George Carwardine's *Anglepoise* light (*c*.1933), the *Fortebraccio*'s graceful and fluent articulation allows its spring-mounted arms a far greater degree of mobility than its classic antecedent. (CF/PF)

Die technisch einfallsreiche Leuchte *Fortebraccio* (1998) von Alberto Meda und Paolo Rizzato war die erste Arbeits- bzw. Tischleuchte mit Halogenlampe und ohne Transformator, die man ohne Gefahr anfassen konnte. Durch ihren praktischen stielförmigen Griff aus Polykarbonat und das innovative ellbogenartige Gelenkstück, das den zweiteiligen Arm horizontal und vertikal drehbar macht, lässt sich die Leuchte besonders leicht in jede gewünschte Position bringen. Die *Fortebraccio* Leuchte ist zwar von George Carwardines Arbeitsleuchte *Anglepoise* (ca. 1933) inspiriert, ihre geschmeidige Gelenkverbindung ermöglicht den gefederten Armen jedoch einen weitaus größeren Bewegungsspielraum. (CF/PF)

Techniquement inventive, la *Fortebraccio* (1998) d'Alberto Meda et Paolo Rizzato fut la première lampe de travail ou de table à ampoule halogène et sans transformateur à pouvoir se manipuler sans risque. Sa confortable prise en forme de poignée en polycarbonate et son articulation centrale coudée qui permet au bras de pivoter verticalement et horizontalement, assure à son utilisateur un très haut degré de contrôle directionnel. Bien que ce modèle soit inspiré de l'*Anglepoise* de George Carwardine (vers 1933), son articulation gracieuse et souple lui assure un degré de mobilité beaucoup plus important que son antécédent. (CF/PF)

Fortebraccio task light, 1998

Polycarbonate head and grip with steel arms and Zamak, 43.7 cm lower arm, 35.5 cm upper arm / Leuchtenkopf und Griff aus Spritzguss-Polykarbonat, Arme aus Stahl und Zamak-Druckguss, 43,7 cm unterer Arm, 35,5 cm oberer Arm / Tête et poignée en polycarbonate, bras en acier et zamak, bras inférieur : 43,7 cm, bras supérieur : 35,5 cm
Luceplan, Milan, Italy

▷ Design drawings and illuminated Fortebraccio *task light showing polycarbonate grip* / *Entwurfzeichnungen und eingeschaltete Arbeitsleuchte* Fortebraccio *mit Griff aus Polykarbonat* / *Dessins de conception de la lampe de travail* Fortebraccio *allumée montrant la poignée de polycarbonate*

Best known for his characterful products for Alessi and his best-selling *Bombo* chair for Magis, Stefano Giovannoni's work is marked by a playful, child-like quality that is highly endearing and connects "with our memory and imaginary world." His *Big Switch* table/wall light (1996) "cartoonizes" the humble on/off switch, while its scale gives the design an ironic out-of-context quality. Giovannoni is well aware that, for a product to succeed in a global market, it must have a strong emotional pull – in other words, it must not only function well, it must also make us smile. (CF/PF)

Die Entwürfe des vor allem durch seine charaktervollen Produkte für Alessi und seinen kommerziell äußerst erfolgreichen *Bombo* Stuhl für Magis bekannten Stefano Giovannoni zeichnen sich durch eine kindliche Verspieltheit aus, die besonders liebenswert ist und an „unsere Erinnerungen und unsere Fantasiewelt" anknüpft. Seine Tisch-/Wandleuchte *Big Switch* (1996) „karikiert" einen simplen Lichtschalter und wirkt durch die Überdimensionierung auf ironische Weise aus dem Zusammenhang gerissen. Giovannoni weiß genau, dass ein Produkt, will es auf dem globalen Markt bestehen, einen starken emotionalen Anreiz haben muss – mit anderen Worten, es muss nicht nur gut funktionieren, sondern uns auch zum Schmunzeln bringen. (CF/PF)

L'œuvre de Stefano Giovannoni, surtout connu pour ses créations pleines de personnalité réalisées pour Alessi et son siège best-seller *Bombo* pour Magis, se caractérise par un aspect ludique et enfantin sympathique, lié à « notre mémoire et à notre monde imaginaire. » Sa lampe de table/applique *Big Switch* (« gros interrupteur ») de 1996 fait de l'humble interrupteur classique un personnage de BD dont l'échelle confirme un humour hors-normes. Giovannoni est parfaitement conscient de ce qu'un produit doit posséder un puissant appel émotionnel pour réussir sur le marché international. En d'autres mots, il doit non seulement bien fonctionner, mais également nous faire sourire. (CF/PF)

△△ ***Big Switch* table/wall light, 1996**
Injection-molded polycarbonate body with injection-molded silicone fittings, 12 cm high / Leuchtenkörper aus Spritzguss-Polykarbonat mit Montierungen aus Spritzguss-Silikon, 12 cm hoch / Corps en polycarbonate moulé par injection, pièces de montage en silicone moulé par injection, 12 cm de haut
Segno, Parabiago, Italy

△ *Segno publicity photograph showing* Big Switch *light in situ / Werbefoto von Segno mit Leuchte* Big Switch */ Photographie publicitaire Segno de la lampe* Big Switch *en situation*

flapflap table and floor lights, 1999

Steel and polypropylene construction, table version: 70 cm high, floor version: 100 cm high / Konstruktion aus Stahl und Polypropylen, Tischleuchte: 70 cm hoch, Stehleuchte: 100 cm hoch / Structure en acier et polypropylène, table: 70 cm de haut, lampadaire: 100 cm de haut
Next, Baldham, Germany

Turning all the laws of weightlessness on their heads, *flapflap* table and floor lights hover in space, as though frozen in mid-air after falling from a table or shelf. *flapflap* was designed in 1999 by Benjamin Hopf and Constantin Wortmann of the Munich design studio Büro für Form and is manufactured by the German firm Next in Baldham, which also produces other Hopf and Wortmann creations. The deliberately traditional shape emphasizes the ironic and distinctly surreal impression created by the apparently floating light. This effect is produced by using reinforced steel cable as the base of the light. (TB)

Alle Gesetzte der Schwerelosigkeit auf den Kopf stellend, scheinbar eingefroren im freien Fall von einem Tisch oder einem Regal, schweben die Tisch- und Stehleuchten *flapflap* im Raum. Entworfen wurden die *flapflap* Leuchten 1999 im Büro für Form in München von Benjamin Hopf und Constantin Wortmann. Produziert werden sie von der deutschen Firma Next in Baldham, die auch andere Leuchtenmodelle der Designer Hopf und Wortmann herstellt. Die gewollt traditionelle Formgebung der Leuchte verstärkt ihr ironisches Erscheinungsbild, das durchaus surreale Qualitäten hat. Ermöglicht wird die Konstruktion durch das unsichtbar mit Edelstahl verstärkte Stromkabel, das den Fuß der Leuchte bildet. (TB)

Inversant les lois de la gravité, les lampes de table et lampadaires *flapflap* flottent dans l'espace, comme figées en l'air après être tombées d'une table ou d'une étagère. La ligne *flapflap* a été dessinée en 1999 par Benjamin Hopf et Constantin Wortmann, de l'agence de design munichoise Büro für Form, et fabriquée par la firme allemande Next de Baldham, qui édite également les autres créations de ces designers. Sa forme délibérément traditionnelle met en valeur l'impression amusante et même surréaliste créée par cette lampe en suspension. L'effet est produit par un câble d'acier renforcé qui joue le rôle de base. (TB)

XXL Dome hanging light, 1999

Fiberglass, metal and stainless-steel construction, 180 cm diameter / Konstruktion aus Fiberglas, Metall und Edelstahl, 180 cm Durchmesser / Structure en fibre de verre, métal et acier
inoxydable, 180 cm de diamètre
Ingo Maurer, Munich, Germany

▷ **XXL Dome hanging lights at the
Westfriedhof subway station in
Munich, 1998**

Aluminum shades, inner surfaces enameled,
380 cm diameter / Lampenschirme aus Aluminium, Innenflächen lackiert, 380 cm Durchmesser / Abat-jour en aluminium, intérieur
laqué, 380 cm de diamètre
Ingo Maurer, Munich, Germany (one-off
production)

Ingo Maurer designed his enormous
XXL Dome hanging lights in 1998 as
part of the lighting scheme for Munich's
Westfriedhof subway station. Nearly
four meters in diameter, the aluminum
domes hover above the platform. In
combination with blue lights installed
onto ceilings and walls, they create
the illusion of a futuristic dream world.
In 1999 Maurer launched a smaller,
mass-produced version, a little more
than half the size of the original. Instead
of aluminum, this version of the *XXL
Dome* uses fiberglass, while the reflector's inner surfaces are enameled fluorescent pink, orange, red or green.
(TB)

Ingo Maurer hat seine überdimensionalen Hängeleuchten *XXL Dome* 1998
als Teil des Beleuchtungskonzepts für
die Münchener U-Bahnstation Westfriedhof entworfen. Mit einem Durchmesser von fast vier Metern schweben
die Lichtdome aus Aluminium über dem
Bahnsteig und sorgen in Kombination
mit den an den Decken und Wänden
angebrachten blauen Leuchtmitteln für
die Illusion einer futuristischen Traum-
welt. 1999 ging eine um etwas mehr
als die Hälfte verkleinerte Version der
Leuchte auch in die Serienproduktion.
Anstelle von Aluminium wird für diese
Version der *XXL Dome* Leuchte Fiberglas eingesetzt. Die Innenseiten der
Reflektoren sind in leuchtendem Pink,
Orange, Rot oder Grün lackiert. (TB)

Ingo Maurer a dessiné ces énormes
luminaires *XXL Dome* en 1998 dans le
cadre d'un projet pour la station de
métro du Westfriedhof à Munich. Leurs
dômes d'aluminium de près de quatre
mètres de diamètre, semblent en lévi-
tation au-dessus du quai. En liaison
avec la lumière bleue sur les plafonds
et les murs, ils créent l'illusion d'un
monde imaginaire. En 1999, Maurer en
a lancé une version plus petite, d'un
peu plus de la moitié de la dimension
originale, produite en série. La fibre de
verre y remplace l'aluminium, tandis
que l'intérieur du réflecteur est laqué
en rose, orange, rouge ou vert fluo.
(TB)

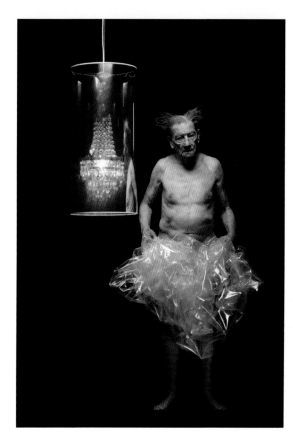

▷ **Light Shade Shade hanging light, 1999**

Semi-transparent mirrored film shade surrounding existing chandelier, small: 47 cm diameter, large: 70 cm diameter / Kronleuchter umgeben von Lampenschirm aus halb transparentem, spiegelndem Kunststoff, klein: 47 cm Durchmesser, groß: 70 cm Durchmesser / Abat-jour rendu semi-transparent par un film translucide sur un modèle, lustre existant, petit modèle: 47 cm de diamètre, grand modèle: 70 cm de diamètre
Droog Design, Amsterdam, The Netherlands (reissued by **Moooi**, Breda, The Netherlands)

◁ Photograph by Erwin Olaf showing Light Shade Shade hanging light / Fotografie von Erwin Olaf mit Hängeleuchte Light Shade Shade / Photographie de Erwin Olaf, mettant en scène le lustre Light Shade Shade

In 2001 Marcel Wanders established Moooi (meaning "beautiful" in Dutch) to get challenging designs by young freelance designers into production. The venture has led to some remarkable products, including Jurgen Bey's Light Shade Shade hanging light (1999). This design fuses the esthetics of the old (an existing chandelier) with the new (the semi-transparent shade) to produce a richly poetic yet tension-filled composition. The outer semi-transparent cylindrical shade is available in two sizes and can be purchased either separately, to put over an existing light of one's choice, or in conjunction with two selected chandeliers, as shown here. (CF/PF)

2001 gründete Marcel Wanders die Firma Moooi (holländisch „schön"), um jungen freischaffenden Designern eine Produktionsmöglichkeit für ihre provokanten Entwürfe zu bieten. Sein Unternehmen hat einige interessante Produkte hervorgebracht, zu denen auch Jürgen Beys Hängeleuchte Light Shade Shade (1999) gehört. In diesem Modell wird die Ästhetik des Alten (eines vorhandenen Kronleuchters) mit der des Neuen (des halb transparenten Schirms) verbunden zu einer poetischen und dabei spannungsgeladenen Komposition. Der Lampenschirm ist in zwei Größen erhältlich und kann allein erworben werden oder in Verbindung mit einem der zwei vorgesehenen Kronleuchter, wie in den hier abgebildeten Beispielen. (CF/PF)

En 2001, Marcel Wanders a fondé Moooi (« magnifique » en néerlandais) pour éditer des projets provocants de jeunes designers indépendants. L'entreprise a donné quelques fruits remarquables, dont le Light Shade Shade de Jurgen Bey (1999). Ce projet marie l'esthétique traditionnelle (un lustre existant) à la plus contemporaine (l'abat-jour semi-transparent) dans une composition à la fois riche en poésie et puissante. Cette protection cylindrique est proposée en deux dimensions et peut s'acheter séparément pour coiffer sur un lustre existant, ou en conjonction avec deux lustres présélectionnés, comme dans ces pages. (CF/PF)

***Holonzki* wall light, 1999–2000**

Holographic glass plate with metal fittings, transformer and fabric covered wire, 56 cm high / Holographische Glasplatte mit Montierung aus Metall, Transformator und Textilkabel, 56 cm hoch / Plaque de verre holographique à pièces de montage métalliques, transformateur, câble gainé de tissu, 56 cm de haut
Ingo Maurer, Munich, Germany

▷ ***Wo bist du, Edison, …?* hanging light, 1997**

Acrylic glass and aluminum construction with 360° hologram, 46 cm diameter / Konstruktion aus Acrylglas und Aluminium mit 360°-Hologramm, 46 cm Durchmesser / Structure en verre acrylique et aluminium avec hologramme à 360°, 46 cm de diamètre
Ingo Maurer, Munich, Germany

Developed by Ingo Mauer in collaboration with the hologram specialist Eckard Knuth, the hanging light *Wo bist du, Edison, …?*, 1997) is the first light ever to be based on a 360° hologram. Lit by a concealed halogen lamp, the shade projects a hologram of an old-fashioned light bulb – a homage to Thomas Alva Edison. The *Holonzki* wall light (1999– 2000) also uses hologram technology to create the illusion of a real light bulb. The name *Holonzki* alludes to the small Russian company that is the world's only manufacturer of the special film used for the photographic plate. (TB)

In Zusammenarbeit mit dem Holographie-Techniker Eckard Knuth entwickelte Ingo Maurer 1997 die Hängeleuchte *Wo bist du, Edison …?*, die weltweit erste Leuchte, die auf einer 360°-Holographie basiert. Angestrahlt durch eine in der Leuchtenhalterung versteckte Halogenleuchte, erzeugt der Lampenschirm das Hologramm einer historischen Glühbirne – eine Hommage an Thomas Alva Edison. Auch die Wandleuchte *Holonzki* (1999–2000) benutzt die Technik der Holographie, um die Illusion einer real existierenden Glühbirne zu erzeugen. Der Name *Holonzki* ist eine Anspielung auf den kleinen russischen Betrieb, der als weltweit einziger Produzent die für die Herstellung der Leuchtenschirme benötigten Spezialfilme herstellt. (TB)

Mis au point par Ingo Maurer en collaboration avec le spécialiste des hologrammes Eckard Knuth, *Wo bist du, Edison, …?* («Où es-tu Edison?», 1997) est la première lampe jamais conçue à partir d'un hologramme à 360°. Illuminé par une ampoule halogène dissimulée, l'abat-jour projette l'hologramme d'une ampoule à l'ancienne, hommage à Thomas Alva Edison. L'applique *Holonzki* (1999–2000) utilise également la technologie de l'hologramme pour créer l'illusion d'une vraie ampoule. Son nom, *Holonzki*, est une allusion à la petite entreprise russe, seul fabricant au monde du film spécial utilisé pour la plaque photographique. (TB)

E.Light 6W task light, 1999
Polycarbonate and Zamak base, brass stem
with polycarbonate head, 32.5 cm high (max.) /
Fuß aus Polykarbonat und Zamak, Teleskoparm
aus Messing, Leuchtenkopf aus Polykarbonat,
32,5 cm hoch (max.) / Base en polycarbonate
et Zamak, tige en laiton, tête en polycarbonate,
32,5 cm de haut (max.)
Artemide, Pregnana Milanese, Italy

Specially developed for computer work-stations, Ernesto Gismondi's 1999 *E.Light 6W* task light uses state-of-the-art microlight technology. Space-saving and economical, it can also provide discreet reading and task lighting for seminar rooms and lecture halls. The lamp has an average life expectancy of 20,000 hours. The height-adjustable telescopic rod and the reflector that can be turned through 360° give it enormous flexibility. The foot and reflector are in translucent polycarbonate in a choice of orange, crystal, dark blue, green, black or silver. (TB)

Speziell für den Gebrauch an Compu-terarbeitsplätzen entwickelt, wendet die Arbeitsleuchte *E.Light 6W* (1999) nach Entwurf von Ernesto Gismondi modernste Mikrolicht-Technologie an. Durch ihre platzsparende und kosten-günstige Ausformung eignet sich die Leuchte aber auch als dezente Lese-und Arbeitsleuchte für Seminarräume oder Hörsäle. Der Leuchtkörper hat eine durchschnittliche Lebensdauer von 20.000 Stunden. Durch den höhenver-stellbaren Leuchtenarm und den um 360° drehbaren Reflektor ist die Leuch-te in ihrer Anwendung extrem flexibel. Die Verkleidung des Lampenfußes und des Reflektors besteht aus transluzi-dem Polykarbonat und ist in den Far-ben Orange, Kristall, Dunkelblau, Grün, Schwarz oder Silber erhältlich. (TB)

Spécialement conçue pour les postes de travail informatiques, la *E.Light 6W* d'Ernesto Gismondi (1999) fait appel à la technologie avancée des microlam-pes. Peu encombrante, économique, elle peut aussi faire office de lampe de lecture et de travail discrète dans les salles de réunions et de conférences. Sa source lumineuse possède une durée de vie moyenne de 20.000 heu-res. Le bras télescopique à hauteur réglable et le réflecteur qui tourne à 360° lui assurent une étonnante flexi-bilité. Son pied et son réflecteur sont en polycarbonate translucide et sont, disponibles en orange, cristal, bleu foncé, vert, noir ou argent. (TB)

Suite 1 and Suite 2 table lights, 1998

Anodized aluminum bases with methacrylate
shades, small: 32 cm high, large: 50 cm high /
Gestelle aus eloxiertem Aluminium mit Lampenschirmen aus Methacrylat, klein: 32 cm hoch,
groß: 50 cm hoch / Pieds en aluminium anodisé,
abat-jour en méthacrylate, petit modèle : 32 cm
de haut, grand modèle : 50 cm de haut
Tronconi, Corsico, Italy

A prolific designer of furniture and domestic products as well as lighting,
Raul Barbieri has worked from his own
studio in Milan since 1989. His collaboration with the lighting manufacturer
Tronconi is of long standing and has
yielded the *Bulbo* table light (1983),
the *Master* desk light (1988) and the
Troller floor light (c.1985), among others. The *Suite* table lights (1998) share
– and indeed exaggerate – the pared-
down esthetic of these earlier works
and seem to look back on earlier, Mod-
ernist-inspired lighting designs. Their
only expressive touch is the delicately
transparent coloring of their methacrylate shades. (QC)

Raul Barbieri machte sich 1989 in
Mailand mit einem Designstudio selb-
ständig und erwarb einen Ruf als
äußerst produktiver Entwerfer von Möbeln, Haushaltsprodukten und Leuchten. Aus seiner langjährigen Zusammenarbeit mit dem Leuchtenhersteller
Tronconi entstanden unter anderem
die Tischleuchte *Bulbo* (1983), die
Schreibtischleuchte *Master* (1988) und
die Stehleuchte *Troller* (ca. 1985). Die
Tischleuchte *Suite* (1998) beruht noch
stärker als seine früheren Leuchtenentwürfe auf einer puristischen Formästhe-
tik und ihr Design erinnert an modernistische Leuchtenentwürfe der 1930er
Jahre. Ihre besondere Ausstrahlung
erhalten die Leuchten durch die zart
transparente Färbung ihrer Lampenschirme aus Methacrylat. (QC)

Designer prolifique de mobilier, de produits pour la maison et de luminaires,
Raul Barbieri possède sa propre agence à Milan depuis 1989. Sa collaboration de longue date avec le fabricant Tronconi a donné naissance, entre
autres, à la lampe de table *Bulbo*
(1983), au modèle de bureau *Master*
(1988) et au lampadaire *Troller* (vers
1985). Les lampes de table *Suite*
(1998) partagent – et amplifient même
– l'esthétique épurée de ses premières
œuvres et semblent renvoyer à un style
d'inspiration moderniste. Leur seule
touche d'expressivité vient de la colora-
tion transparente délicate de leur abat-
jour en méthacrylate. (QC)

Michael Young's *Stick* floor light (1999) typifies his refreshingly original approach to design, which seeks "new yet rational ways of realizing objects." He is interested in simple yet visually striking forms, which often have a strong graphic presence. His engagingly totemic *Stick* light is rotationally molded, a relatively low-tech and inexpensive manufacturing process for plastic products. Serially produced by Eurolounge, the manufacturing company founded by Tom Dixon, the *Stick* light is available in translucent white polypropylene. In 2001 Young also produced a special limited edition of 20 hand-colored *Stick* lights. (CF/PF)

Die Stehleuchte *Stick* (1999) von Michael Young ist ein typisches Beispiel für seinen erfrischend originellen Gestaltungsansatz und sein Streben nach „neuen, und doch vernünftigen Möglichkeiten, Objekte zu realisieren". Er beschäftigt sich mit einfachen Formen, die eine überraschende Wirkung erzielen und häufig eine starke grafische Präsenz aufweisen. Seine faszinierende *Stick* Leuchte wird im Rotationsgussverfahren hergestellt, einer technisch relativ unaufwendigen und kostengünstigen Fertigungsmethode für Produkte aus Kunststoff. Die von Tom Dixon gegründete Beleuchtungsfirma Eurolounge hat die serielle Fertigung übernommen und produziert die Leuchte aus transparentem weißem Polypropylen. 2001 brachte Young darüber hinaus eine limitierte Sonderausgabe von 20 handkolorierten *Stick* Leuchten heraus. (CF/PF)

Le lampadaire *Stick* (1999) de Michael Young est typique de son approche originale et rafraîchissante du design, qui cherche « des façons nouvelles mais rationnelles de réaliser des objets ». Il s'intéresse à des formes simples mais frappantes, qui possèdent souvent une forte présence graphique. Le *Stick*, à la séduisante allure de totem, est moulé par rotation, processus de travail du plastique relativement simple et économique. Produit en série par Eurolounge, l'entreprise de Tom Dixon, le *Stick* est proposé en polypropylène blanc translucide. En 2001, Young a également réalisé une série limitée de vingt *Stick* colorés à la main. (CF/PF)

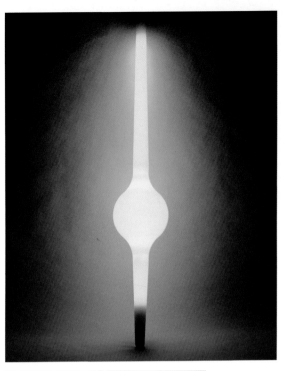

△△ *Stick* floor light, 2001 – hand-colored version
Rotationally molded polypropylene construction, 190 cm high / Durch Rotationsguss hergestellte Polypropylenkonstruktion, 190 cm hoch / Fabrication en polypropylène moulé par rotation, 190 cm de haut
Eurolounge, Norwich, Great Britain (limited edition of 20)

▷ *Stick* floor light, 1999
Rotationally molded polypropylene construction, 190 cm high / Durch Rotationsguss hergestellte Polypropylenkonstruktion, 190 cm hoch / Structure en polypropylène moulé par rotation, 190 cm de haut
Eurolounge, Norwich, Great Britain

△ Astro *nightclub in Reykjavik, Iceland, with* Stick *floor lights, c.2000 / Nachtklub Astro in Reykjavik, Island, mit Stehleuchten* Stick*, ca. 2000 / Night-club Astro à Reykjavik, Islande, équipé de lampadaires* Stick*, vers 2000*

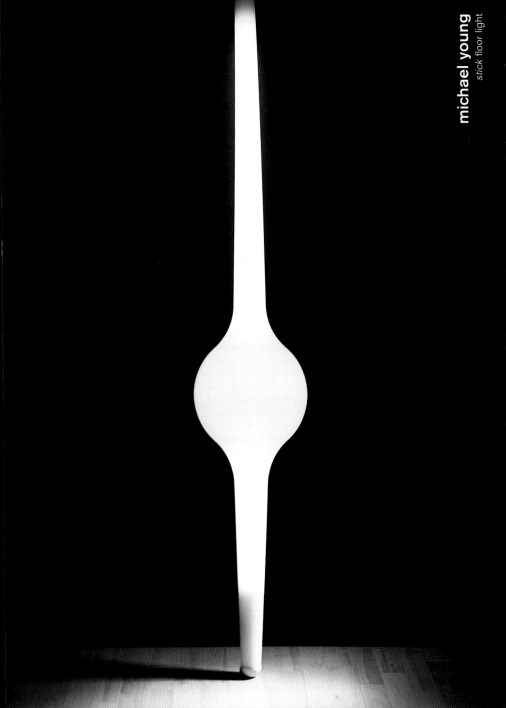

michael young
stick floor light

While still at college, Harri Koskinen collaborated with the Iittala glassworks on a wedding present project. Although unsatisfied with the resulting design – a pair of glasses in a cast glass box – Koskinen was fascinated by the way molten glass glowed when poured into the mold. He subsequently carved a graphite mold using a regular light bulb as a template. Once the form was cast in glass he sandblasted the void so that a smaller-sized bulb could be inserted without being seen. Since the ice-like *Block* light was put into production in 1997 over 15,000 units have been sold. (CF/PF)

Noch während seiner Ausbildung arbeitete Harri Koskinen mit der Glasmanufaktur Iittala an einem Hochzeitsgeschenk-Projekt. Koskinen war zwar mit dem Design, das daraus hervorging – zwei Gläser in einem Behälter aus Gussglas – nicht zufrieden, aber was ihn faszinierte, war das Glühen des geschmolzenen Glases, wenn es in die Form gegossen wurde. Daraufhin fertigte er eine Form aus Graphit an, die einer herkömmlichen Glühlampe nachgebildet war. Er ließ die Form in Glas gießen und bearbeitete den Hohlraum durch Sandstrahlen, sodass eine kleinere Lampe darin Platz fand und aussah, als wäre sie mitgegossen worden. Seit die an einen Eisblock erinnernde Tischleuchte *Block* 1997 in Produktion ging, wurden mehr als 15.000 Stück davon verkauft. (CF/PF)

Encore étudiant, Harri Koskinen avait collaboré avec la verrerie Iittala pour un projet de cadeau de mariage. Bien qu'insatisfait du produit final – une paire de verres dans une boite de verre moulé – il fut cependant fasciné par la façon dont le verre fondu s'illuminait lorsqu'il était coulé dans le moule. Il fabriqua donc un moule en graphique, à partir d'une ampoule utilisée comme gabarit. Une fois la forme prise dans le verre, il sabla le vide pour qu'une ampoule légèrement plus petite puisse s'y loger sans être visible. Depuis le lancement de la lampe de table *Block* (1997), plus de 15 000 exemplaires en ont été vendus. (CF/PF)

Miconos ceiling light, 1999–2000

Chrome-plated metal mounts with transparent blown-glass diffuser, 48 cm drop / Montierung aus verchromtem Metall, Schirm aus klarem, mundgeblasenem Glas, 48 cm lang / Montures en métal chromé, diffuseur en verre soufflé transparent, 48 cm de haut hors tout
Artemide, Pregnana Milanese, Italy

Polyethylene construction, ceiling light: 100 cm drop; hanging light: 40 cm diameter; wall light: 60 cm high / Polyethylen-Konstruktion, Deckenleuchte: 100 cm lang, Hängeleuchte: 40 cm Durchmesser, Wandleuchte: 60 cm hoch / Fabrication en polyéthylène, plafonnier: 100 cm de haut, suspension: 40 cm de diamètre, applique: 60 cm de haut

Next, Baldham, Germany

Liquid-light drop-1 ceiling light,
Liquid-light drop-2 hanging light &
Liquid-light drop-3 wall light, 2000

The *liquid-light* series, designed in 2000 by Benjamin Hopf and Constantin Wortmann offers light "in liquid form." Like luminous raindrops, the *Drop-1* and *Drop-3* lights cling to ceilings and walls, or hover, apparently weightless, in midair like the *Drop-2* hanging light. In 1998, the two designers Benjamin Hopf and Constantin Wortmann set up their Büro für Form studio in Munich, where they are involved in product and graphic design, as well as designing trade exhibitions. Their creations are characterized by perfect functionality and effective ergonomics while also appealing to the emotions and generating a sense of poetry. (TB)

Die Leuchtenserie *liquid-light*, 2000 entworfen von Benjamin Hopf und Constantin Wortmann, präsentiert Licht in „flüssiger Form". Wie zähflüssige, leuchtende Tropfen kleben die Deckenleuchte *Drop-1* und die Wandleuchte *Drop-3* an Decken und Wänden oder verharren scheinbar schwerelos wie die Hängeleuchte *Drop-2* im freien Fall in der Luft. Die beiden Designer Benjamin Hopf und Constantin Wortmann gründeten 1998 das Büro für Form in München. Sie betätigen sich in den Bereichen Produkt-, Grafik- und Messedesign. Neben perfekter Funktion und Ergonomie steht bei ihnen das Erzeugen von Poesie und Emotionen im Mittelpunkt ihrer Designarbeit. (TB)

La série des *Liquid-lights*, conçue en 2000 par Benjamin Hopf et Constantin Wortmann propose une lumière « sous forme liquide. » Comme des gouttes de pluie lumineuses, la *Drop-1* et la *Drop 3* s'accrochent aux plafonds et aux murs, ou flottent apparemment sans aucun poids, comme la suspension *Drop-2*. C'est en 1998 que ces deux designers ont créé leur agence Büro für Form à Munich, qui se consacre au design graphique et produit ainsi qu'à la conception d'expositions commerciales. leurs créations se caractérisent par leur parfaite fonctionnalité et leur ergonomie efficace tout en s'adressant aux sens et en générant une réelle poésie. (TB)

Renowned for its world-class architecture, Foster & Partners also produces innovative industrial designs ranging from door handles and switches to wind-powered energy converters. It is, however, the practice's lighting designs that perhaps best encapsulate the technical inventiveness and strict formal vocabulary that distinguish its building projects. The *Oto* (1997–99) is a comprehensive, flexible and robust system that incorporates built-in housings with differing light apertures that mount onto a rail-like track. In recognition of its design excellence the system won a Red Dot Award in the product design category in 2001. (CF/PF)

Das weltweit bekannte Architekturbüro Foster & Partners ist auch durch innovatives Industriedesign von Türgriffen und Schaltern bis hin zu Energiewandlern für Windkraftanlagen hervorgetreten. Aber es sind die Beleuchtungsdesigns des Büros, die hinsichtlich technischem Einfallsreichtum und strengem formalen Vokabular am ehesten an seine Bauprojekte heranreichen. Das Leuchtenssystem *Oto* (1997–99) verwendet Einbaugehäuse mit verschiedenen Lichtquellen, die auf einer gleisähnlichen Schiene laufen, und ist sehr vielfältig, anpassungsfähig und robust. 2001 wurde das hochwertige Design des Systems mit einem Red Dot Award in der Kategorie Produktdesign ausgezeichnet. (CF/PF)

Réputée dans le monde entier pour ses interventions en architecture, l'agence Foster & Partners s'intéresse également au design industriel et a conçu de nombreux produits allant des poignées de porte à des convertisseurs d'énergie éoliens. Ce sont cependant, ses réalisations dans le domaine de l'éclairage qui se rapprochent le plus de l'inventivité et de la rigueur de vocabulaire formel de ses œuvres architecturales. *Oto* (1997–99) est une système complet, souple et robuste qui comprend des spots de différentes ouvertures montés sur un rail. En reconnaissance de son excellence de conception, le système a remporté un Red Dot Award dans la catégorie design produit en 2001. (CF/PF)

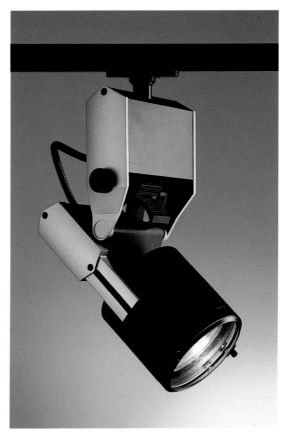

Oto **track lighting system, 1997–99**
Extruded aluminum and die-cast aluminum housings on rail-type track. Oto 130 spotlight: 13 cm diameter; Oto 80 spotlight: 8 cm diameter / Gehäuse aus extrudiertem und druckgegossenem Aluminium auf Schiene. Oto 130 Strahler: 13 cm Durchmesser, Oto 80 Strahler: 8 cm Durchmesser / Spots en aluminium extrudé et fonte d'aluminium. Spot Oto 130: 13 cm de diamètre, spot Oto 80: 8 cm de diamètre
Artemide, Pregnana Milanese, Italy

Photograph by Elliott Erwitt of Oto *track lighting system, c.2000 / Foto des Beleuchtungssystems* Oto *von Elliott Erwitt, ca. 2000 / Photographie par Elliott Erwitt du système d'éclairage sur rail* Oto, *vers 2000*

Hertz 4 suspended ceiling light, 2000

Varnished die-cast aluminum mounts with adjustable polycarbonate diffusers, 31 or 80 cm drop / Montierung aus klarlackiertem Druck-gussaluminium mit verstellbarem Diffusoren aus Polycarbonat, 31 oder 80 cm lang / Monture en fonte d'aluminium vernie, diffuseurs réglable en polycarbonate, 31 ou 80 cm de haut hors tout
Flos, Bovezzo, Italy

One of the most satisfying lighting solutions of recent years, the *Hertz* system (2000) combines excellent functionality with refined esthetic qualities. Designed by Munich-based Konstanin Grcic, the *Hertz* is suitable for both contract and domestic environments. It is available with either two or four separately adjustable spotlights and is supplied as a total integrated unit with the transformer built into the ceiling rose. Like much of Grcic's work, the *Hertz* has a very distinctive structural clarity that is the result of his highly considered, essentialist approach to design. (CF/PF)

Mit seiner Kombination von ausgezeichneter Funktionalität und hoch entwickelter Ästhetik ist das Leuchtensystem *Hertz* (2000) eine der überzeugendsten Beleuchtungslösungen der letzten Jahre. Das von dem Wahlmünchener Konstantin Grcic entworfene System eignet sich sowohl für öffentliche Gebäude als auch für den Wohnbereich. Es ist mit zwei oder mit vier einzeln verstellbaren Strahlern erhältlich und wird als komplette Einheit verkauft, wobei der Transformator in der Deckenrose installiert ist. Wie die meisten Arbeiten Grcics zeichnet sich auch das System *Hertz* durch außergewöhnliche strukturelle Klarheit aus, die sich aus seiner sehr überlegten und essenzialistischen Designhaltung ergibt. (CF/PF)

Une des plus brillantes solutions d'éclairage de ces dernières années, le système *Hertz* (2000) combine une remarquable fonctionnalité à un grand raffinement esthétique. Conçu par Konstantin Grcic, designer installé à Munich, il est conçu pour les environnements professionnels ou domestiques. Il est proposé équipé de deux ou quatre spots réglables séparément et est doté de son propre transformateur logé dans la rosace de fixation au plafond. Comme beaucoup des projets de Grcic, le *Hertz* présente une simplicité de construction particulière qui résulte d'une approche du design très précise, allant à l'essentiel. (CF/PF)

marc sadler
lite table lights

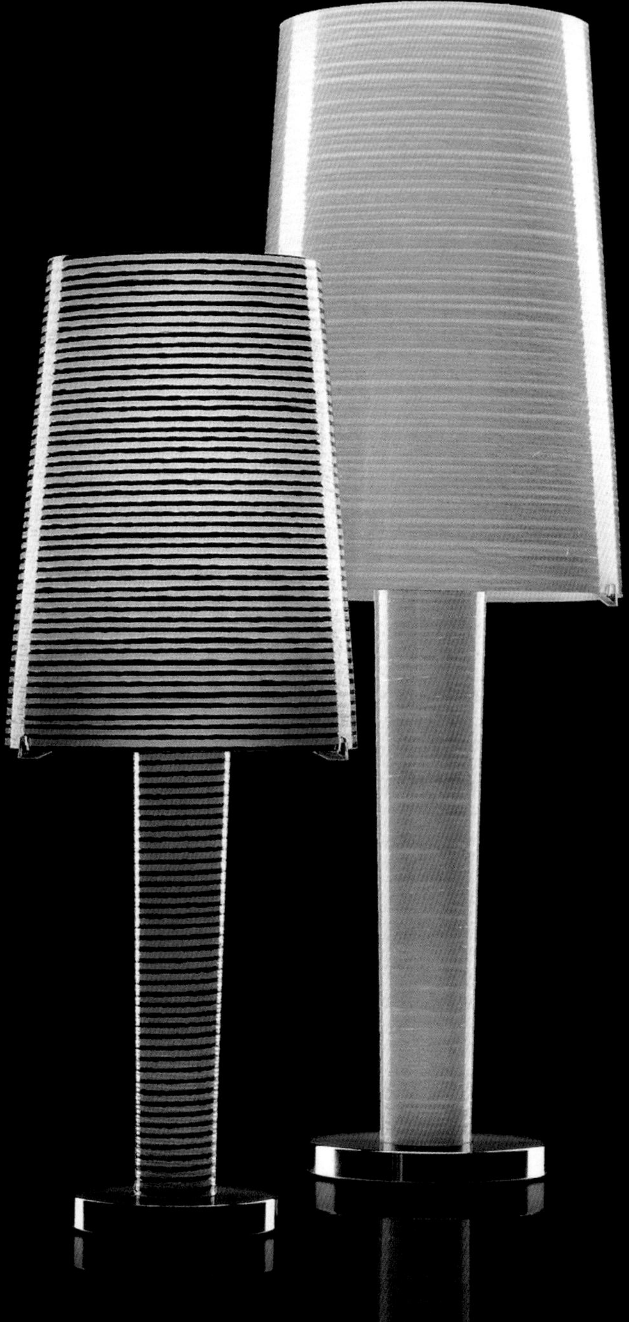

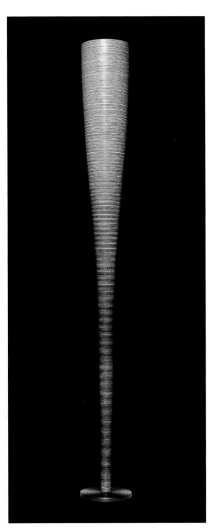

Marc Sadler is renowned for his innovative use of plastic materials and technological processes. In 2001 he won a Compasso d'Oro award for his *Mite* floor light (2000) and *Tite* hanging light (2001), both of which incorporate a composite material offering a high strength-to-weight ratio and are made of fiberglass strengthened with either black carbon thread or gold-colored Kevlar – the latter being used to make bullet-proof vests. This type of High-Tech material had never been used for lighting before, even though it has excellent diffusing properties. According to Foscarini, the simplicity and functionality of the forms chosen by Sadler fulfilled the material's "highest esthetic expression." (CF/PF)

Marc Sadler ist bekannt für seinen innovativen Einsatz von Kunststoffen und technologischen Verfahren. 2001 wurde er für die Stehleuchte *Mite* (2000) und die Hängeleuchte *Tite* (2001) mit dem Compasso d'Oro ausgezeichnet. Für die Konstruktion der beiden Leuchten verwendete er einen Verbundwerkstoff, der ein günstiges Festigkeit-Gewicht-Verhältnis ermöglicht und aus Fiberglas gefertigt ist, das entweder mit schwarzer Karbonfaser oder goldgelbem Kevlar, einem für kugelsichere Westen verwendeten Material, verstärkt ist. Trotz ihrer stark streuenden Eigenschaften waren derartige Hightech-Werkstoffe bis dahin noch nicht für Beleuchtungskörper verwendet worden. Laut Foscarini brachten die von Sadler gewählten einfachen und funktionalen Formen das Material zu „höchster ästhetischer Ausdruckskraft". (CF/PF)

Marc Sadler est réputé pour son recours aux matériaux plastiques et à des procédés technologiques innovants. En 2001, il a remporté le Compasso d'Oro pour son lampadaire *Mite* (2000) et sa suspension *Tite* (2001), tous deux intégrant un composite à rapport poids-résistance élevé, fait de fibre de verre renforcée de fils de carbone noir ou de Kevlar doré comme celui utilisé dans les gilets pare-balles. Ce type de matériau high-tech n'avait jamais été employé pour un luminaire jusqu'alors, bien qu'il possède d'excellentes propriétés de diffusion. Selon Foscarini, la simplicité et la fonctionnalité des formes de Sadler confèrent à ce matériau « le plus haut niveau d'expression esthétique ». (CF/PF)

◁ *Lite* **table lights, 2001**

Chrome-plated metal base with fiberglass stem and shade reinforced with carbon threads, small: 40 cm, large: 55 cm high / Fuß aus verchromtem Metall mit Schaft und Lampenschirm aus Fiberglas, verstärkt mit Karbonfaser, klein: 40 cm, groß: 55 cm hoch / Base en métal chromé, tige et abat-jour en fibre de verre renforcée de fils de carbone, petit modèle : 40 cm, grand modèle : 55 cm de haut
Foscarini, Marcon, Italy

△ *Mite* **floor light, 2000**

Chrome-plated metal base with fiberglass and Kevlar-reinforced stemmed diffuser, 185 cm high / Fuß aus verchromtem Metall mit Schaft und Diffusor aus Fiberglas und Kevlar, 185 cm hoch / Base en métal chromé, tige et diffuseur en fibre de verre renforcé de Kevlar, 185 cm de haut
Foscarini, Marcon, Italy

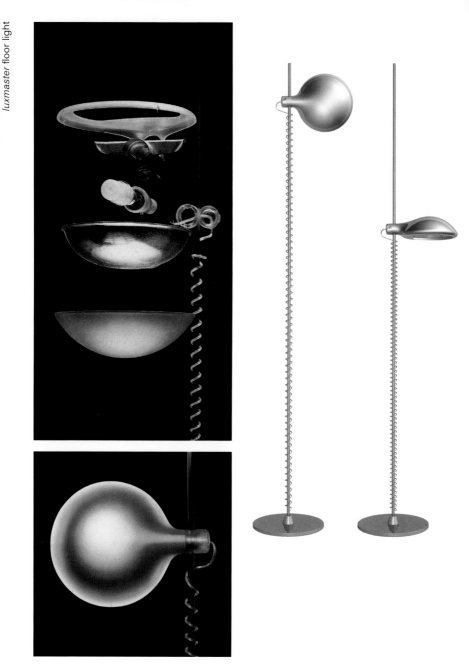

▷ *Metalampo* **table light, 2000**
Enameled Zamak base and enameled aluminum stem with polycarbonate shade, 57 cm high / Fuß aus lackiertem Zamak mit Schaft aus lackiertem Aluminium, Lampenschirm aus Polykarbonat, 57 cm hoch / Base en Zamak émaillé, tige en aluminium émaillé, abat-jour en polycarbonate, 57 cm de haut
Artemide, Pregnana Milanese, Italy

◁ *Luxmaster* **floor light, 2000–01**
Die-cast Zamak base with brushed stainless-steel stem and aluminum reflecting head with polycarbonate diffuser, 190 cm high / Fuß aus Zamak-Druckguss mit Schaft aus gebürstetem Edelstahl, Reflektor aus Aluminium mit Diffusor aus Polykarbonat, 190 cm hoch / Base en fonte de zamak, tige en acier inoxydable brossé, vasque en aluminium réfléchissant et diffuseur en polycarbonate, 190 cm de haut
Flos, Bovezzo, Italy

◁◁ *Details of head and diffuser of Luxmaster floor light / Detailansichten von Leuchtenkopf und Diffusor der Stehleuchte Luxmaster / Détails de la vasque et du diffuseur du lampadaire Luxmaster*

The elegant yet unobtrusive *Luxmaster* (2000–01), designed by Jasper Morrison, was inspired by the work of Joe Colombo, whose *Alogena* (1970) was one of the first domestic lighting products to use a halogen lamp. Morrison's brief from Flos was to design an adjustable uplighter – a lighting typology that had been largely neglected since the 1970s. The power cable of the resulting *Luxmaster* spirals rationally around the stem, allowing adjustment both vertically and laterally. Sharing a similar pared-down esthetic and rational functionality, Adrien Gardère's *Metalampo* table light (2000) has an adjustable shade that allows the light to be efficiently and easily directed. (CF/PF)

Die von Jasper Morrison entworfene Stehleuchte *Luxmaster* (2000–01), ein elegantes und unaufdringliches Modell, ist von Joe Colombo inspiriert, dessen Leuchte *Alogena* (1970) die erste Wohnraumleuchte mit einer Halogenlampe war. Morrison hatte von Flos den Auftrag, einen verstellbaren Deckenfluter zu entwerfen – ein Leuchtentypus, der seit den 1970er Jahren aus der Mode gekommen war. Das Spiralkabel der *Luxmaster* Leuchte ist so um den Schaft gewickelt, dass die Höhe und Neigung des Leuchtenkopfes verändert werden kann. Adrien Gardères Tischleuchte *Metalampo* (2000) zeichnet sich durch eine ähnlich verhaltene Ästhetik und rationale Funktionalität aus. Ihr Schirm lässt sich ebenso effizient wie einfach ausrichten. (CF/PF)

L'élégant et discret lampadaire *Luxmaster* (2000–01), conçu par Jasper Morrison est inspiré de Joe Colombo, dont l'*Alogena* (1970) fut le premier appareil d'éclairage domestique à utiliser une ampoule halogène. Le cahier des charges de Flos portait sur un lampadaire réglable, type « uplighter », moins en vogue depuis les années 1970. Le câble d'alimentation s'enroule en spirale autour de la tige, pour permettre des réglages verticaux et latéraux. Dans le même esprit d'esthétique épurée et de fonctionnalisme rationnel, la lampe de table *Metalampo* d'Adrien Gardère (2000) possède un abat-jour réglable pour orienter aisément et efficacement le flux lumineux. (CF/PF)

andrea anastasio
brezza floor light

The Italian word *brezza* means "sweet," "mild," or "pleasant," and is often used when referring to a soft breeze. There is a remarkable airy quality, certainly, about Andrea Anastasio's series of *Brezza* lights (2000), whose virtually weightless nylon tulle diffusers appear to be floating. With its fragile femininity and wispy lightness, this range of floor, table, wall and hanging lights signals the more poetic and emotional approach to design that has already begun to define many of the lighting products of the early 2000s. (CF/PF)

Das italienische Wort *brezza* bedeutet „süß", „sanft", „angenehm" und wird häufig auch im Sinn einer leichten Brise verwendet. Die Leuchtenserie *Brezza* (2000) von Andrea Anastasio ist ohne Zweifel ungewöhnlich luftig, und ihre praktisch schwerelosen Schirme aus Nylontüll wirken, als glitten sie im Wind dahin. Mit ihrer fragilen Weiblichkeit und bauschigen Leichtigkeit lässt diese aus Steh-, Tisch-, Wand- und Hängeleuchten bestehende Leuchtenserie die poetischere und emotionalere Haltung erkennen, die bereits viele Beleuchtungsprodukte des neuen Jahrtausends prägt. (CF/PF)

En italien, *brezza* signifie « brise ». La ligne de luminaires *Brezza* (2000) d'Andrea Anastasio possède certainement les mêmes qualités aériennes et délicates. Ses diffuseurs en tulle de nylon semblent aussi légers qu'une plume et paraissent flotter en l'air. Par sa féminité fragile et sa légèreté ouatée, cette série de lampes de table, de lampadaires, de suspensions et d'appliques annonce l'approche plus poétique et émotionnelle du design qui commence à caractériser bon nombre des luminaires du début des années 2000. (CF/PF)

Brezza floor light, 2000

Chrome-plated base and stem with polycarbonate diffuser and chrome-plated iron frame supporting cotton and nylon tulle shades, 130–200 cm high / Verchromter Fuß und Schaft mit Diffusor aus Polykarbonat, verchromtes Eisengestell für Lampenschirme aus Baumwolle und Nylontüll, 130–200 cm hoch / Base et tige chromées, diffuseur en polycarbonate, structure en fer chromé soutenant un abat-jour en tulle de coton et nylon, 130–200 cm de haut
Artemide, Pregnana Milanese, Italy

▽ *Design drawing of the Brezza hanging light, c.2000 / Entwurfzeichnung der Hängeleuchte Brezza, ca. 2000 / Croquis de la suspension Brezza, vers 2000*

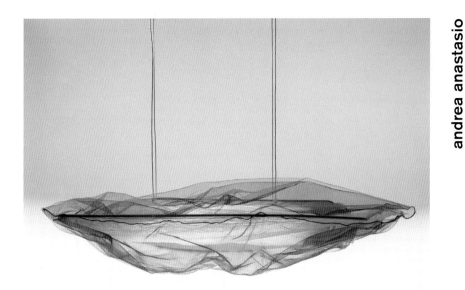

△ *Brezza* hanging light, 2000

Chrome-plated mounts and suspension wires
with polycarbonate diffuser and chrome-plated
iron frame supporting cotton and nylon tulle
shades, 100–170 cm drop / Verchromte Montierung und Aufhängekabel, Diffusor aus Polykarbonat, verchromtes Eisengestell für Lampenschirme aus Baumwolle und Nylontüll, 100–
170 cm lang / Montures et câbles chromés,
diffuseur en polycarbonate, structure en fer
chromé soutenant un abat-jour en tulle de coton
et nylon, 100–170 cm de haut hors tout
Artemide, Pregnana Milanese, Italy

▽ *Brezza* wall light, 2000

Chrome-plated mounts with polycarbonate
diffuser and chrome-plated iron frame supporting cotton and nylon tulle shades, 10.5 cm
diameter / Verchromte Montierung mit Diffusor
aus Polykarbonat, verchromtes Eisengestell
für Lampenschirme aus Baumwolle und Nylontüll, 10,5 cm Durchmesser / Fixation et tige
chromées, diffuseur en polycarbonate, structure
en fer chromé soutenant un abat-jour en tulle
de coton et nylon, 10,5 cm de diamètre
Artemide, Pregnana Milanese, Italy

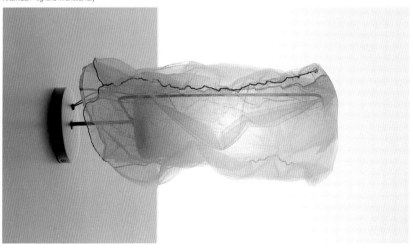

In 2000 Ron Arad presented an exhibition in Milan entitled "Not Made By Hand, Not Made in China," featuring objects created with new RP (rapid-prototyping) technologies – namely SLA (stereolithography) and SLS (laser sintering). Both technologies were used to "grow," rather than assemble or mold, the *Ge-Off Sphere* (2000), which comprises a spiral of polyamide that can be extended by adjusting the tension of the suspension wires. Delighting in the functional and expressive potential of RP technologies, Arad claims that "whatever we can draw, we can make. And we can draw whatever we want." (CF/PF)

2000 stellte Ron Arad im Rahmen der Ausstellung „Nicht von Hand erzeugt, nicht in China erzeugt" in Mailand Objekte vor, bei deren Herstellung neue RP-Technologien (Rapid Prototyping) wie SLA (Stereolithografie) und SLS (Lasersintern) zum Einsatz kamen. Mit diesen Verfahren wurde die Hängeleuchte *Ge-Off Sphere* (2000) gewissermaßen „gezüchtet" und nicht wie sonst aus Bestandteilen zusammengebaut oder in einem Formprozess hergestellt. Die Leuchte besteht aus einer Polyamid-Spirale, die ausgezogen werden kann, indem man die Spannung der Aufhängedrähte verändert. Fasziniert vom funktionalen und expressiven Potential der RP-Technologien, behauptet Arad, man könne damit „alles, was man zeichnen kann, auch herstellen. Und zeichnen kann man, was man will." (CF/PF)

À Milan, en 2000, Ron Arad a présenté une exposition intitulée « Pas fait main, pas fait en Chine », autour d'objets créés grâce aux procédés de prototypage rapide, en l'occurrence la stéréolithographie et le frittage par laser. Ces deux technologies ont été utilisées pour « développer » plutôt qu'assembler ou mouler la suspension *Ge-Off Sphere* (2000), faite d'une spirale de polyamide qui se déploie grâce au réglage de la tension des fils de suspension. Conquis par le potentiel expressif et fonctionnel des technologies de prototypage, Arad assure que « tout ce que nous pouvons dessiner est réalisable. Et nous pouvons dessiner tout ce que nous voulons ». (CF/PF)

Ge-Off Sphere hanging light, 2000
Polyamide construction using stereolithography and laser sintering, 13 cm diameter / Polyamidkonstruktion unter Einsatz von Stereolithografie und Lasersintern, 13 cm Durchmesser / Structure en polyamide, fabriquée par stéréolithographie et frittage par laser, 13 cm de diamètre
Ron Arad Associates, London, Great Britain, for **Gallery Mourmans**, Maastricht, The Netherlands

▷ *Stretched* Ge-Off Sphere *hanging lights / Ausgezogene Hängeleuchten* Ge-Off Sphere */ Suspensions* Ge-Off Sphere *en position étirée*

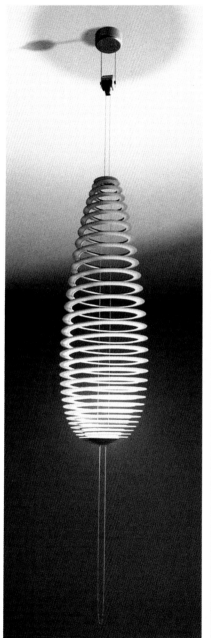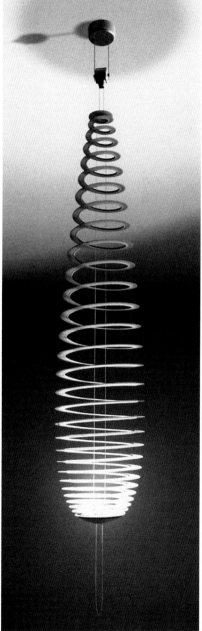

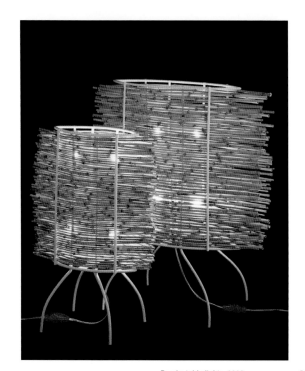

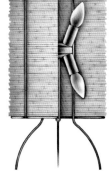

Bambu table lights, 2000
Painted metal frame with woven bamboo reeds,
small: 45 cm high, large: 58 cm high / Fuß und
Montierung aus lackiertem Metall mit geflochtenen Bambusstäben, klein: 45 cm hoch, groß:
58 cm hoch / Structure en métal peint, tiges de
bambou tressé, petit modèle : 45 cm de haut,
grand modèle : 58 cm de haut
Fontana Arte, Corsico, Italy

Diagram showing construction of Bambu *table light, c.2000 / Schematischer Bauplan der Tischleuchte* Bambu, *ca. 2000 / Dessin technique de la lampe de table* Bambu, *vers 2000*

The Brazilian brothers Fernando and Humberto Campana have produced some outstanding designs in recent years, achieving widespread acclaim for their quirky yet poetic furniture and lighting that is both expressive and experimental. Often using found objects and out-of-context materials, their work breaks esthetic and functional boundaries, possessing a delightful sense of freedom. Their *Bambu* table lights (2000) have a very simple construction with thin bamboo reeds functioning as screen-like diffusers – an original treatment of an organic material that provides not only a pleasing light but also a sense of national authenticity and craftsmanship. (CF/PF)

Die Brüder Fernando und Humberto Campana aus Brasilien haben in den letzten Jahren hervorragende Entwürfe vorgelegt und für ihre ungewöhnlichen, aber poetischen Möbel und Leuchten, die expressiv und experimentell zugleich sind, viel Beifall bekommen. Sie verarbeiten häufig Fundstücke sowie Materialien aus anderen Kontexten und brechen in ihren Entwürfen ästhetische und funktionale Grenzen auf. Die Tischleuchten *Bambu* (2000) sind mit ihren dünnen Bambusstäben, die die Funktion eines schirmartigen Diffusors erfüllen, sehr einfach gebaut und verarbeiten auf originelle Weise ein organisches Material, das nicht nur ein angenehmes Licht gibt, sondern auch von nationaler Authentizität und Kunstfertigkeit zeugt. (CF/PF)

Les Brésiliens Fernando et Humberto Campana ont produit quelques remarquables créations au cours de ces dernières années, et se sont fait internationalement apprécier pour leurs meubles et luminaires à la fois curieux et poétiques, expressifs et expérimentaux. Faisant souvent appel à des objets trouvés ou des matériaux « décalés », leur travail transgresse les codes esthétiques et fonctionnelles et offre un délicieux sentiment de liberté. Les lampes de table *Bambu* (2000) partent d'une très simple construction en tiges de bambou formant écran-diffuseur. Ce traitement original d'un matériau naturel procure un éclairage agréable tout en apportant un sentiment d'authenticité exotique et de travail artisanal. (CF/PF)

Shuriken hanging light, 2000

Wappa construction, 55 cm drop, 55 cm wide /
Konstruktion aus Wappa, 55 cm lang, 55 cm
breit / Structure en wappa, 55 cm de haut,
55 cm de large
Modern, Kanagawa, Japan

In 2000, several of Toshiyuki Tani's sculptural lighting designs were exhibited at Designers Block in London. These products, including the *Shuriken* hanging light of 2000 shown here, are made of *wappa* – strips of cedar wood that are used to make the round, wooden lunch boxes traditionally carried by Japanese workers living in the mountains. Exquisitely crafted, Tani's rhythmic designs cast a warm, scattered light that enhances the definition of their elegantly precise proportions. Tani's designs were featured in the December 2000 issue of *Vogue Nippon* but are still largely unknown outside Japan. (CF/PF)

Im Jahr 2000 waren mehrere von Toshiyuki Tanis skulpturalen Beleuchtungskörpern bei Designers Block in London ausgestellt. Diese Leuchten sind, wie die hier gezeigte Hängeleuchte *Shuriken* (2000), aus *Wappa* gefertigt – Zedernholzstreifen, aus denen die runden Holzschachteln hergestellt werden, in denen japanische Arbeiter in den Bergen traditionell ihr Mittagessen transportieren. Die sehr fein ausgearbeiteten, rhythmischen Modelle von Toshiyuki Tani verströmen ein warmes, gestreutes Licht, das ihre eleganten und exakten Proportionen noch besser zur Geltung bringt. Tanis Designs wurden in der *Vogue Nippon* vom Dezember 2000 vorgestellt, sind jedoch außerhalb Japans bis dato weitgehend unbekannt geblieben. (CF/PF)

En 2000, plusieurs lampes sculpturales de Toshiyuki Tani été ont exposées à Londres, Designers Block. Tout comme la suspension *Shuriken* (2000) photographiée ici, ces produits étaient en *wappa*, de fines bandes de cèdre utilisées pour fabriquer les traditionnelles boîtes de repas des ouvriers dans les régions montagneuses du Japon. Remarquablement réalisés, ces objets très « rythmés » projettent une lumière chaleureuse et diaprée qui met en valeur leurs proportions élégantes et précises. Les créations de Tani ont été présentées dans la numéro de décembre 2000 de *Vogue Nippon* mais sont encore largement méconnuse en dehors du Japon. (CF/PF)

tom kirk

spike no. 2 wall light

The young British designer Tom Kirk has produced a number of innovative lighting designs over the last few years. His best-known work is the *Spike* wall light (2000), which as its name suggests incorporates numerous spikes of multi-colored plastic resin that project from an aluminum box-like mount. Producing an ambient diffused light, this batch-manufactured luminaire is a compelling example of the ever-increasing convergence of art and design. As *The Observer* newspaper noted of the *Spike*, "Is it a lamp, or an art installation? Who cares when it looks this good?" (CF/PF)

Der junge britische Designer Tom Kirk hat in den letzten Jahren eine Reihe von innovativen Leuchten entworfen. Seine bekannteste Arbeit ist die Wandleuchte *Spike* (2000), bei der, wie im Namen angedeutet, zahlreiche Spitzen aus buntem Kunststoffharz aus einer tafelartigen Wandmontierung aus Aluminium ragen. Diese serienproduzierte Leuchte erzeugt ein stimmungsvolles, diffuses Licht und ist ein überzeugendes Beispiel für die immer größere Annäherung von Kunst und Design. Die Zeitung *The Observer* bemerkte zur *Spike* Leuchte: „Ist das eine Leuchte oder eine Kunstinstallation? Wen kümmert das, wenn sie so gut aussieht?" (CF/PF)

Le jeune designer britannique Tom Kirk a réalisé un certain nombre de luminaires innovants au cours de ces dernières années. Son œuvre la plus connue est l'applique *Spike* (2000) qui, comme son nom le suggère, comprend de multiples pointes de résine plastique multicolore qui ressortent d'un boîtier d'aluminium. Produisant une lumière d'ambiance diffuse, cette applique fabriquée en séries est un exemple convaincant de la convergence toujours plus grande entre art et design. Au sujet de la *Spike*, le journal *The Observer* a noté : « Est-ce une lampe ou une installation artistique ? Quel est le problème quand elle a aussi belle allure ? » (CF/PF)

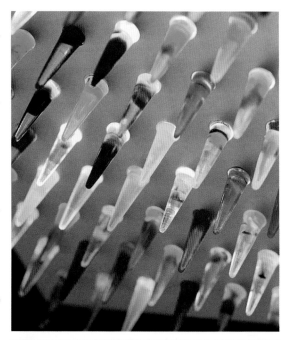

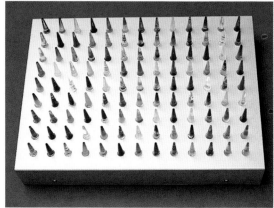

△ **Spike No. 2 wall light, 2000**
Cast polyester-resin diffuser with silver anodized aluminum mount; can be commissioned to any size / Diffusor aus gegossenem Polyesterharz mit Montierung aus silbereloxiertem Aluminium; auf Bestellung in jeder Größe anfertigbar / Diffuseur en résine polyester moulée, monture en aluminium anodisé argent ; dimensions variables à la demande
Tom Kirk Lighting, London, Great Britain

△△ *Detail of* Spike No. 2 *wall light / Detailansicht der Wandleuchte* Spike Nr. 2 / *Détail de l'applique* Spike n° 2

Marcel Wanders's work is often imbued with witty humor and quirky function, which is the result of his thinking outside the design box. His knowing yet playful product solutions can be seen as second-generation Post-Modern – a more refined version of the 1980s style that frequently incorporated mixed references, hybrid themes and ironic messages in designed objects. His *B.L.O.* table light (2001), which is turned on and off by blowing on it, is a tongue-in-cheek contemporary interpretation of a traditional candlestick. Utilitarian yet endearing, this design engages us with memories of life before electricity. (CF/PF)

Viele Entwürfe von Marcel Wanders zeichnen sich durch intelligenten Humor und verdrehte Funktionalität aus, was daraus resultiert, dass er nicht in Designkategorien denkt. Seine klugen und dabei verspielten Produktlösungen können als Postmoderne der zweiten Generation bezeichnet werden – eine verfeinerte Version des Stils der 1980er Jahre, als Designobjekte häufig mit vermischten Bezügen, hybriden Themen und ironischen Hinweisen ausgestattet waren. Wanders' Tischleuchte *B.L.O.* (2001), die sich durch Pusten ein- und ausschalten lässt, ist eine augenzwinkernde zeitgenössische Interpretation des traditionellen Kerzenständers. Dieses utilitaristische und dennoch liebenswerte Objekt weckt Erinnerungen an das Leben vor der Einführung der Elektrizität. (CF/PF)

Le travail de Marcel Wanders est souvent empreint d'un humour délié et d'un fonctionnalisme bizarre, issus d'une réflexion qui sort des cadres habituels du design. Ses créations pertinentes mais ludiques, peuvent être considérées comme du postmodernisme de seconde génération, version plus raffinée de ce style des années 1980 qui intégrait fréquemment des références mixtes, des thèmes hybrides et des messages ironiques. Sa lampe de chevet *B.L.O.* (2001), qui s'allume ou s'éteint en soufflant dessus, est un clin d'œil au classique bougeoir. Utilitaire mais sympathique, cet objet nous renvoie à des souvenirs datant d'avant l'invention de l'électricité. (CF/PF)

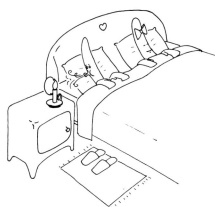

△△ **B.L.O. table light, 2001**
Polycarbonate base with polished aluminum reflector, 19.5 cm high / Fuß aus Polykarbonat mit Reflektor aus poliertem Aluminium, 19,5 cm hoch / Base en polycarbonate, réflecteur en aluminium poli, 19,5 cm de haut
Flos, Bovezzo, Italy

△ *Cartoon by Marcel Wanders featuring the B.L.O. table light, c.2001 / Cartoon von Marcel Wanders mit Tischleuchte B.L.O., ca. 2001 / Dessin humoristique de Marcel Wanders mettant en scène la lampe B.L.O., vers 2001*

In a process not dissimilar to the preparation of the Japanese food of the same name, Tokujin Yoshioka's *ToFU* table light (2000) is created with a "delicate manufacturing and cutting technique." Acrylic resin is poured into a mold, allowed to set and then cut to create a perfectly symmetrical form into which a halogen light is inserted. When lit, the light-carrying potential of the acrylic is fully exploited, with the edges of the plastic block glowing in an otherworldly manner. This remarkable product combines a jewel-like polymer with a strong structural simplicity to create a truly poetic composition that is as much about the object as the space surrounding it. (CF/PF)

Die Tischleuchte *ToFU* (2000) von Tokujin Yoshioka wird mittels eines „komplizierten Fertigungs- und Schneideverfahrens" produziert, das der Herstellung des gleichnamigen japanischen Nahrungsmittels ähnelt: Acrylharz wird in eine Form gegossen und nach dem Aushärten zu einem exakt quadratischen Block geschnitten, in den eine Halogenlampe eingesetzt wird. Im eingeschalteten Zustand kommt die lichtleitende Qualität des Werkstoffs Acryl voll zur Geltung, und die mattierten Kanten des Kunststoffblocks erstrahlen in außerirdischem Licht. Das außergewöhnliche Design erzielt durch seine geometrische Grundform, die wie ein geschliffener Edelstein aus Kunststoff wirkt, eine poetische Wirkung, die sich von der Leuchte ausgehend auch auf ihre Umgebung überträgt. (CF/PF)

Selon un processus qui n'est pas sans similitude avec la préparation de l'aliment japonais du même nom, la lampe *ToFU* (2000) de Tokujin Yoshioka fait appel à une « technique de découpe et de fabrication délicate ». La résine acrylique est versée dans un moule, mise à reposer, puis découpée pour obtenir une forme parfaitement symétrique dans laquelle vient s'insérer l'ampoule halogène. Le potentiel lumineux de l'acrylique est pleinement exploité, les bords du plastique retenant la lumière de façon étrange. Ce remarquable produit combine un polymère brillant comme un diamant et une grande simplicité structurelle, dans une composition authentiquement poétique qui prend en compte autant l'objet lui-même que l'espace qui l'entoure. (CF/PF)

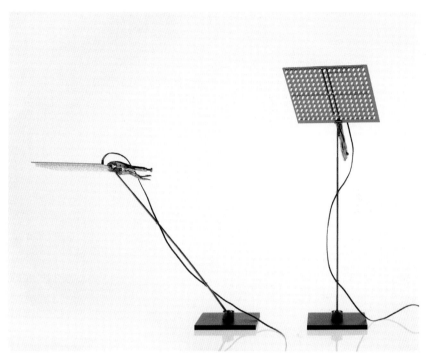

◁ *ToFU* table light, 2000

Cast acrylic diffuser with aluminum mounts and
halogen bulb, 29.5 cm high / Diffusor aus gegossenem Acryl, Montierung aus Aluminium
mit Halogenlampe, 29,5 cm hoch / Diffuseur
en acrylique moulé, monture en aluminium et
ampoule halogène, 29,5 cm de haut
Yamagiwa, Tokyo, Japan

El. E. Dee table light, 2001

Metal base with stainless-steel stem and LED
circuit board, 50 cm high (max.) / Fuß aus
Metall mit Schaft aus Edelstahl und LED -
Platine, 50 cm hoch (max.) / Pied en métal,
tige en acier inoxydable et carte de circuits et
LED, 50 cm de haut (max.)
Ingo Maurer, Munich, Germany

LED lights are among Ingo Maurer's
very latest developments. Light-emitting
diodes of the type that have long been
used by the electronics industry as well
as by motor manufacturers for making
headlights, are mounted on special circuit boards to replace traditional light
bulbs. The *El. E. Dee* table light (2001)
is Maurer's first design working exclusively off light-emitting diodes to go
into serial production. It was a deliberate decision to make it look more like a
prototype than a fully-fledged production model. Maurer believes that LED
technology is in its infancy but is all set
to revolutionize artificial lighting in the
future. (TB)

Die LED-Leuchten zählen zu Ingo Maurers neuesten Entwicklungen. Auf speziellen Platinen angebrachte Leuchtdioden, die bereits seit langer Zeit in
der Elektronik eingesetzt und auch
als Leuchtmittel für Autoscheinwerfer
benutzt werden, ersetzten dabei die
klassischen Glühbirnen. Die Tischleuchte *El.E.Dee* (2001) ist Maurers
erste serienreife Leuchte, die ausschließlich mit Leuchtdioden als
Leuchtmittel arbeitet. Bewusst erinnert
ihr Aussehen eher an einen Prototypen
als an ein ausgereiftes Serienmodell.
Nach Maurers Meinung steht die LED-
Technik erst am Anfang ihrer Entwicklung und wird in Zukunft die Welt des
künstlichen Lichts revolutionieren. (TB)

Les diodes électroluminescentes font
partie des dernières recherches d'Ingo
Maurer. Les LED de ce type ont longtemps été utilisées par l'industrie électronique ainsi que pour les phares
d'automobiles, montées des cartes de
circuits imprimés spéciaux pour remplacer les ampoules traditionnelles. La
lampe de table *El.E.Dee* (2001) est
le premier projet de Maurer utilisant
exclusivement ce type de diodes à être
produit en série. La décision de lui
donner l'allure d'un prototype plutôt
que celle d'un modèle de production
abouti est délibérée. Maurer pense
que la technologie des LED est encore
balbutiante, mais qu'elle révolutionnera
l'éclairage artificiel dans le futur. (TB)

The word *Agaricon* derives from the Greek for "mushroom", and Ross Lovegrove's light (2001) certainly has the appearance of a magical toadstool, culled from a sci-fi landscape. In place of a traditional on/off switch, the light is controlled by touching the extruded aluminum ring that encircles its injection-molded polycarbonate body. Incorporating pigmented raw plastic, *Agaricon* possesses a unique chromatic effect that cannot be achieved through painting or printing a molded plastic surface. The light comes in three different colors – mandarin orange, jade green and milky white. (CF/PF)

Die Bezeichnung *Agaricon* leitet sich von dem griechischen Wort für Pilz ab, und Ross Lovegroves Leuchte (2001) hat tatsächlich etwas von einem Zauberpilz, der in einer Science-Fiction-Landschaft gepflückt wurde. Die Leuchte wird nicht wie üblich durch Betätigen eines Schalters an- und ausgeschaltet, sondern durch Berühren eines Ringes aus extrudiertem Aluminium, der den Leuchtenkörper aus Spritzguss-Polykarbonat umgibt. Durch die Verwendung von pigmentiertem Rohkunststoff wird bei der *Agaricon* Leuchte ein einzigartiger Farbeffekt erzielt, der durch Lackieren oder Bedrucken einer Oberfläche aus gegossenem Kunststoff nicht zu erreichen ist. Die Leuchte ist in drei Farben erhältlich: Orange, Jadegrün und Grau. (CF/PF)

Le nom d'*Agaricon* vient d'un mot grec signifiant champignon, ce qui correspond bien à l'apparence de cette lampe de Ross Lovegrove (2001), sorte de champignon vénéneux cueilli dans une nature de science-fiction. Ce modèle est dénué d'interrupteur, et la commande se fait en touchant l'anneau d'aluminium extrudé qui encercle le corps de la lampe en polycarbonate moulé par injection. En plastique brut teinté dans la masse, l'*Agaricon* produit un effet chromatique original qui ne pourrait être atteint par la peinture ou par l'impression d'une surface en plastique moulée classique. Le modèle existe en trois teintes différentes, orange mandarine, vert jade et blanc laiteux. (CF/PF)

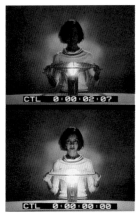

◁ **Agaricon table light, 2001**
Injection-molded polycarbonate construction with touch-sensitive extruded aluminum ring, 41 cm diameter / Konstruktion aus Spritzguss-Polykarbonat mit berührungsempfindlichem Ring aus extrudiertem Aluminium, 41 cm Durchmesser / Fabrication en polycarbonate moulé par injection, commande tactile par anneau en aluminium extrudé, 41 cm de diamètre
Luceplan, Milan, Italy

△△/△ *Luceplan publicity images showing the touch-sensitive mechanism of the* Agaricon *table light / Werbefotos von Luceplan mit Demonstration des auf Berührung reagierenden Mechanismus der Tischleuchte* Agaricon */ Photographies publicitaires Luceplan du mécanisme à commande tactile de la lampe de table* Agaricon

Yin flu floor light, 2001

Methacrylate and polyester construction on
plastic castors, 123 cm high / Konstruktion aus
Methacrylat und Polyester auf Kunststofträdern,
123 cm hoch / Fabrication en méthacrylate et
polyester, sur roulettes en plastique, 123 cm de
haut
Artemide, Pregnana Milanese, Italy

Included in Artemide's *Metamorfosi* range, the *Yin flu* and *Metacolor* floor lights (2001) create, according to the company, "a luminous, colorful setting in which each of us can satisfy his own need for wellbeing, looking after oneself through the use of light that produces and irradiates energy, feeding in emotion, awareness and energy." Certainly, by integrating a remote-controlled system that allows the variation of color and luminosity, the *Metacolor* (a static pillar of polychromatic light) and the *Yin flu* (a mobile light) can be used as light therapy units to create highly evocative atmospheres. (CF/PF)

Laut Artemide schaffen die zur Leuchtenserie *Metamorfosi* gehörenden Stehleuchten *Yin flu* und *Metacolor* (2001) „eine bunt erleuchtete Szenerie, in der sich jeder nach seinen individuellen Bedürfnissen wohlfühlen, sich mit der strahlenden Kraft des Lichts verwöhnen und neue Gefühle, Gedanken und Energien auftanken kann". Da die *Metacolor* Leuchte (eine statische Säule mit mehrfarbigem Licht) und die *Yin flu* Leuchte (eine mobile Leuchte) mit einer Fernsteuerung ausgestattet sind, mit der Lichtfarbe und Lichtintensität eingestellt werden können, sind sie auch lichttherapeutisch zur Erzeugung suggestiver Stimmungen einsetzbar. (CF/PF)

Appartenant à la gamme *Metamorfosi* d'Artemide, les lampadaires *Yin flu* et *Metacolor* (2001) créent, selon leur éditeur, « un cadre coloré lumineux dans lequel chacun d'entre nous peut satisfaire son propre besoin de bien-être, se concentrer sur lui-même grâce à la lumière qui produit et irradie de l'énergie, le nourrit d'émotions, d'une conscience accrue de soi et du monde, et d'énergie. Le *Metacolor* (un « pilier » fixe de lumière polychrome) et le *Yin flu* (lampe mobile) sont équipés de variateurs de couleur et d'intensité télécommandés et dotés, sans nul doute, de vertus thérapeutiques. On peut aisément s'en servir pour créer des atmosphères relaxantes et inspirantes. (CF/PF)

△△ *Metacolor* floor light, 2001

Metal base with opalescent acrylic diffuser and blue, green and red fluorescent tubes, 205 cm high / Fuß aus Metall mit opalem Acrylschirm und blauen, grünen und roten Leuchtstoffröhren, 205 cm hoch / Base métallique, diffuseur en acrylique opalescent, tubes fluorescents bleu, vert et rouge, 205 cm de haut
Artemide, Pregnana Milanese, Italy

△ ◁ / △ ▷ *Details of* Metacolor *floor light's programmable remote control system /* Detailansichten der programmierbaren Fernbedienung der Stehleuchte Metacolor / *Détails du système de télécommande programmable du lampadaire* Metacolor

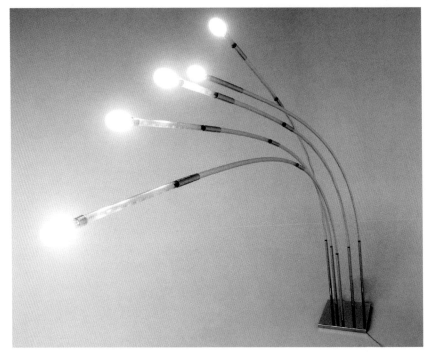

Ray Bow floor light, 2004

Chrome-plated metal mounts with extruded polycarbonate tubes and sliding metal weights, 220–400 cm high / Fuß aus verchromtem Metall mit Röhren aus extrudiertem Polykarbonat und verschiebbaren Gewichten aus Metall, 220– 400 cm hoch / Pied en métal chromé, tubes en polycarbonate extrudé et poids métalliques coulissants, 220–400 cm de haut
Kundalini, Milan, Italy

▷ **Shakti floor lights, 2001**

Laser-cut co-extruded Perspex diffuser on chrome-plated metal base, 200, 250, 320 or 400 cm high / Diffusor aus lasergeschnittenem, koextrudiertem Perspex auf Fuß aus verchromtem Metall, 200, 250, 320 oder 400 cm hoch / Diffuseur en Perspex co-extrudé et découpé au laser sur base en métal chromé, 200, 250, 320 ou 400 cm de haut
Kundalini, Milan, Italy

Founded in 1996, the Milan-based lighting company Kundalini takes its name from the Sanskrit word used in Tantric philosophy for the coiled bio-electrical energy that, when released, leads to spiritual enlightenment. Accordingly, its lighting is intended to connect with users on a deep emotional and spiritual level, while also exploring new materials and technologies. The *Shakti* floor light (2001) – named in tribute to the Great Mother of the Universe – is made from an innovative, two-colored co-extrusion of Perspex. The *Ray Bow* floor light (2004) designed by Gregorio Spini, Kundalini's founder, is similarly poetic and inventive, incorporating stems of tubular extruded polycarbonate. (CF/PF)

Der Name der 1996 in Mailand gegründeten Leuchtenfirma Kundalini ist ein Wort aus dem Sanskrit und bezeichnet die wie eine schlafende Schlange aufgerollte bioelektrische Energie, die, einmal erweckt, zur spirituellen Bewusstseinserweiterung führt. Die Leuchten von Kundalini verkörpern diese Energie und erproben gleichzeitig neue Materialien und Technologien. Die Stehleuchte *Shakti* (2001) – benannt nach der Großen Mutter des Universums – ist aus einem innovativen zweifarbigen, koextrudierten Perspex-Polymethylmethacrylat gefertigt. Die von Gregorio Spini, dem Begründer von Kundalini, entworfene Stehleuchte *Ray Bow* (2004) ist ihr mit ihren Röhren aus extrudiertem Polykarbonat an Poesie und Einfallsreichtum ebenbürtig. (CF/PF)

Fondée en 1996, l'entreprise d'appareils d'éclairage milanaise Kundalini tire son nom d'un mot sanscrit utilisé en philosophie tantrique pour désigner l'énergie bioélectrique en spirale qui, relâchée, conduit à l'illumination spirituelle. Les luminaires sont censés connecter leur utilisateur à un niveau émotionnel et spirituel profond, tout en explorant des matériaux et des technologies nouveaux. Le lampadaire *Shakti* (2001) – dont le nom rend hommage à la Mère de l'Univers – est réalisé à partir d'un procédé original de co-extrusion de Perspex de deux couleurs. Le *Ray Bow* (2004) de Gregorio Spini, fondateur de Kundalini, est tout aussi poétique et inventif, avec ses «tiges» en polycarbonate extrudé. (CF/PF)

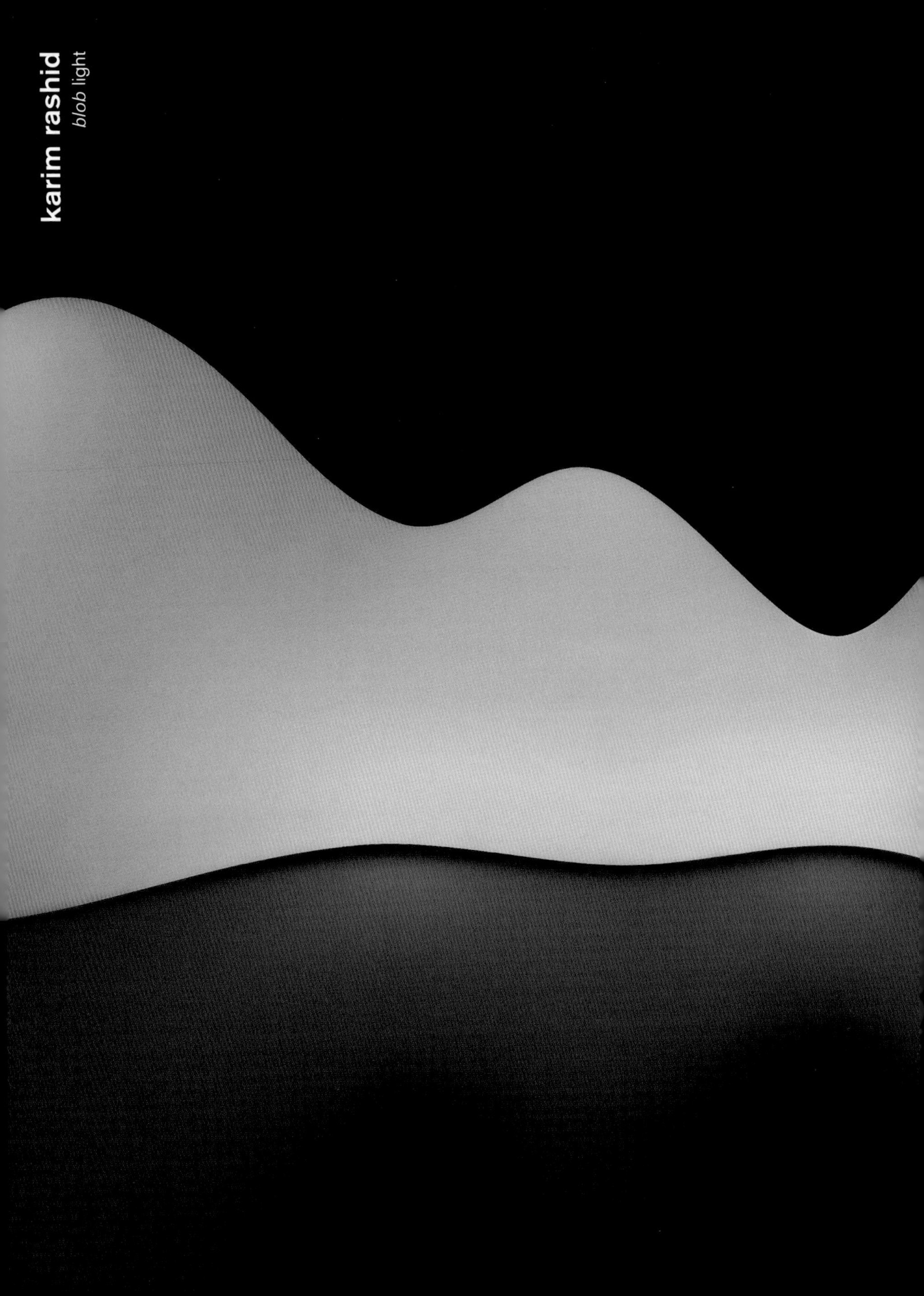
karim rashid
blob light

Karim Rashid has transformed the look of American products with his playful approach to design, perhaps best described as "blobjectivity." Using organic forms for both stylistic and ergonomic purposes, he creates low-cost yet innovative products for the home. Available in three sizes and in either white or yellow, the *Blob* (2002) can be used as a wall, ceiling, table or floor light. As Rashid notes, "Products must deal with our emotional ground," and certainly these lights are ideal for creating an alluring ambient mood. (CF/PF)

Karim Rashid hat mit seiner verspielten Einstellung zum Design, die sich am besten als Blobjektivität beschreiben lässt, das Aussehen von amerikanischen Produkten verändert. Unter Verwendung organischer Formen aus stilistischen und ergonomischen Gründen entwickelt er preiswerte und dennoch innovative Produkte für den privaten Haushalt. Die in drei Größen und in Weiß oder Gelb erhältliche *Blob* (2002) kann als Wand-, Decken-, Tisch- oder Stehleuchte verwendet werden. Für Rashid müssen, so sagt er, „Produkte auf unsere Emotionen eingehen", und diese Leuchten eignen sich ohne Zweifel dazu, eine verzaubernde, stimmungsvolle Atmosphäre zu schaffen. (CF/PF)

Karim Rashid a transformé le look des produits américains avec cette approche ludique du design que l'on pourrait définir comme «l'blobjectivité». Faisant appel à des formes organiques et ergonomiques, il crée pour la maison des objets économiques mais novateurs. Proposée en trois tailles et en blanc ou jaune, la *Blob* (2002) peut servir de lampe de table, de lampadaire, de suspension ou d'applique. Comme le fait remarquer Rashid, «Les produits doivent échanger avec nos émotions». Ces luminaires sont certainement recommandés pour générer une atmosphère d'ambiance stylée. (CF/PF)

karim rashid
blob lights

◁ *Detail of medium-sized* Blob *light / Detail-ansicht einer mittelgroßen Leuchte* Blob */ Détail de la lampe* Blob, *modèle moyen*

Blob lights, 2002

Molded polypropylene construction, 46, 95.5 or 126 cm long / Konstruktion aus geformtem Polypropylen, 46, 95,5 oder 126 cm lang / Structure en polypropylène moulé, 46, 95,5 ou 126 cm de long
Foscarini, Marcon, Italy

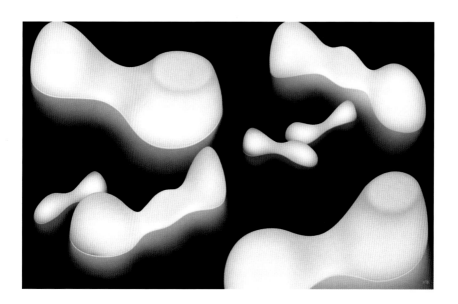

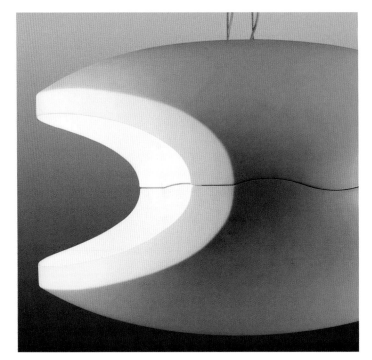

O-space hanging light, 2003

Expanded polyurethane diffuser with chrome-plated fittings, 56 cm diameter, 200 cm drop (max.) / Diffusor aus Polyurethan-Schaumstoff mit verchromter Montierung, 56 cm Durchmesser, 200 cm lang (max.) / Diffuseur en polyuréthane expansé avec pièces de montage chromées, 56 cm de diamètre, 200 cm de haut (max.)

Foscarini, Marcon, Italy

▷ **Nexflex table light, 2002**

Bone-china segmented body with brass and aluminum fittings, 35–40 cm high / Mehrteiliger Leuchtenkörper aus weißem Porzellan mit Montierungen aus Messing und Aluminium, 35–40 cm hoch / Corps en porcelaine, pièces de montage en laiton et aluminium, 35–40 cm de haut

Alva Lighting, London, Great Britain

The *O-space* hanging light designed in 2003 by Luca Nichetto (art director of the Italian glassworks Salviati) and Gianpietro Gai has an arresting sculptural form that appears to change depending on the angle of vision. The soft contours of its polyurethane body reflect the light of a halogen lamp held within, while its aperture provides direct light. Similarly organic and sculptural, David Edgerley's *Nexflex* table light was designed in 2002 as a "niche light" to illuminate dark corners. Made up of four bone-china segments, it can be articulated to direct the emitted light, altering its serpentine form in the process. (CF/PF)

Die 2003 von Luca Nichetto (Art Director des italienischen Glaswerks Salviati) und Gianpietro Gai entworfene Hängeleuchte *O-space* hat eine faszinierend skulpturale Form, die sich je nach Blickwinkel verändert. Die weichen Konturen ihres Polyurethan-Körpers reflektieren das Licht der darin enthaltenen Halogenlampe, während aus ihrer Öffnung direktes Licht strömt. Die ähnlich organisch und skulptural gestaltete Tischleuchte *Nexflex* von David Edgerley wurde 2002 als „Nischenbeleuchtung" für dunkle Ecken entworfen. Ihr Lichtstrahl kann durch Verstellen der vier Segmente aus weißem Porzellan ausgerichtet werden, wobei sich die Form der Leuchte verändert. (CF/PF)

La *O-space*, conçue en 2003 par Luca Nichetto (directeur artistique de la verrerie italienne Salviati) et Gianpietro Gai, possède une forme sculpturale frappante qui semble se modifier selon l'angle de vision du spectateur. Les contours pleins de douceur de son corps en polyuréthane reflètent la lumière produite par l'ampoule halogène qu'il contient, l'ouverture assurant un éclairage direct. Tout aussi organique et sculpturale, la lampe de table *Nexflex* de David Edgerley (2002) a été imaginée comme une « lampe de niche » pour éclairer les coins sombres. Composée de quatre parties en porcelaine, elle s'articule pour orienter la lumière émise, sa forme serpentine se transformant du même coup. (CF/PF)

Although energy-efficient lamps have been around for years, few light fixtures have been specifically designed to house them. An exception to the rule is Sam Hecht's *Light Branches* and *12 Light Years* hanging lights (both 2002), which soften the glare of the compact fluorescent lamps in much the same way as the opalescent glass of a traditional bulb does. These designs also reflect Hecht's quest for simplification and his belief that "the less you see the designer's effort in the work, the better." Both lights simplify the fixing of the shade by either clipping it onto the bulb or plugging it onto a socket. (CF/PF)

Obwohl es schon seit Jahren Energiesparlampen gibt, wurden nur wenige Beleuchtungskörper eigens dafür entworfen. Eine Ausnahme bilden Sam Hechts Hängeleuchten *Light Branches* und *12 Light Years* (beide 2002), die das grelle Licht der Kompakt-Leuchtstofflampen in der gleichen Weise mildern, wie es opales Glas bei einer traditionellen Glühbirne tut. Bei beiden Modellen zeigt sich auch Hechts Streben nach Vereinfachung und seine Überzeugung, dass ein Entwurf umso besser sei, „je weniger man [ihm] die Bemühungen des Designers ansieht". Bei beiden Leuchten ist die Montierung des Lampenschirms so weit vereinfacht, dass dieser nur über die Lampe geschoben oder auf eine Fassung gesteckt zu werden braucht. (CF/PF)

Bien que les lampes basse consommation existent depuis des années, peu de luminaires ont été spécifiquement conçus pour elles. Exceptions à la règle : les suspensions *Light Branches* et *12 Light Years* de Sam Hecht (2002), qui atténuent l'éclat des ampoules fluorescentes compactes d'une façon semblable à celle du verre opalescent des ampoules traditionnelles. Ces créations reflètent également la recherche de la simplification chère à ce designer et sa conviction que «moins vous percevez l'effort du designer dans l'œuvre, mieux c'est». Ces deux lampes simplifient la fixation de l'abat-jour par un système de clips sur l'ampoule ou son branchement dans une sorte de prise. (CF/PF)

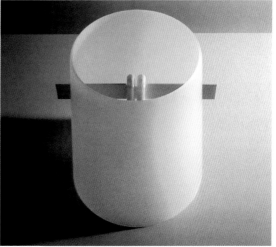

⊿⊿ **Light Branches hanging light, 2002**
Paper shade with polycarbonate fittings, 25 cm high / Lampenschirm aus Papier mit Montierung aus Polykarbonat, 25 cm hoch / Abat-jour en papier, pièces de montage en polycarbonate, 25 cm de haut
Industrial Facility, London, Great Britain

⊿ *Image showing the bulb clip of the* Light Branches *hanging light / Abbildung der Montierung der Hängeleuchte* Light Branches */ Image du système de clips pour l'ampoule de la suspension* Light Branches

12 Light Years **hanging light, 2002**

Injection-molded silicone diffuser, 32.5 cm
diameter / Diffusor aus Spritzguss-Silikon,
32,5 cm Durchmesser / Diffuseur en silicone
moulé par injection, 32,5 cm de diamètre
Droog Design, Amsterdam, The Netherlands

△ *Diagram showing fitting of* 12 Light Years
hanging light / *Montageanleitung zur Hänge-*
leuchte 12 Light Years / *Schéma explicatif*
du montage de la suspension 12 Light Years

Random hanging light, 2002

Epoxy and fiberglass construction, 50, 85 or 105 cm diameter / Konstruktion aus Epoxidharz und Fiberglas, 50, 85 oder 105 cm Durchmesser / Fabrication en époxy et fibre de verre, 50, 85 ou 105 cm de diamètre
Moooi, Breda, The Netherlands

▷ Photograph of Random hanging lights by Erwin Olaf, c.2002 / Hängeleuchten Random, fotografiert von Erwin Olaf, ca. 2002 / Photographie des suspensions Random, par Erwin Olaf, vers 2002

In 1999 Bertjan Pot and Daniel White founded the design studio Monkey Boys in Eindhoven, The Netherlands. For the next three years (until the partnership dissolved) they mainly worked on self-initiated projects. Their best-known design is the Random hanging light (2002), which was exhibited that same year at the Salone del Mobile in Milan and at the Victoria & Albert Museum in London. Having a strong visual presence, the Random light appears magically to defy gravity. It is made of resin-drained yarn, randomly (hence the name) coiled around an inflatable mold, and set into a three-dimensional construction of textile fibers. (CF/PF)

1999 gründeten Bertjan Pot und Daniel White in Eindhoven gemeinsam das Designbüro Monkey Boys. Drei Jahre lang (bis zur Auflösung der Partnerschaft) arbeiteten sie vorwiegend an eigenen Projekten. Ihr bekanntestes Design ist die Hängeleuchte Random (2002), die 2002 beim Salone del Mobile in Mailand und im Victoria & Albert Museum in London ausgestellt wurde. Die optisch reizvolle Random Leuchte scheint auf wunderbare Weise die Gravitation außer Kraft zu setzen. Sie ist aus in Kunstharz getränktem Garn gefertigt, das nach dem Abtropfen per Zufallsprinzip (at random – zufällig) um einen Ballon gewickelt wird und zu einem dreidimensionalen Gebilde aus Textilfasern aushärtet. (CF/PF)

En 1999, Bertjan Pot et Daniel White ont fondé le studio de design Monkey Boys à Eindhoven. Jusqu'à la dissolution de leur association trois ans plus tard, ils travaillèrent principalement sur des projets personnels. Leur projet le plus connu est la suspension Random (2002), exposée en 2002 au Salon du meuble de Milan et au Victoria & Albert Museum de Londres. D'une très forte présence visuelle, la Random semble défier la gravité comme par magie. Fabriquée en fils de résine déposés de façon aléatoire (at random – par hasard) autour d'un moule gonflable, elle fait penser à une construction tridimensionnelle en fibres textiles. (CF/PF)

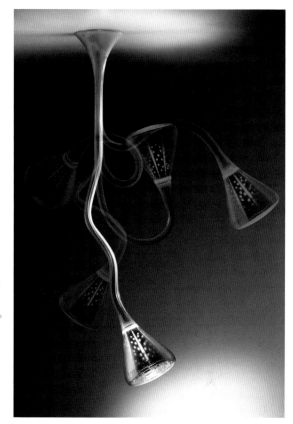

Pipe suspended ceiling light, 2002

Flexible tubular steel stem sheathed in platonic
silicone with perforated aluminum diffuser,
138 cm high / Flexibles, mit Platinsilikon über-
zogenes Stahlrohr und Diffusor aus gelochtem
Aluminium, 138 cm hoch / Tige flexible en tube
d'acier gainée de silicone, diffuseur en aluminium perforé, 138 cm de haut
Artemide, Pregnana Milanese, Italy

◁ *Offices of the Swiss insurance company,
Helvetia Patria, designed by Herzog & de
Meuron, with* Pipe *suspended ceiling lights /
Sitz des von Herzog & de Meuron gestal-
teten Schweizer Versicherungsunternehmens
Helvetia Patria mit Hängeleuchte* Pipe /
Bureaux de la compagnie d'assurance
suisse Helvetia Patria, conçus par Herzog
& de Meuron, équipés de suspensions Pipe

The famous architect duo, Jacques
Herzog and Pierre de Meuron originally
designed the *Pipe* suspended ceiling
light (2002) for the offices of a Swiss
insurance company. With its snaking
flexible stem, this 21st century luminaire
is especially suitable for workspaces
that require the option of both direct
and indirect lighting. Manufactured by
Artemide, the *Pipe* has a micro-perforated cone-shaped aluminum diffuser
sheathed in translucent silicone that
offers non-glaring "dark-light" optic
emission. In recognition of the structural innovation of this beautiful and
supremely functional design, the *Pipe*
won a Compasso d'Oro in 2004.
(CF/PF)

Das berühmte Architektenduo Jacques
Herzog und Pierre de Meuron entwarf
die Hängeleuchte *Pipe* (2002) ursprünglich für den Firmensitz einer Schweizer
Versicherungsgesellschaft. Dieses
Leuchtenmodell aus dem 21. Jahrhundert eignet sich mit seinem schlangen-
artig biegsamen Schaft besonders für
Arbeitsplätze, die zugleich direktes und
indirektes Licht erfordern. Die von Artemide gefertigte *Pipe* Leuchte hat einen
mikroperforierten, kegelförmigen Diffusor aus Aluminium, der mit transparentem Silikon überzogen ist und mit seiner
Darklight-Optik eine blendfreie Lichtemission ermöglicht. Die strukturelle
Innovation dieser Leuchte und ihre
ästhetische und funktionale Brillanz wurden 2004 mit einem Compasso d'Oro
ausgezeichnet. (CF/PF)

Le célèbre duo d'architectes Jacques
Herzog et Pierre de Meuron ont conçu
la suspension *Pipe* en 2002 pour les
bureaux d'une société suisse d'assu-
rances. Grâce à sa tige flexible, ce luminaire du XXIe siècle est particulièrement adapté aux lieux de travail qui ont
besoin d'éclairage à la fois direct et
indirect. Fabriquée par Artemide, la
Pipe possède une diffuseur conique
en aluminium à micro-perforations gainé
de silicone transparent qui délivre une
« lumière sombre » ou *dark light* non
éblouissante. L'innovation structurelle
de ce projet magnifique et merveilleusement fonctionnel lui a valu un Compasso d'Oro en 2004. (CF/PF)

The name of Sebastian Wrong's *Spun* light (2003) makes reference to the manufacturing process used to produce it – metal spinning. This is actually one of the oldest techniques for producing metal hollow-ware and can be dated as far back as Ancient Egypt. Made seamlessly from machined and spun aluminum using High-Tech machinery, "the essence of the *Spun* light," according to Wrong, "is simplicity," while its cylinder-on-a-trumpet form is inspired by the "dynamic fluid esthetics" of its medium. In 2004 Flos launched an eye-catching black version of the *Spun* light. (CF/PF)

Der Name der Leuchte *Spun* (*to spin*, schnell drehen) von Sebastian Wrong (2003) nimmt Bezug auf ihre Herstellung im Schleudergussverfahren. Dabei handelt es sich um eine der ältesten Fertigungsmethoden für Hohlwaren aus Metall, die bereits im Alten Ägypten bekannt war. Die *Spun* Leuchte wird aus maschinell bearbeitetem, schleudergegossenem Aluminium mithilfe von Hightech-Maschinen ohne Naht erzeugt, und laut Wrong besteht „das Wesen der *Spun* in ihrer Einfachheit", während ihre Form – ein Zylinder auf einem Trichter – von der „dynamisch fließenden Ästhetik" ihres Werkstoffs inspiriert sei. 2004 brachte Flos eine schwarze Version der *Spun* Leuchte heraus. (CF/PF)

Le nom de cette lampe de Sebastian Wrong, *Spun* (2003), fait référence à son procédé de fabrication, l'emboutissage du métal. Il s'agit de l'une des plus anciennes techniques de production d'objets creux en métal – un savoir-faire qui remonte à l'Égypte ancienne. Pour le designer, « l'essence de la *Spun*, c'est la simplicité ». Elle est fabriquée en aluminium embouti et travaillé avec des techniques sophistiquées. Sa forme de cylindre posé sur une trompette s'inspire de « l'esthétique de la dynamique des fluides » propre à son matériau. En 2004, Flos a lancé une séduisante version noire de la *Spun*. (CF/PF)

Spun floor and table lights, 2003

Spun aluminum construction, table version: 58 or 68 cm high, floor version: 175 cm high / Konstruktion aus Aluminium-Schleuderguss, Tischleuchte: 58 oder 68 cm hoch, Stehleuchte: 175 cm hoch / Fabrication en aluminium embouti, version de table: 58 ou 68 cm de haut, version de sol: 175 cm de haut
Flos, Bovezzo, Italy

***Reef* wall light, 2002**
Brushed or polished aluminium mount with
white foamed ceramic shade, 12 cm high /
Montierung aus gebürstetem oder poliertem
Aluminium, Lampenschirm aus weißem
Keramikschaum, 12 cm hoch / Monture en
aluminium brossé ou poli, abat-jour en mousse
de céramique blanche, 12 cm de haut
Serien Raumleuchten, Rodgau, Germany

Established in 1991 by Claus Zimmermann and Roland Knieg, Next Space is
primarily concerned with corporate and
commercial design, but also with the
domestic environment. Launched at the
2002 "Light & Building" fair in Frankfurt,
their elegant and restrained *Reef* pro-
gram comprises not only the present
wall light, but also a table light and various single or multiple suspension systems. What has won the design most
attention, however, is its beautiful, coral-
like shade, made of foamed ceramic.
Though delicate in appearance, the
manufacturer Serien Raumleuchten
nonetheless claims that it can be un-
screwed and placed in a dishwasher.
(QC)

Die 1991 von Claus Zimmermann und
Roland Knieg gegründete Firma Next
Space ist vorwiegend im Corporate
und Commercial Design tätig, erstellt
aber auch Entwürfe für den Wohnbereich. Das bei der Messe „Light &
Building" 2002 in Frankfurt vorgestellte
elegante und zurückhaltende Leuchten-
programm *Reef* umfasst nicht nur die
hier gezeigte Wandleuchte, sondern
auch eine Tisch- und verschiedene
Einzel- oder Mehrfach-Hängeleuchten.
Am meisten Aufmerksamkeit erhielt
diese Leuchtenserie jedoch wegen
ihres ansprechenden, korallenartigen
Lampenschirms aus Keramikschaum.
Obwohl er zerbrechlich aussieht, wirbt
die Herstellerfirma damit, dass er ab-
genommen und im Geschirrspüler
gewaschen werden kann. (QC)

Fondé en 1991 par Claus Zimmermann
et Roland Knieg, Next Space intervient
essentiellement dans le design institu-
tionnel et commercial, mais aussi dans
l'environnement domestique. Lancé en
2002 lors du salon «Light & Building»
à Francfort, leur programme *Reef*, d'une
sobre élégance, comprend cette applique mais également un modèle de table
et diverses suspensions à un ou plusieurs réflecteurs. Mais c'est son
magnifique abat-jour en mousse de
céramique imitant le corail qui a particulièrement retenu l'attention. Bien
que d'apparence délicate, il peut néanmoins être dévissé et passer au lave-
vaisselle, selon le fabricant. (QC)

◁ *Diode* **floor lights, 2003**

Metal base and stem with Corian diffusers, three sizes / Fuß und Stab aus Metall mit Diffusor aus Corian, drei Größen / Base et tige en métal, diffuseur en Corian, trois dimensions
Marc Newson, London, great Britain

▷ *Castore* **hanging lights, 2003**

Thermoplastic ceiling mounts with steel suspension wires and frosted glass diffusers, 25, 35 or 42 cm diameter / Deckenrosette aus thermoplastischem Kunststoff mit Stahlkabel und Diffusor aus Mattglas, 25, 35 oder 42 cm Durchmesser / Rosace de plafond en thermoplastique, câbles des suspension en acier, diffuseurs en verre givré, 25, 35 ou 42 cm de diamètre
Artemide, Pregnana Milanese, Italy

Marc Newson created a forest-like installation of lollipop-shaped *Diode* floor lights (2003) for the "De-Lighted" exhibition held in Milan in 2003. Sponsored by the American Corian manufacturer, DuPont, the exhibition also featured specially commissioned pieces by Ross Lovegrove and James Irvine, and dramatically showed how Corian – an advanced composite made of natural minerals and pure acrylic polymer – could be used for applications other than countertops. Sharing a comparable globular and fluid form, Michele de Lucchi and Huub Ubbens' *Castore* hanging lights (2003) similarly reflect the move away from hard-edged minimalism towards a more human-centered approach to design. (CF/PF)

Für die Ausstellung „De-Lighted" zur Mailänder Möbelmesse 2003 gestaltete Marc Newson einen Wald aus seinen Lollipop-Stehleuchten *Diode*. Die von dem amerikanischen Corian-Hersteller DuPont finanzierte Ausstellung zeigte auch zwei für den Anlass in Auftrag gegebene Exponate von Ross Lovegrove und James Irvine und demonstrierte, dass die Anwendungsmöglichkeiten von Corian, einem Hochleistungs-Verbundstoff aus natürlichen Mineralien und reinem Acrylpolymer, weit über Arbeitsplatten für Küchen hinausgehen. In der ähnlich fließenden, kugelförmigen Hängeleuchten *Castore* (2003) von Michele de Lucchi und Huub Ubbens wird ebenfalls das Abgehen vom scharfkantigen Minimalismus und die Hinwendung zu einer mehr auf den Menschen ausgerichteten Designhaltung sichtbar. (CF/PF)

Marc Newson a créé une installation de type forestier à partir de son lampadaire en forme de sucette *Diode* (2003) pour l'exposition « De-Lightetd » tenue à Milan en 2003. Financée par le fabricant américain de Corian, DuPont, cette manifestation présentait également des pièces spécialement réalisées pour l'occasion par Ross Lovegrove et James Irvine qui montraient de Corian – un composite de minéraux naturels et de polymère acrylique pur – pouvait être utilisé dans des applications autres que les habituels plans de travail. Dans le même esprit globulaire et fluide, les suspensions *Castor* (2003) de Michele de Lucchi et Huub Ubbens reflètent de aussi l'éloignement d'un minimalisme pur et dur au profit d'une approche plus humaniste du design. (CF/PF)

Philippe Starck's lighting designs are constantly evolving and he continues to develop his ideas and lighting families. *Miss K* (2003) is a sexier, more streamlined and larger version of *Miss Sissi* (1990). Her transparent base is just a tease: when turned on, her outer diffuser also becomes transparent, revealing the inner diffuser as if to our X-ray vision and providing a touch of voyeuristic pleasure. The *Romeo Hot Hot* (2003) represents a functional addition to the *Romeo* line: ideal for use in kitchens, it includes an integrated fan and air purification filter. (VT)

Philippe Starck entwickelt seine Leuchtenentwürfe ständig weiter und arbeitet auch an früheren Ideen, um seine Leuchtenserien zu verbessern und zu erweitern. Die Tischleuchte *Miss K* (2003) ist eine sinnlichere, schnittigere und größere Variante der Tischleuchte *Miss Sissi* (1990). Ihr transparenter Fuß dient als Blickfang: Beim Einschalten verwandelt sich der äußere Diffusor in einen durchsichtigen Lampenschirm, während der innere wie durch Röntgenaugen sichtbar wird – ein voyeuristisch anmutendes Vergnügen. Die Hängeleuchte *Romeo Hot Hot* (2003) ergänzt die *Romeo* Serie funktional: Sie ist mit einem eingebauten Luftfilter und Ventilator ausgestattet und damit ideal für Küchen geeignet. (VT)

Les créations de luminaires de Philippe Starck évoluent en permanence et il développe sans cesse de nouvelles gammes d'idées et de modèles. *Miss K* (2003) est une version plus épurée, plus grande et plus sexy de *Miss Sissi* (1990). Sa base transparente est trompeuse : éteinte, son diffuseur extérieur devient transparent et dévoile le diffuseur interne comme s'il était passé aux rayons X, offrant une sorte de plaisir voyeuriste. La *Romeo Hot Hot* (2003) est une addition fonctionnelle à la ligne *Romeo* : elle est idéale pour les cuisines et comprend un ventilateur et un filtre de purification de l'air intégrés. (VT)

▵▵ *Romeo Hot Hot* **hanging light, 2003**

White ceramic diffuser with integrated air filter and fan, 22.5 cm high / Diffusor aus weißer Keramik mit integriertem Luftfilter und Ventilator, 22,5 cm hoch / Diffuseur en céramique blanche avec ventilateur et filtre à air intégrés, 22,5 cm de haut
Flos, Bovezzo, Italy

◁/▵ *Miss K* **table light, 2003**

PMMA frame with polycarbonate internal diffuser and transparent polycarbonate external diffuser with high-vacuum aluminization process finish, 43.2 cm high / Leuchtenkörper aus PMMA, Innendiffusor aus Polykarbonat und Außendiffusor aus transparentem Polykarbonat, im Hochvakuum aluminiumbedampft, 43,2 cm hoch / Structure en PMMA, diffuseur interne en polycarbonate, diffuseur extérieur en polycarbonate transparent à finition aluminée sous vide, 43 cm de haut
Flos, Bovezzo, Italy

***Mirror Ball* hanging, table and floor lights, 2003**

Blow-molded polycarbonate globe with metalized mirror finish, stainless-steel stands, 20–50 cm diameter / Kugel aus formgeblasenem Polykarbonat mit hochglanzpolierter Metallbeschichtung, Füße aus Edelstahl, 20–50 cm Durchmesser / Globe en polycarbonate moulé à finition métallisée miroir, support en acier inoxydable, 20–50 cm de diamètre
Tom Dixon, London, Great Britain

Tom Dixon's role as creative director of Habitat has necessarily restricted his independent design work. "I tend to be on the periphery," he comments, "occasionally popping out a product ... mainly through an interest in materials and technologies." The *Mirror Ball* light series (2003) may be one such product. Certainly, its complex construction reflects the technological bent of a designer who has since launched *Fresh Fat Plastic*: spaghetti-like extrusions that can be woven or molded. However, the *Mirror Ball*'s geometric purity also places it in a stylistic continuum with Dixon's earlier designs, such as the *Jack* and *Octo* lights (1997). (QC)

Seit Tom Dixon als Kreativdirektor für die Firma Habitat arbeitet, bleibt für seine Arbeit als freier Designer nur wenig Zeit. Dixon bezeichnet sich selbst als „Grenzgänger, der nur ab und zu ein neues Produkt entwickelt ... eine Tätigkeit, die meinem Interesse an Werkstoffen und Technologien entspringt". Die komplizierte Konstruktion der Leuchtenserie *Mirror Ball* (2003) belegt die Technikbegeisterung eines Designers, der mit *Fresh Fat Plastic* (2000) stranggepresste Kunststoff-Spaghetti entwickelt hat, die man frei weben und formen kann. Die geometrisch klare Formensprache der *Mirror Ball* Leuchten stellt sie in eine Reihe mit früheren Entwürfen von Dixon, so die Leuchten *Jack* und *Octo* (1997). (QC)

Le rôle de Tom Dixon comme directeur artistique d'Habitat a nécessairement réduit son travail personnel. « Je tends à me retrouver en périphérie », explique-t-il, « sortant à l'occasion un produit ... principalement par intérêt pour les matériaux et les technologies. » La lampe *Mirror Ball* (2003) est sans doute l'une de ces occasions. Sa fabrication complexe reflète le penchant pour la technologie d'un designer qui a depuis lancé les *Fresh Fat Plastic*, extrusions de plastique style spaghetti qui peuvent être tissées ou modelées. Néanmoins, la pureté géométrique de la *Mirror Ball* la place dans la continuité des projets antérieurs du designer, comme les lampes *Jack* et *Octo* (1997). (QC)

All iconic designs are quintessentially of their time, and Tord Boontje's lights are very beautiful symbols of the early 21st century. While their design and manufacture would have been inconceivable without recent advances in digital technology, their underlying poetry reflects our yearning for a beautiful arcadia offering respite from an uncertain world. While the *Blossom* chandelier (2002) is encrusted with sparkling crystals, the *Garland* hanging light (2002) is inexpensively yet ingeniously made from laser-cut and acid-etched metal sheet. By scattering a warm dappled shadow of flowers, both lights invite us into a magical child-like world that is both sparse yet homely. (CF/PF)

Design wird zur Ikone, wenn es ein Inbegriff seiner Zeit ist, und Tord Boontjes Leuchten stehen als besonders ausgewogene Symbole des beginnenden 21. Jahrhunderts. Auch wenn sie ohne den Einsatz der modernsten Digitaltechnik in dieser Form nicht realisierbar wären, wird in ihrem poetischen Grundton unser Traum von einem idyllischen Arkadien spürbar, das Zuflucht vor einer unsicheren Welt verspricht. Während der Kronleuchter *Blossom* (2002) mit glitzernden Kristallen verziert ist, wird die Hängeleuchte *Garland* (2002) preisgünstig, aber durchaus kunstvoll aus lasergeschnittenen und geätzten Messingplatten gefertigt. Blumengirlanden streuen ein warmes, schattiertes Licht, mit dem beide Leuchten in eine kindliche Zauberwelt einladen, die wir kaum noch kennen, uns aber dennoch so vertraut erscheint. (CF/PF)

Tous les projets devenus des icônes du design expriment la quintessence d'une époque et les lampes de Tord Boontjes sont de superbes symboles du début du XXIe siècle. Si leur design et leur fabrication auraient été inconcevables sans les récents progrès de la technologie numérique, leur poésie intrinsèque reflète notre nostalgie d'un univers arcadien, un refuge face aux incertitudes du monde actuel. Alors que le lustre *Blossom* (2002) est incrusté de cristaux étincelants, la suspension *Garland* (2002), bon marché, est astucieusement découpée au laser dans une feuille de métal. En projetant des ombres florales diaprées, ces deux lampes nous invitent dans un monde magique et enfantin, à la fois précieux et chaleureux. (CF/PF)

◁ **Blossom chandelier, 2002**
Enameled steel frame with Swarovski crystals and LED bulbs, small: 80 cm wide, large: 150 cm wide / Montierungen aus lackiertem Stahl mit Swarovski-Kristallen und LEDs, klein: 80 cm breit, groß: 150 cm breit / Support en acier laqué avec pendeloques de cristal Swarovski et LED, petit modèle : 80 cm de large, grand modèle : 150 cm de large
Prearo Collezione Luce, Lughetto di Campagnalupia, Italy, and Swarovski, Wattens, Austria

Garland hanging light, 2002
Laser-cut and acid-etched metal sheet construction, 40 cm drop (approx.) / Konstruktion aus lasergeschnittenen und geätzten Metallplatten, 40 cm lang (ca.) / Feuille de métal gravé à l'acide et découpé au laser, 40 cm de haut hors tout (environ)
Habitat, London, Great Britain

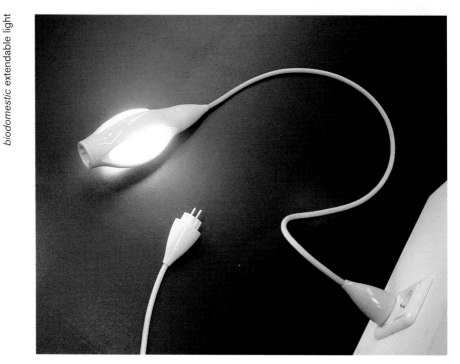

Biodomestic light, 2003

Polyurethane holder with opaline polycarbonate
diffuser and elastomer cable, 28 cm long / Gehäuse aus Polyurethan mit Diffusor aus opalem
Polykarbonat und Kabel aus Elastomer, 28 cm
lang / Support en polyuréthane, diffuseur en
polycarbonate opalin et câble en élastomère,
28 cm de long
Luceplan, Milan, Italy

▽ *Construction of* Biodomestic *extendable
light /* Schematische Darstellung der koppel-
baren Leuchte Biodomestic / *Image du montage de la lampe* Biodomestic, 2003

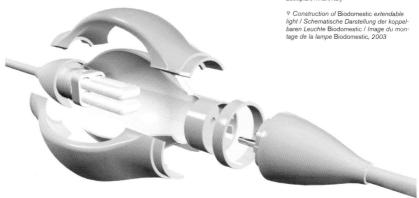

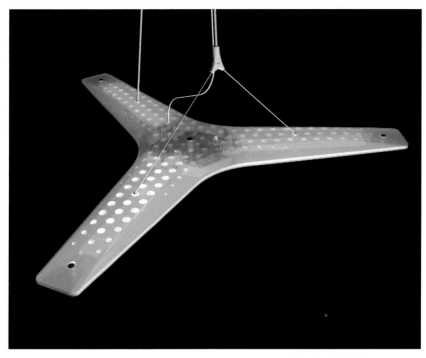

Airco chandelier, 2003
Injection-molded photo-engraved polycarbonate
construction, 100 cm diameter / Konstruktion
aus Spritzguss-Polykarbonat mit Fotogravur,
100 cm Durchmesser / Structure en polycarbonate moulé par injection et photogravé,
100 cm de diamètre
Luceplan, Milan, Italy

The *Airco* and the *Biodomestic* (both
2003) belong to the *Greenlight* series
of energy-efficient lights designed by
the Amsterdam-based team of Willem
van der Sluis and Hugo Timmermans.
The *Airco* was conceived as a futuristic
chandelier, with three interior light
sources refracted through a multitude
of lenses. The *Biodomestic*'s environ-
mental preoccupations, however, run
deeper. Both its boldly organic form
and its ability to "grow" through the
addition of extra units create parallels
with the natural world. And like the
creeping vine it mimics, the *Biodomestic* respects no boundaries, serving
equally well as floor, table, wall or suspended light. (QC)

Die Leuchten *Airco* und *Biodomestic*
(beide 2003) gehören zu der energiesparenden Serie *Greenlight* von Willem
van der Sluis und Hugo Timmermans,
die in Amsterdam als Designerteam
tätig sind. Die *Airco* Leuchte wurde als
futuristische Hängeleuchte konzipiert
und besitzt drei Lichtquellen sowie eine
Vielzahl von Linsen, durch die das Licht
gebrochen wird. Die *Biodomestic*
Leuchte orientiert sich stärker an der
Natur. Sowohl ihre organische Form als
auch die Möglichkeit, sie durch Koppe-
lung mit weiteren Leuchten „wachsen"
zu lassen, stellt dazu eine Parallele
dar. Ohne Grenzen wie eine rankende
Weinrebe lässt sie sich ebenso als
Boden-, Tisch-, Wand- oder Hängeleuchte verwenden. (QC)

Les lampes *Airco* et *Biodomestic*
(2003) appartiennent à la série de luminaires économes en énergie *Greenlight*, conçue par l'équipe amstelloda-
moise formée par Willem van der Sluis
et Hugo Timmermans. L'*Airco* est un
lustre futuriste, à trois sources lumineuses internes réfractées par une
multitude de lentilles. Les préoccupations environnementales de la *Biodomestic* sont plus affirmées. Sa forme
résolument organique et sa capacité
à « croître » par adjonction d'unités
supplémentaires n'est pas sans parallèle avec le monde naturel. Comme la
vigne vierge qu'elle imite, la *Biodomestic* ignore les contraintes, servant aussi
bien de lampe de table, de lampadaire,
d'applique, que de suspension. (QC)

Toric 1 and Toric 2 hanging lights, 2003

Enameled metal shade, small: 38 cm diameter,
large: 50 cm diameter / Lampenschirme aus
lackiertem Metall, klein: 38 cm Durchmesser,
groß: 50 cm Durchmesser / Abat-jour en métal
laqué, petit modèle : 38 cm de diamètre, grand
modèle : 50 cm de diamètre
Tronconi, Corsico, Italy

Patrick Norguet's *Toric* family of hanging, floor and table lights was launched
by Tronconi at "Euroluce" 2003.
Described as the "offspring of an
alliance between fashion and design,"
Norguet has an eclectic resumé. Alongside furniture for Cappellini, he has
designed windows for Louis Vuitton and
Givenchy, and cosmetic containers for
Jean-Paul Gaultier. The wide-ranging
design sensibility that this presupposes
is reflected in Norguet's *Toric* lights. Like
his *Apollo* armchair (2002) and *Rive
Droite* sofa (2001), the *Toric* – with its
color contrasts and smooth, varnished
surfaces – has its roots in the 1960s
and early 1970s. (QC)

Auf der „Euroluce" 2003 präsentierte
Tronconi die Serie der Häng-, Steh-
und Tischleuchten *Toric* von Patrick
Norguet. Der als „Abkömmling einer
Verbindung zwischen Mode und
Design" beschriebene Norguet kann
mit einer vielfältigen Werkliste aufwar-
ten – neben Möbeln für Cappellini gestaltete er Schaufenster für Louis
Vuitton und Givenchy und entwarf
Kosmetikbehälter für Jean-Paul Gaultier. Die dafür erforderliche Sensibilität
im Design zeigt sich auch in den *Toric*
Leuchten. Wie Norguets Stuhl *Apollo*
(2002) und sein Sofa *Rive Droite*
(2001) hat die *Toric* Leuchte – mit ihren
Farbkontrasten und glatten, glänzenden
Flächen – ihre Wurzeln im Design der
1960er und frühen 1970er Jahre. (QC)

La famille de suspensions, de lampadaires et de lampes de table *Toric*, de
Patrick Norguet, a été lancée par Tronconi au salon « Euroluce » 2003. Décrit
comme « un enfant du mariage de la
mode et du design », Norguet possède
un curriculum vitae éclectique qui va
de la création de meubles pour Cappellini à des vitrines pour Vuitton et
Givenchy, en passant par des condi-
tionnements de cosmétiques pour
Jean-Paul Gaultier. La sensibilité variée
que cette carrière présuppose se
retrouve dans ses luminaires *Toric*.
Comme son siège *Apollo* (2002) et
son sofa *Rive Droite* (2001), la *Toric*,
par ses contrastes de couleurs et ses
surfaces vernies satinées, puise aux
sources des années 1960 et 1970.
(QC)

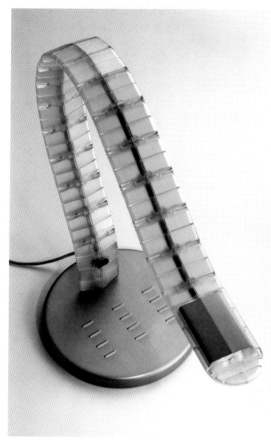

The *Soon* halogen light (2000) is the result of a development process that lasted many years. Comprising a number of identical parts, *Soon* can to be used as a desk or wall light. Two flat steel bands with insulation between them run along the length of the light, providing both support and power supply. The steel bands are held in position by a series of translucent plastic chain links. This cleverly devised mechanism enables the light to be positioned to suit individual requirements – the head being adjusted with the help of a lever. (TB)

Die Halogenleuchte *Soon* (2000) ist das Ergebnis langjähriger Entwicklungsarbeit: Durch unterschiedliche Zubehörteile ist sie sowohl als Tisch- als auch als Wandleuchte einsetzbar. In ihrem Inneren sorgt ein zweischichtiges Stahlband, geteilt durch einen Isolator, für Halt und gleichzeitig für die Stromzufuhr. In Form gehalten wird das Stahlband durch transluzide Kettenglieder aus transparentem bzw. orange eingefärbtem Kunststoff. Ihr technisch ausgeklügelter Mechanismus erlaubt die Positionierung der Leuchte in jeder gewünschten Form. Der Kopf der schlangenartigen Leuchte mit Leuchtmittel und Reflektor ist mithilfe eines Hebels schwenkbar. (TB)

La lampe de bureau halogène *Soon* (2000) est l'aboutissement d'un processus de développement qui a duré de nombreuses années. Composée d'un certain nombre de pièces identiques, elle peut servir aussi bien sur un bureau qu'en applique murale. Deux anneaux plats en acier isolés l'un de l'autre assurent à la fois l'alimentation électrique et la rigidité nécessaire. Ils sont maintenus par une succession de maillons en plastique translucide. Ce mécanisme astucieux permet d'adapter la lampe à la plupart des besoins à l'aide d'un petit levier. (TB)

Soon table/wall light, 2000

Aluminum base (table version) with steel supports and polycarbonate stem and diffuser, 52 cm high (max.) / Fuß aus Aluminium (Tischversion), Arm mit Stahlbändern und Diffusor aus Polykarbonatverkleidung, 52 cm hoch (max.) / Base en aluminium (version de table), tige et diffuseur en polycarbonate et à raidisseurs en acier, 52 cm de haut (max.)
Tobias Grau, Rellingen, Germany

***Angel* floor lights, 2003**

Polycarbonate prismatic bubble diffusers
on steel stems with touch-sensitive dimmer,
128 or 200 cm high / Prismatische, blasen-
förmige Diffusoren aus Polykarbonat auf
Füßen aus Stahl mit berührungsempfindlichem
Dimmer, 128 oder 200 cm hoch / Diffuseur
bulle en polycarbonate prismatique, tige d'acier
avec rhéostat tactile, 128 ou 200 cm de haut
Luceplan, Milan, Italy

"Organic design comes from organic thinking."

„Organisches Design entsteht aus organischem Denken."

« Le design organique vient de la pensée organique. »

– Ross Lovegrove

Goggle wall light, 2003
Polycarbonate mounts and molded polycarbonate diffuser with mirrored film, 32 cm high / Montierung aus Polycarbonat mit Diffusor aus gegossenem Polykarbonat mit verspiegelter Folie, 32 cm hoch / Monture en polycarbonate, diffuseur en polycarbonate moulé avec film miroir, 32 cm de haut
Luceplan, Milan, Italy

Inspired by swimming goggles, Ross Lovegrove's *Goggle* wall light (2003) incorporates a mirrored film of iridescent color that twinkles as it changes from purple to orange, like the eye of some exotic aquatic creature. State-of-the-art materials and natural, organic forms also inspired Lovegrove's *Angel* floor light (2003). Resembling shining wings in motion, the design's gold diffusers are made from polycarbonate prismatic bubbles, which softly filter the light. The lower one (which can be used separately) is mounted at sitting height for reading, while the upper one serves for more atmospheric general lighting. The brightness levels can be altered via touch-sensitive rings. (CF/PF)

Ross Lovegroves von schwimmenden Stachelmakrelen (*goggles*) inspirierte Wandleuchte *Goggle* (2003) ist mit einer verspiegelten Folie mit irisierender Farbe ausgestattet, die aufblitzt, wenn sie von Violett zu Orange wechselt. Auch Lovegroves Stehleuchte *Angel* (2003) ist geprägt von modernsten Materialien und organischen Formen. Die goldenen, blasenförmigen Diffusoren aus prismatischem Polykarbonat erinnern an Flügel, die im Flug schimmern. Der untere Diffusor (der auch allein verwendet werden kann) ist auf Sitzhöhe montiert und kann als Leselampe dienen, während der obere für eine stimmungsvolle Allgemeinbeleuchtung sorgt. Die Helligkeit kann über berührungsempfindliche Ringe eingestellt werden. (CF/PF)

Inspirée des lunettes de natation, l'applique *Goggle* (2003) de Ross Lovegrove comprend un film-miroir de couleur iridescente qui clignote lorsqu'il passe du pourpre à l'orange, comme pourrait le faire l'œil d'une créature aquatique exotique. Matériaux d'avant-garde et formes organiques naturelles lui ont aussi le lampadaire *Angel* (2003). Faisant penser à des ailes scintillantes en mouvement, ses diffuseurs dorés sont des bulles prismatiques de polycarbonate qui filtrent doucement la lumière émise. Le diffuseur inférieur – utilisable séparément – est à hauteur de siège pour la lecture, tandis que le plus grand fournit un éclairage d'ambiance. L'intensité lumineuse se règle *via* des anneaux tactiles. (CF/PF)

Ross Lovegrove's *Biolite Eon* task light (2004) is indicative of the increasingly sculptural quality of his work. Inspired by natural forms, Lovegrove synthesizes ergonomics with new production technologies and materials to create objects that have both logic and beauty. Like the other lights in the *Biolite* range, the *Eon* produces a level of light that is intended to reduce eyestrain. Its form is equally soothing with its sensual contours inviting interaction. When closed the *Eon* has a strong sculptural presence that is reminiscent of Henry Moore's work, yet when opened for use the light reveals Lovegrove's highly refined approach to functional requirements. (CF/PF)

Ross Lovegroves Arbeitsleuchte *Biolite Eon* (2004) offenbart die skulpturale Qualität seiner Entwürfe. Formal bezieht Lovegrove seine Inspirationen aus der Natur und vereint ergonomische Erwägungen mit neuen Produktionstechniken und Werkstoffen zu Objekten, die sich durch Logik und Schönheit auszeichnen. Wie die anderen Modelle der *Biolite* Leuchtenserie erzeugt die *Eon* Leuchte ein augenschonendes Licht. Auch die Form der zur Interaktion einladenden Leuchte mit ihren sinnlichen Konturen ist wohltuend. Wenn sie zusammengeklappt ist, vermittelt die *Eon* Leuchte eine starke skulpturale Präsenz und erinnert an Werke von Henry Moore. Wird sie zum Betrieb aufgeklappt, zeigt sich Lovegroves gekonnte Umsetzung von Funktion. (CF/PF)

La lampe de bureau *Biolite Eon* (2004) de Ross Lovegrove témoigne de l'aspect de plus en plus sculptural de ses créations. Inspiré par les formes naturelles, Lovegrove synthétise ergonomie, nouvelles technologies de production et nouveaux matériaux pour créer des objets à la fois logiques et beaux. Comme les autres modèles de la gamme *Biolite*, la *Eon* offre une intensité lumineuse conçue pour réduire la fatigue visuelle. Sa silhouette aux contours sensuels qui invitent à l'interaction, est tout aussi apaisante. Éteinte, l'*Eon* conserve une forte présence sculpturale qui rappelle l'œuvre du sculpteur Henry Moore. Allumée, elle illustre l'approche raffinée de la fonction pratiquée par son designer. (CF/PF)

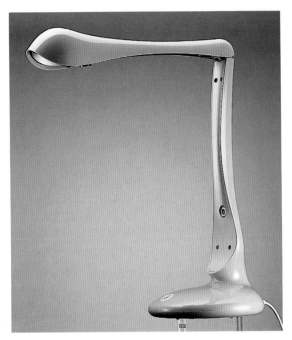

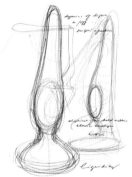

△/▷ *Biolite Eon* task light, 2004

Polycarbonate body with die-cast aluminum base, 47 cm high / Leuchtenkörper aus Polykarbonat mit Fuß aus Druckgussaluminium, 47 cm hoch / Corps en polycarbonate, base en fonte d'aluminium moulée sous pression, 47 cm de haut
Yamagiwa, Tokyo, Japan

◁ *Design drawing of* Biolite Eon *task light, c.2004 / Entwurfszeichnung der Tischleuchte* Biolite Eon, *ca. 2004 / Croquis de la lampe de bureau* Biolite Eon, *vers 2004*

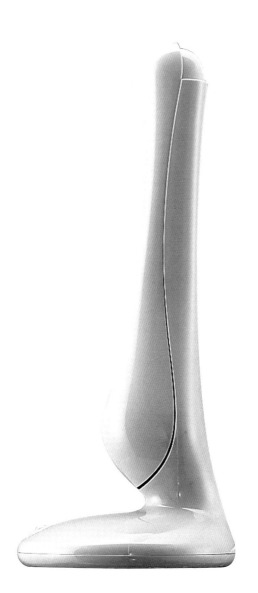

FL/Icon hanging light, 2002

Transparent or sanded methacrylate shade, 52 cm diameter / Lampenschirm aus transparentem oder sandgestrahltem Methacrylat, 52 cm Durchmesser / Abat-jour en méthacrylate transparent ou sablé, 52 cm de diamètre
Kartell, Noviglio, Italy

Ferruccio Laviani has made a considerable impact on the world of lighting, with exuberant designs such as the *Orbital* floor light (1992) and the *Supernova* hanging light (2000), both for Foscarini. A close relationship has also blossomed with Kartell, resulting in a series of lighting and furniture designs expressing Laviani's irrepressible love of shape and color. The *Take* table light (2003), surely drawing its inspiration from Philippe Starck's *Walla Walla* wall light (1994), humorously revisits the classic bedside light, while the *FL/Icon* hanging lights (2002) have been compared to "light, airy, multi-colored soap bubbles." (QC)

Ferruccio Laviani hat die Welt des Beleuchtungsdesigns mit so extravaganten Modellen wie der Stehleuchte *Orbital* (1992) und der Hängeleuchte *Supernova* (2000), die er beide für Foscarini entwarf, spürbar beeinflusst. Aus der engen und fruchtbaren Zusammenarbeit mit Kartell sind eine Reihe von Beleuchtungs- und Möbelentwürfen hervorgegangen, die Lavianis Freude an Form und Farbe zum Ausdruck bringen. Die Tischleuchte *Take* (2003), ohne Zweifel inspiriert von Philippe Starcks Leuchte *Walla Walla* (1994), ist eine humorvolle Neubearbeitung der klassischen Nachttischleuchte. Die Hängeleuchten *FL/Icon* (2002) hingegen wurden mit „leichten, luftigen, bunten Seifenblasen" verglichen. (QC)

Ferruccio Laviani a exercé un impact considérable sur le monde de l'éclairage à travers d'exubérants projets comme le lampadaire *Orbital* ou la suspension *Supernova*, tous deux pour Foscarini. Il a également développé une étroite collaboration avec Kartell, qui a donné naissance à une série de luminaires et de meubles exprimant sa passion irrépressible pour les formes et les couleurs. La lampe de table *Take* (2003) qui tire certainement son inspiration de la lampe *Walla Walla* (1994) de Philippe de Starck, revisite avec humour la classique lampe de chevet, tandis que les suspensions *FL/Icon* (2002) ont été comparées à des « bulles de savon légères, aériennes et multicolores. » (QC)

Take table light, 2003

Batch-dyed polycarbonate construction, 30 cm high / Konstruktion aus Spritzguss-Polykarbonat, 30 cm hoch / Structure en polycarbonate moulé par injection, 30 cm de haut
Kartell, Noviglio, Italy

◁ Take *table light with its easy-to-carry packaging / Tischleuchte* Take *in praktischer Verpackung mit Tragegriff / La lampe de table* Take *et son conditionnement à porter*

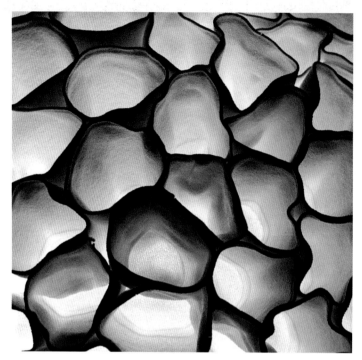

Detail of Styrene hanging light */ Detailansicht der Hängeleuchte* Styrene */ Détail de la suspension* Styrene

▷ *Styrene* **hanging light, 2002**

Heated polystyrene cup construction and steel wire, 65 cm diameter (approx.) / Konstruktion aus hitzebehandelten Polystyrolbechern und Stahldraht, 65 cm Durchmesser (ca.) / Structure en gobelets de polystyrène chauffé et fil de fer, 65 cm de diamètre (environ)
Paul Cocksedge, London, Great Britain

While studying under Ron Arad at the Royal College of Art in London, Paul Cocksedge discovered that when polystyrene cups are heated, they shrink rather than melt, producing beautiful, rigid organic forms, each slightly different from the next. Using wooden pegs, Cocksedge clips the cups into sections and heats them to 150° in an oven. He then joins the shrunken sections to create his *Styrene* hanging light (2002). It is a tribute to his ingenuity that Cocksedge has created something so sculptural and poetic from something as mundane as a disposable vending cup. (CF/PF)

Noch während Paul Cocksedge bei Ron Arad am Londoner Royal College of Art studierte, machte er die Entdeckung, dass Becher aus Polystrol bei Hitzeeinwirkung nicht schmelzen, sondern schrumpfen und dabei sehr schöne und starre organische Formen bilden, die jedes Mal ein wenig anders ausfallen. Mit Holzklammern steckt Cocksedge jeweils mehrere Becher zusammen und lässt sie im Ofen auf 150° erhitzen. Aus den geschrumpelten Elementen entsteht dann die Hängeleuchte *Styrene* (2002). Es spricht für seinen Einfallsreichtum, etwas derart Skulpturales und Poetisches aus etwas so Alltäglichem wie einem Wegwerfbecher zu schaffen. (CF/PF)

Travaillant sous la direction de Ron Arad au Royal College of Arts de Londres, Paul Cocksedge découvrit que, chauffés, les gobelets de polystyrène rétrécissaient au lieu de fondre, produisant de superbes formes organiques, chacune légèrement différente de l'autre. À l'aide de chevilles en bois, Cocksedge attacha les tasses par petits groupes et les chauffa à 150° dans un four, avant de les éléments rétrécis relier pour créer cette suspension *Styrene* (2002). C'est un hommage à l'inventivité du designer que d'avoir su créer un luminaire sculptural et poétique à partir d'un objet aussi banal qu'un gobelet en plastique. (CF/PF)

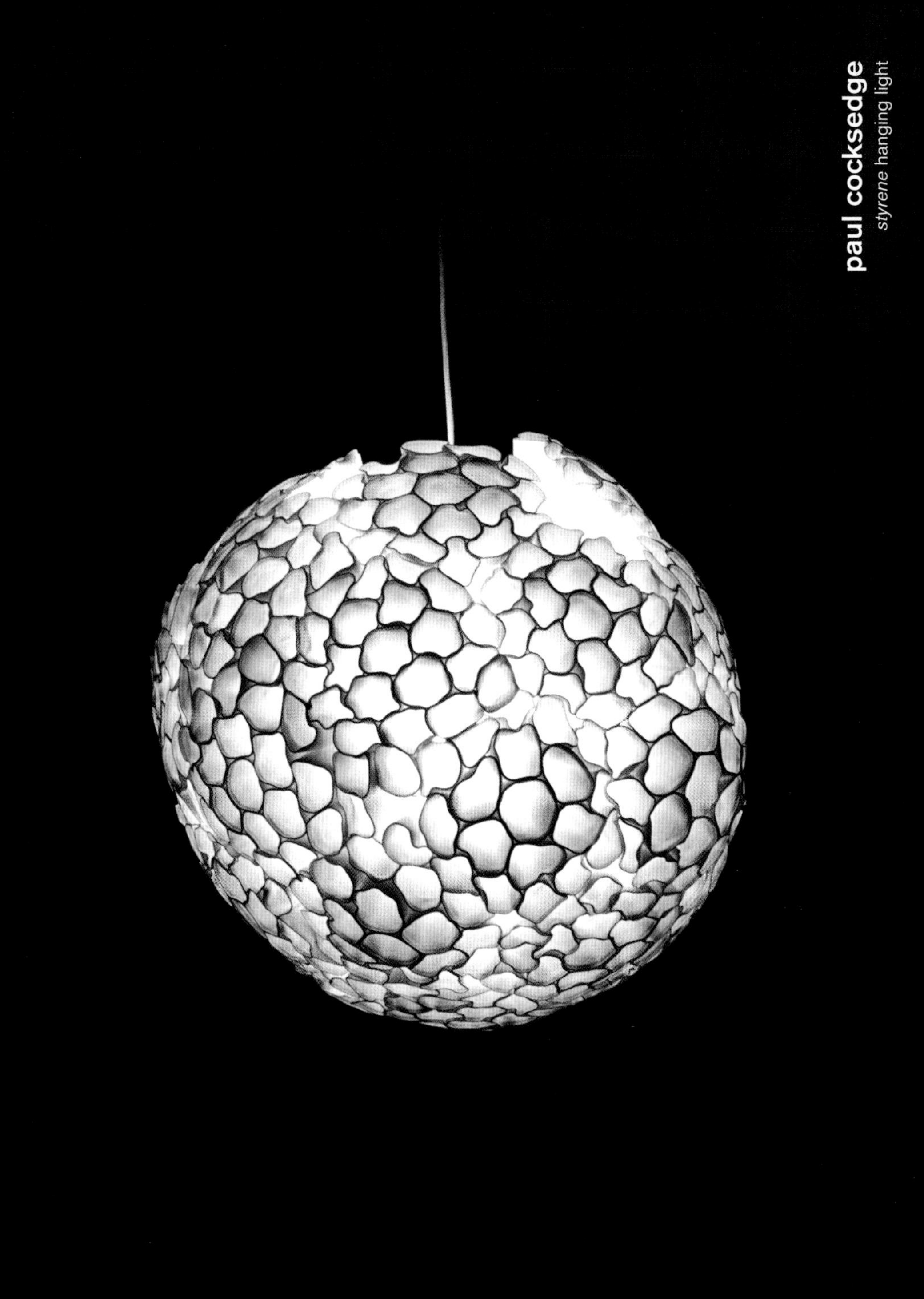

paul cocksedge
styrene hanging light

Manzù, Pio (Italy, 1939–1969) 476–477
   Parentesi suspended pole light, 1970 476–477
Martinelli Luce SpA (Lucca, Italy) 402–403, 440, 472,
   484–485
   Model No. 599 Serpente table light, 1965 484
   Model No. 620 Pipistrello table light, 1965–1966
   402–403
   Ruspa desk light, 1967 440
   Model No. 640 Profiterole table/floor light, 1968
   472
   Model No. 629 Cobra table light, 1968 484
   Ruspa table light, 1969 440
   Model No. 615 table light, 1970 484–485
Martinelli, Elio (Italy, b.1922) 484–485
   Model No. 599 Serpente table light, 1965 484
   Model No. 629 Cobra table light, 1968 484
   Model No. 615 table light, 1970 484–485
Master desk light, 1988 629
Mathmos (London, Great Britain) 374–375
   Astro lava light, 1963 (reissue) 374–375
Matthieu (France) 300
   Floor light, 1953 300
Mattiolo, Giancarlo (Italy, active 1960s) 422–423
   Nesso table light, 1962 422
   MT table/floor light, 1969 423
Maurer, Ingo (Germany, b.1932) 41, 408–409,
   542–543, 574–575, 596–597, 622–623, 626–627,
   649
   Bulb table light, 1966 408–409, 575
   Design M lighting products, c.1970 408
   Bulb Bulb hanging/floor light, 1980 575
   Ya Ya Ho lighting system, 1982–1984 542–543
   One from the Heart table light, 1989 574
   Porca Miseria! chandelier, 1994 596–597
   Wo bist du, Edison, … ? hanging light, 1997
   626–627
   Zettel'z 6 chandelier, 1998 596
   XXL Dome hanging lights, Westfriedhof subway
   station, Munich, 1998 622–623
   XXL Dome hanging light, 1999 622
   Holonzki wall light, 1999–2000 626
   Stardust suspended ceiling light, 2000 41
   El. E. Dee table light, 2001 649
Mawa Design GmbH (Langerwisch, Germany)
   360–363
   Model No. sy1 Ssymmank (Integra) floor light,
   1959 (reissue) 360–361
   Model No. sch1 Schliephacke floor light,
   1959–1960 (reissue) 362–363
Maxim, Hiram (USA, 1840–1916) 22
Mazza, Sergio (Italy, b.1931) 356–357
   Alfa table light, 1959 356–357
Mazzoni delle Stelle, Alessandro (Italy, b.1941) 499
Meda, Alberto (Italy, b.1945) 40–41, 564–565,
   572–573, 589, 618–619
   Berenice task light, 1985 589
   Lola floor light, 1987 564, 589
   Lola wall light, 2001 564–565
   Titania hanging light, 1989 572–573, 589
   Bap task light, 1992 589
   Titania floor light, 1995 573
   Fortebraccio task light, 1998 589, 618–619
   StarLed table light, 2001 40–41
Mefistole ceiling light, 1970 490
Memphis srl (Pregnana Milanese, Italy) 34, 526,
   534–540, 548, 557
   Ashoka table light, 1981 538–539
   Oceanic table light, 1981 534
   Super table/floor light, 1981 535
   Tahiti table light, 1981 534, 536–537
Mendini, Alessandro (Italy, b.1931) 34
Metacolor floor light, 2001 652–653
Metalampo table light, 1983 600, 639
Metallwerke vorm. Paul Stotz AG (Stuttgart, Germany)
   150–151
   Model No. ME78b table light, 1926 150–151
Metamorfosi lighting range, 1996 38–39, 600–601,
   652–653
Mezzochimera table light, 1966 430–431
Mezzoracolo table light, 1970 462–463
Michie, Clay (USA, active 1950s) 262–263
   Model No. 8 desk light, 1950 262–263
Midgard task light, c.1923–1925 148–149
Mies van der Rohe, Ludwig (Germany/USA,
   1886–1969) 362, 33
Miklós, Gustave (Hungary/France, 1888–1967) 236
Milkbottle hanging light, 1991 582–583
Mini-Box table light, 1980 532–533
Mira floor light, 1983 550–551

Mirror Ball hanging light, 2003 671
Mirror Ball table light, 2003 671
Mirror Ball floor light, 2003 671
Miss K table light, 2003 670
Miss Sissi table light, 1990 580–581, 664
Mitchell Manufacturing Co. (USA) 226–229
   Model No. 114 Executive desk light, 1939
   226–227
   Model No. 100 New Student desk light, c.1939
   228–229
Mite floor light, 2000 637
Modern (Kanagawa, Japan) 645
   Shuriken hanging light, 2000 645
Modern Art table light, 1955 323
Moholy-Nagy, László (Hungary/Germany/USA
   1895–1946) 153, 171
Moloch floor light, 1970–1971 492–493
Monkey Boys (Eindhoven, The Netherlands) 662–663
   Random hanging light, 2002 662–663
Monroe, Jay (USA, active 1950s–1960s) 410–411
   Model No. 6500 Tensor student light, c.1960 411
   Tensor student light, c.1960 410–411
Montjuic floor light, 1990 584–585
Moon Phases table light, c.1955 336
Moooi (Breda, The Netherlands) 624–625, 662–663
   Light Shade Shade hanging light, 1999 (reissue)
   37, 624–625
   Random hanging light, 2002 662–663
Morning Glory floor light, 1994 604–605
Morning Glory table light, c.1900 604
Morris, William (Great Britain, 1834–1896) 59
Morrison, Jasper (Great Britain, b.1959) 638–639
   Luxmaster floor light, 2000–2001 638–639
Moser, Koloman (Austria, 1868–1918) 84–85
   Chandelier, c.1900 (attrib.) 85
   Hanging light, c.1902 84
Motozawa, Kazuo (Japan, active 1970s) 513
   Saturno hanging light, 1972 513
Mouille, Serge (France, 1922–1988) 314–319
   Three-arm floor light, 1953 316
   Lampadaire floor light, 1953 316
   Tuyau desk light, c.1953 319
   Seven-branch wall light, c.1953 315
   Antony suspended ceiling/wall light, c.1953 317
   Applique Murale two-arm wall light, c.1953 316
   Saturne wall appliques, 1958 318
   Coquille wall lights, c.1958 318
MT table/floor light, 1969 423
Müller & Zimmer GmbH (Stuttgart, Germany) 200–203
   Desk light, c.1931 202
   Sistrah adjustable suspended ceiling light, 1931
   200
   Sistrah Model No. P4.5 hanging light, 1931 201
   Sistrah Model No. T4 table light, 1932 203
Müller, Karl (Germany, 1888–1972) 167
   Ceiling light, Werkbund Weißenhofsiedlung
   exhibition, 1927 167
Müller, Otto (Germany, active 1930s) 200–203
   Desk light, c.1931 202
   Sistrah adjustable suspended ceiling light, 1931
   200
   Sistrah Model No. P4.5 hanging light, 1931 201
   Sistrah Model No. T4 table light, 1932 203
Multipla floor light, 1970 494
Multipla table light, 1970 494
Murdock, William (Great Britain, 1754–1839) 9
Musa hanging lights, 1994 529
Muthesius, Friedrich Eckart (Germany, 1904–1989)
   182
Muthesius, Hermann (Germany, 1861–1927) 63

Narcissus wall appliques, c.1900 68
Nastro table light, 1983 547
Natalini, Adolfo (Italy, b.1941) 447, 535
Nelson, George (USA, 1908–1986) 246–249,
   260–261, 354–355
   Bubble hanging light, 1947–1950 246
   Bubble hanging light, 1947–1950 247
   Bubble hanging light, 1947–1950 248
   Bubble hanging light, c.1950 249
   Holiday House table light, 1950 260
   Half-Nelson table light, c.1955 261
   Lantern Series hanging light, c.1958 354
   Lantern Series table light, c.1958 355
Nessen Lamps Inc. (New York, NY, USA) 172–173
   Model No. NF987 floor light, 1927 (reissue) 173
   Model No. NT922 floor light, 1927 (reissue) 172
Nessen Studio Inc. (New York, NY, USA) 172–173,
   266–267

   Model No. NF987 floor light, 1927 173
   Model No. NT922 table light, 1927 172
   Anywhere table light, 1952 266–267
Nessie hanging light, 1985 566
Nesso table light, 1962 422
New Lamp (Rome, Italy) 404–405, 439
   Table light, c.1969 404–405
   Quasar table light, 1969 439
New Student Model No. 100 desk light, c.1939
   228–229
Newson, Marc (Australia/Italy, b.1963) 594–595,
   668–669
   Helice floor light, 1993 594–595
   Diode floor lights, 2003 668–669
Nexflex table light, 2002 658–659
Next (Baldham, Germany) 621, 633
   flapflap floor light, 1999 621
   flapflap table light, 1999 621
   liquid-light drop-1 ceiling light, 2000 633
   liquid-light drop-2 hanging light, 2000 633
   liquid-light drop-3 wall light, 2000 633
Next Space (Kassel, Germany) 667
   Reef wall light, 2002 667
Nichetto, Luca (Italy, b.1976) 658
   O-space hanging light, 2003 658
Noce floor/table/wall light, 1972 593
Noguchi, Isamu (USA, 1904–1988) 4–6, 232–233,
   346–349
   Cylinder table light, c.1944 232–233
   Model No. UF4-L10 Akari floor light, 1950s 347
   Model No. UF3-Q Akari floor light, 1950s 347
   Model No. 33S-BB3 Akari floor light, 1960 346
Noll, Alexandre (France, b.1969) 253
   Table light, 1950s 253
Norguet, Patrick (France, b.1969) 676
   Toric 1 hanging light, 2003 676
   Toric 2 hanging light, 2003 676
Norm 69 hanging light, 1969 386
Normann Copenhagen ApS (Copenhagen, Denmark)
   386
   Norm 69 hanging light, 1969 386
Northern Lights (Canada) 37
   SAD-A-LITE light, c.1980–85 37
Nuage table/floor light, 1970 472–473
Nucleo (Sormani) (Arosio, Italy) 498–499
   B. T.2 table light, 1971 499
   B. T.3 floor light, 1971 498–499
Nummi, Yki (Finland, 1925–1984) 322–323
   Modern Art table light, 1955 323
   Hanging lights, 1959 322
   Skyflyer hanging light, 1960 386–387
Nuvola ceiling/wall light, 1966 404
O Luce srl (Milan, Italy) 31, 381, 390–393, 442–443,
   478–479, 522–523, 635
   Model No. 281 Acrilica table light, 1962 381
   Spring floor light, c.1965 390
   Model No. 291 Spider table light, 1965 390–392
   Model No. 3391 Spider floor light, 1965 390–392
   Model No. 2202 Coupé table light, 1967 392
   Model No. 3321 Coupé floor light, 1967 392–393
   Flash table light, 1968 442
   Model No. 2206 Flash table light, 1968
   (re-edition) 442–443
   Alogena floor light, 1970 31, 478, 639
   Alogena suspended ceiling light, 1970 31, 478–479,
   639
   Model No. 761 Alogena wall light, 1970 31, 478,
   639
   Atollo table light, 1977 522–523
Oceanic table light, 1981 534
Octo floor light, 1997 671
Oiseau de Feau table light, c.1920 126
Olbrich, Joseph Maria (Silesia 1867–1908) 83
Oldenburg, Claes (USA, b.1929) 408, 449
Olook hanging light, 1968 447
Olympia floor light, 1984 548–549
Omikron Design, (Milan, Italy) 242–243
   Claritas floor light, 1946 (reissue) 242
   Claritas table light, 1946 (reissue) 243
One from the Heart table light, 1989 574
One-Off Ltd (London, Great Britain) 550
   Tree floor light, 1983–1984 550
Onidia table light, 1992 584
Optiplex lighting system, c.1957 328
Oracolo floor light, 1968 462–463
Orbital floor light, 1992 586–587, 682
Origlia, Giorgio (Italy, b.1943) 518–519
   Area Curvea table light, 1974 518–519
   Area floor, table and hanging lights, 1974 519

AKARI ASSOCIATES, LONG ISLAND CITY (NY), USA
www.noguchi.org

ADELTA, DINSLAKEN, GERMANY
www.adelta.de

AIRAM ELECTRIC AB, HELSINKI, FINLAND
www.airam.fi

ALESSI SPA, CRUSINALLO, ITALY
www.alessi.com

ALVA LIGHTING, LONDON, GREAT BRITAIN
www.alvalighting.com

ANGLEPOISE LTD, WATERLOOVILLE, GREAT BRITAIN (PREVIOUSLY HERBERT TERRY & SONS)
www.anglepoise.com

AQUA CREATIONS LTD., TEL AVIV, ISRAEL
www.aquagallery.com

ARREDOLUCE, MONZA, ITALY
www.arredoluce.it

ARTEK, HELSINKI, FINLAND
www.artek.fi

ARTELUCE SEE FLOS SPA

ARTEMIDE SPA, PREGNANA MILANESE, ITALY
www.artemide.com

ATELJÉ LYKTAN AB, ÅHUS, SWEDEN
www.atelje-lyktan.se

CAPPELLINI SPA, AROSIO, ITALY
www.cappellini.it

DAUM FRANCE SA, NANCY, FRANCE
www.daum.fr

DESIGN HOUSE STOCKHOLM AB STOCKHOLM, SWEDEN
www.designhouse.se

DRIADE SPA, FOSSADELLO DI CAORSO, ITALY
www.driade.com

DROOG DESIGN, AMSTERDAM, THE NETHERLANDS
www.droogdesign.nl

ECART INTERNATIONAL, PARIS FRANCE
www.ecart-international.com

ERCO LEUCHTEN GMBH, LÜDENSCHEID, GERMANY
www.erco.com

EUROLOUNGE, NORWICH, GREAT BRITAIN
www.eurolounge.co.uk

FOG & MORUP SEE HORN BELYSNING A/S

FLOS SPA, BOVEZZO, ITALY
www.flos.com

FONTANA ARTE SPA, CORSICO, ITALY
www.fontanaarte.it

FORNASETTI, MILAN, ITALY
www.fornasetti.com

FOSCARINI SRL, MARCON, ITALY
www.foscarini.com

FRATELLI FRANCESCONI & C. SRL, RONCADELLE, ITALY
www.francesconi.it

GISPEN, CULLEMBORG, THE NETHERLANDS
www.gispen.com

HABITAT, LONDON, GREAT BRITAIN
www.habitat.net

HERMAN MILLER INC., ZEELAND (MI), USA
www.hermanmiller.com

IDMAN OY, MÄNTSÄLÄ, FINLAND
www.idman.fi

IGUZZINI ILLUMINAZIONE SPA, RECANATI, ITALY
www.iguzzini.com

INFLATE DESIGN, LONDON, GREAT BRITAIN
www.inflate.co.uk

INGO MAURER GMBH, MUNICH, GERMANY
www.ingo-maurer.com

JEAN PERZEL LUMINAIRES, PARIS, FRANCE
www.jean-perzel.com

JIELDÉ SA, LYONS, FRANCE
www.jielde.com

KARTELL SPA, NOVIGLIO, ITALY
www.kartell.it

KNOLL INTERNATIONAL, EAST GREENVILLE (PA), USA
www.knoll.com

KUNDALINI SRL, MILAN, ITALY
www.kundalini.it

LALIQUE, PARIS, FRANCE
www.lalique.com

LE KLINT, ODENSE, DENMARK
www.leklint.dk

LIGHTOLIER, FALL RIVER (MA), USA
www.lightolier.com

LOUIS POULSEN LIGHTING A/S, COPENHAGEN, DENMARK
www.louispoulsen.dk

LUCEPLAN SPA, MILAN, ITALY
www.luceplan.com

LUMI SRL, MILAN, ITALY
www.lumi.it

LUMINA ITALIA SRL, ARLUNO, ITALY
www.lumina.it

LUXO ASA, OSLO, NORWAY
www.luxo.com

MARTINELLI LUCE SPA, LUCCA,
ITALY
www.martinelliluce.it

MATHMOS, LONDON, GREAT
BRITAIN
www.mathmos.co.uk

MAWA DESIGN GMBH, BERLIN,
GERMANY
www.mawa-design.com

MOOOI, BREDA, THE NETHER-
LANDS
www.moooi.com

MÜLLER & ZIMMER GMBH & CO.,
STUTTGART, GERMANY
www.muezi.de

NESSEN LIGHTING, MAMARONECK
(NY), USA
www.nessenlighting.com

NEXT, BALDHAM, GERMANY
www.next.de

NORMANN COPENHAGEN APS,
COPENHAGEN, DENMARK
www.normann-copenhagen.com

O LUCE SRL, MILAN, ITALY
www.oluce.com

OMIKRON DESIGN, MILAN, ITALY
www.omikrondesign.com

ONE-OFF LTD. (RON ARAD
ASSOCIATES), LONDON,
GREAT BRITAIN
www.ronarad.com

OZEKI & CO., LTD., GIFU, JAPAN
Tel: + 81 58 26 30 111

PALLUCCO ITALIA SPA,
CASTAGNOLE DI PAESE, ITALY
www.palluccobellato.it

PAUL COCKSEDGE, LONDON,
GREAT BRITAIN
www.paulcocksedge.co.uk

POLTRONOVA SRL, MONTALE,
ITALY
www.poltronova.com

SEGNO SRL, PARABIAGO ITALY
Tel.: +39 0331 55 8202

SERIEN RAUMLEUCHTEN,
RODGAU, GERMANY
www.serien.com

SIRRAH SEE IGUZZINI ILLUMI-
NAZIONE SPA

SWAROVSKI, WATTENS, AUSTRIA
www.swarovski.com

TECNOLUMEN GMBH & CO. KG,
BREMEN, GERMANY
www.tecnolumen.de

TECTA, LAUENFÖRDE, GERMANY
www.tecta.de

TENSOR CORP., CHELSEA (MA),
USA
www.tensorlamp.com

THORN ORNO OY, HELSINKI,
FINLAND
www.thornlight.fn

TOBIAS GRAU GMBH, RELLINGEN,
GERMANY
www.tobias-grau.com

TOM DIXON, LONDON, GREAT
BRITAIN
www.tomdixon.net

TOM KIRK LIGHTING, LONDON,
GREAT BRITAIN
www.tomkirk.com

TRONCONI SRL, CORSICO, ITALY
www.tronconi.com

VALENTI SRL, CUSAGO, ITALY
www.valentiluce.it

VENINI SPA, MURANO, ITALY
www.venini.it

VITRA DESIGN MUSEUM,
WEIL AM RHEIN, GERMANY
www.design-museum.com

WOKA LAMPS, VIENNA, AUSTRIA
www.woka.com

YAMAGIWA CORP., TOKYO, JAPAN
www.yamagiwa.co.jp

ZEUS NOTO SRL, MILAN, ITALY
www.zeusnoto.com

ZUMTOBEL STAFF AG, DORNBIRN,
AUSTRIA
www.zumtobelstaff.com

Abercrombie, S., *George Nelson: The Design of Modern Design,* MIT Press, Cambridge (MA) 1995

Alan, *Serge Mouille Luminaires,* La Nef, Bordeaux 1993

Aloi, R., *Illuminazione d'Oggi,* Ulrico Hoepli/Editore Milano, Milan 1956

Aloi, R., *L'Arredamento Moderno,* Ulrico Hoepli/Editore Milano, Milan 1964

Bangert, A., *Italienisches Möbeldesign – Klassiker von 1945 bis heute,* Bangert Verlag, Munich 1987

Baroni, D., *L'Ogetto Lampada,* Ulrico Hoepli, Milan 1981

Bassi, A., *La Luce Italiana; Design delle Lampade, 1945–2000,* Electa, Milan 2003

Bax, Captain E. I., *Popular Electric Lighting, being Practical Hints to Present and Intending Users of Electric Energy for Illuminating Purposes,* Biggs & Co., London 1891

Benjamin, P., *The Age of Electricity: from Amber-Soul to Telephone,* Charles Scribner's Sons, New York 1887

Binroth, J.A., et al., *Bauhaus Lighting? Kandem Light!; the Collaboration of the Bauhaus with the Leipzig Company Kandem,* Arnoldsche Art Publishers, Stuttgart 2002

Blühm, A. and Lippincott, L., *Light! The Industrial Age 1750–1900,* Thames & Hudson, London 2000

Bowers, B., *A History of Electric Light and Power,* Peter Peregrinus Ltd., Stevenage 1982

Bowers, B., *Lengthening the Day: A History of Lighting Technology,* Oxford University Press, Oxford 1998

Branzi, A., *Il Design Italiano, 1964–1990,* Electa, Milan 1996

Bröhan, T. and Berg, T., *Avantgarde Design 1880–1930,* TASCHEN GmbH, Cologne 1994

Buddensieg, T. and Rogge, H., eds., *Industriekultur, Peter Behrens und die AEG 1907–1914,* Gebr. Mann Verlag, Berlin 1979

Byars, M., *50 Lights: Innovations in Design and Materials,* Rotovision, Crans-Près-Céligny 1997

Casciani, S., *Furniture as Architecture, Design and Zanotta Products,* Arcadia Edizioni, Milan 1988

Castiglioni, P., Baldacci, C., Biondo, G., *Lux: Italia 1930–1990, l'Architettura della Luce,* Berenice, Milan 1991

Cox, J. A., *A Century of Light,* The Benjamin Company Inc., New York 1979

Cox, W., *Lighting and Lamp Design,* Crown Publishers Inc., New York 1952

d'Allemagne, H.R., *Musée du Luminaire à l'Exposition Universelle de 1900,* J. Schemit, Paris 1900

Daum, N., *Daum: Maîtres Verriers,* Edita-Denoël, Lausanne 1980

Dietz, M. and Mönninger, M., *Lights,* TASCHEN GmbH, Cologne 1993

DiNoto, A., *Art Plastic, Designed for Living,* Abbeville Press, New York (NY) 1984

Droste, M., *The Bauhaus-Light by Carl Jacob Jucker and Wilhelm Wagenfeld,* Verlag form, Frankfurt 1997

Duncan, A., *Art Nouveau and Art Déco Lighting,* Thames & Hudson, London 1978

Duncan, A., Eidelberg, M., Harris, N., *Masterworks of Louis Comfort Tiffany,* Harry N. Abrams Inc., New York 1993

Edison Swan Electric Company Ltd., *The Pageant of the Lamp,* Edison Swan Electric Company Ltd., London 1950s

Eidelberg, M. (ed.), *Design 1945–1965: What Modern Was. Selections from the Liliane and David M. Stewart Collection,* Harry N. Abrams Inc., New York 1991

Eidelberg, M. (ed.), *Design for Living: Furniture and Lighting 1950–2000, the Liliane and David M. Stewart Collection,* Flammarion, Paris 2000

Eidelberg, M. (ed.), *Designed for Delight; Alternative Aspects of Twentieth-Century Decorative Arts,* Flammarion, Paris 1997

Favata, I., *Joe Colombo and Italian Design of the Sixties,* Thames & Hudson Ltd., London 1988

Fiell, C. and P., *60s Decorative Art,* TASCHEN GmbH, Cologne 2000

Fiell, C. and P., *70s Decorative Art,* TASCHEN GmbH, Cologne 2000

Fiell, C. and P., *Design of the 20th Century,* TASCHEN GmbH, Cologne 1999

Fiell, C. and P., *Designing the 21st Century,* TASCHEN GmbH, Cologne 2001

Fiell, C. and P., *Industrial Design,* TASCHEN GmbH, Cologne 2000

Fiell, C. and P., *Scandinavian Design,* TASCHEN GmbH, Cologne 2002

Fontana Arte: una Storia Trasparente, a Transparent History, Fontana Arte/Skira Editore, Milan 1998

Franklyn Paris, W., 'Georges Szabo: a Ferronier of the Old School', *Pencil Points,* June 1931

Fullmer, J.Z., *Sir Humphrey Davy's Published Works,* Harvard University Press, Cambridge (MA) 1969

Garner, P., *Sixties Design,* TASCHEN GmbH, Cologne 1996

General Electric Co. Ltd., *The Story of the Lamp,* The General Electric Co. Ltd., London c.1920

General Electric Co., *Factory Lighting Designs; a Practical Handbook for the Installer of Lighting Equipment,* National Lamp Works of General Electric Co., Cleveland 1925

Gramigna, G. and Biondi, P., *Il Design in Italia dell'Arredamento Domestico,* Umberto Allemandi & C., Turin 1999

Gramigna, G., *1950–1980 Repertory, Pictures and Ideas Regarding the History of Italian Furniture,* Arnoldo Mondadori Editore, Milan 1985

Greenhalgh, P., *Quotations and Sources on Design and the Decorative Arts,* Manchester University Press, Manchester 1993

Hiesinger, K.B. and Marcus, G.H., *Landmarks of Twentieth-Century Design, an Illustrated Handbook,* Abbeville Press Publishers, New York (NY) 1993

Italian Look, Federlegno, Milan 1972

Jahr, A. (ed.), *Moderne Klassiker, Möbel, die Geschichte machen,* Gruner+Jahr, Hamburg 1996

Janneau, G., *Le Fer à l'Exposition Internationale des Arts Décoratifs Modernes,* F. Contet, Paris 1925

Janneau, G., *Le Luminaire: Lighting Design, 1925–1937,* Editions Charles Moreau, Paris 1992

Jorstian, T. and Munk Nielsen, P.E. (eds.), *Light Years Ahead: The Story of the PH Lamp,* Louis Poulsen & Co., Copenhagen 1994

Journal of the Royal Institution of Great Britain, London 1802

Kahr, J., *Edgar Brandt: Master of Art Déco Ironwork,* Harry N. Abrams Inc., New York 1999

Keating, P.W., *Lamps for a Brighter America,* McGraw-Hill Book Company, New York 1954

Kita, T., *Washi and Urushi: Reinterpretation of Tradition,* Rikuyosha, Tokyo 1999

Lotz, W., *Licht und Beleuchtung,* Bücher der Form, vol. 6, Deutscher Werkbund, Berlin 1928

Luckiesh, M., *Artificial Light,* The Century Co., New York 1920

Magnani, F. (ed)., *Lampade,* Görliche Editore, Milan 1965

Maril, N., *American Lighting, 1840–1940,* Schiffer Publishing Ltd., Pennsylvania 1995

Mundt, B., *Produkt-Design 1900–1990: Eine Einführung,* Dietrich Reimer Verlag, Berlin 1991

Myerson, J. and Katz, S., *Lamps and Lighting,* Conran Octopus Ltd., London 1990

Noever, P. and Oberhuber, O., eds., *Josef Hoffmann 1870–1956, Ornament zwischen Hoffnung und Verbrechen,* Österreichisches Museum für angewandte Kunst, Vienna 1987

Pasca, V., *Vico Magistretti: Elegance and Innovation in Postwar Italian Design,* Thames & Hudson Ltd., London 1991

Paul, T., *The Art of Louis Comfort Tiffany,* Shooting Star Press Inc., New York 1996

Pope, F.L., *Evolution of the Electric Incandescent Lamp,* Henry Cook, New Jersey 1889

Porcelli, V.L., and Green, D., *International Lighting Design,* Rockport Publishers Inc., Rockport (MA) 1991

Radice, B., *Memphis: Research, Experiences, Results, Failures and Successes of New Design,* Thames & Hudson Inc., London/New York (NY) 1995

Remmele, M. and von Vegesack, A. (eds.), *Verner Panton: The Collected Works,* Vitra Design Museum, Weil am Rhein 2000

Rizzi, R., Steiner, A., Origoni, F. (eds.), *Design Italiano, Compasso d'Oro,* Centro Legno Arredo Cantù, Italy 1998

Romanelli, M., *Joe Colombo: Lighting Design – Interior Design,* O Luce, Milan 2002

Santini, P.C., *Facendo Mobili con Poltronova,* Artigraf Edizioni, Florence 1996

Schweiger, W.J., *Wiener Werkstätte, Kunst und Kunsthandwerk 1903–1932,* Christian Brandstätter Verlag, Vienna 1982

Serge Mouille Luminaires, 1953–1962, Imprimerie J.R., Paris 1983

Skinner, T., *Lighting 2000: a Guide to the Best in Contemporary Lighting Design,* Schiffer Publishing Ltd., Atglen (PY) 2000

Sparke, P., *Italian Design 1870 to the Present,* Thames & Hudson Ltd., London 1988

Storey, Sally, *Lighting by Design,* Pavilion Books, London 2002

Sudjic, D., *The Lighting Book; a Complete Guide to Lighting your Home,* Mitchell Beazley, London 1985

Sulz, G., *Wohnen im Richtigen Licht. Licht, Lampen und Leuchten,* Verlag Gerd Hatje, Stuttgart 1991

Sulzer, P., *Jean Prouvé / Complete Works, Volume 2: 1934–1944,* Birkhauser, Boston 2000

Swan, K.R., *Sir Joseph Swan and the Invention of the Incandescent Electric Lamp,* Longmans, Green & Co., London 1946

Swan, M.E. and K.R., *Sir Joseph Wilson Swan F.R.S.: A Memoir,* Ernest Benn Ltd., London 1929

Uecker, W., *Licht – Kunst: Lampen des Art Nouveau und Art Déco,* Neff, Rastatt 1992

Urquhart, J.W., *Electric Light,* Crosby, Lockwood & Co., London 1883

Wagner, O., *Moderne Architektur,* Getty Center for the History of Art and the Humanities, 1988

Weber, K. (ed.), *Die Metallwerkstatt am Bauhaus,* Bauhaus-Archiv, Berlin 1992

Weitz, C.E., *Electric Illuminants,* International Textbook Company, USA 1938

Westinghouse, *Lighting Handbook,* Westinghouse Electric Corporation, New Jersey 1956

Wilhide, E., *Lighting: A Design Source Book,* Stewart, Tabori & Chang, New York (NY) 1998

Wilhide, E., *Wohnen mit Klassikern: Leuchten,* DuMont Buchverlag, Cologne 2000

EXHIBITION CATALOGUES

Ambasz, E., *Italy: The New Domestic Landscape; Achievements and Problems of Italian Design,* The Museum of Modern Art, New York (NY) 1972

Bauhaus Exhibition Catalogue, Barry Friedman, New York 1988

Bosoni, G., Picchi, F., Strina, M., Zanardi, N. (eds.), *Original Patents of Italian Design, 1946–1965,* Electa, Milan 2000

Centre Georges Pompidou, *Lumières,* Éditions du Centre Pompidou/Editions Hermé, Paris 1985

Ferrari, F. and N., *Light; Lamps 1968–1973: New Italian Design,* Umberto Allemandi & C/ Klaus Engelhorn, Vienna 2002

Ferrari, P., *Achille Castiglioni,* Centre Georges Pompidou, Paris 1985

L'Union des Exploitations Electriques en Belgique, *Eclairage de 1900 à Nos Jours,* Brussels 1967

McKean, H.F., *The Treasures of Tiffany,* Chicago Review Press, Chicago 1982

Mitchell Wolfson Jr. Collection of Decorative & Propaganda Arts, *Light Opera – Virtuosity in Lighting Design,* Miami-Dade Community College, Miami 1987

Museum of Art and Design, *Tapio Wirkkala – Eye, Hand and Thought,* Helsinki 2000–2001

Salone Internazionale del Mobile, *Alla Castiglioni,* Cosmit, Milan 1996

Salone Internazionale del Mobile, *Alvar Aalto,* Cosmit, Milan 1998

Salone Internazionale del Mobile, *Joe Colombo,* Cosmit, Milan 1996

Salone Internazionale del Mobile, *Vico Magistretti,* Cosmit, Milan 1997

Salone Internazionale del Mobile, *Gio Ponti,* Cosmit, Milan 1997

San Francisco Museum of Modern Art, *Sitting on the Edge, Modernist Design from the Collection of Michael & Gabrielle Boyd,* Rizzoli International Publications, Inc., New York (NY) 1998

L'Union des Exploitations Électriques en Belgique, *Éclairage de 1900 à Nos Jours,* Brussels 1967

von Vegesack, A. (ed.), *Ingo Maurer – Light – Reaching for the Moon,* Vitra Design Museum, Weil am Rhein 2004

THOMAS BERG

Thomas Berg, born in Bonn in 1965, studied European and Oriental history of art at Bonn University. He works as a freelance specialist dealing with and writing on 20th-century decorative arts. His particular fields of interest are the Bauhaus design movement and the Vienna Secession. He is a co-author of Taschen's *Avantgarde Design*.

STEFANO CASCIANI

Born in Rome in 1955, Stefano Casciani is a writer, designer and artist. At 24 he was a freelance editor at *Domus* magazine and at 26 art director of the Italian cult furniture manufacturer Zanotta. In 2001 he was awarded a Compasso d'Oro design prize. Since 2000 he has been Deputy Editor of *Domus*. His writings and product designs have been featured in magazines, books and exhibitions in museums and art galleries worldwide.

QUINTIN COLVILLE

Quintin Colville graduated in 1994 from Magdalen College, Oxford, with a degree in modern history. He gained an MA and a PhD in the history of design from the Royal College of Art; and also held research fellowships at Linacre College, Oxford, and the National Maritime Museum, Greenwich. In 2001, he was awarded the Alexander Prize by the Royal Historical Society. He currently works as a researcher for Charlotte and Peter Fiell.

CHARLOTTE AND PETER FIELL

Charlotte and Peter Fiell are leading authorities on 20th and 21st-century design and have written numerous books on the subject, including Taschen's *1000 Chairs*, *Design of the Twentieth Century*, *Industrial Design*, *Scandinavian Design*, *Designing the 21st Century* and *Graphic Design for the 21st Century*. Together they work from London as Taschen's international design book editors.

PHILIPPE GARNER

Philippe Garner has worked since 1971 as an auction specialist and is recognized internationally as a leading authority in his fields of 20th-century decorative arts and design, and photographs. He has published widely, including monographs on photographers Cecil Beaton and John Cowan, and two books for Taschen on *Eileen Gray* and *Sixties Design*.

ESZTER KARPATI

Eszter Karpati was born in Budapest in 1975. She received a BA in History of Art from Camberwell College of Art, followed by an MA in Design History from the Royal College of Art, London. Having worked as a freelance journalist and as an editorial assistant to Charlotte and Peter Fiell, she is currently an editor at a London-based art and design book publisher.

ALEX PAYNE

Born in 1972, Alexander Payne is worldwide head of the 20th–21st Century Design Art Department at Phillips, de Pury and Company. Based in London, he has held successful auctions in both London and New York. In addition to his extensive auction experience he has lectured and written on the history of design and is the editor of Series Books Design.

VICTORIA RODRIGUEZ THIESSEN

Victoria Rodriguez Thiessen is a specialist in 20th-century design at Sotheby's, New York. She received an MA in the History of Decorative Arts from the Cooper-Hewitt National Design Museum before joining the specialist staff in the 20th Century Decorative Arts department at Christie's and later Phillips, de Pury & Luxembourg.

This project would simply not have been possible without the input of many talented and dedicated people. To all those who have helped us we offer our sincere thanks. Special mention must go to our editors at Taschen – Kathrin Murr, Thomas Berg and Viktoria Hausmann – who have managed the complex co-ordination of the undertaking, Sacha Davison whose patient devotion to the book's layout has ensured a beautiful outcome, Andy Disl for his design of the cover, Paul Chave for all his beautiful new photograhy, Karen Williams and Sylvie Ragey-Gracé for their painstaking fact checking, our research assistants Eszter Karpati and Quintin Colville for their excellent picture sourcing, Ute Wachendorf in Taschen's production department and of course our team of contributing writers who have brought their own personal insights to bear on this fascinating subject. We would also like to acknowledge the numerous designers, manufacturers, picture libraries, auction houses and museums that have lent images and assisted with information. We also thank the various collectors and dealers, especially Rick Gallagher, Ross and Miska Lovegrove, Michael and Nancy Krzyzanowski, Mark McDonald, Stella Christie, Sam Kaufmann, Nick Wright and Dan Ostroff, who have kindly allowed us to photograph the lights in their collections. Additionally we must mention the valued contribution of our daughters, Emelia and Clementine, who have become highly skilled at mounting transparencies and image filing. Lastly we would like to give a personal thank you to our friend and publisher, Benedikt Taschen for his enthusiasm and determination to create the best possible work on the history of lighting.

With additional thanks to:

Tina Anderson – Louis Poulsen Lighting ▷ Simon Andrews – Christies ▷ Doug Brackett – Edisionian.com ▷ Torsten Bröhan ▷ Clara Buoncristiani and Azzurra Rodella – Flos ▷ Stella Calvert-Smith and Charlotte Grant – Christies Images ▷ Paul Cattermole – Arcaid ▷ Paul Cocksedge ▷ Lydia Cresswell-Jones – Sotheby's ▷ Linda-Anne D'Anjou – Musée des Beaux-Arts Montréal ▷ Sue Daly – Sotheby's Picture Library ▷ Douglas De Nicola – The Isamu Noguchi Foundation ▷ Klaus Engelhorn and Michael Turkewitsch – KlausEngelhorn22 ▷ Carmen Figini and Annalisa Biliato – Editoriale Domus ▷ Mauro Flamini and Catia Giaccaglia – iGuzzini ▷ Arthur Floss – Quittenbaum ▷ Peter Gössel – Gössel und Partner ▷ Cressida Granger – Mathmos ▷ Rosi Guadagno – Luceplan ▷ Marco Ghilarducci – Martinelli Luce ▷ Thomas Happel – Ingo Mauer ▷ Karen Heath – Bonhams ▷ Frank James – Royal Insitution ▷ Michaela Kreuter – Die Neue Sammlung ▷ Peter Lang-Taucher ▷ David Limberger ▷ Helen Loomes and Martin Krautter – Erco Lighting ▷ Peter and Shannon Loughrey – Los Angeles Modern Auctions ▷ Graham Mancha ▷ John Meiczinger and Peter Macy – Lightolier ▷ Minako Morita – Yamagiwa ▷ Antonella Morlino – O-Luce ▷ Anne Palkonen ▷ Simona Romano – Kartell Museum ▷ Silvia Ros – The Wolfsonian FIU ▷ Jerry Sarapochiello ▷ Jeff Schuerholz ▷ Ayala and Albi Serfaty – Aqua Creations ▷ Sabrina Serra and Giovanna Solinas – Artemide ▷ Sarah Silver ▷ George Sowden ▷ Gregorio Spini – Kundalini ▷ Ara Tavitian – Retro Gallery ▷ Simon Terry – Anglepoise ▷ David Thompson – Science & Society Picture Library ▷ Jean Pierre Vitrac ▷ Richard and Julie Wright – Wright

We are immensely grateful to all those individuals, companies and institutions that have allowed us to reproduce images. We regret that in some cases it has not been possible to trace the original copyright holders of photographs from earlier publications. The publisher has endeavored to respect the rights of third parties, however, if any such rights have been overlooked in individual cases, the mistake will be correspondingly amended where possible. The majority of historic images were sourced from manufacturers' archives and the editors' own picture library.

Adelta, Dinslaken: 387; **AEG Aktiengesellschaft, Frankfurt:** 98 (both); **Alva Lighting, London:** 571, 659; **Aqua Creations, Tel Aviv:** 604, 605; **Arcaid, London:** 100, 568; **Artek, Helsinki:** 312, 313 (top); **Arteluce/Flos, Bovezzo:** 590; **Artemide, Pregnana Milanese:** 34 (left), 35, 39 (both), 40 (right) 356, 357, 377 (both), 414 (both), 415, 418 (both), 422 (both), 427 (bottom), 428 (top), 430, 431 (both), 454 (both), 462 (top), 463, 464, 465 (bottom), 511, 519, 520, 521 (all), 341, 554, 555, 563 (both), 576, 584 (both), 585, 600 (both), 601, 628, 634 (top), 634 (bottom – photo: Elliot Erwin), 639, 640 (both), 641 (both), 652, 653 (all), 665, 669; **Ateljé Lyktan AB, Åhus:** 421 (top); **Bonham's, London:** 256, 296, 311, 317 (top), 366 (top), 416, 449, 495 (bottom), 502, 509, 550; **Tord Boontje, London:** 672, 673 (photo: Habitat); **Büro für Form, Munich:** 621, 633; **Camard Ass., Paris – photo: Renan Cholet:** 335; **Cathers & Dembrosky, New York:** 112; **Christie's Images, London:** 62, 64, 69, 71, 72, 73, 75, 76, 78 (both), 79, 80, 84 (both), 85, 88, 90 (top), 91, 92, 93 (both), 94, 95, 101 (both), 102, 103, 104, 105, 106, 107 (both), 108, 109, 110, 111, 113, 115, 117, 118, 119, 120, 123, 124, 125, 127, 128, 129, 130, 132 (both), 133, 134, 137, 138, 143, 154, 155, 158, 163, 164, 166, 167, 168, 170 (top), 178, 179, 181, 183 (bottom), 188, 189, 190, 193, 194, 195, 197 (bottom), 199 (top), 200, 202 (top), 204 (top left & right), 205, 209, 212, 213, 221, 222, 224, 225, 243, 250, 251, 285 (left & right), 290, 292, 293, 306, 309 (right), 310 (top), 318 (top), 332 (bottom), 333, 336, 338, 339 (top), 350 (top), 351, 380, 381, 404, 440 (top), 446, 448, 469 (top), 470, 471, 472, 486 (top), 490 (top), 491 (top), 493, 535 (top), 340, 548; **Paul Cocksedge, London:** 43, 684, 685; **Crestworth, Dorset:** 374 **Corian/Marc Newson, London:** 668; **Dana-Thomas House Foundation, Springfield:** 90 (bottom); **David Rago, Chicago:** 114; **Michele De Lucchi, Milan:** 528 (both), 529 (both); **Design + Fun** (www.classic-modern.co.uk): 425, 444; **Tom Dixon, London:** 671; **Domus, Milan:** 223 (both), 257 (top), 307, 309 (left), 417, 458, 465 (top), 533, 549, 619; **Driade, Fossadello di Caorso:** 570; **Droog Design, Amsterdam:** 582; **Écart SA, Paris:** 97 (top); **Edisonian Museum** (www.edisonian.com): 54 (all), 55, 56, 57; **Erco, London:** 524 (all), 525 (both), 558, 559 (all), 608, 609 (both), 610, 611; **Fiell International Ltd, London:** 9, 10 (both), 13 (left), 18 (right), 26 (top right), 28 (left), 29 (both), 31, 44–45, 46, 99, 131, 136, 191 (bottom), 326, 453 (top), 507, 535 (bottom); Fiell International Ltd., London – photo: Paul Chave: 22 (left), 27, 58, 165, 216, 330 (right) 375, 388, 401, 419, 427 (top), 429, 443, 510, 518, 562, 581, 632; Fiell International – photo: Paul Chave, courtesy of Anglepoise: 214; Fiell International – photo: Paul Chave, courtesy of Stella Christie (www.stellachristielighting.co.uk): 148, 206, 207 (bottom); Fiell International Ltd. – photo: Paul Chave, courtesy of Eurolounge: 631; Fiell International – photo: Paul Chave, courtesy Michael & Nancy Krzyzanowski: 245; Fiell International – photo: Paul Chave, courtesy of Ross & Miska Lovegrove: 340, 426, 441, 485; Fiell International – photo: Paul Chave, courtesy of Nick Wright: 215, 268; Fiell International Limited – photo: Jerry Sarapochiello, courtesy of Daniel Ostroff: 37, 352, 393, 400, 410, 412, 413, 517, 527; Fiell International Ltd. – photo: Jerry Sarapochiello, courtesy of Ara Tavitian (Retro Gallery): 551; Fiell International Ltd. – photo: Jerry Sarapochiello, courtesy of Jeff Schuerholz: 459; Fiell International Ltd. – photo: Jerry Sarapochiello, courtesy of Sam Kaufmann: 370 (both), 371; Fiell International – photo: Sarah Silver, courtesy of Rick Gallagher: 226, 227, 228, 229, 262, 269 (bottom left & right), 272, 276, 277, 280, 281; Fiell International – photo: Sarah Silver, courtesy of Mark McDonald: 267, 271, 297 (left), 313 (bottom), 384; **Flos, Bovezzo:** front cover, 304, 305 (all), 366 (bottom), 372, 376, 378 (both), 379, 382 (bottom), 383, 432 (both), 476, 477, 503 (all), 530 (both), 531, 567, 569 (both), 580 (both), 591, 592 (both), 593, 594 (all), 595, 635, 638, 647 (top), 666, 670 (all); **Fontana Arte S.p.A., Corsico:** 218, 219 (bottom), 644 (both); **Fornasetti, Milan:** 337, 339 (bottom); **Foscarini, Marcon:** 578, 586, 587 (both), 636, 637, 656, 657, 658; **Alberto Fraser, Milan:** 547; **Fulvio Ferrari, Turin:** 353 (top); **Gallerie Arc en Seine, Paris:** 45; **Ganesvoort Gallery, New York:** 385; Ganesvoort Gallery – photo: Beth Phillips: 175; Ganesvoort Gallery – photo: Eva Heyd: 161, 211, 270, 275; **Philippe Garner, London:** 74 (both), 116 (top), 126 (both); **Habitat, London:** 673; **Sam Hecht, London:** 660 (both), 661 (all); **Holger Strøm/Bald & Bang Aps,**

Copenhagen: 514 (all); iGuzzini, Recanati: 552 (all), 553, 606, 607; Inflate Design, London: 598, 599; Ingo Maurer GmbH, Munich: 41, 408, 342, 343, 574, 575 (both), 596, 597, 622, 623, 626, 627, 649; Isamu Noguchi Foundation Inc., Long Island City: 4–5, 346, 347 (both), 349 (both); Jielde SA, Saint-Priest: 282, 283 (both); Kartell, Noviglio: 682, 683; Kartell Museo, Noviglio: 435; Tom Kirk, London: 646 (both); Klaus Engelhorn 22, Vienna – photography courtesy of Fulvio Ferrari: spine (photo: Mandy Grigg), 394, 405 (bottom), 406, 407, 409, 423, 439, 457, 474, 484, 487, 489, 490 (bottom), 494 (both), 499, 504 (top); Nikola Knezevic, Serbia: 42; Kundalini, Milan: 602 (both), 603, 654, 655; Kurt Versen Co., New York: 210; Le Klint, Odense: 235 (right), 236, 460, 461, 515; Lightolier, Jersey City: 244 (both), 328, 329 (both), 358, 359, 389, 411; Louis Poulsen, Copenhagen: 156, 157 (both), 342 (both), 343, 345 (both); Luceplan, Milan: 40 (left), 176 (left), 560, 561 (all), 564 (both), 565, 572, 573 (both), 589 (both), 614 (bottom left & right), 616, 617, 618, 650, 651, 674, 675, 678 (both), 679; Luxit S.p.A., Presezzo: 588 (both); Luxo ASA, Oslo: 217; Graham Mancha (www.mancha.demon.co.uk): 445, 483; Milo Manara (www.milomanara.it): 482; Marcel Wanders Studio, Amsterdam: 647 (bottom); Mawa Design GmbH, Langerwisch: 360 (both), 361, 362, 363 (all); Memphis, Milan: 534 (both), 536, 539; Metropolitan Museum of Art, New York: 93 (bottom); Modern, Yokohama-Shi: 645; The Montreal Museum of Fine Arts, Montreal: 239 (Liliane and David M. Stewart Collection, photo: Richard P. Goodbody – MBAM/MMFA), 324 (top) (Liliane and David M. Stewart Collection, gift of Mr & Mrs Charles D. O'Kieffe Jr., in memory of Mr & Mrs Charles DeWitt O'Kieffe – photo: Schecter Lee – MBAM/MMFA), 451 (Liliane and David M. Stewart Collection – photo: Giles Rivest (MBAM/MMFA), 556 (Liliane and David M. Stewart Collection, gift of Toshiko Mori – photo: Denis Farley – MBAM/MMFA), 583 (Liliane and David M. Stewart Collection, gift of Murray Moss – photo: Denis Farley – MBAM/MMFA); Moooi, Breda: 624 (photo: Erwin Olaf), 625, 662, 663 (photo: Erwin Olaf); Museo di Arte Moderna, Trento: 177; MY Studio, London (Michael Young): 630 (bottom); Normann, Copenhagen: 386; Anthony Oliver, London / Hunterian Art Gallery, Glasgow: 65; OLuce, Milan: 390 (top), 392 (top), 478 (both) 479, 522, 523 (both); Omikron Design, Milan: 242; Anne Palkonen, Helsinki: 241 (both); Panton Archiv, Basel: 365, 467, 468;; Phillips, de Pury & Co., London: 140, 141, 146, 147 (top), 159, 171, 184, 196, 197 (top), 198, 230, 252, 253, 300, 316 (top), 316 (bottom left), 319, 433, 436 (top), 437 (right), 466, 473, 495 (top), 496, 497, 506, 532, 630 (top); Philips Lighting, Amsterdam: 34 (right), 36 (both), 38 (both); Poltronova, Montale: 33, 405 (top), 436 (bottom), 437 (left), 447 (bottom), 450; Ron Arad Associates, London: 642, 643 (both); Quittenbaum, Munich: 32, 331; Julius Shulman Photography, Los Angeles: 348; Science & Society Picture Library, London: 16, 25, 47, 48, 49 (bottom), 51, 53 (right); Segno, Parabiago: 344, 345 (both), 620 (both); Serien, Rodgau: 667; Sistrah, Stuttgart: 201, 202 (bottom), 203; Sotheby's Picture Library, London: 60, 61, 66, 67, 68, 77, 82, 89 (top), 122, 139, 180, 182, 185, 186, 187, 191 (top), 220, 237, 289, 295, 301, 303, 308, 315, 341, 398, 402, 452, 469 (bottom), 475, 537; George Sowden, Milan: 504 (bottom), 505; Stendig, New York: 382 (top); Stilnovo, Milan: 566; Studio X (Ross Lovegrove), London: 614 (top – photo: John Ross), 615 (photo: John Ross); Hisao Suzuki, Barcelona: 664; Swarovski, London: 672; Taideteollisuusmuseo (Museum of Decorative Arts), Helsinki: 240, 321, 323; Tajan, Paris: 70; Tecnolumen, Bremen: back cover, 150, 152, 546; Tobias Grau, Rellingen: 677 (both); Torsten Bröhan Archiv, Berlin: 145, 169; Tronconi, Corsico: 629, 676; Vitra, Weil am Rhein: 231 (bottom); Jean-Paul Vitrac, Paris: 481 (bottom); Woka Lamps, Vienna: 86, 87 (top); The Wolfsonian-FIU (Florida International University), Miami Beach: 7, 8, 30 (left), 30 (right), 59, 63, 83, 160 (top), 174, 208; Wright, Chicago: 96, 172, 173, 219 (top), 232, 238, 246 (both), 247, 248 (top), 249 (top), 254, 255, 257 (bottom), 258, 259, 260 (top), 261, 264, 265, 266, 269 (top), 273, 274, 278, 279, 284, 286, 287, 288 (top), 291, 294, 298, 299, 302, 318 (bottom), 320, 325, 327, 330 (left), 354, 355, 364, 367, 368 (both), 396 (both), 397, 440 (bottom), 442 (top), 447 (top), 453 (bottom), 455, 480, 481 (top), 498, 500, 508, 526, 538; Yamagiwa Corp., Tokyo: 512, 513, 557, 576, 577, 648 (both), 680 (top), 681; Zumtobel Staff GmbH, Dornbirn: 612, 613

Cover: Achille & Pier Giacomo Castiglioni, *Taccia*, table light, 1962
Spine: Ingo Maurer, *Bulb*, table light, 1966
Back cover: *Model No. HL99*, suspended ceiling light, c. 1900 (reissue)

To stay informed about upcoming TASCHEN titles,
please request our magazine at www.taschen.com or write
to TASCHEN, Hohenzollernring 53, D-50672 Cologne,
Germany, Fax: +49-221-254919. We will be happy to
send you a free copy of our magazine which is filled
with information about all of our books.

This work was originally published in two volumes.
© 2006 TASCHEN GmbH
Hohenzollernring 53, D–50672 Köln
www.taschen.com

Original edition: © 2005 TASCHEN GmbH
© VG Bild-Kunst, Bonn 2006 for the following designers: Jaques Adnet,
Peter Behrens, Edgar Brandt, Marianne Brandt, Walter Gropius, Maurice
Ingrand, Renè Lalique, Yonel Lébovici, Robert Mallet-Stevens, Alexandre Noll,
Jacobus Johannes Pieter Oud, Jean Perzel, Armand Albert Rateau, Gerrit
Rietveld, Raymond Subes, Wilhelm Wagenfeld, Frank Lloyd Wright

Design: Sacha Davison, London; Sense/Net, Andy Disl and
Birgit Reber, Cologne
Cover design: Angelika Taschen, Berlin; Sense/Net, Andy Disl and Birgit Reber,
Cologne
Project management: Kathrin Murr, Florian Kobler and
Ines Dickmann, Cologne
Coordination: Viktoria Hausmann and Thomas Berg, Cologne
Production: Ute Wachendorf, Cologne
German translation: Karin Haag, Vienna; Brigitte Rapp, Vienna
French translation: Jacques Bosser, Paris; Marie Dumont-Agarwal, Brussels

Printed in China
ISBN-13: 978-3-8228-5287-3
ISBN-10: 3-8228-5287-2